WAVELL

THE VICEROY'S JOURNAL

The Viceroy writing his Journal

WAVELL

THE VICEROY'S JOURNAL

EDITED BY

PENDEREL MOON

LONDON
OXFORD UNIVERSITY PRESS
DELHI KARACHI
1973

Oxford University Press, Ely House, London W1X 4AH

GLASGOW NEW YORK TORONTO MELBOURNE WELLINGTON
CAPE TOWN IBADAN NAIROBI DAR ES SALAAM LUSAKA ADDIS ABABA
DELHI BOMBAY CALCUTTA MADRAS KARACHI LAHORE DACCA
KUALA LUMPUR SINGAPORE HONG KONG TOKYO

ISBN 0 19 211723 8

Printed in Great Britain
at the University Press, Oxford
by Vivian Ridler
Printer to the University

CONTENTS

ILLUSTRATIONS

ACKNOWLEDGEMENTS

Before his untimely death on active service in Kenya in 1953, Lord Wavell's only son, Major A. J. A. Wavell (who became Viscount Keren, M.C., and on his father's death the 2nd Earl Wavell), had taken a year's leave from the army in order to go through all his father's papers, intending eventually to arrange for the publication of the Journal. With this in mind he interviewed a number of people who had been closely connected with Lord Wavell during his Viceroyalty, and recorded notes of what they said. With the permission of those interviewed I have made use of these valuable notes.

The very considerable labour of preparing typed copies both of the Journal and of the notes and letters referred to therein and of assembling all the other relevant papers that had been in Lord Wavell's possession, was undertaken by his three daughters, Lady Pamela Humphrys, Lady Felicity Longmore, and Lady Joan Gordon. I am indebted to all of them for this preliminary spadework. I am also greatly indebted to Lady Pamela and Lady Felicity for much essential information and valuable advice and for the promptness and patience with which they have answered a large number of questions.

My thanks are also due to my sister, Mrs. Oakeshott, for reading the whole typescript and making many helpful suggestions; to Sir Evan Jenkins and Sir George Abell for answering some specific questions and for providing useful background information; to Lt.-Gen. Sir Arthur Smith and Lt.-Gen. Sir Reginald Savory for responding to some inquiries about the Breakdown Plan; and to Professor Mansergh and the staff of the Historical Section, India Records Office, for tracing and furnishing copies of two documents that were missing from Lord Wavell's papers.

Documents written by Lord Wavell in his official capacity as Viceroy are Crown Copyright material and are reproduced with the permission of the Controller of Her Majesty's Stationery Office.

PENDEREL MOON

INTRODUCTION

The three and a half years of Lord Wavell's Viceroyalty from October 1943 to March 1947 was probably the most difficult and momentous period of office that any Viceroy has had to face. The crucial significance of these years and the great services that Wavell rendered during them to India and Britain, though recognized to some extent at the time, have not since then received the appreciation that is their due. A shadow has been cast over his Viceroyalty by his summary dismissal from the post and by the brilliance with which, immediately after his departure, Lord Mountbatten wound up the British Raj with the full agreement of all parties. By contrast Lord Wavell's unavailing efforts to bring about agreement between the Congress and the Muslim League can all too easily appear in retrospect to have been fumbling and maladroit and his removal from the scene to have been a necessary preliminary to a final ringing down of the curtain amid general applause. In some recently published books references to his Viceroyalty have been disparaging, even contemptuous. It has been said that he was quite unfitted for delicate negotiations, that he was defeatist in outlook, an advocate of what Winston Churchill would have 'properly described as an ignoble and sordid scuttle', that he was often at a loss what to do and, by the time of his dismissal, at the end of his resources. These judgements are largely based on surmise and have been put forward without reference to all the relevant documents, many of which have not been published. Lord Wavell's Journal, along with some of his own notes and memoranda, should help to correct a number of misconceptions and will lead, perhaps, to a better appraisal of his achievements as Viceroy and his qualities as a man.

The main significance of his Viceroyalty lies in the two fateful political decisions that were, in effect, reached during his tenure of office. One of them, that India should be granted Independence within eighteen months, was taken at his instance, and largely because of his insistence, and was announced before he left the country. The other, that India should be divided, though it was not actually taken and proclaimed by the British Government till some weeks after his departure, had in reality been reached by India's political leaders before he handed over to his successor.

It was not a decision that he willed, desired, or advocated, indeed he greatly regretted it; but, as he realized and told the British Government as soon as he arrived back in England, partition had become virtually inescapable; it was the necessary sequel to the breakdown of his long and patient endeavours to reconcile within a united India the conflicting aims of the Congress and the Muslim League. By the time of his departure the embittered protagonists of these hostile parties had at last agreed at least on this, that they should go their separate ways in a divided India. The key members of the Congress, who had earlier been adamant in their resistance to division, were by now convinced by experience in the Interim Government that collaboration with the League in governing India was impossible and that it was best, therefore, to let the Muslims take those parts of the country that on a population basis they could indisputably claim, and form them into a separate State. Meanwhile Jinnah and the Muslim League had come to accept the position that if they really wanted Pakistan, all they could get would be the truncated Pakistan that population figures would give them, and they were content to take this rather than to have no Pakistan at all. Thus, when Mountbatten became Viceroy, a firm basis for agreement between the parties already existed. He built upon it with superb confidence, decision, and skill; but it was a much easier task than to coax the Congress and the League into some form of united India, as Wavell and the British Government had for one and a half years rightly, but vainly, attempted.

Mountbatten also had the advantage of enjoying fuller powers (for which he had wisely stipulated in advance) than were ever allowed to Wavell. It is said[1] that Nehru was so struck by the air of authority with which he spoke that a few days after his arrival in India he asked him: 'Have you by some miracle got plenipotentiary powers?' 'Suppose I have,' Mountbatten replied, 'what difference would it make?' To which Nehru answered: 'Why then you will succeed where all others have failed.'

Wavell's failure, which paved the way for Mountbatten's success, was certainly not his fault. The task that he was set was a well-nigh impossible one, almost comparable to the hopeless task assigned to him as a military commander to stem the Japanese advance in South-East Asia; and he was hampered throughout by the indecision and weakness of his masters, the British Government. Nevertheless he came very near to success, and it is at least arguable that if he had been given a freer hand or if the British Government had followed his advice and acted with the firmness and

[1] H. V. Hodson, *The Great Divide* (London, 1969), p. 201.

decision that he advocated, the transfer of power could have been effected without the disasters that actually accompanied it.

The political problem occupied Wavell's mind from the first moment of his appointment as Viceroy, and during his last two years of office it came to dominate all else. But there were many other daunting problems that he had to cope with. At the very outset he was confronted with a famine in Bengal and thereafter, right to the end, amid all his other cares he had to meet repeated threats of famine and chronic shortages of food, cloth, coal, and other essentials. As soon as the war ended, there was, as he had foreseen, a renewal of political agitation and the fomenting of popular discontent, and this was followed by mutinies, strikes, outbreaks of disorder, both anti-government and communal, and the threat of rebellion and civil war. Wavell sought to forestall and counteract this turbulence by pushing ahead plans for post-war development and by attempting at the Simla Conference of 1945 to form a Congress–League coalition government before the war ended. This wise and statesmanlike move, which the British Government delayed and obstructed, did not succeed in its object; but in the judgement of the Congress President, Maulana Abul Kalam Azad, it marked the beginning of a decisive and favourable change in Indo-British relations; and it probably helped to keep in check the extremist wing of the Congress during the ensuing dangerous months.

It will be found from Wavell's Journal and the documents mentioned in it that amid all his difficulties and disappointments he never accepted defeat and was never for long at a loss what to do, but that, on the contrary, he was almost invariably in advance of the British Government in prompting and proposing courses of action, and that he was always looking ahead and devising ways of meeting contingencies that they had not begun to think of. The policy of scuttle that has been attributed to him was one that he strongly advised should be avoided. He foresaw that unless there was a complete reversal of policy and a firm decision was taken to remain in India for another fifteen to twenty years, British control could not be effectively maintained for very long. He therefore urged the British Government to fix a date for withdrawal and to make timely arrangements to beat an orderly retreat; and when he found that they preferred just to hope for the best and to scuttle if these hopes were not realized, he pressed his advice upon them with a blunt insistence that was, no doubt, partly responsible for his dismissal. In the end the British Government agreed to fix a date and took the credit for this 'bold and courageous move' that he had for months been vainly advocating.

Indians of all political parties recognized that during his term of office

Wavell worked tirelessly, sincerely, and with great ability for the good of India, for the reconciliation of their internal differences, and for the peaceful transfer of power to Indian hands. He showed himself to be straightforward, just, energetic, firm, and decisive. These were the qualities that Indians associated with the British at their best, and they were pleased to find them in the Viceroy. These qualities are clearly revealed in the Journal.

The reasons that prompted Wavell to keep a Journal are explained in the following short note that he wrote inside the cover of the first volume.

I have never kept a diary or any record of my life other than a small book in which I set down in what part of the world I am in each month.

Since this war began and I have become involved in great events I have regretted that I have not kept a note of certain happenings and conversations. Now that I have been appointed Viceroy I think I will try to put down at the time some note of matters and impressions which may be of interest from the personal or historical point of view.

In accordance with this resolve he kept a regular record of his activities and impressions throughout his term as Viceroy. When he was in Delhi or in Simla or on a visit to London he made entries in the Journal almost every day; when he went on tour to different parts of India he usually wrote up the Journal on his return to headquarters. The labour of this writing after a heavy day's work must have been considerable. The portion of it covering the period of his Viceroyalty fills eleven volumes and runs to over 260,000 words. It is written in his clear regular handwriting with scarcely an erasure.

References in the Journal to personal and family matters are infrequent; some of them have been omitted. There is also comparatively little reference to world or national affairs, and considering the large part that he had played as a military commander from 1939 to 1943, there is not much comment on the progress of the war or on military operations other than those that directly affected India. The great bulk of the entries in the Journal are concerned with his activities as head of the Government of India and with the events of his Viceroyalty.

Inevitably substantial cuts have had to be made, and readers may wish to know the nature of these cuts. Apart from the omission, already mentioned, of a few of the references to personal matters, some of the entries regarding the Viceroy's routine, day-to-day work, and social engagements, including some happy references to members of his staff in connection with social and sporting events, have been omitted. But enough have been retained to give the reader an idea of the wide range of matters which required the Viceroy's personal attention, and to serve as a reminder of his heavy social obligations. Similarly some of the detailed accounts that Wavell wrote of his tours have been omitted or greatly curtailed; but the more interesting or amusing of them have been given in full or with only slight abbreviation.

A number of entries regarding the general problems of the Princely States have been curtailed, and references to happenings in individual States that had no serious repercussions in the rest of India, e.g. the deposition of the Maharaja of Rewa, have usually been omitted altogether. There is also one whole subject, the treatment of Indians in South Africa, almost all references to which have been cut out. This was a subject that in the years 1943–5 bulked large in the deliberations of Wavell's Executive Council; but it is quite divorced from the main themes of his Viceroyalty, and the Council's debates and decisions on it have not much historical significance; for no action that India might take against South Africa could deflect the Government of that country from its basic policies. Wavell sympathized with the feelings of the Indian members of his Council regarding the treatment of Indians in South Africa and did whatever he could to help. As a result of his years of command in the Middle East he had rather a special relation with Smuts, and in a talk with him in London in April 1945 he impressed on him the strength of Indian feeling and the difficulty he was having in restraining his Council from intemperate action. He suggested a conference, but Smuts, who had his own difficulties, thought that this would be premature. The references to this subject in the Journal are fairly numerous, but most of them are fragmentary and would be difficult to understand without a good deal of supplementary noting. It has seemed best not to distract the reader by obscure references to a side issue; and so, except for one self-explanatory entry, they have been omitted altogether.

A few of the Journal's comments on individuals that might be embarrassing to persons still living have been omitted; but most of such comments, both favourable and unfavourable, have been allowed to stand; and despite the risk of giving offence to Indian readers, none of the hard things that Wavell wrote of Mr. Gandhi have been altered or omitted; for Wavell's very unfavourable judgement of him is of some historical interest.

Occasionally Wavell included in his Journal a brief record of his interviews with leading Indian politicians; more often he dictated separate notes of such interviews and referred to them in his Journal, sometimes adding the words 'copy enclosed'. Some of these separate notes have been reproduced either in full or abbreviated; but, to make for easier reading, extracts from some of them have been worked into the text of the Journal, as though they were part of it.

Apart from the omissions that have been indicated and this incorporation in the text of portions of the interview notes,[1] the Journal stands as Wavell wrote it. His spelling of Indian names and his punctuation, at times somewhat erratic, have been left unaltered.

The early volumes of the Journal are comparatively gay, buoyant, and light-hearted in tone; but later, especially after the Simla Conference in July 1945, as the outlook in India became more gloomy and threatening and the work piled up and the strain and stress grew more intense, there is less light relief, the Journal is more and more concentrated on the political scene and towards the end becomes sombre and pessimistic in tone. It is clear that by this time, though Wavell still looked cheerful and continued to be energetic and, as his letters show, still derived some amusement from the manoeuvres of the politicians, he was really very tired; it is probable that, unknown to him and to his doctors, his health had already been undermined by continuous strain and overwork; and he was certainly depressed by the little support or constructive help that he got from H.M.G. The Journal ends on a rather sad, dispirited note.

[1] In one instance on p. 22 a portion of a separate note on a Cabinet meeting has been inserted in the text of the Journal.

Note: The letters I.C.S. or I.P. have been added in footnotes or in the Index after the names of persons who were members of the Indian Civil Service or the Indian Police; but details of honours and titles have not been given.

1
APPOINTMENT AS VICEROY

June 24, 1943

It may be of interest if I set down while the events and impressions are fresh in my mind the history of my appointment as Viceroy from my point of view—rather a detached one up to the climax.

When I came home from India in April,[1] I had of course no idea whatever that the post might be offered to me, but I was naturally interested to know on whom the choice would fall since I should have to work with him as C-in-C India. The last time I spoke to the Viceroy [Lord Linlithgow] before I left India he said he had no idea who his successor would be and did not seem inclined to discuss possibilities (we had been through them at an earlier date before his extension was announced). I had heard one or two people suggest my name but they were not responsible persons and the suggestion merely annoyed me. I had seen enough of the business of the government of India by sitting on the Executive Council, discussions with the Viceroy and others, to convince me that I had no inclination or capacity for that sort of work, and I privately thanked heaven there was no chance of my having to do it, and made up my mind to refuse any Governorship if one was offered me after the war.

The P.M.'s greeting to me when I first met him on return home was far from cordial; and he was very critical and even unpleasant about the Arakan[2] operations, though I pointed out to the War Cabinet their limited scope, that they would never have been undertaken at all if I had had shipping available for a direct assault on Akyab; and that I had at least kept the Japanese busy for a whole campaigning season without much encouragement from home and entirely on my own initiative; while the Chinese, who according to Stilwell would advance in force on March 1,

[1] Wavell, as Commander-in-Chief, India, was in mid April summoned to England by the Chiefs of Staff for consultations along with the Naval and Air Commanders-in-Chief in the India region. He reached England on 22 April.

[2] At the end of 1942 the 14th Indian Division advanced into the Arakan province of Burma with the object of recapturing the port of Akyab. After some initial progress the advance was held up, and although another Division was thrown in, a Japanese counter-stroke compelled the British–Indian forces to withdraw again to the frontier with some loss of men, equipment, and morale.

had never moved at all. Stilwell[1] had only informed me that they did not intend to advance in February. This seemed to go down well with the War Cabinet, but the P.M. did not look pleased. This was on April 29. I had dined with the P.M. the night before (Antony Eden and Admiral Somerville the only two others)—P.M. quite pleasant but not much business talked, except that I said I thought we ought to go to Washington since Stilwell and Chennault were there, and P.M. said he did not think he would trust me to discuss plans alone with the Americans; he or Chiefs of Staff or both should go also. I said I was sure someone ought to go, now that it had been decided that the plan agreed with the Americans in India in February for Burma could not be carried out in full.

During the next few days it was decided that the P.M., Chiefs of Staff, the three Service Commanders from India (Somerville, Peirse and myself) and a large delegation should go to U.S.A. on Queen Mary, leaving London on the night of May 4. On some day before I left I had a message that Eden would like to see me at the Foreign Office. Later I had a message that Amery would like to see me at the India Office before I went to the F.O. When I saw Amery he told me that the P.M. was pressing Eden to become Viceroy, and that Eden wanted to discuss it with me. Amery urged me to do what I could to persuade Eden to go to India as he thought he was the best choice. I heartily agreed, as I like Eden and thought he would be good to work with. When I went over to the F.O., Eden told me that he was being pressed by the P.M. but was in two minds, because the intention was that he should be recommended to H.M. to succeed Winston as P.M. if anything should happen to W. He obviously feared that the break of five years in his political career might put him out of running as P.M.; at the same time he was attracted by the idea of being Viceroy. He said P.M. had agreed to his going as a Commoner, as a special case, and not taking a peerage. I asked who would succeed him at the F.O. and he said Cranborne. Eden wanted to know whether I thought that anything in the way of great political progress in India was possible at the present time. I replied that I was doubtful whether the deadlock could be easily solved during the war; his appointment would obviously arouse great hopes which he might not be able to fulfil; but I hoped that he would take the Viceroyalty for which he was so well qualified. He asked me a few questions about whether the present pomp and ceremony could not be greatly reduced. I said that I thought it certainly could. We talked

---

[1] Lt.-Gen. Joseph W. Stilwell, a U.S. General popularly known as 'Vinegar Joe'. He was Chief-of-Staff to Chiang Kai-shek and commanded U.S. and Chinese forces in India and Burma.

for about half-an-hour and he remained undecided, though I thought he was inclining to acceptance. He said he would have to give a reply when the P.M. returned from U.S.A.

On the Queen Mary on the way to New York, the P.M. discussed the Viceroy's successor with me once; and said, rather to my surprise in view of my talk with Eden, that he had come to the conclusion that Eden could not be spared; and that he thought Oliver Lyttleton would be his choice. This was the last occasion on which he spoke to me about the successor to the Viceroy till he offered me the post a month later.

During the voyage the P.M. continued his critical attitude of the Arakan operations, and in a note by him which was widely distributed to most of the staff of the Mission he used the expressions 'complete failure' and 'deep disgrace' in connection with some remarks on them. This made me furious, and I wrote a letter to him to the effect that, if he considered the operations such a failure and disgraceful, he could remove me from my command, but that as long as he continued to entrust it to me I would not have such remarks circulated to junior officers, some of whom were on my staff. It was rather a good letter; but I then decided to sleep on it and to consult Alan Brooke (CIGS) in the morning. He advised against sending the letter; and said that such remarks were 'common form' with the P.M.; that those who worked with him had become hardened to them and disregarded them; and he asked me not to give the P.M. any possible chance to remove me from India. So I did not send the letter, but when I saw the P.M. alone that day I tackled him about it. He professed complete confidence in me and said he had never intended that his remarks should have such wide circulation. Later, he called in all copies of his note, and amended the offending paragraph, thereby really calling more attention to it.

He found another subject for criticism in the loyalty of the Indian Army. Amery had sent a paper to the War Cabinet calling attention to obvious dangers arising from the expansion of the Indian Army. It was the result of some papers I had had sent home as C.-in-C. We realised the dangers in India, were keeping a close watch on them, but were not in the least alarmed and convinced of the general soundness of the Indian Army. The P.M., however, chose to read into Amery's note the impression that the Indian Army was liable to rise at any moment; and he accused me of creating a Frankenstein by putting modern weapons in the hands of sepoys, spoke of 1857, and was really almost childish about it. I tried to re-assure him, both verbally and by a written note, but he has a curious complex about India and is always loth to hear good of it and apt to believe the worst. He has still at heart his cavalry subaltern's idea of India; just as his military tactics are inclined to date from the Boer War.

He also raised on the voyage the question of the Eastern Command. He gave me two papers, one from the Air Minister on the separation of the air in India from the C.-in-C.'s control, the other by Amery on the creation of a new Command to control all operations in S.E. Asia, separate from C.-in-C. India. I wrote out my comments on both of these and sent them to P.M. I pointed out the constitutional difficulties of having a separate air command in India, quite apart from the military disadvantages and the difficulties of working with the Americans if we have an entirely different set-up to theirs. I strongly advocated a Joint Anglo-American command on the lines of Eisenhower's command in North Africa or MacArthur's in Australia. The P.M. sent no reply to these papers, which were actually sent to him after we got to Washington, nor referred to them in any way. I showed Peirse the paper on the Combined Command and he agreed generally.

I did not see much of the P.M. in Washington, and he was not very cordial when I did. At a luncheon at the White House in the President's study, at which there were only the P.M., the President, Harry Hopkins and myself, the P.M. took occasion to make some rather caustic references both to the Arakan operations and to the Indian Army, which annoyed me, as the President was being very pleasant and had not raised either topic. I ignored the Arakan remarks but defended the Indian Army with some heat, and the P.M. said no more. A day or two later he sent the CIGS a memo asking some questions on the Arakan operations and referring to them in most scathing terms, using the expressions 'discreditable', and 'disgraceful'. I sent the CIGS an indignant reply, but I don't know how much of it he passed on to the P.M. He again said that those who worked closely with him became hardened to such minutes and took little notice of them.

I wanted to go practically straight back to India from Washington, but the CIGS told me that the P.M. wanted me to stay in England till he could discuss the set-up of Command in India with me. The P.M. confirmed this just before we left Washington. I could not quite understand why we did not raise and discuss the Joint Anglo-American command in Washington; but I sensed that there was something working in the P.M.'s mind which he was not prepared to discuss or mention to me at present. Alan Brooke swore that he did not know in the least what was in the P.M.'s head about the Command.

So when we left Washington on May 26, I resigned myself to waiting a week or more in London till the P.M. returned from North Africa and settled up the Command. Alan Brooke went to Africa with P.M. The P.M. had said he would discuss the Indian Command on his return. The DCIGS and CIGS (on his return) accepted my views practically without amendment; and later the Chiefs of Staff, after some discussion, put forward these views as a C.O.S. paper, recommending a Joint Anglo-American Command, with a Supreme Commander. Without vanity, I could consider that I was the obvious choice for Supreme Commander, but I was also quite certain that the P.M., for some reason, did not want me there: I asked Alan Brooke if he knew how his mind was working. He said he had no idea except that P.M. had mentioned that he thought he would like to appoint a good young Corps commander from North Africa, such as Oliver Leese, to take charge of the operations from India. I warned the CIGS that if operations were removed from C-in-C India, and placed under a comparatively junior commander, the P.M. could hardly expect me to remain as C-in-C India merely to administer the Indian Army. CIGS said there was no question of that; if that happened Auchinlek would be C-in-C.[1]

This must have been about June 9 (the P.M. and CIGS had returned on June 6). I had no idea what was in the wind, or that there was any question at all of appointing me Viceroy; and spent a good deal of my time visiting military and Air Force establishments in various parts of England, when I was not dealing with matters concerning the Army in India at the War Office or India Office. I considered, rather vaguely, the possibility that the P.M. might intend to bring me home to take charge of the Forces for the invasion of the Continent, but thought this improbable as it would be a waste of my Eastern experience; in fact I did not quite see how the P.M. could avoid the conclusion that a Joint Command and a Supreme Commander was the right solution for the East Asian theatre; or that I was the obvious choice as a Supreme Commander. But I thought he might have broached this to the President at Washington and met objections owing to the way the Arakan operations had been misrepresented—largely by himself—as a complete failure; and their importance exaggerated. I was also quite certain that the Air Force were trying hard behind the scenes either to get complete independence from the control of a soldier or to get an Airman appointed as Supreme Commander. On the whole, however, I felt pretty confident that I should go back to India, and be appointed Supreme Commander if that went through.

I asked someone (I think Amery) after I got back from Washington if

[1] General (later Field Marshal) Sir Claude Auchinleck became Commander-in-Chief, India, when Wavell was made Viceroy.

it was true that Eden had definitely decided against the Viceroyalty, and was told he was still considering it. Since the P.M. showed no sign of life as far as I was concerned, I went away for the week-end on Saturday June 12. I concluded that the P.M. was still making up his mind about the question of the higher Command in India and wished he would get on with it. I intended to go to my sisters in the New Forest for the week-end; but Amery had asked me several times to go to the house that Lord Moyne had lent him near Chichester and I had always refused, so I thought I would propose myself for a night and then motor on to my sisters and return to London on Tuesday (Monday was Whit-Monday). Amery asked me to motor him down on Saturday evening. The whole way down he talked Indian politics. I took a languid, even somnolent, interest. I do not much like talking in a car, Amery is a little deaf and so am I, and I had made up my mind that whatever happened to me I should not be bothered with Indian politics much more. If I was appointed Supreme Commander in S.E. Asia, I should be dealing mainly with operations and someone else would be C-in-C India, presumably Auchin-leck. If someone else was made Supreme Commander, CIGS had said that there was no intention of keeping me on as C-in-C India to run the Indian Army. So I am afraid that I did not listen to Amery's monologue on future appointments to the Viceroy's Council and other matters with the attention that I might have done had I had any inkling of what was in store.

Next morning, Sunday, I went for an hour or so's walk with Amery. We again talked mainly of India, but I talked entirely from the military angle. I asked Amery if the Viceroy had yet been chosen, he said 'not yet, but it had reached the semi-final stage'. I did not ask the names of the semi-finalists, as he did not sound inclined for discussion (he, of course, knew the P.M.'s decision, and was being very discreet). Soon after we got back to the house, the P.M.'s Secretary telephoned and asked me to go and dine with the P.M. on Monday night. This was rather tiresome as it made my stay with my sisters a very short one. I had promised to lunch with the Head-master of Winchester on Monday and had intended to return to my sisters for Monday night; now I should have to go straight on to London from Winchester. I imagined that the P.M. had come to some decision on the S.E. Asian Command and wanted to discuss it with me, but thought that, having kept me waiting so long, he might now have waited till Tuesday.

I motored on to Ringwood on Sunday afternoon. I remember wonder-ing for a moment why the P.M. should send for me at such short notice; and the thought did cross my mind that Amery's attitude to me had shown a rather more proprietary shade than before, was it conceivable that the P.M. meant to sound me on the matter of the Viceroyalty? I dismissed the idea at once and concentrated on putting together a few ideas to deliver to the School at Winchester next day. When I got to Little Somborne, my sisters said Lord Cranborne had rung up and was very anxious I should go over and see him. I knew the Duff-Coopers were there, I had offered myself to Lady Diana for lunch on Sunday at her farm and she had told me they were to be at Cranborne, and had asked me to come over there to see them, so I imagined she was partly responsible for the invitation. My sisters and I motored over there after tea. Bobbety Cranborne's greeting to me was: 'Well, are we to congratulate you?' I said 'What on earth for?' and he said 'Oh, I thought they might have offered you a new appointment, I'm sorry I spoke' or something like that. There were about 8 or 10 people with the Cranbornes, and I thought the atmosphere seemed rather constrained. Lady Diana looked at me so fixedly that I asked her whether she had anything on her mind about me, but she said no. (I have since realised that probably everyone in the room, except myself and my sisters knew that the choice for Viceroy had fallen on me).

Next day I motored to Winchester with my sisters, spoke to the School and lunched with the Headmaster. It was not until after tea (which I had in Sixth Chamber in College with the School Officers), when I was motoring up to London that Bobbety's greeting at Cranborne came back to me and I really started thinking about it. It then occurred to me that he was unlikely to know about a fresh military appointment, such as Supreme Commander in S.E. Asia, but might well know about the selection of a Viceroy, in fact almost certainly would. For the first time, during that drive to London, I really began seriously to consider the possibility of the Viceroyalty being offered to me, and to wonder what I should do about it. As I have said I had made up my mind some time before that I had no taste for the cares of Governorship and that I should refuse any offer of such when my military career ended. I saw, however, that it might be rather difficult to refuse the Viceroyalty offered to me as a war appointment. It would mean that Eden had finally declined; and that the P.M. had decided that I would be of more value to the side as Viceroy than as Supreme Commander of S.E. Asia which was the post I had hoped for. I had always gone where I was told during the war without protest, and had decided to make none if the P.M. wished to remove me from the Command in India to some other military command, or to put me on the shelf. I thought I was possibly as suitable as one or two of the candidates for the Viceroyalty I had heard mentioned. Anyway, I have the bad (or good?) habit of never worrying much about my fences till I come to them. If the P.M. was seriously considering me for the Viceroyalty he would presumably give me time to think it over as he had the others. So I did not reflect very long or deeply about it all, beyond wondering what my wife would say; she would obviously make an excellent Vice-Reine.

I changed into uniform and went to 10 Downing Street at 8.30 p.m. on June 14. I was kept waiting about quarter of an hour in the basement where the P.M. dines during the war. I noticed the table was laid for two only. I employed the waiting time looking at the P.M.'s library in the sitting room. When the P.M. came in, he went straight to the point. He said something like this (I cannot recall the exact words): 'I have decided that you will have to give up your appointment as C-in-C India; but when you hear what I have to propose to you I am sure you will agree. I propose that you should be Viceroy. How does that strike you?' I said that it was a surprise to me, that I was very honoured by his considering me fit for such a post, but that I should have preferred to remain in a military appointment. He made some complimentary remarks, seemed to assume that I should accept, said that he had obtained His Majesty's approval on a signed document before H.M. went to North Africa, as he wished to make the announcement at once. He said: 'You will have to become a civilian, and put off uniform'; and after the conversation had only lasted a few minutes said 'We will now go and have dinner'. He was very pleasant during dinner, and talked about India and the proposed set-up of Command etc., as if I had already accepted. Towards the end of dinner, he asked me: 'May I assume that you accept?'. I said: 'Well, I must at least ask my wife, she has a heavy task to shoulder also'. He said: 'Certainly, send a telegram tonight, I will get Pug Ismay over to send it for you'; and he forthwith rang for his Secretary and told him to get Ismay over. I felt I was being rushed. Ismay came over and the P.M. said goodnight shortly afterwards. I wrote out a telegram to Queenie and gave it to Ismay. I had stipulated that she should be flown home at once, if I accepted, and the P.M. said 'Of course'. Incidentally, he said I should have to take a peerage. He also said it would probably be a war appointment only and that he would make a political appointment after the war; he indicated three years as the limit of my tenure.

My wife's reply came two days later, and I then wrote to the P.M. formally accepting the post.

July 3

Not very much to record; I've lunched and dined with a lot of people, worked a good deal at the India Office, mostly answering letters and seeing various people, and have attended one or two Cabinet meetings. I had a trying day on June 22 when I had a Press meeting and had to make my first public pronouncement, naturally an important occasion. I have a weakness that I can seldom bring myself to do anything till the last possible moment. Though I had fair warning of this Press Conference and had meant to write out my address during the previous weekend, I did something else less important; and actually only wrote it late at night the day before the Conference. It was quite good and went down well, but I suppose it might have been better if I had done it earlier and given more time to it. I must try to cure this weakness but I have done the same thing all my life and perhaps it is inevitable and it seems to work well on the whole.

On Friday July 3 there was a special Cabinet on Palestine, due to a pessimistic report by the Minister of State on increased Arab–Jewish tension on the approach of April 1944 when by the White Paper of 1939 Jewish immigration becomes dependent on Arab sanction. I knew Winston was a confirmed Zionist, but had never quite realised the lengths to which he was prepared to go, in speech at any rate, or the strength of the pro-Jewish feeling in the Cabinet. No-one seemed prepared to say anything at all on the Arab side. So at last I spoke up, and said that no-one ever seemed to remember the second part of the Balfour Declaration or the other pledges given to the Arabs. I said everyone spoke of protecting the Jews, but that if Arabs and Jews were left to fight it out in Palestine without outside interference I had no doubt that the Jews would win, and that it was the Arabs who required protection. The P.M. had talked of all we had done for the Arabs. We had done a good deal for the Jews in introducing half a million into a country whose inhabitants did not want them. The P.M. said the Arabs had done nothing to help us in the war. I said that Ibn Saud's friendship had been invaluable and that his enmity might have done us much harm; after all the Jews, as a race, had not helped us. The P.M. took my remarks better than I expected.

July 5

I saw Morrison (Home Secretary) and Cripps[1] in the morning. Morrison spoke of India, about which he really knew little. His idea seemed to be to encourage the masses against the classes by factory legislation, spread of education and mechanisation of farming on the Soviet model, but he had little idea of the problem, and thought the 'depressed classes' and 'untouchables' were merely another name for the poor, and seemed hardly

[1] Sir Stafford Cripps was at this time Minister of Aircraft Production.

to have heard of the caste system. I pointed out the differences from Russia where all at least spoke a common language and had a common religion (or lack of religion). He is a nice little man, and I like him, but I hope that the Labour Party generally know more of India.

Cripps also spoke of social legislation to counteract political agitation. He does at least realise the difficulties of the Indian problem.

July 9

Meeting with Amery and Mudaliar,[1] to hear M.'s views on constitutional progress:

M. said, in effect:

Gandhi and Congress will not retract August resolution,[2] though there is considerable revolt inside Congress against G.'s negative policy.

G. rejected the Cripps offer because he thought Japan would win, and his policy of non-violence was inconsistent with support of war.

Best possibilities for Government are to do something to remove sense of frustration of political India, and to encourage reaction against Gandhi.

No possibility during war of such Constitutional change as removing Viceroy's powers, as was suggested during Cripps' negotiations. It would hand over India to irresponsible oligarchy.

M. himself is convinced of H.M.G.'s intentions, but India still lacked confidence in them. We agreed that some preparatory work on designing a Constitution for India might be undertaken, and some body appointed to consider various forms of Federation (e.g. Swiss, U.S.A., Dominion). This body, which should be academic rather than political in composition, could define Pakistan and consider its effects on defence, finance, communications, etc.

M. then spoke of Indianisation of Council, i.e. present criticism that all key posts (Home, Finance, Communications) are held by British. He thought unnecessary to have Council completely Indian, provided principle established that keyposts could be held by Indians. He thought there was no difficulty about communal feeling if Indian appointed Home Member, and that Hindus would accept Moslem Home Member.

Lunched with Elibank, and then went to College of Arms about my title. I wanted to be 'Viscount Wavell of Winchester and the Middle East' but Garter King at Arms raised objections to both. I pointed out my family's long connection with Winchester and that I was being made a

[1] Sir A. Ramaswami Mudaliar, at this time Member for Supply, Governor-General's Executive Council
[2] The 'Quit India' resolution that led to the rebellion of 1942.

freeman of the city and he gave way on that, but after a long discussion I accepted Cyrenaica in place of Middle East. So I am going to be 'Viscount Wavell of Cyrenaica and of Winchester in the County of Southampton'.

July 14

Q.[1] arrived in England early morning with Felicity.[2]

July 15

Mass for Sikorski at Westminster Cathedral. $1\frac{1}{4}$ hours of usual R.C. flummery and ceremonial, (taking on and off a vast bishop's mitre, lighting and blowing out of candles, processions, genuflexions etc) not at all impressive or very well done, but Polish troops were good, steady, rigid, tough-looking. I would prefer not to be buried by any priest, even of my own religion (except for one or two like McKew or Thom) and would like to be put away as simply as possible and with no ceremony or mourning, nor in a cemetery, if there is an unhallowed hillside somewhere available. If the Abbey were ever suggested, I should like my ashes to be near Allenby's; but do not feel worthy of either Abbey or Allenby. However, I shan't really be interested in what happens to my vile corpse.

July 16

A man called Thompson came to see me. Author, professor of economics in Bengal for many years, historian, fellow of Oriel College, good soldier in last war with 7th Indian division, left-winger, friend of Nehru, well acquainted with Gandhi. Quite interesting, but little knowledge of political difficulties of government.[3]

July 21

Lunched at Buckingham Palace with King and Queen. No party, only Their Majesties and my wife and self, and no ceremony. H.M. complained about the length of the Viceroy's telegrams and hoped I would keep them shorter.

Joan and Simon[4] arrived this evening from India in quite good trim.

[1] Lady Wavell.

[2] Wavell's second daughter, now Lady Felicity Longmore.

[3] About a year later Edward Thompson sent some books to Lord Wavell with the request that he would pass them on to Nehru, who was then in gaol. Wavell, who as Commander-in-Chief had met Nehru once, forwarded them to him with a private letter, and having learnt from Thompson that poetry was one of Nehru's chief interests, he enclosed a copy of his own anthology, *Other Men's Flowers* (London, 1944).

[4] Wavell's third daughter, Joan, married Captain the Hon. S. N. Astley, 7th Hussars, in 1943.

July 22

Government lunch for me to meet some Americans. Anthony Eden took chair and proposed my health. I asked him the day before what he proposed to say and what he wanted me to say. He wrote in effect: *no politics*; talk about India's *past* war effort; be polite about American assistance; and pay compliment to Mudaliar. Then after lunch he got up and said 'F. M. Wavell will now talk to you about his future policy in India'! I protested loudly and spoke on his original lines. I have no intention of declaring a policy to anyone at present, and Eden must have known quite well that I couldn't. I might, for all he knew, have embarrassed the Government by setting out a policy quite at variance with their aims.

Court Circular announced that 'Viscount' Wavell had had audience with H.M., so began to use title instead of 'Sir Archibald'.

July 24

Lunched with Arthur Wauchope.[1] That curious person Hugh Dowding[2] was there. He has now taken up spiritualism and has written a book on it. Has no doubt about there being a future life, but seems to have no evidence that such a life is worth while, there is nothing in this life so incredibly dull as the glimpses of future life that spiritualists produce. Hugh Dowding said he was never really military in his outlook and that the only reason he went to Army Class at Winchester was to avoid being taught Greek— a curious confession for one who has acquired a peerage by military (air force) talent.

July 27

Cabinet at 6 p.m. on Lease-Lend problems mainly. It gave P.M. opportunity to hold forth for nearly an hour and a half with intervals on the scandal of the fact that we already owed India £800 million. He hates India and everything to do with it, and as Amery said in a note he pushed across to me 'knows as much of the Indian problem as George III did of the American colonies'. Winston drew harrowing picture of British workmen in rags struggling to pay rich Indian mill-owners; and wanted to charge India the equivalent of our debt to her for saving her from Japanese invasion. He was in his most intractable form. Amery stood up to him very well and pointed out how it stood from the Indian point of view.

[1] General Sir Arthur Wauchope, High Commissioner, Palestine, 1931–8. He was one of Wavell's closest friends. Wavell succeeded him as Colonel of the Black Watch.
[2] Air Chief Marshal Lord Dowding, who was head of Fighter Command during the Battle of Britain.

When Winston's fireworks were over, Cabinet quietly agreed to Chancellor's proposals about Lease-Lend. My only contribution to discussion was to point out that India had defended us in the Middle East in the first two years of the war rather than we defend India.

July 28

Took my seat in House of Lords. Trenchard and Lee of Fareham were my supporters. It all went off quite smoothly and was not really a very alarming ceremony.

Dined at Grays Inn with the legal profession. The Lord Chancellor [Simon] was there and Amery and Brendan Bracken, Lord Greenwood, Caldecote (Inskip that was). Winston came in a little late and was seated opposite me. He was in good form and held forth during and after dinner on a variety of subjects—post-war democracy, the Battle of Britain, expected surrender of Italy, financial settlement after last war, necessity for strong Poland. He is a good and interesting talker. He left early for a Cabinet meeting at 10.30 p.m., and unfortunately had a bright idea that I should attend it, so goodbye to a quiet evening talk with the Dills which I had arranged.

The Cabinet meeting lasted nearly $2\frac{1}{2}$ hours in a hot and stuffy room. It was after midnight before we got to the subject I was interested in, operations from India. Auchinleck had asked for more to take Akyab than I ever had and had put off date. The outlook for Eastern campaign is gloomy and it looks like rows ahead with America and China.

July 31, Bailiffscourt

Walked with Amery for $1\frac{1}{2}$ hours in morning. We talked of Indian affairs. Amery thought I should 'build up' prestige of present Viceroy's Council by good publicity; thought that Russian village system might be worth study as model for Indian local government; and said that a nucleus of the three Supreme Court judges (one of whom is Zafarullah[1] Khan) might be a suitable nucleus for a fact-finding body for Indian Constitution. He said Halifax and Eden both favoured Bajpai[2] being given diplomatic status as Indian representative in Washington, but Viceroy was opposed, so matter had been dropped.

[1] Sir Muhammad Zafrulla Khan, later Foreign Minister of Pakistan.
[2] Sir Girja Shankar Bajpai, I.C.S., Agent-General for India, Washington, 1941–7. After Independence he became Secretary-General, Ministry of External Affairs.

August 1

During another walk with Amery, we talked of Roman evacuation of
Britain—à propos of eventual British evacuation of India. This led to the
Arthurian legend, which Amery thought arose from some Romanised
mail-clad Britons holding the Saxon invaders at bay for a spell; and then
to the legend of Troy. We then went on to speak of our failure to mix
with the people of India; Amery thought that intermarriage might have
been no bad thing, and that the ban we put on the Indian Princes marrying
English women was wrong. I said that perhaps it was the marriage customs
of the Hindus and Moslems rather than the colour question that had
prevented intermarriage, and the difference of religion. Amery finished
up on the Lords debate on insemination. He has usually an interesting and
up-to-date point of view on any question, and is always well-informed.
He is certainly not the obstinate Tory die-hard that Indian, and some
British, papers and politicians are fond of depicting. He has usually very
liberal views about India.

August 4–17

I spent this fortnight in Scotland at St. Andrews and Dalmeny.

August 20

Woke up at about 3 a.m. with some ideas about possible procedure in
India and feeling wakeful wrote them out. Q. approved them next
morning but I doubt whether official opinion will or whether my ideas
are really practicable.

> *This original, if somewhat naïve note, which is given in full at Appendix I,*
> *was the genesis of the proposal, put forward in September to the Cabinet*
> *Committee on India, for forming a Coalition Government of Congress and*
> *Muslim League leaders. The note was addressed to Mr. E. M. (later Sir Evan)*
> *Jenkins, as Private Secretary to the Viceroy Designate (P.S.V.(D.)).*
> *Mr. Jenkins advised that the chances were five to one against the success of such*
> *a meeting of Indian political leaders as Lord Wavell had suggested, but was not*
> *opposed to attempting it.*
>
> *Sir Evan Jenkins was an outstanding member of the Indian Civil Service,*
> *who had been Chief Commissioner of Delhi, 1937–40, and Secretary, Depart-*
> *ment of Supply, 1940–3, before being selected to be Wavell's Private Secretary.*

Went to see Halifax, got nothing particularly fresh from him. He did
not find Gandhi a practical person to deal with when he was Viceroy and
thinks he is probably worse now but he said his experience was that he did

keep faith over frank conversations 'off the record'. He had no great opinion of Nehru. He said Bajpai was doing good work and approved the idea of his being made Indian Minister with U.S.A., to which Viceroy had objected.

August 23, 1943

Cabinet meeting with 2nd XI present, practically all 1st XI being still in Canada. Proposal to appoint Mountbatten to the S.E. Asia Command, with Stilwell as Deputy, and Giffard[1] as commander of Land Forces, was announced. There was some criticism but general feeling was that appointment should be accepted since Chiefs of Staff and Americans approve.

P.M. is still in Quebec. I hear that Wingate[2] has apparently 'sold himself' well there and his ideas are to have a good run. I expect P.M. will now claim him as his discovery and ignore the fact that I have twice used Wingate in this war for unorthodox campaigns and that but for me he would probably never have been heard of. I gather they are at last realising the difficulty of communications in Assam and Burma which I have been trying to impress on P.M. for nearly two years.

August 26

Amery came up from Bailiffscourt and I had half an hour with him. Viceroy is thinking of moving Jack Herbert[3] from Bengal, he has apparently had difficulties lately with his Ministry and the food problem etc. I suggested to Amery that if he did he should try to get Lumley[4] back to India to replace him. Mountbatten as Supreme Commander was Amery's own idea, it appears; I think it should be good, if he has a level-headed C.G.S. to check any wild ideas, I think a little boldness was badly needed in planning from India, I could never get James Somerville to back anything that wasn't 100% safe, and Richard Peirse and the Air always seemed to me to want a large safety margin. I pointed out many times that the Japanese would never have invaded Malaya or got anywhere if they had planned on our conservative lines.

August 31

Saw Louis Mountbatten and heard about Quebec Conference which seems to have gone quite well. I advised him to take an American as Chief

---

[1] General Sir George Giffard, who became Commander-in-Chief of 11th Army Group in South-East Asia.

[2] Brigadier (temporary Maj.-Gen.) Orde Wingate who commanded the 'Chindits'—the name given to troops flown into Burma to operate behind the Japanese lines.

[3] Sir John Herbert, Governor of Bengal, 1939–43.

[4] Sir Roger Lumley, later Earl of Scarbrough, Governor of Bombay, 1937–43.

Administrative Officer, in spite of anything the QMG might object; Wheeler[1] would do him quite well, and it will make it easier to get things from U.S.A.

September 1

Jack Herbert is ill, appendix and internal ulcer. Viceroy has decided in any event to replace him. Amery approached Lumley but he refused quite definitely to consider going out again. The P.M. being away, Amery spoke to Attlee about a successor and put forward some suggestions. Attlee said it must be a Labour man, as the other Governors were Conservatives. Absurd that Politics should enter into it at all, we want best possible man. Amery asked Attlee whom he proposed. A. said he would think it over.

September 6

Holiday now over and I have almost unending lunches, dinners, speeches, discussions and such like functions from now till I go out. I have done hardly anything of what I intended to do in August, I have not read the books, drafted the speeches, written the articles or thought out the plans that I purposed to do, I shall be driven as usual to improvise at short notice.

Amery told me Attlee had mentioned Jack Lawson[2] as possibility for Bengal. He was best of that Parliamentary Mission that went to China, but he is 62 and I wonder if he is good enough for Bengal, which seems to be in an awful mess. Nothing will be decided, I imagine, till P.M. comes back and that may not be for another fortnight.

September 8

Two strenuous days of functions.

Today, after several interviews at India Office, lunch with Thirty Club (Press Management), about 90 people, another speech. Amery there and spoke well about India's future. He has the qualities for success, perhaps in greater measure than Winston—ability, well-arranged and accurate knowledge, great courage, command of words. But he has an unimpressive personality, and is too much of a gentleman for the rough and tumble of high-power politics.

Found it impossible to buy a tooth-brush today, even from a very friendly chemist.

---

[1] Maj.-Gen. (U.S.) Raymond A. Wheeler was in charge of a large number of American maintenance services in India. Wavell's advice was taken and General Wheeler was a great success.   [2] J. J. Lawson, M.P., Secretary of State for War, 1945–6.

September 10

A pretty full day, starting with a visit to Letchworth to see Indian Bevin boys which entailed walking round machinery for a couple of hours and a short address to Indians. Then lunch in City to meet Lord Catto, formerly a Calcutta merchant, now financial adviser to the Treasury. He did not seem particularly alarmed by present rise of Indian sterling balance.

After lunch, meeting with S. of S., Munster,[1] Monteath,[2] & Co., about future policy in India. Amery prepared to talk for an hour or so on Indianisation of Council, powers of Federal Court, etc; and I rather threw a spanner into works by demanding first of all a clear-cut policy on constitutional progress; was I or was I not to make an effort to get political leaders into the Government? After 1½ hours talk general opinion seemed to be that it was rather tiresome of me to be so direct, but that perhaps we should make the effort, though it was most unlikely that the Indian leaders would accept. Jenkins, who supported me well, is to draft a paper for War Cabinet.

E. Grigg[3] then came to see me over my second volume of Allenby of which he has asked to see the proof. He was rather perturbed at criticism he thought it might cause in Conservative circles. I don't think I mind if it does, I am not very much in sympathy with the right-wing Conservative, and I doubt if Grigg is a very good judge of public opinion.

September 14

Discussion again on policy in India. Jenkins had drafted a very good memorandum for Cabinet Committee to consider. Amery obviously is rather for sitting tight and carrying on with present Executive Council, while making some academic exploration into possible future Constitutions. I am sure this will not resolve present deadlock. If the end of the war finds us with no further progress and another year or two of frustration in political India, we shall be in a poor position. We decided to put the amended draft up to a Cabinet Sub-Committee on Friday.

The draft memorandum was lengthy and underwent several revisions. In the form in which it reached the Cabinet Committee on India it recommended

    (i) *that H.M.G.'s immediate aim of policy in India should be the establishment of a Coalition Government of party leaders at the Centre, working under the existing Constitution and willing to support the war effort,*

[1] Earl of Munster, Parliamentary Under-Secretary of State for India, 1943–4.
[2] Sir David Monteath, Under-Secretary of State for India, 1941–7.
[3] Sir Edward Grigg, M.P. (later Lord Altringham).

(ii) *that the method of establishing such a Government should be by inviting selected political leaders to a meeting to discuss the matter,*

(iii) *that it should be left to the Viceroy's judgement to decide when to make a move and issue invitations.*

September 16

Lunch with the Pilgrims Society, a considerable ordeal. Nearly 300 present and most of them distinguished. I have no idea how my speech got across, I think the matter of it was reasonable and I did not forget my words, but I have a very great deal to learn about the technique of public speaking. I doubt whether I ever shall learn it.

September 20

On Friday 17th, I had the last of my Press lunches, with the Foreign Press representatives. I sat between a Russian and a Swede. I had got so bored with speeches that I prepared nothing and trusted to the inspiration of the moment. Actually the Chairman (Russian) gave me a handle by saying in his introductory speech that if the Indian political problem were solved, hundreds of thousands more Indians would join the Army. I confuted this nonsense and told them something of the Indian Army. Not a very effective address, but it appeared to interest them.

Then to a Cabinet sub-Committee on my paper about policy in India. Attlee presided and the others were Amery, Halifax, P. J. Grigg, Sir John Anderson and Simon. Amery and Halifax supported my proposals without much enthusiasm; P. J. Grigg[1] said that no progress was possible till Gandhi died; John Anderson[1] and Simon opposed. Nothing very conclusive came out of the discussion, which ended with an instruction to us to make some amendments to the note and re-submit it. What I want is some definite policy, and not to go on making promises to India with no really sincere intention of trying to fulfil them.

September 21

At a reception given by the East India Society, which was one of my engagements in much too full a day, Amery spoke and said that the sagacious elephant always tested the strength of a bridge before he crossed it. I said, when I spoke, that 'this sagacious elephant has first to find a bridge!'

[1] Sir James Grigg, Secretary of State for War, and Sir John Anderson, Lord President of the Council, were both originally Home Civil Servants with Treasury experience, but both had served in India, Grigg as Finance Member, Governor-General's Executive Council, 1934–9, and Anderson as Governor of Bengal, 1932–7.

September 23

Another long day. Motored down to Winchester for presentation of freedom—one speech at presentation of freedom, one at lunch. The first prepared, the second short and impromptu. Directly after lunch back to London in time for reception of Empire Societies.

September 24

India Office in morning till 12.30, then to Buckingham Palace to be sworn of the Privy Council, a slightly complicated ceremony but a silent one on the part of the P.C. Q. and I lunched with King and Queen; H.M. presented her with insignia of Crown of India and self with G.C.S.I. and G.C.I.E. and gave us their portraits. We lunched alone with King and Queen, nothing very much said. H.M. again referred to undue length of Viceroy's telegrams and told me to make them shorter.

After lunch went to Cabinet meeting on food for India in P.M.'s room at House of Commons. P.M. spoke scathingly of India's economic inefficiency which made it necessary to supply it with food which otherwise might not be needed. 100,000 tons of barley from Iraq had been arranged and 50,000 tons of wheat from Mediterranean, but more could not be provided without taking it from Egypt and Middle East where reserve was being accumulated for Greece and Balkans. Apparently it is more important to save the Greeks and liberated countries from starvation than the Indians and there is reluctance either to provide shipping or to reduce stocks in this country. I pointed out military considerations and that practically the whole of India outside the rural districts was more or less engaged on war effort, and that it was impossible to differentiate and feed only those actually fighting or making munitions or working some particular railways, as P.M. had suggested. I left Amery still battling for more wheat, and motored very fast down to Aldershot to inspect Canadian Black Watch—a fine looking lot. Tea with officers and then motored on to Winchester to stay night with H. T. Baker, the Warden.

September 25

Ad Portas ceremony, Latin speech by Prefect of Hall and my reply in Latin. Went to service in Winchester Cathedral for Land Girls in Hampshire, and read lesson. Motored on to Ringwood. So ends a pretty strenuous week.

September 27

Saw Amery in morning. Cabinet on Friday resulted in about 200,000 tons being allotted for India up to end of year, further supplies being left for consideration later. Amery thought we might get my paper on Indian policy through Cabinet to extent of getting permission to explore possibilities; he said Mountbatten had read and approved my paper.

September 29

Started at 10 a.m. with Cabinet Sub-Committee on Indian policy to reconsider my paper as amended. Attlee, Cripps, Amery, Simon, John Anderson, P. J. Grigg. Support for my proposals was very limited, otherwise attitude was negative or opposed. After a good deal of rather desultory discussion I read out my original sketch[1] for a conference of Indian leaders out of which the paper had developed. It was decided to submit proposal to Cabinet for instruction to Viceroy to 'explore avenues'. Rather a depressing experience. I do not believe these men face their fences honestly, they profess anxiety to give India self-government but will take no risk to make it possible.

> *The recommendations made in the paper for the Cabinet Committee on India (see p. 17) were transformed into a more vague recommendation. It was proposed that the Viceroy-Designate should be given general authority to study the possibility of attempting to break the present deadlock in some such way as he had suggested, and to approach the political leaders in India as and when he considered it desirable, but that he should consult the War Cabinet first.*

September 30

Another long day. Lord Lytton[2] spent half an hour telling me that from the point of view of the Governor of Bengal it was inconsiderate if the Viceroy always made his visit to Calcutta about Xmas time and stole the limelight from the Governor just at the time of all the big social events (he said Reading was very inconsiderate about this). I don't like limelight or Calcutta or big social events, as far as I am concerned the new Governor can have them. He then went on to expound at some length that it was a good thing for the Viceroy to see the Agents of the States and to hold conferences of the Governors and keep them in the picture. These are things I should have done in any case as far as practicable.

Then a deputation of three shipping magnates who explained to me the importance of British shipping and the necessity to see that no sort of discrimination was made in India against British shipping. I asked them whether if India should become a Dominion they agreed that she would

---

[1] Appendix I.   [2] Governor of Bengal, 1922–7.

have the right to regulate her coastal shipping as other Dominions such as Australia have. They agreed somewhat reluctantly. I fancy their idea of 'no discrimination' is really 'special privileges'.

Phillips[1] the American then came in, charming as ever. He says the President does not propose to send him back to India unless I say I want him. He was complimentary about my Pilgrim speech and said American opinion and the President are very anxious to see another attempt by us to solve the deadlock even if it fails. Mountbatten followed him. He and the Chiefs of Staff have been having, I gather, a very difficult time with the P.M. over plans for Eastern campaign, and the P.M. has been trying to play him off against Chiefs of Staff. He had seen my paper on Indian policy and supported it warmly. He was full of dynamic energy and optimism as usual. I fear he will find some shocks in India. He said P.M. had a blind spot about India, and was most unreasonable and 'riding for a fall' over it.

October 4

After two days shooting at Melton Constable—my last holiday—got back to London on Monday night.

Meeting of the Sub-Committee on India at 4.30 p.m. at which we got a submission to the Cabinet on policy passed in reasonable shape. I would have preferred something more definite but Amery thought we had done well. P. J. Grigg is at least honest and whole-hearted in his opposition. I wish I could think the others were as honest and wholehearted in support.

October 5

Gave Lady Oxford (Margot Asquith) tea at my Club. She is still very intense and intelligent. Her chief theme was what a poor Government Winston had got and how bad his Home policy was. I had only met her once before: she is still vital, at eighty odd, and nothing to spend her vitality on. Great, pathetic, restless: a woman who has played a great part and aspired to play a greater. Nothing short of being Queen Elizabeth would really have satisfied her, and God help her Essex. But I am glad to have met her. She said Winston always wrote his speeches and learnt them by heart; she used to hear him when he stayed with her husband, reciting them loudly in his bedroom at any hour; on the other hand she remembers as a girl Joe Chamberlain (whom she did not like) saying that he used to practise his speeches in front of a mirror but gave it up because he looked such a fool.

[1] William Phillips, American representative in India, 1942–3.

October 6

Government farewell dinner to me at Claridges. P.M. very angry about
the paper on Indian policy (I believe he almost refused to come to the
dinner) and told me he could not possibly accept it. He was, however, quite fairly pleasant at dinner and said nice things about me in
his speech. About India he eulogised what the British had done and
said he was unfashionable enough not to believe in the present policy.
My speech went down well with some, I think not well with the
Conservatives.

October 7

Paper on India seems to have caused some flutter. P.M., Lord Croft[1] and
P. J. Grigg have put in condemnatory notes, the supporters of the India
Sub-Committee are lukewarm and I shall obviously have a rough passage
in the Cabinet this afternoon. Talked to Amery about it, he will support me.

Cabinet at 6 p.m. on India, worse even than I had expected, not because
of opposition, but because of spinelessness, lack of interest, opportunism.
Amery did his best but talked too long and allowed himself to get tied up
on points of detail by P.M. P.M. managed the discussion well from his
point of view, as he drew each speaker away from principles onto matters
of detail and waved the bogey of Gandhi at everyone. Anderson and
Attlee gave rather lukewarm support. Grigg stood pat on his diehard
paper. Smuts and others spoke on the thesis 'Quieta non movere'. [I said
that to put the whole constitutional and political business into cold storage
so long as the war lasted, as recommended by Grigg, was a perfectly
logical and understandable policy with considerable short-term advantages:
but if we proposed to adopt it, I thought we should say so clearly and
definitely. I did not agree with this policy because I thought that it would
land us in considerable difficulties at the end of the war. I considered that
if it was possible to make political progress during the war, we should most
certainly make a sincere attempt to do so in spite of the difficulties. I said
that I had no intention to rush matters, but I did propose to examine
seriously whether any fresh effort to solve the political deadlock was
possible, and I only wanted Cabinet approval for me to judge whether and
when a fresh attempt could be made on the lines I proposed. Probably the
best opportunity would be some time early in 1944 while the effect of a

---

[1] Parliamentary Under-Secretary of State for War, 1940–5. Before being raised to the
peerage he was Brigadier-General Sir Henry Page-Croft, a well known 'die-hard' in the
inter-war period.

new Viceroyalty was still present.][1] Morrison and Bevin were frightened over the Gandhi bogey and talked vaguely of social progress and setting the poor against the rich. Eden also spoke as if I was proposing to enthrone Gandhi. Somewhere about here the P.M. worked himself up to a tirade against Congress and all its works and then digressed into the dangers of the Indian army becoming politically minded and anti-British. It ended with the P.M. promising to draft a directive for me to be discussed tomorrow. Something face-saving will be produced, designed to carry them on and get me out there, but with every intention of blocking any progress. The more I see of politicians, the less I respect them; or is Lady Oxford right in considering this a contemptible Cabinet?

October 8

Had short discussion with S. of S. on economic progress. Meanwhile Winston had cancelled 3 p.m. Cabinet on India and proposed to see me alone at 3 p.m.: he had produced a formula for a directive which was mostly meaningless, e.g. it exhorted me to get on with the war, to improve the lot of the Indian, to make peace between Moslem and Hindu, and indicated right at the end that political progress during the war was not barred. Amery on reading it said: 'you are wafted to India on a wave of hot air'. P.M. was menacing and unpleasant when I saw him at 3 p.m., accused me practically of playing to the gallery, misrepresented what I had proposed, and indicated that only over his dead body would any approach to Gandhi take place. I resented this and I am afraid rather replied in kind. I think what it really amounts to is that he fears a split in the Conservative Party and trouble in Parliament over any fresh political advance in India, so is determined to block it as long as he is in power. In the end we parted on an outwardly friendly note, but he has always really disliked me and mistrusted me, and probably now regrets having appointed me. He will do his best to discredit me when I have gone. He told me Simon had come to him after the last Cabinet and entirely withdrawn his support for my proposals; I just held my tongue and refrained from saying 'So I should have expected'. I never counted Simon a supporter, he is a man of straw, of legal ability but no character. On the whole I am sure I was right to raise the issue. I have discovered that the Cabinet is not honest in its expressed desire to make progress in India; and that very few of them have any foresight or political courage. I put down Cranborne as the best, courageous, and sensible but he lacks ambition and drive, I think.

[1] The portion within square brackets is taken from a separate note that Wavell recorded of this Cabinet meeting and is not part of the Journal.

When I went to say goodbye to the girls who had done all my typing work at the India Office, one of them said: 'Do you mind if we girls give you a piece of advice? Trust your own judgement and don't worry too much about Whitehall'.

October 12 (in plane between Gibraltar and Cairo).
On Sunday evening (10th) there was a phone call from 10 Downing Street to ask me to go and see Smuts on Monday. I had an hour with him, he had come up from Chequers, and had, as I had expected, been turned on by the P.M. to reinforce his views about India and to counter mine. He repeated, very pleasantly, what the P.M. had said to me rather unpleasantly on Friday. I exposed my point of view about looking ahead to the end of the war; and reminded Smuts that he should surely be the man to see the virtue of a generous settlement, such as was made after the South African war, if possible; and spoke of what had happened in Egypt at the end of the last war and Allenby's solution. I told him he could assure the P.M. that I was not going to act hastily or start negotiations with Gandhi as soon as I arrived. I think Smuts was speaking on a brief from the P.M. rather than from his own convictions. He came out at the end with what is really the truth, that the P.M. is not thinking beyond the end of the war—about India, or I believe anything else—and is alarmed lest, by raising the Indian issue I should split the Conservative Party and Parliament and cause him trouble. He is a great war leader, but otherwise thinks in terms of politics not statesmanship. Here is the main problem, to try to do my best for a future settlement of India without embarrassing our war leader in the present.

Looking back on the 3 or 4 months since I was appointed Viceroy, during which I have been through a fairly testing time for one quite unused to public or political life, I think I have come out of it fairly well, though I have made mistakes and might have used my time better. I think I spent too much time on detail, on seeing comparatively unimportant people and on social engagements and left myself too little time for constructive thinking. However, people like seeing one and being seen, and like having their letters answered, and I like seeing fresh people. And I am lazy mentally and don't care about thinking until I have to. I don't flatter myself that my speeches were impressive, I know they weren't, but I hope they left some impression of a reasonably clear and honest mind. I remember two comments on them which I got second-hand: an American after an address I made in Washington on operations against Japanese and the Indian army, remarked: 'The British always *will* tell the truth'—and

Bill Astor said of my talk to some M.P.s 'We hear quite enough people in Parliament who can speak, and it is refreshing to hear someone who has no pretence to be an orator'.

I ought to have raised the issue of policy in India rather earlier, I think, and perhaps been less provocative about it; but one has to deal with matters fairly forcibly with the P.M. or one simply gets browbeaten. I am sure the decision to raise the issue was the right one.

We had quite a party to see us off in the afternoon: H.M. and P.M. represented; of Government: Amery, John Anderson, Cripps, Simon, Cranborne (all with wives), Devonshire, Selborne, Leathers, Croft, Munster, Creedy, the Ranganadhans and others.

Lord Wavell was accompanied by Lady Wavell, Felicity Wavell (his second daughter) and the following members of his personal staff:

Sir Evan Jenkins	*Private Secretary*
Major Peter Coats ('Peter')	*Comptroller*
Captain the Earl of Euston ⎫	*A.D.C.s*
Captain the Hon. Simon Astley ⎭	

Other members of his personal staff who joined him in India when he assumed office were:

Mr. G. E. B. (later Sir George) Abell ('George')	*Deputy Private Secretary*
Lt.-Col. A. F. W. Humphrys, ('Francis', married to Lord Wavell's eldest daughter, Pamela)	*Military Secretary*
Captain W. Henderson ⎫	
Captain G. Crookshank ⎬	*A.D.C.s*
Captain B. Fortune ⎭	

Randolph Churchill was at Gibraltar on way home after being with Commando at Salerno. I always find him pleasant and intelligent to talk with and do not see the unpleasant traits he is credited with by most people. He said I went to India with one great advantage over the last few Viceroys: they had to decide whether and when to lock up Gandhi, I should find him already locked up.

Cairo, October 15

Landed in Cairo about 3 a.m. on October 13. Stopped with Jumbo Wilson[1] at Maadi. Found Antony Eden and Pug Ismay on their way to Moscow, neither looking forward to it especially. Saw Indian troops at

---

[1] Field-Marshal Lord Wilson of Libya, at this time Commander-in-Chief, Middle East.

Mena one morning. They all seem in good heart and were pleased at my visiting them. Cairo has not altered much. Nor has Jumbo, he is imperturbable as ever.

Talked with Casey,[1] Minister of State, about food situation in Middle East, since it concerns India. Casey pessimistic about general world food situation, says Australia has had very bad harvest and has little surplus, Canada can do no more than supply U.S.A. and G.B. deficiencies, and that Argentine burnt her surplus of 2,000,000 tons of wheat as fuel on railways since she could not get coal, of which there also seems to be a world shortage.

[1] R. G. Casey, later Lord Casey, an Australian, was Minister of State in the Middle East and Member of the War Cabinet, 1942–3, Governor of Bengal, 1944–6, and Governor-General of Australia, 1965–9.

2
FIRST MONTHS AS VICEROY

Except for one short break early in 1942 when he was Supreme Allied Commander in South-East Asia, Lord Wavell as Commander-in-Chief, India, had been a Member of the Viceroy's Executive Council since July 1941 and so was fully conversant with the current Indian situation. He had been in Delhi in March 1942 when Sir Stafford Cripps flew out to India with an offer of complete independence at the end of the war under a constitution of India's own making. The Congress had rejected this offer mainly because, with the Japanese threatening invasion, the whole outlook seemed uncertain and because the British were unwilling to make any immediate constitutional changes, but also partly because the offer gave individual Provinces the right to stand out of the projected Indian Union and to frame constitutions for themselves. This was a concession to Muslim opinion, but the Muslim League also rejected the offer on the ground that the demand for Pakistan had not been fully conceded.

Following their rejection of the Cripps offer the Congress had launched in August 1942 the 'Quit India' rebellion, thereby seriously disrupting Wavell's plans for the defence of India against Japanese attack. In consequence of this rebellion all the Congress leaders had been put in gaol and so when Wavell became Viceroy, Gandhi, as Randolph Churchill remarked, presented for the moment no problem, since he was already locked up. There was a lull in political agitation and most of the country was happily engaged in making money out of the war, final victory in which seemed by this time to be assured.

The temporary eclipse of Congress had left the political field open to Jinnah and the Muslim League and they made good use of this opportunity to vilify and discredit Congress and to rally all Muslims to the League's support. Jinnah represented the 'Quit India' rebellion as an insidious plot to coerce the British to surrender India to Congress, quite regardless of Muslim interests; and he claimed that the League was the Muslims' sole defence against Congress, i.e. Hindu, domination in the future.

Jinnah and his principal henchmen in the League pointedly refrained from any active assistance of the war effort, but, unlike the Congress leaders, they did not positively obstruct; and Jinnah permitted the Muslim League and Muslim League Coalition Ministries, which now, thanks partly to the absence of Congressmen in gaol, existed in five out of the eleven Provinces, to co-operate fully in all measures required for winning the war.

The Provinces of India had been granted by the Government of India Act of 1935 what was virtually parliamentary self-government. Ministers responsible to the Provincial legislatures in accordance with the British parliamentary system were to form the governments of these Provinces. The Governors were to be in the main 'constitutional' Governors, accepting the advice of their Ministers, however unpalatable it might be to them. But for certain specific purposes, e.g. to prevent any grave menace to the peace of the Province, to protect the legitimate interests of minorities, and to safeguard the statutory rights of civil servants, the Governors were empowered, if they thought necessary, to set aside the advice of their Ministers and act in accordance with their individual judgement. They were also authorized in the event of failure of constitutional machinery to assume to themselves all the powers of the Provincial Government. The Section of the Act which gave them this authority was Section 93, and it is frequently referred to in the Journal. Its first clause ran as follows:

'If at any time the Governor of a Province is satisfied that a situation has arisen in which the government of the Province cannot be carried on in accordance with the provisions of this Act, he may by Proclamation (a) declare that his functions shall, to such extent as may be specified in the Proclamation, be exercised by him in his discretion, (b) assume to himself all or any of the powers vested in or exercisable by any Provincial body or authority.'

The need to invoke Section 93 had arisen shortly after the outbreak of World War II when the Congress Ministries holding office in seven[1] of the eleven Provinces resigned and no other Ministries could be formed which would command majorities in the legislatures. In these Section 93 Provinces, as they were called, the Governors carried on the government with the aid of official I.C.S. Advisers and constitutional government remained in abeyance. However in one of the Congress Provinces, Orissa, seven Congress members of the Assembly changed their allegiance in 1941 and joined the anti-Congress group in forming a Coalition Ministry; and in May 1943 it proved possible to form a Muslim League Ministry in the N.W.F.P. So when Wavell became Viceroy, Ministries responsible to the legislatures were in office in six Provinces, viz. Bengal, Punjab, Sind, Assam, Orissa and N.W.F.P., while in the remaining five Provinces the Governors were in full control under Section 93.

The names of the Governors in October 1943 and also of the Premiers in Provinces in which Ministries were functioning are given below.

	Governor	Premier
Bengal	Sir Thomas Rutherford, I.C.S. (acting)	Sir Nazimuddin (Muslim League)
Punjab	Sir Bertrand Glancy, I.C.S.	Sir Khizar Hyat Tiwana (Unionist–Muslim League)

---

[1] A Congress Coalition Ministry in an eighth Province, Assam, also resigned, but it proved possible to form another Ministry under a Muslim Premier.

	Governor	Premier
Sind	Sir Hugh Dow, I.C.S.	Sir Ghulam Hussain Hidayatullah (Muslim League)
Assam	Sir Andrew Clow, I.C.S.	Sir Muhammad Saadullah (Muslim League)
Orissa	Sir Hawthorne Lewis, I.C.S.	Maharaja of Parlakimedi (anti-Congress)
N.W.F.P.	Sir George Cunningham, I.C.S.	Sardar Aurangzeb Khan (Muslim League)
Bombay	Sir John Colville	Section 93
Madras	Sir Arthur Hope	,,
United Provinces	Sir Maurice Hallett, I.C.S.	,,
Bihar	Sir Frank Mudie, I.C.S. (acting)	,,
Central Provinces	Sir Henry Twynam, I.C.S.	,,

When the 1935 Act was drawn up, it was hoped that the Provinces and Princely States of India would be brought together in a Federation; but owing to the hesitations of the Princes it had proved impossible to inaugurate the Federation and bring into operation the federal part of the Act by the outbreak of war, and thereafter efforts to do so were suspended. Consequently the Central Government and Central Legislature of British India, constituted in accordance with the provisions of an earlier Act of 1919, continued substantially unchanged. The Governor-General (Viceroy) and the members of his Council were the Executive Government. The Governor-General had power to override his Council, but in practice this power remained in the background and the Council functioned much like a Cabinet. If there was a difference of opinion, the opinion of the majority prevailed.

The Council was not responsible to the Legislature. Though not un-influenced by its views, it was not dependent on it, and any Bill which the Governor-General considered essential in the interests of India and which the Legislature rejected, could be 'certified' by him and ipso facto became law. The annual finance bill had frequently to be passed by certification.

The Legislature consisted of two chambers, the Legislative Assembly and the Council of State, in both of which elected members predominated; and so the Governor-General and his Council, despite the presence of a number of official and nominated non-official members, could not always count on a majority in the Legislature; but they endeavoured so far as possible to avoid defeat.

From 1921 until 1939 the Governor-General's Executive Council was generally composed of seven members in addition to himself, four of them

British, including the Commander-in-Chief, and three of them Indian. No immediate change was made on the outbreak of war, but in 1941 and again in 1942 the Council was enlarged by the appointment of additional Indian members, and when Wavell took office it consisted of fourteen members, of whom ten were Indian and four British. The Indians were all non-officials. Many of them had previously been Ministers in Provincial Governments and some of them were prominent politicians—one of them had been Congress Premier of the Central Provinces—but not one of them was at this date representative of either of the two major political parties, the Congress and the Muslim League. Of the four British members one was the Commander-in-Chief, General Auchinleck, two were I.C.S. officials, and the fourth, Sir Edward Benthall, a businessman. The Members of the Executive Council are constantly referred to by name in the Journal. Those holding office in October 1943 are listed below.

Members of the Governor-General's Executive Council

General (later Field Marshal) Sir Claude Auchinleck, Commander-in-Chief
Sir Reginald Maxwell, I.C.S., Home Member
Sir Jeremy Raisman, I.C.S., Finance Member
Sir Ramaswamy Mudaliar, Member for Industry and Civil Supplies
Sir Sultan Ahmed, Member for Information and Broadcasting
Sir Firoz Khan Noon, Defence Member
Sir Edward Benthall, Member for War Transport
Sir Muhammad Usman, Member for Posts and Air
Dr. B. R. Ambedkar (representing the Depressed Classes), Member for Labour
Sir J. P. Srivastava, Member for Food
Sir Jogendra Singh, Member for Education, Health, and Lands
Sir Aziz-ul-Haque, Member for Commerce
Dr. N. B. Khare (at one time Congress Premier of the Central Provinces),
　　Member for Commonwealth Relations
Sir Asoka Roy, Law Member

At the time of Lord Wavell's Viceroyalty the population of India was just over 400 million and was rising at the rate of 4–5 million a year. Nearly 100 million were Muslims; almost all the rest were Hindus. The Sikhs, in origin a reformist sect of Hindus, numbered about 6 million and were mainly concentrated in the Punjab.

More than a fifth of the population were inhabitants of the Princely States which, over 500 in number and scattered over the country, covered two-fifths of the total area. The great majority of these were little more than petty estates; only about 15 of them were of significant area and population, but the largest, Hyderabad, was about the size of Italy with a population of 16 million.

About 80 per cent of India's population lived in villages and were dependent, directly or indirectly, on agriculture. Most of them were entirely illiterate, extremely poor, and comparatively uninterested in politics. The total annual revenues of British India were equivalent to less than ten shillings per head of population and of this only about tenpence were spent on health and education.

The British had never supplied more than a small fraction of the officials required for the administration of this huge country. The overwhelming majority of them had always been Indians, and after World War I Indians had been freely admitted to the highest ranks of the services. In Wavell's time there was only a tiny handful of British officials serving in India—about 500 in the Indian Civil Service, about 200 in the Indian Police, and much smaller numbers in Medical, Engineering, Forest, and other Services. The British were wholly dependent on Indian co-operation for the Government of the country.

The immediate problem that faced Lord Wavell and his Council when he took office was economic. Though the war was bringing prosperity to the peasantry, large profits to traders and businessmen, and fuller employment to all classes, there was a famine in Bengal. For some years before the outbreak of war India had ceased to be self-sufficient in foodgrains, a small exportable surplus of wheat being more than offset by imports of rice, mainly from Burma. The annual overall deficit, quite small in relation to total consumption, averaged rather over one million tons. Some regions of the country, for instance the Punjab and Sind, had considerable surpluses, others were more or less self-sufficient, while others, notably Bombay, Madras, the States of Travancore and Cochin, and Bengal, were deficit.

With the occupation of Burma by the Japanese imports of rice from that country were cut off, nor could they readily be made good from elsewhere as the Japanese now controlled all the rice-growing areas of South-East Asia. This was the basic cause of the Bengal famine. The overall shortage was relatively so small that it should have been possible to avoid actual starvation in any area. But a number of factors combined to aggravate the shortage. Owing to full employment and war-time prosperity large classes of the population somewhat increased their consumption of foodgrains; to extend rationing to the whole rural population was impracticable, it had to be more or less confined to urban areas; surplus Provinces were reluctant to submit to any rationing at all for the benefit of deficit areas or to release their surpluses except at high prices; procurement by Government of the surplus grains of innumerable small cultivators was not easy to organize; and lack of confidence and greed led to hoarding. In spite of these difficulties all the deficit Provinces and States, except Bengal, were able by administrative action to avert disaster, though there was a good deal of distress. In Bengal an inefficient and probably corrupt Muslim League Ministry and an administration that, compared with that of other Provinces, was for a variety of reasons rather weak, failed to grapple with the problem. There was a delay in introducing rationing in Calcutta and in arranging for the movement of supplies to deficit rural areas. Large numbers of *destitutes, mainly old men, women, and children, drifted from the villages into Calcutta, where there was inadequate provision for giving them food and shelter, and they began to die like flies from starvation and disease.*

Wavell realized at once that the most energetic action was required to retrieve the situation. Within six days of assuming office he personally visited Bengal and induced the Ministry to agree to move the destitutes out of Calcutta into camps, to accept assistance from the Army for the movement of foodgrains to deficit rural areas, and to bring into operation a rationing scheme for Calcutta. His prompt personal intervention made a great impression at the time and undoubtedly mitigated the disaster; and thereafter his dogged persistence in extracting foodgrains from an indifferent British Government, though less widely known, was largely responsible for preventing its repetition. More than a million people are believed to have died in this Bengal famine. Wavell was determined that it should not happen again. As the Journal reveals, the threat of a shortage was a constant anxiety throughout his term as Viceroy.

Another step that he took within six days of assuming office was to call a conference of Governors, mainly to discuss the food problem and post-war reconstruction. Such a conference had not been held for many years, partly because, after the introduction of Provincial self-government in 1937, it was thought that a gathering of 'constitutional' Governors might attract criticism. But with nearly half the Provinces under Section 93 regimes this objection had less force. All the Governors welcomed the conference.

The Journal contains occasional references to Wavell's personal staff. A list of the more important of them at the time that he assumed office has been given on p. 25.

October 19. Viceroy's House, New Delhi

Arrived at Karachi on Sunday evening, October 17. From now on, red carpet and ceremonial till I leave India again, I suppose.

Lunched at Jodhpur on way to Delhi yesterday. The Maharaja is a nice little man but has little to say for himself. Comparatively quiet arrival at Delhi, but two guards of honour—one at airfield, one at Viceroy's House. Q. and I dined alone with Viceroy and Lady Linlithgow, and after dinner I talked with him until 1 a.m. Following are main points of our conversation so far as I remember them:

Linlithgow does not like Winston but agreed that he was a magnificent war leader, and that our strategy had been good.

He was pleased at having recently had arrested one of the principal Congress agitators still at large, Jai Prakesh Narain.[1]

---

[1] A Congress leader from Bihar of extreme views and at this date addicted to violence. He had a considerable following. After Independence he became a sincere believer in Gandhi's creed of non-violence.

He spoke at length of the possibilities of the political situation, at my request. He showed me Gandhi's final letter to him and his reply. He does not believe any real progress is possible while G. lives, and believes we shall have to continue responsibility for India for at least another 30 years. We could not for the peace of the world allow chaos in India. He referred me to his talk with G. and Jinnah in August 1940 when he tried to induce them to join a National Government. He said the fundamental difficulty was that they all regarded representation in such a Government as pre-judging the final constitutional settlement, and therefore would not play except each on their own terms which were irreconcilable. He said the problem of removing British control from India was that of getting a three legged stool (Hindu, Moslem, British) to remain stable with one leg removed. He doubted whether it was advisable to make another effort till Burma had been reconquered, because of the danger of arousing communal dissension which might affect the Indian Army.

He said we must be careful that we did not get into a position when we could not get out of India because of the chaos it would cause but were unable to control and administer it if we remained. It was essential to maintain the morale of the I.C.S. and Police, whose financial future should be guaranteed whatever happened. He thought it might be possible to make a fresh appeal in say 6 months time before the influence of the new Viceroyalty was lost, but it would require very careful consideration and would not be likely to succeed. The chief factors of the problem of Indian political progress were the stupidity of the Indian and the dishonesty of the British; we should not be able to get away with it much longer.

He told me that before the Cripps proposals were made, the British Government suggested that the National Defence Council[1] should become the Constitution-making body and should also assist to run the war. Linlithgow said he would resign rather than accept this, and the Cripps proposals followed. He said that Cripps did not play straight over the question of the Viceroy's veto and Cabinet responsibility and did make some offer to Congress through the American Louis Johnson.[2] He said Cripps was crooked when up against it.

Linlithgow's view of Amery was the same as mine, he admired his qualities but said he was quite unable to get his stuff across in Cabinet, or I think in Parliament.

[1] The National Defence Council (N.D.C.) was formed in October 1941 as a consultative body on defence, and consisted of thirty persons, nominated by the Viceroy, representative of both British India and the States.

[2] Colonel Louis Johnson, President Roosevelt's personal representative in India at the time of the Cripps Mission.

On military situation he thought Mountbatten ('the Boy Champion' he called him) would have some rude shocks to his optimism. Linlithgow does not believe the Chinese mean to fight seriously. Nor do I.

Of the food problem Linlithgow says chief factor morale. In July he expected that deaths in Bengal might be up to 1,000,000 or $1\frac{1}{2}$ million, and that we looked like getting off better than he had thought possible.

He advised against further Indianisation of the Council, and agreed that Maxwell's[1] health would not stand an extension, and thought that Twynam[2] should be appointed. He said Mudaliar was not running straight, which is disappointing, I had hoped he could be trusted.

Other matters Linlithgow spoke of were Gandhi's fast and how glucose was administered as soon as it was obvious that Linlithgow meant to stand firm; and the election of a new Chancellor of the Chamber of Princes. Linlithgow thought Bhopal was likely to be elected, and acknowledged his ability, but said he was sometimes like a mischievous boy with a catapult.

Linlithgow said he proposed to stand outside politics for a time when he got home and try to educate opinion on the Indian question.

I have the greatest admiration for Linlithgow, he is a wise strong man and very human really. I wish we had had several days together and that I had been better prepared for this talk. It is an unsatisfactory take-over, this one talk late at night. However, one can only really take over a job by doing it. I can't say that L.'s exposition of the situation was encouraging: after $7\frac{1}{2}$ years experience his opinion of Indian efficiency and reasonableness is certainly not high.

October 20

Sworn in as Viceroy. Ceremony went off all right.

October 21

Saw Hutchings[3] about food, he is a good man, sensible and resolute and should help to produce a solution if anyone can. He says Srivastava[4] is doing quite well.

Raisman[5] next, he is good and sound. Anxious to know about his

---

[1] Sir Reginald Maxwell, I.C.S., Home Member, Governor-General's Executive Council, 1938–44.
[2] Sir Henry Twynam, I.C.S., Governor of the Central Provinces, 1940–6.
[3] Sir Robert Hutchings, I.C.S., Secretary to Government of India Food Dept., 1943–6.
[4] Sir J. P. Srivastava, Member for Food, Governor-General's Executive Council.
[5] Sir Jeremy Raisman, I.C.S., Finance Member, Governor-General's Executive Council, 1939–45. Later Chairman of Lloyds Bank.

future, whether he is likely to be extended and wants several months leave home if he is.

Wylie[1] talked about the main problems of the Princes. He agrees with me that the Princes cannot resist reform pressure if we are firm; their only card is that the faith of the British Crown is involved in honouring their treaties.

October 22

Masses of paper and interviews all day. Saw Somervell, head of Supply Branch U.S. Army, about the war in S.W. Pacific and the problem of developing the capacity of the Assam railways to take increased American aid to China and to support large scale operations into Burma, which the Americans claim can be done if U.S.A. take over railway and eliminate Indian inefficiency.

I talked to Maxwell, Home Member, about the political situation. He agrees we should make progress if possible and hopes there may be a break away from Gandhi's leadership. I doubt if this is probable.

October 29

Returned from 3 days at Calcutta, in the course of which I saw all the Ministers, a number of officials and non-officials; went round the streets of Calcutta by night to see how the destitutes were sleeping and by day to see them being fed; and spent one day in the Contai district of Midnapore, which is supposed to be one of the areas worst affected by the famine. I found things on the whole much as I had expected from what I had read and heard—widespread distress and suffering, not as gruesome as the Congress papers would make out, but grim enough to make official complacency surprising; I don't think anyone really knows the whole situation or what is going on in some of the outlying areas, but obviously we have got to get to immediate grips or it may get out of hand altogether. I saw all the Ministers yesterday evening, told them they must get the destitutes out of Calcutta into camps, which should have been done long ago, got them to accept a Major-General and staff to help with the transport of supplies and the assistance of the Army generally. I also urged them to get on with their rationing schemes, and put before them the proposal to take Calcutta out of the Bengal food problem and feed it from outside. This last proposal seemed to meet with some doubts, but

[1] Sir Francis Wylie, I.C.S., Governor of the Central Provinces, 1938–40, Political Adviser to the Crown Representative, 1940–5, Governor of the United Provinces, 1945–7.

I am advised it is the only possible solution that will restore confidence in
the rural areas and bring prices down.

Three pretty hectic and distressing days. I wonder if my intervention
will do any good. The Ministry is obviously a very weak one, and the
acting Governor (Rutherford) rather disappointed me—no fire in him.

November 3

Three days with National Defence Council just finished. They went off
all right.

Hance, the Director General, Indian Medical Service, came to see me
on Nov. 1. I asked him about the drug position in Bengal; he said with
an air of conscious rectitude: 'I am going down there on Nov. 8 to see for
myself'. I said 'and why not on Nov. 2 or Nov. 3?' he was somewhat
taken aback and said 'But I have to go to Simla for a meeting of the
Sanatorium Committee'. At that I gave him to understand in very clear
terms that sanatoriums at Simla could wait but the Bengal famine would
not. He would go to the A.O.C. in C. at once, I told him and get the first
possible plane to Calcutta.

November 7

A heavy routine week last week, with nothing very special. This afternoon
Mayne, G.O.C.-in-C. Eastern Command, was brought to me by C-in-C
about situation in Bengal. Army has got down to it well and has already
increased outflow of foodgrains from Calcutta to rural districts from 900
to 2,000 tons p.d. But Mayne was very depressing about the medical
situation, and says cholera epidemic is most serious. Hance, D.G.I.M.S.,
whom I sent down there 4 or 5 days ago, has apparently done a very good
job of work, but has found a very great deal to be done, as I suspected.
Mayne also said that pilfering and misappropriation of foodstuffs on way
to population in need is very widespread, and Courts are inflicting only
trifling fines on offenders.

November 10

Ordinary routine business for last 2 or 3 days, except for an emergency
meeting of Council on November 8 over a resolution in the Assembly
asking for an Enquiry or Royal Commission on the Food question, in
which it looked as if we should have the whole Assembly against us if we
opposed. I was quite clear that it would be disastrous to have any Enquiry
now, and that we should hang an awkward millstone round our neck (and
embarrass H.M.G. probably) if we gave any undertaking for an enquiry

in future. I had no difficulty with Council over the question of an immediate enquiry—except Firoz Khan Noon who delivered one of the outbursts without thinking which he sometimes gives tongue to—but the majority, including Auchinleck and Benthall, were for some sort of pledge on a future enquiry. We agreed that Food Member should accept an Enquiry in principle but refuse to commit Government on form, date or scope. Next day the difficulty was postponed temporarily by the motion being dropped on consideration of an extra day for food debate. But the demand for an Enquiry will certainly be made in the debate.

November 14

Plenty of work but nothing in particular last week. But on Saturday evening Mountbatten came to tell me about proposed meeting of the Four Great Ones in Cairo. He then spoke of the future plans of S.E.A. Command, and indicated, as politely as he could, that the general attitude of the Indian Government was obstructive, and that India would really have no difficulty in fulfilling all his fresh demands if she took a more realistic attitude to the war. I did something to try and disabuse him of this idea, and to point out some of India's economic difficulties. He mentioned a requirement of eleven large new airfields in the Calcutta area which the Americans had put forward. He asked me for help over a large increase of supply dropping parachutes to be manufactured in India.

November 17

M.B. came again on 15th to tell me about the Cairo meeting (Sextant) and that Chiang Kai-Shek and Madame proposed to pass through India under American auspices without a word to me or the Government of India, stopping a night at Agra. It seems to me the height of international bad manners on the part of both Americans and Chinese, but since H.M.G. has not seen fit to inform me that a conference is taking place at all, on matters which vitally concern India, I can hardly complain. M.B. also mentioned intelligence pointing to the possibility of a Japanese sea-borne raid on India. We also spoke of the parachute demand; he still seems to think that to double the demand (from 100,000 to 200,000 [per month], the original demand having been 35,000) is a mere trifle for India; as it only meant giving up 2% of total cloth: I pointed out that 2% of India's population was 8,000,000 which was quite a large number to go short of clothes.

Wingate left today after convalescing here for a week. He a little reminds me of T. E. Lawrence but lacks his sense of humour and wide knowledge, is more limited but with greater driving power.

November 18, 1943 (This would have been my father's 100th birthday). Having had an almost continuous series of interviews with Members and their Secretaries, I think I have now heard most of their pet schemes, some very interesting, some practical, some unpractical.

November 21

Finished yesterday a two-day conference with the eleven Governors. I think it was valuable and that they enjoyed it (no conference of Governors had been held since 1930), and it gave me a good chance to size up my Governors.

Arthur Hope (Madras) I found surprisingly good, but I suppose Madras is comparatively easy. Colville (Bombay) is attractive and sensible but knows little of India yet; he should be very good. I was confirmed in my view that Rutherford (acting for Bengal), a good enough administrator in normal times, is no use now for rough stuff. Maurice Hallett (U.P.) is thoroughly sound, wise and courageous; but conservative and perhaps a bit disillusioned. Glancy (Punjab) knows his job but lacks drive. I have not quite sized up Twynam (C.P.) of whom I had been given so high a character, he is certainly able. Mudie (acting for Bihar) is quiet and sensible. George Cunningham (N.W.F.P.) very good where he is and entirely reliable. Lewis (Orissa) willing but not first-class. Dow (Sind) knows his provinces to the finger-tips and has it well in hand; he made more telling and pertinent observations than any of the others, but was provocative at times. Clow (Assam) reminds me of the remark of a very celebrated golfer on one of his weaker professional brethren: 'a nice little golfer, Sir, a nice little golfer—you know what I mean'.

We had a whole day on the Food problem, and half a day on Post-War reconstruction. At the end I gave them my general mind on the political situation, and they gave me theirs. Nothing very constructive or encouraging emerged. They were all for periodical conferences of Governors, and I am sure the meeting has done good.

I got Pandit Kunzru[1] to come and see me since he had been touring Bengal and expressing himself strongly on the famine. He used to be on my Defence Committee when I was C-in-C, and I have always liked the little man; though he is an uncompromising critic and opponent of Government, he is earnest and sincere. He was obviously very upset at the conditions in Bengal, and also at the lack of civic spirit of his countrymen in Bengal and the inefficiency of the Bengal Government, who are still more

[1] Pandit H. N. Kunzru, a highly respected moderate Nationalist politician.

concerned in their political rivalries than with the famine (I really believe there is more anxiety and sympathy about the Bengal famine in England than anywhere in India).

November 23–30

Visit to Punjab and N.W.F.P. My main object in Punjab was to get Ministers to agree to statutory price control of food and rationing. They liked neither, and had committed themselves to their Assembly not to accept them. I made clear the necessity for both, and that I was determined to enforce them, and in the end I think the price was the only real difficulty. I left a price of Rs. 9.4 as maximum for next rabi crop for them to consider. I think Hutchings, the Food Secretary, had rather queered the pitch by giving the Chief Minister the idea that he would accept the current price (about 10.8) as the maximum (when I got back to Delhi the Food Member, Srivastava, indicated politely that he thought Rs. 9.4 was much too high and that he hoped to get prices down to 7–8). I doubt if any of these 'experts'—Srivastava, Gregory,[1] Raisman or Hutchings—really know how prices will go, or whether statutory price control will work. I liked Khizar,[2] the Punjab Chief Minister, attractive, straight and courageous, I should say. Rest of the Ministry of no great account, but Chhotu Ram[3] is quite a personality though not very wise, I suspect.

I enjoyed visit to N.W.F.P., I have always liked Peshawar since I was stationed there nearly 40 years ago. All they want at present is a really stout Governor, which they have got at present. They are just beginning to play at politics and I suppose will before long be as political as anyone.

December 1

A very trying day. At Council meeting Braund, Regional [Food] Commissioner, gave a very depressing account of the situation in Bengal administration—apathy, inefficiency and lack of public spirit—in the matter of food; this only confirms what I already knew or suspected; we want a new Governor and some new men at top; but how to galvanise the corpse of Bengal administration will be a problem for the best man.

Just before lunch Mountbatten came to see me about results of Cairo conference. He was more tired and depressed than I have seen him. He had had a difficult time at Cairo with P.M. and with Generalissimo and they had not got much settled. M.B. said there was little mention of India

---

[1] Sir Theodor Gregory, Economic Adviser to the Government of India, 1938–46.
[2] Sir Khizar Hyat Khan Tiwana, Premier of the Punjab, 1942–7.
[3] Sir Chhotu Ram, the most prominent Hindu member of the Unionist Party and for many years a Minister in the Punjab.

and her economics and he did not show P.M. my memorandum on
India's capacity; but he did (rather unwisely, I think) touch on the political
problem and the P.M. blew up and damned not only him but me and all
my works.

Otherwise it was paper, paper all the day. A curious old thing called
Sir Eric Teichman[1] dined, he looked as if he was all falling to bits, but had
come from Chungking via Chinese Turkestan and Russian Turkestan
(some 7000 or 8000 miles), looking at supply route into China. He made
one quite good remark. I said 'Chinese economy is very rocky, isn't it?'
He replied: 'You don't rock much when you are sitting on the bottom.'

December 2

Started morning with Council on Punjab announcement about price-
control and rationing. It went quite well and Council supported me on the
9.4 price against the Food Member's desire to wait in hope of fixing a
much lower price.

December 7

M.B. dined and we had a cinema—Casablanca, a typical film story of the
sentimental-thriller type. The others seemed to like it but I was neither
touched nor thrilled and said so to M.B. afterwards. He is a great film fan
and was horrified. He apparently has one most nights—'so much easier
and quicker than reading a novel' he urged; 'But I seldom read novels'
I said. 'But what do you read then for relaxation, from your writing it is
obvious that you do read sometimes'. I replied that I read biographies and
poetry rather than novels. 'But don't you like musical films?' 'I fear I am
not musical'. 'But you don't need to be musical to enjoy musical films,
with just cheerful songs and dancing'. He is still youthful and I am afraid
received the impression that I was a cheerless kill-joy not to like films.

December 10

There is too much routine work, interviews etc. to give the Viceroy time
for constructive thinking or the relaxation which is essential to a lazy man
like myself. Today was an awful day; interviews, conferences, papers,
visitors to all meals etc. literally from 10 a.m. to 10 p.m.; and my only
relaxation was a ride 7.30–8.30 a.m. What a life. I have been struggling
for the last 48 hours to find even a short space to compose the speech
I have got to make at Calcutta.

[1] Travelled extensively in China and Central Asia. Originally in the Consular Service in
China.

P.S. We held a parade of the Viceregal Servants the other day, some 150 of them were there and it represented only just over half. They mostly come from the U.P. apparently.

December 22

Got back yesterday from 10-day tour of Orissa, Assam and Bengal. It was very strenuous and we had little or no let-up. Orissa is rather an attractive, friendly, backward province; full of malaria and other diseases, liable to flooding, proud of its old history, and of the Oriya traditions, but with little future, unless the contiguous Eastern States, which are reported to be full of coal and minerals, join up and provide industrial wealth. Even so, I doubt whether the population would have energy enough to take advantage of it. There has been considerable distress in parts which seems to have been tackled quite well on the whole. Lewis, the Governor, is a pleasant sincere personality; I think he runs his province quite well. He had much to do with Gandhi at one time and has no great opinion of him. The Chief Minister, the Maharaja of Parlakimedi, has not very high-powered brains but seems honest. He is at odds with the next biggest landowner of the province, the Raja of Kallikote (a member of N.D.C.), who was burning to pour into my ear all his rival's iniquities.

We went on to Assam and spent three days at Shillong, probably the most attractive hill station in India but very out of the way, it takes five hours in a car to reach a railway or airfield. I saw all the Assam Ministers and chief officials, not a very impressive lot, except the chief minister, who is a shrewd and competent politician, though how he would do in better company I am not sure. Assam is a small province which seems to rub along all right, but it is not in any way go-ahead. The native Assamese are lazy and likely to be ousted by more pushing but less attractive Bengali Moslems. The chief political problem is the desire of the Moslem Ministers to increase this immigration into the uncultivated Government lands under the slogan of 'Grow more food'; but what they are really after is 'grow more Moslems'.

We flew from Assam to Dacca and spent a night there—an unpleasant place I thought, but I do not like Bengal. Dacca District has suffered badly in the famine and is still suffering much from disease. Little sign of Government energy or of confidence in Government, but the troops are running a good show.

We arrived in Calcutta on Sunday morning (19th) and went to a Memorial Service for Jack Herbert.

Spent the afternoon in interviews, and early part of the next morning. Then went to make my first important public speech as Viceroy at the Chambers of Commerce. As usual, though I had known of the speech for two months I had put off writing it till the last moment, and was still in labour with it the evening before. My staff had wanted it finished, vetted by Departments, printed and ready for issue to the Press before I left Delhi on the 11th, but I can't do things that way; and it seems absurd that a speech should become public property days before it is delivered. I think it wasn't a bad speech, given the conditions in India. It has had on the whole a good Press, but has naturally disappointed the political elements, who care little for the economic conditions of the country except as it provides material to attack the Government.

> *At the conclusion of this speech Wavell said that he had made no mention 'of the constitutional or political problems of India, not because they are not constantly in my mind; not because I have not the fullest sympathy with the aspirations of India towards Self-Government; not because I consider political progress impossible during the course of the war . . ., but because I do not believe that I can make their solution any easier by talking about them just at present.' The speech was mainly devoted to the problems of food, coal, inflation, and Post-War Reconstruction.*

In the afternoon visited the 24 Parganas District South of Calcutta—hospitals, food kitchens, camps for destitutes etc. It looked a bit better than Dacca but pretty grim. The Army is doing a fine show. On return I saw the principal Bengal Ministers, and spoke to them pretty straight about the state of Bengal, the delay in rationing Calcutta etc. They said little, even Suhrawardy.[1] I don't think they have any intention really to get down to things, or the ability to do so if they had the intention. And Rutherford has no longer the will to drive them, and is only thinking of getting away on leave. Bengal is most depressing, and I sent a strong telegram to S. of S. on return; they have wasted at least two critical months in appointing a Governor, and do not seem even now to have any sense of urgency.

On the way back to Delhi yesterday I landed at Asansol and went down a coal-mine, had about 5 miles walk underground. Mine was only being worked at half capacity owing to shortage of labour. The conditions above ground in the way of housing and amenities were thoroughly bad and I do not wonder that mines find it difficult to keep labour.

---

[1] Mr. H. S. Suhrawardy, a prominent Muslim Leaguer, at this time Food Minister, and later Chief Minister, Bengal. After Independence he was for a time Prime Minister of Pakistan.

A very hectic tour and I was glad to get back to Delhi. 'Be it ever so humble, there's no place like home.'

Discussed food and coal problems at Executive Council this morning. Both present urgent and difficult problems. The problems about coal include where to procure more labour, how to induce mine-owners to work mines to capacity (some of them are undoubtedly going slow because of Excess Profits Tax); how to prevent bribery and dishonesty in the distribution of the available coal; which industries to put on short rations; and many others.

December 23

Since I returned from tour the spate of paper has been unending, and I have had not a moment for constructive thinking, for any work outside the ordinary routine, private correspondence or recreation. In fact, the whole pace of these first two months of my Viceroyalty has been much too hot, and I see little prospect of its slowing down.

I had a talk to M.B. and C.-in-C. There seem to be six or seven Japanese divisions in Burma now. An attack on Jap positions in the Chin hills failed, as my attacks on Donbaik and Rathedaung did last winter; M.B. says no Japanese entrenched position has yet been taken by assault, and that the Jap position in New Guinea and elsewhere in S.W. Pacific were blasted out of existence by weight of metal rather than taken by assault. I wonder if this is correct, it is as regards India, though I still think we should have succeeded at Donbaik with 6th Brigade, if the attack had been carried out as I intended and directed.

December 26

Work continued all over Xmas.

Food and coal situations continue unsatisfactory, and no rain has yet fallen in the Punjab. Casey's appointment as Governor of Bengal has been announced but there is no immediate prospect of his arrival, and now Mrs. C. is seriously ill.

December 29

Bernard Fergusson[1] turned up unexpectedly yesterday evening for a night, and I had a talk with him about his experiences with 77 Bde in Burma. He says the venture was well worth while, and that Wingate's theories

[1] Brigadier Sir Bernard Fergusson (now Lord Ballantrae), Governor-General of New Zealand, 1962–7. Served with the Wingate expeditions into Burma, 1944–5. A.D.C. to Wavell at Aldershot, 1935–7. Author of *Beyond the Chindwin* (London, 1945), and of *Wavell: Portrait of a Soldier* (London, 1961), and other books.

are right, though the troops did not do all that Wingate claimed that they did. He said Wingate was, and is, extremely difficult—impossible at times —and he had many rows with him, but he still believes in his ideas. He was apprehensive about his forthcoming role, if he had to go in and come out again as he did not feel we could abandon the Burmans who helped us to the vengeance of the Japanese a second time.

The Executive Council this morning has as its only item the weekly Food summary, but it was made the occasion by practically every member present to propose that the Central Government should make itself responsible entirely, or in a greater degree, for the food problem in Bengal; and the majority obviously favoured Section 93 Government. They were all Hindus, except Mohammed Usman, who would not be sorry to see the fall of a Moslem League Ministry; but I think their chief feeling was that the Central Government would be held responsible anyhow if things went wrong in Bengal, so that we might as well take the bull by the horns.

I already had the constitutional problem under examination and the possibility of having to take over. But the S. of S. seems by his last tele- gram to have got cold feet over Section 93 Government in Bengal; and the Governor and his chief officials are at present a weak instrument. I shall probably have to get assistance from the Army. It's a misfortune that they have delayed so long at home over the appointment of Casey.

December 31

A long day but mainly routine. Interviews all morning, a Raja to lunch, meeting of War Committee on coal in the afternoon. A fairly typical end to 1943.

Summary of 1943

It has been a hectic, and surprising, year for me. I think an unmerited share of opprobrium was cast on me for the Arakan operations, which were quite unsupported by the War Cabinet, misunderstood, and mis- represented by the P.M., partly owing to his pro-American bias (and there is no doubt that Stilwell and the Americans in India did their best to malign me to Washington—partly to cover their own failure to move the Chinese), and partly because he has never liked me. So that my military career ended under the shadow of failure.

A very curious chain of circumstances then forced on him my appoint- ment as Viceroy as the only way out of a difficult place; he was pleased to find it well received, and then horrified to find I had liberal views about India and was prepared to express them.

I accepted the Viceroyalty in the spirit of a military appointment—one goes where one is told in time of war without making conditions or asking questions. I think I ought to have treated it in a political spirit and found out what the policy to India really was to be and I think I could have made my own conditions, for I think Winston was really hard put to it to find someone. However, here I am and I must do my best, though I am frankly appalled at the prospect of five years—hard to the mind and soft to the body.

I certainly do not look forward to 1944 and its problems. The food, coal and inflation problems do not look any lighter; there seems likely to be little progress in the war on the Burma front; and I see no prospect of any advancement in the political field.

Note: Almost the last, if not the last, book I read in 1943 was Phoenix, by Mr. H. G. Wells, which a rather intellectual young officer gave me. He stayed in the house and was full of ideas about the welfare of soldiers in this war and of the world at large after the war. I am afraid I found most of Wells' book sheer nonsense. The trouble with most of these intellectuals is that they have little knowledge of ordinary human nature and no experience of government and administration. They are apt to regard the mass of human beings, not only in their own country, but in all lands, as sensible people moved by reason instead of ignorant people swayed by prejudice and sentiment. Intellectuals have often started a revolution by their theories, but have never yet in history been able to control it, so far as my study goes, and I am pretty sure that the disciples of Mr. Wells will not. His scheme of life, as set forth in this book, seems to me like a magnificently equipped and fitted up Rolls-Royce, for which the motive power, petrol—human nature—is lacking. I believe the world will continue to go on in its rattle-trap patched up old Ford which will run. What a wonderful teller of stories Wells was, it is in a way a pity he took to inaccurate history and unpractical social theories.

3

THE FIGHT
AGAINST FAMINE

January 1, 1944

I remember a Latin couplet from my schooldays:

> Perturbabantur Constantinopolitani
> Innumerabilibus sollicitudinibus[1]

I feel the same way as the citizens of Constantinople at the dawn of this New Year. But I am not going to make any new-year resolutions about it. I shall carry on in my rather haphazard, opportunist, almost Micawber-like way, working on certain guiding principles which have by some surprising good (?) fortune brought me to this high position.

January 5

The food problem, coal crisis and inflationary threat continue to be our main anxieties. The Food Department and my staff urge me towards dismissing the Bengal Ministry as incapable of dealing with the food question, and going into Section 93. I want to be convinced first that the Ministry is really incapable, under the firm direction (so I hope) of Casey when he arrives, to deal with the problem; and secondly that a Section 93 regime could make certain of putting things right. I sent my D.P.S.V., Abell, down to Calcutta yesterday to put these questions to the Governor. Casey has cabled to say that he hopes to be in Delhi by the 16th.

I have sent a strongly worded telegram to S. of S. about imports of food grains, to ask for a definite guarantee of 1,000,000 tons during 1944.

Nothing very much otherwise. I have concocted my first letter to H.M. the King; made a short and fairly light-hearted speech ('not long enough or dull enough for a Viceroy' was P.S.V.'s comment on the draft) to open the Indian Science Congress; and presented 2 V.C.s at a parade outside Delhi Fort—quite an impressive ceremony in a fine setting, with a good crowd.

Mountbatten seemed a bit overworked and depressed when I saw him last. His resources are gradually, or not even gradually, being taken away

---

[1] 'The people of Constantinople were beset by countless anxieties.'

and he sees little prospect of accomplishing much of what he had planned this winter.

January 6

Discussed with Jenkins and Abell result of latter's visit to Calcutta, and approved despatch of telegram to S. of S. recommending Section 93 administration for Bengal. It is against my principles to take over from an Indian Government when they are in difficulties; they will never learn to rule themselves if they are not compelled to face their responsibilities and difficulties. But this Government has been given a good run, and too much is at stake. I think they might have been all right with a Governor who was prepared to take a stronger line with them two months ago, when they were thoroughly frightened; but Rutherford has not done so, either through weakness of character or ill-health. (Thorne,[1] who knows him well, says he has always been disinclined for firm action). He also professes scruples over Section 93; he remarked to Abell that the late Viceroy was inclined to be too meticulous about the Constitution but that the present one seemed too prone to disregard it.

January 9

Cabinet have turned down my proposal to appoint an Indian as Finance Member.[2] I gather from S. of S. that John Anderson and Winston torpedoed it. Cabinet also obviously very perturbed over my recommendation to go into Section 93 in Bengal. They are considering it on Tuesday (Jan 11); I also am a bit worried over it but am sure it is right.

> In a private telegram to the Secretary of State dated 7 Jan. Wavell said that he was prepared to await Casey's arrival, if the latter felt that immediate action would embarrass him.

January 10

I saw Nazimuddin,[3] the Bengal Premier, and told him I was dissatisfied with the state of Bengal. He said things would be all right if his Ministry was given a chance and supported against his political enemies. I rather like him and think he is straight but incapable. I have little opinion of his Food

---

[1] Sir John Thorne, I.C.S., Secretary to the Governor-General (Public), 1938–44. He officiated as Home Member of the Executive Council on the retirement of Sir Reginald Maxwell in 1944 and held the post again in 1945.

[2] To replace Sir Jeremy Raisman who was due to retire. Owing to difficulty in selecting a successor, Raisman was given a year's extension till April 1945.

[3] Sir Nazimuddin who was later Governor-General (1945–51) and Prime Minister (1951–3) of Pakistan.

Minister, Suhrawardy, who is also in Delhi and was inclined, at first, to be truculent in an interview with Jenkins.

In the afternoon made a tour of some villages round Delhi, to see medical and veterinary establishments, cattle, schools, consolidation projects (the process of simplifying land tenure) etc. I walked through one village and it seemed fairly clean and prosperous. N.W. India is a much better proposition than Bengal.

January 12

I have decided to alter the method of business. At present I spend my whole mornings in interviews, some of which are interesting and valuable but in many of which time is wasted, since I think that Indian Members of Council with an interview feel that they must fill in their whole time, whether they have any real business or not. And the morning is far my best time for constructive work. So in future I shall see Members only once a fortnight as a routine interview, in the afternoon; but shall encourage them to ask for special appointments in the morning whenever they have anything of importance to discuss.

At Council I raised the question of a Commission of Enquiry into the Bengal famine. Majority were in favour of early enquiry. I cabled S. of S. accordingly.

In afternoon visited Delhi University of which I am Chancellor. Sir Maurice Gwyer[1] is an enthusiast and has done much work on the project— a group of colleges on the site of the old Viceregal Lodge. I think education is probably the thing we have done worst in India, both from our own point of view and that of the Indians. We have allowed a bad system of advanced education to grow up—unpractical, no development of character, concentration on examinations (which are often very dishonestly run).

The Delhi project should be good, if ever carried through, and so long as a good man like Gwyer is in charge.

January 13

The War Cabinet has turned down my proposal for Section 93 in Bengal; they say Casey must be given a chance to press Ministry into adequate action. I do not think they are capable of taking it, or of restoring confidence and reasonable honesty into the Province. I cabled S. of S. pointing

[1] Sir Maurice Gwyer, Chief Justice of India and President of the Federal Court, 1937-43. Since the Federal Part of the Act of 1935 was never brought into operation, he had little judicial work and so devoted his time to Delhi University, of which he was Vice-Chancellor from 1938 to 1950.

out that Cabinet had now twice disregarded my advice and that I hoped they would not do so again on the demand for imports.

First day of National Defence Council meeting. The discussion on food showed, I think, that we should have had public opinion very largely behind us in taking a strong line in Bengal.

January 16

The National Defence Council went off much as usual. The food problem was the one which aroused most interest, and one and all urged strong action on the Centre.

War Cabinet have proposed an unknown, young and apparently, from the description given by S. of S., tactless and ambitious Canadian as Finance Member, having turned down my recommendation for an Indian on the plea that they must have someone really outstanding. I cabled a strong protest.

Wavell conveyed his 'strong protest' both in cables and in a letter, and said in the course of them:

'Cabinet's lack of imagination in dealing with India is sometimes astonishing. They turned down my recommendation for appointment of an Indian on plea that they must appoint man of "acknowledged and outstanding qualifications". Person now proposed is certainly not this. Surely you cannot suppose that selection of young and almost unknown Canadian, whose name does not appear in any book of reference and who has no experience of India, will be easy to defend. Your colleagues must stop trying to have everything both ways. Cabinet should either find me a really outstanding man from U.K. or reconsider my recommendation.'

Jamna Das Mehta[1] stayed for the National Defence Council meeting. Obviously very flattered. Peter went to see him to enquire whether he was comfortably housed. He complained that there had been a rat in his room during the night. Peter rose to the occasion: 'Ah, a rat, sir, those are for our most distinguished guests, the others only get mice'.

M. B. tells following story. A propagandist of S. C. Bose's[2] army on the Arakan front shouted across the lines: 'We shall be in Delhi in ten days'. A sepoy, recently returned from leave, shouted back 'Not on these ruddy railways, you won't'.

---

[1] A former member of Congress and ex-Mayor of Bombay.

[2] Subhas Chandra Bose, an extremist Congress leader from Bengal, escaped from detention after the outbreak of war and made his way to Germany and thence in 1943 to Japan. The Japanese made him Commander-in-Chief of an Indian National Army (I.N.A.) that they formed from such of the Indian prisoners of war as they could induce to join. The I.N.A. took part, somewhat ingloriously, in the Japanese operations against Eastern India in 1943–4. Subhas Chandra Bose was killed in an air crash in 1945.

January 17

My first visitor this morning was M. N. Roy, the Social Democratic leader. Has been a Bengal terrorist, a worker for Germany, Indian representative of the Comintern, expelled from France, imprisoned in India; and is now trying to form a People's Party in India to oppose Congress. Has apparently rather got round Home Member who actually suggested this stormy petrel as a candidate for a seat on my Executive Council. He impressed me quite favourably, rather more to him than most Indian politicians, more independence, more guts perhaps. But I doubt whether he has much following or is likely to have much.

Saw the Service Chiefs—Auchinleck, M. B., Peirse. I talked to C-in-C about Finance Membership, he entirely agrees with me that it ought to be an Indian. Peirse agreed with me about the necessity to give Indians participation in any Empire air crews on imperial routes and saw no reason why they should not make good.

January 30

Got back last night from a tour of U.P., Bombay and Udaipur—strenuous but interesting.

The U.P. is well run. Maurice Hallett, in spite of his rather vague demeanour, is a first-class administrator and a firm one, and gets things done without fuss or friction or eyewash. I went to Gorakhpur (first time a Viceroy had visited it, they said) and saw the Gurkha headquarters and recruiting depot, an interesting and well-run show; and a big Labour Depot where labour gangs were recruited for the mines, docks etc. The scheme, which seemed to be working very well, is due to an enthusiast, one Moss, formerly a soldier now in I.C.S., very fat and like some fat men full of energy and drive.

At Lucknow there were the usual interviews, a garden party, dinner parties, luncheon parties, which are inevitable I suppose, but do not lead to much business, for one like myself who is slow of thought and sparing of speech. I made the acquaintance of two prominent Liberals and 'elder statesmen', Sir Tej Bahadur Sapru[1] and Sir Maharaj Singh.[2] Both full of culture and pleasant to meet, but to my mind of little weight as political leaders. I did not talk politics with Sapru, only Boy Scouts of which he is

[1] Sir Tej Bahadur Sapru, Advocate and Zemindar (landlord), at one time a member of the All India Congress Committee, Law Member of the Viceroy's Executive Council, 1920-3, President of India Liberal Federation.

[2] Raja Sir Maharaj Singh, an Indian Christian and distinguished retired Government official who had been Agent General for India in South Africa, 1932-5, President of the National Liberal Federation, 1943-4, and after Independence was Governor of Bombay, 1948-52.

head (I think he was disappointed that I did not talk politics, but it seemed to me it would have been of little value). Maharaj Singh admitted all the mistakes of the Congress leaders but merely adjured me to release them. His wife criticised violently all that we had done or were doing in a talk to me after dinner but had again no constructive solution. I met another of these old Liberals, Jayakar,[1] in Bombay and he gave me much the same impression. I feel that the cause of India's political troubles may be our failure in the past to make more of these Liberals and to take them into our confidence and give them responsibility many years ago, with the result that they mistrusted our sincerity and honesty, and the leadership passed into irresponsible unpractical hands. Now they realise the futility with which they have been led, but with the sensitiveness of Indians can see nothing but the 'insult' of their 'chosen leaders' being in detention, and will not embark on a more practical policy, even if they had the power to command a following. The only hope now seems to be in getting younger and more vigorous men to co-operate; I have only seen two possibilities so far—Sir Chhotu Ram in the Punjab and M. N. Roy the ex-terrorist—excluding Khizar the Punjab premier who might be very good if he has the spur to enter all-India politics.

Generally, the political situation in the U.P. is, I think, back to some years ago, twenty or more. Officials and police seemed well on top of their work; they all said U.P. would remain perfectly peaceful provided Gandhi and Working Committee of Congress were kept behind bars.

I thought poorly of the Talukdars of Oudh, a degenerate lot of absentee landlords living in the city instead of on their estates and asking Government to raise their rents. But I may be unfair to them, or to some of them. I daresay a collection of our country gentlemen might make a poor impression on a progressive foreigner.

In Lucknow I saw the rationing scheme which seemed to be working well, and an Indian military hospital, quite good. I take some credit to myself for the improvement I made in military hospitals and medical arrangements in India during the two years I was C.-in-C. They would have improved anyhow in the natural course of progress, but I pushed them on faster than the Medical people or staff would have done by themselves.

And so to Bombay (January 22 to 27). We started with an hour or so at the races—a proper Maharaja's day, they won, I think, 6 of the 8 races.

I met the Bombay advisers—Knight, Bristow and Collins, and asked

[1] Mr. Jayakar, a leading lawyer and politician from Bombay, Judge, Federal Court, India, 1937-9.

Bristow about the main political prisoners. He said Gandhi seemed quite content to remain where he was; the Working Committee was still under his influence, they would never co-operate. I saw the Food Committee—Bombay is very proud of the way it has handled its food problem—they insisted on the necessity of imports to form a reserve.

The other two days in Bombay included the usual interviews, parties, visits to ration offices. I also paid a completely surprise visit to the poorer parts of Bombay, saw a City Police Station and went round the docks. I saw Brelvi of the Bombay Chronicle, one of the most violent of the Congress papers, he is not a bad little man, he tried to persuade me to allow Devadas Gandhi[1] to talk politics to his father when he visited his mother[2] who is very ill. Sir Francis Low[3] of the Times of India was interesting about a conversation he had had with Rajagopalachariar[4] who is getting very tired of the present situation and wants to start something on his own if Gandhi won't, and has asked how to approach Jinnah with a view to Jinnah and Gandhi getting together. I doubt whether Jinnah will play. I did not get on very well with young Tata with whom I had a short talk after dinner, a pity as I think he is able and influential about Indian business, but he seemed to me conceited and unhelpful, I expect I didn't take him the right way.

From Bombay we flew to Belgaum on 25th, and spent the day looking into District administration system and saw a Forestry Depot. We motored 200 miles to and through the Bijapur District over rather bumpy and dusty roads on a hottish day. I was garlanded 45 times, had large numbers of people presented to me, and altogether was pretty busy from 8 a.m., when we left Belgaum till 7.30 p.m., when we got into a train at Sholapur. Bijapur is a historic old city with many fine ruins and I should have liked more time to see it. I visited a village a few miles out who put up a very good reception and entertainment but I think that the talent had been largely imported; in fact I was almost reminded of Catherine the Great's tour of Russia when Potemkin, her favourite and chief Minister, had a touring company of artistes complete with effects and scenery, to represent happy villagers wherever Her Majesty went.

Casey had turned up on the 19th (at Lucknow) and I had an evening with him; he seemed in good heart and not depressed by the somewhat gloomy picture I painted to him. He said no one in Cabinet except Amery supported my proposal about Section 93 in Bengal.

---

[1] Gandhi's fourth son.
[2] Mrs. Gandhi had elected to share her husband's confinement.
[3] Editor of the *Times of India*, 1932–48.
[4] C. Rajagopalachari, ex-Premier of Madras.

I had a telegram from Winston a couple of days ago (first communication from him since I left U.K.) thanking me for a New Year letter I sent him to congratulate him on his recovery. He expressed approval of what I was doing, said Casey would be most useful to me, and expressed himself optimistically about the new battle on Italian front.

February 2

Two long days in office. A series of interviews and two big conferences. One on 1st with C-in-C and Benthall on Calcutta Port organisation and military control of Assam railways. Americans are a little difficult in these matters; if anything is not to their liking, instead of discussing it with authorities on the spot they are inclined to send a high-power telegram to Washington demanding action from Chiefs of Staff. Calcutta Port is rather a mess but it is at least partly due to Americans failing to fulfil their promises about materials; and I don't feel like dismissing tried officials simply because the Americans don't like them. But the Port certainly wants reorganisation. I said we would get up Elderton, the Port Commissioner, the man the Americans dislike, to discuss it. I accepted the proposal for military control over railway movement.

On 2nd we had a long Council mainly on a proposal to raise railway fares in the Budget. Members didn't like it much but accepted it by a small majority provided the proceeds were earmarked to improve passenger amenities. I think they may go back on it when the Budget proposals as a whole are discussed on Saturday.

February 7

The Council meetings on the Budget on Saturday evening and Sunday morning went off quite well on the whole. I had to begin by reading the riot act on the matter of secrecy since I was informed on unimpeachable evidence that the result of the meeting on railway fares and the way individual members spoke was known to the Press almost at once. Although Indians cannot keep their mouths shut, I am not sure that New Delhi is very much more indiscreet than Whitehall. Raisman was very good, explained his proposals clearly, was patient and tactful in meeting opposition and conciliatory. Mudaliar let off fireworks and a lot of not very well considered opposition to the proposals, but quietened down after Raisman's convincing but quite tactful refutation of his arguments; Srivastava was very concerned about his dividends but on the whole glad to get off lighter than he expected (he is a very rich man); Ambedkar, always a bit muddle-headed, suggested that we should stop inflation by the simple process of issuing no more currency; old Jogendra Singh wanted reconstruction to be financed as well as the war without increasing taxation. The chief opposition was to the taxes on tea, coffee and betel nut, because it was realised that they would be unpopular and would be criticised as taxing the poor man's little luxuries. But Raisman justified broadening the basis of taxation in preparation for post-war reconstruction, and his proposals went through with only a few minor concessions.

Two conferences this afternoon, one on wages of Indian seamen, a thorny problem we have discussed before. Indian seamen get about £5 a month, Chinese about £15, and British £22. 10. 0. The liberal man says: 'this is racial discrimination, why should men doing the same work be paid differently because of the colour of their skins'. Actually to pay a lascar at anything approaching even Chinese rates would throw the whole Indian wage scale out of gear. We agreed on a moderate increase, since shipping companies were likely to grant it in any case, or lascars were likely to strike.

At other conference we got agreement on new organisations for Calcutta port and Assam L of C, no mean achievement in view of American attitude. I take some credit to myself for refusing to decide organisations purely on paper and insisting on getting up Elderton, the Chairman of Port Commissioners from Calcutta.

February 9

Flew to Lalitpur, near junction of U.P. and C.P. to see Archie John[1] and 2nd Battalion[2] training there in jungle warfare. Talked to them extempore for about ¾ hour and then had picnic lunch, which we had brought, with officers.

Archie John, C.O. and officers all say it will be very difficult to maintain morale unless battalion has a go at the Jap this cold weather.

Got back to find telegram to say Cabinet seemed to be taking an unfavourable view of my request for grain imports, so sent strongly worded telegram to S. of S. and to P.M.

> In the course of his telegram Wavell said:
>
> 'Bengal famine was one of the greatest disasters that has befallen any people under British rule and damage to our reputation here both among Indians and foreigners in India is incalculable. You are better able to judge effect at home and abroad.

[1] Major A. J. A. Wavell, the Black Watch, Wavell's only son.
[2] The Black Watch, Lord Wavell's regiment.

'*Attempt by His Majesty's Government to prove on the basis of admittedly defective statistics that we can do without the help demanded would be regarded here by all opinion British and Indian as utterly indefensible. Please warn your colleagues once more that rigid statistical approach is futile and that my views are based on personal discussions with all Governors and visits to seven of the eleven Provinces.*

'*I warn His Majesty's Government with all seriousness that if they refuse our demands they are risking a catastrophe of far greater dimensions than Bengal famine. They must either trust the opinion of the man they have appointed to advise them on Indian affairs or replace him.*'

February 10

Flew to Jullundur and spent day driving a hundred odd miles round that part of Punjab to see work going on in Sewalik hills and Hoshiarpur district against soil erosion.

My Military Secretary tells me I have flown over 10,000 miles in the DC3 since landing at Karachi in October, as well as 400 by train and 1000 by car during tours—total average 3000 miles a month touring.

February 14

During week-end held investiture in Durbar Hall, cleared off arrears of paper work, finished draft of my speech for the Legislature, and started sitting to Simon Elwes for a portrait. Had a letter from M. N. Roy, the Radical Democratic leader whom I saw lately, practically demanding seats for himself and some of his party on the Executive Council, and a subsidy; my comment to P.S.V. was that I was Viceroy and did not propose to be vice-Roy. Brelvi, editor of the Bombay Chronicle, has been making persistent efforts to draw me on the release of the leaders, by a manifesto signed by all the nationalist editors. I told them they must wait for my speech on 17th. That speech will please no-one of the politicians, but it is the best I can say in present circumstances, I think; it has been passed by S. of S. at home with only textual emendation.

February 16

I found some of my colleagues on the Executive Council rather shaken by my remarks the other day about disclosures to the Press and anxious to explain their own clear conscience.

Lord Knollys, come out on behalf of BOAC, adopted the official BOAC attitude on Indian participation in Empire air route across India, i.e. that Indians in crew would not enjoy confidence of public and would prejudice BOAC competition with Dutch air lines. I disabused him of idea that BOAC would get away with an Empire air line across India in which Indians had no share.

Today, I had to spend a good deal of the day dealing with a telegram telling me the Cabinet had turned down flat my demand for food imports in 1944. I concocted a somewhat spirited riposte warning H.M.G. of the consequences, and got C-in-C and Mountbatten, whom I called into conference, to back it. It will be interesting to see result.

> *In the course of his 'spirited riposte' Wavell said that he regarded it as a practical certainty that there would be large-scale disaster in India if imports were refused.*

Council meeting was fortunately short but meantime boxes and boxes of papers came in, and I was up till midnight dealing with them.

February 17

My address to the Legislature. On the whole I think it went as well as could be expected, though I shall have a bad press with the politicians. Srivastava and Mohammed Usman sent congratulations and Dr Khare whom I saw in the evening seemed genuinely to like it.

> *In this speech Wavell stressed that India was a natural unit within which the two great communities must decide how to live together, as communities differing in culture or religion had contrived to do elsewhere. He reaffirmed the Cripps offer, i.e. full self-government at the end of the war under a constitution formed by Indians themselves and meanwhile co-operation in the Government of India under the existing constitution. He regretted that one important element, which contained 'much ability and high-mindedness', was standing aloof. He would like 'to have the co-operation of this element in solving the present and the future problems of India'. But he saw no reason to release those responsible for the Quit India rebellion until he was convinced that the policy of non-co-operation and obstruction had been 'withdrawn—not in sackcloth and ashes, that helps no one—but in recognition of a mistaken and unprofitable policy'.*

Hutchings the Food Secretary came back from Bengal in rather more optimistic mood. He thinks main part of crop is still in hands of cultivators and has not yet got into hands of speculators. Rationing in Calcutta is not going too badly. Crux is to get stocks of food into districts in time. He spent much time with Suhrawardy and found him rather more co-operative than before. He says Casey is a great success but looks a sick man. He thoroughly approved of my telegram home yesterday about food imports.

March 3

Returned yesterday from tour to Madras and C.P. Madras visit lasted from February 18 to 25. I saw the Collectors of all 23 Districts of Madras Province and had the usual large numbers of interviews with more or less prominent persons, so I got a fairly good but hasty impression of the whole Presidency.

Of interviews the most important was three-quarters of an hour with Rajagopalachariar. He certainly does not give the impression of a forcible character—very few Indians do—but was pleasant and intelligent. He said he had read my speech and saw in it some desire to make progress. He admitted previous mistakes of Congress and asked what sort of progress I had in mind as a possibility. I said that to speak quite frankly and off the record, what seemed to me required at the moment was a Council of 'All the Talents', of men chosen for their eminence who would be recognised as representative of the best elements in India, who would work out India's problems under the present Constitution without paying attention to communal politics but in the interest of India as a whole. I said I would not accept a 'National Government' with so many nominees of Congress and so many of Muslim League, who took their orders from outside. I had expected R. to ask for permission to visit Gandhi, but he said it was no use his doing so until he had a definite proposal. He said G. was useless as an administrator but as a politician was more capable of compromise than the Working Committee. We parted on quite good terms and he asked if he could come and see me in Delhi, but I doubt whether he really has much influence or the leadership to command a following. All these Indian leaders seem to me to want everything handed to them on a plate and their hands held.

I also saw an ex-Congress Minister Subbarayan, really more interested in cricket than politics. He admitted that the British were sitting pretty and could get all the co-operation they required to end the war, without making any political move; and it was this knowledge and fear that British would use it that was causing such frustration and bitterness in Indian political circles.

I had a long day at Coimbatore on February 22, full of surprises and problems. The programme did not at all prepare me for all that was coming. One does not expect to find a naval guard of honour drawn up for one on an aerodrome several hundred miles from the sea. Then I had shortly afterwards to remark on the points of the village stud bull, to grasp the rationing system of a village, to see the village dispensary. Immediately afterwards I had to interview the Collectors of 5 Districts, each much larger than an English county, and learn in a few minutes some of the particular problems of each; to receive a deputation of planters representing rubber, coffee and tea and in ten minutes hear the grievances of the three widely differing interests; to listen to an impassioned tirade against Brahmins by an old bearded gentleman with a rather sketchy knowledge of English; and to deal with one or two telegrams. Then a quick change into uniform to lunch with the Training Centre of the Madras Regiment (50 officers and some 60 V.C.O.s to shake hands with and say something polite to). On the return journey visit a village and inspect a village temple —oranges and lemons being handed one by the priest, while a drum and two horns represented the bells of St. Clements—followed by the explanation of an irrigation scheme by a nervous and not very lucid engineer.

Then an hour's 'rest', during which P.S.V. produced a box of papers, after which the programme called simply for a drive through Coimbatore. Actually this involved driving through all the streets of the town lined apparently by the whole population of C (problem, does one wave one's hat or one's hand or nothing to a large stolid crowd lining streets to look at one?) We stopped at a rationing centre where the rationing scheme was explained at some length; at the Town Council where 32 Councillors were presented, a garland hung round my neck and a speech of welcome made; at an Agricultural College where the Principal would gladly have talked agriculture for hours; and then, suddenly, at a Refugee Settlement, of refugees from Malta, Burma and other portions of the British Empire, where one had a most loyal reception, and had to inspect Boy Scouts, a canteen, a living quarter etc. and to listen to another speech of welcome. Back to the Collector's bungalow just in time for a small party in which one had to talk or listen to more planters, another rabid anti-Brahmin, an ultra-loyalist Indian, a mill-owner, etc. Who says that the Viceroy doesn't earn his salary?

So on to Nagpur and C.P. on Feb. 25. Much the usual programme.

C.P. seems an attractive Province and getting on all right. Twynam has produced an appreciation of the political situation, which he handed in just as we left. It suggests leaving Congress to stew in their own juice and backing the Muslim League and Rajagopalachariar. Hardly practical politics, I think.

The usual frantic effort since to catch up on papers, hampered by a number of interviews and a luncheon party and necessity to deal with food situation. While I was on tour H.M.G. again refused to send any imports of food, and after discussion with Hutchings, C-in-C, and Mountbatten I sent off yet another telegram.

March 6

Birla,[1] the millionaire supporter of Congress, came to see me this morning. We had quite an interesting talk on industrial and agricultural development of India. He recommended a Member of Council for Development (did he see himself in that role?). He only touched on politics at the end, and admitted the mistakes of Congress but said the problem was mainly psychological and that my predecessor with all his qualities had lacked the personal touch.

Archie John was flown in, having been laid up with tick typhus, not looking well but will soon recover, I hope.

March 9

The tide of paper steadily rose against me on 8th, on evening of which we had long Council of 2½ hours mainly on the vexed matter of the increase of railway fares. Council always disliked it, knowing it would be unpopular, and having had an adverse vote in the Assembly are now all for dropping it.

March 10

On March 3 I sent another telegram home emphasising my urgent need of imports and recording offer by C-in-C and M.B. to give up part of their imports of military stores in favour of food. I said that as this was not nearly enough I proposed to ask M.B. to get Americans to do the same. This drew two immediate telegrams from S. of S. and P.M. that on no account was I to approach Americans until War Cabinet had further considered matter.

March 11

H.M.G.'s only reaction so far to my last telegram about food imports is a proposal that I should *export* 25,000 tons of rice per month to Ceylon in return for a similar quantity of wheat and flour several months later. I sent back a quick and stuffy one. I really think they are crazy at Whitehall, or else they never trouble to read one's telegrams.

March 16

Back from a short visit to Sind, two days at Karachi, a day and a half in Upper Sind. The usual sort of programme. There was hardly half an hour that was not occupied. Interviews I find trying—to see a succession of

[1] G. D. Birla, a highly successful financier and industrialist who contributed liberally to Congress funds and in interviews with successive Viceroys often conveyed to them the Congress thinking on various matters.

people for ten minutes each and to try and get any real information out of them or to raise their morale is not the sort of thing for which a rather slow-working brain like mine is adapted.

Generally speaking, Sind prospers. It is an agricultural country, with no food problem, and the only anxiety of the Zemindars is that their opposite numbers in the Punjab may be making more money still out of the high prices of grain, since the Sind Governor has managed to keep prices down to a reasonable level. Though there is a Ministry, Dow the Governor exercises a very strong personal control. He knows Sind and all the tricks and corruptions of his Ministers—which probably are no worse than those of English politicians 100 years ago.

Meanwhile Government has had three defeats in the Assembly on the budget, and I wonder what sort of heart I shall find my Council in.

March 18

Saw both M.B. and Henry Pownall[1] and talked to them of situation on Burma frontier. It shows the respect they have for the Japanese tactics and fighting that though they have something like twice the Japanese strength available on the Chin Hills–Chindwin–Manipur front and have known for months that the enemy were about to attack, they are both feeling rather apprehensive of the result; and have taken aircraft off the ferry route to China to fly into Manipur another division from Arakan. The 17th Division is being pulled back from Tiddim area by Japanese action against their communications, although in numbers we must be superior. How does the Jap do it? The simple answer is that we have a very ponderous L of C and the Jap has practically none at all; we fight with the idea of ultimate survival, the Jap seems to fight with the idea of ultimate death and contempt for it, when he has done as much harm as possible. The flying in of Wingate's two brigades seems to have been a remarkable performance after an initial set-back in which there were about 150 casualties from crashed or lost gliders. But so far the Jap appears to have taken no notice of this force in his rear, his independence of communications is remarkable.

M.B. is prepared to back me up on food problem and agrees that Americans must be told the situation officially if H.M.G. will not find imports.

The apprehensions of Mountbatten and Pownall were well justified. The Japanese advanced with amazing boldness and skill through wooded and

---

[1] Lt.-Gen. Sir Henry Pownall, at this time Chief of Staff to Lord Mountbatten.

almost trackless mountains to the plateau of Imphal; and by the end of March they had cut the road from Imphal to Kohima leading to the railway at Dimapur, were threatening to break through at Kohima and to cut the railway itself, and had hemmed into a narrow area around the town of Imphal the three British-Indian divisions that were originally holding this front and a fourth that was flown in as a reinforcement from Arakan. For many weeks the position was critical. The large British-Indian force at Imphal had to be supplied by air which, with the onset of the monsoon, became exceedingly difficult. But the Japanese were also in difficulties; after much hard fighting they were held at Kohima and they failed to break the resistance at Imphal and to capture the stores there with which to support themselves. At the end of June casualties, exhaustion, and lack of supplies compelled them to withdraw their famished forces to Burma—a disastrous defeat for them, as recorded in the Journal entry for 14 August.

March 19

A comparatively quiet Sunday. I drafted a reply to the letter sent me by Mr. Gandhi, but shall probably not be allowed to send anything so direct and open. I don't, however, see why I should refer home at all. Perhaps I am unwise to enter into correspondence with Mr. G., but I have not provoked it, and I must send some answer to his letter, and do not like the sort of grandmotherly stuff the Home Department produces. Political India is a very tiresome adolescent, but the I.O., Home Department and others still persist in treating it as a naughty child.

The nature of this correspondence with Gandhi is explained on p. 73.

March 24

I had another food telegram from H.M.G. after another Cabinet meeting; they now offer me 250,000 tons for 1944 and again repeat their suggestion of exporting 150,000 tons of rice in exchange for 150,000 tons of wheat. S. of S. even makes the suggestion that I should announce the import of 400,000 tons wheat and conceal for the time being the export of 150,000 tons rice; I shall certainly do nothing so dishonest or stupid. And I shall not let H.M.G. think they have solved India's food problem for 1944 by 250,000 tons when I have told them all along that 1,000,000 is the minimum. I think I may have to resign to bring the situation home to them. They refuse to approach the Americans for shipping.

Farewell dinner to the Maxwells in the evening, he made a witty speech. He will be a considerable loss to the Council.

March 25

Conference with Caroe[1] and Gould[2] on N.E. frontier problems—all three of us Old Wykehamists. We discussed Gould's visit to Tibet and possibility of stiffening up Tibetans to resist any Chinese encroachment, and also pushing up to McMahon line on northern frontier of Assam.

March 28

Last day or two comparatively quiet, usual interviews and papers, but I have actually managed to find a little time to work on the despatch I ought to have written as C-in-C last year.

Griffiths,[3] M.L.A., who has just returned from U.K., where he has been lecturing and talking about India, spoke to me for some time on the political situation. He found, as I did, that there is a very general wish at home to grant India self-government at once but no conception of the difficulties; Muslim League case is hardly known at home, only Gandhi and the Congress. Griffiths' main point in this country was the difficulty of persuading Indians that we really did mean to give them self-government, and were honest in our professions. He said an unequivocal declaration by the P.M. might convince them.

Rowlands[4] is just off home, sent by Supreme Commander to raise questions of civil supplies for Burma, and Political Warfare. I briefed him on food imports and inflation, I think he is sound on these though the Food Member seems to doubt it.

Firoz Khan Noon came to say goodbye before leaving[5] for U.K. I briefed him as well as I could. He expressed some apprehension that Khizar might quit politics now his father was dead, and that he was fighting a losing battle against Jinnah and the League for control of the Punjab Government.

The Budget was defeated by one vote, the Congress leader of the Assembly, [Bhulabhai] Desai, turned up to speak after $3\frac{1}{2}$ years absence, a measure of their apprehension, I think, of Congress being side tracked.

The C-in-C spoke of the fighting on the Assam border where the Japs seem to be making headway. Large numbers of our troops are being

[1] Sir Olaf Caroe, I.C.S., Secretary, External Affairs Dept., 1939–45, Governor North-West Frontier Province, 1946–7.

[2] Sir Basil Gould, I.C.S., Political Officer in Sikkim and for Bhutan and Tibet, 1935–45.

[3] Sir Percival Griffiths, retired from the I.C.S. in 1937, went into business in India and became a member of the Central Legislature.

[4] Sir Archibald Rowlands, a Home Civil Servant, came out to India in 1943 as Adviser to the Viceroy on War Administration. He had previously been in India (1937–9) as Financial Adviser, Military Finance. He was later Finance Member of the Executive Council (1945–6).

[5] To be Indian Representative at the War Cabinet.

Governors' Conference, November 1943

Seated: Sir Bertrand Glancy (Punjab), Sir Thomas Rutherford (acting Bengal), Sir Arthur Hope (Madras), the Viceroy and Vicereine, Sir John Colville (Bombay), Sir Maurice Hallett (United Provinces).

Standing: Sir Hugh Dow (Sind), Sir Andrew Clow (Assam), Sir Henry Twynam (Central Provinces), Sir Francis Mudie (acting Bihar), Sir George Cunningham (North-West Frontier Province), Sir Hawthorne Lewis (Orissa).

In a North-West Frontier village

concentrated in Assam, including I think 2nd Division; this will throw a very heavy strain on communications.

Was told later in the morning that Wingate was missing from an air trip over Burma. I heard later that he had almost certainly been killed in an air crash between Imphal and Silchar.

March 29

Council meeting in evening showed, I think, effect on members of Assembly being in session. Hindu members, led by Srivastava, attacked food policy of Bengal Government. I am told that this may be the effect of lobbying by Hindu members of the Legislature from Bengal, some of whom would go to any lengths, even risk of another famine, to defeat present Muslim League Government in Bengal.

Meanwhile Jinnah's pressure on the Punjab has obviously shaken Khizar, and I gather that Jinnah regards me as an enemy of the Muslim League and is determined to be as much of a nuisance as he can. He does not really represent solid steady Moslem opinion (in fact J. himself is hardly a Muslim) but he can sway opinion, and no one seems to have the character to oppose him.

> *Khizar Hyat, like his predecessor, Sir Sikander Hyat-Khan, and many Muslims of the Unionist Party—a provincial party, representing agricultural interests, with Muslim and Hindu members—was at heart opposed to the demand for Pakistan, and he was unwilling to accept Jinnah's directives in regard to the conduct of the Punjab Government. Jinnah claimed that as the Muslims, who constituted the majority of the Unionist Party, were also members of the Muslim League, the Punjab Government was a 'League' Government and subject to his control as President of the League. Khizar retorted that his Government was a coalition government with Hindu and Sikh members, and not a League Government. Khizar, with many misgivings, resisted Jinnah's attempts to dictate to him and was dismissed from the League in the middle of 1944. The Muslim members of the Unionist Party were then forced to choose between loyalty to Khizar and the Unionist Party and loyalty to Jinnah and the League.*

March 30

Assembly is discussing Baluchistan today, anxious to give it modern democratic government instead of its present old world feudal rule. Poor Baluchistan, I suppose it will have to 'passer par là, comme les autres' some day, but it will not be yet. The Government proposal, I gather, is to have one nominated member from Baluchistan in the Council of State;

the trouble is to find one who can speak and understand English, but it is urged that this does not really matter!

Dickie Mountbatten came to dinner and was in very good form, vital and amusing. M.B. asked me what I thought about his flying into Burma to see the Wingate columns. I said I was all for Commanders getting as far forward as possible, but he had no business to take serious risks unless there was really something to be gained—discussion of a change of plan, estimate on the spot of the state of morale or possibilities of an operation. I also reminded him that if anything happened to him, Joe Stilwell[1] would be left in command.

March 31

Debate in Council on the vexed question of increase in railways fares. Finance Member proposed $12\frac{1}{2}\%$ instead of 25%. We had bare majority in Council for this, but majority of Indian members were obviously against it, and to the disgust of the Finance Member I said we would drop the proposal. Firoz Khan Noon sent me a note directly afterwards: 'The Persians have a proverb: "the bow that can bend shoots the arrow a long way": Y.E. has shot a long arrow tonight'. I think I was wrong really in letting the original proposal go through.

April 13

Returned yesterday from twelve days in Bihar and Bengal. These tours are interesting but Governors are inclined to fit in rather too much. It is the number of 10-minute interviews to a succession of persons which is killing. Some of them are just 'courtesy' visits by local notables, but some are officials or non-officials who might have a tale to tell if one could establish real contact, which is beyond me in a short time. I may with experience acquire the knack, or I may manage to alter the system.

I had a Council Meeting immediately on return and re-assured Members on the Bengal situation, or at least persuaded them that interference by the Centre would not help.

April 14/15

Out riding at 7 a.m. this morning the dhak tree (flame of the forest) was in full bloom in the jungle on the Ridge and the green parrots were in full bloom on the dhak trees for which they seem to have a great taste. It was a beautiful sight, but betokens the coming of the hot weather.

[1] He had been appointed Deputy Supreme Commander, South-East Asia in August 1943.

Heard in the evening of an explosion in Bombay Dock, which sounds a very bad show but have no details yet.[1]

Mountbatten came to dinner. I don't gather from him or from Henry Pownall whom I saw this morning that the Assam battle is really going very well—at least the initiative still seems very definitely with the Japs, and M.B. thinks that at best it will take them 5 or 6 weeks to clear the Japanese out.

He told the story of the visit of the Maharaja of Benares to Rampur. The Maharaja is an ultra-orthodox Hindu and conceives it necessary for his spiritual health that a cow should be the first object he sees every morning. At Rampur the guest rooms are on an upper-floor, but Rampur got a crane from a sugar factory and rigged up a platform on which a rather astonished cow was elevated every morning to His Highness' bedroom window.

Mountbatten was attractive as usual but he is having a hard passage, what with the Japs, the P.M. and the Americans, and has lost that first fine careless confidence that caused my predecessor to call him the Boy Champion.

Fire at Bombay has put two docks out of action, lost us a number of ships and 50,000 tons of food, a bad business but a little better than it looked at one time.

April 16

I got momentarily up-to-date with my work and had time to write a few letters. Even Jenkins ran out of papers and took an afternoon off. He sent me a formal little note: 'If Your Excellency approves, I will take the afternoon off'. I wrote on it the informal and undignified comment: 'Hooray, hooray, when the cat's away the mice will play'; and went off to the golf links.

I wrote a letter to H.M. the King, and drafted one to Amery on relations with the Princes.

April 17

We started a session of the National Defence Council but it only lasted about ¾ hour because Benthall who should have dealt with two subjects was still in Bombay—and Jamna Das Mehta was absent. Later the Food

[1] Fire had broken out on a ship lying in Bombay docks loaded with cotton, timber, and ammunition and caused an explosion in which 500 people were killed, 2,000 injured, and large amounts of shipping, food, and stores destroyed.

Member came to see me, rather depressed. He had been badly heckled at Bombay over food imports; and was even more worried by attacks on him from the Bengal Muslim side, evidently due, as he said, to a leakage about what had been said in Council on March 29. I tried to comfort him, this leakage from Council is disturbing but is no new thing. Jenkins heard from India Office that Rowlands failed to make any impression on the Committee on food imports.

Mookerjee, a Calcutta business man and member of the National Defence Council held forth to me at lunch on the behaviour of American troops in Calcutta, and implied almost that India was beginning to regard the British as comparatively civilised.

April 18

National Defence Council went along well. The Food Department actually had quite a lot of bouquets thrown at it, in contrast to the heckling of the last meeting. The only grouses were about black market prices, mainly by Kunzru, but it was apparent that the real trouble is that so many of the public will pay blackmarket prices if they want something and not take action to report the offender.

April 19

National Defence Council ended very quietly—rather a dull session, and absence of Jamna Das Mehta probably meant 2 or 3 hours less talk. Member for Sind, being furthest from any operations, was most bellicose and talked of the high morale in Sind and its desire to supply recruits— it has supplied less than any other Province.

April 20

A busy day. In the morning sat to Simon Elwes again, and then a large number of interviews, ending with Sir Ardeshir Dalal[1] of Tatas, one of the authors of the 10,000 crore scheme,[2] which had been debated that afternoon with members of the Government; the discussion seemed to have been satisfactory. I offered him the post of Member of Council for Reconstruction. He said he must ask Tatas and Delhi did not suit his health.

Finally a Council meeting, only about half numbers and quick decisions.

---

[1] After a distinguished career in the Indian Civil Service Sir Ardeshir Dalal became a Director of Tatas.

[2] Known as the 'Bombay Plan', an ambitious outline plan for economic development.

April 21

A Sikh landowner, Sir Datar Singh,[1] was rather grudgingly allowed by my staff to see me this morning, with the intimation that he didn't amount to much. I found him most interesting on the subject of cattle-breeding, much above the usual run of my 'courtesy' visitors, intelligent and talked clearly and well. Young Tata came to lunch. When I met him down at Bombay I found him rather a supercilious and tiresome young man, but got on with him rather better today. Sir Ardeshir Dalal had spoken to him about the offer I made him yesterday. I think Tata was pleased that the offer had been made but was doubtful whether the firm could spare him. Srivastava, whom I told about my intention to have a Development Member last night, is obviously rather upset; he has been Vice-President of the Reconstruction Committee of Council up till now, and thinks it a reflection on him. He is very sensitive to criticism. Both I and P.S.V. have explained to him no reflection on him is intended but that Reconstruction has become a full time job.

April 25

Returned from a short trip to Bombay to see damage to docks and go down area caused by recent explosion and fire. On the whole Bombay has come well out of it. Damage may amount to £50,000,000 or more, we have lost about 70,000 tons of shipping, 40,000 tons of food and a great quantity of valuable stores. But it might have been very much worse. If position had not been taken in hand efficiently, and if wind had not been favourable, we might have lost the principal dock, Alexandra Dock, or the oil tanks might have caught fire, or a large part of the city might have been burnt. Morale is good, and Bombay is feeling rather proud of itself. Civil and military worked in well together. Fire brigade and A.R.P. did well, and all Services co-operated whole-heartedly. Relief of homeless and sufferers was well organised, and Bombay rather feels that it can 'take it'. All the authorities are however concerned on the question of who will pay for the damage; there is no doubt that safety precautions were broken for war reasons, and that explosives ought not to have been unloaded where they were. The liability of the Insurance Companies and their capacity to pay is doubtful. We got the principle of an Enquiry, with the Chief Justice of Bombay as President, provisionally agreed; and can probably announce this almost at once.

---

[1] He established a reputation as an authority on cattle-breeding and later, both before and after Independence, held various posts in the Ministry of Agriculture.

Got back late in evening to find a message from Governor Punjab to say that Khizar had decided to stand up to Jinnah, and asking leave to dismiss Shaukat from the Ministry. Shaukat is Sikander's (the late Premier) son, and has been a great disappointment.[1] I told Governor I approved the dismissal and would support him.

April 26

Rowlands came in the afternoon; he had not made much impression in London on the Cabinet Committee on India food grains—little wonder when he told me the composition: that old menace, the Professor (Cherwell); Leathers, an interested party, only concerned to hang on to his shipping; P. J. Grigg, who is always mischievous about India; and Llewellyn, the Food Minister, who knows nothing of India and is concerned to preserve his food supplies at home. Attitude simply is that there is no shipping and Americans can't be asked to supply some in case they do so but deduct it from allotment for U.K. Grigg and Cherwell said the remedy was to lock up all grain merchants. Chiefs of Staff are sympathetic but can not move War Cabinet. The conclusions arrived at by the Committee on April 6, after hearing Rowlands, were that the courses open were: (a) to supply the shipping; (b) to ask the Americans for it; (c) to tell the Viceroy to supply the Army's needs and let the Indian people starve if necessary; and that the War Cabinet must decide. I wonder what has happened since then. I think they would adopt course (c), if they had any real hope that the Viceroy would consent to carry it out. I expect the P.M. is regretting that he ever appointed me.

The Caseys arrived, he looks better.

April 27

Another longish day in office. An hour with Srivastava, who was very worried about personal criticism of himself, especially in Bengal. I don't think he and Casey had had a very successful interview. He was also upset by my decision to appoint a Reconstruction Member, and thought it implied failure of himself. I got him to talk of his previous career and achievements in science, business, and politics; and I think this cheered him up. He dislikes democracy and Congress, and adjured me to get rid of this headcounting business as quite unsuitable for India. So it is. But will authority ever really have the courage to say so? I like Srivastava, he has some character and courage and independence, though I think his business is always at the top of his mind.

[1] He did not stand by Khizar in his struggle with Jinnah but sided with the latter.

April 28

Woke up feeling rather rheumatic, and then had a fall off my horse on to my back, so have been rather stiff and lame all day. Sat to Simon Elwes, who is making a good picture, I think, but rather deliberately. Then a very long day in the office. Jogendra Singh came in the morning and gave most of his favourite hares a run. He finally suggested, as he left, that the Viceroy should see more of his Council informally and discuss general questions with them; I think this was complimentary and meant to indicate that they consider me sympathetic and liberal and that my views carry some weight. I must think it over. Bombay reported some concern about the health of Gandhi whose blood pressure has suddenly dropped; and I found a little to my surprise that we have no real policy for action if the old man gets dangerously ill or should hand in his checks.

April 30

Abell came in with a telegram in the evening, giving the text of a very good letter from P.M. to President asking for help for India in shipping for imports of wheat. It ought to ring the bell. He has put India's needs at 1,000,000 tons. This represents a considerable success for my persistency. I had in the morning sent off a letter to the P.M. on the general state of India, the first I have written to him.

May 1

A long day in the office. Mohammed Usman as usual had nothing to say about his Department, but delivered himself of political views that even a hardened Tory might regard as reactionary—'God never meant India to be independent' and so forth. Next visitor was Mr. Pothan Joseph (which sounds slightly reminiscent of Egypt in the bad old Biblical days), the editor of Dawn a cheerful ruffian. He has mainly worked for Congress papers, is now Muslim League and is actually by religion a Christian. He cross-examined me on the difference between civil and military responsibility, and I said there wasn't much difference but that the civilian, politician or statesman, was always on active service and the soldier only occasionally. I don't think he understood what I meant. Then the Finance Member who is off home shortly. Finally a conference on the Bombay enquiry, but as everybody had agreed beforehand it did not take long.

May 8

I got back yesterday from a short tour to Sikkim. A long days travel on May 2; left Delhi 6 a.m., landed Hassimara about noon and then had to cross a river by elephants, a flood having taken the bridge. Then a long motor drive to Gangtok where we arrived at 9 p.m.

The only official ceremony laid on during my stay was a visit to the girls school being built in memory of the Maharaja's eldest son who was killed while serving in the I.A.F. The programme called for a simple visit to the school, but I found that Gangtok had laid itself out to produce some ceremony. I was met by a guard of warriors in old Bhutanese costume, gay coloured silks, two swords apiece, shields of rhinoceros hide, old steel helmets of roundhead pattern, a band and dancer to lead them. Then a monastery band greeted me, with monks in silk robes, long 12-foot horns, chanters, conches and other strange instruments, and a display of banners carrying prayers printed on them. There was also the Maharaja's retinue in the picturesque Lepcha costume, and another band, and then a modern police guard, and a parade of boy-scouts, and the school-girls singing. The actual inspection of the school did not take long as it is only half-built; and then we sat under a dragon-embroidered shamianah and drank tea and watched a Lepcha dance (treading out the harvest) and a Tibetan dance (slow and solemn) and a Nepalese dance (rather ribald). A picturesque and friendly performance.

On the morning of May 4 Gandhi interrupted the peace. George Abell brought me a telegram at 2.30 a.m. to say that the doctors (Roy and the Bombay surgeon-general Candy) thought very poorly of his health and that he might die at any moment. Bombay Government, Home Department and most of the Governors recommended immediate release and P.S.V. wanted my approval to a telegram to S of S to say that we proposed to release him 24 hours later. Personally, I could not see that we gained much credit by releasing him at the point of death; and if he was not at the point of death there was no need of such hurry. I did not entirely trust the medical opinions. However, it was difficult to disregard them, and Thorne's opinion was very strongly in favour of release. And Jenkins was not likely to make a panic proposal, and said that doctors views indicated that G. would not be a factor in active politics again. On the other hand, I should have liked to consult my Council and should certainly have done so had I been in Delhi. I talked it over with Abell for about an hour before cabling consent.

I left Gangtok on May 6th and flew to Sylhet in Assam. I spent the night at Sylhet and visited H.Q. 3rd Indian Division—the headquarters of what were Wingate's raiding columns, now Lentaigne's.[1] Lentaigne is good,

[1] Maj.-Gen. Lentaigne, succeeded Wingate in command of the 'Chindits' and after Independence became Commandant of the Indian Staff College.

I think, more orthodox and less highly strung than Wingate, who possibly was killed at the right moment both for his own fame and the safety of the division. But he was a remarkable man and I am glad that I was responsible for giving him his chance and encouraging him. My dealings with him, in three campaigns, were almost entirely official and I never knew him well enough as a man to like or dislike him.

I had hoped to see Archie John but he had flown into Burma a week before. Tired of waiting for vacancy in the Black Watch he had taken one in the South Staffords. I believe the column he has joined is likely to be flown out soon, but I expect Archie John will try to stay on with his own regiment or some other column. I hope his health will stand it. I saw Bernard Fergusson, complete with bushy beard, whose brigade had just been flown out. He was well, but a little upset by his failure to win his first pitched battle, at Indaw against the Jap airfield. He had had a hard time marching down from Ledo through the jungle, said it was surely the only recorded instance of a brigade marching 250 miles in single file.

We had a long fly back, nearly 7 hours, as we were in a slow machine, and did not reach Delhi till nearly 7.45 p.m.

May 12

May 10 was long day in office and May 11 much longer, work seemed to be accumulating all the time. At Council on May 10, some of my colleagues were rather upset that I had not consulted them over Gandhi's release; they all agreed that it was the right thing to do but resented that the credit of the release should all be given in the Press to the Viceroy and not to the G of I; they had had the odium of putting him in prison but no kudos for releasing him. Fortunately I had taken the initiative by explaining to them what had happened before they raised the point. I think they were fairly happy in the end. Amery unfortunately had said that he 'left the decision to Lord Wavell' instead of 'to the Government of India'.

Reports on Gandhi's health seem to show that he is really ill and P.S.V. seems to think that his memory and headpiece may be affected.

Had long talk with Bernard about his Operations in Burma. He had obviously been considerably tired and strained by this second expedition into Burma and said he had not realised how much the first expedition had taken out of him. He said no one over 40 stood up to it. I imagine Bernard does not spare himself; but the physical effort of carrying at least 50 lbs continuously in heat and jungle must be great. I hope Archie John will stand up to it.

May 17

I asked Dr. Khare yesterday what he thought of Gandhi's health and his view was he was duping us, or the doctors were, and that he would recover. My own bet is that the old man is still pretty ill. Coal labour is still causing much trouble, odd that the amount of coal we can get varies inversely with the goodness of the rice. Last one was a bumper crop, so the miners left the mines to cultivate their fields.

May 23

Mainly visitors and interviews and one short Council. George Giffard came to see me on May 20th. He has fallen out with MB who is going to replace him. I am very sorry, George is a good soldier. He says the battle is going well but slowly.

Thorne, Home Member, was very strongly against Gandhi's request to see Governor of Bombay being granted. We also discussed the publication of Gandhi's correspondence, and agreed that if we took the initiative in publication we should give G. due warning of our intention.

May 29/31

Got back today from a short holiday at Naini Tal with the Halletts to which I had been much looking forward.

We have at last got out the settlement for the Bombay disaster, after some prolonged negotiations with the Insurance companies. It has taken just a month, since I came back from Bombay.

Had a telegram from P.M. to acknowledge my letter of April 29. It was friendly and complimentary but finished up with a diatribe against Gandhi, he is obviously disturbed by the idea that I may start negotiating with him.

May 31

For the first time since I became Viceroy I was almost short of work this morning but this afternoon a long telegram from Casey about his Ministry which he fears may collapse over the Education Bill. His Chief Minister has not the energy or courage to force a difficult matter through and the Speaker of the Assembly seems definitely to have sided with the Opposition. Bengal politics are bitter and dirty. It looks as if Casey may be forced into the Section 93 regime which I recommended six months ago.

June 1/2

I don't feel altogether happy about the Assam and North Burma operations. There is not much progress being made anywhere, especially in the vital task of reopening the Kohima–Imphal road. Meanwhile the supply by air to Imphal and to the 3rd Division columns in North Burma is causing anxiety.

Inside Burma our raiding columns seem to be getting into difficulties. I hope Archie John is all right.

June 4

The President has turned down flat the P.M.'s request for shipping for food for India, so I sent home yet another telegram. This is disappointing, after waiting 5 or 6 weeks for a reply. I had gathered from a letter I had from Jack Dill that the request was likely to be favourably considered.

June 7

Work has been much less the last few days, and there has not been much of interest. Sir Ardeshir Dalal[1] came to see me yesterday, he has very firm ideas of what he wants and I can foresee some rows ahead with Council Members, some of whose work and staff he will want to appropriate. However, I must back him, even if it means trouble, but I warned him not to go too fast. He seemed sensible about the political situation and India's needs. He said the Bombay damage settlement had been very well received. He thinks Gandhi still a sick man. Hydari[2] talked about the political situation, he said no progress was possible till both Gandhi and Jinnah were underground, first time I have heard an Indian say so, but I expect a good many of the sensible ones think it.

A short Council meeting today with few members. The Gandhi correspondence did not cause much discussion. We decided the best tactics would be to publish the whole of the political correspondence if G. wished to publish any of it.

> Gandhi in a long, argumentative letter had shown that he still stood by the 'Quit India' resolution. Wavell in a courteous reply said that while he absolved the Congress of any deliberate wish to aid the Japanese, he felt that they must have been aware that the 'Quit India' resolution would hamper the prosecution of the war, and that, in his view, the greatest contribution that Congress could now make towards India's welfare was to abandon the policy of non-co-operation. In the course of some further correspondence Wavell said that if, on reflection, Gandhi had some more constructive policy to offer, he would gladly consider it.

[1] He had accepted the post of Member of Council for Development offered to him on 20 April (see p. 66).

[2] Sir Akbar Hydari, I.C.S., Secretary Industries and Civil Supplies, 1943–5, Member of the Executive Council, 1945–6, Governor of Assam, 1947–9.

June 10

Came up to Simla yesterday. It is always a wearisome drive up from Kalka, and the twists do not suit Her Ex.[1] I had a talk with Glancy this morning, he seemed a bit harassed, he had a very difficult time putting enough backbone into Khizar and his Ministers to stand up to Jinnah. Although Jinnah is a most unorthodox Moslem (to say the least of it) he seems to be able to wave the banner of religion and frighten them all to heel with it. We shall have more trouble with J. and his private army, the Moslem National Guards. I went round some of the houses being used on the Viceregal Estate for a soldiers' leave camp. A very nice lot of men and they seem happy and appreciative.

June 12

Had a telegram this morning to say that Archie John was seriously wounded, no details. His column was last reported south of Mogaung. I am afraid that there is no air strip available and that evacuation may be very difficult. I am not even sure whether they have a doctor with those forward columns.

Went to dine with Glancys at Barnes Court. On return had more optimistic news which showed they were hopeful of getting A.J. out by plane at early date.

June 13

News this morning that A.J. has lost a hand, but is not considered to be in danger. We will go down to Delhi today and fly to Assam tomorrow to wherever he is.

Had a long talk with Khizar, the Punjab Premier, and tried to hearten him up for his conflict with Jinnah. He is very apprehensive of two things, Jinnah's private army, and the maulvis[2] which he says J. is bringing in from outside to preach and stir up communal feeling.

Left Simla about 1 p.m. and reached Delhi about 6 p.m. Decided to get on early next morning to Dinjan, to which Archie John may be flown out.

June 19

Returned this evening from expedition to N.E. Assam to collect Archie John. We stayed with Gregory, a tea-planter, a nice person who treated Viceroys as human beings, and there was no ceremony of any kind, a

---

[1] Lord Wavell referred to Lady Wavell in his Journal as 'Her Ex' more in fun than in ceremony. He never wrote 'Her Excellency'.

[2] 'Learned men', an honorific title applied to those believed to be learned in religion and Muhammadan law.

welcome change. It rained almost the whole time, and we had some trying rather monotonous days of waiting. A.J. was not flown out till 17th, partly owing to weather, mainly owing to his own refusal to be evacuated till all cases he considered more serious had gone. In spite of an amputated left hand and slightly damaged right hand, he seems to have kept on his legs and carried on helping in the administrative work. He is in remarkably good shape and heart, considering his injury.

I only got a very limited amount of work from Delhi, from a letter from the S of S, I gather they have definitely refused shipping for food imports, and will make fatuous suggestions that we reduce the Indian Army (as if that would help) or import food instead of military stores.[1] But the official telegram from the War Cabinet has not yet arrived, and from a private telegram it looks as if the Chiefs of Staff had seen the absurdity of the War Cabinet proposals, and were considering means to find the shipping. Meanwhile these discussions have been going on for six months, with deliberate obstruction on the part of certain members of the Government. Casey is still in trouble over Bengal politics and recognises the possibility that he may have to go into Section 93. Gandhi has published his correspondence with me, or rather he gave the Press typed copies and they insisted on publishing it. So we are publishing the whole of the Gandhi correspondence. I don't think it will do us any harm or G. any good, it seems to me to show him as verbose, petty-minded, and quite devoid of any constructive statesmanship, bent only on his own self-justification.

June 21

Two fairly quiet days. I had a letter from Mr Gandhi asking to see the Working Committee and to see me. I am replying that as our recent correspondence has shown radically different points of view, I see no value in our meeting or in his meeting the Working Committee, until he has something more constructive than Quit India to propose.

June 23

Two quiet days. So many reports have reached me that a member of my Council is disclosing financial information gained in Council to his friends for business purposes that I thought it better to warn him when I saw him yesterday that his name was being connected with disclosures. He took it quietly, said it was a great surprise, but did not protest his innocence with any vehemence.

[1] This had been considered before. See entry for 10 March, p. 59.

The India Office or the F.O. or both are being maddeningly slow over deciding on giving Bajpai, India's representative in U.S.A., ministerial status, which I thought was practically decided more than six months ago; and are also being pedantic about allowing our representative in China the appellation of 'Honourable Mr'.

Simon Elwes asked for a final sitting,[1] as he was unhappy about my hands. He got them to his liking at last. He has put a thundercloud behind my head, I asked whether it was symbolical. He said partly technical to put the left side of my face in shadow and partly symbolical of the storms that might burst over my Viceroyalty. They surely will.

June 24

I wired two days ago to S of S to say that I must really have a decision about food imports and that I must send a personal wire to P.M. if no decision was yet reached. From reply today it is evident that they are still fiddling and procrastinating, so I sent the P.M. a personal appeal, drafted by Jenkins but pepped up by myself.

I had a talk with George Giffard about the Assam war. Jap resistance on the Imphal road collapsed quickly in the end and they got it open quicker than expected. It has been bloody fighting on the E. Frontier. Our casualties in some six months in Arakan and Assam approach 25,000; while the Jap losses are estimated at 30,000 to 35,000, with a very high proportion of killed.

George is feeling very sore at the American attitude of constant criticism and denigration of the British effort. We agreed that no other nation would take so calmly and good humouredly the American insults and carry on co-operating with them on friendly terms; and that we were a very great nation, greater than the American, and would remain so.

June 26

I have won another round over food with H.M.G. A telegram yesterday promised to ship another 200,000 tons in the next 3 months and to reconsider our further needs in August and then again in November. This telegram crossed my telegram to the P.M., which India Office suggested need not now be delivered. I wired back that it should be and that I did not consider the situation satisfactory yet. Still we are getting on, I have extracted 450,000 tons since the War Cabinet regretted that nothing could be done.

---

[1] The portrait now hangs in Rashtrapati Bhavan (formerly the Viceroy's House) in Delhi, together with the portraits of other Viceroys.

Carton de Wiart[1] came and spent a night, mainly, I believe, to tell my son how well he had managed without a hand. He is a charming person.

June 29

A lot of visitors the last few days. Henry Pownall came from home, Mountbatten and some of his staff from Ceylon, and Casey from Calcutta, the latter to discuss the political situation. After six months experience of Bengal politics and administration, he is burning to take over the Province under Section 93. It is a curious reversal of form. Six months ago I advocated a Section 93 Government for Bengal and was turned down by H.M.G., I think largely because Casey, who was then at home, wanted to have a chance of making a success of Ministerial Government. When Casey arrived in India about the middle of January and I saw him in Lucknow, I painted him rather a gloomy but I think realistic picture of Bengal affairs, but he was full of hope. Now he is aghast at the virulence and corruption of Bengal politics and the inefficiency of the administration, and wants to run the Province under Section 93. Six months ago, when famine and disease were raging in Bengal, we should have had, I think, almost the whole of public opinion behind us in taking over the Province. Now we should be criticised from every quarter. I don't worry much about public opinion, but we shall never get on in India if we take over from Indians every time they get into trouble. Six months ago the lives of many hundred thousands of Indians were at stake; and in the hope of saving them I was prepared to neglect or override constitutional forms. But today there is no immediate prospect of famine in Bengal, and I am trying to get Indians to learn to ride the horse before we hand him over. We agreed that Casey should keep his present Ministry in office if possible, that no alternative Ministry was possible, and that I would prepare the ground in London for the possibility of Section 93. What a nice fellow Casey is, and a very good and keen administrator.

June 30

A lot of files but nothing much in them. The Nationalist papers are making a great play over my refusal to see Gandhi, and the News Chronicle correspondent, Gelder, is trying to advertise himself by seeking an interview with me to persuade me to see Gandhi. I refused to see him. Nor have I any intention of seeing Gandhi unless he shows some unmistakable sign of a great change of heart, which seems unlikely.

[1] Lt.-Gen. Sir Adrian Carton de Wiart, V.C., special military representative with General Chiang Kai-shek, 1943–6.

4

PROPOSAL FOR
A POLITICAL MOVE

July 1

A quiet day. Since Gandhi was employing his usual technique of putting out such portions of correspondence as suited him, I gave orders for the publication of our recent exchange of letters.[1]

It has been very hot indeed the last few days, and the monsoon seems late and light so far, I hope it is not going to fail us.

July 4

A comparatively quiet time recently. Thorne tells me our issue of the Gandhi correspondence has become a best-seller, and that a further edition is being called for. Congress supporters are obviously very annoyed that their plan of publishing such portions of the correspondence as suited them has been upset by our prompt publication of the whole. They were doing the same with the last two letters, and the Hindustan Standard had an angry leader today because I had published them in full.

July 5

I sent P.S.V. a note yesterday on preparations for the possibility of the war ending within a year. I think we must have a plan, political and otherwise, in case there is a sudden collapse of our enemies. After all, no one in July 1918 believed for a moment that the war would be over in November. At the moment we seem somewhat stuck in Normandy and I fancy the flying bombs are being rather more of a menace than we have admitted. However, the Russians seem to be sweeping on fast.

Winston sent me a peevish telegram to ask why Gandhi hadn't died yet! He has never answered my telegram about food.

July 11

The correspondence between Jinnah and Rajagopalachariar published yesterday is curious, so are the various interpretations put on it by the Press and the various political parties. Jinnah is a mass of vanity and no

[1] See entry for 21 June, p. 75.

Famine relief, Orissa

At Bhubaneswar Temple, Orissa

statesman, but he is much too wary to accept the rather vague proposals put forward by R. without more definition. It is not quite clear how far Gandhi himself is committed to these proposals, but the Hindustan Times seems to consider they have his full approval. We are undoubtedly in for a period of political manoeuvring which may lead to trouble. I wonder if we shall ever have any chance of a solution till the three intransigent, obstinate, uncompromising principals are out of the way: Gandhi (just on 75), Jinnah (68), Winston (nearing 70).

> *Rajagopalachari put forward a 'formula' which, he said, Gandhi was prepared to recommend to Congress, if Jinnah would accept it. Under this formula 'contiguous districts' in the North-West and East of India in which Muslims were in an absolute majority were to be demarcated and these would constitute Pakistan. Arrangements were to be made by mutual agreement between Pakistan and the rest of India to safeguard defence and commerce, and communications, and for other essential purposes. Jinnah replied that he could not accept the 'formula' on his own responsibility and would have to refer it to the Muslim League, which he would be ready to do, if Gandhi would deal with him direct. Later he arranged to meet Gandhi, but he denounced the formula as offering only a maimed, mutilated, moth-eaten Pakistan. It was the Pakistan which in the end he had to accept.*

Old Jogendra Singh came in yesterday in tremendous form, full of gratitude to me for backing his agricultural schemes and saying it had given him a new lease of life. He's a nice old boy, though woolly-pated.

I read the proceedings of the Dominion Premiers conference in May. You would hardly know from them that India existed or had any importance at all. Iraq and Persia received more mention. Curious that neither Australian nor South African Premiers seem to take any interest in a country whose future must greatly influence their own problems.

July 14

Came up to Simla yesterday for a fortnight, unless Mr. Gandhi should necessitate my return. He is putting forth a series of statements to the Press and seems determined to raise a political turmoil if he can.

July 17

A fairly quiet time up here so far. On Saturday (15th) I saw Sir Chhotu Ram[1] still rather suspicious of the Government of India and all their works but more friendly, I think, and less suspicious than when I first met him

---

[1] Sir Chhotu Ram died six months later, a severe loss to Khizar and the Unionist Party.

in the Punjab some six months ago. Punjab are now, I fancy, rather proud of having 'seen Jinnah off', and more confident of the eventual issue.

Her Ex has had a busy time with Red Cross work. She had a Committee meeting today, morning and afternoon, and seems to have managed it very cleverly.

The leave camp here in the Viceregal grounds, the idea of Her Ex and arranged by Peter Coats, seems to be a great success.

July 19

Chief business in the last day or so has been drafting telegrams to S. of S. about Mr. Gandhi's activities. There is likely to be a debate on India in House of Commons on July 26, and Amery is likely to have a rough passage, especially in explaining why Gandhi should not be allowed to see the Working Committee. I have tried to give him ammunition but I am afraid that nothing he says goes down very well. It would in any event be difficult to convince a large section of the House that Gandhi's motive is not really for a settlement but to secure the release of the Working Committee as a prelude to further political agitation.

I am a bit bothered about the monsoon, it is late and weak so far, I hope it is going to play the game.

Woodhead,[1] President of the Famine Commission, arrived. One of his members seems to be running out already. I had the arrangements for this Commission started in January, as a result of a resolution passed in the Legislature in November, with the idea of getting it started in March! It will be lucky if it does any business before mid-August, I think the delay this time has been mainly at the Whitehall end; and from my experience of the last year or so I should say that on the whole Whitehall is slower at getting anything done and more verbose even than New Delhi.

July 22

I was told today of a secret conference on Palestine held in Cairo last May. The subject was the decision by H.M.G. to partition Palestine and the probable military repercussions. I hear that with one exception everyone there, civil and military, expressed themselves in very strong terms against the Partition proposal. I wonder if the views of the men on the spot will have any influence on H.M.G.

It will be noticed that, though India has over 90 millions of Moslems, many of whom feel very strongly about Palestine, H.M.G. did not even think fit to inform me of this conference.

---

[1] Sir John Woodhead, I.C.S. (retd.). He had served in Bengal.

July 23

I have had another letter from Gandhi, to which I replied calling Mr. Gandhi's attention to my statement in my previous letter that I was willing to consider a definite and constructive proposal if it were submitted to me.

I saw a letter from Kirby[1] our Food Controller, who is at home, describing in pessimistic terms the way in which Indian affairs are treated in the Cabinet and especially our requests for food imports; and the complete failure of the India Office to make their weight felt. The Committee on food imports is a packed committee headed by that old fraud and menace, the Professor, seconded of course by Leathers.

July 24

A very busy day for my last in Simla. Many visitors, and finally Khizar, Punjab Premier, who was in much better heart than last time I saw him, and advocated a Centre Party but did not explain how it was to be formed. I like Khizar very much but he is not a strong character any more than his predecessor Sikander Hyat Khan was. Odd that these big Punjab landlords should be so dominated by a down-country lawyer like Jinnah.

July 26

At Council meeting this morning I informed my colleagues of my recent letter from Gandhi and my reply, and discussed G's statements and my attitude to them. Council unanimously supported my attitude, and no one had a good word to say for Gandhi. Council was anxious that S. of S. in speaking to Parliament should make G. of I. responsible for any refusal or acceptance of negotiations with Gandhi and not merely the Viceroy.

July 31

I had an hour with Bhopal in the morning, listening to the grievances of the Princes. Bhopal himself is modern and shrewd, but he is only a Princeling really, and in no position to call the tune for the Princes as a whole, who are for the most part concerned mainly with maintaining all their privileges, position and prestige untouched, and whose attitude is inclined to be: the British Crown must either continue to protect us or cease interference with our affairs.

In the afternoon I had the C-in-C, then Md. Usman, then Rowlands, and finally Mudie, the new Home Member, with a draft reply to Gandhi's

[1] W. H. Kirby, Assistant Secretary, Board of Trade, loaned by the British Government as rationing adviser to the Government of India.

last letter which I must take time to consider. I am quite sure that he is keeping one objective in mind as his immediate aim, to secure the release of the Working Committee. I doubt if he is really one whit nearer compromise on his idea of a Congress Raj.

> *In this letter Gandhi said that as a constructive proposal he was prepared to advise the Working Committee that Mass Civil Disobedience as contemplated by the resolution of August 1942 could not be offered and that Congress should give full co-operation in the war effort, if India was immediately declared independent and a National Government formed responsible to the Central Assembly, subject to the proviso that military operations should continue under British control, but without involving any financial burden on India. This proposal, as Gandhi well knew, was totally unacceptable. A similar proposal had been put forward at the time of the Cripps Mission in 1942 and had been rejected.*

August 2

I have been busy the last day or two in writing a quarterly letter to H.M. and in drafting a reply to Mr. Gandhi's latest, which has now been cabled home for approval—rather reluctantly on my part, I dislike this reference to Whitehall on every detail.

August 4

One of my Departments told me the other day that I had reduced the number and length of telegrams by 50%. I wish I could think it was true. Srivastava came in this morning, ostensibly to discuss the food problem, really to talk about politics. I like Srivastava, and usually manage to send him away in quite a cheerful mood, but I think he is harassed at home (his wife is quite a strong Nationalist) and has a difficult time, since he feels that if anything goes wrong with food he will have to bear the brunt; and he is very sensitive to criticism.

The P.M. wired me that the Cabinet was very perturbed that I had entered into negotiation with Gandhi, who should be dead—at least politically—according to the medical reports cabled home. I fortunately remembered his directive of last October,[1] and wired back that I was not negotiating with G, merely informing him that negotiation on his basis was impossible; that I had carried out the injunctions of his directive; and that the only provision of his directive which I had been unable to carry out was 'to divert shipping to carry food grains', since H.M.G. would give me neither shipping nor food grains.

[1] See p. 23, entry for 8 October.

August 9

Got back this afternoon from a short tour to Manipur and Assam to see some of the troops and the recent battlefields. I was 'back to the Army again' for some days, which was pleasant, but it was quite strenuous.

I flew to Calcutta on the 5th and stopped a night there. Had about 2 or 3 hours talk with Casey. He is now very set on Section 93, and regrets that my recommendation of last January was not accepted.

On the 6th I flew to Imphal and did a heavy programme of inspection of military and R.A.F. units.

I stopped the two nights at Imphal with Gimson,[1] he still had not had his bathroom window repaired (broken in May 1942); his wireless still gave forth unintelligible sounds; and his cat had had kittens. In fact he was as cheerfully inefficient as ever. (When my predecessor, Linlithgow, stopped there, he always claimed that a cat dropped on his bed from the ceiling during the night. My M.S. mentioned this story to Gimson, who said quite unconcernedly: 'I don't think it can have been a cat, quite probably a rat, though'!)

On the 8th I motored up the Dimapur road and saw representatives of 6th Brigade and 2nd Division, both of which I formerly commanded. I presented some decorations and made a short speech to them. I then went on to Kohima.

I was told that 15 or 20 Nagas would come to meet me at Kohima, actually 200 to 300 turned up, a picturesque sturdy looking people. They brought gifts of spears and headdresses and woven cloths and chickens and eggs. I had brought rum and cigarettes for them but there were a great many more than we had expected. The Nagas did us extraordinarily well in the recent fighting.

After a picnic lunch I motored on to Dimapur and found another longish programme which was not finished till 7 p.m.

I had been 12 hours continuously at it, and had motored over 150 miles. Rather to my horror I found that I was booked to go to an Ensa entertainment after dinner. It was not very good and went on till after 11 p.m. During it a bag arrived, so that I had to attend to one or two letters and telegrams before going to bed.

Next morning, the 9th, we were booked to take off from the ground at 6 a.m. We got back to Delhi at 3 p.m.

My apprehensions at referring my reply to Gandhi home were fully justified. I got back a revised draft exactly the same in principle, but intransigent and discourteous in tone. It seems to me one of our great

[1] Mr. C. Gimson, I.C.S., Political Agent in Manipur.

mistakes in this country is not to have realised the importance to the Indian mind of good manners and an appearance at least of consideration. I drafted a cable back, proposing revision of the Cabinet's draft. P.M. will be furious.

Wavell's draft reply to Gandhi's letter, after restating the proposals that Gandhi had made, continued as follows:

2. Since your letter was written you must have studied the statement made by Mr. Amery in the House of Commons on 28th July, and will know that this proposal is not acceptable to His Majesty's Government as a basis for discussion. It is very similar to the proposal made by Maulana Kalam Azad to Sir Stafford Cripps in April 1942, and His Majesty's Government's reasons for rejecting it are the same as they were then.

3. Although His Majesty's Government cannot accept your present proposal, and I do not think that we should make progress if we met in order to discuss it, I must assure you that they are most anxious for a settlement of the Indian problem. The war is now moving fast, and unless we can reach agreement on lines satisfactory to all parties, India can hardly take her proper place at the Peace Conference, and our plans for post-war economic and social development will be hampered.

4. I do not wish to prejudge any proposals that may later be made to me, but if the leaders of the Hindus, Muslims and other important minorities were willing to co-operate in a transitional government which would be established and would work within the framework of the present Constitution without modification by convention or otherwise, I believe we could make progress. It is quite clear that until the war is over the responsibility for Defence and Military operations cannot be separated from the other responsibilities of Government and that until the new Constitution takes shape His Majesty's Government and the Governor-General must retain their responsibility over the entire field. If the transitional government is to succeed there must, I think, be agreement before it is formed between Hindus and Muslims and the other important minorities as to the general basis of the new constitution and as to the method by which it should be framed. This agreement seems to me a matter primarily for the Indian leaders. I should be glad to help them to achieve it if I thought I could do anything to help; but I doubt if I can do anything until they have come closer together than they are now. I beg you to remember that minority problems are not easy. They exist in many countries and have caused much unhappiness and even civil war. It is a mistake to say that the minority problems in India have been created by the British; they are real and can be solved only by patience and generosity. The period after the war is over for which the transitional government would last would

depend on the speed with which the new Constitution could be framed. I see no reason why work on the Constitution should not begin as soon as the transitional government takes office, and if the parties had arrived at a genuine agreement as to the method of framing it, I do not think the period need be very long.

5. You and Mr. Jinnah have my good wishes for your approaching discussion.

This draft reply was friendly in tone and evinced very clearly a desire to open the door to negotiations, whereas the Cabinet's draft gave the impression of a desire to keep it closed. Wavell's draft was, in the Cabinet's view, 'much too forthcoming and conciliatory', and they decided to 'stiffen its tone'. They cut out, therefore, all friendly and gracious touches, for instance paragraph 5; and they introduced a new paragraph which by stressing the conditions attaching to the 'offer of unqualified freedom after the cessation of hostilities', particularly the need to safeguard the interests of racial and religious minorities and the Depressed Classes, seemed to suggest that freedom might be postponed indefinitely.

August 10

A long day of files and visitors with little to show for it.

In the evening had a letter from S. of S., in which he said that the P.M. 'stormed incoherently for about an hour' over my letter from Gandhi. I wonder what he will do when he gets my come-back.

I have just read rather an interesting book 'The Bear of Britain' by a man called Frankland,[1] which gives a realistic and savage version of the Arthurian legend, much nearer the truth of course than Malory's Knights. I have been trying to find out something about the Roman evacuation of Britain and the state of the country afterwards, but nothing much seems to be known.

August 11

Patiala came to see me and stayed to lunch.

Out of the long list of subjects which Political Department suggested H.H. might wish to discuss, only one was raised by him, he wanted a war medal, for which he hadn't qualified, but other more fortunate Princes had!

August 12

My telegram home about Gandhi letter has perturbed the poor S. of S. Winston himself seems to have drafted the Cabinet version in a very

[1] Edward Frankland, *The Bear of Britain* (London, 1944).

stormy meeting, and now Winston is in Italy. S. of S. wanted me to issue a short reply of 'nothing doing'. I have stuck to my guns and said I am quite prepared to issue my draft and incur Winston's displeasure. I wonder what they will do now.

August 14

I had a long talk with George Giffard on the war in Burma. He thinks the Japanese will have a very difficult job to reform their Army and to reinforce. They have practically given up using Rangoon, owing to the threat of our air force and it is reckoned that they can only bring in a division a month over the Bangkok railway. They will require at least 75,000 reinforcements to reform their shattered divisions, they have lost practically all the artillery of three divisions and almost the whole of their Tank regiment. George hopes to get Kalewa before the end of the monsoon. I wonder what will happen to George himself, it will be a little difficult for them to remove him after such a great victory; on the other hand there is little hope of the Americans consenting to serve under him.

August 15

H.M.G. or at least, Ministry of War Transport, is furious at the Bombay Explosion Enquiry Report and has sent us a very intemperate statement on it.

The Cabinet refused to play over the Gandhi letter, except for one small amendment, so I have sent their draft, as it is not a big enough issue for a head-on collision, which I think is bound to come sometime, if the Cabinet continue their negligent and hostile attitude to the affairs of India.

The Secretary of State had urged Wavell not to issue his own draft and incur Churchill's displeasure, as this would involve a head-on collision which would not be justified by a mere difference about wording. Wavell agreed that 'this occasion is not one for a head-on collision', but he expressed his dissatisfaction to the Secretary of State in strong terms:

'I feel that many of our troubles in India, both administrative and political, are due to ignorance and prejudice among your colleagues. It is discouraging work to serve an obviously hostile Cabinet, who seem to have no confidence in my judgement on any matter. They have now turned down my recommendations for (a) Indian Finance Minister; (b) Section 93 in Bengal at the beginning of the year; (c) Bajpai's status; (d) the form of my reply to Mr. Gandhi; and (e) my requests for food imports, of which my great persistence has produced an inadequate amount.'

He was also intensely annoyed at the attitude of the Ministry of War Transport to the findings of the Commission of Enquiry into the Bombay explosion. The Ministry wanted to make a foolish and 'ill-tempered attack on the Commission', which had been headed by the Chief Justice of Bombay with a distinguished Admiral as a member. 'The Ministry,' he wrote, 'is hardly on a good wicket in trying to defend a very minor official by impugning the impartiality of two very distinguished Government officials.

'His Majesty's Government must really give up trying to treat the Government of India as a naughty and tiresome child whose bottom they can smack whenever they feel like it.'

I am sure that the G–J meeting will result in a demand for the release of the Working Committee, but I doubt whether it will have any other result.

Following his correspondence with Rajagopalachari, Jinnah announced that he had agreed to meet Gandhi. After several postponements they met on 9 September.

August 16

Quiet Council meeting. I read out the reply to Gandhi and there was little comment. Firoz Khan Noon signalled his return by a characteristic outburst of eloquence in favour of high prices for food grains to support the farmers, with his usual disregard for accurate facts and the exact issue under discussion.

August 22

The result of the Cabinet's amendment of my reply to Gandhi's letter has been as I warned them. The reactions have been virulent and have concentrated on the tone of the letter—'rude' and 'arrogant' it was called—, on the dragging in of the Depressed Classes and the apparent additional conditions above the Cripps Offer before a transitional Government was formed, and on the fact that the letter was published immediately on its receipt by Gandhi—all of which were due to the Cabinet's amendments and would not have been vulnerable in my original version. In fact Cabinet has destroyed at one blow my reputation for fairness and good temper in my correspondence with Gandhi, and has thus weakened my usefulness in any eventual dealings with Congress. This was probably the P.M.'s intention. It has also increased the likelihood of a Congress–League coalition against us.

I have just finished reading Dorothy Sayers 'Man Born to be King',[1] very well done and very interesting. Curious to think that if Gandhi were a saint, instead of a very shrewd and rather malignant politician (which is possibly how the Sanhedrin thought of Jesus at the time), or became transformed into a saint by history; and if he died on my hands, as he might well do, if he fasts again, I might go down to the readers of 2000 years hence with the same reputation as Pontius Pilate; my Council would play the part of the Sanhedrin; and perhaps one of the Princes could be cast for Herod.

I was amused to see that since the Americans took over the Assam Railways, there have been 33 derailments and 6 collisions, whereas during the Congress troubles in 1942 all attempts at sabotage caused only 6 derailments.

August 31

Governors' conference for last 3 days, which means a pretty hectic time, since ordinary routine work does not stop. We discussed food problem, post-war development, war allowances for civil servants, and the political situation. Perhaps the chief feature of the food discussion was the desire for central control, both now and after the war. In post-war development, Bombay, Madras and U.P. are well ahead with their schemes, but I doubt whether others have done very much.

The discussion on the political situation was interesting. I made a short statement of my views, i.e., that we could quite easily hold the present situation till the end of the war if necessary; but that if nothing was done before the end of the war, we shall find ourselves in a very dangerous position; and that an opportunity might occur for a move at the end of the European War and should be taken. Governors were unanimous in supporting me in this, though there was some difference on the form of approach. On the question of progress in 93 Provinces, no one favoured the summoning of the Legislatures, but Madras was quite anxious to have non-official advisers, and Bombay and U.P. did not object. Rutherford even thought he might be able to form a Ministry in Bihar, but he was woolly about it as usual.

Outside the Conference I had talks with all the Governors.

Casey agreed rather reluctantly that he must try to keep a Ministry going in Bengal and forego the delights of Section 93. He told me Nazimuddin had got back several followers, one by typical Bengal methods.

[1] D. L. Sayers, *The Man Born To Be King* (London, 1943).

These Governors meetings are valuable, but have aroused the wrath of the Congress Press, and the Hindustan Times had a cartoon of me as an octopus, stretching my tentacles (the Governor's head at the end of each tentacle) all over India. Firoz Khan Noon too, in his usual slap-dash way, wrote suggesting I was trenching on Executive Council's work and by-passing it. He was easily pacified.

September 7

Mountbatten came up to Simla today, but as he only arrived just before midday and departed at 5 p.m., our talk was rather hurried. He said P.M. was as intractable as ever about India, seemed to regard sending food to India merely as 'appeasement' of Congress; and it was only the efforts of the Chiefs of Staff, who realised the necessity for feeding India if it was to be a stable base for operations, which produced any food at all. My impression was confirmed that there was really plenty of shipping but that Leathers would not part; and that the Indian Food Imports Committee was a packed body. P.M. was quite furious about Gandhi's release and subsequent activities, and in fact quite impossible about India. Leo Amery, who does stand up to him, had accused P.M. of a 'Hitler like attitude' to India, and had got a first-class rocket.

We discussed welfare and nurses and medical help and all the other amenities for which India has been asking and has been denied for years; now Press and Parliament have turned their eyes East and are shouting to high heaven at the scandalous inefficiency of India for not having all these things. They will be sent now, but nothing will ever be said of all that India has done with the scanty resources allotted to her.

September 15

Got back to Delhi from Simla yesterday evening. I saw Raisman the evening before I left Simla and heard about the Bretton Woods conference, sterling balances problem etc. He agreed that the raising of pay and allowances for the troops in the East would have very serious repercussions on India's finances and that it was monstrous that we had not been consulted. (I had already sent an indignant telegram to S of S.)

H.M.G. suddenly intimated that the pay and allowances of British forces serving in the East were to be increased. Despite the fact that under the defence expenditure settlement the cost of the increases would mainly fall on India and would almost inevitably involve corresponding increases in the pay of Indian forces, the Government of India was not consulted—a typical example of

H.M.G.'s cavalier treatment of India to which Wavell was always objecting. The War Department of the Government of India sent a vigorous protest. One of Wavell's private telegrams of protest to the Secretary of State was improperly allowed to come to the notice of Churchill and, as will be seen, roused his wrath.

September 16

Two days discussions with the Princes went quite well. Bhopal put his points clearly and temperately, and the rest hardly spoke at all. I said a few words at the end about the necessity to face changes after the war, and the idea of a united India. They received these remarks in silence and I don't think that anyone of them like the idea of change.

I had a talk with C-in-C yesterday, he approved 100% my proposal to make a political move, and even said he was prepared to work under an Indian Defence Minister.

September 18

Some time ago I asked Caroe's 'Brains Trust'[1] to produce a comparison between India and China as future Great Powers, e.g. in material resources, man power, political stability, organization. They produced an interesting paper which I read today. The general conclusion was that there was not much in it, but that China was tougher and had been through the fire both of internal revolution and of external invasion, while India had not and was softer. Curiously enough, Dalal, whom I asked this afternoon what he thought about the future of the two countries, said at once that he thought India was too soft and would have to go through the fire before she was able to be as fit for future power as China.

September 21

I got off to S. of S. yesterday my proposal[2] for a political move. I have no idea what the reactions of the P.M. and H.M.G. will be—wholly unfavourable, I imagine. Its despatch coincided with the arrival of a singularly stupid letter from Gandhi to the P.M., he had apparently written it some time back and practically accused us of suppressing the original

[1] A small study group, composed mainly of British officials, that studied various problems likely to confront India in the post-war world.

[2] This proposal was for the formation of a Provisional Government at the Centre representative of the main political parties and for the calling of a small conference of political leaders with this object in view. The reasons for making such a move well before the end of the War were very cogently stated and were later given more briefly in a letter to the Prime Minister dated 24 October 1944 which is reproduced on pp. 94–9.

(I should think his secretary or followers had probably not sent it, realising how silly it was).[1] I think it shows that Gandhi's mental powers are failing; and it will not improve the prospects of the P.M. approving any negotiations.

In the afternoon I saw Sir Henry French (Permanent Secretary, Ministry of Food in U.K.) who having toured India for six weeks now realises that our view of India's food problems and requirements is justified and that Whitehall's ïdeas of them are all wrong. I suppose they will listen to him, after having refused to listen to the Viceroy for 9 months. So perhaps we shall now get our Food import problem settled on reasonable lines.

September 30

The Gandhi–Jinnah talks ended on a note of complete futility. I must say I expected something better. I did not expect statesmanship or a practical solution, but I did think the two would have got down to something, if only the best way to embarrass the G. of I. Anything so barren as their exchange of letters is a deplorable exposure of Indian leadership. The two great mountains have met and not even a ridiculous mouse has emerged. This surely must blast Gandhi's reputation as a leader. Jinnah had an easy task, he merely had to keep on telling Gandhi he was talking nonsense, which was true, and he did so rather rudely, without having to disclose any of the weaknesses of his own position, or define his Pakistan in any way. I suppose it may increase his prestige with his followers, but it cannot add to his reputation with reasonable men. I wonder what the effect on H.M.G. will be, I am afraid it will increase their dislike of any attempt at a move.

> *Gandhi offered Jinnah the maimed, mutilated Pakistan of the Rajagopalachari formula, but without real sincerity or conviction. Jinnah rejected the offer and bluntly told Gandhi that the division of India was only on his lips and did not come from his heart.*
> *Moreover Gandhi insisted that any division of India could only take place after the British had left, which was in line with the general Congress aim of wresting control from the British first and settling with the Muslims, Princes,*

---

[1] Gandhi's letter was as follows:

Dear Prime Minister, You are reported to have the desire to crush the 'naked faqir', as you are said to have described me. I have been long trying to be a faqir and that naked— a more difficult task. I therefore regard the expression as a compliment, though unintended. I approach you then as such and ask you to trust and use me for the sake of your people and mine and through them those of the world.

Your sincere friend, M. K. Gandhi

etc. afterwards. Jinnah believed that once the British had gone, the Hindus would never agree to the division of India and that the Muslims would have to fight a civil war to get even a mutilated Pakistan.

October 4

Mostly routine business. The P.M. sent me rather an insulting telegram, because in a private telegram to S. of S. I had, in protesting against India not being consulted on the pay increases, said that Council might take the view that if the British Government had to bribe the British soldier to fight in the East, India should not be saddled with the cost. Unfortunately the telegram was seen by the P.M. who seized the opportunity to get at me of which he is always glad, and wired what amounted to an accusation against me of insulting the British soldier. I wired back an explanation, and added that I thought my record of service might have saved me from his insinuation. I am afraid this exchange will not improve his views on India or the relations between us. (October 6.—Rather to my surprise he cabled me a polite acknowledgement.)

October 11

For the first time for something like 10 years, I have been in bed for 2 or 3 days with a fever. I felt rotten on Saturday, had a temperature of over 102 and a head—chill on the tummy I think. Was all right by Monday, but left first two days of N.D.C. to C-in-C and only presided at final session this morning. We discussed food, Srivastava had been well briefed by Hutchings and was quite good. We had got the day before telegram from S. of S. giving us 300,000 tons for last quarter and Srivastava was able to announce this. After nine months hard struggle I have got 700,000 tons for India *after* H.M.G. had twice said no imports were possible at all (no mean achievement for India, I think).

　　Had long telegram from S. of S. urging every possible objection and difficulty against my proposed political move, all of which I had of course considered before making it. He makes a fatuous counter-proposal which Linlithgow turned down with a bang nearly three years ago. I thought they would refuse to face it.

　　The Secretary of State suggested that the National Defence Council should be utilized for discussing the basis of a future constitution for India and framing proposals. Wavell replied that this was quite impracticable and would lead nowhere. Gandhi and Jinnah held the keys of the situation and could not be bypassed.

October 20

For the last week I have been up and downstairs and in and out of bed, running high temperatures for a short time, having headaches and indigestion, never very bad but enough to make work difficult and life depressing. I am feeling better today and hope I am all right. I have, however, cancelled my tours to Baluchistan and N.W.F.P.

We had a difficult and unfortunate Council meeting on 18th over the application to India of the War Service pay and Japanese campaign pay which H.M.G. sprang on us without consultation or warning. The results have been disastrous. The C-in-C demanded similar benefits for Indian troops including the indefensible allotment of Japanese campaign pay to Indian troops serving in India. If I had been fit and had more time, I would certainly have stopped this. C-in-C said he would not be responsible for the morale or discipline of the Indian army unless the increases were granted and all the Indian members of Council naturally supported him. C-in-C also demanded pay rises for Indian Commissioned Officers and this was also passed. He admits privately that Japanese pay inside India is illogical, and that so also really is the extra pay for I.C.Os. But once the issue of racial discrimination is raised, it is not possible to restrain Indian members. F.M. came to me next day and practically threw his hand in.

I have been Viceroy a year today, the hardest year's work I have done. In some ways I have done reasonably well, the food problem and getting some sort of a move on post-war development. I have found H.M.G.'s attitude to India negligent, hostile and contemptuous to a degree I had not anticipated, or I think I might have done more. Still the more one sees of the political problem and of the Indians, the more one realises that there are very dark days ahead for India, unless more wisdom and good will are shown, and I think they will have to begin from the top, from Whitehall.

I have made some mistakes. I don't think the release of Gandhi was one, though I always mistrusted the medical opinions on which he was released. I wish I had been firmer with the C-in-C over increases of pay though I think most of them have been justified.

Rowlands came in on return from U.K. He says the forcible tone of some of my telegrams has made P.M. furious and made it difficult for other members of Cabinet to help; on the other hand if they had not been forcible P.M. would have taken no notice. General Election is apparently inevitable in spring, on strictly party lines, and the issue doubtful. I have proposed Rowlands for Finance Member of the Executive Council and sounded him this evening.

October 25

I have answered S. of S. objections to my proposal for a political move, saying that I fully realised the difficulties and risks but that we should never get on unless we faced them. He has now wired proposing that I should consult Governors, he is obviously in a dither at the idea of having to put my proposals up to the Cabinet. Meantime I have written a letter to the P.M. on the occasion of my completing a year as Viceroy, stating my views on India, and have taken as text his directive to me of a year ago—but the P.M. won't like it.

With approval from home I offered Rowlands the job of F.M., he asked for time to consider but did not definitely turn it down.

On 24th I presented 4 V.Cs and a G.C. on quite an impressive parade just outside Delhi Fort; and yesterday we had 500 Indian soldiers to tea (the V.Cs and their relatives and the men of the Guards of Honour and other troops on parade), quite a good party—Her Ex's idea.

The letter to the Prime Minister with the omission of a few paragraphs mainly about the background of conditions in India, is reproduced below.

24th October 1944

My dear Prime Minister,

I have now completed one year in the high and responsible office for which you did me the great honour of recommending me to His Majesty; and I feel I should write and give you some account of my stewardship and of the views I have formed on the present and future of India.

I propose to write entirely freelyand frankly, as I know you would wish. I have served you now for over five years and we should know one another reasonably well. I know you have often found me a difficult and troublesome subordinate. I have not always found you an easy master to serve. But I think you realise that I have always served loyally—and I may say with unqualified admiration for your courage and your strategy—and that I have always told you the truth as I saw it without fear of consequences. I propose to do so now.

I will begin by saying that my primary reason for writing is that I feel very strongly that the future of India is the problem on which the British Commonwealth and the British reputation will stand or fall in the post-war period. To my mind, our strategic security, our name in the world for statesmanship and fairdealing and much of our economic well-being will depend on the settlement we make in India. Our prestige and prospects in Burma, Malaya, China and the Far East generally are entirely subject to what happens in India. If we can secure India as a friendly partner in the British Commonwealth our predominant influence in these countries will,

The Governor-General's Executive Council, 22 March 1944

Seated: Sir Edward Benthall, Sir Sultan Ahmed, Sir Jeremy Raisman, General Sir Claude Auchinleck, the Viceroy, Sir Reginald Maxwell, Sir Ramaswami Mudaliar, Sir Firoz Khan Noon, Sir Mohammed Usman.

Standing: Sir Evan Jenkins (P.S.V.), Sir Asoka Roy, Sir Aziz-ul-Huque, Sir J. P. Srivastava, Dr. B. R. Ambedkar, Sir Jogendra Singh, Dr. N. B. Khare, Sir John Thorne (Secretary).

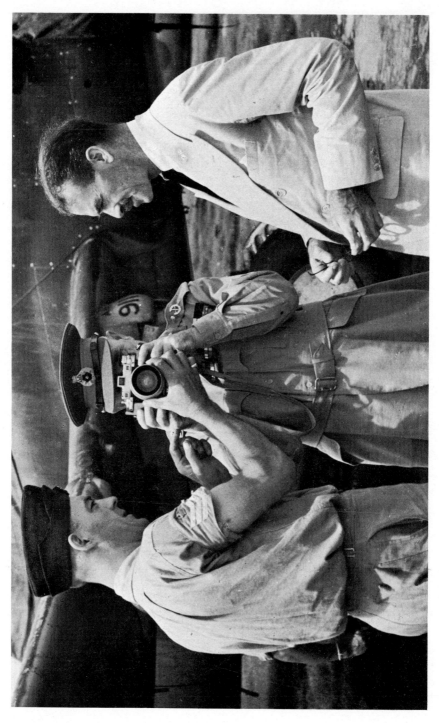

Lord Wavell (centre) at Alipore with Mr. R. Casey (right), Governor of Bengal, August 1944

I think, be assured; with a lost and hostile India, we are likely to be reduced in the East to the position of commercial bag-men.

And yet I am bound to say that after a year's experience in my present office I feel that the vital problems of India are being treated by His Majesty's Government with neglect, even sometimes with hostility and contempt. I entirely admit the difficulty of the problems, I know the vital preoccupations of the European war. I agree in the main with what I think is your conviction, that in a mistaken view of Indian conditions and in an entirely misplaced sentimental liberalism we took the wrong turn with India 25 or 30 years ago; but we cannot put back the clock and must deal with existing conditions and pledges; and I am clear that our present attitude is aggravating the mischief.

May I give you a few instances of what seem to me a neglectful or unfriendly attitude to India and her problems.

I read the proceedings of the meetings of the Dominion Premiers. India, one of the most vital problems of the Commonwealth, was hardly mentioned, either from the strategic or political point of view.

At the last big debate on India in the House of Commons, I am told that there were hardly ever more than 40 members present.

In spite of the lesson of the Bengal famine, I have had during the last nine months literally to fight with all the words I could command, sometimes almost intemperate, to secure food imports; without which we should undoubtedly be in the throes of another famine, and probably of uncontrolled inflation, since without these imports I could hardly have held food prices from soaring as they did last year.

The recent increase of soldiers' pay, which have added some £50,000,000 to our inflationary position, already precarious, and a considerable part of this sum to the Indian tax-payer's burden, were introduced without any consultation of India at all, or even warning; though we could have suggested means of easing the burden both for the British and Indian tax-payer; and Indian Members of Council would have felt no resentment if they had been consulted in advance.

The obloquy now being heaped on India for the lack of amenities for soldiers is mainly due to disregard of repeated requests during the past three years or more for doctors, nurses, medical comforts, and goods of all kinds.

Having got that off my chest, I will try to give you a picture of the Indian problem as I see it.

I will take as a text the directive you gave me on October 8th last year, before I left for India. This directive required me, in brief:

(i) to secure the defence of India against the Japanese;

(ii) to rally all classes to the support of the war effort;

(iii) to establish and maintain the best possible standard of living for the largest number of people;

(iv) to appease communal differences; and

(v) to make proposals for political advance as occasion warranted, subject to the demands of (i) and (ii) above.

. . . .

. . . On the first two tasks given in your directive, I have carried on my predecessor's work, to meet the development of the campaign. The S.E.A.C. has been firmly established; and Mountbatten has expressed his complete satisfaction at the support in men and material given to the 14th Army during the recent operations on the Eastern frontier; and in the preparations made for future plans. Transportation is perhaps our most serious single problem; and we also need special help to improve the welfare of British troops. The strain on Indian economy generally is serious; and additional burdens without relief in other directions will risk a breakdown.

The third task in your directive concerned standards of living, and is a most difficult and complicated problem. The Bengal famine of 1943 was a very serious disaster, and disclosed the weaknesses in our food administration. These weaknesses are due partly to an absolute shortage in a country which is permanently under-nourished; and partly to the human qualities of fear, selfishness, greed, and provincialism. My chief aims in food administration during the past year have been to restore confidence, to improve the procurement and distribution of food, to extend rationing, and to get more food grown. It was absolutely essential to secure food imports on a large scale, and I am afraid I had to be importunate about this, since my first requests were received with much the same astonished incredulity as Oliver Twist encountered on a well-known occasion. I have tried to break down provincialism, both by personal visits to all Provinces, and discussions with those concerned in food administration; and by conferences of all the Governors. I think I can claim a certain measure of success; for example, I induced the Punjab to accept both rationing and price control after their Ministers had publicly announced that in no circumstances would they do anything of the kind. And there is certainly a great deal more confidence throughout the country than there was a year ago, with a very wholesome effect on prices. With the help now being accorded by His Majesty's Government, we should be able to hold the food position, but only just. We are, and shall remain, on a knife-edge until normal trade conditions are restored. The danger areas are at present Bengal, parts of Madras, the Travancore and Cochin States, and the Bombay Deccan; at the moment the Travancore and Cochin States and the Malabar district of Madras form the most urgent problem. The difficulty, almost impossibility, of persuading the rice-eating South to eat the hard Northern grains will be well known to you, and you will realise how it complicates the problem.

Apart from the food problem, I have endeavoured to stimulate planning for post-war development over the whole administrative field, both in industry and agriculture, so as to secure a better standard of living for the Indian people; and I have appointed a special additional Member of Council to deal with the problem. This is an immense task, perhaps impossible of accomplishment under the present Government of India. Success will require either complete autocracy on the Russian model, or effort and self-denial of a kind only possible under imaginative and popu- lar leadership. Indians have not so far shown themselves any keener than other people on austerity and high taxes. But I think I can claim that the Government of India is stimulating ideas in the direction of development as far as possible.

The fourth and fifth tasks you gave me together constitute the political problem. I cannot claim to have made any progress with them, but they are of vital importance. The following seem to me to be the essential factors of the problem:—

(i) When we started, 20 or 30 years ago, on the political reform of India, we laid down a course from which we cannot now withdraw. It may have been a mistaken course, and it would probably have been better to have prescribed economic development first; but I am afraid it is too late to reverse the policy now. And the general policy, of giving India self- government at an early date, was confirmed not long ago in the Cripps offer.

(ii) Nor do I think that in any case we can hold India down by force. Indians are a docile people, and a comparatively small amount of force ruthlessly used might be sufficient; but it seems to me clear that the British people will not consent to be associated with a policy of repression, nor will world opinion approve it, nor will British soldiers wish to stay here in large numbers after the war to hold the country down. There must be acquiescence in the British connection if we are to continue to keep India within the Commonwealth.

(iii) India will never, within any time that we can foresee, be an efficient country, organised and governed on western lines. In her development to self-government we have got to be prepared to accept a degree of in- efficiency comparable to that in China, Iraq, or Egypt. We must do our best to maintain the standards of efficiency we have tried to inculcate, but we cannot continue to resist reform because it will make the administra- tion less efficient.

(iv) The present Government of India cannot continue indefinitely, or even for long. Though ultimate responsibility still rests with His Majesty's

Government, His Majesty's Government has no longer the power to take effective action. We shall drift increasingly into situations—financial, economic, or political—for which India herself will be responsible but for which His Majesty's Government will get the discredit. We are already in the position that Indian Members of Council have a controlling voice, and are increasingly aware of their power. The British Civil Services, on which the good government of the country has up till now depended, might almost be described as moribund, senior members are tired and disheartened, and it will be extremely difficult after the war to secure good recruits.

(v) If our aim is to retain India as a willing member of the British Commonwealth, we must make some imaginative and constructive move without delay. We have every reason to mistrust and dislike Gandhi and Jinnah, and their followers. But the Congress and the League are the dominant parties in Hindu and Muslim India, and will remain so. They control the Press, the electoral machine, the money bags; and have the prestige of established parties. Even if Gandhi and Jinnah disappeared tomorrow (and I do not think that Gandhi today would be described by Insurance companies as a good life) I can see no prospect of our having more reasonable people to deal with. We have had to negotiate with similar rebels before, e.g., De Valera and Zaghlul.

(vi) When we should make any fresh move is a difficult problem. I am quite clear that it should be made some considerable time before the end of the Japanese war. When the Japanese war ends, we shall have to release our political prisoners. They will find India unsettled and discontented. Food will still be short; demobilisation and the closing down of the war factories, and overgrown clerical establishments, will throw many people out of employment. They will find a fertile field for agitation, unless we have previously diverted their energies into some more profitable channel, i.e., into dealing with the administrative problems of India and into trying to solve the constitutional problem. We cannot move without taking serious risks; but the most serious risk of all is that India after the war will become a running sore which will sap the strength of the British Empire. I think it is still possible to keep India within the Commonwealth, though I do not think it will be easy to do so. If we fail to make any effort now we may hold India down uneasily for some years, but in the end she will pass into chaos and probably into other hands.

(vii) To be effective any move we make must be such as to capture the Indian imagination. If India is not to be ruled by force, it must be ruled by the heart rather than by the head. Our move must be sincere and friendly, and our outlook towards India must change accordingly. I am prepared to put up proposals for a move, which will involve risks, but which I think constitute the best chance of making progress.

What I have in mind is a provisional political Government, of the type suggested in the Cripps declaration, within the present constitution, coupled with an earnest but not necessarily simultaneous attempt to devise means to reach a constitutional settlement. Amery knows my views, and I drafted a paper for the Cabinet, which I have asked him to withhold for the present.

But the real essential is a change of spirit, a change which will convince the average educated Indian that the British Government is sincere in its intentions and is friendly towards India. It will not be easy to do, there is very deep-rooted feeling of suspicion to overcome, but certain steps could be taken which would help to reduce the mistrust and enmity now generally felt. In fact, if we want India as a Dominion after the war, we must begin treating her much more like a Dominion now. If certain measures, which I would suggest, were taken by His Majesty's Government, and I were permitted within a policy approved by His Majesty's Government to try and convince India of British sympathy, I believe it would be possible to effect a considerable improvement.

I should like to add that the view that something must be done before long is not merely my opinion. It is the considered opinion of the Commander-in-Chief, of all eleven Governors of the Provinces of British India, and of all the senior members of the Services with whom I have discussed the question. I do not think His Majesty's Government can afford to ignore the entire weight of British official opinion out here.

If the Cabinet is opposed in principle to any move during the war, I think a clear statement to that effect should be made so that we may all know where we stand. But if it is a matter of timing and of method my advice is entitled to due weight. I think the failure of the Gandhi–Jinnah talks has created a favourable moment for a move by His Majesty's Government.

It is easy to condemn any plan for betterment of the Indian situation on the ground of risk or probable failure. If we are to make any progress, we must take risks and be prepared for failure; but a move made generously and honestly, even if it failed, would do good.

I have, as you know, no axe to grind. I did not seek this appointment or wish it; but since I have been placed in a position of such immense responsibility for the future of the British Commonwealth which we serve, I am bound to place my views in front of you; 'without partiality, favour or affection'.

[592/9]   Yours sincerely,
                                                    WAVELL

October 29

Simon (Astley) left for home this morning after 2½ years as ADC. He is about the quickest witted and most efficient ADC I have had, and has in many ways an attractive personality.

I got Maurice Hallett and Colville up here to discuss the proposal for a political move, and sent George Abell to Lahore to consult Glancy. Hallett and Colville entirely support me, Glancy taking a Provincial view, is afraid that move may affect Punjab Ministry and Unionist Party and strengthen League.

November 9

Back to-day from a short tour to the Punjab. As usual, a pretty strenuous performance. There were interviews with all the Ministers and some of the officials; a reception of about 150 or so people; and inspections and tours.

Meanwhile I had to deal with the usual spate of official papers from Delhi; and to keep abreast of the discussions going on between Srivastava, the Food Member, who had come to Lahore to try to smooth out differences on food prices etc. with the Punjab Ministers. These seem to have gone fairly well, but there are still some difficult problems: Punjab want parity of rice prices with U.P. and priority of movement for their surplus grain and one or two other things.

On my way to the plane this morning I paid a surprise visit to the Lahore Gaol.

On return I had a long interview with C-in-C. On the issue of Japanese Campaign pay to Indian troops in India, which the S. of S. wants reconsidered in council, I found Auchinleck very stubborn. I don't mind the financial effect, but I don't want at this juncture to be turned down by H.M.G. on an issue on which we are in the wrong, and have not a leg to stand on logically.

November 11

A long day with lots of files and a very difficult conference with C-in-C and Finance Member over Japanese campaign pay which lasted for an hour and a half. I got C-in-C just a little more accommodating. We are sending telegram to S. of S. to elucidate certain matters and C-in-C's final attitude will depend on his reply.

No reaction from P.M. yet about my letter, but S. of S. has cabled that it has arrived. Rowlands has accepted Finance membership provisionally, asking for certain conditions which are quite acceptable.

November 13

Lunch party today included two Ministry of Information officials (Redman and Bamford) and I tried to impress on them how to get over British propaganda in India, which Bamford admitted the M.O.I. was unable to do. My theme on propaganda to India was this: the M. of I. approach is to boost British achievements etc., with the implication that India is very lucky to be able to belong to the British Commonwealth. I said that the approach must be to boost Indian achievements, with the implication that the British Commonwealth is very lucky to have so valuable a member.

November 16

Bulabhai Desai, leader of the Congress party in the Assembly, came to see me yesterday evening—I had asked to see him. Rather an attractive person with a pleasant voice. He was all sweet reasonableness in his proposals for measures to ease the present situation, in fact his ideas seem to bear a distinct resemblance to the recommendations I have made to H.M.G. He wanted a National Government under the present constitution formed of members drawn from the existing legislature—and of course the release of the Working Committee and replacement of Section 93 Governments.

November 20

A moderately quiet weekend but any number of files. I have to make 4 or 5 speeches shortly—to the Chamber of Princes, to the Naval training ship at Bombay (Dufferin), to the Chamber of Commerce at Calcutta, at Cawnpore, and possibly when I visit the Army at Imphal. I am not very good at speeches, I hate being hurried over them, but seldom finish them in good time.

Sapru's proposed Committee, announced this morning, will be hailed with delight by H.M.G. as an excuse to postpone consideration of my proposals. I have told P.S.V. to draft a wire to S. of S. to ask that my proposals may be considered, even if they have eventually to be postponed till Sapru's Committee has reported.

At Gandhi's prompting the veteran Liberal politician, Sir Tej Bahadur Sapru, was induced to set up a Committee of his Non-Party Conference— a moribund political body—to study the constitutional problem and attempt a solution of it. Nothing important came of this.

November 26

I think Indian 'political circles' have guessed that there is something afoot, or ought to be. G. D. Birla, Jinnah and Mirza Ismail[1] have all been around taking soundings. Birla had a long talk with Jenkins, who gave nothing away. It all really amounted to the fact that they are most anxious in all political parties for H.M.G. to move, and I think prepared to accept something on the lines of my proposal to H.M.G. I don't think there can have been a leakage, but it does look as if they knew or guessed something.

November 28

The house has been full of Governors' wives and others for W.V.S. and Red Cross conferences, run by Her Ex. who must be having a frightful time. There has also been a conference of Railway managers, all of whom came to lunch.

Meanwhile I have been struggling with six speeches which I have to deliver in the first half of next month, the one to the Chambers of Commerce at Calcutta being the important one.

The routine work too has been heavy.

The P.M. has acknowledged receipt of my letter in a telegram which I am sure indicates his determination to do nothing whatever till the war is over. I shall obviously have to make some very determined move if India is to have consideration in the near future.

November 30

Srivastava in a discussion with me today told me that, after the Congress success at the polls and assumptions of office in U.P. in 1937, the leading industrialists—all I think Hindu—got together and decided to finance Jinnah and the Muslim League and also the Mahasabha, as the extreme Communal parties to oppose Congress who they feared might threaten their financial profits. I said I considered it a most immoral proceeding, and Srivastava merely said: 'but politics are immoral'.

I have been speech-bound for the last 10 days trying to write my speeches for the forthcoming tour, especially the Calcutta speech, but am still practically speech-less.

December 3

Work has been heavy but nothing sensational.

On the matter of extra pay for Japanese campaign, S. of S. has sent a series of most confused and illogical telegrams. I could make neither head

[1] Sir Mirza Ismail, Dewan of Mysore, 1926–41, Prime Minister of Jaipur, 1942–6, Prime Minister of Hyderabad, 1946–7.

nor tail of them but P.S.V. has managed to interpret their meaning. The result is even more illogical than before and will really satisfy nobody.

H.H. of Bhopal came to see me this morning just before a meeting of the Standing Committee of the Princes. He expressed himself disappointed at the answer I had sent to their representations at the September meeting. He came again at 2.30 p.m. said his Standing Committee meeting had lasted till 1.20 p.m. and that they wished to resign. I said he must have had a difficult meeting, that it was tiresome for him to lose his Committee at this time, and that I must await the receipt of their formal resignation.

Later, at dinner time I got the formal resignation of the Chancellor, Pro-Chancellor and whole Standing Committee. I wonder what the next move is.

The September meeting with the Princes, which is briefly referred to in the journal entry for 16 September, had apparently passed off without any particular difficulty. The Princes were mainly apprehensive about schemes that were being put forward for grouping smaller States together for administrative purposes or for attaching them to larger States. One such 'attachment scheme' in Kathiawar had been put into force, despite objections by some of the Rulers, but had later been held by the Courts to be illegal; whereupon the illegality was summarily cured by Act of Parliament without the Princes being consulted. They were upset and alarmed by this procedure.

A letter was drafted, and approved by the Secretary of State, dealing with representations that they had made on this and other matters at the September meeting. Though it was conciliatory in tone and said that the Kathiawar Attachment Scheme would not be repeated, it did not grant the Princes any special concession. Their disappointment at this letter was the pretext for the resignation of the Standing Committee.

December 5

The resignation of the Princes has of course made a sensation. It will be exploited by the Nationalist Press and enemy propaganda, and is a tiresome affair; but it is surely a blunder from the Princes' point of view and I think they will soon realise it.

We had a big party from 7 to 9 p.m. for the Princes. Wylie tells me he has good information that the 'crisis' was the work of Bhopal and the Jam Sahib who forced or bluffed the rest of the Standing Committee into signing.

December 6

A very long day. I had an interview with Bhopal who gave a most disingenuous account of the resignation of the Standing Committee. It is now clear that he and the Jam Sahib deliberately engineered the 'crisis', and forced the Standing Committee to resign, without even telling them the result of his interview with me or of the contents of the Political Department's reply to their representations, or anyway giving them time to digest it. I discovered that when he saw me at 2.30 p.m. on December 3, and professed himself unable to control his Standing Committee, he had already had in his pocket the resignation document which he had himself signed and forced the others to sign. I told him that I thought the Princes had made a very serious blunder, and had shown grave discourtesy to the Crown, and had done themselves no good by bringing their affairs into public discussion. He was obviously ill at ease, and professed himself willing to do anything to retrieve his blunder.

I had an hour's talk with Jinnah. He showed his attractive side and was friendly and sensible. He professed himself willing to come into any Provisional Government under the present Constitution, although he said he could convince me that Pakistan was necessary and desirable. He is certainly intelligent.

December 16

Got back from tour this evening. A strenuous affair. We went to Bombay on 7th, a long day 6 a.m.—11 p.m. Next morning I went down to the Docks to see the repairs after the explosion, very well done; and about midday took off for Hyderabad.

We spent December 8–13 in Hyderabad. It was very strenuous but in some ways easier than I had expected. The Nizam, of whose eccentricity and personal habits I had heard so much, was in some ways an agreeable surprise. We had a long drive together from the airfield to the Falaknuma Palace where we were quartered. This pretty well exhausted my small talk, for H.E.H. was not very helpful. Then we paid one another State visits and this involved sitting side by side on ceremonial chairs with our staffs in long and silent lines on either side, and making formal conversation for 10 or 15 minutes. We managed quite fairly well, but I had to do practically all the conversation, and it does not come easy to me.

Three long days of official engagements followed, and on Tuesday, the 12th, the Nizam had a long talk. He began with a very fast yorker, as he said that since all the requests he had to make were in a printed 'yellow book' which he had sent to me, he need not go into them in detail. I had to say that though I was aware generally of H.E.H's hopes, I knew nothing of a yellow book. (Wylie of whom I hastily enquired later had also no idea what H.E.H. meant but concluded that he referred to a document of several years back). However, the Nizam did not press the subject, and then went on to enquire about the dispute with the Princes and resignation of the Standing Committee, on which he was obviously well informed. I told him frankly my view of the Princes' action. He then went on to ask about my interview with Jinnah and the general political situation. He is no fool and shrewd in a self-interested way. The Nawab of Chhatari who followed him obviously spoke to a brief given to him by H.E.H. on the great merits of Hyderabad's war effort and the need to reward them substantially.

There were some rather comic incidents. One was H.E.H. and the champagne. Before the visit the Nizam had written to the Resident expatiating on the high price of champagne and enquiring whether I expected it to be served to me. I told the Resident to relieve H.E.H's mind by telling him that I thought champagne was out of place in war time. However, on this last night the major-domo came to me shortly after dinner began and said the Nizam wished me to drink champagne with him. A champagne glass was placed before me, but no champagne followed and I heard agitated colloquies of the servants with H.E.H. on my left. It turned out that the first bottle opened was flat or corked, and it took some courage to suggest to the Nizam that a second bottle should be broached. This too proved flat and there was consternation. Finally someone was found hardy enough to suggest the opening of a third bottle and the Nizam regretfully agreed. But that too was wrong and champagne was given up, the Nizam explaining to Her Ex. and myself the high price the champagne had cost him and the sorrowful waste of his money. (The major-domo, a European, explained to me later the H.E.H. had bought the champagne years ago and had kept it standing upright with fatal results.)

This visit was rather an ordeal. All sorts of tiresome questions of etiquette cropped up, and the Nizam rather delighted in being awkward about them. I hate these problems, it is difficult to steer between the Scylla of being pompous and the Charybdis of letting down the dignity of the office. Another problem is the matter of gifts. The Nizam sent some round shortly before we left. There was his photograph and a book of his own poems, but there was also a necklace of problematical value for Her Ex. There does not seem any very strict guide about these presents, I was told that the practice was to accept them, and place them in a sort of public treasure chest, whence they were sold and proceeds used to purchase gifts which Viceroy had to present.

Hyderabad is a freakish place, a curious mixture of modern and mediaeval, of progress and of stagnation, under the despotic rule, except so far as British influence restrains him, of an odd personality. But the Nizam was less odd, more shrewd and less physically debilitated than I had been led to expect.

We got to Calcutta in the early afternoon of the 13th. Casey seemed to have fewer problems than usual. He has an 'embarras de rice' at the moment and would very gladly part with large quantities if we could guarantee to replace it in the second half of 1945. I like the Caseys very much and they are doing a great job of work in Bengal and actually seem to like Bengalis.

Next day I inspected the Calcutta Light Horse before breakfast; and made my speech to the Chambers of Commerce at 11 a.m. On the 15th I flew to Imphal and knighted Slim, Christison, Scoones and Stopford. Mountbatten, Leese and Browning were there.

On December 16 we flew back to Delhi, stopping at Cawnpore on the way to open the Hallett hospital, quite a good building.

December 20

I had a long talk to Wylie on 18th. He says visit to Hyderabad was a success and that Her Ex. in especial created a great impression. He persuaded me, rather against my own judgement, to cancel the visit to Bhopal. My instinct was to carry it out despite all Bhopal's tiresomeness. It looks as if I might be in for a show-down with the Princes, and I am not quite sure that I am ready for it.

Srivastava was very grateful for my remarks in the Calcutta speech on the work of the Food Department.

December 22

The usual routine for the last few days. The meeting with C-in-C and F.M. over the Japanese Campaign Pay went better than I had expected. We all agreed that the S. of S.'s half-rate proposals were quite illogical and unacceptable and that either all ranks of the Indian Army should receive at full rates in India or none, British or Indian. We all agreed that everyone should receive them east of a certain line.

December 25

Nothing of great importance lately except a telegram from S. of S. to say that the War Cabinet would make no move about India until I went home and advocated it myself. From his telegram it was obvious that they would much sooner I didn't hurry, and he used the Sapru Committee as an excuse for delay and suggested that I should wait till that had reported. I think the sooner I go the better. But I shall think it over for a day or so; I can't go before the end of January because of the visit to Nepal.

December 31

A quiet week, one of the quietest I have had since I became Viceroy, but all the same my trays were never really empty.

I have cabled S. of S., proposing to go home about January 25 for a fortnight.

So ends 1944. On the whole not a bad year for India. I have kept her on a fairly even keel, and can claim credit for some successes. I think it was quite an achievement to get 1,000,000 tons of food almost, after H.M.G. had twice at least declined flatly to send any more. And I have had some progress made with post-war economic development, though not nearly as much as is required or as I had hoped. The machine is desperately slow and cumbrous, and few of the personnel are really first-class. I don't know whether I could have done more to improve the coal situation, I did realise the need for action at once and tried my best to remedy the defects in organization and to increase production.

I think I did well in getting a quick and generous financial settlement after the Bombay explosion.

On the political side we have made no progress; and I have undoubtedly disappointed the hopes of political India which were raised by Gandhi's release.

I think his release was correct; though I am still not quite sure that he would have got out so easily if I had been in Delhi, I should certainly have insisted on another medical opinion. I believe his release has done good on the whole. I am sure I have been right not to see him until he could show some reasonable proposal; and anyway H.M.G. would never have allowed it. I think I have been right to back up Khizar in the Punjab against Jinnah's attempt to disrupt the Unionist Ministry.

I have now at least put a definite proposal to H.M.G. and have made them take notice of it. 1945 will show whether I can get it across with them; and if I can, whether I can get it across with the Indians; and in the unlikely event of these two improbabilities happening, whether I can make it work and set India on the right road. I am afraid that the hopes are slender, I have less opinion than ever of Indian capacity for leadership and statesmanship and commonsense; nor do I think that I have a strong enough personality to put through the almost superhuman task of persuading India to be a nation. I conceive that my two main objects must be: first, to try and persuade Indians that they have it in them to be a great nation; and secondly to persuade Whitehall of the paramount importance to British prestige, British security and British prosperity to secure a satisfactory but generous settlement of the Indian problem.

The trouble about the first is that there is hardly any sense at all of nationhood in India or of leadership likely to produce it: few of them see beyond their own personal or sectional interests. There is no greatness about India yet, I wonder if there ever will be. Even the Princes have no leaders nor dreamers of dreams, they too seem to be thinking only of personal pomp and prestige or personal gain. Has India a great future or is her great future already behind her?

In Whitehall there is ignorance and prejudice to overcome, it is curious how little they seem to know or to care about India and her problems. Official circles still treat India as a naughty child, whereas she has reached the more tiresome age of adolescence—I am speaking in regard to British rule—and will leave the parental protecting home of the British Commonwealth and perhaps go wrong altogether, unless given a latch-key, sympathy and a good deal of freedom.

Even if I manage to hold down this job for my full five years, I could make little impression on the situation; but the above are the general principles I should like to work on.

Evan Jenkins has been a great mainstay, and I have leaned heavily on him. His extraordinary capacity for work, clear-headedness and detailed knowledge have been invaluable, and I could not have got on without him.

It is hard to say how we have done on the social side, all right I hope. Her Ex. is of course an outstanding success as Vicereine. I think the atmosphere in the Viceroy's House is friendly without loss of dignity, and the Staff have done their work well, I have heard a good deal of testimony to the way the A.D.Cs. look after guests. But it is hard work and very easy to make a bad mistake, we may have made some already.

Someone (was it Dr. Johnson?) defined golf as the art of directing a small ball into a hole with instruments singularly ill-adapted to the purpose. It would serve as quite a good description of Indian politics.

5

THE FIRST VISIT TO LONDON

January 3
1945 has opened quietly. Practically the only discussion in Council today was on the glut of rice in Bengal and measures necessary to get it turned over and prevent its deterioration.

January 5
Little Menon[1] spoke of an interview he had had with Sapru, who was apparently of the opinion that I was completely opposed to progress. Menon said he satisfied him that I was not, and Sapru said that a move by H.M.G. would be welcome even if his Committee had not reported.

January 7
S. of S. has wired that War Cabinet will not have time to see me at home before March owing to meeting between the Big Three. They obviously want to delay as long as possible the moment when they have to take a decision about India. I suspect they will find other reasons for delay by March.

January 11
We had a National Defence Council on the 8th, 9th and 10th. Rather a tame affair, even little Jamnadas Mehta had little to say and the proceedings were rather dull.

Council lasted all morning today. It looks as if Bengal might have to export 200,000 tons of rice in order to turn over the stocks they have accumulated, but I am not sure that they will have the nerve to do it. Old Jogendra Singh gave his free-trade hare its usual run, and Aziz-ul-Haque chased it as usual.

January 13
We had another Council meeting yesterday on the status of our High Commissioner in South Africa.

[1] Rao Bahadur V. P. Menon, Reforms Commissioner, 1942–7, an Indian official of outstanding ability who played a leading role in the final Transfer of Power and in the subsequent Integration of the States.

Meanwhile P.S.V. was seeing Bulabhai Desai, the Congress Leader of the Assembly, who represented that he had the agreement of both Gandhi and Jinnah to propose a Coalition Government at the Centre, and similar Governments in the Provinces under the existing Constitution as a war time measure; in fact his proposals are very near what I have put to H.M.G. I have cabled to H.M.G. that I propose to see Desai on my return from tour, and that this approach cannot be disregarded. They will be convinced that I have engineered it, to force their hand, since I have seen both Desai and Jinnah recently. I think it may be an advantage in some ways that the approach has come from the Indian side. But I shall have some lively passages with H.M.G.

January 19

Got back this evening from five days camp in Nepal Terai with Maharaja. The party shot twelve tigers and six rhino. It was good fun and a very pleasant change in an attractive part of the country.

We were very comfortable and the atmosphere was very friendly. The old Maharaja (Joodha) was very well and in good form, I liked him. There was a ceremony (spring festival) on the morning of the 18th, at which H.H. and his family wore their gorgeous headdresses, solid with diamonds, pearls, emeralds and rubies and topped with birds of paradise; and H.H. and suite came in after dinner on last evening to make a short speech and propose my health to which I replied and proposed the Maharaja's: otherwise there were no social contacts and we lived in separate camps.

A huge pile of work on return. War cabinet very annoyed at my seeing Desai tomorrow—I had refused to cancel the appointment made before I went on tour—but gave a grudging consent.

January 20

I had two important interviews this morning, with Khizar and Desai. Khizar was in good heart, in spite of Chhotu Ram's death; he warned me against the machinations both of Congress and the League. In fact K. is really quite content with things as they are, and has really no great wish to sever the British connection.

I had 45 minutes with Desai, mainly asking him questions about his proposals, to ascertain exactly what he had in mind and what real support he had. He was all sweet reasonableness in his answers to my questions and seemed frank and friendly; but how much backing he really has I cannot say, I wired home a summary of my talk, and said that I must see

Lady Wavell

A. J. A. Wavell at Dinjan, June 1944

Jinnah if H.M.G. are prepared to go further with the proposal. I doubt whether they are, but they may find it a little difficult to say so.

Meanwhile I have to cope with a curious (Stafford Cripps called it 'startling', Amery says) proposal which S. of S. has evolved and put to War Cabinet. It practically amounts to giving India Dominion status under present Constitution and present Executive Council. It seems to me quite unworkable, both for constitutional and psychological reasons. S. of S. has a curious capacity for getting hold of the right stick but practically always the wrong end of it.

January 25

This afternoon I saw Jogendra Singh, charming and rather woolly as usual. He is the most attractive character of my Executive Council, I think, and has the right ideas but not a very practical grasp of realities. Hydari on the other hand who was my next visitor is a very practical young man, and I think on the whole more 'English' in his outlook than any official Indian I have met. Ronald Adam, A.G. at the War Office, turned up in the evening, he was as full of gossip as ever and told me of the next meeting-place of the Big Three and approximate date. P.M. will be in a much less dominating position than at previous conferences, both President and Stalin have realised their superior strength—of their national power for the time being, I mean. I wonder if P.M., who is the biggest man of the three, will still be able to assert his dominant personality. A great triumph if he can, the oldest man of the three with the weakest hand to play.

January 28

Returned this evening from a weekend at Bikaner. The usual sand grouse shoot, small duck shoot and bustard shoot.

H.H. asked for my help on a few private matters, and then mentioned the resignation of the Standing Committee, though I think he had not originally intended to do so. I think they all realise now that they made a bad blunder and want to get out of it with as little loss of face as possible.

On return I found the usual mass of files, and two important telegrams from Cabinet on the Desai proposals, mainly raising petty and unimaginative objections of detail; but they are biting at the proposal all the same.

January 30

I sent three telegrams to the Cabinet yesterday on the Desai proposals, answering the two they had sent me. The first two were drafted by P.S.V.

and dealt succinctly and effectively with the points they had raised; the
third was a personal message drafted by myself to the effect that they had
the best chance they have had for a long time, or were likely to have, to
make a moderate advance in the Indian problem and that they had better
take it at once and not worry too much about details or comparisons with
the Cripps offer, etc.

January 31

Council meeting this morning. The only subject that aroused much discussion was Ambedkar's proposal to re-impose the ban on women working in the mines by a fixed date. All members except Srivastava professed
sympathy with the proposal but agreed that in view of the coal situation
and the war we could not impose the ban within any foreseen period.
Srivastava said frankly that he thought the women would resent the re-
imposition of the ban, that he saw no reason against their working in the
mines if they wanted to, and that he thought they should be allowed to as
long as they liked. (At an early stage in the proceedings Srivastava caused
some amusement by complaining that Shankar, the Hindustan Times
cartoonist, always drew him with no clothes on, except a towel, because
he had once met him in a Turkish bath).

February 17

Came back this evening from a fortnight's tour to Mysore, Travancore
and Cochin. Very strenuous as usual, and on the whole rather less interesting than I had expected.

The Mysore visit was quite a pleasant one. I liked the Maharaja, courtly
and cultured but very shy and reserved; he would be a source of strength
to the Princes if he would come out of his shell a bit more; but his fatness,
due to some gland trouble, seems to have made him almost impenetrably
self-conscious. But he is one of the best of the Princes.

I had a lot of talk with him during the visit, and tried to encourage him
to come out more, but I doubt whether it will be effective.

The Maharaja of Travancore is entirely overshadowed by his mother,
the Junior Maharani, and by the very forcible Dewan, Sir C. P. Ramaswami Aiyar. He is not altogether a fool, but does not have a chance with
these two dominant personalities; there is no doubt that Travancore is
a one-man show, and the one man is Sir C. P. There is no doubt about his
efficiency, his charm when he chooses to exert it, or his determination to

get his own way. How good the State administration really is behind its impressive façade it is hard to say.

On February 15 we motored on to Cochin and spent the next two days there. Cochin has a very close affinity to Travancore, but is more old-fashioned and less well advertised. The Maharaja is an old gentleman of nearly 80 with a very limited command of English. His prospective successor is over 75; and owing to the working of the matriarchal system of succession—and I suppose the philoprogenitiveness of the Cochin Royal family—there are some 200 in the succession line now alive, and little prospect of a Ruler succeeding much under the age of 70 for any foreseeable period ahead. This matriarchal method of succession is peculiar to Travancore and Cochin—and I believe the Malabar coast—but no one seems able to explain its origin—even Frazer's Golden Bough is silent and the Encyclopaedia Britannica vague; but I imagine that it must derive from a practice of polyandry. Its present operation seems to result in the Maharajas being only figureheads and the power resting with Dewans—possibly no bad thing, if they are wisely chosen.

Just before I started on tour, S. of S. sent another long telegram of Cabinet hesitations, doubts and objections on the Desai proposals. I cabled that I would see Jinnah and Desai on return, to which H.M.G. had given a grudging consent, and then report results; but that I must know earliest date when H.M.G. could see me, as a long interval might be fatal.

February 20

As usual on my return from a tour I have been busy clearing off arrears of work and getting up to date with events. Except for mercy petitions from murderers of which I must have dealt with at least 50 in the last few days, the accumulations of work were not heavy, but there have been two Council meetings and the ordinary routine has been quite heavy.

The two Council Meetings, yesterday evening and this evening, were on the Budget proposals. A proposal to introduce a Death Duties Bill and to make a motion for its circulation aroused a good deal of feeling, though Dalal pointed out that fresh sources of taxation must be found if any social progress was to be made. But feelings were too heated, so I broke off the meeting and said we would meet again this evening.

When the Council met this evening, all went like clockwork. Finance Member agreed simply to introduce the Bill and to make no motion for circulation. This would avoid opposition in the Assembly, as a motion to introduce is never opposed. Otherwise the Budget proposals, which were not in any way drastic, had an easy ride.

February 26

Bhopal has written on behalf of the Princes after their Bombay conference to request me to hold bye-elections to re-constitute the Chamber. I wrote back and suggested that it would be much simpler if they withdrew their resignations. I don't know how they will receive this, I think they will prefer to show the firmness of their front by getting themselves all re-elected.

On the political side I found Jinnah was in Bombay, and not likely to come to Delhi for some time; so I got Colville to see him and ask him his attitude to the Desai proposals. He disclaimed all knowledge of Liaquat's[1] talks with Desai, an obvious falsehood I am sure; but said that he was prepared to consider an offer and would be in Delhi on March 6. He is playing his usual slippery game in fact. Meanwhile the Sind Government seems to be revolting from League control, the N.W.F.P. Government likely to fall, and the Unionist Ministry in the Punjab consolidating itself.

> *Bhulabhai Desai claimed that in informal talks with Liaquat Ali Khan the latter had agreed to his proposals for a Congress–League Coalition Government at the Centre and for similar Governments in the Provinces. Later Liaquat denied this in the Assembly, but told Desai privately that he was obliged to deny it for political reasons. Jinnah was believed to have been annoyed with him for having talks with Desai.*

February 28

I had three quarters of an hour with Sapru, who came to lunch, and he told me of the progress of his Committee. I doubt whether he really expects anything approaching a solution from it. He ended by saying that if Indians fail to agree, H.M.G. must impose a solution. I asked whether he expected us to force a United India on the Moslems, if that was our solution, or Pakistan on the Sikhs, if we decided to divide India. He merely said that we were the men in possession and that it was up to us to find the way out.

Leathers has declined to find shipping for more than 40,000 tons of wheat a month, about half what we need, and it looks as if we may soon be back at the old struggle for food.

March 1

Longish Council meeting this evening, mainly on the question of the safeguards in the Constitution to protect British business. Everyone is

---

[1] Nawabzada Liaquat Ali Khan, the *de facto* leader of the Muslim League in the Central Assembly and Jinnah's No. 2. He was later Prime Minister of Pakistan.

agreed they should go, and H.M.G. has promised that they will not be included in a fresh Constitution. It was a question of tactics to be adopted in an Assembly debate tomorrow which demands immediate action by the G. of I. to get the safe-guard Sections removed and for the appointment of a Committee of the Legislature to examine the question. S. of S. has warned us that H.M.G. would not agree to remove the Sections until a new Constitution was made and that any attempt on our part to do so would be most unpopular and meet with a rebuff; while a Committee would be likely to embarrass both ourselves and H.M.G. So our problem was to show our full agreement with the House but to avoid becoming committed either to immediate demand for their repeal or to a Committee. I think we got a fairly satisfactory decision in the end; but what will happen in the actual debate today is a little doubtful.

March 3

I presented five V.C.s to Indian soldiers or their widows this morning; and we gave tea to about 500 or 600 Indian servicemen, who had provided the guards on the parade, this afternoon. How smart and well-turned-out the Indian soldier always is, compared with the rather casual British.

A Council meeting on Japanese Campaign Pay went well, and we settled at last this controversial issue. Rather surprisingly, the telegram conveying H.M.G.'s decision began with three paragraphs of apology for the way G. of I. was treated by the original decision being taken without consultation. I almost believe I am beginning to put India on the map of Whitehall.

Patiala and Bilaspur were staying for the V.C. parade, since two of the recipients came from their States. A curious contrast; of all the present Princes I suppose Patiala looks most like a Maharaja, and Bilaspur least like a Raja. I rather like Patiala though I would never trust him very far, and he is, in his rather arrogant way, a magnificent looking man. Bilaspur dresses and looks like an insignificant looking trader or attorney; and has rather Uriah-Heep-like manners; but I fancy he is shrewd.

March 10

Jinnah who was to have seen me on March 7 is sick, I am told that he has a touch of pleurisy and may be laid up for some time. Meanwhile I cannot get a date from H.M.G. for my visit home, I don't think the P.M. wants me at all and will procrastinate as long as possible. I don't intend to let them use Desai and Jinnah as reasons for delay. After all, the principle of

my going home for a discussion was accepted long before Desai's proposals came up; and it is the mind of H.M.G. that I want to know
rather than the minds of Desai and Jinnah. I shall send S. of S. a cable this
weekend.

My Government continue to be beaten in the Assembly, and are I think
getting a little rattled. Desai and Liaquat are obviously out to show me
that I had better get rid of my Executive Council and give them the
loaves and fishes. I am told that Desai has been offering portfolios to his
friends. That sort of thing is not the best way to do business with me.
I have made up my mind not to see Desai again before I go home.

March 13

Council this evening on Sargent's[1] Education report. Not a very satisfactory performance, the Communal Spirit being given full play. Firoz
Khan Noon, having as usual read none of the papers, delivered a most
forcible denunciation of the Report from the point of views of Muslims in
general and the Punjab in particular, which he said would never accept the
principles of it. He was only momentarily disconcerted when it was
pointed out to him that the Report was signed by the Punjab Minister of
Education and another Punjab representative, and that the Punjab
Government as a whole had since then accepted the principles of the
Report. Firoz Khan Noon said he would have to speak to Khizar about
this. Ambedkar of course delivered a harangue in favour of the Depressed
Classes and also of the Criminal Tribes. Srivastava was discursively reminiscent of his days as Education Minister in the U.P.; Aziz ul Huque, who
likes talking, prattled along for some time on nothing in particular; and
only Dalal really got back to business. I had to ask the Member, Jogendra
Singh, to put up another Summary giving Council some really definite
points for decision in order to get the Education business started. But
obviously feeling is going to run high.

March 14

S. of S. still cannot get date for my visit from P.M. but is going ahead
with arrangements, e.g., the official announcement. The proposed wording suggests that it is a sudden decision by H.M.G. I am insisting that it
should be made clear that the suggestion was made by me six months ago;
otherwise it will appear as if it was due to Desai's move.

[1] Sir John Sargent, Educational Adviser to the Government of India.

March 15

S. of S. cabled this morning that as Attlee would be busy with the San Francisco conference they must postpone my visit till June. I cabled an indignant protest but shall not get any change. The discourtesy of the thing annoys me. No apology, no explanation, just a contemptuous wave of the hand—'Tell India to wait till it's more convenient'.

Two Muslim League Governments have been in trouble, Sind and N.W.F.P. In Sind Hidayatullah has managed to emerge still in charge, after a most unsavoury exhibition of disloyalty and intrigue by all concerned. In N.W.F.P. Aurangzeb was defeated, he is less adroit a politician than Hidayatullah. Congress under Dr. Khan Sahib has taken office,[1] I wonder how long that will last.

March 17

H.M.G. came back quickly on my cable and said that since I felt strongly on the matter I had better come home at once, and that a plane would be at Karachi ready to take me on the morning of the 21st.

March 20

We are off home this afternoon. All rather a rush. I informed Council yesterday evening, I believe that Desai has made them believe that I am pledged to him and that I am going to put Congress straight into power on my return, which is certainly the last thing I intend. I wonder whether I shall get any policy at all out of H.M.G.

Colville arrived about midday to act for me while I am home, and I put him into the picture as far as possible.

Cairo—March 21

Left Delhi 2 p.m. yesterday and arrived Karachi about 7 p.m.

Dow was as caustic as usual about Sind Politics and Sindhis in general. Hidayatullah the Premier, whom I think he trusted to a certain extent, double-crossed him and his own colleagues during the recent crisis, which has made Dow even more cynical and disillusioned than usual. He said the Ministry had appointed an anti-corruption officer but that his chief job was to keep an eye on the few honest ones and see that they did not give trouble. He spoke of the general weariness of the European side of the administration, and the general subserviency of the Provincial administration to the Ministers, since the Province was so small that the Ministers

---

[1] This was the first Congress Ministry to take office after all of them had resigned in 1939.

could, and did, put their fingers in every pie. Dow is very provincial and does not take a wide outlook, but he knows his Sind pretty well.

In Cairo Miles Lampson (Killearn) at the Embassy seemed in very good form and put us up to date with the latest Cairo gossip. I asked him about Palestine and he told me that H.M.G. had proposed partition last August, very secretly, but that everyone on the spot had objected. He agreed that it was scandalous that India with 90 million Muslims should never even have been informed of this proposal.

March 23

Arrived Poole 2.30 p.m., Amery, Linlithgow, and others met us at Victoria and we went to Dorchester where a suite had been booked for us.

March 24

Talked with Linlithgow for an hour in the morning. He was as usual very sensible and practical on Indian affairs but a bit dry and cynical. I think his trouble in India was that he is too wedded to efficiency to make allowance for Indian inefficiency, and never grasped that the Indian thinks and acts a great deal more with his heart than his head. He said that he had kept entirely clear of politics and any expression of views on India since he came home (except for the address to a Parliamentary body which he sent me); he thought it was the duty of any ex-Viceroy to do this, in justice to his successor. He asked whether I would care to tell him anything of my ideas, and I showed him my letter to Winston. He approved of it as a statement of the case but said he thought I was rather too optimistic in my estimate of the possibilities of making progress. He then detailed the obvious risks and objections, which I had already considered; and finished by asking in an indirect way whether I was prepared to go to the lengths of resignation if the P.M. proved intractable; and had I considered the possible damage to the war effort and general position that such action might cause. He spoke of the interests of big business in maintaining something like the status quo in India. He was friendly as always and I like him.

In the afternoon I had an hour and a half with Amery. I felt that we had 'great argument about it and about but evermore came out by the same door as in we went'. I don't think there was anything fresh that came out. We finished by an almost heated argument about Palestine, he upholding the Zionist point of view, I arguing the interest of the Indian Muslims in the problem and the Arab case.

March 26

Two hours with Cabinet Committee on India this morning. Attlee, Amery, Cripps, John Anderson, Simon, Grigg, R. A. B.[1] Butler; Gilbert Laithwaite[2] as Secretary, Listowel[3] in attendance. I made a statement on situation in India and outlined my proposals. I was then cross-questioned, mainly on personalities and matters of detail, and on the risks involved. The atmosphere generally was friendly, no one seemed to have any alternative proposals though they stressed the dangers and difficulties of making any move. After two hours, they decided to think it all over and have another meeting at 10.30 p.m. tomorrow. Simon, who had been making a lot of legalistic and constitutional points which had really not very much bearing on the question at issue, took me aside afterwards and said that he was really only trying to be helpful and sympathetic, but was apprehensive of the risks involved. I told him that no one realised them more than I did but that one could get nowhere without taking risks. He asked about withdrawal of Quit India resolution and I said that I considered that dead but that to try and bury the corpse might revive it. He asked what I proposed to do about a pledge to forward the war and I said I proposed to get a new Council, if one was formed, to issue a statement that they would fully support the war.

Finished day by seeing Gielgud's Hamlet, a very fine performance.

March 27

Spent the morning at India Office. S. of S. said he thought yesterday's meeting went very well.

We had another meeting of the India Committee at 10.30 p.m. It got us little, if any, further after $1\frac{1}{2}$ hours discussion. What it comes to is that they none of them like my proposal and see and raise all the obvious objections. But none of them seem to have an alternative. Simon as usual raised lawyer-like and constitutional points of detail; John Anderson spoke of the responsibility of the House of Commons, which my proposals do not alter, and of the sins of Congress generally; Attlee inveighed against my proposals as un-democratic; I pointed out that the body I proposed was certainly more democratic so far as any democracy at all existed in India, than the present Executive Council. There was a lot of indeterminate

[1] Wavell always wrote R. A. B. Butler (for R. A. Butler) because he was familiarly known as 'Rab' Butler.

[2] Sir Gilbert Laithwaite, an India Office official, who had been Private Secretary to Lord Linlithgow when he was Viceroy.

[3] Earl of Listowel, Parliamentary Under-Secretary of State for India, 1944–5, Secretary of State for India, 1947.

skirmishing between Cripps and Attlee and Grigg; and nothing very definite. However, we are perhaps making progress of a sort in allowing everyone to get the position clear. It was finally decided that anyone who wished should put up an alternative solution, and that we would meet again after Easter. I drove R. A. B. Butler back to the Dorchester, and he said that on the whole I was getting on well and having a comparatively calm passage.

March 28

Quiet morning at India Office. Went to see H.M. at Buckingham Palace at 1 p.m. He had, I think, been told by P.M. that I was casting spanner into works over India but did not press his questions on it very far, and then went into general conversation. Q. and I lunched afterwards with the King, Queen and the younger Princess. They all seemed in very good heart, and they make one feel at home, especially the Queen; she takes a great interest in the Regiment. The King told me before lunch that he had wanted to visit the troops in India this last winter but that the P.M. had not wished it.

Went to see Laurence Olivier's Richard III, a marvellous piece of acting.

March 29

After lunch I went to Downing St. and had an hour and a quarter with P.M. He began by apologising for not seeing me earlier and explained he had been at the Front and had then had to prepare a funeral oration for Lloyd George. He said he had had no time to consider India but eulogised the India Committee as a very strong and representative body who would advise him. He then said 'you must have mercy on us', and proceeded to state all the problems they had to consider, and the reasons for delay in considering India, which he thought could be kept on ice. He mentioned probability of early General Election. I said quite firmly that India was very urgent and very important, that the problems would be just as difficult in all parts of the world at the end of the war as now, and that I could see no reason to postpone the issue. The P.M. then launched into a long jeremiad about India which lasted for about 40 minutes. He seems to favour partition into Pakistan, Hindustan, Princestan etc., has very old-fashioned ideas about the problem, and seems to see no ray of hope. He talked as if I was proposing to 'Quit India', change the Constitution, and hand over India right away; and I had to interrupt him a number of times. He was friendly on the whole, but I thought he seemed depressed and lacking in fire.

Then I went back to I.O. and saw Cripps. He said the whole India Committee were now in favour of making some move, except Simon. They were however afraid in my proposal that the Executive Council might be too much swayed by party caucuses. John Anderson was putting up a proposal for an Advisory Council elected from the Central and Provincial legislatures, out of which the Viceroy would select his Executive Council. I said we should obviously have to consider such a proposal. Cripps seemed to think prospects were considerably brighter than they had been before I came home.

Next I had 45 minutes with Leathers. We talked first of the P.M.'s health, then he spoke of all the shipping and transport difficulties. He said there was sufficiency of wheat but that transport was lacking to get the wheat to the ports and from the ports to destination. He said India's food requirements and S.E.A.C.'s military requirements could not both be met and that there would have to be a cut in the Eastern shipping. I asked where all the ships were, and the answer seemed to be, mainly in the Pacific, where 6 to 7 million tons is absorbed in shipping used simply as storehouses. I impressed on him the necessity for 1,000,000 tons of wheat per annum for India. I then asked for more passages to India to enable the Civil Service to get home for leave before the post-war period. He seemed a little more hopeful about this—after V.E. Day.

I finally mentioned Indian shipping and its post-war aspirations.

April 4

Cabinet meeting in the evening. Smuts, Forde and Evatt (Australia), Peter Fraser (the N.Z. Prime Minister) and Firoz Khan Noon were there besides the ordinary attendants. The P.M. spoke of the difficult and unfriendly attitude of Russia since the Yalta conference; of the mighty military power of the U.S.A.; and hence the need for Empire unity. Each of the Dominion representatives then made a little speech, beginning with Smuts who stressed the possibilities of India as a great Eastern power and the need to keep her in the Empire. Then the P.M. surprised me by asking me to say a few words and prefacing it by a eulogy of my military achievements. I spoke shortly about the services of India to the War effort, her importance to the Empire's security and welfare and the need for solving the Indian problem. Firoz Khan Noon said rather optimistically that everyone in India was united in wishing to remain in the Empire.

I then went to dine with Amery and found Attlee there. We had about an hour and a half after dinner on the Indian problem. The India Committee wants to make a move but wants me to arrive on my new Council by a complicated method of election. I pointed out the difficulties—the time it would take, the release of all political prisoners which it would involve as a preliminary, the danger of getting an entirely unsuitable body out of which to make a selection, the difficulty of arriving at the numbers to be elected by each Province etc. I stressed the advantages of my proposal as being quicker and giving more scope for private negotiation as against public discussion in the Press. I don't think Attlee was convinced but he realised the difficulties of his proposal, I think. Amery proposed that I should have Indian members for Defence (instead of C. in C.) and External Affairs, neither of which appealed to me; and produced one or two other red herrings.

At 5 p.m. there was a Cabinet Committee on Food for India. A new crisis has arisen in India and we want a substantial quantity of wheat at once. The discussion showed what I suspected was the value of Leathers' professed friendliness last week, i.e. nil. He declared himself unable to find any shipping and seemed indifferent to the possibility of famine in India. The Committee, on the basis of Cherwell's fatuous calculations, simply tried to show that we already had enough food in India, whereas it turned out that we had in fact for some months past been getting only half of what we should have had, which again was only half of our requirements. An unsatisfactory meeting. Went straight on to see Gielgud's Midsummer Night's Dream, a fine performance.

April 5

India Committee this morning at which an extraordinarily woolly proposal was put up as the Committee's idea. I don't think anyone ever really believed in it. It proposed quite unnecessary constitutional changes and an absurd Grand Council of India with very nebulous origins and responsibilities. I stated all the objections, and in the end we were back much where we started. From their criticisms both of my proposals and of my draft broadcast it was obvious that some members of the committee had not read the papers I had put up, or had forgotten them. I suppose these discussions are essential steps towards progress, but we seem to me to be going round in a circle.

Conference at I.O. at 6 p.m. with Amery, Cripps and all the I.O. officials. I thought we were only going to talk about technical questions, i.e. amendments to the 1935 Act necessitated by my proposals and those of India Committee; but they re-opened this morning's discussion, so I stuck very bluntly to my point and refused to budge. I am sure these are the right tactics.

April 6

Started the morning by sitting to Epstein for a bust. He is an odd, untidy, rather aggressive, self-opinionated little man whom I found attractive and intelligent. His method of working intrigued me, I imagined that a sculptor would start with a lump of clay and mould it to shape, but he starts from nothing and builds up the head outwards, sketching all the time, so to speak. Went on to I.O. S. of S. seemed to think political talks were going quite well but was all for compromising on the principle of some method of election for my council, in order to appease Attlee's democratic ideas. I stuck quite firmly by my own ideas and instanced the precedent of the Cripps Mission, when no one suggested that the leaders with whom Cripps negotiated (nor the Council, if the proposal had been accepted) should be subject to any form of election. I am not going to budge from my position if I can help it.

Another food crisis seems to be blowing up in India, and I shall obviously have to have at Leathers again.

April 9

Even Evan is rather depressed today and thinks we are heading for an impasse in the discussions with the India Committee. Nothing at all happened about it all day except that Sir John Anderson asked me to come and see him this afternoon. He explained that what bothered him was that in practice the G.G.'s powers were bound to be curtailed by the existence of a political Executive Council, and that therefore it would be better to admit it at once by legislating for less power or by admitting in a statement in Parliament that the power would be weakened. I tried to get him to see that this would make my task more difficult since it would mean pressure on me; and that until it was certain that I could form a political Executive Council it would be folly to give away anything. He said it would make it much easier to get a scheme through the Committee if I agreed to his proposal. I left unconvinced but rather unhappy.

A dull Cabinet, but it brought home to me the very different attitude towards feeding a starving population when the starvation is in Europe. In this case it is Holland which needs food, and ships will of course be available, quite a different answer to the one we get whenever we ask for ships to bring food to India.

April 10–11

No progress at all.

Flew over to Germany to Monty's headquarters in a schloss east of

Osnabruck. Had about 5 hours with Monty, during which he talked pretty continuously.

April 12

Nothing much doing in the morning. India Committee still preserving a deep inertia and silence.

Cabinet meeting on War criminals.

Had half an hour with S. of S. afterwards mostly on some minor points but I impressed on him that I must be kept informed on Palestine. He seemed to think the discussions with the India Committee were going all right. They met again this evening but did not invite me.

April 14

Amery told me that the India Committee had produced a scheme which he thought not too bad, considering all the difficulties. He showed it me later; and I think that subject to my being allowed freedom of action on certain points, e.g., when to release political prisoners, and method of selecting new Council, it may be acceptable.

April 15

Took a walk with Leo in morning and had some general discussion. He is hopeful of proposed solution and thinks it may be the beginning of a reasonable settlement of Indian affairs. But it is the first step that counts, and that is going to be a very difficult one, I think perhaps more difficult than Leo realises. However, we have got the India Committee a long step on the road.

April 16

Went to the Treasury with Amery to talk to Sir J. Anderson about sterling balances. Sir J. A. drew the picture of our financial situation. Our overseas liabilities are £3000 million and may rise to £5000. We owe India £1000 million which may rise to £1500. Amery entered into a rather lengthy technical disquisition. I simply emphasised the political and psychological factors in India, and asked that India should at least be treated sympathetically as one of the family. I said a statement about the balances, i.e. that we would not repudiate them, and an early discussion with Indian representatives were desirable.

Then discussed India Committee's draft solution with Jenkins and

Menon, who thought poorly of it, and went along to S. of S. who was discussing complacently minor textual amendments with his officials. I stated my objections, briefly but cogently; and we fixed a meeting for 10 a.m. tomorrow. I then dictated a note stating my views, to be ready for tomorrow's meeting.

The India Committee's 'scheme' or 'draft solution', referred to in the Journal entries of 14 and 16 April, seems to have consisted of proposals for modifying Wavell's plan in two important respects.

1. *In order to provide more 'democratic' backing for the new Executive Council it was proposed that its members should be selected from a panel chosen by the Provincial and Central Legislatures.*

2. *Since the appointment of an Executive Council representative of the main Indian political parties would make it in practice (though not in constitutional theory) much more difficult for the Governor-General to override his Council, it was proposed that this should be plainly recognized and the fields defined in which the Governor-General could disregard the advice of his Council.*

Wavell realized that to both these proposals there were considerable objections, and his reluctance to accept them was confirmed by the advice of Jenkins and Menon. The first proposal would bring no tangible gain and would lead immediately to the demand (which could hardly be resisted) for the release of all Members of the Legislatures under detention so as to enable them to take part in choosing the panel. It was not desirable at the outset of negotiations, which might come to nothing, to be forced to make this concession. Moreover, it was likely that persons particularly well-fitted to be Members of Council, e.g. Rajagopalachari, the ex-Premier of Madras, who was temporarily in disfavour, would not be included in the panel.

The objections to the second proposal were even stronger. A change in the Governor-General's powers as contemplated would involve complicated legislation and consequent delay; would at once provoke controversy, as the Congress would demand that the Governor-General's powers should be whittled away altogether; would alarm and alienate the Muslims and other minorities who looked on the Governor-General's powers as a protection for themselves; and, once again, would give something away before negotiations started. The desire of politicians in England to advertise the fact that the appointment of a 'political' Executive Council would in practice mean a diminution of the Governor-General's powers and hence, ultimately, of Parliamentary Control, was due to a fear that Parliament would later complain that the position had not been properly explained to it. From the point of view of Delhi the supposed need to protect Parliament from its own impercipience was far outweighed by other considerations.

April 17

Meeting with S. of S. and officials at 10 a.m. My note was accepted with little discussion and will go to Committee. Jenks later in the afternoon was gloomy about the whole thing and says I shall have a very rough passage in the Committee tomorrow, fixed for 9.30 a.m. and a still rougher one in the Cabinet.

April 18

Meeting of India Committee, to consider my objections to the proposed draft statement. Most unfavourable. Attlee started attacking me at once, complaining that I had rejected their whole scheme out of hand. John Anderson complained that I would not admit that I was making a radical change in the Constitution. Cripps was absent, Grigg and Simon were definitely hostile and Butler very unhelpful. Leo Amery supported me manfully and quite skilfully, and I stuck to my guns, in fact kept on firing them. An hour and a half of desultory and rather acrimonious discussion got us nowhere, but Amery at the end thought we had not done too badly. I wish I could agree with him, I felt depressed and ruffled.

April 19

Evan depressed this morning and thinks we have failed, but S. of S. still optimistic. Evan says I.O. officials are against my proposal and do not support their own S. of S. properly. They are a poor lot anyhow I think.

April 23–25

On 23rd, 1½ hours with India Committee, with Simon in the chair instead of Attlee who had gone to San Francisco. An untidy, uncontrolled discussion which led nowhere; but Leo Amery seems to regard such methods as inevitable, and leading gradually in the right direction.

Today, 24th, Leo Amery, Cripps and self met, with Laithwaite, I.O. officials and Jenkins and Menon; and proceeded to produce yet another draft for the Committee. On the whole satisfactory, and we agreed that if we three stood pat on this, it would be difficult for India Committee or Cabinet to override us; but there will be some difficult passages still.

On 25th the India Committee met, but without me, they find my presence troublesome apparently and prefer to come to decisions without me. Then they get annoyed if I raise objections to their work later on. However, I hope Amery and Cripps stood pat.

Lord Wavell: a drawing by Augustus John, 1945

May 9.

A critical day with a dramatic denouement.
We began by passing an answer from S. of S. to
Jinnah. Then there was an almost heated
argument between S of S and myself over the
method of selecting representatives to the Constituent Assembly, so as to get over the injustice to
the Muslims in their majority Provinces owing to the
weightage to minorities in the Communal award.
The S of S was all for accepting the weightage,
arguing that anything else would antagonise Congress, I argued strongly that the population basis
must be taken into account as the fairest and,
I contended, the most 'democratic' method (it

A page from Lord Wavell's Journal

April 26

Another fruitless tiresome day, so far as business went. Leo told me the results of yesterday's meeting. Cripps and John Anderson were absent for the first hour and he had to face alone the attacks of Simon, Grigg and Butler, all of whom want to do nothing. When the other two arrived, I gather that the draft statement was more or less approved, except that the Committee insisted on including Foreign Affairs [i.e. in the subjects to be handed over to an Indian member], and that John Anderson put in some phrase about the limitation of the Governor-General's powers. Simon will now apparently draft the report of the Committee and send it to the Cabinet, I think without letting me see it. I am getting tired of being treated as an Untouchable in the presence of Brahmins, and shall say so shortly. Grigg wants to drag in something about the Indianisation of the Army, I believe.

April 27

Saudi Arabian Minister called in the morning to give me an invitation from King Ibn Saud to visit him at Rijadh on my return journey, if possible. I shall try to do so.

Lunched with R. A. B. Butler at the Oriental and had 40 minutes with him afterwards on my proposals. He raised the usual objections, negotiations with Congress, alienation of our friends, wouldn't it be better to do nothing for a while, etc. I don't know how far I succeeded in countering his objections but he said I had stated my case very clearly.

April 29

A quiet rather depressing weekend. I feel I have failed to make H.M.G. realise the importance and urgency of the Indian problem or the real facts of the position. We have been talking for 5 weeks, in a very disconnected way. The matter could have been settled in a week if they had really taken it seriously and wanted to. Now I think we have missed the bus in any case. The sudden complete collapse of the Germans, and the approaching reoccupation of the whole of Burma will make Indian politicians much less accommodating than a few months ago. If I got my own way now, I feel it would be too late.

April 30

Another wasted day so far as India is concerned. The Cabinet is meeting on India at 10 p.m. tonight but don't want me. I have not even been allowed to see Simon's report of the India Committee's conclusions. I saw Leo this morning, still optimistic. What a gallant, loyal, straight little man he is, but a little detached from realities and more occupied with ideas and theories than persons and facts.

May 1

A little routine work in morning. Saw S. of S. in afternoon who told me they had talked in Cabinet for $2\frac{1}{4}$ hours last night without result.

A Cabinet Committee meeting on food, it was proceeding on the usual lines of Leathers having no shipping, Cherwell saying that India had plenty of food if they only managed their affairs properly, and everybody suggesting avenues to be explored and stones unturned at considerable leisure, when I thought it was time to ginger them up. So I told them I had saved them from a famine last year by my importunity of which they complained, and that they would have one this year if they didn't do something about it. They didn't like this transgression of the usual polite prolixities and postponements of official debate; but I think it will do no harm. I am tired of Leathers' smooth evasions and false promises.

May 2

Spent morning reading Cabinet papers on Palestine. In afternoon went to see H.M. the King. He had obviously been studying the papers of the India Committee discussions and seemed to consider it settled that my scheme would go through.

May 4

Had a talk with Auchinleck who arrived yesterday. Things quiet in India but the long delay is not improving the prospects of political settlement. He approves the draft now before the Cabinet. Food prospects in India seem to be a little brighter.

May 8 (V.E. Day)

Saw Leo Amery in afternoon and blew off steam about the way I was being kept hanging about. He counselled patience, said P.M. was very busy doing Foreign Secretary (in Eden's absence) in addition to other business and also occupied with election prospects. India Committee had discussed Dalal's request for revision of Commercial clauses of 1935 Act,[1] but had not even thought fit to ask views of Viceroy.

[1] See entry for 1 March, pp. 114–15.

Linlithgow dined with me, friendly but rather pessimistic and disillusioned as usual.

Today had interview with Dalal and told him not to get upset and disheartened because he didn't get all he wanted at once—he complained of an unsympathetic reception by Leo Amery. Went to House of Lords to hear announcement of end of European war and to service in Abbey afterwards.

Peace in Europe is very welcome but has come too soon for my plans in India, or rather H.M.G. has been so slow that the opportunity has been missed.

May 11

Today I discovered the reason of Dalal's discontent. Without even informing me, the India Committee had held a meeting on the proposals Dalal had brought home and had shot them down at once. What extraordinary people they are! One would think that with the Viceroy at home and available they would have asked his opinion on an important matter of great political significance which had been approved by the Governor General in Council instead of contemptuously dismissing it without even informing him. Amery should have refused to accept the decision without my having been given an opportunity to express a view. Instead, he simply saw Dalal and told him that there was nothing doing, which naturally upset Dalal. I have now put in a note to the Committee giving my views and asking that they should be given a hearing. What a crew they are for a perilous voyage!

May 14

On Monday morning a meeting of the India Committee on the safeguarding Commercial clauses—my first official contact with or communication from the Committee for exactly three weeks. Leathers was there and Summers of Board of Trade, to reinforce the opposition. I made a statement on the whole problem of India's industrial development and claimed sympathetic hearing and treatment for the Government of India's proposals. Amery tried to make out that the hampering effect of the safeguard clauses was hypothetical and that we should wait till a difficulty actually occurred. He was prolix and unconvincing and was shot down from all sides. Cripps produced his usual conciliatory compromise draft, suggesting an announcement that while legislation was impossible H.M.G. would give sympathetic consideration to any special cases. Grigg then made a fiery statement condemning the whole policy of Indian industrialization as wrong, fulminating against Birla & Co., and talking of betrayal of Indian people, etc. Amery replied at full length and as usual soon bored most of the Committee, he took nearly 15 minutes to say what could have been said more effectively in 5. Then John Anderson practically supported Grigg and said that the proposals were not in the interests of the Indian masses and that the Indian aim was really the elimination of British business and British personnel. Cripps spoke sensibly on the historical and psychological aspects, pointing out that it was not for us to tell the Indians what they wanted. Butler merely reiterated what he has said before that it would be much better to settle the Indian problem as a whole and not piecemeal and to wait for a Constitutional agreement. (Of course it would if it were possible, but it is not and R. A. B. Butler knows it). Leathers then spoke from the point of view of big business and was of course for maintaining the clauses. Summers for the Board of Trade was more conciliatory. I asked to be allowed to reply, and said that to be tough with India and to continue to treat her as a Colony was a possible policy if H.M.G. was prepared to provide the force to support it, and to controvert or ignore public opinion in this country and abroad; but in the long run it would be disastrous. The alternative was to treat Indian aspirations with sympathy and good will; we should have some shocks, considerable loss of efficiency and perhaps temporary damage to our interests, but in the long run we should gain, morally and materially. But at present we were professing a policy of freedom for India and in practice opposing every suggestion for a step forward; and such a mixture could only lead to trouble. I pointed out that it was futile to talk of protecting the Indian masses against the policy of industrialization (as Grigg and Anderson had) when improvement in the standard of living and social services could only be gained by increased wealth, and when all vocal opinion in India was in favour of it. In the end the Cripps formula was accepted, and I suppose I have gained that much at least. I ended by pointing out that the Committee had completely ignored me for three weeks and that I had now been home for 6½ weeks without any decision. Simon made a smooth but inoperative reply.

May 15

Lunched with S. of S., Cripps, Dalal, Raisman. Object of party was to show Dalal that we were sympathetic to his projects. Cripps was good and persuasive, Leo very friendly and very prolix, and I think Dalal realised that the atmosphere was not unfriendly.

Gave Bevin dinner at the Athenaeum and had a long talk with him. He is quite sympathetic about India, but not I think very knowledgeable, and promised to help. He said he was held up with his work until P.M. decided about election. Labour Party had told P.M. they would continue Coalition Government till end of present Parliament if he wished; but that P.M. might decide for party reasons to have an election at once. He said that he thought Labour would get into office very soon and would then hold power for 20 or 30 years. He professed optimism about Labour's attitude, about agreement with employers, about the standard of living, abolition of unemployment etc., which many other knowledgeable people do not share. He said that in 5 years of war we had only lost $4\frac{1}{2}$ million working days through strikes and absence—mainly in the mines—against some 28 million in the last war. I got him to talk about his early career—he had been agricultural labourer, page boy, tram conductor, shop assistant and in other employment before becoming a trade union official. I asked him which of his professions had interested and amused him most; he grinned and said: 'agitation'. I liked Bevin, I think he is genuine and quite shrewd, though not I should say very clever. I wonder whether he is straight and courageous, I should think so.

May 23

S. of S. told me this morning that Government had resigned. He was still, however, hopeful of getting a solution next week, though not even knowing whether he would still be S. of S.

Food Committee in afternoon. Woolton, Llewellin, Cherwell, Amery, Leathers, Listowel. Atmosphere much more friendly to India than before, only Leathers, as usual hostile and making heavy weather. But when they talked of 'concessions on both sides' in the arrangement proposed, I had to point out that all the concession was on India's side, as she was getting much less than the minimum asked for, and was being asked to supply rice for Ceylon and groundnuts for this country.

May 24

A long day but some movement at last or hope of movement. I began the day by writing to the P.M. to point out that I had been 8 weeks at home, that I had had nothing from India Committee for 4 weeks or from himself for 7 weeks, and asking for a decision. After seeing S. of S. I toned it down a bit. He said that Antony Eden had sent him a message that the P.M. was going to agree to the proposed draft statement in Parliament and that now the question of dates arose as the statement would have to be made before Parliament dissolved on June 15. Colville had wired that Council expected to be consulted before the announcement was made; and it worked out that I should have to leave England about 11 days before the statement. Eden had suggested June 8 for the statement in Parliament which meant my leaving almost at once. I protested strongly at this, at being hurried off at short notice after being kept waiting for 4 weeks—especially as Q. was ill. I arranged to see Antony Eden in the evening on the question of date.

I had 40 minutes with Birla in the morning, the industrialists[1] having at last reached England. He said they had had a good journey and seemed pleased at the friendly reception they had had from the British business associations they had met so far. He then talked politics hard and mentioned the views of 'the man in the street'. I asked to what section of Indians he applied this term, and it turned out that he really meant the educated Hindu. He recommended a business Government and more than hinted that he was ready to assist me in forming one or indeed to take part in the Government. I said he had better carry on with his valuable industrial mission. He tried to persuade me that Gandhi was not anti-British and very ready to compromise; I said I could only judge by his actions and speeches and found this assertion hard to believe. Birla then tried to justify Gandhi's actions in 1942, and spoke of the bitterness caused by our action. I countered by giving some of the reasons for bitterness and mistrust on our side, as I had no intention of his getting over on me that Gandhi was a saint or statesman. I then said both sides would have to try and forget the past if we were to progress in the future. Birla is able but he obviously would like to have a finger in the political pie, and it would be of the Jack Horner type. He spoke slightingly of Nehru whom he obviously fears as left-wing.

I also saw Claude Auchinleck who starts back for India on Saturday. He told me that Beaverbrook had asked to see him, and that he had found Brendan Bracken there too. Beaverbrook obviously wanted to find out how far Auchinleck was behind me in supporting my proposals. Claude left him in no doubt about this, and said that Beaverbrook seemed to agree with the idea of a move, but that Brendan Bracken was obviously hostile.

Had half-an-hour with Antony Eden before dinner. He was dining with the P.M. and seemed confident that he would accept the India proposals; and he promised to try and postpone statement in Parliament to June 12, so that I need not leave England before June 1.

---

[1] The visit of a group of Indian industrialists to England had been planned early in 1944, but for various reasons the visit had been delayed.

May 25

No definite decision, but Leo said I should make arrangements on assumption that I should leave on June 1.

Spent most of the morning trying to draft a broadcast for India on my return, not very successfully.

May 26

No word from P.M. or Eden or anyone.

Went and stood in a queue outside a News Theatre with Pam and Francis, and the feeling was quite familiar after all these weeks of waiting on Ministers. But we did get into the theatre in the end; while I am still in the queue for a decision on India.

May 28

Evan told me he had seen the India Committee's report to the Cabinet, which I had not been allowed to see; Turnbull[1] imagined I had, so gave it to him. Committee were against any move but said that if a move was decided my proposal was the best. Later in the morning I had a very stuffy reply to my letter to the P.M. He said in effect that he had not wanted me home but that I had insisted on coming and they had done their best for me. He said he would give me Cabinet's decision by the end of the week. I saw S. of S. in morning and again in the afternoon, and he said it was all right, I could make all arrangements to start on Friday. So I sent off telegrams to Colville and to Mudaliar in Washington, giving former the expected date of return and asking latter to try to get to Delhi by June 15.

Saw Dalal in morning, who had been, I think, a little tactless in giving practically the whole of the White Paper on Indian industrial development to the F.B.I. and other business associations, and I warned him to go slow and be as tactful as possible.

I continued to make all arrangements to leave on June 1, but am still entirely without official intimation.

In the afternoon Godfrey Nicholson M.P. and a man called Richter came to see me about a proposal to hold an exhibition of Indian art at Burlington House in 1947. I said I thought it an excellent idea, but I was a little perturbed to find that their proposal was to have a purely British Committee to run it in this country, and said that Indians must be on the Committee.

During the day I got most of the necessary drafts completed for the

[1] F. F. (later Sir Frank) Turnbull, an official of the India Office, at this time Principal Private Secretary to the Secretary of State.

return to India, a letter to Governors, invitations to those concerned, etc.
I also got Leo's amendments to my draft broadcast, some of them quite
sensible but very verbose, and if adopted would have quite spoilt the whole
spirit of the broadcast which was direct and simple. Leo never can make
a point and leave it at that, he always over-elaborates. We also discussed
at some length the release of the Working Committee prior to the
Conference of leaders and finally agreed to leave the point to be discussed
with my present Executive Council.

May 30

A critical day. The Cabinet met at 11.30 a.m. on India, but I was not
invited to be present and had an idle morning.

Later went to I.O. and saw S. of S. He said Cabinet in morning had
agreed to my proposals after only 40 minutes discussion; but that P.M.
had telephoned in the afternoon that his conscience was troubled and
that he wanted the matter re-considered at a Cabinet at 6.30 p.m. I said
that P.M. could not expect me to return to India empty-handed, and that
surely it would be unfortunate if from an electioneering point of view
India came into party politics, which could hardly be avoided if I was
turned down since Attlee, Cripps and Bevin all knew of the proposals.
Leo said he could hardly hold office if my proposals were rejected, but was
obviously very worried.

Went off to Athenaeum to dine with Eden and hear result of Cabinet.
I got a message to say Antony E. would be late, and waited till about
8.40 p.m. when Leo Amery rang up, very worried, and said Cabinet had
gone badly on India, but that they had decided to have another at 11.30
a.m. tomorrow at which I should be called on to state a case. Antony
turned up at 9 p.m. having been called down to the House about Syria
and Lebanon which are in a proper mess. He said we had decided to take
over in Syria. We then discussed India at length, and I explained what
I proposed to do and corrected some misapprehensions. He said that if
what I had told him had been put to Cabinet he thought it would have
gone through, but that Leo had not put the case well. What had happened
in the morning was that the whole decision had been taken, when someone at the end remarked that he didn't like it but that since the India
Committee had recommended it, he would accept, whereupon certain
members of the Committee had said they had not agreed with the proposed solution. He said Winston was very tired and realised it himself.
He had proposed possibility of Eden taking Defence Ministry after the
election and P.M. himself becoming Leader of the House.

May 31

I prepared a draft statement for the Cabinet and discussed it with Amery who approved it. Cabinet began with a long polemical statement by P.M. against my proposals. He said I should lose a good Council and get a bad one; there was no democratic foundation; the workers would be victimised by the capitalists, the agriculturalists ruined by the money lenders, the Untouchables would remain untouchable, etc. etc. He then invited me to make a statement. I began with the genesis of the proposals, my Governors conference last August, the views of the C. in C., Home Member, Political Adviser etc. and why I had pressed to come home now. The P.M. gave me a good run and did not interrupt. There was not a great deal of discussion, it was almost a duologue between the P.M. and myself. At the end Leo made a long statement on the origin and nature of the political deadlock—he never can leave well alone. No one paid any attention and the P.M. interrupted and stopped him before he had finished. The P.M. finished with a rather irrelevant dissertation on the methods of officering the Indian Army. He then said he was prepared to agree to my proposals, if the India Committee suitably amended the draft since it did not completely square with what I proposed to do. It was agreed that the Committee should meet at 3.15. P.M. was quite pleasant to me, indeed complimentary.

The India Committee met at 3.15. Only John Simon, Oliver Stanley, Leo Amery and P. J. Grigg (Butler came in at the end). Simon produced two additional paragraphs about the de facto limitation of the Viceroy's powers which after some considerable amendment were accepted. I read my broadcast which Simon approved. P. J. Grigg sat rather glowering apart, and contributed a hate against Birla on the score of his being given an official lunch: but, as Simon pointed out, this was hardly a matter which came into the amendment of the draft statement. We finished at 4.30 p.m. Simon gave me a word of congratulation. The amendments were to come before a Cabinet before or after dinner.

The climax of my visit was an extraordinary one. At the meeting of the Cabinet at 10.30 p.m. the P.M. made just as forcible an address in favour of my proposals as he had made in their damnation this morning. In particular, he cut out of the draft statement the two paragraphs about the de facto limitation of the Viceroy's powers on which John Anderson had insisted and to which I had always objected. He made me read my draft broadcast and approved it entirely with one or two minor exceptions, and in fact exuded good will towards India and myself at every pore. He will change again but I suppose I can claim in the meantime some sort of personal triumph. I think that what really happened was that he saw that the logic of facts was against him (possibly Beaverbrook reported his conversation with Auchinleck) and that with the Election looming up he could not possibly risk India becoming a party issue, and decided to give way with good grace. What an extraordinary man he is! And so at 11.30 p.m. I got my decision, just twelve hours before my train was scheduled to leave Victoria. It all ended in an atmosphere of good will and congratulations—only temporary, I fear.

June 2. Cairo

Not many to see us off yesterday, thank heaven, but old Lady Simon turned up and several times called down on me the blessing of St. Patrick and all the saints.

6

THE SIMLA CONFERENCE

June 3 and 4 (Visit to King Ibn Saud)

A very long but interesting day. Left Embassy at 3.30 a.m. and flew to Jiddah (about 4 hours), where the Minister (Graffety-Smith) met us and one of the King's sons from Taif. We breakfasted and changed into Arab dress—long pyjama-like drawers, shirt, cloak, headdress—and then flew on to a landing ground near Rijadh, a bumpy fly of $3\frac{1}{2}$ hours. G. Smith and the King's son came with us, and the King had sent his own plane to escort us. The drive to Rijadh, to a palace a few miles the other side of it, took nearly $1\frac{1}{2}$ hours, though our Arab friends (two more of the King's sons had met us) optimistically called it 40 minutes, an illusion in which they unfortunately persisted next day for the return journey. The reason for the distance away of the landing was not that the ground was unsuitable elsewhere—one could have landed practically anywhere right up to the town itself—but that the King did not wish to offend his subjects by having an aeroplane, still suspect as a contrivance of Ebli's or unbelievers, within sight of his capital.

We reached Rijadh at about 3 p.m. The Crown Prince met me and we had about 10 minutes formal conversation; he was pleasant but looks studious rather than forcible and it seems doubtful whether he will be able to hold together all his father had won and to rule the many other sons, some of whom probably have ambitions and backers. After a large lunch and a short rest we went to pay our first visit to the King.

The King greeted me in a large chamber in his Palace. He is most impressive in appearance and manner, and is obviously a big man. He was very friendly but we only talked compliments and formal conversation at this meeting. We went back to our residence and I had time for a bath before going back again to the Palace for the evening meal. This was in the form of a feast Arab fashion, sitting cross-legged on the ground, everything laid out before one, sheep roasted whole, eating with one's fingers, etc. I did not distinguish myself, I simply cannot sit cross-legged with any comfort, did not very much like the food and was given too much of it, and did not realise that the meal should be eaten at pace, tried to make conversation and kept everyone waiting at the end. After the meal, the King took us inside his private quarters for a few minutes to show them to us; and we then sat in an open-air hall on the roof and talked for about an hour. The King presented to me a large collection of sons and grandsons, I think he has about 30 sons and 30 grandsons in all. We talked a bit about education, and agreed that it was the Turks who had ruined the original Arab reputation for science and learning; he spoke of the lack of consumer goods in Arabia and asked whether I could help from India, and a few other matters. He did not mention the troubles in Syria, or Palestine, or politics at all. At the end I asked him to tell me the story of his capture of Rijadh some 40 years ago, the fight which was the turning point of his fortunes. He did so, and ordered one of his sons when we left the Palace to show us the scene of the fight. While I was undressing for bed, two of his suite arrived with his gifts—a sword, a dagger, several suits of Arab clothes, two carpets, a very handsome present. My rather modest return gifts—two old well-bound hand-written copies of the Koran, a bound copy of 'Allenby in Egypt',[1] and my photograph in a silver frame—are to go round next morning. I hope they will be a success.

At frequent intervals throughout the day Arab bitter coffee was served in tiny cups. It is boiling hot but the right thing is to drink at once in one gulp, whereupon a servant at once comes to refill it; the custom seems to be to drink about 3 or 4 cups and when one has had enough to waggle the cup when returning it to the servant.

June 6

We got to Karachi in the evening of June 4 and stayed the night with the Dows at Government House.

I heard on landing how Desai had been putting about that he had me in his pocket and that I should at once send for him.

I gave Dow the outline of the plan and he approved. He thought his Premier, Hidayatullah, would attend the conference and would be reasonable. He was as usual caustic and amusing on politics: he said that if Gandhi, Jinnah and Amery made identical announcements the Nationalist Press would term them respectively: a clarion call, a crazy outburst, and imperialistic humbug.

I found John Colville at Delhi in good heart, and having I think enjoyed his time as Viceroy.

Met Council in evening and disclosed the proposals: they met with a very cold reception, and no one except Archie Rowlands fully supported them, and hardly any Member had a good word to say for them. What it

---

[1] Vol. ii (London, 1943), of *Allenby, a Study in Greatness*.

really amounts to is that, as at home, nobody really wants to move at all. Some suggested elections at once, nearly all proposed the immediate release of the Working Committee, so as to get the Kudos for it. Nobody had any constructive suggestions. Practically all were against any Members of Council attending the proposed conference. A discouraging reception. I adjourned until this morning.

Before the meeting this morning all the Indian Members of Council, except Mohamed Usman and Roy, got together and produced a written indictment of the proposals, recommending Dominion status at once (without the foggiest idea, as it turned out, of what this really involved), general elections at once, immediate release of political prisoners (only the Working Committee, they explained later), and that the conference should be confined to those supporting the war. Of the members who had not signed this document, Benthall was as usual rather prolix and woolly and stressed all the obvious dangers and difficulties; Mohamed Usman said he did not like the proposal but would support H.M.G. and myself to the end; Roy wanted an election at once; and Mudie and Rowlands supported me. I broke off the meeting until this evening and decided to see Sir Sultan Ahmed in the afternoon.

I saw Rowlands after the meeting. He supports me and thinks my proposals have a chance of success.

I saw Mudie, Rowlands, and Benthall at 3.0 p.m., latter still a little unconvinced—but ready to support the proposals. I then had a long talk with Sir Sultan Ahmed on the proposals. I asked him whether he did not agree that any publication of the document he had given me must involve the resignation of the members who had signed it. He agreed instantly and heartily and said the Members had no intention of publishing it or of resigning, and would support me in making the proposal though they did not agree with it. About an hour later I found that the Associated Press of India had put out a summary of discussions in Council this morning and of the proposals made by the seven members. What an impossible people to do business with.

I met Council again at 6.0 p.m. and began by disclosing the leakage. I think most of them were genuinely horrified, and asked that steps should be taken to stop the A.P.I. message and to discover the culprit (I thought F. K. N. looked a little embarrassed). I then said that, subject to H.M.G.'s agreement, I proposed to continue the plan; and I think Council were genuinely relieved that someone had taken a decision, and discussions ended in a friendly spirit, but Ambedkar and Benthall had both to add a little more wool to an already well-filled Woolsack.

I was a little surprised at Council's uncompromising opposition, though I had expected difficulties. But they have been subject to intense pressure while I have been away, and Desai in particular has been a nuisance by proclaiming that the initiative for a settlement came entirely from him, that he would be asked to form a Government, etc. I suppose I made a mistake in seeing him at all last January when I had already put forward my own proposals; but I thought I had better hear what he had to say, and I was most careful not to commit myself.

June 7

A worrying day. The Hindu members of Council—Ambedkar, Khare, Srivastava—sent in a written protest against the proposal to have equal numbers of Hindus and Muslims on the Council; and later Ambedkar sent in a passionate protest about the representation of the Depressed Classes, and more than hinted at resignation.

June 8

A long day, perhaps a little more encouraging. It looks as if the attitude of the Executive Council and their indiscretions had rather had the effect of predisposing Nationalists to give them [the proposals] a chance. I began by seeing Ambedkar who required at least two seats in the new Council for the Scheduled Castes and wanted this made clear in the announcement of the new proposals; otherwise he threatened that they would boycott the whole scheme and even hinted vaguely at revolution. I told him there was nothing in the proposals to prevent the Scheduled Castes getting two or even three seats on the Council; but that I did not think that H.M.G. would be prepared to announce any number to be reserved.

Sandwiched in between my afternoon visitors came Srivastava. After some talk of his health, he began to explain away the document signed by the seven members, and said the demand for Dominion status was only meant to bring to my notice the importance of the long term issue, and that the other matters—general elections and release of prisoners—were points on which there might be two opinions.

June 11

Casey arrived this afternoon for a short visit. He seemed well and in good heart. He is delighted with the Section 93[1] administration, says it has

---

[1] The Muslim League Ministry in Bengal was defeated at the end of March while Wavell was in England, and since no alternative Ministry could be formed commanding a majority, the Governor took over under Section 93.

enabled him to make a great difference in a short time and is popular with the people. He says I was absolutely right to recommend it at the beginning of 1944 and wishes H.M.G. had accepted it then. He would like to keep it on till the end of the year and then have elections.

He read the Parliamentary announcement and my broadcast, approved both and thinks that the move has a good chance of success.

Casey wants to go next year, in March for choice, back to Australian politics.

June 12

Nothing very much on the political front. All the minorities wire in and ask for representation.

I saw Khare, who tried to persuade me that the Mahasabha had supported the war effort on the curious argument that 24 Hindus had got V.C.s; I said that the present leader of the party, Dr. Mookerjee, most certainly had not supported the war.

June 13

A comparatively quiet day. The Caseys went off in good heart, Casey having had an interview with Aziz ul Huque on the nakedness of Bengal due to shortage of cloth, but having hardly moved him a dhoti, I gathered.

Routine Council meeting, with few attendants, most of my colleagues having decided that as their time may be short they would be foolish to spend it in working at Delhi in the heat, and that it is wiser to 'recess' in the hills, and certainly pleasanter.

After Council I saw Ambedkar on the matter of Depressed Castes representation at the Conference on which he was now quite reasonable.

June 14

In the evening, my broadcast on the political proposals. It came through quite well, I am told. Afterwards I had to undergo the ordeal of repeating the performance, or most of it, for an American cinema unit, rather a hot and trying business under the scorching glare of powerful lights. P.S.V. meanwhile took a Press Conference and said it went quite well and that they were not unfriendly.

In his broadcast Wavell said that he proposed to invite Indian political leaders to take counsel with him with a view to the formation of a new Executive Council more representative of organized political opinion, and including an equal number of Caste Hindus and Muslims. Except for the Viceroy and

Commander-in-Chief it would be an entirely Indian Council, and for the first time the 'Home', 'Finance', and 'Foreign Affairs' portfolios would be in Indian hands.

The Council would work within the framework of the existing Constitution, and one of its main tasks would be to prosecute the war against Japan to a successful conclusion; but its Members, when they thought it possible, would also have to consider the means by which agreement could be reached on a new permanent constitution. H.M.G. had not lost sight of the need for such an agreement and the present proposals were intended to make it easier to reach one.

Wavell also announced that orders had been given for the immediate release of the members of the Working Committee of Congress who were still in detention.

And so is launched a fresh attempt to help India to political freedom, which I initiated with a note to H.M.G. just 9 months ago. I suppose it is something of an achievement to have got it thus far, but whether it will crash on Indian intransigence, like the Cripps and other proposals, remains to be seen. I have certainly got a very difficult time ahead; and I do not pretend to be a diplomatist.

June 16

While the proposals have had quite a favourable reception in the Press, Gandhi and Jinnah are behaving like very temperamental prima donnas, and the latter is publishing his telegrams in the Press before I even receive them; Gandhi at least had the courtesy to ask whether I agreed to publication. Jinnah wants me to explain my proposals in detail to him and then to have Conference postponed for a fortnight while he consults his Working Committee. Gandhi insists on the fiction that he is not a member of Congress and cannot represent them; he also objects to the term Caste Hindus, and wants me to revise my broadcast to include 'independence'. I am replying as patiently and courteously as I can, but whether I shall ever get my Conference together, Lord knows. Rajagopalochariar is about the only invitee, except the European representative, who has sent a cordial and unequivocal acceptance.

This is thirtieth anniversary of the fight at Bellewarde, in which I lost my eye. I hope the one eye will continue to last me out, it has done so fairly well up to date.

June 18

The Principals, Gandhi and Jinnah, are still engaged in manoeuvring for position, and I have sent them both telegrams refusing to be drawn into

Simla Conference, 1945

Above: the Viceroy greets Malik Khizar Hyat Khan Tiwana (Dr. Khan Sahib and Mr. Bhulabhai Desai looking on).

Below: Master Tara Singh.

Simla Conference

Pandit Pant, Mr. M. A. Jinnah, Mr. Rajagopalachari, Sir Mohammad Saadulla, Maulana Abul Kalam Azad, Khwaja Nazimuddin.

preliminary discussion and asking for a definite yes or no. Evan compares
it to trying to get mules into a railway truck. It is a depressing business
and doesn't augur very well for the success of the Conference. But I doubt
whether it is increasing the reputation of either Gandhi or Jinnah in the
eyes of any except their bigoted followers.

June 19

Not much moving. Gandhi's daily telegram threatened to ban the Conference unless the stipulation of parity between Hindus and Muslims was
removed, but at the same time said the way seemed now open for the
Conference. I refused to be drawn and sent a short non-committal but
polite (I hope) answer. Evan is rather depressed today and thinks we shall
not get the Conference assembled.

June 20

Bhopal arrived in response to my invitation to discuss solution of Chamber
of Princes resignations six months ago. The upshot of a long talk in the
course of which he said that he approved the political proposals was that
he would be prepared to advise the Standing Committee to withdraw
their resignations if I could write him a face-saving letter to say that I was
quite open to further discussions on certain points. There should be no
great difficulty about this.

A lull on the political front, pending the Congress meeting in Bombay
on the 21st. It looks as if they would come up to Simla anyway unless
some last-moment issue arises.

June 21

The lull on the political front continues, pending the Congress Meeting
in Bombay. In the morning I had a War Board meeting on the coal
situation at which Benthall drew a very gloomy picture of the railways
running out of coal altogether by the end of the year, unless practically all
coal to industry was stopped or drastically curtailed. I think he is pessimistic, at least I hope so.

In the afternoon I had a long talk with Wylie. He is off on leave in
a week or two, and this was probably his last interview as Political
Adviser.[1] He is wise and steady but possibly a little too drastic with the
Princes; anyway they don't like being ridden on his rather tight rein and
with his rather sharp spurs.

[1] He was giving up this post to become Governor of the United Provinces.

June 23

Came up to Simla yesterday. Had difficult interviews this morning with Glancy and Khizar who are entirely opposed to the proposals. Glancy has always been completely provincial and has never taken a very broad view. He says that the Unionist Ministry will not last unless a Unionist Muslim gets a seat on the Executive Council.

Khizar was very upset and said he had the gravest misapprehensions over what I was doing. He spoke about the loyalty of the Punjab, that there had always been a Punjab Muslim in the Executive Council since 1919, and that my approach to Congress and the League was a slap in the face for all co-operators. He said I was handing over power to the enemy, that my veto was 'dead as mutton', and prophesied chaos and disaster all round. But he had no practical alternative, like the objectors at home, had no answer to my saying that the difficulty had to be faced some day and that to do nothing was merely to postpone it. I believe that Khizar in his heart of hearts would really like the British to stay on, for a long time anyhow. His only suggestion was that the present Conference should consider the long-term solution before going to the interim government.

On the lighter side, I had a letter this morning from a Parsee at Karachi, to ask me, now that I have been elected Chancellor of Aberdeen University (I have no information that I have), would I recommend for the Nobel prize for idealistic literature his work entitled 'Can a Prostitute go to Heaven?'.

June 24

A long trying day of interviews with Azad,[1] Gandhi and Jinnah. Azad came first in the morning accompanied by Pant (Ex-Premier U.P.) as interpreter. (Azad understands English well but is shy of speaking it). We had a talk of $1\frac{1}{4}$ hours, it would have been much longer, but I broke it off at lunch time, as the conversation was getting well away from the Conference. It was quite friendly, and nothing original was raised.

After lunch I had $1\frac{3}{4}$ hours with Gandhi, the first time I had met him. He was rather vague and discursive but on the whole gave his blessing to the proposals. I began by making a short statement on the objects of the proposals of H.M.G., the spirit in which they were conceived and the spirit in which I hoped they would be accepted and worked. I emphasised the necessity for full support of the war, and that it was essential that the political parties should put in their very best men, determined to

[1] Maulana Abul Kalam Azad was at this time President of Congress.

concentrate on the economic and other problems of India, and not merely to enter the Government in a party spirit.

Mr. Gandhi then made a long, tortuous and prolix statement, which dealt with the history of the Congress, British rule in India, British character, the qualities of a good soldier, and many other more or less relevant subjects. It lasted over half an hour, and ended with a sort of general blessing on the proposals, which he said he had recommended to the Working Committee.

He then went on, referring to some notes, to deal with certain other points. I think this was a list prepared for him as a result of the discussions by Congress Working Committee. The main points were as follows:—

(a) That it would have been much better if I had ordered the release of all the political prisoners and not merely the Working Committee.

(b) That the term 'Caste Hindus' should not have been used, as his great aim was that there should be no question of caste inside Congress; he would have preferred the term 'Non-Scheduled Hindus'.

(c) He then went on to the question of Coalitions in Provinces, obviously with the idea of trying to establish that the Minorities should be represented by members of their body belonging to Congress.

(d) He referred to the matter of parity, and said he had been under very severe pressure as regards this, but that he was prepared to accept it. He indicated that it would be open to Congress to put forward the names of Muslims or Scheduled Castes, and I agreed but said that the principle of parity between non-Scheduled Hindus and Muslims must be maintained.

(e) He then digressed into a long story about members of the Indian Army who had wished to see him but had been compelled, like Nicodemus, to come to him by night and in mufti. I said that the one thing which was disastrous for any Government was if the Army became political; that the Indian Army had a Commander-in-Chief in whom they had full trust; that their reputation never stood higher and that I could assure him that the Indian Army was on the whole a thoroughly contented body. He agreed to all these statements.

(f) He then started on the question of the Indian States. I said that the Conference dealt entirely with British India, and that I was not prepared at this stage to enter into a discussion of the Indian States. He agreed that it had nothing to do with the Conference and was not appropriate for discussion at the moment.

I asked Mr. Gandhi at the end, whether he proposed to attend the Conference in person. He said that he represented nobody except himself, and that though he would be prepared to attend the Conference if I wished, and sit in a corner, he strongly advised me that his presence at the Conference was undesirable. He said that he would hold himself at my disposal for as long as I wished, but that if I had nothing on which I had to consult him he would propose to leave Simla tomorrow. I said that I would let him know.

The interview was mainly a discursive monologue by Mr. Gandhi, interspersed by numerous digressions, such as a most graphic description of the death of his Private Secretary, and the relation of his carrying down the wounded General Woodgate from Spion Kop in 1899. My general impression of him was that he was friendly for the time being, but perfectly prepared to go back at any time on anything he had said.

A little later I had $1\frac{1}{2}$ hours with Jinnah, who is much more direct than Gandhi, but whose manners are far worse.

Mr. Jinnah began by saying that whatever happened the Muslims would be in a minority. I pointed out that he assumed, rather gratuitously, that all the Minorities would vote against the Muslims, and that there was at the back always the veto of the Viceroy. He said that the Minorities, e.g. Sikh and Scheduled Castes, would be Hindus and would vote with them, and that the Viceroy would be extremely reluctant to exercise his power of veto. I said that I could not agree with these assumptions. He then proposed that if on any matter the majority of the Muslims were opposed to it, it should not go by vote. I said that this was quite unacceptable and was contrary to all principles of Government. I think he realised that this was rather a forlorn try-on, and said little more.

He then went into the matter of nomination of Members of the Executive Council and claimed that the Muslim League had the right to nominate all Muslim Members. I said that I could not accept this proposition. He then began a long history of all the bye-elections of the last two years, claiming that the Muslim League candidate had always been successful and that therefore the Muslim League represented the whole of the Muslims of India. He seemed to think that I was thinking of nomination of Muslims by the Congress. I said that I had also in mind the nomination by the Unionist Party of the Punjab of a Muslim. This led to a long diatribe to the effect that the Unionist Party were traitors to the interests of the Muslims, and that the fact that they had been able to run a coalition Ministry in the Punjab for so long was solely due to the sufferance of Mr. Jinnah. I merely maintained that I would not give a pledge beforehand that all the Muslims on the Executive Council should be nominated by the Muslim League.

He asked me whether Mr. Gandhi was coming to the Conference. I told him that Mr. Gandhi had said that he represented nobody and had advised me that it would be better that he should not attend the Conference. Mr. Jinnah seemed rather upset at this and said it was another trick of Gandhi's, he pretended not to belong to the Congress when it suited his book, but when necessary appeared as the Dictator of Congress which everyone knew he was.

Mr. Jinnah said at the end that he would have to consult his Working Committee, but gave no indication that the Muslims would not attend the Conference; in fact he seemed to assume that they would, but that there would be ructions inside the Conference. I think he is probably having a difficult ride with his followers. It struck me that Mr. Jinnah was rather depressed and not sure of his position.

June 25

First day of the Conference. On the whole I think it went pretty well, though Jinnah was a little difficult. I think he has the hardest task of any leader as he has certainly not got the grip on his followers that Congress has. The level of discussion was not high, and I was rather appalled at the quality round the table. Jinnah has a good legal brain, so I think has Rajagopalachariar. Of the rest, perhaps Kher for the Congress and Saadullah for the League are the best, but they are second class. The remainder are poor stuff, I think. If we can build a self-governing India on this sort of material, we shall have emulated the legendary rope-trick.[1]

June 26

On the advice of Evan Jenkins, I put up to Conference[2] today the points

---

[1] These unflattering remarks clearly do not represent Wavell's considered opinion. He already had considerable regard for Khizar Hyat Khan and later he formed a high opinion of Liaquat Ali Khan.

[2] *List of Delegates to the Simla Conference:*

Maulana Abul Kalam Azad, President of Congress

Dr. P. N. Banerjee, Leader of Nationalist Party in the Central Assembly

Bhulabhai Desai, Leader of the Congress Party in the Central Assembly

M. K. Gandhi (he did not attend the Conference on the ground that he was not a member of the Congress Party, but he remained in Simla so as to be available for consultation)

Sir Ghulam Hussain Hidyatullah, Premier of Sind

Hossain Imam, Leader of the Muslim League in the Council of State

M. A. Jinnah

Dr. Khan Sahib, Premier of N.W.F.P.

B. G. Kher, ex-Premier of Bombay

for decision under two heads, i.e.:—A. if we could reach agreement on the composition of the Council, were the general principles under which it would work—programme outlined in my broadcast, parity of Hindus and Muslims, present constitution, etc.—acceptable; B. if above principles were acceptable could we reach agreement on composition of Council and names to be recommended.

This scheme was approved, and we reached general agreement on A.

The Conference then said they would like time for private consultation and discussion on B., and we adjourned until tomorrow morning. Atmosphere today was friendly and debate on quite a good level, but B. is of course the real crux of the whole matter. Jinnah was in much better mood today. Press reactions on first day's proceedings seem to be good.

June 27

Not a fruitful day. I had heard overnight that discussions between the parties were not going well, and it became obvious this morning that no progress had been made. After about three-quarters of an hour, during which there was some skirmishing between League and Congress which almost burst into open conflict twice, we agreed to adjourn till Friday morning to give parties an opportunity of private negotiation.

In the afternoon Baldev Singh[1] came to see me. He has two of the Congress (Kher and Sinha) staying with him. He said the Punjab would be quite satisfied if they had 1 Sikh and 1 Punjabi Mussulman in the Council.

At 5.30 p.m. Jinnah came, after having had tea with Q., and stayed till

Malik Khizar Hyat Khan Tiwana, Premier of the Punjab
Nawabzada Liaquat Ali Khan, Deputy Leader of the Muslim League in the Central Assembly
G. S. Motilal, Leader of the Congress Party in the Council of State
Khwaja Sir Nazimuddin, ex-Premier of Bengal
Pandit Govind Ballabh Pant, ex-Premier of the United Provinces
Maharaja of Parlakimedi, ex-Premier of Orissa
C. Rajagopalachari, ex-Premier of Madras
Sir Henry Richardson, Leader of the European Group, Central Assembly
Sir Muhammad Saadulla, Premier of Assam
Rao Bahadur Siva Raj, representative of the Scheduled Castes
Pandit R. S. Shukla, ex-Premier of the Central Provinces
Sri Krishna Sinha, ex-Premier of Bihar
Master Tara Singh, representative of the Sikhs

Secretaries
Sir Evan Jenkins, P.S.V.
Rao Bahadur V. P. Menon, Reforms Commissioner.

[1] Sardar Baldev Singh, a wealthy Sikh industrialist who was at this time a Minister in the Unionist Government of the Punjab. He was *persona grata* with the extremist group of nationalist Sikhs, known as 'Akalis', and subsequently played a prominent part, as the representative of the Sikhs, in negotiations for the transfer of power.

7.15 p.m. I began by telling him that while I appreciated his difficulties, I had to consider Provinces as well as parties, and was very conscious, as no doubt he was, of the importance of the Punjab, which was supplying so large a proportion of the food and of the soldiers of India. I, therefore, considered it essential that there should be a Punjab Muslim in the new Executive Council, as indeed there always had been for some time past; and I hoped that he agreed to the necessity for this. What I had in mind was someone who would represent the interests of the Punjab but without strong party affiliations, either to the League or to the Unionist Party.

Mr. Jinnah, who seemed rather worried and ill at ease, was a great deal more prolix and less business-like than usual. He went off into a long description of the 1940 offer, of the composition of the Unionist Party in the Punjab, of his own reception in the Punjab during his journey down from Kashmir as showing that he really commanded the allegiance of practically all Muslims in the Punjab, and so on.

I finally got him back to business by asking what the result of his conversations with Pant had been. He said they had been completely negative; that Congress had claimed the right to nominate two Muslims out of the Muslim quota to the Council, and that they had got no further than this.

I asked whether they had discussed the strength of the Council. I gathered that they had not done so in any detail. He said he wanted a Council of 14, with 5 Hindus, 5 Muslims, one Sikh, and one Scheduled Caste.[1] He said this was the only Council in which the Muslims would stand a chance of not being out-voted on every issue. I said that he was assuming that every vote would be taken on communal lines, and that if this was the spirit with which the Muslim League would enter the Council the whole purpose of it failed. I said that I had now had four years on the Executive Council, and that I did not recall a single issue which had been settled on purely communal lines. On what sort of issues did he expect the Muslims to be out-voted? The only thing he mentioned was post-war industrial development.

I finally asked what was his position regarding the nomination of the Muslim Members to the Council. He said that his position was that they must all be nominated by the League and must all be Leaguers. I said that, as I had told him at our first meeting, this was entirely unacceptable to me, and asked him bluntly whether he proposed to wreck the whole Conference on this issue. After considerable discussion I gathered his position to be this: that the League claimed the right to nominate all Muslim

[1] The Viceroy and Commander-in-Chief would bring the number up to fourteen.

Members to the Council and that they must be Leaguers; but that if I put it to him that I would not accept this point of view and that out of the Muslim quota I would allow the League only so many and would nominate the others myself, he would be prepared to put this position to his Working Committee.

June 28

While the political parties were consulting, I had a number of interviews.

Firoz Khan Noon, who has really very few political principles, now told me he supported the political move. He tries to trim between Jinnah and Khizar, and is I think trusted by neither.

Parlakimedi put before me Orissa's problems and claims, but really only showed animation when I spoke of the exploits of his horse Philanthropist and discussed its breeding and qualities and his hopes of winning the King-Emperor's and/or Viceroy's Cup. His heart is in racing, not politics.

In the afternoon I saw Banerjee who spoke of Bengal's claims. He is an educationalist and has really little idea of practical politics, but is an earnest and well-meaning person.

Next came Jogendra Singh and Sargent on the Education report, discussion of which I began in Council last March before going home. Colville, for some reason did not continue the discussion, as I had intended and hoped, and nothing more has been done on this important and rather controversial subject. I doubt whether I shall now get my present Council to take any decision and meanwhile work is being held up. Jogi was as charming and woolly as ever.

So far as I can hear, the discussions between Congress and the League are not going well and promise little result.

June 29

When the Conference met this morning, it was obvious that the two main parties had failed entirely to agree. I, therefore, proposed my own alternative line of approach, i.e. that party leaders should send in panels of names to me, and I should try to form an acceptable Council from them. After some discussion all agreed to do so, except Jinnah and Siva Raj who said they could not agree to submit a list without consulting their Working Committees. (Siva Raj came to see me afterwards and agreed to submit a list after consulting his Committee). Congress said they must consult the Working Committee before submitting names. Jinnah was very difficult and argumentative, trying to corner me on some lawyer's point and refusing to give a straight answer: at last I had to say to him:

'I am no dialectician and do not propose to argue, I have put you a simple proposal which everyone else seems to understand, are you or are you not prepared to submit me a list of names?'. He then asked for the proposal in writing, which I had sent to him in the simplest possible terms. I am not sure whether he means to break up the Conference but his attitude seems to be hardening.

We decided to adjourn till July 14. I am not very hopeful of success, unless there is a change of spirit. One of the troubles is that none of the principal leaders—Gandhi, Jinnah, Nehru, Liaquat, Patel—have any administrative experience; and they do not understand how the machinery of Government works in practice; and think entirely on the lines of all questions being decided by party votes.

June 30

I saw two of my Council Ambedkar and Sultan Ahmed, this morning. Both now profess to welcome and support the political move they opposed so hotly. In fact not one of the 'mutineers' has had the courage to adhere to his opposition, now that they have seen that the proposal has on the whole been popular. But I am told that they are going about in private, claiming that they were deceived and ill-used by me and that I never gave them any inkling that my journey home had any political significance. This although I held a special Council[1] meeting before I went to inform them that I was going to discuss the political situation with H.M.G. I feel some sympathy with them, but they have played their cards badly, and know it. And I don't feel that I have been crooked with them.

Ambedkar was bitter against Jinnah and the League, and said that if this failed he recommended Pakistan. He has the curious theory that after a few years experience of Pakistan, the Muslims would want to rejoin Hindustan. He then entered on a long diatribe against Congress and their method of capturing Scheduled Caste seats. He made it clear that whatever happens he would like to retain his portfolio of Labour, and suggested that an extra seat in the Council should go to Siva Raj and should be Education.

Sultan Ahmed had not much to say, except to inveigh against Jinnah's bad manners and the absurdity of his claim to represent all Muslims.

July 1

Walked for about three hours today up in Catchment area, and had a picnic. About the first real exercise I have had since I came to Simla, that

[1] See entry for 20 March, p. 117.

is one of my chief reasons for disliking the place. It was the first time I had been outside the grounds since I came up, and I found the first mile or so stiff with Police and thought that the local authorities had been officious on my behalf, as they used to be in Delhi; however, it was not for me, I found, but for the arrival of Nehru. N. is coming to see me tomorrow; Gandhi wrote and asked if I would see him, I meant to anyhow.

(My son-in-law, Francis, who went to hear the announcement on India in the House of Commons on June 14, tells me in a letter that there were never more than about 30 members present, which shows the measure of interest taken in the Indian problem at home).

July 2
I had a long talk with Nehru, he rather ranged at large over economics and history, and it was not easy to get him down to practical politics, though he was not quite so entirely unpractical as when I saw him three years ago at the time of the Cripps offer. He said Congress would do their best over the present offer although it was far short of necessities. He was quite friendly and pleasant, except at the end when I warned him that I could permit no victimization of public servants for action taken during the disturbances of 1942. He stopped to tea with Q., Archie John and the staff; and they all liked him.

July 4
A rather mixed dinner party this evening included Jogendra and Lady Singh (old Jogi was in great form and told Q. she had 'a gracious motherly face').

July 6
Two comparatively idle days. Master Tara Singh came to inform me that at the insistence of his Committee he had placed his own name at the head of Sikh nominees for Council (the other two names are complete duds!) This may be awkward, since Tara Singh would be a poor member of Council. He also tried to draw me on what my attitude would be if the Muslim League refused to put forward names, or to accept my proposals for Council.

July 9
I had 1½ hours with Jinnah yesterday evening which left us where we began. He spent practically the whole time trying to get me to agree that none except himself as head of the Muslim League could nominate the Muslims on the New Council. I refused to accept this, and he finally

refused to give me his list of names, though he left himself a loophole at the end by asking me to write to him, which I have done this morning. He was obviously in a high state of nervous tension, and said to me more than once; 'I am at the end of my tether'; he also said 'I ask you not to wreck the League'. He is obviously in great difficulties; but they are largely of his own making by his arrogance and intransigence. He fears now to be made the scapegoat for the failure of the Conference; and yet will not give up anything of his claim to represent all Muslims.

The Congress list of 15 names is disappointing, a great proportion of them are 'stooges' for Congress from the minorities; and Azad's covering letter is aggressive and speaks of 'independence' as the immediate goal after the defeat of Japan. The lists sent in by Banerjee and Siva Raj are unimportant. Khizar has been hanging in the wind with his list till he knew what the M.L. were doing. He is bringing them personally this afternoon. Altogether, the omens for success are unfavourable.

Khizar was friendly and seemed more confident and less upset than last time I saw him. He asked me the position about the Muslim League and I told him that Jinnah had so far refused to let me have names. He said that the parties would be foolish indeed to refuse 'an offer so liberal that it made many of us shudder'. He gave me his list of 4 names, the leading one, Sir Muhammad Usman Khan, Nawab of Kot, a leading Punjab land-owner, who has been a soldier, may make quite a reasonable member. I then asked him if he had any views about Sikh representation. He obviously knew all about Tara Singh's list, which he described as 'Tara Singh and two dummies'. He said Baldev Singh could not be spared from the Punjab; and that Datar Singh, though honest and capable, would not be acceptable to the Sikhs, as he belonged to a non-agricultural tribe and was not an Akali.[1] Khizar seemed in good heart, and though he said my move would probably stir up a lot of trouble I might possibly have been right to make it. He remarked that the P.O. must be reaping a great revenue from the Conference, to judge by the number of telegrams he was receiving.

In the evening I got a letter from Jinnah definitely refusing to send in names. I cabled home my provisional selection (including four Muslim Leaguers) for approval by the Cabinet; and if I get approval shall confront the leaders with them, as a last effort to get agreement. I think it is unlikely but at the same time they may find it a little awkward to refuse. I hope the Cabinet will back me up and will not haver or delay.

[1] The Akalis were the most powerful Sikh political party, representing extreme Sikh nationalism.

July 11

I fear I have to record the definite failure of the Conference and so of this fresh effort to make progress in Indian self-Government. I had a Cabinet telegram yesterday evening giving general approval to my 'shadow' Council if I could secure its acceptance by leaders. I, therefore, saw Jinnah this morning, gave him the proposed composition of the Council by parties and communities, the names of the four Muslim Leaguers I had selected and of the Punjab Muslim with whom I proposed to make up the Muslim quota. He refused even to discuss names unless he could be given the absolute right to select all Muslims and some guarantee that any decision which the Muslims opposed in Council could only be passed by a two-thirds majority—in fact a kind of communal veto. I said that these conditions were entirely unacceptable, and the interview ended.

I saw Gandhi an hour later. He took the news of the breakdown calmly, but said that H.M.G. would have to decide sooner or later to accept either the Hindu or the Muslim point of view, since they were irreconcilable.

So ends my attempt to introduce a fresh impetus and a fresh spirit into Indian politics. I am afraid that the result may be an increase in communal bitterness and agitation in India. I wonder what comes next. I have asked all Governors to meet me in Delhi at the beginning of next month to discuss the situation and the next move.

July 12

I saw Khizar this morning and explained the position to him. He is obviously relieved on the whole that the proposals have failed, but he said I had done my best and vindicated good intentions of H.M.G.; he thought the problem was intractable and must be left to destiny and time!

Azad and Pant came in the afternoon and I explained the position to them. They were obviously very disappointed and inclined to be bitter; they said Congress had made greater sacrifices and gone farther than ever before to reach agreement; and was one party always to block progress? I had to remind them that the attitude and mistakes of Congress had blocked progress on more than one occasion.

July 13

In the afternoon I saw two of the Congress—Dr. Khan Sahib[1] and

---

[1] Dr. Khan Sahib, the Congress Premier of N.W.F.P. was the brother of Khan Abdul Ghaffar Khan, known as the Frontier Gandhi. He had close ties with all-India Congress Leaders, but was also on friendly terms with many English officials.

Rajendra Prasad[1]—to make their acquaintance. Khan Sahib seems a pleasant sensible person, rather attractive. Rajendra Prasad seems quite ordinary and friendly and not very formidable or outwardly bitter.

The Cabinet, by the way, has been very prompt in answering my cables and giving approval to the course of action I have recommended, and have sent me two complimentary messages.

July 14

The final session of the Conference passed off more easily and smoothly than I had expected. Azad made quite a temperate statement, Rajagopalachariar exhorted me to form a Government without the League; and then Jinnah made a long exposition of the League point of view, its claims to Pakistan and its mistrust of Congress; he seemed at one time to raise his claim to parity inside the Council with *all other parties combined*. If he really meant this, it shows that he had never at any time an intention of accepting the offer, and it is difficult to see why he came to Simla at all. It is possible that his attitude hardened during the discussions.

So my efforts to bring better understanding between the parties have failed and have shown how wide is the gulf. Whether I have done more good or harm by trying, only time will show. In the outside world certainly Congress stock will go even higher and Jinnah's stock will go down, I imagine. Congress will claim to have been all sweet reasonableness. But actually their list would have given complete domination of the Council by Congress; and I very much doubt whether they would have accepted my provisional list. I think Jinnah made a tactical blunder in not bringing the matter to an issue. Whether his position with the Muslims will be strengthened I am not sure, but I imagine that it will be. Congress will be encouraged to try and win over Muslims from the League by all possible methods; and any elections will be bitterly fought.

I had a long talk with Nehru after lunch. I put to him that the only hope for India to make best use of the opportunities before her, and to win self-government without disruption or civil war was for the Hindus and Muslims to make friends. He was quite friendly and reasonable, the theme of his discourse was that Congress represented a modern nationalistic point of view and the League a narrow mediaeval conception; and that the eventual cleavage when India's freedom was secured would be between classes rather than communities, between poor and rich, between

---

[1] Dr. Rajendra Prasad, a member of the Congress Working Committee and later President of India.

peasant and landlord, between labourer and employer. Nehru is honest
and sincere but a theorist and doctrinaire rather than a practical politician.

*In his final address to the Conference, announcing its failure, Wavell said,
'I wish to make it clear that the responsibility for the failure is mine. The main
idea underlying the Conference was mine. If it had succeeded, its success would
have been attributed to me, and I cannot place the blame for its failure on any
of the parties. I ask the party leaders to accept this view, and to do all they can
to ensure that there are no recriminations.'*

*Azad, Jinnah and other speakers all spoke appreciatively of Lord Wavell's
efforts and said that he had done his best. Gandhi in a letter to him said, 'This
time you have taken the blame on your shoulders. But the world will think
otherwise. India certainly does.'*

*The root cause of the failure was, of course, Jinnah's intransigence and
obstinacy, but Wavell recognized that this intransigence 'represents a real fear
on the part of the Muslims, including those who do not support Jinnah, of
Congress domination, which they regard as equivalent to a Hindu Raj'.*

July 17

I returned to Delhi from Simla yesterday. Delhi is very sticky but I always
dislike Simla where I can get little exercise and feel shut off. It is good to
be able to get on a horse again.

I discussed with Rowlands the possible re-construction of Council, he
suggested the resignation of the whole Council to enable me to get rid of
the unsatisfactory members.

July 19

My old munshi from Peshawar, Ahmed Jan, treated me to a long harangue
—addressed, he said, to Lieut. Wavell of 40 years ago not to the Viceroy
of today—condemning all politicians and adjuring me to use the big stick
to both Congress and League.

As a footnote to the Conference I am told that both Bulabhai Desai
and Rajagopalachariar got properly told off by the Working Committee;
the former because he had not made his proposals dependent on the
release of the Working Committee, the latter apparently for having
instigated Gandhi to the discussions with Jinnah last autumn.

*The Simla Conference, though it ended in failure, may be regarded in some
ways as the greatest achievement of Wavell's Viceroyalty. The idea of holding
it, undoubtedly a right one, was entirely his, and it was his dogged persistence
that overcame the resistance of H.M.G. Once he had obtained H.M.G.'s
approval, he encountered little difficulty in assembling the Conference, and
skilfully got it off to an excellent start in a general atmosphere of goodwill;*

for his initiative had been warmly welcomed in India, and he himself had made a favourable impression on some of the Congress leaders, notably on Abul Kalam Azad, who has recorded[1] that he was much struck by Wavell's frankness and sincerity and his obviously genuine desire to open a new chapter in the relations between Congress and the Government.

Nevertheless the Conference failed. Although Wavell took responsibility for its failure, clearly the fault was not really his. Some critics have, however, contended that by capitulating without a struggle to Jinnah's intransigence and abruptly bringing the Conference to an end, he needlessly abandoned a great chance of setting India on the road to united self-government.[2] This conclusion implies that if he had ignored Jinnah and continued negotiations with the other parties, Jinnah would have had to give way, since he could not afford to see a new Council formed without the League; or, alternatively, that if he had still refused to come in, he would have lost his hold over the Muslims and more moderate leaders would have come to the fore.

These were possibilities, but hardly much more; and if Wavell was to take advantage of them, such as they were, he had to be prepared to accept, if necessary, a Congress-dominated Council. Would this have been advisable? One of his main objectives in trying to form a new Council was to facilitate a long-term solution of India's constitutional problems by getting Congress and the League to collaborate in the actual task of governing India. If he went ahead without the League, this objective would have to be foregone; indeed the communal problem was likely to become even more intractable. Apart from this, the war with Japan was still in progress and was expected to last at least one or two years more. In the prosecution of the war a Congress-dominated Council was likely to be a grave embarrassment, perhaps even a positive menace. Most of the Congress leaders had only recently been released from imprisonment on account of the 1942 rebellion and were still viewed with considerable suspicion. Wavell hesitated, therefore, to risk having to form a new Council without the participation of the League. But he did not entirely rule it out, and on 30 June, realizing that Jinnah was likely to prove intransigent, he consulted all the Governors by telegram on the advisability of going ahead without him. The Governors were about equally divided in their views, but among those who considered that it would be unwise to form a new Council without the League were the Governors of the important Muslim-majority Provinces of Bengal and the Punjab.[3] This tended to confirm Wavell's hesitations.

There was another important consideration. Churchill, who was still Prime Minister, and many of his Ministers had only reluctantly consented to the Simla Conference being held at all. They would have been outraged if its upshot had

---

[1] *India Wins Freedom* (Bombay, 1959), pp. 106–7.

[2] See H. V. Hodson's, *The Great Divide* (London, 1969), p. 126, where this criticism is discussed.

[3] On the other hand the Governors of the small Muslim-majority Provinces of Sind and N.W.F.P. both favoured disregarding Jinnah.

been a proposal to form a Congress-dominated Council unbalanced by the League. Wavell was well aware that there would be small chance of H.M.G. agreeing to such a proposal, if he had decided to make it.

In the circumstances there was no way in which he could meet Jinnah's obduracy except by persuasion; and so when he found that Jinnah would not yield to persuasion, he was obliged to admit failure and bring the Conference to an end. As Khizar put it, he had done his best and vindicated the good intentions of the British Government. He had also won the goodwill of those who attended the Conference. In the next few difficult months when extremist elements in Congress were itching to repeat the 1942 rebellion, this goodwill seemed to be largely dissipated; but the Congress President, Azad, retained full confidence in Wavell and consistently threw such influence as he possessed on the side of moderation. He said later (in a letter to Lord Wavell) that by calling the Simla Conference Wavell had rendered India and Great Britain a service which had few parallels in history and that the new possibilities of Indo-British friendship were due to that step.

Simla Conference: Sir Evan Jenkins and Lord Wavell

Mr. Gandhi leaving Viceregal Lodge, 11 July 1945

7

END OF THE WAR AND
SECOND VISIT TO LONDON

July 26

So there has been what is called for some reason 'a landslide' in favour of Labour at the elections. It was obvious by this evening that they would have a majority of about 200. It is too big, I had hoped for something like a balance between the two main parties, with a revived Liberal party holding the scales. I am afraid there will be a lot of foolish, inexperienced and rather wild legislators amongst the 400 odd of Labour. However there were very many stupid and tiresome Tories in the late Conservative majority. I think Labour is likely to take more interest in and be more sympathetic towards India, but they will have some weird ideas about it.

July 31

My Governors arrived today, all except Hope, whose plane broke down or was delayed by weather; and I had interviews with some of them.

I wrote a letter to Winston a couple of days ago. I thanked him for having entrusted me with such responsibilities and said what a privilege it had been to serve under so great a man. I have never quite known, though, how he really considered me, sometimes I think more as a liability than an asset. He has certainly, as I know, often said some very biting and critical things of me, though never, so far as I remember, to me. I am pretty sure that when he appointed me Viceroy it was with the intention and expectation that I should simply keep things quiet in India till the war was over. I should have saved myself a lot of trouble and should perhaps have served my own interests best, had I done so. Then I could have claimed to go back home at the end of the war, and to leave the political imbroglio in India to some ambitious politician. But I doubt whether I could have accepted this role, my instincts are for action and not to sit still over a problem, and my tendencies are progressive. I undoubtedly shook Winston by my proposals, and I think there were times when he wished he had appointed someone else. However, there it is, and I must go on now and do my best for my new masters. But how pleasant it would be if I could look forward to demobilization at the end of the war.

I am told that H.E.H. the Nizam's reaction to the British election results was: 'how awful, I must now begin to economise'.

August 2

The Governors Conference went well on the whole. No one produced any original ideas as to the solution of the problem, but there was almost unanimity of recommendation as to the next moves. Only one Governor (Colville) advocated by-passing the League and forming a political Executive Council without it. On the other hand only one favoured reconstruction on an 'efficiency' basis; the others all thought I should carry on with my present Council, with any changes I could make in the ordinary course, unless and until I could get a political Council. All, except Glancy, favoured Elections as soon as possible to the Central Assembly; and all, again except Glancy, wanted Provincial elections this winter; but practically all Governors of Provinces under Section 93 thought elections should precede the formation of Ministries, though they agreed that should any leader come forward meanwhile who could form a stable government and give satisfactory assurances as regards support of the war effort it would not be easy to debar him from forming a Ministry; and then it would be necessary for the governor to consult him about elections.

No one found much difficulty on the general policy of releasing political prisoners, except the dangerous ones, and lifting the ban on Congress organisations.

I pointed out that elections were probably inevitable but that they did not amount to a policy, and might, after some months dislocation of administration and communal agitation, leave us exactly where we were, if Congress still refused to take office in the Provinces unless a political Government was formed at the Centre. Some Governors were in favour of bringing Pakistan into the open by means of a Conference, Committee or Mission—Indian, British or International—to determine its advisability and practicability. I said that the difficulty was that Jinnah and the League would almost certainly boycott any such enquiry unless they were given some such unacceptable pledge—of the fate of certain Provinces or areas being determined by the Muslim vote alone—as Jinnah demands.

Everyone approved my suggestion of the formation of a Council—to be called perhaps the Planning and Development Council—composed of the Premiers of Provinces, when Ministerial Government has been restored in all or the great majority, and some representatives of the States. They also all agreed that the National Defence Council should be continued till the end of the war with Japan, but need not meet so frequently.

We also discussed in a general way, Food, coal, cloth, resettlement of soldiers, shortage of personnel, pay of government servants.

August 3

My Governors have either left today or leave tomorrow morning. They all profess themselves pleased with the meeting, and I think genuinely; they get a chance of seeing one another and exchanging views and of doing a good deal of business with Departments of Government. I have had interviews with them all, their Provinces all seem to be running reasonably well and they had nothing very much to tell me about them.

Council meeting in evening, only routine items of Food and Coal, and Summary. At this time of year the Food and Coal prospects can seldom both be good; if the monsoon is favourable a very large proportion of the labour in the coalfields goes off to cultivate the land and we lose coal; if the monsoon is bad we may get more coal but shall lose food.

August 6

I know nothing of the new S. of S. Pethick-Lawrence, I fear he may have fixed and old-fashioned ideas derived mainly from Congress contacts. I wonder what the policy of the new Government to India will be, I have no indication at all yet.

I had a discussion this morning with C.-in-C., Home Member and Finance Member over the treatment of the re-captured I.N.A. The general policy is all right I think, to detain the 'Blacks' and try the worst of them by court-martial, to discharge the 'Greys', and to return the 'Whites' to their units. The main point at issue is the financial treatment of the Greys; when I saw him some days ago C.-in-C. intended to discharge them *with their pay during the whole time they had been Prisoners of War*. I told him that I really could not stand for our paying men to fight against us, and that it was not fair on men who had remained loyal, and that he must think again. He now proposes to pay them gratuity earned by previous service and to give them the leave on full pay that they would normally be entitled to on discharge. I again think, and Finance and Home Members agree, that these terms are too generous. Claude Auchinleck promised to reconsider.

Of some 70,000 men of the Indian Army who fell into Japanese hands as prisoners of war about 20,000 defected to them and joined the I.N.A. (Indian National Army). This was at first commanded by a Sikh officer, but he fell out with the Japanese and the I.N.A. became more or less moribund until the autumn of 1943 when Subhas Chandra Bose (see footnote on p. 49) arrived and took over command.

Militarily the I.N.A. was of little use to the Japanese, but it had some propaganda value. Many of the 20,000 military personnel who joined it did so primarily to get better treatment; but some of them were imbued with genuine patriotic fervour and were persuaded by Bose to believe that they were serving the cause of Indian freedom.

The 'Blacks' were considered to have entered wholeheartedly into the movement and to be quite unrepentant. They numbered over 7,000. Some of them had been guilty not only of waging war against the King, but also of appalling brutality to many fellow-prisoners who remained loyal and refused to join them. Consequently there was very strong feeling against the I.N.A. among some of the loyalists. The decision to try a few of the worst offenders by court-martial gave rise to a great deal of agitation a few months later.

August 7

So the atomic bomb has come, a surprise to me, though I think I have known or suspected the majority of the war secrets. I knew vaguely that they were working at it, but had no idea it was near going into use. The correspondence there has been about the Travancore mineral salts (Monasite, etc.) is connected with it, I fancy. A very dangerous scientific development, since I doubt whether man has yet the wisdom to use it wisely. It may end war or it may end civilization. It is not a weapon that any thinking man would willingly have put into the hands of the present-day world. It has shown it cannot be trusted with a box of matches, is it reasonable to think it can play with a Mills grenade and not pull the pin out?

August 8

Routine Council this morning, nothing much except that the food situation will deteriorate again unless we get some heavy rains soon. Sir John Woodhead is staying with me, he has written an efficient but dry rather dull report on the food problem.

I had a telegram from Winston thanking me for the letter I wrote him on his ceasing to be P.M., he seems quite pleased with it.

August 11

Habet Nippon, so now for the horrors of peace. The first one will be that I must write a victory broadcast, I suppose.

August 14

The last few days have been spent waiting for the formal surrender of Japan. Wheeler[1] came to see me on Sunday. Americans are always quick off the mark, and he was already starting to get home the 200,000 Americans in India and Burma and the 60,000 in China. S.E.A.C. are sending a commando to Penang to take over the port and airfields there, and a division from Rangoon to Singapore. I wonder how many of our British and Indian Prisoners of War we shall recover.

In the Departments of the G. of I. we are not nearly ready for peace, but I doubt whether we ever should have been. P.S.V. and I are trying to stir up Departments but it is a hard job.

August 18

Nothing much to record. I gave my broadcast on the 15th on the defeat of Japan, not a very good one, but adequate I suppose.

A telegram from the S. of S. today, the first real sign of life, indicated that H.M.G. intend to take the India problem in hand at once and seriously. They agree to elections and the general programme[2] I put home after the Governors' Conference, but obviously mean something further; and S. of S. says another telegram will be sent me early next week after further discussion in Cabinet.

August 19

Thanksgiving Service this morning. I was sent the choice of three most inappropriate and rather dreary pieces of scripture to read as the lesson, so I said I would read the song of Deborah. I was told that this would be most out of keeping with the spirit of the Service but it seemed to me entirely in keeping with the celebration of victory; and I duly read it. It was a good service, but the Bishop is not a good preacher.

Monteath sent Evan Jenkins a private wire indicating that I am likely to be called home at short notice for consultation.

Basil Gould took leave, he goes home tomorrow after 37½ years in India. We went to Summerfields together over 50 years ago and on to College at Winchester. He certainly did well in Sikkim and the people up there loved him.

---

[1] General Wheeler had become Deputy to Mountbatten in succession to General Stilwell.
[2] This was the programme for elections, release of political prisoners, lifting the ban on Congress organizations, etc., agreed to at the Governors' Conference.

August 20

F.K.N. told me that if elections were to be held early next year he wished to leave Council and go back to Punjab politics. He has in fact gone over to Jinnah and the League and against his cousin Khizar. He will be no loss to Council.

August 22

The present Government certainly moves quicker than its predecessor. They want me to start home the day after tomorrow or as soon after as possible. And they announced it straight away, also the holding of elections. I had to call a special Council yesterday at very short notice, to let them know before the public announcement. Felicity will go with me and Menon, and George Abell will meet me in London.

Azad has sent an indignant wire about my ordering elections without consulting the convenience of Congress, who apparently want more time to organise, and will also use elections as another lever to try to get their remaining criminals out of jail.

A private telegram from the S. of S. indicates that they propose to go back to the Cripps offer. This won't do, I am sure, it is much less likely to be accepted by the parties now than before.

August 24

Left Delhi at noon.

Dow at Karachi was in his usual rather cynical form. We spoke of the acquittal of his ex-Minister Khuhro, who will now probably become Premier before long; to be suspected of murdering one's enemies, or even to be known to have done it, is a qualification rather than a hindrance in Sind politics.

Dow thinks that some sort of a Constituent Assembly, or preliminaries for one, is now necessary, but agrees that an inquiry into the question of Pakistan is probably an essential preliminary.

I wonder if the Japanese announcement of Subhas Chandra Bose's death in an air-crash is true, I suspect it very much, it is just what would be given out if he meant to go underground. My first reaction when I heard it was to tell P.S.V. to ask S.E.A.C. to make most careful enquiries into the story as soon as they could. If it is true, it will be a great relief. His disposal would have presented a most difficult problem.

I am not very much looking forward to this trip. I shall find it difficult, I think, to persuade the Labour party of the realities of the Indian situation and that they must go slow. However, it will be easier to do it in person than by exchange of telegrams.

August 26

Arrived London this evening. The S. of S. met us and I motored with him to Claridges. He looks old, is pleasant and amiable. George Abell tells me that Cripps is the only man in the Government who is really in a hurry over India, and he wants to get back to the Cripps offer. The remainder of the Government, George thinks, are in no hurry, and the rank and file of the Labour party and the country at large take little interest in India.

August 27

I had 1½ hours with S. of S. He outlined the reasons that were impelling the Labour Government to early action—the pronouncements of Labour leaders; the end of the war; the fact that the Foreign Ministers of Great Britain, U.S.A., and Russia are meeting early next month and Bevin would like to show progress in India; and the fact that Congress seemed to be in an accommodating mood. He said that if progress was to be made, the alternatives seemed to be the Cripps offer or a modification of it, or some new line of approach. He then spoke of the Pakistan issue and the attitude of the Muslims. Finally, he said that while the Constitutional issue was being settled there would presumably be a time-lag during which the business of India had to be carried on, and suggested means for forming a provisional Executive Council from a Provincial panel.

I said the reasons impelling the Government to an early settlement were understandable, but did not justify action that might throw India into chaos or turmoil. Besides the political issue, we had responsibility to the minorities other than the Muslims, to the workers vis-à-vis the factory owners, and to the peasants vis-à-vis the landowners, and for India's post-war problems; we must not overlook these in the hope of appeasing a few political leaders. I said the spirit and objectives of Congress had not really changed, they were in a comparatively reasonable mood at present because they were anxious to get back into power. I did not believe a fresh Cripps offer would be acceptable to any of the parties; and I thought we had to face the Pakistan issue and bring its real implications into the light before we could get any further. I agreed the time-lag would be consider-able and might amount to 5 or 6 years. I outlined the possibilities of an Executive Council during this interim period—a political Council if one could get one; an 'efficiency' Council; or the present Council. I reminded him that he had not even mentioned the States but that they were a considerable part of the Indian problem, and warned him of the dangers that might result, especially in the Punjab, if it were said that the Cripps offer would be enforced (he had hinted at this). I spoke of India's social, economic, and financial problems that had to be faced and must not be neglected in concentrating on the political settlement. I emphasised the Indian lack of leadership. Some talk followed on Jinnah's attitude and demands and the difficulty of fitting the Punjab with any Pakistan scheme. P.L. gave me the impression that he had no wish to be in a hurry himself but was being pressed by Cabinet and Party.

After lunch had another 1½ hours with S. of S., and the Under Secretary, Henderson, was present. We talked at considerable length of the detention Ordinances which the Labour Government want abolished; the H.I.Fs., and J.I.Fs.,[1] of whose crimes and dangerous proclivities they seemed unaware; of the meeting of Foreign Ministers and India's interest in the problems they might discuss (Palestine, the future of Italian East Africa, Persia, Siam); of Bajpai's status; and other matters.

In the evening I dined with the P.M. in the flat in the War Cabinet buildings, P.L. was the only other present. We talked rather at large on India and Indian personalities without getting down to anything definite. Dinner was at 7.30 p.m. and the party broke up at 9.45, Winston would have had dinner at 9 p.m. and talked till 2 a.m.

August 28

Busy at I.O. practically the whole day. I went to have a talk with S. of S. in morning on assumption that we had finished with the political situation for the moment and that he wanted to discuss Governorships and other matters. But I found that his mind was entirely engrossed with producing some definite scheme for tomorrow's meeting of the India Committee; and he asked me to outline a draft announcement to be made, which would go as far as possible to meet forward opinion in the Cabinet and would not embarrass me in India. This was a very quick one for which I was not in the least prepared. I thought on the whole I rose to the occasion rather effectively. I outlined the heads of a possible announcement on general policy towards a settlement, which S. of S. said he thought would do admirably. He asked me to produce a draft announcement by 5 p.m. I put George Abell, Menon and Turnbull on to producing a draft, and went off to give George Giffard lunch.

---

[1] J.I.F.s, i.e. Japanese Inspired Fifth Column, were the men of the I.N.A. The H.I.F.s, i.e. Hitler Inspired Fifth Column, were the very much smaller number of prisoners of war in German hands who had agreed to collaborate with them.

George Abell produced a short and simple draft, which the S. of S. approved in substance but then started to try his hand at drafting. So we had another discussion at about 6 p.m., I didn't like his draft, so we left it till next morning.

August 29

Final draft was produced at I.O. this morning, and I got through a certain amount of miscellaneous work.

At India Cabinet Committee in afternoon were P.M., Cripps, Ellen Wilkinson, Stansgate (Wedgwood Benn that was), Pethick-Lawrence, Henderson and Listowel. I made a general statement on the present position and the causes and result of the failure at Simla and said it now seemed that we must clear the Pakistan issue before we could go any further. I said I did not think the Cripps offer would now be accepted by the parties, and Cripps said that Birla, Shiva Rao[1] and others had told him that the Hindus would accept it.[2] The draft drawn up by S. of S. and myself was criticized by P.M. and Cripps as reactionary; and it became evident that Cripps was, mainly I think for reasons of personal prestige, set on enforcing the original Cripps offer, which he said was now H.M.G.'s policy. About three-quarters of an hour inconclusive talk followed; at the end of which it was agreed to think again. This is a set-back to my hopes of early return.

I sent off a telegram to Colville, asking him to consult Hallett, Glancy, Casey, Hope and Corfield[3] on implications of a renewal of Cripps offer.

August 31

Went to War Office and saw new S. of S., Lawson, whom I had known in 1942 when he came to India with the Parliamentary Mission to China. We had about 20 minutes of goodwill, I impressed on him the necessity for a quick decision on officering the I.A. and put him wise about Hifs and Jifs problem.

Then to F.O. and had half an hour with Bevin, who I thought was very sensible about Palestine, about the status of India's representatives at

[1] B. Shiva Rao, a distinguished journalist writing mainly for the Madras paper, *The Hindu*.

[2] It would not have been accepted by the Muslim League. The Cripps offer had given individual Provinces the right to stand out of an Indian Union, but the Muslim majorities in the important Provinces of Bengal and the Punjab were so small that the League could have no assurance that in these two Provinces there would be a vote in favour of standing out of an Indian Union.

[3] Sir Conrad Corfield, I.C.S., who had succeeded Sir Francis Wylie as Political Adviser.

Washington and Chungking, about Indian representation whenever the Dominions were represented, and other matters. He was anxious to get some announcement out about progress on the Indian political situation before Sept 10, when he meets Foreign Ministers of U.S.A. and Russia.

I went to see the S. of S. whose drafting I dislike more every time I see it. We discussed his fresh draft for India Cabinet Committee and agreed to meet again at 5.15 p.m., and then went on to the matter of détenus in Bengal, S. of S. feels very strongly about detention of people without trial, it is of course indefensible in principle, but almost certainly the only way to keep law and order in some parts of India.

I had an hour with Winston from 4 to 5 p.m. He was friendly and in good form, is just off on a holiday to Italy, to a villa near Lake Como where he will paint. He gave forth his usual jeremiad about India; warned me that the anchor (himself) was now gone and that I was on a lee shore with rash pilots; revealed that the only reason he had agreed to my political move was that the India Committee had all told him it was bound to fail!

When I got a bit tired of his diatribes on India, I asked him whether he was going to write the history of the war, he disclaimed any intention of it, said he was too old and might leave notes to be put into shape after his lifetime. He spoke of the shock of the election; how in one day in 1940 he had been elevated to P.M. when the enemy was at the gates, and in one day in 1945 when the war was over had been thrown out.

We talked of the strategy of the war, of the fall of Singapore, of the Greek campaign which he still regarded with disapproval; of Cairo and Moscow in August 1942; and then of the atomic bomb, it was not till Potsdam that they knew it was a success. Winston said if he had known it was going to come off and that the Japanese war would be over so soon he would not have had the election till October; he admitted, however, that the result would probably have been much the same. He was very friendly, and I think genuinely pleased that I had been to see him. His final remark as I closed the door of the lift was: 'Keep a bit of India'.

I had a short session with the S. of S. and told him his last draft was the worst of all and that I couldn't accept it. I agreed to produce an alternative by Monday and that the India Committee should not meet again till Tuesday.

September 3

I seem to have reached rather a crisis with H.M.G. After seeing the telegrams from Colville giving the views of Governors—which agreed generally with my own—early this morning, I drafted a note for the India Committee stating the objections to trying to impose a Constitution Making Body on India without further consultation with Indians, and took it round to S. of S. He was rather shaken, but I told him quite clearly that I meant to stick to it, and suggested that I should see the P.M. I saw him again in the afternoon when he had made a rather feeble attempt to water down my draft announcement, 'in order to make it easier to get it past the India Committee'. I told him that it was perfectly easy to draft something that would get past the Committee, but that if it promised something we could not fulfil it would be dishonest, and if it was completely unacceptable to one of the two principal communities it would be highly dangerous, and that I would not consent to either.

These people hate to be brought up against realities and made to face their fences squarely. Birla and Shiva Rao and other Congress propagandists are, I know, seeing Cripps and Attlee, and they are taking all they say as gospel.

That was pretty nearly all the business of the day, except a certain number of routine telegrams, but it took quite a time.

September 4

A very busy and not very profitable day. Sir R. Maxwell came to see me, his only suggestion on the India problem was an enlarged franchise, rather a surprising one from him, he must know better than anyone the ignorance of the present electorate.

At 4 p.m. I had an hour with P.M. He was quite friendly but did not convince me about the advisability of imposing a Constitution Making Body on India; I don't think I convinced him of the inadvisability, but I left him in no doubt about the dangers. At the back of it all he made it clear, without intending to do so, that the Cabinet was thinking more of placating opinion in their own party, and in U.S.A., than of the real good of India. He said in the end that the India Committee would discuss it among themselves that afternoon.

Then went to dine with Cripps. He tried to persuade me on the same lines as the P.M., and I was equally firm on the dangers of trying to force the pace and impose a Constitution Making Body. He also revealed in what he said that at the back of his mind was pledges to the party tail and fear of their pressure, instigated by Congress propaganda, rather than the real good of India. I made no secret of my views as to the dangers of the course they proposed and the extent to which they were disregarding the good of the people. However, they are obviously bent on handing over

India to their Congress friends as soon as possible. They will try to get me to accept some compromise formula of words that they will interpret their way. I may have to decide whether to refuse to be a party to their plans to Quit India, or to go back and try to keep them out of disaster as much as possible. Afterwards Cripps talked more sensibly on India's economic problems, and then on the question of Governorships.

September 5

Just before lunch S. of S. produced yet another draft, and I discussed it with him for over an hour in the afternoon. He is a most charming old gentleman but not a very skilful drafter. I think this latest effort may do with a few alterations, but it really leaves all the loose ends untied.

September 6

Meeting of the Cabinet India Committee went well. The latest draft announcement was passed with only a few textual amendments, it was agreed that it would be a good thing if I supplemented it with a broadcast; and the P.M. would also probably broadcast at home. I then made a statement, warning H.M.G. of the rocks ahead and emphasising that a mere expression of their intentions, however good, did not solve the Indian problem and that there were many awkward questions to be answered and decisions to be made before C.M.B. could come into being, much more before a Constitution could be agreed. I outlined some of them— the composition and procedure of the C.M.B., the secession issue, the pledges to the Princes, the rights of minorities. It was agreed that there should be a discussion of these points before I went back.

The announcement, which Wavell made on behalf of H.M.G. on 19 September after his return to India, was as follows:

'As stated in the gracious Speech from the Throne at the Opening of Parliament, His Majesty's Government are determined to do their utmost to promote in conjunction with the leaders of Indian opinion the early realisation of full self-government in India. During my visit to London they have discussed with me the steps to be taken.

'An announcement has already been made that elections to the Central and Provincial Legislatures, so long postponed owing to the war, are to be held during the coming cold weather. Thereafter His Majesty's Government earnestly hope that ministerial responsibility will be accepted by political leaders in all Provinces.

'It is the intention of His Majesty's Government to convene as soon as possible a Constitution-making Body, and as a preliminary step they have

authorised me to undertake, immediately after the elections, discussions with representatives of the Legislative Assemblies in the Provinces, to ascertain whether the proposals contained in the 1942 declaration are acceptable or whether some alternative or modified scheme is preferable. Discussions will also be undertaken with the representatives of the Indian States with a view to ascertaining in what way they can best take their part in the Constitution-making Body.

'His Majesty's Government are proceeding to the consideration of the content of the treaty which will require to be concluded between Great Britain and India.

'During these preparatory stages, the Government of India must be carried on, and urgent economic and social problems must be dealt with. Furthermore, India has to play her full part in working out the new World Order. His Majesty's Government have therefore further authorised me, as soon as the results of the Provincial elections are published, to take steps to bring into being an Executive Council which will have the support of the main Indian parties.'

September 11

The Secretary of the India Society, Richter, came to see me about the proposed exhibition of Indian Art at Burlington House and I found that almost nothing had been done since I was home last. So I wrote a note to the S. of S.

The Cabinet Committee discussed all the difficulties in front of us a little languidly, since they were not immediate. Cripps was always ready with a form of words, but even he realises that words, however skilfully chosen, will not solve fundamental differences. Still the atmosphere was friendly, different to the India Committee of the last Government, who were, however, more alive to the practical difficulties. Compared with last time, I have had to raise my right foot—the one on the accelerator pedal—and put down my left foot—the brake pedal one—gently but firmly.

September 12

The usual last day hustle included a meeting with the Secretary of State on Commercial safeguards and discrimination against British firms and several other matters—a mixed bag.

Sitwell, the gunner whom I left in command on Java in February 1942 came to see me. He has been a Jap prisoner ever since. He seemed in very good heart, as he was when I handed him over that very forlorn hope. He told me the story of his adventures. When the Japs landed Sitwell was ordered by Ter Poorten to surrender. The Japs beat him up really thoroughly at the start, to try and get from him where the Australian I Corps was, he told me he was left on the floor for ten days with his hands tied behind his back, for six days without food. Afterwards they (the officers) were subjected to a policy of degradation in front of their men— a policy which did not pay from the Japanese point of view, as it only aroused the fury and indignation of the men. He said the morale of our men was much better thant hat of the Dutch and Americans. Sitwell impresses me by his vitality and courage, as he did when I put him in command.

September 14 (Cairo)

Usual party to see me off yesterday. Arrived Cairo about 8 p.m. and went to Paget—our old house on Gezira.

The Caseys turned up for dinner and I had half an hour with him. He was furious over the release of Sarat Bose,[1] apparently it was done without consulting him. He wants to leave Bengal in January, rather to my disappointment he had no very definite ideas about a successor.

September 16

Back to Delhi by lunch time. Evan Jenkins had as usual prepared a succint and illuminating note on all the principal developments in my absence.

So ends another stage or incident of my Viceroyalty. I think it was worthwhile to go home and make contact with the new Government. I appear to have for the moment the confidence of H.M.G. and of people generally, and hope I have introduced some sense of realities into the people to whom I have talked on the Indian situation.

It has been fairly grilling work and I am a little weary.

[1] Left-wing Congress leader from Bengal, brother of Subhas Chandra Bose.

8

THE EDGE OF A VOLCANO

Lord Wavell had predicted that the end of the war would be a testing time in India, and he was right. The left-wing extremists in Congress, many of whom had recently been released from jail, were itching to launch a fresh 'Quit India' rebellion, and during the next few months this seemed to be the intention of the Congress leaders, judging by the violence of their public utterances. Gandhi was said to favour moderation, but Gandhi's influence was on the decline.

*The first trials of members of the I.N.A. began in November and aroused great excitement, fomented by the Congress leaders, some of whom were thinking of employing I.N.A. officers and men as the spearhead of a rebellion. The trials were a source of great anxiety to the Government of India. On the Army's insistence and against the advice of the Home Member, they were unwisely held in the Red Fort at Delhi in the fullest glare of publicity; and in retrospect it is clear that the policy, adopted later, of only sending for trial those against whom charges of brutality could be **proved**, should have been followed from the outset; but it is difficult to see how these trials could have been avoided altogether.*

Another source of anxiety at this time was the possible need to use Indian troops against the Indonesians. If the impression was created that the Indian Army was being used to restore 'colonialism', this would intensify political trouble in India and might excite disaffection in the Army itself.

However, by the end of the year the worst dangers were over. The important Congress leader, Vallabhbhai Patel, seems to have come round to the view that Independence could be gained quite soon by peaceful means and that it would be foolish to stir up trouble and create disorder in the country. He therefore began to throw the weight of his great influence in favour of keeping the peace.

September 20

Council meetings on last two days. On the evening of 18th I held a special meeting to communicate the result of my discussions at home and to read the proposed announcement of H.M.G. In contrast to the last occasion when I came back, the proposals had a very good reception, and the comments of members were sensible and friendly.

After dinner I made my broadcast of H.M.G.'s announcement, and then had to do it all over again in front of an American film unit, whose machine kept breaking down with the result that I was kept about 40 minutes in front of those blazing lights. I remarked to the American in charge that I did not wonder that film stars became temperamental, he merely replied 'You are lucky, you haven't got any make-up on'.

September 21

According to the Japs at Singapore, S. C. Bose definitely is dead, but I shall be sceptical till further confirmation.

I told Caroe and Trivedi about their Governorships[1] and they seemed pleased. Mudie has accepted Governorship of Sind.

September 22

Ceremonial parade this morning when Wheeler presented Legion of Merit to C.-in-C. and myself. We had a number of Americans to lunch later on. Parade went well and I think Wheeler was very pleased, he has been a great co-operator with the British and genuinely liked by everyone.

I saw two correspondents this morning—Moraes of the Times of India, who tried to draw me on my political intentions and drew a blank; and Holburn of the Times. Sultan Ahmed also came and expressed a wish to resign from Council and take up a post as Muslim Adviser to the Chamber of Princes.

September 28

Back this morning from a fairly strenuous 4 days at Dehra Dun. I saw the 2 Gurkha Training Depot and battalions of 2nd and 9th Gurkhas back from P.o.W. camps in Malaya. 9th Gurkha battalion put up an impressive performance by turning out on parade very smart for inspection in spite of being a very sick and debilitated lot of men. Both battalions had brought back more men and in rather better shape than I expected; both were exceedingly bitter about the I.N.A. from whose hands they had had worse treatment than from the Japs.

September 30

A pretty busy day Saturday was succeeded by a very 'Green-box', Sunday, and I got no week-end rest at all. Bengal is getting very worried about food, and it looks as if we might have a situation comparable with 1943, unless we are careful.

[1] Sir Olaf Caroe, I.C.S., who had been Foreign Secretary, was appointed Governor of the N.W.F.P., and Sir Chandu Lal Trivedi, I.C.S., who had been Secretary, War Department, was appointed Governor of Orissa.

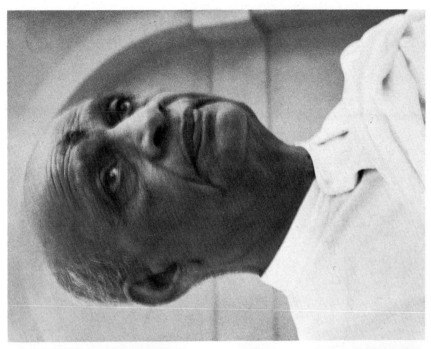

Sardar Vallabhbhai Patel

Pandit Jawaharlal Nehru

Viceroy's House: the ballroom

October 1

I began with an hour with Lawson, the S. of S. for War, who arrived last night. I tackled him over passages home for the large numbers of civilians, Service and commercial, who have been abroad for 7 or 8 years. He was, perhaps naturally, impressed with the necessity of clearing the block of soldiers waiting to go to the U.K. where trade is suffering from lack of labour.

I then had two of the Diwans of big States—Ramaswami Aiyar of Travancore and the Nawab of Chattari from Hyderabad. The former talked of his plan for Regional grouping, of the necessity to form an Interim National Government, of proposals to bring the Princes into consultation over industrial and economic questions, of Pakistan and how to elucidate it. He has clear and sound ideas of what should be done but no intention, as he showed a year or two ago, of descending into the dust and strife of the arena himself.

The Nawab of Chattari with a bad cold was even less audible and intelligible than he usually is to me. He was charged by his formidable and importunate master to suggest that H.M.G. should enter into a separate treaty with Hyderabad as an independent State and give her an outlet to the sea by permitting or helping her to buy Marmagoa from the Portuguese; also that H.E.H. should be given a resounding title and be released from all restrictions as a reward for his services in the war. I was not encouraging about either proposal.

Then I had a talk with Archie Rowlands for an hour on the reorganisation of the Finance Branch; the decimalization of the coinage; India's ratification of the Bretton Woods agreement; and several other matters.

Next an hour with C.-in-C. on various matters. He wants a big Victory parade and military week in February, which seems a bit late; and the Africans, East and West, removed from India as soon as possible—especially the West Africans.

Finally, a big dinner party of 70 or so, largely Princes.

October 4

The 19th and final session of the N.D.C., which has been in existence for just four years, ended today. It has been, I think, a useful body; but it has sometimes been rather a wearisome one. We discussed a number of matters and then at the end an officer P.O.W. from Malaya, Major Bahadur Singh of the Hyderabad Regiment, spoke of his experiences and sang a hymn of hate against the I.N.A. His obvious sincerity and the obvious sufferings he had been through made a considerable impression. It was a good session and ended with farewell complimentary remarks by myself, the Jam Sahib, and Sir C. Jehangir.[1]

We had two biggish parties, an At Home on the evening of the 2nd for Lawson to meet the N.D.C. and a farewell dinner tonight for the N.D.C.

Peter Coats departed yesterday morning with Lawson, he has been with me for nearly six years, as ADC, P.S. and Comptroller. I shall miss his stimulating company and quick wit.

Outside the N.D.C., there has been plenty of paperwork and a number of interviews. I had a long session with Corfield on the difficult problem of war rewards for the Princes, on which it will be very difficult to satisfy them. It looks as if we should have to agree to Mirza Ismail going to Hyderabad to replace Chattari—a vain, untrustworthy but clever man for an honest but stupid one.

Dalal saw me today, full of difficulties and complaints of the slow functioning of other Departments, says he can get no decision on Agricultural policy, Educational policy, policy to deal with unemployment (roads, etc.). I hold no brief for my Members in charge of these Departments, they are maddeningly slow; but Dalal is rather soft and faint-hearted and cannot stand up to difficulties or criticism. I tried to hearten him a little. He said he had seen Gandhi and Vallabhai Patel in Bombay. Gandhi had now no objection to promotion of heavy industries, though he still wished for cloth to be produced by village industry. Vallabhai Patel was very bitter about the dissolution of the Assemblies by Governors and claimed that Congress should have been given the chance to form Ministries, though he said they would not have done so. I suppose what they wanted was to be asked to form Ministries so that they could have refused or demanded conditions. I am told that there is a considerable struggle going on inside Congress between the advocates of co-operation (on Congress terms) and violence. Vallabhai Patel of course advocates the latter.

October 6

A considerable number of interviews. Sir Cowasjee Jehangir talked on the political situation. He had been talking to Jinnah and was possibly sounding me on Jinnah's behalf. He said communal feeling was worse than ever, and adjured me to form a Central Government before the elections with parity between Moslem League and Congress. I said that we were a little tired of making efforts at solution and finding them rejected

[1] A prominent Parsee, who represented the City of Bombay in the Central Legislative Assembly, 1930–47.

and that Jinnah had said at Simla that nothing less than Muslim equality with all other parties at the Centre would satisfy him; and that I thought he was playing his cards badly. C.J. said there were dissensions in Congress and that Gandhi was losing his influence, and that the immoderates were gaining ground.

I talked to Mudie about law and order during the elections, about which Rutherford had been rather panicky, and told him to impress on everyone that to appease the Congress at the expense of loyalists was *not* my policy.

October 17

Got back this evening from a visit to Kashmir and Rawalpindi. The visit to Kashmir was comparatively peaceful; my only official duties were the opening of an (unfinished) hospital and interviews with Ministers; but social occasions were many. We had three shoots and a round of golf at Gulmarg.

The hospital was a very complete piece of camouflage; it was unfinished and would not take patients for many months; but a complete staff of doctors, nurses, orderlies, etc., had been assembled, the finished wards were complete with beds, blankets, flowers, and every detail; instruments, X-ray apparatus, operating tables and so on had been installed in their proper places; the dispensaries had an entire stock of medicines; even the offices were full of stationery, ash-trays, etc., as if in use. Next day I suppose it was all moved back to the other hospitals from which it had been taken. I made a short speech and the ceremony did not take long.

I liked H.H., he is shrewd, has quite a sense of humour, and is liberal-minded—for an Indian Prince. He means well by his State and subjects, and does not seem to be very extravagant—except on his wife's jewellery. But he is energetic only by fits and starts and will not really put himself out.

I quite fell for the Maharani who is attractive and has obviously a good deal of character. Her jewels must be seen to be believed; she wore a fresh set every day we were there.

The new Prime Minister, Kak, a Kashmir Pundit with a British wife, is clever, plausible, and quite useless in a crisis, I should say. He has been the power behind the throne for some time and is said to have ousted the last two or three P.M.'s by his intrigues. Kashmir is likely to be the seat of political trouble before long; there are two factions, both Muslim (80% of the population is Muslim), one of which supports and is supported by the Congress, the other Muslim League. Nehru, Azad and Jinnah have all visited the State lately and have agitated.

We had four days of official engagements in Rawalpindi, military and otherwise.

I had longish talks with Glancy and Khizar; both were very anxious that H.M.G. should announce a definite policy about Pakistan, i.e. what they really meant by permission to secede from the Indian Union which was promised in the Cripps offer. F.K.N. and Jinnah are firing in strong accusations, both to the S. of S. and myself, that Glancy and Khizar are using officials to support the Unionist party and to influence the elections.

October 19

A long day of green boxes, interviews and a Council meeting. The Council meeting was the long-postponed one on Education. It was less difficult than I expected though I don't think it really gets us anywhere. The Indian tendency to think with the heart rather than the head was evident. All the Indian members disregarded Finance Member's warning that the full scheme was quite impossible to finance; and practically all insisted that it was the really backward classes that must get the most attention and money, although it is quite obvious that India's real need at present is technicians and leaders; and that half-educated sweepers and bhistis and wild men of the hills can contribute little or nothing to the removal of India's poverty. Sargent was very good, clear and conciliatory, and we arrived at some sort of general approval of the report. Curiously enough, it was Ambedkar alone of the Indians who advocated that money should be spent on leaders, technicians and businessmen rather than on the most backward.

October 24

Normal day of papers and interviews. Depressing reports continue to come in from Provinces of the intemperate attitude of Congress, their attempts to intimidate the Services by threats of revenge when they come into power, and so on. Nehru, in particular, seems quite unable to restrain himself, and perhaps imprisonment has quite upset his balance which was never his strong point. Thorne[1] agrees that I should see him and warn him about his speeches.

Council meeting this morning was a longish one. There was an encouraging telegram from S. of S. about Food imports; and apparently on the strength of it, Jogi gave his de-control hare a canter round the track but could find no one to chase it. We decided to restore the ban on women working underground in mines on February 1, 1946; on the summary,

[1] He had succeeded Sir Francis Mudie as Home Member.

Members of Council voiced their apprehensions on the law and order situation, and are obviously getting a little rattled.

October 26

Dr. Khan Sahib, Congress Premier of N.W.F.P. lunched yesterday. He is pleasant but not perhaps a very strong character. Hutchings, who has lately returned from leave home, said that the atmosphere in the Food Ministry at home was quite changed and now much more friendly to India.

October 31

I had C.-in-C. and Thorne in and told them to be prepared for trouble and possibly for a fresh struggle with Congress as in August, 1942, in view of the obvious intention of Congress leaders to stir up a mass struggle.

George Cunningham arrived in the evening and I had some talk with him about the Frontier Province.

Next day a conference with the C.-in-C., George Cunningham and Olaf Caroe on the Frontier problem. The C.-in-C. committee on Frontier defence had been divided on the issue of disarming the tribes. The majority had held, quite rightly I think, that disarmament could only come by economic penetration and improved social conditions, obviously a matter of time. The President, Tuker[1] and the R.A.F. member recommended a policy of immediate disarmament as an essential. The C.-in-C. insisted on disarmament as the key. Cunningham and Caroe supported the majority opinion. After a good deal of time the C.-in-C. promised to produce a plan for the substitution of Armed police for troops in Waziristan and the Khyber. So the old see-saw of frontier policy goes on, much as it has gone on for the last 100 years, without getting any nearer to a permanent solution.

November 2

Wild speeches by Nehru and Patel, threatening a mass movement after the elections, unless they get all they want (i.e. Quit India), continue, and Smith,[2] the D.I.B., was gloomy yesterday.

P.S.V. saw Holburn of the Times today and put him into the picture, he had just come back from Burma and said that serious trouble was brewing there.

---

[1] Lt.-Gen. Sir Francis Tuker, G.O.C.-in-C., Eastern Command, India.

[2] Sir Norman Smith, I.P., Inspector-General of Police, Bombay, 1942–4, Director Intelligence Bureau, Government of India, 1945–6.

Had a farewell lunch party for Sultan Ahmed today, who has resigned from Council to take up a job with the Princes.

November 3

I had an hour with Nehru this morning. I told him that no Government could continue to tolerate indefinitely incitement to violence or threats to its officials; and that the future of India must depend on some compromise between Hindu and Muslim.

He replied that Congress could make no terms whatever with the Muslim League under its present leadership and policy, that it was a reactionary body with entirely unacceptable ideas with which there could be no settlement.

He practically admitted that he was preaching violence and said that he did not see how violence could be avoided, if legitimate aims could not be attained otherwise.

I left him in no doubt that the Government were bound to take the necessary measures to prevent violence. I don't think it will do any good. Though his attitude was quiet and friendly throughout and I cannot help liking him, he seems to me to have reached the state of mind of a fanatic and is quite incapable of considering any views that do not coincide with his own. I think he knows he is heading for trouble but feels he can rouse the country sufficiently to make it difficult for us to suppress it. The situation gets to look more ugly every day and the tone of the Nationalist Press more virulent. We shall before long be faced with the issue of another violent suppression of Congress, with weaker and rather demoralised forces perhaps, if their intimidation of officials and police continues unchecked and they succeed in dividing the I.A. over the I.N.A. trials; or of capitulation to them.

Ivor Jehu[1] came to dinner and I had an hour with him afterwards. He is always interesting. He is very worried over the policy of his paper, the Times of India, i.e. what line to take about the Congress. He agrees that the policy of Congress is now almost openly violence. He thinks they will take office after the elections, get rid of the British officials, paralyse the administration and start a mass movement. I.J. has had talks with Vallabhai Patel whom he regards as the strong man of Congress and says they are determined to get rid of British power altogether in a year or two. He wanted to know what line Government proposed to take with Congress. He agrees with me that our propaganda and publicity over the

---

[1] I. S. Jehu, at this time acting-editor of the Times of India.

I.N.A. was fatally slow and ineffective, and that we have given Congress a weapon which they have been not slow to use, and very unscrupulously.

November 5

A long, rather depressing day. Old Mohamed Usman at his interview today was really upset at the prospect of the British leaving India, the dear old boy is a real die-hard Imperialist and quite contemptuous of the ability of his own countrymen to rule. He said we were losing all our friends, that no one in India ever worshipped the setting sun, only the rising one, and that was now Congress. He deplored the general tide of world politics, which perhaps made our attitude inevitable.

I had a long talk in the evening with Alan Brooke (now Alan Alanbrooke) who arrived this afternoon. I showed Alan the note I proposed to send H.M.G. on the Indian situation, he agreed that I ought to send a warning but had no idea where the troops would come from if we wanted them.

The note sent to H.M.G. is given below:

We are now faced in India with a situation of great difficulty and danger, in which I require support and guidance from His Majesty's Government.

2. Since the session of the All India Congress Committee (21st–23rd September) the Congress leaders everywhere, but particularly Vallabhai Patel in Bombay and Nehru and Pant in the United Provinces, have been making statements and speeches which can only be intended to provoke or pave the way for mass disorder. They began by taking the credit of the 1942 disturbances; asserting that the British could be turned out of India within a very short time; denying the possibility of a compromise with the Muslim League; glorifying the I.N.A.; and threatening the officials who took part in the suppression of the 1942 disturbances with trial and punishment as 'war criminals'. From these general attempts to excite racial and communal hatred, they have now passed to a disclosure of their programme, which is, briefly, to contest the elections, to serve an ultimatum on H.M.G., and, in default of its acceptance, to organise a mass movement on the 1942 lines but on a much larger scale.

3. The Congress, as a body, would almost certainly deny, in spite of the speeches of members of the Working Committee, that violence is any part of their official creed. But either there is a secret policy which includes use of violence, or the more extreme leaders are out of control. Gandhi's influence is believed to be on the side of moderation but he has said and done practically nothing for weeks, and his friends are believed to be

seriously worried about his health. Whether he will attempt later to control the extremist Congress leaders I do not know; but if, as I suspect, they are taking their line from the rank and file of the party, he may be unwilling or unable to do so.

4. At any rate there is nothing secret about the intentions of Nehru and Patel; and as they are, after Gandhi, by far the most influential of the Congress leaders, the others are taking their line from them. In a recent speech at Bombay, Patel said that 'Congress was not going to sit quiet after the elections and wait on the convenience and pleasure of the British Government. The Congress would demand an immediate and final solution. . . . If such a solution was not forthcoming . . . sure as day follows night there would follow another struggle. . . . When the time for action comes and the time for action may come soon, we must be able to act as one man'. . . . Nehru said a day earlier that 'revolution is inevitable'.

5. In order to make sure that there was no misunderstanding I saw Nehru on 3rd November, and pointed out to him the danger of the course he and other leaders were advocating. He made it clear that he thought violence inevitable, and shortly after our interview delivered an inflammatory speech of the usual kind. I believe that the Congress are counting on the I.N.A. as the spear-head of their revolt; they would suborn the Indian Army if they could, and they hope that their threats will impair the loyalty and efficiency of the Police. They have been encouraged by events in French Indo-China and Indonesia which they are watching carefully; and a good deal may depend upon what happens there and in Syria and Palestine.

6. The object of the rising the Congress leaders have in mind would be the expulsion of the British. Whatever the leaders themselves might say publicly, there would be organised attacks on the railways and public buildings, treasuries would be looted and records destroyed. In fact Congressmen would attempt to paralyse the administration, as they did in 1942; they would also attack and possibly murder any officials, British and Indian, on whom they could lay their hands. In a recent speech Nehru has given special praise to the people of Ballia, a District in the United Provinces, in which the rioters managed to paralyse the administration for a few days in 1942; he named and threatened five British officials who restored order there.

7. It is in my judgment unlikely that the Congress leaders will attempt their *coup* until all the Provincial elections are completed, unless events force their hand. I doubt if they are much interested in the elections as such; what is more important to them is the opportunity afforded by the elections to revive and re-organise the Party, and they are already taking full advantage of this opportunity. The tone of the nationalist Press has

perhaps never been worse, and there is no doubt about the growth of Hindu enthusiasm for the Congress. It is probable that there may be communal disorder on a large scale before the Provincial elections, and it is possible that in Provinces such as the U.P. and Bihar, anti-Government disorders may begin before the Congress leaders intend.

8. I must accordingly, with the utmost gravity, warn H.M.G. to be prepared for a serious attempt by the Congress, probably next spring, but quite possibly earlier, to subvert by force the present administration in India. Half measures will be of no use in dealing with a movement of this kind, and the choice will lie between capitulating to Congress and accepting their demands—whatever they may be—and using all our resources to suppress the movement.

9. The main Congress demand would, I suppose, be the grant of immediate independence to India under a Government selected by the Congress High Command. This has been the aim of Congress policy for years, and it is clear that nothing short of it would satisfy Nehru and Patel. I do not imagine that His Majesty's Government will wish to yield to force or threats of force; nor can we lightly divest ourselves of our obligations to the minorities. I assume therefore that there will be no question of the acceptance of a Congress ultimatum.

10. If this assumption is correct, we must be prepared to suppress the movement, and to suppress it this time with great thoroughness. I am aware of the extreme difficulty of this course; it would involve the use of a considerable force of British troops; probably the declaration of martial law over parts of the country; the detention of a large number of persons without trial or trial by special courts; and the suppression for an indefinite period of the Congress Party. All this would be most unsatisfactory, but the alternative is to hand India over to a single party—admittedly the strongest and best organised in the country, but consisting mainly of caste Hindus and experienced in nothing but agitation. If we handed over British India, it would be impossible for us to fulfil our obligations to the States, the rulers of which have loyally supported us.

11. We should be justified in moving against the Congress now, on the information already available. The Party is not yet fully re-organised and its immediate suppression would be relatively easy. Moreover, immediate action would rally those Indians who have hitherto supported us, and would put heart into the Services. The British members of the I.C.S. and I.P. are dispirited and discontented; the Indian members of these services are uneasy about the future and under strong political and social pressure; while the Indian subordinates on whom the administration so largely depends are naturally reluctant to make enemies of the future masters of India.

12. But I do not recommend immediate action, unless it is forced on us before the elections by actual disorder. To abandon our programme now would be to invite criticism all over the world, and to stimulate the general doubts about our good faith. I am afraid that we must wait for the present, and prepare to act quickly as soon as we are compelled to do so. The dangers of inaction are grave, since the capacity of the administration in rural districts to stand up to serious disturbances is largely a matter of morale, and service morale is now bad in many districts and is being steadily undermined.

13. I am convinced that His Majesty's Government should at some very early date make it clear (i) that they are aware of the gravity of the Indian situation; (ii) that they do not intend to permit the use of force by any political party and will suppress disturbances by every means; (iii) that they will support against political attack officials who have done their duty; and (iv) that they will provide me with the resources I require to keep the peace. A statement on these lines might bring some of the less hysterical Congressmen down to earth, and would certainly put heart into the Services. It is in fact essential, in my view: and it is just possible that it might bring Congress to its senses and prevent the violent movement which I apprehend.

W

6–11–1945

November 8

Council meeting yesterday lasted under half an hour. The members present unanimously approved keeping Ordinance III (Arrest without trial) in force till September 1946, instead of withdrawing it next month as had been proposed; and made some gloomy comments on the law and order situation.

S. of S. cabled that Archie Nye[1] was being offered Madras, if I approved. I agreed.

V. P. Menon, optimistic as usual, said that he thought Nehru had quietened down a bit since his interview with me; I can see little sign of it. Azad sent what was, I think, meant to be a conciliatory reply to my last letter to him.

November 15

Back this evening from U.P. It was the dullest tour I have done, tiring, depressing and hot.

---

[1] Lt.-Gen. Sir Archibald Nye, Vice-Chief of Imperial General Staff, 1941–6, Governor of Madras, 1946–8, High Commissioner for the U.K. in India, 1948–52.

On return I held a short Council meeting on some matters in connection with the Assembly; and started on the weary business of catching up on the work which always seems to accumulate, however many green boxes one deals with on tour.

Gandhi wrote a malevolent letter to P.S.V., admitting that Nehru's speeches were 'hot' but putting forward the curious argument that if the British really meant to grant freedom to India it did not matter how hot they were; if the British were not in earnest they ought to be hotter; and that 'forgive and forget' could not be held to apply to our action in suppressing the 1942 rebellion. He is a malignant old man.

November 17

Evan Jenkins went off yesterday,[1] I shall feel his loss greatly. He had an extraordinarily clear and quick brain, and was a sympathetic personality in spite of his rather detached outlook.

Archie Rowlands discussed his visits to the Provinces and the big schemes of expenditure they would need to prevent heavy unemployment. He said G. D. Birla was alarmed at the virulence of Congress speeches.

November 21

I returned from a few days in Gwalior which I hoped were going to be restful but turned out to be exhausting.

Tuesday was supposed to be given up to a tiger shoot. It didn't turn out the least as I had expected. There was one short beat and no tiger and that was all the shooting. The beat for tiger was about 20 miles away. While we were collecting at the rendezvous two male elephants started a fight while being loaded up and delayed proceedings for nearly an hour, and the noise probably disturbed the tiger; anyway he was not in the beat which was down a narrow ravine. Then we motored another 20 miles for lunch, after which we motored on another 40 miles to Shirpuri to visit the tombs of H.H.'s ancestors. There was something rather incongruous about this; we were all in shooting clothes, it was quite unexpected, and some of the items were unusual; for example there was outside a fine marble tomb a small cheap bath-mat with the word 'welcome'; and a sentry with fixed bayonet stood and presented arms while we inspected a shrine to Rama and Hanuman (the monkey god). The tomb of H.H.'s father was a fine one with inlaid marble after the fashion of the Taj Mahal, and silver doors. At his grandmother's tomb there was a figure of the old

---

[1] He was proceeding on leave preparatory to taking over as Governor of the Punjab. George Abell took his place.

lady, which was, H.H. informed us, treated as living, and washed and fed. The immense gulf between the Hindu religion and mentality and ours, and the Moslem, is the real core of all our troubles in India; and this visit in a way brought it home to me. After it, we motored to a lake and rushed about in American speed-boats and were then offered an enormous tea. A weary drive home of 70 to 80 miles ended a curious day.

I like the Maharaja, but he has never quite grown up. A long minority, with a domineering mother, has given him an inferiority complex and a suspicion of interference or advice. But he has the right ideas, no vices, and a very attractive Maharani.

November 22

Long Council meeting in the morning 10.30–1 p.m. Food member gave quite an encouraging report from Bengal but coal had had a bad week.

Rowland's plan for decimalisation of coinage went through, with instructions to keep the term 'anna' and to avoid 'cent'. The rest of the morning was taken up by discussion of 5 bills which Ambedkar wishes to introduce in next session—a Working Hours in Factories bill, a Minimum Wages bill, an Amendment to increase the Compensation for injuries, a bill to compel employers to post up conditions of employment in all factories, and a bill for the recognition of Trade Unions. Ambedkar had not quite thought them all out, but on the whole got a good deal of his programme through, a bit mangled.

I had over an hour with C.-in-C. on political situation and internal security precautions; I.N.A. trials; the proposal that the Victory Week in Delhi should be cancelled (C.-in-C. and I agreed that it should not); and one or two other matters.

November 23

The paper on the situation in India which I sent home about a fortnight ago has obviously shaken up the Cabinet. I had a long telegram last night from S. of S. which I discussed with Home Member this morning. H.M.G.'s proposals are: (a) to send out a Parliamentary Delegation at about the end of the year (b) that I should see Gandhi and ask for his assistance in counselling moderation (c) that Nehru and Jinnah should be invited to London (d) that H.M.G. should make a statement when the visit of the Parliamentary Delegation is announced, re-affirming their intention to press on with a Constitution Making Body after the elections, and making clear their attitude towards disorder and their intention to protect Government servants. In my reply I welcomed (a) and (d), and discouraged (b) and (c), which I am sure would do no good. Later I got a sensible letter from S. of S. which he had written after seeing my paper.

Of my visitors, Kharegat[1] was as dry as ever, but rather more interesting than usual, about locusts, afforestation, etc.; he knows his stuff but is a pure pen-pusher, I am sure, and will never get results. Hutchings was hopeful about the food situation after his visit to Bengal but gloomy about the political outlook, and pointed out that interruption of communications on anything like the August 1942 scale might mean famine.

November 24

I have given up hoping for any relief at week-ends. I have been struggling to draft a speech for Calcutta, but have hardly had a clear five minutes. George Abell brought in some papers and expressed his concern about the I.N.A. trials; then Srivastava asked specially for an interview and came in with one of his periodical attacks of cold feet, over the I.N.A. trials again, suggesting that I should call them off. He was followed by B. N. Rau[2] about the Madras–Orissa boundary dispute and the work he is doing on the preparation of a draft treaty between Britain and India. Then came the C.-in-C., also about the I.N.A. trials, on which he is putting up a modified policy; he is now definitely worried about them and the possible effect of them and Indonesia on the loyalty of the Indian Army. He has sent in the appreciation which H.M.G. asked for as the result of my reports on the political situation—quite a good one but not very comforting.

> *The trial of I.N.A. officers afforded Congress leaders a splendid opportunity of arousing popular feeling against the Government which they were not slow to exploit. They set up a strong defence committee under Bhulabhai Desai which included Nehru and the veteran Liberal Leader, Sir Tej Bahadur Sapru. Not to be outdone in patriotism the Muslim League also associated itself with the defence of the accused.*
>
> *The trial of the first batch of officers, a Hindu, a Muslim, and a Sikh, who were accused of waging war against the King and of murder or abetment of murder, opened at the Red Fort, Delhi, in November. It was the signal for widespread demonstrations which in Calcutta led to serious rioting. Over thirty people were killed, several hundred injured, and a large number of cars and police vehicles destroyed or damaged.*

[1] Sir Pheroze Kharegat, I.C.S., Secretary to the Government of India, Department of Agriculture.

[2] Sir B. N. Rau, I.C.S., Puisne Judge of the High Court, Calcutta, 1938–44; on special duty with the Government of India, 1945; Constitutional Adviser to the Constituent Assembly of India in 1946; Permanent Representative of India to the U.N., 1949.

A very good and illuminating letter that Sir George Cunningham, Governor of the N.W.F.P., wrote to Lord Wavell at this time on the subject of the I.N.A. trial is reproduced below:

Peshawar, November 27th, 1945

Dear Lord Wavell,

I am going somewhat outside my proper sphere in writing to Your Excellency about the I.N.A. trial, but the matter is one on which I have been trying to gauge opinion of all sorts and I have now come to a definite conclusion. It is that the C.-in-C. should at once announce that, as Indian opinion is opposed to the trial of these persons, he wipes the whole thing out and takes no further proceedings against anyone. No one can do it but the C.-in-C., of his own volition and on his own responsibility. Done by anyone else, even by the King, it will not have the same effect—particularly on the Army.

Some Army Officers of great experience with whom I have discussed the matter—Dick O'Connor was one—have said that leniency at this stage would have a disastrous effect on the Army. I do not believe that that is true. Some Indian officers and soldiers, whose relations or close friends have suffered under the I.N.A. leaders, are no doubt thirsting for their blood. But I am certain that they are comparatively few and that their resentment at any clemency shown now would not affect Army discipline as a whole. Most Indian soldiers who have said to me 'Hang the lot' have, in my opinion, said so because they thought it was what I wanted to hear; and this applies to comment by Indians on most occasions.

The thing is daily becoming more and more purely Indian versus British, and less and less ill-disposed Indians versus British-cum-well-disposed Indians. I think that every day that passes now brings over more and more well-disposed Indians into the anti-British camp and, whatever the outcome of the trial may be, this anti-British bias will persist in each man's mind. The only way of stopping the rot is by a clean cut, as I have said; and at once.

I dislike saying this intensely. It is tantamount to surrendering to threats, and no reasonable man doubts for a moment that the worst of the I.N.A. leaders ought to have been shot out of hand. Congressmen—Dr. Khan Sahib among them—have said to me 'If only they had been shot in Rangoon or Singapore, everyone would have been pleased'. But that feeling has gone and cannot now be revived.

I feel terribly for Your Excellency and for Claude A. in this. It is the most difficult problem to tackle that I have ever known in India. But I am certain, from what I have heard from a very wide variety of people here, British and Indian, that the best thing to do is to cut our losses.

Yours sincerely,
G. Cunningham

Lord Wavell replied:

The Viceroy's House, New Delhi
November 30th, 1945

My Dear Cunningham,

Many thanks for your letter No. 271 of 27th November about the I.N.A.
trials. It was good of you to write, and I was glad to have your view. It is
about as difficult a case as one could want. But we have, after considering
all opinions in the last few days, decided on a policy, and a communiqué
will be issued before you get this letter. No future trials will take place
except where there are allegations of gross brutality against the accused.
We have advisedly said nothing about the present cases, but it is intended
that these will continue. Council considered the policy and approved this
morning. We shall no doubt continue to suffer from distorted publicity,
but I think in the long run it will be recognized that we have given the
accused a fair trial and that though we have gone to the very limit of
clemency, we have not entirely forgotten the 40,000 out of 60,000 of the
Indian Army who were loyal to their allegiance and refused to give way
to pressure and join the enemy.

2. I hope you will not think that I have failed to appreciate the strength
of the arguments you put forward. I do appreciate it, but I think the policy
on which we have decided is the right one.

Yours sincerely,
WAVELL

November 25

After lunch the Caseys turned up, and I had a long talk with him about the
Calcutta riots. It was his first experience of civil disorder and he was
obviously surprised but not at all shaken. He said the police staff-work
was thoroughly bad, a good deal of the firing unnecessary, and most of
the Bengal officials useless. The crowd was quite hysterical and he could
get no sense out of any of them, though he went down to them personally
without molestation. The tactics of attacking transport and putting up
road-blocks proved difficult to deal with. Casey wanted the troops to act
as additional police, armed with truncheons, and I pointed out the difficulties and dangers of this. Later in the day he had a talk with C.-in-C.
and with Smith of the D.I.B. Latter explained to him Bombay police
methods of dealing with crowds and riots, and Casey decided at once to
send one of his police officers to Bombay to study them.

Casey said he was going to ask for some more of Bengal officers back
from the Centre, I doubt whether we can afford to let them go. On the
general political situation, I showed him my paper of November 6 to the

S. of S., and he said it was a masterly statement. He spoke of Burrows,[1] whom he had met, said he was a good stout-hearted man; but he thought he would be all at sea in Bengal and in the hands of his officials for the first six months.

November 27

A comparatively quiet day, except for the general current of uneasiness about the I.N.A. trials which practically all my visitors express or imply. I am sure it would be disastrous to stop the present trials as I am being urged to do; and I am not much in love with the C.-in-C.'s idea of putting out a fresh communiqué. I think the harm is done now and that we should stick to our guns.

November 28

A frightful day, after a pretty solid 10 hours or so at the desk I had barely kept abreast of routine work and had to leave important things still undone. That is the worst of this job, one so seldom has time at all to think out the next move, or even to give one's mind a rest.

Council took three hours. The rest of the day was spent with papers, interviews and an At Home to the Irrigation Board. I went to bed with papers still unfinished, an exhausted mind, and a sense of having accomplished nothing useful at all.

November 29

I had a letter from Evan Jenkins on his interview with the S. of S., he had certainly painted the picture in dark colours.

I had a conference with Claude Auchinleck on the I.N.A. trials. He had proposed a new policy for trying only those guilty of brutality and had drafted a communiqué which neither George Abell nor anyone else liked much, and as the matter had to come before Council tomorrow morning, I wanted to discuss. He was a bit vague on the number of officers involved, the legal method of dismissing officers, etc. We decided to meet again at 9.30 a.m. tomorrow before Council and try to improve the Press Communiqué.

Then to a Railway Board cocktail party. The one bright moment was when I asked the wife of some Railway Manager whether she had a family, and she replied; 'No, I've tried frightfully hard, but I've only got dachshunds'.

---

[1] Sir Frederick Burrows, Company Sergeant-Major, Grenadier Guards, President National Union of Railwaymen, 1942–4, Governor of Bengal, 1946–7.

November 30

The Council meeting on I.N.A. trials went quite well, I saw C.-in-C. before the meeting and we got a communiqué drafted; and Council accepted the policy and the communiqué with little alteration suggested to latter.

Two out of the first three I.N.A. officers put on trial were acquitted of all charges except that of waging war against the King. Some months later Lord Wavell admitted that 'it was undoubtedly a serious blunder to place on trial first men against whom no brutality could be proved'.

December 4

We got back just before lunch from three days in Bahawalpur. Quite a pleasant trip but rather mobile, we never slept more than one night in the same place, and one place was a train, and we did a lot of motoring over not very good roads.

The usual job in catching up with papers this afternoon, but no interviews. Casey rang up about his talks with Gandhi, he is seeing him again tonight. He thinks one of G.'s main objects is to try and ascertain how far Congress will be allowed to go in incitement during the elections without the arrest of the leaders. Casey claims to have private information that Nehru and Patel are determined on violence in 1946.

December 5

I had an interesting letter from Evan Jenkins on a visit to Chequers, at which he was attacked by Attlee, Morrison and Jowitt on the inefficiency of the Indian Government. They obviously know little about India, do not care very much, but are very worried and have no real idea what to do.

December 6

Dalal has sent in his resignation, I have been expecting it for some time. He has little stamina, physical and moral, and is not the man to take the knocks of politics, especially in an unpopular administration. Nor I think has he got on well with his colleagues; in fact he said when I saw him that only my support had enabled him to get on at all, that the others were jealous, especially Mudaliar, who had wanted the job himself. D. suggested M. should now be given it. D. wants to time his resignation so that he will not have to face the Assembly at the end of January.

D 169   O

December 15

Returned this evening from a tour to Calcutta, Assam and Bihar. On Monday I delivered my address to the Associated Chambers of Commerce, which has somehow come to be the Viceroy's annual review of the economic and political position in India; I don't think it is a good convention that such an address should be delivered to a commercial and British audience, and I think I shall try to find some other occasion. I am not a great admirer of the British business man in Calcutta. I think the speech was not a bad one in the prevailing conditions, the Nationalist Press is rude about it of course, but not so rude as might be expected; and secret information is to the effect that it made some impression.

In the course of this speech Lord Wavell appealed for moderation and a sincere effort to reach agreement. 'The British Government and the British people', he said, 'honestly and sincerely wish the Indian people to have their political freedom and a Government, or Governments, of their own choice. But . . . it is not a simple problem; it cannot and will not be solved by repeating a password or formula. "Quit India" will not act as the magic "Sesame" which opened Ali Baba's cave. It cannot and will not be solved by violence. . . . There are various parties, . . . who must somehow or other reach a measure of agreement amongst themselves—Congress, the largest political party in India; the minorities, of whom the Muslims are the most numerous and most important; the Rulers of the Indian States; and the British Government. The objective of all is the same—the freedom and welfare of India. I do not believe an agreed solution between the parties is impossible; I do not believe it would even be very difficult, given goodwill, commonsense and patience on all sides. . . . I do appeal most solemnly and earnestly at this critical moment of Indian history for goodwill on the part of all leaders. . . . It is a time when every man in any position of responsibility must determine to do all in his power to bring about a just and lasting solution of India's problem without plunging this great land into conflict.'

After that I interviewed a deputation of the European Association. They voiced their apprehensions of the present political situation, and of the safety of isolated Europeans, especially in Bihar. They also deplored the departure of Casey and change of Governors at this critical moment. I told them that it was quite impossible to put a police guard on every European's house which they seemed to expect; and that the change of Governors had to take place some time and that no one could tell quite when the crisis would come.

They were followed by Gandhi—with whom I had 40 minutes. I deplored the recent speeches of Congress leaders and said that the preaching of violence could only lead to violence, especially with the inflammable

material in India, of young students and goondhas (the Indian equivalent of hooligans); and that fomentation of racial and communal
hatred would not produce the atmosphere in which a solution could be
produced in next year's discussions. He admitted the violence of Congress
speeches and indicated that he was trying to get the tone lowered. I said
that an agreement of some kind between Hindu and Muslim was necessary,
even if it was an agreement to part. He said he had always tried for a settlement but was frustrated by the British policy of divide and rule. I said this
was nonsense, we tried our best to bring them together; that the increase
in communal feeling was mainly due to the action of Congress Ministries
in 1937–39 which had made Muslims feel they would not get a square
deal from Congress and had caused the rise of the Muslim League and the
idea of Pakistan. He defended the Congress Ministries at some length, and
said all Governors had admitted their fairness. I said there was no doubt
about the psychological effect on the Muslims, whatever the facts may
have been; and he admitted this. I then said that the British were accustomed to abuse and misrepresentation from Indian Nationalists, but
that there was a limit, and that it seemed hardly wise to antagonise us at
this moment when we were trying our best to bring about a settlement,
and that India after getting her freedom would want Britain's co-operation
in defence and in commercial development. I added that if any disorder
resulted from the hatred now being stirred up, it would of course be my
duty to suppress it, and I should do so by all means in my power. He
assented to this; and then said that India needed no help from Britain in
trade or defence. She would develop her trade in her own way, and her
defence would be the moral force of non-violence, which would eventually conquer the world and bring about universal peace. I said I did not
think either of us would live to see this desirable issue, and that the
immediate point was to prevent violence in India during the next year or
so. We left it at that. He was quite friendly though woolly, and seemed
in good health. He then went off to see Arthur Smith,[1] who found him
querulous, malicious and quite unimpressive, so he told me at the airfield
next morning. He told Arthur that he had no trust at all in the British, that
they always broke their word, that I had broken mine at Simla (he based
this on the grounds that I had said I meant to make the Conference succeed, if possible, and then had not done so!), and went back to the Mutiny,
etc. He has not changed and never will.

Casey seemed in quite good heart. He told me of his talks with Gandhi,

---

[1] Lt.-Gen. Sir Arthur Smith, G.O.C.-in-C., Eastern Command, India, 1945–6, Chief of
General Staff, India, 1946.

Nehru and Patel. He did not think much of Nehru and judged him a weak character. He said Patel was a proper 'tough' and the real driving force behind Congress' aggressive policy.

I went on to Assam on the 11th, to see the northern frontier and the tribes there. We landed at Tezpur about midday and motored to Charduar where I lived in the Political Officers' bungalow. Next morning we went out to the Bareilli River for a picnic, seeing an elephant camp on the way with several recently captured wild elephants. In the afternoon there was a parade of the Tribesmen of the Balipara Frontier Tract, a picturesque and rather attractive looking lot who did ceremonial dances and some national sports, an interesting performance.

Next day we flew east over the Himalayan foothills and tribal country, and then up the Lohit valley, through some magnificent mountain gorges over Walong, a frontier post at the N.E. corner of India on the borders of China and Tibet.

I had a long talk on the N.E. frontier and the future of the tribes with Mills, the Governor's adviser for tribal areas, and Godfrey one of the Frontier Political Officers, both sensible people, who knew and liked the tribes. They wanted a policy for frontier organisation, a road policy, and information about the possibility of continuing to supply the frontier posts by air. The drop last month was on the whole successful, but I gather the R.A.F. thought it risky. It is difficult to see any good future for these simple unsophisticated, probably quite happy, wild men; one cannot stay the advance of civilization or pretend that it brings unmixed blessing; and what will happen when Indians take over is not pleasant to contemplate, few of them are likely to have our sympathy with wild men and wild life. Mills and Godfrey both thought the policy of advance to the MacMahon line correct.

I went to Bihar on the 14th. We flew for an hour and a half to see the depredations caused by the erratic behaviour of the Kosi river which has moved some 30 or 40 miles in the last 15 years or so, destroying large areas of fertile land. Then I went and looked at a Medical School and two hospitals, attended a Garden Party given by the Maharaja of Dharbanga,[1] with whom we were staying, had an hour of interviews, and finished up with a ten-course dinner at Dharbanga's palace, followed by an exhibition of dancing. It was a long day, I had caught a cold in Calcutta and it was now at its worst.

This morning I motored 40 or 50 miles (terribly dusty roads) to see some of the Kosi river floods at close quarters. We went out in a boat to

[1] An exceedingly wealthy landowner, *not* a Ruling Prince.

a flooded village, and got a good impression of the damage done. The villagers politely assured me that their troubles would now be over since I had come and taken the matter in hand; a very voluble, intelligent and candid gentleman, who was the local Congress leader, explained the position to me in an extraordinary mixture of Hindustani and English, and said that plenty of people had been to look at the floods but no one had done anything, he hoped I would really get something done.

December 19

Arrears of work for several days and the house full of visitors.

I finished a note on the political situation and a possible way of dealing with it. I also went into the question of getting a survey, by air and on the ground, of the Kosi river where it leaves the hills in Nepal, and also a survey of levels in the flood area. I am not quite clear why nothing has been done before. Reports and recommendations have been made but have been pigeon holed and ignored.

Today, quite an impressive parade outside the Red Fort, at which I presented a number of V.C.s. The Chief Commissioner of Delhi had begged me not to hold it, as he feared a demonstration in favour of the I.N.A. I absolutely refused to pay any regard to his protests. There was a large and orderly crowd, a very good parade and no demonstration of any kind.

In the afternoon we had a soldier's party at V.H. for the men on the parade, and there were about a thousand.

One way and another—parades, parties, green boxes, red carpet— Her Ex. and I earned our keep today.

December 20

I am feeling definitely overworked. I have been at it all day and have not even kept abreast of the routine stuff, let alone several important things I have to do—appreciation for Cabinet, speech for Engineers at Calcutta, letter to the King—and private correspondence.

Council meeting was fortunately short. Both Food and Coal positions are deteriorating rapidly. We decided to adhere for India to the Bretton Woods agreement, which has to be done by 31st December if India is to obtain the advantages and prestige of original membership. This means breaking our pledge to consult the Assembly first, for which we shall be heavily criticised; but if we don't do it, they will criticise us for not securing India a place.

I gave Council an account of my meeting with Gandhi, and Md. Usman made characteristic comments.

My last interview today was with Dr. Khan Sahib, Congress Premier of the N.W.F.P., whom I like and find sensible though not perhaps a very good administrator. We spoke of economic penetration of the Tribal area. He agrees with me that any policy of forcible disarmament of the Tribes would be folly.

December 22

The last two days have been a steady struggle against files, with the files gaining ground. I have been trying to complete two jobs, a political appreciation for the Cabinet and a speech for the Engineering Institution which I have to give at Calcutta next week. I am also due to write a periodical letter to the King, but have not had time even to begin it. And private correspondence continues to accumulate.

Lord Wavell sent the 'political appreciation for the Cabinet' to the Secretary of State on 27 December along with a 'programme for political action'.

Appreciation of political situation

1. Our immediate objectives for 1946 are:

(a) to secure a reasonably efficient Executive Council with representatives of the principal parties on a proportional basis, which will carry on the government of India during the interim period;

(b) to form a Constitution Making Body which will produce a workable and acceptable constitution;

(c) to bring about Governments in the Provinces, on a Coalition basis as far as possible.

2. The chief factors we have to take into consideration are the aims and policies of the Congress, the Muslim League, and the Ruling Princes. We have also responsibilities to the numerous minorities, and a general responsibility to ensure that India is not thrown into chaos and civil strife before, during or immediately after our hand-over of power.

3. The objective of Congress, the principal political party, is undoubtedly to seize power for their organization, i.e. the Caste Hindus, and to destroy British influence in India as soon as possible. They will go to any lengths to achieve this if they feel strong enough; and will use violence if necessary.

Congress commands the support of practically all Caste Hindus, and of certain other elements in India which tend to follow their rising fortunes. They have the support of nearly the whole of the Press; they have the best organised—in fact the only well organized—political machine; and they command almost unlimited financial support. Almost all educated Hindus, and especially the student class, are their enthusiastic followers, and they can always raise mob passion and mob support, and do not hesitate to use the worst and most violent elements in the population for their purposes.

Indian business magnates, although strongly pro-Congress, are anxious for a solution without conflict and disorder.

Most of the big landowners dislike and fear Congress and would like to support Government, but few of them can probably now be relied on to give active aid. They have never organized opposition to Congress with any success, and are on the whole rather a poor lot.

There is generally speaking no organized opposition to Congress amongst Hindus in British India (except possibly in the Punjab) and nothing to put in its place if we suppress it. Neither the Communist Party nor M. N. Roy's Social Democrats have any influence. The Scheduled Castes are divided and many of them support Congress. The only real opposition to Congress comes from the minorities, of which the Muslim League is of course the principal but represents entirely sectional interests and not all-India. The League, though strongly anti-Congress, is not pro-government or pro-British, and would support us only to the extent of remaining neutral in a conflict between Government and Congress.

Pakistan will remain inflexibly the League policy, so long as Jinnah controls it, though many of his supporters, perhaps the majority of those who really think, realise the difficulties and disadvantages of Pakistan.

4. At present the Government can probably count on the support of the Officials, Police and Army, in a conflict with Congress, though there might be some defections amongst the junior officials and perhaps junior police officers. It would certainly not be wise to try the Indian Army too highly in the suppression of their own people. As time goes on, the loyalty of Indian officials, the Indian Army and the police might become problematical. A large number of British officials will probably take the first opportunity to retire.

5. The attitude of the Princes is on the whole that they would like to be rid of the British if it were not for their fear of Congress. They would, certainly for the most part, support us in a show-down with Congress. The Princes are not organized and do not normally show a common front. The Chamber of Princes is by no means representative.

6. The general conclusions I make on this part of the appreciation are:

(a) That Congress commands the support of practically the whole of articulate Hindu opinion; and could undoubtedly bring about a very serious revolt against British rule;

(b) That we could still probably suppress such a revolt, after a considerable amount of bloodshed;

(c) That if we do have to suppress Congress we have nothing to put in
its place, and should be driven to an almost entirely official rule, for
which the necessary numbers of efficient officials do not exist.

In other words, we shall be placed in a quite untenable position, unless
we find a solution, and we must do so by some means or other. Our chief
problem is to find some bridge between Hindu and Muslim.

Probable course of events

7. The present Congress policy seems to be to avoid conflict at any rate
until the elections are over; while taking full advantage of the licence they
are being allowed during the elections, to increase their influence and
prestige, to stir up racial hatred against the British and communal feeling
against the Muslim League, and to complete their organization for a mass
movement, unless their demands are satisfied after the elections. They will
go as far as they feel they safely can without provoking a premature (from
their point of view) conflict with Government. Meanwhile they will do
their best to weaken Government by intimidating officials and all non-
official supporters of Government, and by endeavouring to suborn the
Indian Army.

8. After the elections, which will undoubtedly show overwhelming
success for Congress, they will, unless we take the initiative, present their
demands in some form or another, with the threat of a mass movement if
not fulfilled. These demands may include:

(a) Immediate establishment of a Central Executive, on which Congress representation will be proportionate to their success in the
elections;

(b) Abolition of the Governor-General's power of veto, or a convention
that it will not be used;

(c) Formation of a C.M.B. on which Congress representation will be
proportionate to their success in the elections; and a pledge from
H.M.G. that the decisions of this body will be accepted without
further discussion or amendment;

(d) Possibly, a refusal to take office or cooperate in any way, unless
Indian troops are withdrawn from Indonesia and/or all I.N.A. men
released.

9. What we have to decide now is:

(a) The method by which we are to attempt the formation of a new
Executive Council; by a conference as at Simla, or by direct

invitation by the Governor-General to certain individuals to assume office; or by any other method;

(b) How far we are prepared to go to secure Congress cooperation in a Central Executive; the two crucial issues will be:

    (i) to what extent we are prepared to over-ride or by-pass Jinnah and the Muslim League;

    (ii) whether we will consent to any restriction of the Governor-General's power of veto;

(The above are inter-related to the extent that any weakening of the Governor-General's veto will increase the reluctance of the Muslim League to cooperate)

(c) How we are to form the Conference on the C.M.B.

The 'programme of political action' that Lord Wavell suggested was designed to forestall Congress demands and enable him to seize the initiative. He said that he wished to attempt to form a new Central Executive as early as possible, i.e. towards the end of February; for by then the results of the elections in the Punjab would be known and these would show the measure of success that the Muslim League had won. He proposed to avoid a conference on the lines of the Simla Conference, and simply to see the Presidents of the Congress and the Muslim League and to ask them to let him have panels of names from which he would choose the Congress and Muslim League members of the Executive Council. He would, if necessary, make it clear to them that if any party refused to co-operate he would go ahead and form an Executive Council without them.

If the Punjab elections went well for the Muslim League, he intended to assure Jinnah, (a) that the Muslims would have parity with the Hindus other than Scheduled Castes in the Executive Council; (b) that the Muslim seats would be filled by Muslim Leaguers; (c) that the Muslim League could have two out of the four key portfolios, viz. War, External Affairs, Home, Finance. He envisaged a Council of fourteen composed as follows: five Hindus other than Scheduled Castes; five Muslims; two Scheduled Castes; one Sikh; one Indian Christian.

As soon as the new Executive Council was formed, he proposed to put before them suggestions for holding a Preliminary Conference to reach decisions about setting up a Constitution Making Body. He furnished detailed papers, drawn up by V. P. Menon and Sir B. N. Rau, regarding the composition of this Conference and its agenda.

Lord Wavell also sent to the Secretary of State on 27 December an important Memorandum showing how he proposed to proceed in regard to the Pakistan issue. If, at any stage, the Muslims brought about a deadlock by their inflexible demand for Pakistan, he would tell Jinnah that if they persisted in this attitude,

H.M.G. would have to take a decision themselves and their decision would be based on the principle that large non-Muslim populations could not be included in Pakistan against their will. This would mean that Western Bengal including Calcutta and at least two-fifths of the Punjab would have to be excluded from Pakistan and Jinnah would be left, in his own words, with only 'the husk'. Lord Wavell thought that if Jinnah was confronted with this prospect, there was at least a chance that he would set to work to secure the best possible terms for the Muslims within a united India.

H.M.G. acknowledged these proposals, but did not comment on them in detail, for the decision, taken in January, to send to India a Cabinet Mission caused them to be set aside. It will be found, however, that in dealing with Jinnah the Cabinet Mission more or less adopted the line that Lord Wavell suggested, offering him only a truncated Pakistan as an alternative to some form of all-India Union, and that Jinnah, faced with this bleak prospect, opted, to begin with, for a loose union.

December 23

Cleared up arrears and had one visitor, Pandit Kunzru, an old friend or enemy—earnest, sincere, austere, rather tiresome sometimes. He is going to Malaya as an unofficial delegation, to enquire into the difficulties of Indians there under arrest or at liberty. He spoke at some length on the political situation, and stated the problem with admirable lucidity, but had no solution to offer.

December 30 (in Calcutta)

I had two long talks with Casey, on the lessons of the Calcutta riots, the use of troops in civil disturbances, tear gas, Australian politics, etc. He has enjoyed his two years in Bengal, but leaves with a liking for the Bengali but a very poor opinion of him as a politician or citizen.

A serious food crisis seems to be developing again as H.M.G. is going back on all its promises about imports, and the situation in Bombay and Madras is worsening. I thought that Food was going to be one of the few things in India I should not have to worry about in the next six months.

So ends 1945, a busy and eventful year for me. The important periods were of course my visit home in the early part of the year and long struggle for permission to make an attempt to end the Indian deadlock, and then my failure at Simla to do so. Then came two rather unexpected developments, the Labour success in the Election and the sudden ending of the war with Japan, both of which had of course considerable effect on my problems out here.

I am sure that I was right to try for a solution, and I think it was something of an achievement to have got it past Winston's Government. I have wondered many times whether I could have avoided the Simla failure, by a different handling of Jinnah or by by-passing him when he was obstinate. I doubt it.

The end of the war brought on my difficult period sooner than I had expected; but a Labour Government has on the whole made things easier, since rather more attention is paid to India and the outlook is rather more sympathetic.

And so to 1946, to which I am not very much looking forward. I think we may have passed the first crisis, an immediate outbreak of violence or such a threat of it as would have necessitated a fresh conflict with Congress. But all the difficult and dangerous factors still remain; and I shall consider myself very fortunate if I am writing with any cause for satisfaction at the end of 1946.

9

THE DANGER RECEDES

I am not very much looking forward to 1946, and shall be surprised and very pleased if we get through without serious trouble. But I believe everyone wants a solution; and everyone really expects H.M.G. to produce it; and that works down to me, I suppose; and I very much doubt whether my brain-power or personality are equal to it. I shall just have to keep on trying, but I shall, as I say, be very pleased and surprised if it comes out right.

New Year 1946

January 2

I opened the year yesterday with discussions on two important problems—with Hutchings on Food and the C.-in-C. on I.N.A. trial sentences.

Hutchings was not as perturbed at the food situation as I had expected, he hoped we should be all right till end of March—with U.P. the immediate danger—provided we had some rain shortly in the Punjab and managed to get rice out of Nepal. The shortage was fortunately worst in our best-administered Provinces—Bombay and Madras.

The C.-in-C. told me of the sentences in the first I.N.A. trials[1] and his proposals to commute them.

Today's Council meeting went quite smoothly. There was an almost unanimous decision for the Government to remain at Delhi for the summer and not go to Simla.

January 5

I had over an hour with Jinnah in the morning. He was rather less difficult in manner than at Simla but just as uncompromising in substance.

The Parliamentary Delegation[2] turned up many hours late, and rather tired, having been delayed four hours at Bahrein by a damaged float. On first impressions, quite a pleasant body with little knowledge of India but anxious to learn.

[1] All the three accused were sentenced to transportation for life, and to be cashiered and lose all pay and allowances while with the Japanese. General Auchinleck remitted the sentences of transportation.

[2] The proposal to send out a Parliamentary Delegation had been made in November, see p. 186.

The following list of Members of the Delegation was inserted in the Journal:

Professor R. Richards (Leader of the Delegation), M.P. (Lab)
Mr. R. Sorensen, M.P. (Lab)
Mrs. Muriel H. Nichol, M.P. (Lab)
Mr. A. G. Bottomley, M.P. (Lab)
Major Woodrow Wyatt, M.P. (Lab)
Mr. Godfrey Nicholson, M.P. (Cons)
Brigadier A. R. W. Low, C.B.E., D.S.O., M.P. (Cons)
Mr. R. Hopkin Morris, M.P. (Lib)
The Earl of Munster
The Lord Chorley of Kendal

January 6

A dinner party for the Delegation to meet Executive Council went quite well, I think. I think the Delegation had had rather a critical reception by some of the Press at a conference in the evening, and seem to have acquitted themselves quite well.

January 7

I spent an hour and a half in the morning, giving the Delegation a short talk on how the Government of India functioned and on the economic problems, and answering their questions. This went quite well.

Then Md. Usman delivered his usual homily on the folly of the British in leaving India; and Roy the Law Member, who had been away sick for some months without anyone noticing it very much, told me all about his illness.

In the evening we had a mixed bag party for the Delegation. It went quite well. I talked to the local Muslim League leader, who thought I was one of the Delegation and was rather shocked when I told him I was the Viceroy; I think the personnel of the Delegation is on the whole very well chosen for goodwill purposes.

January 12

Back this evening from a short tour to Ahmedabad, Bombay and Poona. Quite interesting but strenuous. Ahmedabad, a big industrial centre, a great Congress stronghold and an interesting city from the old and the modern point of view, had not been visited by a Viceroy for 17 or 18 years. I saw some of the old buildings in the morning.

I was garlanded at a Hindu temple near the Bhadra fort; by the Jews of Ahmedabad, by the calico printers, and by the Dyers. This garlanding habit is much practised in Bombay Presidency, and is tiresome; an Englishman feels a fool and looks a fool, when a very large garland of wet flowers is hung round his neck and a large tight bouquet of flowers pressed into his hand and a platoon of photographers crowd round to take photographs. It is a little difficult to decide at what stage one is entitled to remove the garland, which is usually dripping down one's neck and soaking one's collar, and hand the bouquet to an A.D.C. I have decided that as soon as the photographers have recorded the event, the garlander is quite satisfied and the garlandee can remove the garland.

January 16

I had the usual interviews and a Council in the morning which went quite smoothly.

I then had an hour or so, first with Dickie M.B. and then with him and C.-in-C., chiefly on the danger of trouble in Burma in which Indian troops might be involved. I do not share Dickie's enthusiasm for Aung San, the Burmese leader, first of an army of Burmans for the Japs and against us, next for us and against the Japs, and now of a political party. I doubt if I should place much trust in the gentleman, but victory seems to make us acquainted with some strange bedfellows.

January 17

The first day of the Chamber of Princes, entirely formal for the most part, except for certain passages in my opening speech, warning the small States that they must, by amalgamation or otherwise, form themselves into unities capable of running a reasonable administration. Bhopal came to me after the day's Session, and said he was in difficulties with the smaller States, to whom his election as Chancellor was chiefly due; they opposed any form of amalgamation or reform; and Bhopal, while professing to be entirely out of sympathy with them, said he would have to represent their views. He said that some of them were threatening to merge with British India if they had to lose their independence; and B. suggested that Nehru had got at them (I fancy that a number of the larger Princes, including Bhopal himself, have been in touch with Congress as to the terms they might expect in a Congress-ruled India). Bhopal's ways are tortuous; he spoke vaguely of resignation, but I imagine that he does not want to repeat his mistake of last year.

January 18

Session of Chamber of Princes concluded quietly today, I think the tone was perhaps more realistic than usual, the Princes have realised that they must move with the times.

January 19

I saw Vallabhai Patel for the first time this morning. Not an attractive personality and uncompromising, but more of a man than most of the Indian politicians I have met. I began with some talk about Ahmedabad, where he lives, which I had lately visited—its buildings, its industries and history. We then had some talk of the scarcity of rain in that part of India and of the food situation generally. We passed on presently to the political situation, and the need for a settlement between Hindu and Muslim. Patel at once began with allegations that the British were supporting Mr. Jinnah and the Muslim League, that Jinnah had been allowed to wreck the Simla Conference, that his manners to Azad had been intolerable, and so on. He then went on to make a grievance of the Provincial Legislatures being dissolved before Congress ministries could take office, and alleged that this had been done at the instance of Jinnah. I combated this and said that Congress had had ample time and opportunity to make up their minds if they wanted to form Provincial ministries after Simla, and to approach Governors; but that they had shown no sign of doing so, in fact I thought that one prominent Congress leader had said that they had no intention of forming ministries before the elections. I told him that at the Governors' Conference, which I had held after Simla, it had been agreed that if any approach had been made to Governors for the formation of ministries they would be accepted; it was only after there was no sign of any intention of the political leaders to come forward that Legislatures were dissolved, as a matter of administrative convenience in view of the approaching elections. Patel seemed to be determined to make a grievance of this and an instance of British support of the Muslims, but did not speak with any great bitterness about it.

He said that he did not see how there was ever going to be a settlement between Hindu and Muslim while the British were in India, and that the British should clear out and leave Indians to settle matters themselves. I said he really could not expect us to leave India to chaos and civil war, and that there must be some sort of settlement. I did not introduce the issue of Pakistan, as the tone of his approach did not seem to favour it, and merely said that it was my business to see that law and order was maintained until some new form of Government was settled. He agreed with this.

He was polite, and certainly quite as friendly as I expected, but obviously uncompromising.

January 24

A period of comparative quiet was succeeded by a real blizzard of work, a whole number of awkward problems seeming to arise at once.

Council meeting in the evening lasted nearly two hours, of which $1\frac{1}{4}$ hours were on food. The complete failure of the rains in the South has created a famine position in parts of Madras, Bombay and Mysore; and the lack of winter rains in the north has entirely dried up procurement in Punjab and Sind. Also rice is not coming out of Siam quick enough or in sufficient quantity; how far this is due to H.M.G. insisting on 1,500,000 tons being supplied free as reparations is uncertain; but it will undoubtedly be the subject of bitter criticism here. There will be a debate in the Assembly next week.

Meanwhile a telegram came in from H.M.G. to say that they propose to send a delegation of three Ministers to negotiate a settlement of the Indian problem, to arrive middle of February. I wonder if this is a wise move, they are under an illusion if they think a week or two of discussion is going to be sufficient. From my own point of view, it relieves me of some of the immediate load of responsibility, I suppose; but may increase it in the end, as I suspect that I may be left with all the loose and awkward ends to tie up, and perhaps to implement a policy with which I do not agree. It depends a great deal whom they send. I am afraid that I would not wholly trust Cripps as a negotiator.

I also saw Smith, D.I.B. His information is that Congress is in militant mood and out gunning for the Muslims, confident that they can down them. He thinks they are prepared to take office in the Provinces without waiting for the Centre,[1] and will then secure control of Government servants and make action against Congress impossible, by dismissal or persecution of any officials not amenable to their ideas. A dangerous policy for us, and also I think for themselves in the long run.

I saw Liaquat Ali Khan in the evening, he is rather an attractive person, much pleasanter and easier to talk with than Jinnah. His general theme was that Hindus and Muslims would never agree and that the British would have to face the Pakistan issue and produce a solution. I said that if we imposed a solution we should have to stop in India to enforce it, and he

[1] This was confirmed by Azad during his interview with Lord Wavell on 25 January.

said that in any event we should have to stop for many years yet, and that the Muslims were not at all anxious that we should go; India could not stand alone and would only get some worse master.

January 25

Another very full day. I saw Hydari and asked him to take over Planning and Development Department from Dalal, as Mudaliar, having been elected President of an important Committee of U.N.O., was not likely to be available for some months at any rate. Hydari was delighted.

After lunch I had 1½ hours with Azad and Asaf Ali[1] the latter acting as interpreter. I entirely refused to accept their thesis that Congress was entirely right in all it said and did. I think these Congress leaders live as little tin gods in their immediate entourage and never hear criticism and are entirely autocratic, so that a little plain speaking does no harm.

In the course of this meeting, at which a number of subjects, e.g. the release of détenus, were discussed, Azad informed Lord Wavell that after the elections the Congress would form governments in all Provinces in which they had a majority and would not expect a new Executive Council at the Centre to be formed till after this. Lord Wavell told him that he was discussing with H.M.G. the best way of forming a good Executive Council to carry on the administration while constitution-making was in progress. Azad suggested that the Premiers of all the eleven Provinces should be asked to nominate two persons and that out of this panel of twenty-two the Viceroy should select the Executive Council. In reply to an inquiry whether the Viceroy would have complete freedom of choice in making his selection Azad said that it would be a matter for negotiation.

January 26

I hear Congress do not mean to attend the Assembly when I speak on Monday.

I spoke to A.J.'s soldiers on India, a difficult thing to deal with one of the world's most complicated problems in 40 minutes.

January 28

This morning I addressed the Assembly. Congress did not attend and apparently considered it rather a concession that the President[2] did.

Then we had a Council on Food, found ourselves at least a million tons short, decided to send a deputation to London, and to Washington if necessary, and to take certain other measures.

---

[1] A Congress Muslim from Delhi and member of the Congress Working Committee.
[2] The President, i.e. Speaker, who had just been elected, was a Congressman.

January 29

Sargent spoke to me about the long-delayed letter to the Provinces on Education policy. I took this up in March 1944 just before I went home, did not finish discussion in Council; Colville would not touch it while he was acting for me; when I came back the Simla conference occupied my whole attention for a month or so; then I could never get a quorum of my Council sufficiently large to deal with it till October; we passed the policy in October; and since then Finance branch has held up issue of the policy by a dispute on the financial implications. Such is the difficulty of getting anything important settled and issued in this country.

February 1

A quiet day. I saw an American correspondent, Jones of the New York Times, and suggested that Americans might show their sympathy for the Indian war effort and India's aspirations for freedom by allocating more food. He didn't seem to realise that there had been an Indian war effort but seemed to think the matter of food shortage was worth a message. Srivastava has accepted to lead the Food deputation to London and Washington.

The food problem continues an anxiety. Congress politicians seem determined to make capital out of it, by denouncing the British Government as entirely responsible and by demanding pressure on the Muslim Provinces, Punjab and Sind to produce surpluses. I had a business-like letter from Colville, who seems to be dealing with the problem as efficiently and cheerfully as possible, and a very gloomy one from Glancy, who is obviously a tired and depressed man.

The M.P.s returned, and I had an hour with them before dinner, they have not found any solid answer to the problem and are, I think, as puzzled by the complexities and personalities as anyone else. No one seems to have been impressed with Jinnah, or rather they all seem to be impressed with his intransigence, but practically all think that the Pakistan issue has to be tackled. I fancy a good number of them are disillusioned with Congress and the Indians—certainly Morris, Richards and Bottomley seem to be, and probably Mrs. Nichol. I have not seen Wyatt yet, I am seeing them all again tomorrow evening.

> *Through no fault of its members the Parliamentary Delegation did not arouse much interest in India and had little effect on the course of events; but some of its members probably did succeed to some extent in bringing home to the Labour Government that Jinnah and the League would not easily be persuaded to drop the demand for Pakistan.*

February 9

Back this afternoon from short visit to Bangalore to see the drought affected areas of Madras and Mysore. Three strenuous and rather depressing days. The drought is quite unprecedented, and the seriousness could not be known till the end of the year as rains even in December would partially at least have saved the situation.

On Thursday 7th I did a tour of the Madras areas. We flew to Arkonam and had a meeting on the airfield there with the Collectors of North Arcot, Chingleput, Nellore, Chittor, Anantpur, Salem, who told me their tales of shortage. Then I motored for about two hours round some of the adjacent affected areas with Dixon, Madras Commissioner of Civil Supplies, ex-Diwan of Cochin, a good man, and the Collector of N. Arcot, Ahmed Ali, who obviously knew his District extremely well and was efficient.

We then flew on to Tanjore, lunched with the Collector, and had another Conference with the Collectors of Trichinopoly, Tanjore, South Arcot and Ramned, and the English Diwan of Pudukkottai State and the Rajah.

Yesterday, February 8, I flew for an hour over North Mysore, to see the dryness of the land. The tanks on which irrigation depends in this part of the world seemed even drier than in Madras on the previous day. H.H. excused himself from coming on this tour as the air did not suit him; but accompanied me on a 200-mile drive round the same area, almost, which we began after a quick breakfast with the R.A.F. The drought was even more evident and more complete than in Madras; and it did not seem that the administration was as adequate; in one area the inhabitants claimed to be subsisting on 4 to 5 oz. a day, though it was quite obvious from their appearance that they had not done so for long.

We got back at 4 p.m., and at 5 p.m. I held a Food conference which lasted nearly two hours. One of the chief matters discussed was an all-India cut of the grain ration to 12 oz. On the whole the Conference went well.

February 11

I had decided after the Bangalore trip to try and enlist the co-operation of the principal parties in the food problem or at any rate keep them off agitation about it. So I asked Gandhi and Jinnah to come and see me. Gandhi professed to be too unwell to travel, so George went off to Nagpur early this morning to see him at Wardha. He heard by telephone that G. seemed to be in a most unaccommodating mood. However, George must have been diplomatic and persuasive, for he came back this evening with quite a satisfactory reply, although G. had at first appeared to demand an immediate change of government at the centre. Congress has its knife into J. P. Srivastava for some reason. George said G.'s secretary, Pyarelal, and Amrit Kaur[1] who was there, were helpful.

I had about 45 minutes with Jinnah in the evening. He was quite reasonable and sensible about the food situation; but then started a violent attack on the I.N.A. policy, in fact gave me a summary of the speech he had just delivered in the Assembly. I don't know whether he had any real hope in his mind that I would stop all the I.N.A. trials in return for his attitude about food; when I made it quite clear that the two subjects had nothing to do with each other, he promised to play, though he kept up his usual dramatic manner and ended with an indictment of Congress.

In the afternoon I had a walk round the garden and cup of tea with Burrows the new Governor of Bengal who had just arrived, an attractive person, steady, sensible, straight with a slow West Country speech. He will do well, I think.

After Jinnah, I finished the evening with Thorne who spoke chiefly of the immediate request of the Assam Ministry for the release of all political prisoners. This will of course be the first request of all Congress Ministries —as it was in 1937—and will not be easy to resist.

February 12

Benthall talked to me of the prospects of a railway strike; hitherto we have always been able to rely on the Anglo-Indian element, but in view of the approaching constitutional change they are unlikely to court unpopularity in India by standing out from the rest. I asked B. to consider how an emergency food service could be run if there were a strike. He said the attitude of the Assembly had been less hostile than expected over the I.N.A. debate and Mason[2] had put the Government case well. Jones[3] also mentioned the possibility of a general strike—Posts and Telegraphs this time; and said the Assembly Committee on the Bretton Woods agreement had been quite unable so far to reach any conclusion. Spence[4] discussed the situation that would arise when Ordinances became invalid in September and the best way to replace the essential ones by legislation.

[1] Rajkumari Amrit Kaur, a member of a distinguished Indian Christian family, at this time one of Gandhi's entourage. After Independence she became Health Minister in the Government of India.

[2] Philip Mason, I.C.S., Joint Secretary, Govt. of India, War Department, 1944–7, and author of many books on India.

[3] Sir Cyril Jones, I.C.S., Secretary, Govt. of India, Finance Department, 1939–47.

[4] Sir George Spence, I.C.S., Secretary, Govt. of India, Legislative Department, 1935–47.

Finally, an hour or so with the C.-in-C., who had two important problems: a reply to a telegram from the C.I.G.S. about the possibility of sending more British troops to India—there are none available except by taking them from elsewhere; and the organization of divisions in India, he wants to pull out the British element and organize it into purely British groups. I told him I should want time to think over both these problems. Meanwhile news came in of fresh rioting in Calcutta on a large and violent scale, again with the idea of getting I.N.A. men released apparently.

S. of S. has told me of the Ministers to come out. Cripps, Alexander and himself. I am afraid that Cripps will be the operative element, and I think he is sold to the Congress point of view, and I don't think he is quite straight in his methods. I wonder what these three Magi will achieve. I cannot so far get from H.M.G. any definite policy.

February 13

Dickie Mountbatten was my first visitor. He proposed to hand over Malaya, Singapore and Borneo to civil government on April 1.

Then came Brailsford, the aged left-wing journalist, a round-faced benevolent-looking grey-haired old man who brought in his comparatively young wife, dressed in a sort of semi-Tyrolese costume. He had nothing very special to say or ask, while her main contribution was a suggestion that if we built enough small fishing boats we could feed the people—the miracle of the loaves and fishes came irreverently to my mind, and I wondered whether she cast Gandhi or myself for the principal role.

Council in the evening was almost entirely on the proposed reduction in the food ration. My colleagues were rather slow and woolly over it, but recognized its inevitability in the end.

Rioting in Calcutta continues and seems to be serious.

February 14

I had an hour with Glancy, who looked better but is a tired and depressed man. He thinks Muslim League may get 60 out of the 87 Muslim seats, but will not have a clear majority, Congress will have 45 to 50 seats. Khizar (who has won two seats and is standing for a third, it seems an odd electoral law that allows this) is apparently toying with the idea of a Unionist–Congress coalition, but Glancy thinks it would be unwise.

I told him of H.M.G.'s intention to send out 3 Ministers and of our proposed breakdown plan,[1] which he thought reasonable if one had to concede Pakistan in any form.

I then had a long talk with Wylie[2] on much the same lines as with Glancy. One of his chief troubles will be a demand from a Congress Ministry for an enquiry into the suppression of the 1942 disturbances and punishment of the officials they have already named. Wylie says the suppression really was drastic and that some indefensible things were done, but we must protect our officials. He does not think any sort of Pakistan should be conceded, that there must be some sort of Federation.

Calcutta seems to have quietened down and the Burrows go off to-morrow. I think they will do it well, anyway they go in a calm and confident spirit and will have a good try.

February 16

In the afternoon I had over an hour with Asaf Ali, acting for Azad who is ill at Calcutta. I spoke to him about the food situation and asked for co-operation of the Congress party. He made a tentative sort of suggestion for a change in my Executive Council as a necessity, but I think without any real hope. He then went off into a long diatribe about the way the food situation had been mismanaged in the last 7 or 8 years, how many thousands of acres had been allowed to lie waste, which Congress would certainly have brought under cultivation etc. etc. He then criticised the publicity which had been given to the scarcity and pointed out how publicity created panic and led to stocks, going underground and such platitudes. I interrupted him on this, and told him he was wasting time, did he really think Government could succeed in concealing the fact that the monsoon had failed, or that grain-dealers and other interested persons did not know the exact state of affairs; and reminded him that his own party had criticised Government in the food debate for not disclosing the full facts earlier. I showed him the text of the broadcast on Food I was to make that evening which dealt with most of the points he was raising, and asked him if he had any suggestions. He merely asked that I should alter one or two words: I had said that any attempt to make party capital out of the food situation would be 'folly and wickedness', and he asked me to cut out the 'wickedness'. Asaf was quite friendly, but is a poor sort of creature, without much ability or character but a very exaggerated idea of his own talents. However, I think Congress are bound to play, after Gandhi's lead, though it will not stop them taking party advantage if they see a chance.

---

[1] Wavell is here referring to his plan for dealing with a deadlock over the Pakistan issue explained on pp. 199–200.   [2] At this time Governor of the United Provinces.

By the way, I referred at the end to a speech of Nehru, which implied an attempt to suborn the Army, and said that there could be no greater folly than to introduce politics into the Army on the eve of a settlement. Rather to my surprise he agreed at once.

I broadcast in the evening, not very effectively I am afraid. I lack the fire or conviction for public speaking.

(The one light touch in the election campaign so far has been a petition from the Santals in Bihar, of which the Governor has sent me a copy. They objected to the date fixed. 'Surely Y.E. is aware' they said in effect 'that about this date is the great tribal holiday and that we are all drunk for a week and unable to attend to any business.')

The Elections to the Central Legislative Assembly and to the Provincial Assemblies had to be spread out over the cold weather of 1945–6. In the Central Assembly the Muslim League won all the Muslim seats and the Congress most of the other seats. In the Provincial elections the Congress won the great majority of the non-Muslim seats and the League a majority of the Muslim seats except in the N.W.F.P.

February 18

I wrote a private letter to the S. of S. to warn him that I did not propose to be treated as a lay figure in the forthcoming negotiations.

Personal and Confidential The Viceroy's House
New Delhi
17th February 1946

My dear Pethick-Lawrence,

I feel that I should let you know that I am becoming a little concerned as to what is in the minds of H.M.'s Ministers on the method of conducting the forthcoming negotiations. While it is claimed and announced that the Viceroy will be an equal party in the discussions, I have been given no information whatever, since I sent home proposals early in January,[1] of how the mind of the Cabinet is working; and the latest telegrams about accommodation seem to give the impression that the Ministers wish to conduct the negotiations at some distance from the Viceroy's House, in order to ensure 'informal contacts'. What does this really mean, is the Mission expecting people to come to them like Nicodemus? I can assure you that wherever they are, everyone who comes to see them will be noted by the Press and parties. If the idea is to give the impression that the negotiations are not being influenced by the Viceroy or his advisers, why announce that he is one of the negotiators?

We can probably find a suitable house or houses outside the Viceregal

[1] These were the proposals dispatched from Delhi on 27 December, see pp. 196–200.

Estate, but it will be some distance away (one of the Princes' Houses might be most suitable), one or two miles; so that if the intention really is to negotiate in close consultation with the Viceroy, it will obviously be most inconvenient, especially in hot weather.

I may be quite unjustified in my suspicions that there is an intention, not on your part I am sure, to treat the Viceroy as a lay figure, and to keep him more or less outside the discussions, as was done at the time of the Cripps offer. If so, I should like to know.

Incidentally, I may say that knowledge of the Mission has been fairly general knowledge, to the Press at least and other well-informed people in Delhi, by advices from London, for some time past, though I am not allowed to inform my Governors till tomorrow.

I have thought it right to let you know this privately. If it is the wish of H.M.G. that I should be responsible for implementing in India any settlement to be negotiated, I must really and genuinely be consulted.

Yours sincerely,
Wavell

21st February 1946

My dear Wavell,

I am in receipt of your confidential letter of 17th inst. and hasten to send you a personal reply.

I am indeed sorry that my delay in giving you any detail with regard to our projected personal plans and to our own discussions here on tactics of negotiation should have led you to think that we have any intention of acting separately from yourself.

I can assure you that that is not the case. It is the firm intention of my colleagues and myself that the negotiations shall be undertaken by you and ourselves acting together as a team. But it has been felt that that should not preclude some personal contacts which will be more easily made outside Viceregal Lodge, perhaps at private dinner parties.

As to our tactical approach to the actual problem we are devoting the coming week-end at Chequers to a full discussion of the fundamental issues involved and I hope to be able very shortly afterwards to give you a full account of our reactions to them and to your own plan.

My difficulty has been that until we have had a proper time to deliberate away from the incessant interruption of other business it has not been possible for me to get any coordination of views which it would be profitable to communicate to you or even to clarify my own mind.

I hope this explanation and reassurance will allay the suspicions which I can quite appreciate you may not unreasonably have entertained but which are in fact quite without foundation.

Sincerely yours,
Pethick-Lawrence

February 19

A day of alarms but not excursions. I saw Porter,[1] all for capitulation to the I.N.A.; Bewoor,[2] about a postal strike; Carr,[3] the A.O.C.-in-C, about R.I.A.F. mutiny; Griffin[4] and Conran-Smith[5] about a railway strike; and finally the C.-in-C., most gloomy of all, about the R.I.N. mutiny at Bombay and the I.N.A. trials; though he talked about sticking to our principles, he was really hoping hard that I would give a lead to recommend to H.M.G., surrender to public opinion and total abandonment of I.N.A. trials. I refused to play and said we should stick it out. What a cheerful day—prospect or reality of three mutinies and two strikes! However, I got in 18 holes of golf with Pompey Howard in between and played well.

February 20

I had an hour with Rutherford, who was fairly re-assuring about the law and order position in Bihar, though he said everyone expected a serious outbreak sooner or later.

Council went quietly. The C.-in-C. gave an account of the mutiny of the R.I.N. at Bombay and Council was clear that it should be dealt with firmly and the ringleaders severely punished.

February 21

The Aga Khan came and talked of the necessity for Pakistan and the impossibility of Hindus and Muslims agreeing; he said Jinnah was willing to concede Amritsar, Ambala etc, in the N.W., and the Hindu districts of Bengal and Assam but *not* Calcutta.

Smith D.I.B. had no special intelligence, everyone seemed to agree that an explosion might come at any moment but no one could see immediate signs.

Then C.-in-C. came in just before lunch with serious news of the R.I.N. mutinies at Bombay and Karachi. Fire seems to have been opened on the troops who were confining the mutineers to barracks. According to C.-in-C. there was some suggestion of parley, but he and I entirely agreed that there could be no question of parley and that nothing else than unconditional surrender would be accepted.

[1] A. E. Porter, I.C.S., Secretary, Govt. of India, Home Department, 1945–7.
[2] Sir Gurunath Bewoor, I.C.S., Secretary, Govt. of India, Posts and Air Department, 1942–6.   [3] Air Marshal Sir Roderick Carr, A.O.C.-in-C., India, 1946.
[4] Sir Arthur Griffin, Chief Commissioner of Railways, India, 1944–6.
[5] Sir Eric Conran-Smith, I.C.S., Secretary, Govt. of India, War Transport Department, 1945–6.

Later: R.I.N. mutiny at Bombay is apparently in hand, no news from Karachi.

A hunger strike by some ratings of the Signal School in Bombay on grounds of inadequate pay and racial discrimination touched off a mutiny by other ratings who took possession of their ships and threatened to open fire on the military guards. Ratings at Karachi followed their example. Sympathetic strikes and demonstrations were organized in the city of Bombay and serious disturbances ensued in which about 200 people were killed. The mutiny had been fomented by political agitators, but the Congress leaders had not encouraged it and were alarmed by the disorders. Vallabhbhai Patel personally intervened to induce the ratings to surrender.

There was also unrest at this time in the R.I.A.F. and in some of the technical units of the Indian Army.

February 23

Came back this evening from Patiala, to which I had gone yesterday, meaning to return on Monday. But events in Bombay and Karachi and the obvious 'flap' in Whitehall determined me to get back to Delhi, as I had already fulfilled the two principal functions at Patiala.

I opened a Soldiers Club, attended an Agricultural and Industrial Show, of the usual type, and presented a colour to the Training Battalion—a very good ceremonial parade, including the unusual feature of a State elephant bringing on the Granth Sahib (Sikh bible), to which HH and I presented flowers, which were afterwards hung on the colours.

I like HH of Patiala, I think he is really keen on making a good show of his State, and that its interests are his principal concern in life at present.

February 25

I had a long talk with Thorne in the morning. He is anxious to see all the I.N.A. trials dropped, but admits the difficulty of doing it. He complains that War Department did not keep Home Department sufficiently in touch about the trials.

In the afternoon I had an hour with Azad and Asaf Ali. They were quite pleasant and friendly.

They discussed the formation of an Advisory Food Committee on which both the Congress and the Muslim League would be represented. Azad seemed to indicate that the Congress would be willing to co-operate.

They also discussed the prospects of coalition governments in the Provinces. Azad said that the difficulty was going to be the refusal of Jinnah to permit the League to take part in any government of which a non-League Muslim was a member.

February 26

The Raja of Khallikote,[1] whom I nominated to the Assembly to his great delight, came to see me. I spoke somewhat strongly to him about his proposed absence during part of the Budget debate, to perform the 'thread ceremony' for his son; he said the ceremony was most important, the date auspicious, and the guests invited, and assured me that he would only be away during the debate, he would be back in time to vote!

Next came the Editor of the Amrita Bazar Patrika, whose paper is about the most virulent and poisonous of all the Indian papers in English with any circulation. He is the new President of the Editors Association. He was quite pleasant to talk with. He began by asking my assistance to secure more newsprint and some additional machinery for his paper. 'So that you may have greater scope to abuse my Government and the British, I suppose,' I enquired. This aspect did not seem to have occurred to him. I then took him to task for the unbridled intemperance of the Press in the last six months, which had naturally resulted in out-breaks such as at Bombay; and warned him strongly of the harm being done to India's future. He merely said: 'we felt so frustrated after the Simla Conference'! He then asked for guidance on the food question.

February 27

A comparatively quiet day but somehow rather a depressing one. It becomes increasingly obvious that the students and mobs are out of hand and that the so-called political 'leaders', who are really only political agitators, cannot control the passions they have aroused by six months unbridled incitement during the election period. They have often condemned 'police rule', but it is at any rate better than student rule or mob rule, as they are beginning to find out.

Council agreed this evening to the establishment of an Advisory Food Committee.

Our chief item was the measures proposed by P & T Department to stop a threatened strike. Nobody liked them much, though everyone recognised that the P & T people had some grievances, but the Department put up a good case and they were passed in the end, with a warning that they would probably lead to pressure from the Railways for similar concessions. Ambedkar, whose sudden rather unaccountable reactions sometimes take himself by surprise just as much as his colleagues, held an unexpected one-man indignation meeting over the proposals, proclaiming

---

[1] A rich landowner from Orissa, not a Ruling Prince, see p. 41.

with vehemence that the Labour Department had never been consulted. As the proposal before Council had apparently been drawn up by the Labour Commissioner and backed by the Labour Member himself, it was a little difficult to accept his contention that he had not been consulted; nor could I understand his explanation of the apparent inconsistency. I have given up expecting logic from Ambedkar, when something touches off his touchiness. His 'lone wolf' mentality is engendered by much brooding on the wrongs of the Depressed Classes, I imagine. In his way he is quite a fine character.

A long telegram came from S. of S. about their plans for conducting the negotiations, it seems really to amount to having no plans but hoping to collect some out here by a long series of talks.

March 1

I took over Colonelcy of The Black Watch today.

Another very busy day, with never a moment's pause to allow of any constructive thinking, private business or recreation.

In the evening I presided at a meeting of the Coordination Committee of Council which Benthall had asked for urgently to consider Council's decision on the threatened P & T strike in relation to the railways. The Committee upheld Council's decision and decided that the threat of a railway strike must be dealt with as a separate issue.

March 4

I spent all Sunday morning answering S. of S. telegrams about the delegation's plans and directive. I suggested that they must have some more definite ideas about Pakistan, their objective and their time-table than they appeared to have or had disclosed to me. I pointed out that Pakistan issue affected not only India but the whole Empire, since it might lead to a conflict with Muslims; that they had not mentioned in their telegrams a Constitution Making Body, but had talked of 'final' settlement, so that I was left in doubt whether a C.M.B. still formed part of their plans; and that India was expecting something rather more dynamic than prolonged discussions followed by a recess to Simla to think them over. I wonder whether they really have no plan at all, as would appear from their messages, or whether they have come to some fairly definite conclusions and do not wish to disclose them to me.

H.M.G. were very anxious to preserve the unity of India and hoped to devise some basis for agreement between Congress and the Muslim League that would make this possible. Beyond this it is doubtful whether at this stage they had any very definite ideas. Wavell was, no doubt, somewhat put out by the fact that H.M.G. had put aside, almost without comment, all the plans that he had sent them on 27 December.

One of my visitors was Devadas Gandhi who was outwardly all sweet reasonableness; he made a rather vague suggestion of International arbitration if Hindu and Muslim failed to agree, and said it would give us 'moral support'. I pointed out that we should still be left with the job of enforcing a decision with which perhaps we did not agree; and that we were getting rather tired of holding international babies.

I asked whether he would like Russia taking a hand in deciding the fate of India, as she would certainly want to do if an International body was formed. He professed great anxiety not to break the British connection and to remain in the Empire.

March 5

Comparatively quiet day. Porter of the Home Department was rather depressing. It is quite true that the situation must be depressing as seen from the angle of the average District officer, and we are of course running big risks. But I do not believe that further concession to agitation by dropping all the I.N.A. trials, as Porter advocates, is the right answer.

March 6

Liaquat Ali Khan, who was due to see me on the Food Advisory Council, was too busy with politics at Lahore. I am afraid that the Punjab like Sind will have an uneasy and unstable Ministry.

Council in the evening went quite smoothly. We usually have long and difficult Councils when the Assembly is sitting and all members are present; but Mudaliar is away and Rowlands, Jogendra Singh and Srivastava are sick, so we are fewer than normal. Council decided practically unanimously to give notice to South Africa of the termination of the Trade agreement in retaliation for their Bill against the acquisition of land by Indians. I have managed to keep this in abeyance for about two years, but with the war over, it is essential to make this concession to Indian feelings. It is not likely to do any good at all to India or to Indians in South Africa, but it has become a matter of national prestige to the Indians.

March 7

There was a Co-ordination Committee of Council on control of capital issues, on which I understand little, but I suppose it helps to get decisions if I preside.

In the afternoon was the Victory Parade, a really magnificent show by a very fine lot of men, and well organized. The only failure was the fly-past by the R.A.F. which was very poor. It was a bit wearing for me, as I had to stand at attention for 1½ hours and at the salute nearly all the time.

It is a measure of the unutterable folly of the politicians that they decided to boycott the parade of the men who have saved India and have given her greater prestige abroad than ever before, and to incite their followers to demonstrate against it. The result was that the mobs got out of hand in Delhi and burnt the Town Hall and other places. The Police had to open fire and there have been casualties. It will recoil on the heads of the political leaders some day that they have chosen to exalt and glorify the few thousands of traitors of the INA, who were mostly the cowards and softlings; and to neglect the magnificent men who really fought for them.

In the evening there was an indifferent firework display.

March 8

Interviews all day and finally Liaquat Ali Khan came to see me. He readily agreed on behalf of the League to the proposed Food Advisory Council, and then spoke for some time of the disappointment of the League at not being asked to form a Ministry in the Punjab and of the partiality of the Governor. I merely said I was sure that the Governor had done his best in a difficult position. I then spoke to him very straight about the previous day's events in Delhi. I said I had seen the most magnificent parade and the finest lot of men in my 45 years service as a soldier, and had come away feeling very proud of my connection with the Indian Army—to learn that these men had been hooted and derided by their compatriots; and that a mob, incited to demonstrate against the parade by the political leaders, had broken loose and burnt and looted in Delhi; it made me disgusted with Indian politics and despairing of India's future that her leaders could commit such incredible folly, which could only injure her prestige and credit with the United Nations, to whom she was at the moment appealing for food. I did not mince my words. Liaquat took it well and attempted no defence. He is a gentleman and likeable.

One of the League's most striking electoral successes had been in the Punjab where Khizar and the Muslim Unionists, who had previously been in a great majority, were reduced, after a few defections, to a mere handful of ten, while the League held 79 seats. Though the League was the largest single party, it did not command an absolute majority and was unable to arrange an alliance with any of the other parties. Khizar was, therefore, allowed to take office as the leader of a Unionist–Congress–Akali Sikh coalition and Muslims found themselves under what was virtually a non-Muslim Government in a Muslim-majority Province. This caused intense resentment.

Muslim League ministeries could be formed only in Bengal and Sind. Elsewhere, apart from the Punjab, Congress ministries were installed.

March 10

I had an hour with Azad and Asaf Ali this morning. I began by speaking about the proposed Food Committee, telling the Maulana the proposed composition and asking whether he had any suggestions, and saying that I should be very glad to receive nominations from the Congress Party. He said he agreed generally with the idea of the Food Committee and the numbers; there would be a meeting of the Congress Working Committee at Bombay on March the 12th, and he would put the proposals before them and let me have suggestions and nominations. He said that his idea was that the Committee would be a committee of people who had the ability to advise the Government on food matters, and that it should not be a question of party representation but of individual qualifications. I said that the reason why I had suggested a certain number of nominations for the Congress party and the Muslim League was that it was important to secure the general support of the main political parties for such steps as it would be necessary for the Government to take. He said he would let me have the views of the Working Committee by the 14th.

I then went on to say that since he was meeting the Working Committee, I hoped that he would represent to them the necessity for the greatest possible moderation during the present period. I said that I was still very disturbed at the tone of some of the political speeches, and instanced particularly those of Sinha[1] and Nehru. Recent events have shown the folly of inciting people to violence, and I hoped that he would impress on the Working Committee in the strongest possible way the necessity for moderation in tone. He professed to agree entirely with what I said and asked whether I had noticed the moderation of tone since the meeting of the Working Committee at Calcutta. I said that while the tone of the speeches made showed a slight moderation after the Calcutta meeting, there were still a number of very violent things being said by a great many people, and that it was only in the last week or two that the political leaders had shown any real sign of responsibility and desire to refrain from any incitement; and some of them had still not lowered their

[1] Sri Krishna Sinha, Congress Premier of Bihar.

tone, I instanced particularly Sinha's recent speeches in Bihar. Azad said that it was his desire to maintain a calm atmosphere and that he hoped things would be kept quiet.

I spoke to them very straight about the anti-Victory demonstrations on Thursday and they listened in silence. Azad said that while Congress had been unable to approve of the Victory celebrations, they had issued instructions that people should not stage demonstrations against them, and it had been other elements which had caused the trouble. He fully realised the danger of undermining the morale of the armed forces. I said that I was glad to hear it, but that the whole tone of the press which supported Congress had been to belittle the achievements of the Indian Army and the part they had played in saving India from invasion; and that there had been no sign at all that the political parties took the least pride in the exploits of their magnificent soldiers. Azad said there was no official Congress Press, and that he was not responsible for what the papers said. I replied that if the political leaders had taken the line of giving the armed forces credit for what they had done, the press would certainly have followed them.

I went on to point out the harm that had already been done to the morale and discipline of the army by the Congress attitude in the I.N.A. trials, in which I said they made heroes of people who, for the majority, formed the worst and not the best elements in the Indian Army. I hoped that they would not continue to condone or praise indiscipline in the armed forces, they would certainly regret it subsequently if they did.

Azad then spoke of the situation in the Punjab, which he admitted was most difficult; he said that he had been quite prepared to form a coalition Government with the Muslim League, but that the Muslim League would not agree. He did not strike me as being very confident of the stability of the present Government, but said that there was no better alternative.

I finished by referring to Nehru's visit to Malaya, and said that there had been considerable opposition to the visit, but that I had told the Supreme Allied Commander that I was sure Nehru would honourably observe the understanding on which he was allowed to go to Malaya, i.e. that he would not indulge in political agitation or speeches against the existing administration. I was not likely to be able to see Nehru before he went, so I hoped that Azad would impress this on Nehru. He said that he would do so.

The general tone of the interview was friendly, and I think they are really anxious to preserve the peace, and realise that it is essential to moderate the tone. But I doubt if they are really able to do it.

In the afternoon we had a party for the soldiers who had come to Delhi for Victory Week, it went quite well.

March 12

I had a visit to the Delhi Waterworks arranged for 7.15 a.m. but before going there I visited the Town Hall which was burnt out in last Thursday's riots, all the municipal tax records being destroyed amongst other things, presumably a Communist attempt to make Government impossible.

The Nawab of Bhopal was my first visitor of the morning. I told him about the food situation and the proposed Committee and H.H. promised full support to any measures taken by the Government and outlined what was already being done in the States. He said he would discuss the question of nominations to the Food Advisory Committee with Political Adviser.

The interview took a rather wider scope than I had expected when H.H. asked about arrangements for the Cabinet Ministers to see representatives of the States and for my advice on what the Princes should do in the forthcoming negotiations. I said that if he really wanted considered advice I should want time to think it over but that the aim of His Majesty's Government was a united and self-governing India, with a constitution arrived at by Indians, remaining within the British Commonwealth as a willing partner. In such an arrangement the Princes would obviously have a place but some re-grouping, such as small States joining a larger one, or of other States into Unions, would have to be considered. It was His Majesty's Government's desire that the Princes should find their rightful place within an Indian Union and they would give them every assistance to do so. They had announced that they would not transfer Paramountcy to an Indian Government without the consent of the Ruler. H.H. asked that nothing should be done or said by His Majesty's Government which would weaken the power of the Princes to negotiate with a new Indian government. I said that we had impressed this on His Majesty's Government.

In the afternoon, a rather surprising interview with Jinnah. I have never known him in such a reasonable mood, he seemed an entirely different man to his normal rather aggressive self. He was very courteous, listened to argument and seemed much more human and likeable than in any previous contacts with him.

They discussed the Advisory Food Committee. Jinnah said that it would not help and suggested that Gandhi should be asked to come to Delhi and 'sit in close conference with him, for as long as was necessary, to advise the Government on the matter of food'. He said that he thought that this was the only

*effective way of dealing with the threatened calamity; both Congress and
League organizations would be available all over the country to help the
implementation of Government's measures; and the country would feel that the
problem really was being tackled and that the leaders were behind it. He said,
'The responsibility will of course remain yours and the Government's, but the
moral responsibility will be ours.' He agreed that the Nawab of Bhopal should
sit with them to represent the States. Lord Wavell said that he would put the
proposition to Gandhi.*

*They also discussed the I.N.A. Jinnah listened attentively to what Lord
Wavell had to say and at the end said that he fully appreciated his point of view,
but that the I.N.A. business was poisoning relations to such an extent that they
must try to find a way out. Lord Wavell suggested that he should have a talk
about it with Sir Arthur Smith, Chief of the General Staff.*

March 18

Back this morning after a tour to Jaipur and Alwar.

Before I left Delhi on the 12th, I had commissioned P.S.V. to go to
Bombay and put Jinnah's proposition to Gandhi. The Working Committee had already turned down the proposal, made by Azad to me, that
Congress should participate in a Food Advisory Committee. Gandhi
turned down Jinnah's proposal, on his usual convenient plea that he is not
a member of Congress and cannot represent it. George flew to Jaipur on
the evening of the 14th to tell me of the result. So the political leaders will
not forego any item of party advantage even in face of famine. I don't
think I could have done more to persuade them.

On the morning of the 17th, [at Alwar] just as I was about to get up and
go riding, came the news of my son-in-law Simon's death in an accident
at Quetta. We motored to Palam [Delhi airport], 100 miles, as soon as we
could get ready and flew to Quetta, for the funeral. We stopped a night in
the Residency and flew back this morning.

I spent all the rest of the day getting square with arrears of work, and
in the evening had another interview with Jinnah on the food situation.
He asked me why I could not carry on without Congress cooperation.
I said that I was afraid that this might make matters worse, and that I could
do nothing more at present. He went on for some time in the strain of his
entire disinterestedness and desire to place the matter of food entirely
above all party or personal consideration. I got rather tired of this after
a bit and said: 'I entirely appreciate your attitude Mr. Jinnah, may I ask
whether you would be prepared to sit in the Committee if the Congress
were to nominate Azad as their representative?' He then began explaining
that though he had nothing personal against Azad, he was only a mere

puppet of Congress, and so on and so forth; that it was not a fair proposition to put to him. I said that I had merely put it since he had adopted the attitude that no considerations of any kind would prevent his cooperation. I then asked whether he would be prepared to sit in a Committee with Patel as the Congress representative; he said that he would agree to this, but said that Congress would never agree.

March 19/20

Ivor Jehu, who had come up from Bombay on business for the Times of India, had seen Jinnah and had found him, as I had, much more reasonable than before. He agreed with my proposition that if we offered the leaders all they asked—Congress, complete independence; Jinnah, some form of Pakistan—they would be likely to ask us for help from the consequences. He said that the Congress leaders knew that in view of their age this was their last chance; if they did not reach a settlement, leadership of a mass movement would pass into younger, more violent hands. He also told me that they were finding the I.N.A. and their demands for money an intolerable burden.

Arthur Smith told me of recent talks he had had with Jinnah. J. had covered much the same ground on the I.N.A. trials as he had with me and had practically the same answers. It is always refreshing to talk with Arthur, he has such a courageous outlook and such a nice sense of humour.

March 21

The D.I.B.'s secret and open intelligence pointed to everyone wanting a settlement except the extremists; to control having rather got out of the hands of the Congress leaders, to their great alarm; to the obvious fact that we were living on the edge of a volcano, but that on the whole morale seemed steadier than some months ago; and that Congress could raise much more trouble than the Muslim League if dissatisfied.

10

THE CABINET MISSION: OPENING DISCUSSIONS

The Journal entries for the next three months are mainly devoted to the Cabinet Mission. A short summary of events may assist the reader to follow the thread of the long, complicated negotiations of which the Journal gives Lord Wavell's account.

The task of the Mission was to seek agreement with Indian leaders on the principles and procedure to be followed in framing a new constitution for an independent India. It was also envisaged that simultaneously, the Viceroy, in consultation with the Mission, would open negotiations with the two principal political parties, the Congress and the Muslim League, for the formation of a new 'Interim' Government which would hold office while the constitution was being framed and would include no British member except the Viceroy himself.

Since the proclaimed objectives of Congress and the League were diametrically opposite, the Mission's task of bringing them to an agreement was a difficult, indeed a seemingly impossible one. The Congress wanted a united India; the League wanted India to be divided and the Muslim-majority Provinces of the North-East and the North-West formed into a completely independent and sovereign State of Pakistan. But the Mission believed, not incorrectly as it proved, that the League might accept something less than complete independence for Pakistan; and it was in this belief that they went to work.

After two weeks of discussion which led nowhere, the Mission told Jinnah that if he insisted on a fully sovereign Pakistan, it would have to be of the truncated variety, excluding most of Assam and half of Bengal and the Punjab, since it would be impossible to include in an independent Muslim State large areas in which Hindus were in a majority. A truncated Pakistan did not appeal to Jinnah. But the Mission put to him as an alternative a proposal for a three-tiered constitution—Provinces, Groups or sub-federations of Provinces, and a Union—under which the Groups of Provinces that he claimed for Pakistan would have a large measure of autonomy and would be joined with the rest of India in a Union confined to the control of Defence, Foreign Affairs, and Communications. To sweeten this proposal it was indicated that in the all-India Union the Hindu-majority and the Muslim-majority Groups of Provinces might have equal representation, and that there might be provision for a Province to have the right to secede from the Union after a period of years.

With considerable reluctance Jinnah and the Congress were induced to accept this proposal (often termed by Wavell the 'breakdown award') as a possible basis for negotiation and to agree to send representatives to Simla to discuss it. The Mission moved out of the heat of Delhi to the cool climate of Simla at the beginning of May and the second stage of their work began.

The negotiations at Simla soon broke down, and since the parties could not be brought to an agreement, the Mission decided to elaborate and perfect its proposals for a three-tiered constitutional structure, to add thereto proposals for constitution-making machinery whereby all the details could be worked out, and to issue the whole as a kind of award in the hope that both parties would accept it. This they did in a Statement published on 16 May (Appendix II) immediately after their return from Simla to Delhi. This Statement was, on the whole, well received throughout the country, Gandhi himself remarking that the Mission had produced the best document that was possible in the circumstances. But neither the Congress nor the League showed much inclination to accept it, and a further short Statement was issued on 25 May (Appendix V), clarifying certain points in answer to questions that they had raised.

Both these Statements made references to the 'Interim' Government that it was intended to form. Wavell had opened negotiations about it with Nehru and Jinnah while still in Simla and continued them on his return to Delhi. They dragged on until the middle of June. As with the long-term constitutional problem, no agreement could be reached between the Congress and the League; and so in this matter also Wavell and the Mission at last decided to make their own proposals and hope that they would be accepted. Accordingly in a Statement dated 16 June (Appendix VI) it was announced that the Viceroy had issued invitations to fourteen persons (whose names were given) to serve as members of the Interim Government. Paragraph 8 of this Statement seemed to imply that if either the Congress or the League rejected these proposals, the Viceroy would go ahead without them. This gave rise to a good deal of controversy later.

The Muslim League had decided on 6 June to accept the Statement of 16 May; and it was believed to be fairly certain that they would also in due course accept the proposals for an Interim Government. But the Congress continued to hesitate and to haggle. At last on 19 June it was reported that their Working Committee had decided to accept at any rate the proposals for an 'Interim' Government. Hopes rose high, but were dashed by the last-minute intervention of Gandhi, who insisted that a Nationalist (Congress) Muslim must be included as a member of the Interim Government. Wavell and the Mission had avoided the inclusion of a Nationalist Muslim as they knew from the experience of the Simla Conference that it would be quite unacceptable to Jinnah. They took a gamble—which very nearly came off—that the Congress would reconcile themselves to this.

Congress while conveying on 24 June their rejection of the proposals for an Interim Government, intimated at last their acceptance of the Statement of

16 May. Something, therefore, seemed to be salvaged from the wreck of the Mission's hopes. But the Congress's acceptance was qualified and disingenuous —worse in Wavell's opinion than an outright rejection. So though the Mission on their departure for the U.K. on 29 June appeared to have achieved a partial success, in actual fact their two months' work was largely in ruins and Congress and the League were no nearer agreement than at the time of their arrival.

Moreover, when they left, Jinnah was in a very angry mood. As soon as he knew that Congress had rejected the proposals for an Interim Government, he had got the League to accept them, believing that in accordance with Paragraph 8 of the Statement of 16 June, the Viceroy would proceed to form a Government without the Congress but with the League. The Viceroy and the Mission, however, put a different interpretation on Paragraph 8, and decided that a Caretaker Government of officials should be installed pending fresh negotiations for the formation of a government representative of the political parties that had accepted the Statement of 16 May. Jinnah was bitterly disappointed and resentful.

Wavell had told the Secretary of State that he did not intend to be a lay figure in these negotiations, and it will be seen from his Journal that he played a leading role in them throughout and not merely in those relating to the Interim Government, for which he was primarily responsible. He and Cripps were, in fact, the two chief protagonists on the British side with Pethick-Lawrence generally following Cripps's lead and Alexander that of Wavell. The Journal reveals that there were at times fairly serious differences of opinion within the Mission and also brings out rather forcibly the inadequacy of Pethick-Lawrence.

The three members of the Cabinet were able to devote all their time and thought to the negotiations. Wavell had to sustain in addition the whole burden of the Viceroy's day-to-day work. It was an enormous load. Even Cripps, who when he left Delhi was not on very cordial terms with Wavell and did not trouble to say goodbye to him, later paid a tribute in Parliament to 'the amazing way' in which through three months of Delhi hot weather he carried this double burden.

Wavell was also constantly thinking ahead. Quite early in the negotiations he pointed out to his colleagues that they must be ready with a plan to put into operation if the Congress and the League failed to agree or if either or both rejected the Mission's proposals. He himself drew up a Breakdown Plan to meet these possible contingencies and got the Mission to accept it and send it home, but H.M.G. declined to commit themselves to it. Later, when the Mission seemed to be on the point of success, he reminded them that even if the Congress and the League were shepherded into an Interim Government and a Constituent Assembly, there were many pitfalls ahead, and that circumstances might arise that would compel them to fall back on his Breakdown Plan, unless something better could be suggested. This Breakdown Plan—which several writers have quite misrepresented—was to be a recurrent theme during the rest of his time as Viceroy.

March 24

The three Magi[1] have arrived. They are pleasant and friendly but I am still doubtful whether they have got any definite plan in their heads.

March 25

Meeting in the morning with the Delegation on their statement to the Press conference which is colourless and quite all right. But they also produced at the meeting proposed answers to certain most important supplementary questions which were bound to be put, and which wanted consideration. I hope they will not make a practice of deciding on a line between themselves and then confronting me with it at short notice. Mine is not a quick-working brain.

Council meeting in the evening, preparatory to meeting the Delegation tomorrow. Benthall made a statement giving the general views of Council as voiced at a private meeting they had had yesterday. There was nothing new in it: it emphasised the need for a fresh popular Government; that it was essential to reach a settlement, since the alternative seemed to be civil war, and that no progress could be made without facing the Pakistan issue. There was rather a defeatist view of the loyalty of the Indian Army and Police. Old Muhamed Usman said little, he really dislikes the whole idea of change. Ambedkar held forth on the necessity of safeguards for the Scheduled Castes; he advocated Pakistan, but thought that the Muslims would be sick of it in ten years and would rejoin. Srivastava was rather defeatist but agreed with the general statement made by Benthall. So did Aziz ul Huque, but rather diffusely and not very lucidly.

Khare introduced a lighter touch by declaring that he would leave Council 'singing like a lark', when a new Government took over; he then made quite an oration, in which he suggested a re-distribution of India into Provinces which would include all Mahrattas into one; and strongly insisted that the Mahasabha ought to be represented before the Delegation. Roy put forward the Congress thesis that Provincial Governments should submit a panel from which I should select my new Council. Rowlands was brief and explicit: we must get a settlement, we must recognise the League as representing Muslims generally, and we must concede the principle of Pakistan. Thorne said little except that we could not now begin with the formation of a new Executive Council, as he had once hoped to do. Hydari was practically alone in saying that he would not accept Pakistan in principle, but would invite Mr. Jinnah to define it.

[1] Lord Pethick-Lawrence, Secretary of State for India, Sir Stafford Cripps, President of the Board of Trade, and Mr. A. V. Alexander, First Lord of the Admiralty.

March 26

I had an hour or so with the Cabinet Ministers this morning. Satisfactory on the whole. H.M.G. realise the weakness of our position and the necessity for a settlement; and they seem to have sensible views on the Pakistan issue. For some reason they seemed to think that the Muslim League had joined hands with the Communists. They saw their task as to get an interim Government into office and a Constitutional Making Body or Bodies into being. They expected the process of Constitution making to take a year. I expressed doubts of the possibility of keeping a Council together for that time on the existing set-up, and suggested that something must be done to give the transitional Government a greater feeling of power and independence—had the abolition of the India Office been considered, for instance?

S. of S. brought out the stock I.O. arguments against it, that it would only be camouflage which would deceive no one, etc; but Cripps to my surprise put forward the possibility of a solution on Amery's lines—the Viceroy's independence of the I.O. This was thought a bit too radical, but I insisted that the control of the I.O. over every detail of Indian administration and of finance should be removed or lessened. It was agreed that the Secretaries should consider this.

At Council's meeting with the Delegation in the evening they all said much the same as the evening before.

March 27

The discussion with the Delegation this morning began with S. of S. raising the best means of approaching the Pakistan issue in the discussions with Provincial Premiers, by direct or indirect means. I said that the Delegation need hardly worry about this, the issue would crop up quickly enough, in whatever means they approached the Premiers. I suggested that we might have a short meeting before each discussion at which we could get the background and general character of the men we were to meet and decide the best line of approach; also that the Secretaries might draw up an outline of the matters which it would be wise to discuss with them. This was agreed.

We then discussed a proposed statement to the effect that British troops could not be left in India for internal security purposes or to guarantee Pakistan vs Hindustan or vice versa, if India were divided. It was decided, after some amendments of the statement, to cable it to C-in-C for his comments. Finally, we discussed the advisability of releasing Jai Prakash

Narain, on which S. of S. is keen. I said we ought to consult the governor of the Province (Bihar) to which J.P.N. belongs.

Only routine items for Council; but the Congress Press (Tribune and National Call) made it clear that there had been a complete leakage of last night's meeting with the Delegation, and Home Member was instructed to try and trace it.

March 28

A full day of 14 hours practically continuous work. All the Governors arrived this morning. Three hours in the morning with the Delegation, mainly on States problems, the chief issues being how to dispose of Paramountcy—hand it over by consent, bury it, transfer it to the new Government of British India?—and the effect on the States of the draft aide-memoire on British troops in India. Cripps' proposal was apparently that the States should regain 'independence', when we gave up para-mountcy—a proposal which rather shocked the S. of S. The aide-memoire seemed to bristle with so many difficulties that I questioned the wisdom of issuing it, or indeed of giving out anything on paper, if we could avoid it; this view was I think generally accepted in the end. We also discussed the representation of the States on the Constitution Making Body or Bodies, and how they were to be divided if there were two.

Then I had a short talk with Glancy about Punjab politics and a wheat levy: after which the American Press Association insisted on coming in to take photographs of me at work.

After lunch $2\frac{1}{4}$ hours meeting of the Governors with the Delegation. Nothing very fresh was said but the views of the Governors were quite interesting. After half an hours interval I had nearly another two hours on a Food Conference with the Governors, rather a waste of time.

March 29

Delegation had two hours with Governors in the morning. The main subject was the use of the Governors' powers vis-à-vis popular Ministries and anticipated difficulties. On the whole Governors seemed reasonably happy.

March 30

Two hours with Delegation in morning, almost entirely on the question of the S. of S.'s control and G.G.'s powers of veto. My plea was that while I recognised the necessity for S. of S. control in the interim period I hoped that it would not be exercised in quite such a heavy-handed manner. Cripps was inclined to suggest some whittling down of the G.G.'s powers, and I think that he may be dangerous over this. None of them much liked my Big Stick note (see below) and Cripps said it was quite unthinkable to exercise sanctions against India, and would never be accepted by the present Parliament. I retorted that if British lives were lost or property destroyed on any substantial scale, the British people on all previous form would see to it that something fairly tough was done about it, Parliament or no Parliament.

Note for the Cabinet Delegation

There is a point which I should like to bring before the Delegation, before the beginning of the talks with political leaders.

We are going into these negotiations with an extremely difficult hand to play, owing to the necessity to avoid the mass movement or revolution in India which it is in the power of the Congress to start, and which we are not certain that we can control. It is obvious that Congress will use the threat of such a movement to secure as much as possible of their demands, even unreasonable ones.

We have one high trump in our hand, the Big Stick. We can in the last resort make things practically impossible for India by various kinds of sanctions, of which the principal would be a blockade. We could cut off India from all supplies of oil, kerosine, and imports of all kinds. We could also exact reparations for any damage done to British property or loss of British life, by impounding sterling balances to such amount as we considered effective.

Obviously the last thing we want to do is to make a threat of this kind; but there may possibly come a moment when it will become our last resource; and I think we should consider the implication.

I should like to discuss this with the rest of the Delegation.

W
29.3.1946

April 1

The opening day of our discussions with the Indian leaders, I shall not note them fully here, as there will be an official record, only my general impressions.

We began with Dr. Khan Sahib from N.W.F.P., who is an attractive personality but very definitely woolly in his ideas. He had obviously not really thought out the problems of Pakistan and refused to consider its possibility. Nor had he considered what Hindu domination at the Centre might entail. He talked in fact entirely from the Provincial angle, as if the

Pathans were a separate nation living in Pathanistan. He contributed little of value.

In the afternoon we had Bardoloi, the Congress Premier of Assam, a more forcible and quicker intelligence than the Khan Sahib, but not a very pleasant personality. He put out the general Congress thesis on a settlement —transfer of power at once, Jinnah must not be allowed to stand in the way, Centre should be formed from a panel chosen by Provincial Assemblies, etc. He then launched into a history of Assam, trying to make out it had been a great independent kingdom before the British came; I had to point out gently that the British had rescued it from Burmese rule. He said Assam was badly treated by the Centre, who took all the profits on Assam's oil and tea; denounced the Muslim theory that there were many large tracts of uncultivated land to be colonised; and claimed that all the hill tribes wished to belong to the Province and be administered directly by them. He said Assam would be quite prepared to hand over Sylhet to Eastern Bengal.

I spent the evening clearing up the routine work. Cripps I believe went slumming with Gandhi.

April 2

10 to 11 a.m.	Chancellor Ch. of Princes. H.H. Nawab of Bhopal
11 to 12 noon	Leaders of Opposition (N.W.F.P. Abdul Qaiyum; Assam: Sir Mohd. Saadullah)
12 to 12.30 p.m.	Leader of Opposition, Punjab: Nawab Iftikhar Hussain, Khan of Mamdot
12.30 to 1 p.m.	Leader of Opposition, Sind: G. M. Sayed.
2.30 p.m.	Delegation visit Sir Tej Bahadur Sapru (4 Hardinge Avenue)
4 to 5 p.m.	Nawab of Bhopal, Maharaja of Gwalior, Maharaja of Patiala, Maharaja of Bikaner, Jam Saheb of Nawanagar
5.30 to 7.30 p.m.	Tea with Standing Committee of All-India Newspaper Editors Conference. (Imperial Hotel)

The Chancellor made quite a good impression, he was clear and sensible. As I had warned the Delegation when we discussed the question of the States, he wanted very considerable modifications of paramountcy[1]

---

[1] Paramountcy was the term used of the relationship of the British Crown as suzerain to the Princely States of India. On India's attainment of independence this relationship would necessarily come to an end; and the Cabinet Mission, with the approval of H.M.G., stated plainly that Paramountcy could neither be retained by the British Crown nor transferred to

during the interim period, including the right to require a Committee of Enquiry on all matters of dispute, or rather Court of Arbitration.

The two Muslim League leaders from Assam and N.W.F.P. were not very convincing. Saadullah was obviously very tired after five days travel, and not at his best. He laboured details about the number and affiliations of hill tribes (in direct contrast to what Bardoloi had told us), to prove that Muslims were really in a majority in Assam; and was not very clear on the main issue—Pakistan. Abdul Qaiyum was a rather unpleasant looking tough, only converted from Congress to Muslim League a few months ago. Like Dr. Khan Sahib, he was convinced that the Provincial administration could manage the tribes much better than the Political Department; and advocated a N.W.F.P. made up with the addition of the Tribal territories and a part of Baluchistan, which he professed to believe could stand on its own and defend itself.

The Nawab of Mamdot was a pleasant looking young gentleman but almost entirely dumb, and S. of S. did most of the talking. Mr. Sayed of Sind on the other hand held forth in an almost uninterrupted monologue. His record shows him a quite unscrupulous politician but he is certainly intelligent and has a sense of humour, I should say (he reminds me a little of the Sind Premier who was murdered some years ago, Allah Bakhsh). His main theme was that none of the economic problems of India were receiving attention owing to the concentration on party politics—or polemics.

So ended the morning. The S. of S. is not a very good negotiator or questioner, he is inclined to be sloppy and long-winded and makes little speeches instead of asking questions. Cripps is of course an expert and incisive cross-examiner; but for some reason he makes lengthy notes all through an interview, which must distract his attention, at least it would mine; it seems pointless when a Secretary is doing it already. Alexander does not speak much, I think he takes it in but his knowledge of Indian affairs is scanty.

S. of S. told me he had had a letter from Gandhi after the interview he had with him yesterday, making three immediate demands:

> Release of all détenus
> Abolition of salt tax
> Dismissal of Ambedkar

a new Government of India. In practice, however, the transfer to a new authority of the powers and resources of the Government of India—and these included control of the railways, the major ports, and the armed forces—was bound automatically to put that new authority in a position to establish its Paramountcy vis-à-vis the States.

That comes of all this slopping good-will all over the place. It doesn't really pay, and will make things very difficult later.

In the afternoon we went to see old Tej Bahadur Sapru, who had said he was too ill to come. He looked frail. He talked platitudes with the air of wisdom of an Elder Statesman which he fancies himself to be; I have always thought him rather an old fraud.

Then we had an hour with the Princes' Standing Committee—Bhopal, Jam Sahib, Patiala, Bikaner, Gwalior. Bhopal at the end of the morning session had left a long string of searching questions, which he obviously did not expect to be answered without some long interval. Rather to my horror, S. of S. proceeded to answer them, in a long diffuse monologue, very prolix and woolly, I thought; and he gave away much which I should certainly not have done at this stage—he is no poker player. The Princes with their charming manners made a good impression.

Then to tea with the Editors' Standing Committee—Ghosh, Brelvi, Devadas Gandhi, etc. S. of S. made quite a good little impromptu speech. I made work an excuse to get away early, and left the rest of the Delegation to face the Editors.

April 3

S. of S. spoke of Gandhi's demands which I said were impertinent; but he was still hankering after the release of Jai Prakash Narain.

Maulana Azad was less suave and well-mannered than on the other occasions I have met him, and frequently walked up and down the room in obvious tension. Asaf Ali interpreted. S. of S. began as usual by giving away independence with both hands, and practically asking Congress to state their highest demands.

He cannot ask a question without making a little speech about it and presenting his interlocuter gratuitously with every point. He is a charming old gentleman but no man to negotiate with these tough Hindu politicians. However, perhaps his naive benevolence makes an impression.

Azad put out a scheme for Indian Federation, in which there were two lists of Federal subjects—compulsory and optional. He also admitted the right of a Province or Area to stand out altogether under certain conditions. He produced a novel theory that if there were a division, Muslims domiciled in Hindustan and Hindus in Pakistan would be 'aliens', which Cripps said was juridically impossible. I am sure Azad only meant it as a debating point against Jinnah—towards whom he showed great animosity— because Jinnah had made some rather foolish remark about separate nationalities. He produced the Congress claim that the Centre should be chosen by Provincial nomination which would obviously give Congress a nine to two majority over the League, but conceded that there might be 'adjustments'.

I thought the interview with Gandhi, naked except for a dhoti and looking remarkably healthy, was rather a deplorable affair. S. of S. began with his usual sloppy benevolence to this malevolent old politician, who for all his sanctimonious talk has, I am sure, very little softness in his composition. He began with the demand for the abolition of the salt tax, which he led up to by a lot of rather hypocritical sob-stuff. (In the five years I have been in the Government of India I have never heard from anyone but Gandhi a suggestion that the salt tax was really oppressive, and it brings in 9 crores; but G. wants it removed as a sop to his vanity, because he went to prison over it 15 years ago.)[1] He rambled on in his usual rather vague way, approaching the Pakistan issue by the way of his drunken son who had become Muslim for a while in the hope that it would cure him of drink: spoke of his efforts to meet Jinnah by Rajagopalachariar's formula and his Bombay talks; and finished with the meant-to-be plausible proposal that Jinnah should be asked to form a Ministry—the catch being that he would be subject to the Hindu majority in the Central Assembly (I had heard this idea put forward before). As usual, G. refused to be pinned down to details. The interview closed by a little speech of S. of S. expressing 'penitence' for Britain's misdeeds in the past!

I was frankly horrified at the deference shown to Gandhi, when he expressed a wish for a glass of water, the Secretary was sent to fetch it himself, instead of sending for a chaprassi; and when it didn't come at once Cripps hustled off himself to see about it. Besides being undignified, I am sure this sort of thing does not pay; and will leave an unenviable legacy for the Viceroy and officials. G. is a remarkable old man, certainly, and the most formidable of three opponents who have detached portions of the British Empire in recent years: Zaghlul and de Valera being the other two. But he is a very tough politician and not a saint.

Almost immediately afterwards I had to go to a Committee of Council on the price of cotton. Immediately afterwards came a meeting of Council.

Finally, a small party for the Political Residents who are holding a conference.

---

[1] The tax on salt, which dated back to long before the advent of the British Raj, was so light that no individual was conscious of it as a burden. But its abolition was one of Gandhi's fads; and he had made defiance of the Salt Laws and illegal manufacture of salt—its manufacture was a Government monopoly and the tax was included in the price at which it was sold to the public—the main feature of his Civil Disobedience movement in 1930.

April 4

The Delegation began the morning by deciding not to go to Simla, which some of them had been rather hankering after. Then we had three hours of Jinnah, of which at least two were, to my mind, entirely wasted. I should have started at once on the boundaries of Pakistan; but the Delegation gave J. his head and he talked for one hour on the history of India (largely fanciful) and the cultural differences between Hindu and Muslim (also somewhat fanciful). Then S. of S. made a speech lasting exactly 15 minutes and ending in one question which could have been asked in 15 seconds. Over an hour more was spent in discursive discussions about the possible contents of a supposititious treaty between a hypothetical Pakistan and Hindustan, with analogies and comparisons of U.N.O. which didn't seem to get us much further; and Jinnah stonewalled obstinately against some not very fast or skilful bowling. After about $2\frac{1}{2}$ hours I demanded to know Jinnah's ideas about the boundaries of Pakistan; and we had a more interesting half-hour though we got nothing much out of J.

Talk with Hutchings about Food and with the C.-in-C. about I.N.A. trials, Jubbulpore mutinies and various other matters.

Then back to Conference. Dungarpur and Bilaspur did well for the little Princes, the former read out a long statement advocating federation of the smaller States; while Bilaspur made an eloquent speech about the survival value of small States—especially his own. Dungarpur then asked some pertinent questions about the future.

April 5

Sikhs this morning. Tara Singh brought two others, who did most of the talking. It was not very illuminating, calculations of figures to show that there were more Sikhs than generally supposed and that anyway they ought to count double because they were such fine fellows. Pakistan was absurd of course, but if India was to be divided, the Sikhs would want a large share of the Punjab.

Baldev Singh said much the same in a more polished manner and with greater assurance. The division of the Punjab was quite simple: the Sikhs should have it, except the Rawalpindi and Mooltan divisions and some adjustment elsewhere. The Sikhs were entitled to a large share of the Army, Civil Service and everything else, whatever form of India was set up. All this did not get us much further except to emphasise the difficulty of the Sikh problem in any form of Pakistan.

Ambedkar started quietly on the claims of the Scheduled Castes and gradually worked himself up into a really spirited denunciation of the wrongs they suffered. I sympathise with A., but I am afraid that the uplift of his people will not easily be brought about, whatever the provisions of the Constitution.

I saw Thorne after lunch, mainly because S. of S. worries me daily about the release of Jai Prakash Narain: I told Thorne to telegraph the Governors of Bihar and U.P. about it; I expect we shall have to let him go and there are so many blackguards being let out now that I suppose one more won't make much difference, except that he is an intelligent blackguard.

Then came a cheerful Baluchistan Sardar, whom I nominated to the Council of State some time ago. It was decided that Baluchistan must have a representative and he was put forward as one of the very few presentable Baluchis: it was urged that his almost complete lack of knowledge of English would not matter much, as he could be trusted to vote with Government on every subject! He looked a good type of country gentleman, and talked voluble Hindustani at me, quite regardless of my telling him I had forgotten all my Hindustani. I gathered that his theme was that Baluchistan had equal contempt for Congress and the League, and wanted to be left alone.

Khizar was our final interview in the Delegation. He made a very good impression and was frank and sensible. It was obvious that he had no belief in Pakistan; and said in effect, as he had to me at Simla, that the British had no business to go till they could hand over to something much better than Congress.

I had half an hour with Bourne,[1] who goes off to Assam tomorrow, and was then able to get down to the days routine papers at about 7 p.m.

April 6

Five Congress Premiers this morning—Kher, Pant, Sinha, Shukla and Mahatab. They are not a very inspiring or inspired lot and not very certain of themselves really behind their façade of being the great tribunes of the Indian people. I like Kher, who is I think genuine and honest with a sense of humour; Pant is also honest and well-meaning but not I should say very capable; Sinha is the least pleasant, rather an aggressive agitator type; Shukla probably the least capable, of a not very capable lot; Mahatab also is not impressive. They all of course put forward the Congress demand— immediate transfer of power at the Centre on the basis of each Provincial

[1] Sir Frederick Bourne, I.C.S., Chief Secretary of the Government of the Punjab, 1941-5, Acting Governor of Assam, 1946, Governor of Central Provinces, 1946-7, Governor of East Bengal, 1947-50.

Premier nominating one, not necessarily from his own Province, a
Congress High Command list in fact, and then let them make the Constituent Assembly and the Constitution. They mostly wanted a strong Centre,
on the understanding of course that it was a Centre dominated by Congress; and expressed the usual righteous indignation at any suggestion that
Congress had ever given the Muslims the slightest ground for suspicion
of unfair treatment, in fact they had given them far more in every way
than they were entitled to have.

S. of S. made his usual little speech of how they had come out to transfer
power as soon as possible, our politicians are the only people who have
given away points, and they have given them away with both hands;
while Gandhi and Congress, so far from giving away anything, have increased their demands; and Jinnah has not conceded an acre of Pakistan.

Mahatab's chief subject was the necessity for the States contiguous to
Orissa to be handed over to the Province. They all professed to believe
that food and cloth would at once become plentiful all over India, once
they got control. They were, however, quite friendly.

April 8

After a comparatively quiet Sunday, the Delegation mixture as before.
I raised the general question of the continuous appeasement of Congress
and leading them to suppose that they could get what they wanted by
demanding it. I pointed out that it was not fair on the people who would
be left behind—the Governors, the Services, the Police, the troops—and
would probably have to be tough at some time to keep law and order,
that concessions should be made all the time, and that Gandhi and Co.
should be led to think that they owned India already. Alexander I think
agreed with me, S. of S. and Cripps were rather silent.

Suhrawardy of Bengal was our first visitor. I have always regarded him
as one of the most inefficient conceited and crooked politicians in India,
which is saying a good deal. He made a very bad impression on the
Delegation. He put forward all the stock arguments about Pakistan; and
was allowed by the Delegation to argue about small technical points, of
citizenship, etc., instead of keeping him to broad principles. When I did
tackle him on the defence of Eastern Pakistan, it was obvious that he had
never given it a moment's thought, and he tried to ride off on generalities:
that no country could defend itself alone nowadays, and so on. He then
indulged himself with a hymn of hate against Hindus, claiming that the
greater broadmindedness of Muslims made them much better administrators: he went on to claim that Bengal had been deliberately starved

out by the other Provinces in 1943, and that this proved that there was no unity in India.

He was succeeded by four leaders of Muslim League oppositions in Bombay, U.P., C.P., and Madras. They too were not very impressive. They claimed that Pakistan would help the Muslim minorities in Hindu Provinces, but after an immense amount of verbiage—mainly from Bombay (Chundrigar) with U.P. (Chaudri Khaliq-uzzam) a close runner up—could adduce no real argument, except vague phrases such as balance of power, prestige, psychological effect, but a good deal of hate against Hindus. Madras (Md. Ismail) and C.P. (Syed Abdur Rauf Shah) echoed the same sentiments very volubly, whenever they got a look-in or rather speak-in; and the session had very little of value in it.

The Nawab of Chhatari came to see me after lunch, his chief object being to reiterate his Exalted master's desire to be relieved of all restrictions on his powers.

Later came the Premier of Orissa, Mahatab, to plead in rather a simple and engaging manner, for benefits for his poor Province—a grant-in-aid of 5 crores for development and education was the chief item, for which he seemed almost to expect me to write him out a cheque on the spot. He spoke of food smuggling, of the aborigines and their education, of his desire to send officers to be trained at the Centre and one or two other matters. I rather liked him.

Tuesday April 9

I had three-quarters of an hour with S. of S. before the interviews. What I had said yesterday about the salt-tax and Congress appeasement had obviously gone home; and he made a long exculpatory statement. I pointed out in reply the position of Governors, the Services, the Police and isolated Europeans; our responsibility for law and order, and the danger of leading Congress to suppose they could get anything they asked for. I admitted that our position was weak and that we were conducting a retreat; that the first military rule in making a withdrawal was to show as much strength as possible, and that the weaker one was, the more important it was to keep up a strong appearance, we seemed to be advertising our weakness unnecessarily. Gandhi had great power still, but he was at heart an implacable enemy of Great Britain and would take advantage of every concession and be encouraged to ask for more. S. of S. ended with his daily request for the release of Jai Prakash Narain and I said I was not going to do so without consulting the Governors concerned.

We then interviewed the three best-known Diwans of States. Chhatari of Hyderabad, C.P. Ramaswami Aiyar of Travancore, and Mirza Izmail of Jaipur. Chhatari brought Walter Monckton[1] and an official from Hyderabad; he said nothing unexpected and voiced Hyderabad's desire to maintain an independent position and relations with the British crown; to recover Berar;[2] and to obtain a port. He wanted some special body to deal with economic arrangements between the States and Centre in the Interim period.

C.P. delivered quite a brilliant lecture on the Indian problem in about 40 minutes, nothing very new, but all very lucidly set forth. He said that the States should not insist much on existing treaties; that the exercise of paramountcy would require revision for the interim period and there should be a body of advisers to the Viceroy appointed by the States; that the States should group themselves into viable units (if the standard was a population of 1,000,000 and one crore of revenue there would be about 20 to 25 such units; with a standard of 3,000,000 population and two crores of revenue, there would be about 10); they should have some form of popular government but with a non-removable Executive. He then spoke of the Communist danger to India, of the defence of India, and of the Constituent Assembly. He is of course a strong upholder of a united India. He spoke well and made a good impression. He is one of the cleverest men in India, of course.

Mirza Ismail showed up very poorly in contrast. He has no fixed principles, except to look after Mirza Ismail, and faces all ways. He put forward a quite impossible scheme for forming a Central Executive (2 representatives of Congress out of 8) and Constituent Assembly (5 Congress out of 27) and showed no grasp of realities at all.

In the afternoon Gandhi came to see me about the salt tax. He professed to be coming purely as a friend of Britain, so that the British would get the credit of removing this unjust tax, before the National Government came into power and did so. The old humbug, I wonder whether he suspects that a National Government would do nothing of the sort and that the British are easier to bounce. I refused, naturally, to commit myself in any way, and merely said I would look into the matter. (He had sent Amrit Kaur to see Q. and try to influence her in helping bounce me). He then asked for the release of Jai Prakash Narain, whose wife is apparently one of his followers ('adopted daughter', he called her). I did not commit

[1] Sir Walter Monckton (later Viscount Monckton of Brenchley) was legal adviser to the Nizam of Hyderabad.

[2] Berar was a tract of country that had once formed part of the Nizam's dominions, but its administration had been taken over by the British in 1853 as part of a financial settlement, and in 1902 it was leased in perpetuity to the Government of India.

myself, though I expect we shall have to release him shortly. Gandhi then started on the I.N.A. and I told him exactly what the I.N.A. were—the weaklings and cowards of those captured in Malaya—and what folly it had been for Congress to make heroes of such men and to neglect those who had remained true in spite of starvation, ill-treatment and torture. When we parted I gave him a warning that the threat of mass movement by Congress was a dangerous weapon, there were still a great many thousand British soldiers in India, who did not subscribe to his doctrine of non-violence, and might be very violent if British lives or property suffered. He took this with a grin; and was very friendly throughout.

Cripps has produced a scheme with alternatives A and B. A is a grouping into three blocks—the Hindu Provinces, the Muslim Provinces, and the States, with a Federal Centre on which all three blocks will be equally represented; B is a truncated Pakistan. We are going to discuss it tomorrow.[1]

April 10

We discussed Cripps' paper and our future tactics in trying to bring about a settlement. After $2\frac{1}{2}$ hours quite useful discussion, we decided provisionally to see Jinnah early next week and put the two alternatives in Cripps' paper to him; and to see Congress and make it clear to them that paramountcy would not be handed over to them, and that any Interim Government would be on the present Constitution; and also to obtain their views on the Constitution Making Body. It was agreed that the original discussions on the composition of the Interim Government should be between Congress and myself, not the whole Delegation.

It was also decided to put out a Press note to state that we were getting on with the job; and to draft a telegram to the Cabinet stating Cripps' alternatives. I wanted to see C.-in-C. and ask him about the possible effect of the proposals on the I.A., but he was laid up, so I sent P.S.V. to see him. He agreed generally with the line we were taking.

Saw Maharaj Singh and the Indian Christians in the afternoon who produced nothing new, and then had a longish meeting of Council. We decided to release Jai Prakash Narain, which will make the S. of S. happy and encourage Gandhi to ask for more.

April 11

We began the morning with a Delegation discussion on the telegram home and Press statement. I had complained that at previous meetings drafts were placed in front of me at the opening of the meeting which

---

[1] The alternatives are given in a somewhat fuller form in the 'brief for interview with Mr. Jinnah', see p. 245.

I had had no time to consider, and requested that I should have plenty of time to consider the drafts before the meeting. The Press statement was produced at the meeting itself.

Our interviews in the morning were a pure waste of time. Two members of the Indian Federation of Labour—a cheerful looking old girl called Maniben Kara, and Karnik the Secretary, a little clerk type anxious to please, were interviewed for no other reason, I imagine, than that the representatives of a Labour Government could say that they had seen the representatives of Indian labour. The total membership of the Federation is, at the Secretary's optimistic estimate, about 400,000, and they have no political influence. They proposed that the Central Executive should be handed over to them, or at least that their programme of social reform should be enforced on it; and that immediate fresh elections should be held on the basis of adult franchise. They did not expect this to be taken seriously, did not take it seriously themselves, nor did anyone else. The S. of S. delivered a little lecture on adult franchise and we parted with mutual smiles.

Mrs. Hansa Mehta, President of the All-India Women's conference, about 25,000 members, said that the sooner the British gave India independence and cleared out, the better; but she said it quite politely. The S. of S., as a protagonist of Women's rights, was interested, and another half-hour or so was wasted.

Then came Jayakar, who delivered an hour's speech for the prosecution of the Muslim League, precisely as a lawyer speaking to a brief. It was well delivered, laboured the obvious, contained nothing new, and ended with a recommendation of the scheme of the Sapru Committee, and for the removal of separate electorates. He never paused for the whole hour, and the S. of S. closed his eyes to hear better. I thought it a sorry exhibition of the partisan spirit by one who likes to be considered as an elder statesman of India; there was no atom of compromise in it or recognition that the other side had a case. Jayakar really provided as good an argument for Jinnah's attitude as I have heard.

Finally came K. S. Roy[1] from Bengal, a typical heavy widespread Bengali, with an expansive jowl. He had little to say, except that Bengal should be increased by adding to it the districts of Manbhum and Singbhum from Bihar, and Sylhet, Cachar and Goalpara from Assam! Pakistan was nonsense, of course.

Cripps told me this morning that the younger members of both Congress and Muslim League had got together and brought a joint scheme to

[1] Leader of the Congress in the Bengal Legislature.

Cripps in great secrecy, which he thought might produce a solution acceptable to both sides. I don't like this kind of secret negotiation, but I can't do anything about it.

April 12

Sarat Chandra Bose was the first visitor. A stupid man, with an egg-shaped head, he put forward the usual Congress propaganda, no Pakistan, strong Centre, and the Muslims will come to heel all right.

Griffiths, leader of the European Group was good, and talked very sensibly for over an hour. He said nothing very original but put the general situation and the European case clearly and well.

Hossain Imam, League leader in the Council of State, was more French in appearance and gesture than any Indian I have met previously; he had a little imperial on his chin and moustaches à la Napoleon III and gesticulated like a Frenchman. He merely repeated Muslim League Propaganda, and was a striking example of the precept that you can't argue with a state of mind.

Last came Kunzru, clear and logical and moderate, but with nothing fresh to say. (I should be quite glad to have Kunzru in the Executive, as Foreign Minister or War Member, but I am afraid Congress would think him too moderate.)

April 13

A comparatively quiet day. We met in the morning to consider the brief for Jinnah on Tuesday. Then I had a Committee of Council on food; we decided to try and persuade Congress High Command to instruct the new Ministries not to take independent action about prices for the present. I said I would get into touch with them.

In the evening the First Lord came to dinner, and then sat down at the piano and played and sang for a couple of hours, he has an endless repertoire.

April 15

A quiet Sunday, and I managed to cope with some arrears of private business. I sent to Washington a personal message to the President, asking for an assurance that the promised supplies of food for India were not being reduced.

I do not think our official talks of the last fortnight have got us very far; in fact from my point of view they have mostly been waste of time. The Congress and League briefs have been repeated by a variety of persons—

cleverly or stupidly; clearly or obscurely; with conviction or without conviction; often at great length, very seldom succinctly. Congress has not abated one tittle of its 'democratic' claims as a majority, Jinnah has not conceded an acre of Pakistan. No Hindu has said a word to suggest that the Muslims have a case, no Muslim has admitted the possibility of fair treatment by a Hindu. The Princes and their diwans have been by far the most businesslike, the most sensible and the most lucid. On the surface the omens are not good, but there has been a great deal of talk going on behind the scenes, and Cripps and his minions (Wyatt and Short)[1] have been working hard, to what effect I have no idea; but Cripps seems satisfied. And we have got a paper by Cripps which gives a basis for negotiation. Perhaps it will turn out all right, but I do not think that any settlement we get will be a good one or a lasting one.

We saw the representatives of the Zamindars this morning—Darbhanga, Parlakimedi, Burdwan, Vizianagram, and Nawab Sir Muhammad Yusuf. They began by stating that they had selected Darbhanga to be their spokesman; but he hardly got in half-a-dozen sentences in the whole hour the interview lasted. Yusuf, whom I had met in Lucknow last December, would not stop talking, and Vizianagram was nearly as bad. At one time all except Darbhanga the spokesman were speaking together. And they had nothing to say, except that they had always been loyal to the British and now wanted protection, or at any rate plenty of representation on the C.M.B.

After they had gone, we had an hour's rather rambling discussion on the line to take with Jinnah tomorrow and with Azad on Wednesday.

In the brief for the interview with Jinnah it was stated that the full claim for Pakistan had no chance of acceptance but that progress might be possible in one of the following two ways.

(1) *Agreement might perhaps be reached on a separate sovereign State of Pakistan consisting of Sind, the N.W.F.P., the Muslim majority districts of the Punjab, except perhaps Gurdaspur, the Muslim majority areas of Bengal, and the Sylhet district of Assam. Whether there would be any chance of agreement on Calcutta being a free port was doubtful. Its inclusion in Pakistan could not be justified on any principle of self-determination.*

(2) *The most promising alternative would be for the Congress and the League*

---

[1] Major Woodrow Wyatt, M.P., who had been a member of the Parliamentary Delegation, and Major J. McL. (Billy) Short, a retired officer of the Indian Army, who had a great knowledge of the Sikhs and was in close touch with their leaders. Cripps had brought them out with him from England as assistants.

to try to evolve an agreed scheme for an Indian Union. If the League accepted a Union Centre to control only essential subjects (say, as a minimum, Defence, Foreign Affairs, and Communications) it might be possible to include in one Federation the whole of the Provinces of Sind, Baluchistan, N.W.F.P., the Punjab, and Bengal (plus perhaps Sylhet), while the Hindu Provinces would form another Federation. In such a Union the Muslim and Hindu Federations might have equal representation.

Wavell sometimes refers to this alternative as the 3-tier solution.

April 16

Before the interview with Jinnah we had 20 minutes Press photography, sitting round a table and very obviously not talking business, I thought. I dislike this modern craze for publicity.

The critical interview with Jinnah went about as badly as it could, I thought. I told the S. of S. before it started that I thought he ought to be tough with his approach to Jinnah and make him see clearly that what was being put to him was the best offer he could possibly hope for. S. of S. snubbed me and said he was convinced that the velvet glove was essential. He began with ten minutes rambling platitudes, would-be sympathetic stuff, about the 'welfare of the world', 'advancement of India's interests', etc., which had not the slightest effect on Jinnah, who listened without any sign of interest till S. of S. got down to the brief paper and the alternative solutions suggested. Then J. started taking notes. Once he had grasped the two offers, he merely repeated all his old arguments, maintained that any form of Union or unity was impossible in India, and re-iterated his claim to all 6 Provinces and complete sovereignty. At the end of nearly two hours we had made no progress whatever. Obviously J.'s intention is to drive us into an award and to hope we shall remain in India to enforce it. At the end he said that if Congress admitted the principle of Pakistan he was prepared to discuss its boundaries. No advance at all in fact. I said nothing during the whole discussion, except to ask Jinnah, when he was holding forth about 'unity', what sort of unity he expected in his Pakistan. I expect it is pure conceit on my part, but I believe I could have got Jinnah to move further or at least could have put him firmly up against the alternatives and left him under no illusions that he could expect a better offer. But that would have been too direct and brutal for these politicians. Cripps was rather hankering after going off to see Jinnah and getting him to himself this evening. I don't think he approves of S. of S.'s methods or of mine, but hoped that a lawyer-to-lawyer approach would be successful.

In the afternoon I saw Patel on the food question. He was quite friendly, promised full co-operation, said he would see that Pant came into line, and that a meeting of Premiers or reference to Azad was unnecessary.

April 17

We had a morning meeting of the Delegation, to discuss the method of conducting the interview with Azad. We also had some talk on the Punjab wheat levy, the possible content of a treaty with India, and the proposed arrest of Aung San in Burma. I did not much like the proposed brief for Azad, so I dictated after the meeting a suggested brief. This was later accepted by the S. of S. but failed in the end to keep him on the lines.

> *In this brief it was proposed that Azad should be told that certain suggestions had been put to Jinnah for bridging the gap between the League and the Congress, but that until his reaction to them was known, the Delegation would prefer to say nothing further about them.*
> *There were, however, other matters to be discussed with Azad, e.g. the future of the Indian States—he was to be told that there would be no transfer of Paramountcy, and the formation of an Interim Government—it was to be made clear that this would have to function under the existing Constitution.*

The talk with Azad went badly, according to my ideas. S. of S. read out brief I had suggested without embellishment and I hoped he would stick to it. Azad asked result of talk with Jinnah and was told we could say nothing at present. On the States, he said nothing on the Paramountcy issue, but proposed that the Political Adviser should be an Indian.

Then Azad began on the powers of the Executive Council in the interim period and said they must be 'plenary' and that there must be no control by Viceroy or India Office. Now things began to go all wrong from my point of view. We had agreed in our preliminary conferences that we must stand firm on the question of maintaining the existing constitution during the interim period; but the S. of S. instead of saying so definitely embarked on his responsibility for the I.C.S. as a reason—the worst possible example; he then went rambling on about the files at the India Office (!) and the difficulty that would arise if they were not available (!) He was deplorably woolly, said that all could be arranged with goodwill, and used the phrase 'it takes time even to arrange terms of surrender for a beaten force'. The result was a long inconclusive argument, which ended by S. of S. leaving Azad to think that the matter was open to discussion and that we should probably give way. We then talked for a while on Federal and Union Centres and the constitutional variations possible— Cripps and Azad. I then had a talk with Azad myself about the Punjab wheat levy. He was prepared to help but obviously didn't like the idea of bringing too much pressure on the Punjab Government and risking its break-up.

From here I went straight to Council, and found them discussing this matter of the levy. P.S.V. had had another message from the Governor to say that he was sure that the Ministry would break up if we forced them to a levy; and the Council decided we could not do it.

I finished a long day by writing a note to the S. of S. to say that we must stand firm on the constitution in the interim period.

April 18

Began with a meeting with Cabinet Delegation. Cripps reported that his talk with Jinnah last night had been completely abortive. J. had refused to budge one inch in the direction of a common Centre, and had indicated that H.M.G. would have to make an award which would of course be abused by all parties but might possibly be accepted. Cripps had since seen Gandhi and told him that J. was immoveable. G. had said it was no use, he was sure, his meeting J., agreed that J. would not meet Azad, but told him that he might perhaps meet Nehru, though he was sure that it would lead to no result. Cripps and the other Ministers thought that there ought to be a meeting between Jinnah and Nehru, not with any hope of agreement but purely for publicity value, to show that we had done our best to secure agreement. I was rather doubtful of a meeting on such terms and thought it would do no good, but raised no objections if the others thought it necessary. I said that if Gandhi had been informed of the position, which would soon become public property, the Princes should be informed and that I thought I should see Bhopal and tell him of the progress, or rather lack of progress, of the talks. S. of S. objected, but Cripps and Alexander backed me. S. of S. then went on to the Interim Government, he did not mention my note to him, but had obviously been disturbed by it and tried to make out that he had been firm on the principle of the Constitution with Azad yesterday. I stated my views again very clearly and definitely, and said I did not think we should argue about it, merely stand firm. Alexander backed me and Cripps did up to a point but would, I think, give way to Congress if they threatened a breakdown; in fact I should never be surprised to learn that he had already promised Congress some satisfaction on this point, as he did in the 1942 negotiations.

After a good deal more talk, the following rough time table was agreed:

Delegation returns from Kashmir[1] morning April 24; we will have a meeting that afternoon; Nehru will meet Jinnah on April 25 for a 'Breakdown' talk; it will then take us about 4 days to draw up our award and another 4 days to obtain H.M.G.'s approval; we shall then see the leaders of Congress, Muslim League and Princes about May 2 and present them with the Plan.

Cripps produced at the table an outline of a proposed award, the others have read it, I think, but I have not had time yet.

So ends the Delegation's second round with political India, with no more progress made than in the first. It is clear that we shall have to make an award: and Cripps' paper is quite a good basis for an award. I and my staff will have to turn it over in the next few days and so no doubt will the Delegation. Whether when they come back we shall be able to produce anything acceptable is problematical. So far all the gifts of these Magi—the frankincense of goodwill, the myrrh of honeyed words, the gold of promises—have produced little. Indian politicians are not babes even if they do wear something like swaddling clothes.

April 21

The most peaceful week-end I have had for a long time with the Delegation off and the Easter holiday on.

The C.-in-C. came to see me in the evening. He thinks that Cripps' paper is a good basis for a settlement, or at least as good as we are likely to contrive. He says Asaf Ali expects to be War Member, God forbid, I have the lowest opinion of his character and abilities. We discussed Frontier policy in connection with the forthcoming Peshawar Conference, on which he was sensible; internal security—there is now a plan 'Madhouse' and another 'Bedlam' which allow for the I.A. becoming unreliable or hostile; and some other minor matters.

Today I received an invitation to go home for the Victory parade on June 8. I think it is unlikely that I shall be able to get away but I should like to be there.

April 22

Busy days again after a brief respite.

Master Tara Singh came and poured all the sorrows and apprehensions of the Sikhs once more out of the back of his throat through his thick grey

[1] The Delegation paid a visit to Kashmir simply in order to have a rest and get away from the extreme heat of Delhi.

beard into my ear where it arrived a bit muffled but I had heard it all so many times before that I could pretty well have said his piece myself. The Sikhs are naturally anxious at the possibilities of Pakistan or the division of the Punjab or even more of the Indian Army on which they are so dependent. But they are too scattered all over the Punjab to form a compact homeland of their own.

Hutchings told me of the Singapore Food Conference. Siam is full of rice but owing to the delays and muddlings of H.M.G. over the treaty, and terms and price, nothing has come out yet; Hoover[1] arrives here tomorrow and we must convince him of our plight. On stocks at present available or in sight, our whole system will break down in June or July. Hutchings is not quite convinced that we should not have insisted on a levy in the Punjab, but I am sure it would not have succeeded.

Then Thorne, Menon and George Abell discussed with me Cripps' draft. Subject to elucidation of certain points, we thought it made the best of a very difficult business, and none of us could suggest anything better, though Thorne does not think it will be accepted by either party.

Meanwhile to work on the Honours list, always a tiresome and rather depressing business.

April 23

Bhopal came at 12.30 and stopped to lunch. He was obviously quite well informed of what had been taking place; he had flown Nehru back from Bhopal this morning. He said that the Princes would do their best to help in a solution and would support one which appeared reasonable. Nehru had indicated to him that they would wish to put an Indian Politician in charge of the Political Department but he had told Nehru quite definitely that the Princes would not accept this. If the political parties were as practical as the Princes, we should get along much better.

Meanwhile the Hoover Mission turned up, 7 or 8 of them. After lunch they had a conference with the Food officials, which I gather went quite well; and then I had a talk with Hoover. He is not a forthcoming type, and I think I can understand his failure as President, apart from his bad luck in being in office at the time of the great slump. But he is obviously a fine character and a very capable man. He likened himself to the retired family doctor called back for consultation, but six months too late. I thought it would be a good thing for him to see the party leaders; and Gandhi and Nehru are coming to see him tomorrow. Jinnah refused, but

---

[1] Ex-President of the U.S.A., Chairman of President Truman's Famine Emergency Committee.

said that if Hoover came down to his office, he might fit in a few minutes for him between other engagements! Manners were never Jinnah's strong suit, but it is surprising that he should antagonise an important American in this way.

April 24

Hoover left for Bombay, after seeing Gandhi and Nehru, he did not seem particularly interested in either of them and is obviously aloof from politics. He seemed to think India had done all she could about food and that he could help us. He will hear plenty more about our needs at Bombay and Bangalore.

I then had nearly two hours with the Delegation returned from Kashmir. The reason for the new suggestion of a solution which was cabled from Kashmir was that Cripps had heard from Nehru before they left that the Congress Working Committee would not accept a solution on the lines of his proposal which he left behind; and this new line[1] was suggested by some Muslim Leaguer from the Punjab. I dislike all this hole-and-corner private negotiation of Cripps, and I am sure that he both gets led down the garden path and gives away points. I do not believe in this kind of negotiation and am quite sure we should have done better, and still will do, if we make a plan and stick to it. But these people won't do that, they put their suggestions to one side or the other, who turn them down and hope for something better; they are very bad poker players. We finally decided that Cripps should put the Kashmir proposal to Jinnah privately this evening; and that if he rejected it we should tell him officially at a meeting with the whole Delegation that we could do no more for him and should have to negotiate the best terms for the Muslims that we could get from Congress. The fact is that all this goodwill and pussy-footing has got us nowhere except into a more difficult position, and we should have done much better to be stiffer and more determined from the first.

April 25

The first official business which reached me this morning was a telegraphic summary of the disastrous report of the Palestine Commission. The Americans seem to have insisted on the Jewish point of view being accepted, which will ruin our policy and prestige all over the Middle East, but will do nothing to help us. We seem to have lost the will and courage

---

[1] Since this new solution was not acceptable either to Jinnah or the Congress, it was dropped and its details are not important. It envisaged a complicated system of voting which would probably have resulted in a truncated Punjab similar to what was ultimately agreed to.

to support our own point of view. The results here will be bad and will harden the Muslims in favour of Pakistan. A bad business.

Nearly two hours this morning with the Cabinet Delegation. Cripps found Jinnah most unreceptive, he said he had said all that he had to say and now it was up to us to take our decision. Finally he agreed to put the new proposal to his Working Committee, if the Congress accepted it. I stated my objections both to this form of negotiation and to the proposal itself, which would mean about two months delay and would increase communal tension. But I agreed eventually that since Jinnah had given provisional, very provisional, acceptance, it must now be put to Congress, and it was agreed that Cripps should do so at once. We then had a longish discussion on whether and how we should make an award, what we should do if it was refused and how we should meet a complete break-down. We then discussed Cripps' pre-Kashmir paper and how far we could modify it. The fact is that the Delegation's methods of appeasement and negotiation have completely failed. My blunter and more direct proposals could anyway have had no worse fate.

Shortly before lunch Cripps rang me up to say that Nehru had turned down the new proposal flat. So that's that. The sands are running out and we are no nearer a solution. I drafted a new pre-amble to the draft of an award which Cripps is preparing, and we shall meet tomorrow to consider it.[1]

April 26

Two hours with Delegation in morning. Cripps had seen Jinnah again, and said he had got him to agree provisionally to the '3-tier' Constitution as a basis of negotiation if Congress would. We decided, myself rather reluctantly, that Cripps should put this proposition to Congress, he was seeing Azad before lunch and Gandhi in the evening. We then discussed various types of Constituent Assemblies and Constitutions. This was interrupted by a report that Azad had resigned the Presidentship of Congress and that Nehru had been elected in his stead (it turned out later that he had merely said that he would not stand for re-election on May 17 and recommended Nehru as his successor).

Before lunch Corfield came in and told me that Bilaspur has reported to him on the meeting of the Standing Committee of the Chamber yesterday. Apparently Bhopal had told them that it would help me, and that I had said so, if they recommended the appointment of an Indian as

---

[1] This redraft of the preamble was accepted at the morning meeting of the Delegation on 26 April.

Political Adviser in the interim period! Really the tortuous ways of Bhopal are beyond me.

In the afternoon another meeting with the Delegation. Azad had proposed to Cripps a meeting of 4 from Congress, 4 from the Muslim League to meet Delegation and negotiate on the 3-tier solution—our breakdown award in fact—but not in Delhi, as he could stand the heat no longer. We agreed that Cripps might try this on Jinnah. I said that if Jinnah did not accept the negotiation idea, we should stop all this to-ing and fro-ing by Cripps, and get down to an award. Alexander approved I think, but the S. of S. did not.

April 27

Another discussion with Delegation this morning. Cripps had had another talk with Jinnah who had at first taken up the odd attitude that everything he had said previously had been his personal opinion and not necessarily that of the League. He had eventually agreed to put to the Muslim League the 3-tier proposal as a basis for negotiation. We accordingly drafted a letter to be sent to Azad and Jinnah, asking them to delegate four persons each to meet the Cabinet Delegation at Simla for negotiations on a 3-tier basis. Cripps was anxious to show the draft letter to Azad before it was sent, but I re-acted firmly, and said I thought we had had enough of this private negotiation. I have a suspicion that Cripps does not put quite the same proposition to Azad and to Jinnah, or at least he puts it in such a way that each thinks he is getting a different proposal, more favourable to himself; and I think it is time that we got things on a paper and official basis rather than on an oral and unofficial one. We then discussed the formation of the Interim Government for a while, the S. of S. being against any negotiation till we had a settlement of the main issue, I insisting that we should not waste time; Cripps and Alexander supported me.

We agreed that we must carry on with drafting our breakdown award; and S. of S. informed us, rather to my consternation, that he was drafting the whole document personally: from previous experience I consider him a weak, woolly and wordy drafter. However, we shall see.

April 28

A short meeting in the morning with the Delegation to consider Azad's answer, which rather tends to confirm my suspicion that Cripps has been saying slightly different things to different people. We had no difficulty in replying to Azad.

Azad, in replying to the invitation to send negotiators to Simla, had objected to the three-tier proposal on the ground that it was wrong to form Groups of Provinces on a religious or communal basis and to weaken the Union by the creation of sub-federations. In reply the Delegation informed him that acceptance of the invitation would not be taken to imply full approval of the proposals that had been put forward. They were a possible basis for a settlement which Congress and the League were being invited to discuss.

In the evening S. of S. draft began to come in—woolly, except where he has followed Cripps' draft or mine.

April 29

Two drafting meetings with the Delegation, morning and afternoon. We rather tore to pieces S. of S. draft, dismissed the operative part as much too vague, and agreed to discuss a new draft of Cripps tomorrow. S. of S. sat mostly in rather pained silence.

Meanwhile both parties have accepted the invitation to meet at Simla, though both maintain their position and are still poles and poles apart, and have both interpreted the basis quite differently. Still it is something of a success for the Delegation to have got them to meet. It would be quite unwarranted vanity on my part to reflect that I got them to Simla in a week last year, and it has taken the Delegation more than four weeks.

There was some trouble over the original letter to Azad, who apparently showed a lack of frankness with his Working Committee and did not show it to them, and then wanted a different letter sent which he could show them. I don't quite know how or whether it got straightened out, Congress are by no means a united body.

We decided to let the Princes and Governors know how matters were going.

April 30

Two and a half hours with the Delegation this morning on the draft of the breakdown award and various constitutional devices and formulae. We have got a very long way to go yet.

I had a short meeting of Council in the evening to acquaint them with the progress of negotiations. They were naturally concerned chiefly with their own future, and when they were likely to be replaced by a new Government, and what notice they would get. Then I had a talk with C.-in-C. about new I.N.A. trials and a letter that he had received from Nehru about them.

11

THE MISSION'S PROPOSALS

May 2

We came up to Simla yesterday and had a quiet afternoon. Jinnah is not coming up till Saturday, so we cannot have the first conference till Sunday. This is typical of Jinnah's manners, he originally said he would not come till Sunday, and the Delegation had to ask him to hasten his arrival. But it is a good thing that he did not come up at once; we have a lot to do still before we are ready for the Conference, as our meeting this evening showed. Alexander is not well, and was not at it. S. of S. and Cripps seemed to me to be set on avoiding all the awkward fences and proceeding on lines of indefinite discussion; I said that we really must get down to business, have a definite agenda and face our fences at last. I am sure that both parties really want us to do something definite and make a decision, and are tired of all this endless discussion.

Nehru said as much when I saw him today mainly about some INA trials, about which the C.-in-C. had asked me to speak to him. He said he considered that the last month had been entirely wasted, instead of things becoming more clear-cut and definite they were getting vaguer and more nebulous. All the facts and the attitudes of the parties concerned had been known long ago, nothing fresh had come out, and time was being wasted.

I told him that the INA cases, about which he had written to the C.-in-C., would be dropped, but asked him not to make public that he had written to the C.-in-C. and sought to influence him. He promised not to do so.

I also said that I thought it was an act of folly on the part of the political parties to have glorified the INA men, who were for the most part the weaklings and softlings of the prisoners of war and had joined to obtain better treatment or to avoid hardship. The real heroes were the 45,000 men who had remained staunch, in spite of starvation, ill-treatment, and torture; 15,000 of them had perished as a result of this, while the casualties of the INA had been relatively small, and they had done little real fighting.

Nehru listened quite quietly and said he realised that some of the INA men had not joined from the best of motives and were not the best type of men, but he had met many of them who were of a good type.

He was very friendly and is undoubtedly an attractive character.

May 3

Conference on procedure at first meeting with Congress and League. S. of S. wanted to address it on long and woolly lines; and Cripps tried to find some non-controversial, even if irrelevant issue on which friendly relations might be established. I insisted, perhaps a little brusquely, that we must really get down to business.

After lunch the Delegation gave general approval to my proposed method of trying to form a new Council.

Wavell proposed to see the Congress representatives first and to inform them that the new Council (Interim Government) would be entirely Indian, except for the Viceroy, and would function under the existing Constitution. He had in view a Council of twelve consisting of five Congress (including one Scheduled Caste), five Muslim League, one Sikh, and one Anglo-Indian or non-League Muslim.

Bhopal wants to come up with some representatives of the States and sit in at the discussions. We agreed that he should come up but that we could not let him sit in at the discussions at present.

May 4

Three long meetings of the Delegation. We began in the morning by passing my draft as a basis for the S. of S. opening speech, it is short and business like but I am sure the S. of S. will expand it into something discursive and rather nebulous. We then seemed to have finished, and the three Cabinet Ministers were prepared to break up; but I insisted on getting down to the details of how we were going to issue our 'award', if we have to make it as we almost certainly shall. Cripps was all for still trying to haggle with the Parties over it, but I said very firmly that the whole essence of an award was that it was something we meant to stick to, and that it would be quite fatal to begin the whole process of bargaining over again. Alexander backed me, the S. of S. agreed a little reluctantly, and Cripps most reluctantly (I suspect he will give his Congress friends advance notice all the same). Then I raised the mechanics of the move: timing, publicity at home and abroad, announcement in House of Commons, broadcasts, printing, etc. Just as well that I did, they hadn't thought of it at all, and it will be a most complicated business; and none too much time to arrange it. I secured that we should send Governors at once an outline of the proposed award and get their re-actions as soon as possible. We also agreed to consult the C.-in-C. We decided to return to Delhi before issuing the award, I said this was essential from my point of view. Provisionally we thought we might return to Delhi on the 13th and issue the award on the 15th or 16th. I think the Delegation was a little sobered to realise how much had to be done in the way of staff work before they could get out the plan.

After the rest of the Delegation had gone, the S. of S. suggested that I might require some additional staff, also that Corfield had not impressed them as Political Adviser. I suspected the hand of Cripps in this and said so. S. of S. admitted that Cripps had criticised Corfield as re-actionary, apparently because he had, quite naturally and rightly, refused to discuss behind the back of the Princes the amalgamation of the Orissa States with Orissa Province with Mahatab, the Premier of Orissa, whom Cripps had sent to him. I suspect the idea of extra staff is his too. His activities in the wings are too often mischievous, I wish he would confine himself to drafting which he does admirably. I wonder whether some of his Congress friends have complained that the I.C.S. influence me too much.

In the afternoon we discussed the award which Cripps had drawn up with Rau and Menon. It is ingenious and probably about the best we can do but there are some obvious snags. After two hours on it we broke off to let Cripps draft it in a revised form, to be telegraphed to the Cabinet, which we would discuss after dinner. After another two hours beginning at 10 p.m. we ran aground about midnight over the question of a final arbitration Court, to decide matters on which there was not the requisite two-thirds majority in the final Constituent Assembly. No one could see how to get afloat again, and we were all tired, so we decided to sleep on it.

May 5

My 63rd birthday, is it auspicious or not that we begin the critical negotiations on it? We have not made too bad a beginning, rather better than I expected. Jinnah began by refusing to shake hands with Azad, who was obviously annoyed. Then we settled the hours of sitting: 11.30–1.30, 4–6.

Azad began by asking was the basis of the discussions the independence of India, and was re-assured. Azad and Jinnah then asked that their letters of acceptance, in which they laid down their respective reservations, should be read. This was done. We then decided to start on the composition of the Union, instead of on the Groups, as we had proposed, since Congress wanted it so, and Jinnah agreed. The first point of controversy arose over the financial powers of the Union Centre, Congress wishing it to have powers of direct taxation and to be self-supporting, while Jinnah advocated that it should be given a lump sum and should have to go to the Groups if it wanted any more. Jinnah's method was obviously an unpractical one and he did not argue very convincingly on it. We then went on to the question of a Central Legislature; again, Congress of course wanted one and Jinnah did not, but his arguments were even weaker and more unconvincing. He was certainly not at his best. We broke off the morning session here. The Delegation was I think a little unduly optimistic at the result; but it certainly might have been much worse.

We held a short meeting before the afternoon session, as I wanted to get our tactics clear. When the Conference met, S. of S. tried to corner Jinnah on the matter of a Legislature and to make him admit that there must be one at the Centre. J. stonewalled obstinately but produced no good arguments. We therefore went on to the composition of a Central Legislature on the assumption that there was one; and eventually got J. to admit that parity of representatives from the two British India groups would be 'the least objectionable'. We then spent some time discussing the manner in which the States might join a Union Legislature. Finally it seemed to be generally agreed—at least J. did not dissent—that a Central Judiciary would be necessary. That ended the session.

In the evening I had a talk with C.-in-C. He approves of our 'award' scheme, and thinks it will not upset the Army in any way. We discussed the question of getting the award understood by the Army so that it would not be stampeded by a hostile Press.

May 6

A long discouraging day. We had two hours discussion in the Delegation, 9.30–11.30, before the Session, mainly about the timing of publicity. Just before the session began, we had a letter from Azad, to say in uncompromising terms that Congress entirely disapproved of all that had taken place the day before and that the only issue was the immediate independence of India and the withdrawal of the British.

At the Conference Azad did not raise this, though he had brought copies of the letter and was obviously prepared to do so. We did not refer to it. We discussed the Group organisation, which of course Congress condemned and Jinnah supported. J. was better and clearer than on the day before. We finally got down to an announcement by J. that he would accept the Union Centre if Congress would accept Groups. Nehru said something very near acceptance of J.'s proposition, and Patel's face of cold angry disapproval was a study. The session ended here. They face us as follows from left to right: Ghaffar Khan,[1] large, rugged, bearded,

---

[1] Khan Abdul Ghaffar Khan, brother of Dr. Khan Sahib, the most prominent Congress leader in the N.W.F.P., popularly known as the 'Frontier Gandhi'.

obviously hostile, silent, in rough Khadi which he wraps over his head at times, a stupid but obstinate man: Patel, also in Khadi, but wearing it more like a Roman toga and with rather a Roman face, powerful, clever, uncompromising, very seldom speaking but listening with obvious disapproval: then Azad, looking rather worried, occasionally getting up and standing behind his chair; then Nehru who does all the talking for Congress, able and clear in statement and reasonable, except for occasional bursts about the struggle for freedom and the rights of India. On the League side, there is Liaquat, solid, pleasant, speaking only occasionally, to echo Jinnah, but quiet and reasonable: Jinnah himself, dapper in European clothes which Liaquat also wears: Ismail Khan, small with rather a monkey face but may be clever, he occasionally interjects a remark: and Nishtar, biggish, dark, may be quite capable, silent.

We had an hour with the Delegation after lunch, first the C-in-C came in and gave us his picture, reassuring on the whole about the state of the Army; and then a short discussion on how to handle the afternoon Conference, on the Constitution Making Machinery.

This went much as expected, but Jinnah did agree to a single C.M.B. meeting as one to begin with and then splitting into groups. The final incident of the session was the discussion of a point which Jinnah had raised at the end of yesterday's session after I had left the room, whether there would be any provision for the revision of the Constitution after a fixed period of years. It had not been discussed then and was raised now. At one moment Jinnah seemed to claim the right of a Group to secede after 5 years; and Patel exclaimed triumphantly 'there we have it now, what he has been after all the time'. We finally got it down to an agreement that there would be some provision, arranged by the C.M.B., for the possibility of revising the Constitution, either at fixed periods or by the desire of a certain proportion. But the damage had been done in Patel's mind, and he had been given a handle for his contention that the League are not really in earnest about entering a Union and mean to get out as soon as possible.

Immediately after the conference I had a talk with Azad and Nehru over the possibility of a railway strike about which he had written to me. I told him it was easy enough to buy off the railwaymen temporarily, but would leave a legacy of great embarrassment for a new Government.

We had decided early in the afternoon that it would be a good thing to see Gandhi at once and enlist his support for the proposed solution, as Cripps was confident he could do. For some reason the Delegation wished him to be asked merely to see the Viceroy, and they would drop

in later, which is all rather in a line with their methods of indirect approach.
It was G.'s day of silence which he could not break till 7.50 p.m. He came
at 7.30 p.m. and I spoke a monologue for 15 minutes or so, telling him
generally how things were going. Then the Delegation came in, just as his
silence was up, and the S. of S. and Cripps started their explanations and
blandishments. The result was a shock to them. G., who had been living
with Ghaffar Khan and Patel, the two malcontents, had adopted entirely
their point of view, said the proposed solution was 'worse than Pakistan',
and he could not recommend it to Congress; we must either adopt
entirely the Congress point of view, if we thought it just, or Jinnah's
point of view if we thought it juster; but there was no half-way house. G.
seemed quite unmoved at the prospect of civil war, I think he had adopted
Patel's thesis that if we are firm the Muslims will not fight. Though
Cripps and S. of S. kept at G. for an hour, till 9 p.m. they quite failed
to move him.

So to a waiting dinner party.

May 7

Spent most of day on drafts—10–12 in morning, 2.30–4.30 and 6–7 in
afternoon—a wearisome business, as it was mostly technical matter on
Constitutional arrangements. At 12 I saw C-in-C and told him how far
we had got, he thought that what we were doing was on right lines and
would be accepted by the Army.

At 7 p.m. I had over an hour and a half with Jinnah, to see how far
I could get him towards agreement on the proposals we intended to put
to the Parties tomorrow. It was not very far. He was friendly but showed
his deep and utter mistrust of Congress and all their works. He is convinced of their intention to split the Muslims and secure Hindu domination, and instanced their bringing two Muslims, Azad and Ghaffar Khan,
to the Conference. I put to him very strongly the results of a failure to
secure agreement, especially the splitting of the Indian Army and the
probable partition of the Punjab. He said finally that we must do what
we think just and fair, but must not press him too hard. He ended with
thanks for stopping the I.N.A. trials but a plea for the release of those
convicted.

Meanwhile Cripps had been seeing Gandhi, and came down triumphant
to say that he had secured G.'s full approval of our outline proposals, and
that G. had suggested that we send them with a letter to both Parties and
postpone our meeting for 24 hours. This S. of S. proposes to do. I went to
bed unhappy all the same. I sympathise with the Muslims rather than

with Congress, and I am not convinced that our document is quite fair to them. Also I had a message just before going to bed that Menon and Rau had said the proposals were unworkable. Also I do not quite trust Cripps and wholly mistrust Gandhi, and would back the latter every time to outsmart C., clever man though C. is. I am not at all persuaded that C. had led G. up to the altar, I believe it is more likely that G. has led C. down the garden path.

May 8 (I have 45 years service today)
Such a day. I began at 9 a.m. with Azad and Nehru on the Interim Executive Council (they want to call it something else, the National Government, I said I had not the slightest objection, if so doing did not invalidate its proceedings). Rather to my surprise they did not raise the issue of the Viceroy's veto, but said that the Government ought to be responsible to the Assembly. I said that it was impossible to make it so by act of law, but that there was nothing whatever to prevent them resigning if they were defeated in the Assembly on a major issue. They then raised the question of nominated members, I said that the official nominated members were supposed to vote with the Government, or could be directed by the Government to abstain from voting. This seemed rather a new idea to them. I told them that the non-official nominations were usually discussed by the G–G with Governors who would naturally consult their Ministers. We then discussed portfolios, the composition and the method of arriving at a list of names quite amicably. On the whole this talk went reasonably well.

At 11 a.m. I saw Vallabhai Patel. He was to begin with uncompromisingly hostile to any settlement except on the basis of complete Hindu supremacy; and said that they were bound to have it out with the Muslims sooner or later, and that it was better to have a conflict now and get it over. I pointed out to him as strongly as I could what the results would be of plunging India into chaos at this time, and that surely it was a bankrupt policy to precipitate civil war when it might be averted by commonsense. I have no idea whether I shook him at all (Cripps told me later that his information was that V.P. was a bit shaken), but he was quite polite and friendly. But his nature is fascist and he is always likely to be on the side of direct action and if necessary violence.

At 12 I saw Corfield and discussed the Princes representation which is going to be a complicated business. He says Bhopal has lost the confidence of the smaller States—and I don't think he ever had that of the larger ones like Hyderabad and Kashmir.

After lunch I saw Bhopal who seemed worried, and gave him a copy of the draft agreement we have put to the parties.

At 6 p.m. more drafting. We have got into a muddle over method of representation in the Constituent Assembly by election from Provincial Assemblies. The natural method of proportional representation of parties does not work owing to the weightage[1] which the Communal award of the 1935 Act gives to minorities.

Just before dinner, Cripps received a letter from Gandhi saying in effect that the draft proposals for settlement, of which Cripps had claimed that he accepted every word last night, were unacceptable in several respects; while S. of S. received a letter from Jinnah to the effect that he never had agreed to anything which was in the document and could not agree to it. These letters are no surprise at all to me, it simply means that the political leaders are running true to form and are quite incapable of statesmanship of any kind. We held a meeting in Cripps' room after dinner; and decided that Cripps should see Azad and that I should see Jinnah tomorrow morning, and see whether we can move them at all. But we shall not. Simla Conference history will repeat itself.

May 9

A critical day with a dramatic dénouement. We began by passing an answer from S. of S. to Jinnah. Then there was an almost heated argument between S. of S. and myself over the method of electing representatives to the Constituent Assembly, so as to get over the injustice to the Muslims in their majority Provinces owing to the weightage to minorities in the Communal award. The S. of S. was all for accepting the weightage, arguing that anything else would antagonise Congress, I argued strongly that the population basis must be taken into account as the fairest and, I contended, the most 'democratic' method (it is not often that I introduce democracy as an argument!). Alexander supported me but S. of S. was unconvinced until Cripps came in from seeing Azad and supported me. He said Azad had raised strong objections to certain features of the proposal, especially to parity at the Centre and to pre-determined Groups, but had not been unreasonable.

At 10 a.m. Bhopal turned up with a formidable looking typewritten document from which he asked questions, sensibly and to the point. The

---

[1] Under a system of 'reservation' and 'weightage', a fixed proportion of seats was reserved for each community, but 'weightage' gave the minorities more seats than they would have been entitled to on a numerical basis. This meant that in Provinces like Bengal and the Punjab, where the Muslims were numerically only in a small majority, this majority was further reduced in the Provincial Assemblies by 'weightage'.

Princes are naturally anxious that we are committing them by our negotiations without fully consulting them, and there is much force in their contention. We did what we could to reassure him.

At 12 I had three-quarters of an hour with Jinnah. He has been much more reasonable, easier to talk with, and more likeable in the interviews I have had with him lately. He was quite helpful over several points we discussed—grouping of Provinces, meeting of Constituent Assembly, etc.

At 3 p.m. the Delegation met again to hear my report on the talks with Jinnah and to decide on our tactics at the Conference this evening. Since these seemed rather indeterminate and woolly, I offered to dictate a brief, and did so in about 10 minutes, a quick bit of work and not a bad one. The Delegation approved it, practically without alteration.

In this brief the points of agreement and of disagreement between Congress and the League in regard to the draft proposals were listed and it was suggested that the Secretary of State should put these before the parties and then propose that the points of disagreement should be discussed with each party in turn with a view to seeing how they could be resolved.

At the Conference at 5 p.m., S. of S. spoke on my draft, giving the points of agreement but not of disagreement. After a short discussion Nehru made the proposal on behalf of Congress that Congress and League Delegations should meet with an umpire to settle points of difference, whose decision would be accepted as final. Jinnah replied that he would be pleased to meet any *Hindu* representatives of Congress. There was a pregnant silence for a minute or so; and then Nehru suggested that he and Jinnah should meet there and then and see whether they could decide on an umpire.[1] We adjourned for 40 minutes and most of us strolled about the lawns to the obvious curiosity of some Press men while N. and J. talked. When they came back, they merely proposed that the Conference should adjourn for 48 hours, till 3 p.m. Saturday while they had further talks. This was agreed.

I had a talk with Evan Jenkins and he stopped to dinner. He was in good heart, but said the Punjab was in an inflammable state, and he could get little work out of his Ministers.

So the Conference has a death-bed reprieve, but is still on the danger-list.

May 10

Spent a good deal of the day (10–12.30; 6–7) drafting our breakdown award. It is curious what a lot of snags there are in making out these

[1] The official record says that Jinnah agreed only to sit with Nehru and 'consider whether this proposal could be accepted, and if so, who the umpire should be'.

constitutional proposals, especially when one has to steer between the Scylla of Congress and Charybdis of Jinnah. We are not nearly ready yet. Cripps, who cannot keep his finger out of the pie, had heard from Nehru that the talks with Jinnah were not hopeful, as J. absolutely refused to meet any Congress Muslim. Tiresome of J. but Congress have been very provocative in bringing up here two Muslims out of four, when they are almost entirely a Hindu organization.

May 11

A really dreadful day from my point of view, since I think it has gone far to destroy most of what we have accomplished up here. I may be wrong and unduly depressed but I have had to sit and watch what seemed to me a deplorable exhibition of failure to face facts on the part of the S. of S. and I think partisanship on the part of Cripps.

We began with an hour or so's drafting, the main point being the numbers to be summoned to the Constituent Assembly. We decided eventually to 'double the number we had first thought of', which will make the total up to about 400, an unwieldy number but it apparently enables us to avoid certain anomalies. We have now practically speaking completed the revise of our Statement. Meanwhile Cripps who is in close correspondence with Nehru hears that the negotiations between him and Jinnah are unlikely to be successful. We agreed unanimously that at the afternoon's meeting we would strictly confine the discussion to the question of an umpire and on no account allow all the old questions to be raised again. Cripps was particularly strong on this.

Meanwhile I had a peevish letter from Gandhi about the salt tax, the propaganda he has put out about the imminent abolition of the tax has naturally upset all the salt trade so that a salt famine is likely, and Finance Member says it can only be averted by a communiqué which Gandhi describes as 'discreditable'. I arranged to see the old man at 7 p.m.

Just before the 3 p.m. Conference Cripps produced a letter from Nehru to the effect that Jinnah had run out, and claimed with some emphasis that we must definitely pin the responsibility on Jinnah.[1] I countered this strongly and said that it would be entirely disastrous to any hope of settlement to do so, and S. of S. and Alexander agreed, to the obvious disappointment of Cripps.

The Conference itself was a disastrous affair. The first quarter of an hour showed that the attempt to decide on an umpire or arbitrator had failed

---

[1] Jinnah maintained, apparently correctly, that he had not agreed to the appointment of an umpire, but only to consider this proposal.

and that Jinnah had gone back to his original standpoint that he would do nothing unless the division of India was recognised. Nehru said that it had been proposed that the arbitrator should be Indian but not Hindu, Muslim or Sikh, and that international arbitration had also been in his mind. We ought to have broken off the Conference here, as we had agreed that the arbitration issue was the only one we would consider. But the S. of S. and Cripps would keep on—Cripps, I think, because he wanted to pin the onus for failure on to Jinnah, S. of S. because he has a sort of pathetic idea that if he keeps on talking vague and benevolent generalities long enough it is bound to get him somewhere; and he is constitutionally unable to be brief and keep to the point. The result was quite disastrous. All the old ground was gone over again with increasing divergence of opinion and acerbity; every inch of ground gained in the first two days was lost; and I am afraid that our own proposed Statement was hopelessly prejudiced by the two sides being driven into extreme positions. I tried hard to stop it, but S. of S. would not listen, and we went on till nearly 6 p.m., though the Conference had been dead at 3.30 p.m. Even then they would not recognise it, and did the worst thing possible, by asking Jinnah to put his demands on paper, which means that he is bound to put them in extreme form, and will then have to stick to them. We meet again at 5 p.m. tomorrow, to bury the corpse.

After the conference, I expressed myself strongly to the Cabinet Mission on what had happened, and told S. of S. and Cripps that I considered that they had seriously prejudiced the chances of our own solution being accepted and had made the situation much worse and lost all the ground we had gained. Alexander told me afterwards that he had already said the same thing to them.

At 7 p.m. Gandhi came to see me about his wretched salt tax. I told him that if a complex administrative process was suddenly reversed, after it had lasted for hundreds of years, without proper preparation, chaos was bound to result and consequent suffering to the poor. But nothing would persuade him that it could not all be done with the stroke of a pen. He was quite friendly, and contributed some extremely woolly ideas on how to solve the food crisis.

What a day, I am afraid it has sunk the hopes of settlement.

May 12

We spent a good deal of the day (9.30–11.30; 3.30–5 p.m.) completing our Statement. It will not be an impressive document from the point of view of presentation, there have been too many hands at it and it is too much of a patchwork. But it does contain, I believe, a reasonable way for India to make a Constitution. If it had not been for yesterday's disastrous meeting, or if we had got it out earlier and not come up to Simla at all, I believe it would have had a good chance of success. Now I believe that the chances of acceptance are slight.

From 11.30 a.m. to 1 p.m. I saw Patiala, C.P. Ramaswami Aiyar, and Corfield. Patiala was chiefly concerned with the Sikhs. He said that they were hopelessly disunited (Akali group, Congress group, Communists) and had no leader or outstanding personality, and usually came to him in a difficulty. They were holding a meeting on the 14th, to decide, I gather, whether they would break away from the Coalition Government in the Punjab. It is probably undesirable for H.H. to play with Sikh politics, but he thought they would inevitably consult him. I could only say that I thought the Sikhs, if they played their cards well, could exercise an influence in the Punjab far beyond their numbers. But they do not usually play well, and are too fond of cheating (this I did not say to H.H.)

C.P. was his usual suave, self-confident omniscient self. We talked about the States' negotiating Committee. He deplored how many of the Princes were still living in a fool's paradise, and how few really got down to business. Otherwise they might be the balancing power in India.

I discussed with Corfield amendments on behalf of the Princes to the draft Statement; the amendments he puts forward are all sensible and reasonable.

After lunch the Delegation saw Bhopal about the draft Statement, we only showed him the one paragraph which referred to the States, and gave him the Aide-Memoire about paramountcy prepared some time ago. He seemed satisfied but worried.

The letters from Jinnah and Nehru came in during the day. As I knew would be bound to happen, both sides had stated extreme views, and were further apart than 2 days ago.

At 6 p.m. meeting of the Conference, it was obvious in ten minutes that life was extinct, and that no amount of the artificial respiration attempted by S. of S. and Cripps would be of any use; but we took over another hour to compose the obituary notice. Jinnah said at once that the disagreement with Congress was fundamental and could not be resolved; while Nehru said that Congress had gone as far as possible and could not go further. J. then said that Muslim League had gone a long way, while Congress had not moved.

It was obvious that there was nothing more to be done, and we should have ended there by saying that we were putting out a Statement on

Thursday and asking both sides to hold their hands till then; and that those wretched letters which S. of S. and Cripps had forced Jinnah and Nehru to write should not be published, at any rate till after our Statement. If this had been done clearly and directly, all would have been well. But S. of S. is constitutionally incapable of being brief, direct or decisive. The result was a long and unedifying wrangle over the publication of the letters, Jinnah wishing to publish, Congress quite willing not to do so. (As an example of the unwillingness of S. of S. to say anything direct, he said that we were 'contemplating' the issue of a Statement, knowing full well that the Statement was written and the date settled, as I imagine most of those present knew). (A statement by Nehru seemed to me to indicate that he had already a fairly intimate knowledge of the contents of the Statement; he mentioned representation on a population basis of one per million). Eventually it was agreed that publication should be withheld till the end of the week, but we became committed to eventual publication, which I think unfortunate. The discussion became almost heated at one time, with Jinnah saying that the whole Hindu Press would be mobilized to put him in the wrong.

So ends the second Simla Conference with much the same fate as the first. I was always very doubtful about it, I have never attached the same importance as the Mission to Congress and the League reaching agreement, as I was pretty sure that they never would. I still think we would have done better to put our plan out at a much earlier stage. However, this is a political show and my soldier's judgement and direct methods seem crude and clumsy to them; though I still think I was right. The Conference I think did good up to that fatal meeting of the 11th, in my view. Again, perhaps I am wrong. Also I think Cripps' continued and daily contacts with the Congress camp are all wrong.

The S. of S. told me rather to my horror that he was seeing Nehru tomorrow morning, I am afraid that he is going to try to get him to agree to concessions about the Executive Council which he failed to extract from me; and that the S. of S. may be weak.

May 13

I saw Nehru and Jinnah this morning. A note of these discussions is enclosed.

The talk with Nehru was confined to administrative matters such as the proposal of some Provincial Governments to enlist I.N.A. men in the Police. In the talk with Jinnah, who 'looked tired and ill', Lord Wavell outlined to him his proposals for a new Executive Council (Interim Government), viz. a Council of twelve (five from the Muslim League, five from Congress, including a Scheduled Caste representative, one Sikh, and one other). He said that he did not know whether H.M.G. would accept this, but if they did, he thought 'the Muslim League would be well advised to accept so favourable a proportion'. He also expressed the hope that Jinnah would reflect carefully before refusing to sit with a Congress Muslim because as there was a Congress Ministry of Muslims in the N.W.F.P. it might be difficult to resist Congress on this point.

'Jinnah listened carefully but made little comment. He seemed inclined to agree with me that the Defence Member should be neither a Hindu nor a Muslim. . . . He said that whether or not the Muslim League came into the Interim Government would depend on whether our Statement seemed likely to offer a solution of the long-term issue. His fear was that the Congress plan was to get control of the Central Government, to shelve the fundamental long-term issue, and concentrate on getting control in the Provinces. He could not come into the Government unless it was on a basis of a long-term settlement satisfactory to him being in view.

'I think this is the nearest I have ever got Mr. Jinnah towards accepting the possibility of entering an Interim Government. He did not commit himself in any way, but he did not adopt an entirely unreasonable and non possumus attitude as has so often been his practice in the past.'

Just before lunch we had three-quarters of an hour on the final draft Statement and publicity arrangements. After lunch I saw Short about the Sikhs and Evan Jenkins about the Punjab. Both thought Baldev Singh the best bet as a Sikh for Council.

Evan Jenkins seemed to think the Punjab could be kept in order. Khizar thought the offer of the Cabinet Mission would merely add to the 'constitutional wreckage' already lying around India. We talked for an hour on the situation in general. He seemed to think the Punjab would produce a reasonable amount of surplus food by the methods he was putting into force, and it was no use forcing matters by an Ordinance or Direction by the Centre.

Just before dinner I had at the S. of S. He had, as I suspected, been very woolly with Nehru over the Executive Council and was woolly now. I told him I could not remain responsible for India unless I had something definite.

May 14

I saw Nehru for $1\frac{1}{2}$ hours (8.30 a.m.–10 a.m.) about the Executive Council but did no more, I fear, than discourage the hopes the S. of S. had obviously given him yesterday that we would give in on the parity issue and make a convention depriving the Viceroy of his powers and handing over supreme control to the Interim Government. I am sure we should have been all right on both these questions if we had been firm and definite from the start, but the S. of S.'s vagueness and Cripps' continuous courting, flattery and appeasement of Congress have led them to believe they can get what they want. Nehru talked of 'vital forces' at work in the country which must be taken into account; I said it was the business of a Government to control and direct 'vital forces' and 'mass sentiment' and 'fundamental issues' (which were the sort of phrases he used) and not to follow them blindly, they were usually ignorant and often misleading. I told him my father's favourite story of a French mob rushing on to some foolishness which was obviously wrong, and a spectator stopping a man who was following the mob and asking him why he did so: his reply was: 'mais il faut que je les suive, je suis leur chef'. I don't know whether I moved Nehru at all but I made it quite clear that I was quite definite and not proposing to compromise.

We went down the hill after an early lunch and got back to Delhi at 6 p.m. I saw C-in-C for a few minutes, he wanted to know the publicity arrangements.

Alexander and George Abell dined with me in my study and we talked till 11.30 p.m., partly about the course of action if the Parties reject our Statement and partly reminiscence about Winston, etc. A. is first class company and very sensible, I wish he had been leading the Delegation.

May 15

A long Indian day. Delegation met at 9.30 a.m. to consider final publicity arrangements. What with Wireless, broadcasting, Press requirements, the House of Commons, the time factor in three countries (India, U.K., U.S.A.) all requiring to be considered and satisfied, and a slip-up likely to bring down the wrath of Press in any one of three countries, or of House of Commons, or of B.B.C. or A.I.R., it is a complicated business. While we were still considering it, the Cabinet's proposed amendments came in. They were obviously dictated by apprehension of what Winston and the Opposition might say, and tried to re-iterate the possibility of independence within the British Commonwealth, the necessity for common defence measures, the benefits to India from British rule—all calculated to arouse suspicion of British intentions which the Delegation had been so careful to allay. Cripps and even the S. of S. became quite bellicose about it and even began to talk of resignation. Finally, I was deputed to draft a reply to the P.M., which went over the teleprinter at about 1 p.m. and we sat and waited for an answer till about 2 p.m. when I got hungry and went to lunch. At 3 p.m. they called me back—to say that P.M. had said that he would answer before 4 p.m. They were still feeling rather bellicose and inclined to send the P.M. an ultimatum, but quite glad to be advised that it was unnecessary and injudicious. So I walked back again, and heard about 4 p.m. that the P.M. had given the all-clear.

At 5 p.m. I saw that pleasant old gentleman the Nawab of Chhatari, who said that Simla was not all loss:—we had narrowed the issue between Congress and the League, got Pakistan defined at last, and proved H.M.G.'s sincerity; made his usual request (or rather his master's) for Berar and a port; and asked that if British troops were removed from Secunderabad they should not be replaced by Indian.

At 6 p.m. another meeting with the Delegation. We spent some time over the publication of the Simla letters—which Congress and M.L. want to issue on Friday. I reaffirmed my view on the disastrous effect this might have, and we agreed to try and defer it a few days. Then we considered the reply to a rather plaintive telegram from the P.M. over our refusal of the Cabinet amendments. Finally I dropped or threw a large brick in the pool of their complacency by demanding a discussion on the action to be taken if one or both parties turned down our proposals. Cripps said in effect 'scuttle'; but I demonstrated that this was just as bad a policy as repression, and—the important thing from their point of view—likely to be fatal to the Labour Party. We then had a very useful hour on the grim realities and awkward alternatives if our proposals were turned down. They had never considered them and I had to be brusque and challenging to make them face them. I tried to stiffen them to be firm with Congress over our Statement and to make it clear that if they turned it down they would not get a better offer. S. of S. was a little pained and shocked at my attitude, but I am sure it did good.

Finally, Francis Low came to dine, and I showed him the Statement. He thought that though rather clumsy it was quite a good proposal and might be acceptable as a long-term policy; but Congress was really interested in the short-term policy, the Interim Government. I explained to him my views on this at some length. He has some influence with Congress and will be helpful, I think.

May 16

D-Day for the Delegation's Statement.[1] We began by two hours rather inconclusive discussion on a paper by George Abell about the action to be

[1] Appendix II.

Lord and Lady Wavell in the Mughal garden at the Viceroy's House

The Cabinet Mission, June 1946—Sir Stafford Cripps, Lord Pethick-Lawrence, and Mr. A. V. Alexander with the Viceroy (Sir George Abell is behind Lord Wavell)

taken in the event of a deadlock and a mass movement by Congress. C-in-C was called in, but beyond deciding that neither repression nor scuttle were practicable policies we did not get very far.

The rest of the morning I was trying to write a broadcast which always bothers me and which, as usual, I had left till too late. The result was universally condemned by my staff, mainly on the ground that it contained one or two reminders of difficulties ahead and did not foster the illusion that independence was just round the next corner. My reaction was that there has been quite enough, and more than enough, appeasement and pandering of Congress and that it was time realities were faced. I was reminded of Kipling's couplet:

'No doubt but ye are the People—your throne is above the Kings
Whoso speaks in your presence must say acceptable things.'

At 4.30 p.m. Alexander and I saw Bhopal. He had little to say on the Statement.

Then came the Sikhs (Baldev Singh and Master Tara Singh). Baldev said little and I believe was relieved on the whole, but Tara Singh launched into a declamatory jeremiad on the wrongs and oppressions of the Sikhs and their need for an area completely their own, which is impossible.

Finally, Azad and Nehru from Congress. Azad said little and seemed reasonably satisfied, or else was content to withhold judgement. Nehru seemed to me worried and nervous and therefore a little inclined to be aggressive. He concentrated mainly on the States, said the provisions about them were vague, was dissatisfied with the idea of the Rulers appointing the representatives or even the negotiating Committee, and obviously has it in mind to get rid of Princely rule as soon as possible. I warned him against too hasty attempts at democratization. He also said the document was not definite enough on independence. I pointed out that it was the whole keynote of the Statement and was mentioned in the first paragraph and in the last. But it turned out that what Nehru was thinking about was immediate independence, in the Interim period, in fact he disclosed almost nakedly the real Congress objective—immediate control of the Centre, so that they can deal with Muslims and Princes and then make at leisure a Constitution to suit themselves. I warned him again that there could be no change in the present constitution till a new one was made. He passed over the joining of Assam to Bengal without much comment, accepting the explanation that geographical reasons made it necessary. Finally they said they would send Congress views in writing in a couple of days. Then that business of the publication of those wretched letters from Simla came up. Azad and Nehru said they would be agreeable to postponement if Jinnah agreed.

Meanwhile S. of S. and Cripps had been seeing Gandhi and the Muslim League. They reported it had gone fairly well, but I have a strong suspicion that Gandhi was offered more incense of appeasement. The Simla Delegation, less Jinnah, represented the League and apparently took it seriously and quietly. They asked whether Bengal and Assam would be able to join the N.W. Group if they wished, and whether there would be any power to secede from the Union.

Then at 7 p.m. to a rather hostile Council, who had just read the Statement. Ambedkar was grimly dissatisfied that the Scheduled Castes had not received better treatment; Azizul Huque voiced the personal grievances of Members at not knowing the date of their demise; old Md. Usman sang a hymn of hate against the Punjab for not delivering grain to his starving Province; and Rowlands was brusquely negative to Benthall over possible means to avert a railway strike. Not a pleasant Council, but nothing to what I am likely to have with a new Council.

May 17

Revised broadcast and wrote a warning to S. of S. to be firm and definite about maintaining the present Constitution in the Interim period at the Press conference they are attending.

Broadcast went not too badly, I think.

May 18

Hutchings came to see me before Council meeting, and we discussed the food situation generally, especially as regards Punjab procurement.

In Council on food we decided to send a letter to the Punjab pressing them to take certain measures, but it is really more to save face than in hope of practical results. We then discussed the latest estimate, which seems to show we may hold out till September anyway if all goes well and that a cut in the ration may not be necessary.

Delegation had met at 12 noon, they had had several hours with Gandhi, they always think—or Cripps does—that they swing the old man, personally I believe it is the other way about; and that if only they were firmer and more definite we should have less trouble. I delivered myself of a small but vigorous oration on the danger of letting Congress have their own way and on their objectives in the Interim period, i.e. to obtain control of the Centre rather than constitution-making. I wondered at the time whether I had been a little aggressive, but Turnbull told George afterwards that I was perfectly right to warn them.

May 19

Jinnah sent a message late last night that he hoped to call his League general body about the middle of June, and could take no decision till then, and why were we in such a hurry! So we arranged for Liaquat to come and see Delegation at 11 a.m. Liaquat[1] came and said it was impossible for the League to meet any earlier as by its Constitution members had to have a fortnight's notice. Cripps and S. of S. argued at length that such constitutional rules could and must be broken in an emergency and that they could not possibly wait for a month. Liaquat after 'being silent to a brief' for some time agreed to telephone Jinnah and press him.

Cripps then told me very briefly the result of about seven hours talk with Gandhi, whose main points had been: (a) whether the procedure of the Constituent Assembly could be modified without the consent of the two main parties; (b) that paramountcy should be terminated at once; (c) the position of the N.W.F.P. and Assam; (d) whether Europeans in Bengal would join Constituent Assembly; (e) removal or anyway non-use of British Troops in Interim period; (f) parity in Executive Council; (g) representation of Baluchistan in Constituent Assembly. Cripps claimed to have satisfied him on every point without giving away anything; but I have strong doubts, and kept on emphasising the need to be firm and definite. I elicited from Cripps that he did think the Governor-General's powers could be limited by convention; and I am quite sure that he has encouraged Congress in this belief. We decided that I should go on with the negotiations for Interim Government.

Liaquat came again at 5.15 p.m. after a talk to Jinnah on the telephone, and said that J. was calling the Working Committee of the League for June 3 and 4 and the Council for June 5, and begged not to be hurried as it would take time to persuade his people to accept the proposals. The Delegation had to agree rather reluctantly. They then produced a letter from Gandhi, the first of the Congress efforts to wreck the Groups of Provinces. This is what the Delegation has let itself in for by not standing firm and definite on our Statement; they have had seven hours with Gandhi, and this is the result, the clever attempt of an able and unscrupulous politician to torpedo the whole plan. I told the Delegation in plain language that we were sunk if we qualified the Statement or argued about

---

[1] Jinnah was ill at this time.

it on lawyers' points, our only chance was to stand firm, and refuse to argue. But they won't do it, I fear.

> In his letter Gandhi referred to Paragraph 15 of the Statement which provided, inter alia, for Provinces forming Groups with their own executives and legislatures, and inquired whether those who welcomed the Statement but disliked Grouping could honestly seek to educate the country and the Constituent Assembly against the provisions for Grouping; and, if the answer was 'yes', whether it would not follow that the Frontier and Assam delegates would be free to abstain from joining the Sections of the Assembly to which they were arbitrarily assigned.
>
> Wavell noted in the margin: 'The answer must be a very definite and decided "No".'

May 20

A really dramatic morning. Delegation met at 9.30 a.m. to consider the reply to Gandhi's letter. Cripps produced a long argumentative reply, Alexander a shorter but also giving reasons, I recommended two brief paragraphs returning a negative answer on both points raised by Gandhi. I kept warning them against Gandhi and of the danger of being drawn into argument with him and how he would twist your words and that the only chance was to be firm and definite. I drew rather a heated reply from Cripps, while S. of S. looked at me rather sadly, thinking obviously what a rough blimpish soldier I was, and how unjust my suspicions of Gandhi. Just then he was handed a further letter from Gandhi and read it out. I have never seen three men taken more aback by this revelation of G. in his true colours. Cripps and S. of S. were shaken to the core, while Alexander's reactions were pure John Bull at his most patriotic and in-sular. After sitting for a while—Cripps quite 'ahuri', S. of S. sadly dis-illusioned, Alexander boiling with indignation, and myself refraining with a little difficulty from saying 'I told you so', we agreed to think it over and meet again at 3 p.m. If it were not so tragic and dangerous, it would also have been amusing to see the sudden change in the three men.

> In this second letter (Appendix III) Gandhi discussed at some length the other points that he had raised in talks with Cripps and the Secretary of State and on which Cripps claimed to have satisfied him. It was very clear that Gandhi was far from satisfied. The Secretary of State said that this letter greatly misrepresented what had passed in their interview with him and he was now convinced that nobody should see Gandhi apart from other members of the Delegation and without a note being taken. Alexander said that Gandhi clearly

did not want a settlement on the basis of the Statement and that his letter grossly misrepresented the Delegation's position.

I then saw Benthall about Europeans joining the Constituent Assembly; and the railway strike, which he hopes to avert by negotiation. He was followed by Ambedkar about his proposal to raise the percentage for Depressed Classes in government service.

From 3–4.30 p.m. we discussed the reply to Gandhi, and while we were doing so a letter from Azad arrived containing the official Congress reply and raising most of G.'s points. We sent a fairly stiff reply to Gandhi and decided to sleep on Azad's letter.

Then I had 1½ hours with Nehru about the Interim Government. He kept on about the necessity for immediate independence and the impossibility of parity; and I kept steadily on our determination (mine really) not to give way on these issues. I don't know whether I made any effect; I did in the end get him down to reluctant discussion of names. He kept talking of 'vital forces' and I insisted on jobs to be done and men to do them.

Then to a party for Provincial Premiers and Development Ministers who were holding a Conference. Finally I had the S. of S. to dine and tried to bolster him into firmness about Azad's letter, and then suggested that a holiday would do the Delegation good.

May 21

Delegation met 10 a.m.–12 noon, and did not get very much further with the reply to Congress letter, none of us much like the others' drafts, and Cripps, our chief drafter, is in hospital, with dysentery. We decided to think it over and meet again tomorrow.

May 22

We had two hours with Delegation, 10–12, on the draft reply to Azad, and with some difficulty arrived at a new draft to be retyped and discussed again after lunch. We met again at 2.30 p.m. and in about 40 minutes or so passed a final draft—a small mouse after all these mountainous labours of drafting, but one which I hope the Congress cat may find it difficult to get its claws into.

A crucial passage in this letter was the following: 'You are aware of the reasons for the grouping of the Provinces, and this is an essential feature of the scheme which can only be modified by agreement between the two parties.'

S. of S. then raised the question of our action in case the offer was not accepted and things went badly. I gave an impromptu appreciation which was quite well received but which I shall now have to reduce to writing.

This morning just after lunch I saw Mahtab, Premier of Orissa, about his proposed conference with the Orissa States. He is a reasonable and rather attractive person, who is on the Working Committee and he told me that Congress had decided to accept the Scheme.

Council went off quietly, this Council is practically moribund now, and I think in a mood to pass almost anything.

May 23

Azad and Nehru for $1\frac{1}{4}$ hours over Interim Government. I put a list of names to them to which they did not offer very much comment but said they would write to me after consulting Working Committee. They kept on again about the Independence question, i.e. that the new Government should be virtually a sovereign government, answerable only to the Central Assembly—'the will of the Indian people'—and I kept steadily stonewalling. They were quite friendly.

Corfield came later in the morning to show me a letter from Bhopal expressing his wish to abdicate at an early date in favour of his daughter. I wonder what that old fox has in mind, I don't think he has cold feet or is tiring of ruling, he is an ambitious man.

At 4 p.m. we had $1\frac{1}{2}$ hours in the Delegation over the draft provisions for elections to the Constituent Assembly. The S. of S. was making very heavy weather over it all, and the First Lord was also rolling and pitching a bit. S. of S. is very worried over the European vote in Bengal, which is an awkward problem. I rather suspect that he and Cripps committed themselves to Gandhi rather further than they admit.

> In Section C (Bengal/Assam) of the projected Constituent Assembly the numbers were going to be very evenly balanced (36 Muslims and 34 non-Muslims), and therefore the voting of the few Europeans might be crucial. The Muslim League wanted the Europeans to vote so as to ensure their majority in this Section. The Congress objected to Europeans taking any part both on principle and because it would diminish their chances of preventing a Muslim League majority. The Europeans were quite willing to refrain from voting, but were afraid that if they disclosed their intentions too soon it might discourage the Muslim League from accepting the proposals.

Burrows, Governor of Bengal, arrived to stay, in good and refreshing form. He says he gets on well with Suhrawardy, who is straight with him—after trying it on once or twice and realising that B. was not to be bounced, I gather—but that he would not trust him as far as across the street. He thinks S. is determined to remain in office, 'at least till he can re-coup the election expenses', and will press Jinnah hard to accept the offer. He believes it will be fatal for Europeans' interests if they elect themselves to the Constituent Assembly and says he has advised them to that effect and that they agree.

May 24

1½ hours in morning with Delegation and Burrows, B. explained the general reactions to the Statement in Bengal, which were on the whole favourable. He thinks that whatever happens the Hindus will control Bengal within a few years of a new Constitution coming into being. We then discussed at some length the position of the Europeans and Burrows repeated what he had said to me last night. There is little doubt in my mind that the S. of S. and Cripps really committed themselves pretty deeply over this matter of the Europeans in their talks with Gandhi—those fatal 7 hours.

Letter from Azad in evening, enclosing Congress Resolution on lines of his previous letter, not very helpful.

> In their Resolution of 24 May, the Congress Working Committee stalled, saying that 'in the absence of a full picture' they were unable at this stage to give a final opinion on the Delegation's proposals. They reiterated the objections that they (and Gandhi) had previously raised to these proposals; in particular they claimed that, according to their interpretation of the Delegation's Statement, it was not obligatory on a Province to enter the Section in which it had been placed. (They had been expressly told that their interpretation was incorrect and that Grouping was an essential feature of the scheme.)
>
> They also said that the Interim Government (which they termed the Provisional National Government) must function as a cabinet responsible to the Central Legislature and must be in fact, if not in law, virtually independent. They said that the status, powers, and composition of this Provisional Government would have to be defined to enable them to come to a decision on the Delegation's proposals.

May 25

Spent nearly all day drafting—by myself an appreciation[1] for the Delegation, with the Delegation a statement[2] in answer to the Congress statement

[1] This important and farsighted appreciation of the situation that was likely to arise if the Delegation's proposals failed, and of the general policy to be adopted in that event is given, with some abbreviation, in Appendix IV.

[2] This statement is given in full as Appendix V. Paragraph 8 and Paragraphs 10–12 were of considerable importance.

—concise, clear and firm, I hope, but it will not please Congress. Two more letters from Azad in the evening and one from Nehru—I fancy they are quite in a fuss and jam too, trying to counter the left wing—Jai Prakash Narain & Co.—and a very peevish Gandhi I gather.

These letters were mainly concerned with the Congress demand that the Interim Government should have the status in fact, if not in law, of a truly national government and function like a Dominion Cabinet.

May 26

S. of S. came and woffled for an hour, about nothing special, mainly the Interim Government and powers of G-G. Then I had over an hour with Nehru, to reply to his letter. It went much as usual, and was quite friendly but I don't know whether either of us persuades the other much, though we get on quite well. The more I see of Nehru, the better I like him.

Otherwise a quiet day. Cripps is still in hospital. Alexander has gone off to Trincomalee to see the Fleet, the Congress Working Committee has broken up, Jinnah is still in Simla.

In the evening a dinner of my Council, to say farewell to Rowlands and Thorne. Short speeches by self, Benthall, Rowlands and Thorne.

The following 'Note for talk with Pandit Nehru' indicates what Wavell said to him:

I regret all our talks seem to have led to nothing apparently except a feeling of frustration and disappointment on your part. Our outlook is of course bound to be different: quite apart from the question of race and traditions, I look at the immediate future of India from the practical point of view, while you seem to be entirely sentimental. My whole life has been devoted to keeping law and order and peace as far as possible, your outlook is that of a revolutionary.

I must also say that I feel depressed and disappointed in the conversations, disappointed at what seems to me a complete lack of reality in the Congress attitude. To be quite frank, they seem to me to be thinking much more of party politics and party advantage, than of the good of India as a whole.

Congress are practically asking us to hand over India to a single party, a party which is deeply distrusted by all Muslims, by Rulers of States and quite a proportion of their people, and by quite a number of other people in India.

We are asked to guarantee complete independence to a Government under the control of this party, BEFORE we know whether it and the

Muslims can work together, and while its objective in the States seems to be to cause agitation against the Rulers.

We are bound to have some suspicion that the objective of Congress is to secure control of the centre, entirely eliminate British influence, and then deal with the Muslims and States with a high hand. We are asked to guarantee independence and to hand over complete control to a Government responsible to a Central Legislature which has a Hindu majority.

Such a policy seems to us bound to lead to a complete refusal of the Muslims to co-operate, to break up the Indian Army on which the defence of India depends, and to cause chaos in India which may lead to another World war. We feel we are bound to see that there is a good prospect of order and peace in India before we hand over control completely.

Our attitude is not, as you seem to suspect, prompted by a desire to retain power for power's sake; but to give India the best possible chance of success as an independent nation. We are giving you a chance of a United India, and I think it may be the last chance, and are prepared to give every possible help to you to obtain it. But we are not prepared simply to abdicate to one political party.

If you are unable to see the difference between the proposed new Council and the old one, I am afraid that I cannot help you, it seems to me to be an entirely different thing. And I can assure you that H.M.G. will treat a coalition Government working for the good of India as a whole, with a very light hand. But it does seem to us that the only possible chance of getting such a Government is that it really should be a Coalition Government in which the Muslims will feel that they are not at the mercy of a Hindu majority. This will undoubtedly entail concession to the Muslims in the matter of numbers.

As regards the States, I do not propose to defend the Rulers as a whole or the present system as a whole. But to carry on agitation against the Rulers at this juncture seems to me an extremely foolish procedure. Any Government is bound to react against agitation against itself. And we surely do not want disorderly revolution in the States at the present moment. It can only harden the whole attitude of the Princes.

May 28

Benthall came in at 10 a.m. about the Railway strike threat. The railway-men are opening their mouths very wide. We decided to get Nehru and Liaquat, who were in Delhi, and discuss the matter with them. This was done at 4 p.m., they did not commit themselves but seemed to realise the unreasonableness of the men's demands and the danger of giving way to them.

Claude Auchinleck came in the evening, and said that he agreed entirely with my appreciation [Appendix IV] and would have the measures necessary to implement it examined.

May 29

A long meeting of Council in the morning, three hours. Food, coal, demobilization, control of minerals, lend-lease agreement with U.S.A. all took a certain amount of time, but were not very controversial: then came the very difficult question of the threatened railway strike. I was sure we must face it and refuse to be blackmailed any further; but some of Council were rather timid and woolly. In the end we got only a fairly satisfactory solution, to offer some compensation in the lower grades and a very limited adjudication if they refuse it.

Old Md. Usman came to say good-bye after Council, he is departing to Madras, to await the formation of a new Government. He has been a loyal old thing and entirely disapproves of the new order.

May 30

In the afternoon I had a short session with the S. of S. over the draft letter to Azad about the Interim Government and the protests of the Sikhs. S. of S. wanted to reply to Azad by inviting him and Nehru to come and discuss the whole matter again, but I refused resolutely to propose it. I have a feeling, however, that S. of S. will, sooner or later, have such a talk and will commit himself to something vague and woolly. We decided that nothing much could be done for the Sikhs except to try and persuade them.

A letter was sent by the Viceroy to Azad on 30 May and is of importance as it was the basis on which the Congress subsequently entered the Interim Government. It is reproduced below:

I have received your letter of 25th May on the Interim Government.

2. We have discussed this matter on several occasions and I recognise the importance that you and your party attach to a satisfactory definition of the powers of the Interim Government and appreciate your reasons for asking for such a definition. My difficulty is that the most liberal intentions may be almost unrecognisable when they have to be expressed in a formal document.

3. I am quite clear that I did not state to you that the Interim Government would have the same powers as a Dominion Cabinet. The whole Constitutional position is entirely different. I said that I *was* sure that His

Majesty's Government would treat the new Interim Government with the same close consultation and consideration as a Dominion Government.

4. His Majesty's Government have already said that they will give to the Indian Government the greatest possible freedom in the exercise of the day to day administration of the country; and I need hardly assure you that it is my intention faithfully to carry out this undertaking.

5. I am quite clear that the spirit in which the Government is worked will be of much greater importance than any formal document and guarantees. I have no doubt that, if you are prepared to trust me, we shall be able to co-operate in a manner which will give India a sense of freedom from external control and will prepare for complete freedom as soon as the new Constitution is made.

6. I sincerely hope that the Congress will accept these assurances and will have no further hesitation in joining to co-operate in the immense problems which confront us.

7. In the matter of time table you will be aware that the All-India Muslim League Council is meeting on June 5th, at which we understand decisive conclusions are to be reached. I suggest therefore that if you summon your Working Committee to reassemble in Delhi on Friday the 7th, it may be possible for final decisions to be made by all Parties on all outstanding questions early in the following week.

May 31

Benthall came in about the strike, and I suggested certain points to be brought out in propaganda. I gather the men's leaders expected us to give way and are a little shaken.

From 5–7.15 p.m. we had an almost interminable meeting with S. of S., Alexander and C-in-C over a very lengthy telegram the Delegation wishes to send to the P.M. with proposals for action in the event of a breakdown. It was very sticky going, and it was decided to re-draft the telegram very materially. We also discussed the objections of the Sikhs to the Delegation Statement and their threats of action against it; and a telegram from Bombay about a proposal to enlist I.N.A. men in the Police.

Finally a largish dinner party, after which C-in-C tried to object to my instruction that the Home Department should see the summary of evidence in the proposed R.I.N. court-martials. I am not going to have a repetition of the I.N.A. mistakes if they can be avoided.

One of my first C.O.'s, Chumpy Maxwell, over 40 years ago, used to sing a song: 'The long, long Indian day'. I am having plenty of them.

So end two months of negotiation without any decision. Perhaps we shall get one in June, and very much good work has been done by the Delegation; but I shall not alter my view that a more firm and definite line, and less pandering to the Congress, would have produced quicker and better results.

I am disappointed to miss the Victory Parade in London, but it is impossible to get away. I am feeling stale and over-worked; not sleeping very well, and waking up depressed and worried. I think the strain of seven years heavy responsibility without a proper rest is beginning to tell on me. However, I expect I shall manage to carry on, though without much enthusiasm for the work. Indian politics and Indian politicians are disheartening to deal with; and we British seem to have lost faith in ourselves and the courage to govern at present. But we have *seemed* to do that often enough before in our history, and recovered. And I have seen too many dark and apparently hopeless situations turn out all right since 1939 to lose hope over this one.

12

THE MISSION'S FAILURE

June 1

Wylie and Twynam, from U.P. and C.P. came for week-end. I saw them at 4 p.m.; and at 4.45 the S. of S. and Alexander came and we talked till nearly 7 p.m. Afterwards, S. of S. wanted to know about the railway strike and also talked about the Interim Government. I am convinced that he and Cripps have in some way committed themselves to Congress over this; and that is why we are having all this trouble.

June 2 (Sunday)

I talked to Wylie and Twynam in the morning. Wylie was very certain that any withdrawal from India would be disastrous and that we could deal with a revolt. But like everyone else he had no idea of where we went from there, after repression, unless we were prepared to govern on the old terms for another 10 or 15 years. He was worried about the large number of Europeans who would be isolated at Naini Tal in case of trouble. He hoped that the food problem would be all right and did not take as gloomy a view as J. P. [Srivastava] did the other day, but said that the complete inefficiency of his Government was a hampering factor. His Home Member Kidwai was a thoroughly bad man.

Twynam had not a great deal to say about the C.P., but all his I.C.S. people would retire as soon as possible, he thought, and were anxious about compensation terms.

At 11.45 a.m. the Delegation came, and we spent nearly two hours on the draft telegram to the P.M., without reaching any final decision except that practically all the courses open to us in the event of a breakdown were disastrous and unworkable. We decided to think it over till tomorrow.

I wrote a note to P.S.V. on a possible breakdown plan.

This note, somewhat abbreviated, is reproduced below:

I have been thinking again over the problem of our action if the present proposals break down; but have not managed to arrive at anything much more definite. It is very difficult to choose a line of action, until one is able to see how the crisis is brought about.

2. If the breakdown comes through the refusal of the Muslim League to take part in the Interim Government or Constituent Assembly, or if they make impossible conditions, Congress will undoubtedly expect us to go ahead without them. If we do not fulfil their expectations, they will accuse us of bad faith, and I should expect a crisis to arise almost at once.

I think that all we could do would be to call the leaders together and make one last effort to get them to see reason. We should inform the Muslim League that we must go ahead with handing over independence to India, in spite of their intransigence; and that while we do not intend to assist Congress to enforce Hindu domination, we have no intention at all of assisting the Muslim League to a complete Pakistan. We should remind Congress of their repeated assertions that they will allow independence to those parts of the country which desire it; and that we propose to maintain the present position in the Muslim-majority provinces until we can consider further. The other Provinces (and I suppose these must include the N.W.F.P. and Assam) will be summoned to the Constituent Assembly; and will proceed to devise their Provincial constitutions, and any groups they may wish to form, but not at present a Union Government.

The choice for the Interim Central Government would be between a purely official Government, and a Government of Congress with Muslims represented by officials or non-League Muslims.

I do not think that this arrangement would satisfy anyone, but it might possibly gain us a little time for further consideration.

3. If the Congress refuse, while the Muslim League agree, it will mean that the Congress left-wing has gained the upper hand. In this event, we should obviously have to allow Muslims to go on with their own constitution-making in Groups B and C; I think we should have to stick to our grouping, and if N.W.F.P. or Assam refuse to send representatives to the Group Constitution-making-bodies, carry on without them.

In the rest of India, we should invite the Provincial Assemblies to elect representatives to a Constituent Assembly for the Hindustan Provinces, to decide on the Provincial constitutions and any grouping they wished.

The plan would in fact be to try and carry on with the Constitution for the Provinces and Groups, leaving the Centre in abeyance.

I think the Central Government would have to be an official one, I do not think it will be feasible to have Muslim League leaders on it with no Congress representatives.

I should not expect this plan to succeed; there would be widespread communal outbreaks all over India—in the Muslim provinces as well as in the Hindustan provinces, I think; and it would become increasingly difficult to maintain law and order.

4. In the end, we are really faced with the same alternatives—repression or withdrawal. If it is decided that repression is not a practical proposition, we are left with the various alternatives of withdrawal: a complete and immediate withdrawal from all India, which is unthinkable; withdrawal by a certain date, which is I think equally impracticable; and a partial withdrawal, to northern India.

There is in fact *no* alternative, which is in any way satisfactory, to obtaining agreement; and we must exercise every possible resource at our command to do so. But lack of resolution is the most fatal possible thing; and we *must* make up our minds what our policy is to be.

5. What then are we to say to H.M.G., and what policy are we to decide on? I think that something on the lines of the present draft telegram will do; but the telegram should lead up to the conclusion that if repression is ruled out and complete withdrawal equally so, a partial withdrawal to the Muslim-majority Provinces of North-West and North-East India is the only practicable course we can see, but that it is not a good one and must be avoided if possible.

6. I have been unable to think of anything better than the above so far. Will you come down and discuss it with me after golf has cleared our minds, I hope?

> *A telegram substantially on these lines was sent to the Cabinet on 3 June. It was proposed, in the event of a break with Congress, to give, in effect, independence to Southern and Central India and to maintain the existing position in North-West and North-East India. This was what Wavell had recommended in Paragraphs 11–12 of his appreciation dated 30 May (Appendix IV).*

June 3

I saw Jinnah at 10 a.m., he seemed to be in good heart. He said he could not give me names for the Interim Government until after he had seen his Council, but I got the impression that the M.L. would probably come in. He asked about the correspondence with Azad which had been reported in the Press, and I showed him a copy of my last letter to Azad.[1] He made no comment, except to discourse on the way Congress always continued to haggle and ask for concessions. He then went on to complain that the Muslims had not been given parity in the Union Legislature, and stressed the very great concession he had made in agreeing to a Union at all, with a disquisition on the Canadian Constitution. He then asked what we

[1] The letter dated 30 May, see p. 280.

should do if the M.L. came in and Congress refused. I had anticipated this query and had consulted S. of S. through P.S.V. I told him that the M.L. would certainly not suffer by its readiness to work the Delegation scheme, and that the intention was to go ahead with the scheme as far as possible with any party who would work for it. He asked for something more specific before he met his Working Committee at 6 p.m. and I said I could do nothing more without consulting the Delegation. He said the matter was of very great importance and asked me to do so. We then had some further talk about the Sikhs and Pathans, and he left after an hour. (By the way, Ian Scott[1] told me out riding this morning that Bhopal had told his doctor that the reason he was preparing to abdicate was that he might become Defence Minister in the Interim Government!)

At 11 a.m. we had over two hours again on the draft telegram to the P.M. on action in the event of a breakdown, it seems to get longer and woollier the more we work on it. I got permission to give Jinnah a verbal assurance that we would work with the M.L. if they accepted and Congress refused, so summoned him again for 4 p.m. After lunch I dictated a form of assurance to Jinnah. In this I told him that though the Delegation could not give him a written assurance of what its action would be in the event of the breakdown of the present negotiations, I could give him, on behalf of the Delegation, my personal assurance that we did not propose to make any discrimination in the treatment of either party; and that we should go ahead with the plan laid down in our statement so far as circumstances permit, if either party accepts; but we hoped that both would. I asked him not to make this assurance public, but simply to say to his Working Committee, if necessary, that he was satisfied on this point.

The Delegation approved the assurance and also produced one from Cripps, which amounted practically to the same thing. I showed them to Jinnah at 4 p.m. and he seemed satisfied. He then asked me one or two questions of detail: would it be obligatory on the Chairman of the Constituent Assembly to accept the opinion of the Federal Court—on which I read him Spens'[2] opinion; could provincial Assemblies nominate anyone outside the Province for the Constituent Assembly, to which I said yes; and was there any objection to members of the Interim Government being also members of the C.A.—which was one I had not thought of. He then went on to the election of a representative from Baluchistan,

---

[1] Ian (later Sir Ian) Scott, I.C.S., had succeeded George Abell as Deputy Private Secretary to the Viceroy.

[2] Sir Patrick Spens, who had succeeded Sir Maurice Gwyer as Chief Justice of India in 1943, gave the opinion that acceptance of the Federal Court's advice should be obligatory on the Chairman of the Constituent Assembly.

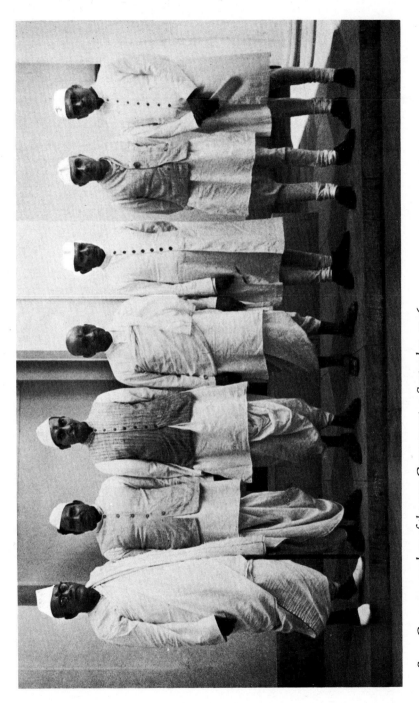

Some Congress members of the new Government, 2 September, 1946

Left to right: Mr. Sarat Chandra Bose, Mr. Jagjivan Ram, Dr. Rajendra Prasad, Sardar Vallabhbhai Patel, Mr. M. Asaf Ali, Pandit Nehru, Syed Ali Zaheer.

The new Government reconstituted to include Muslim League nominees, 26 October 1946

Left to right: Sardar Baldev Singh, Dr. J. Matthai, Mr. C. Rajagopalachari, Mr. Jagjivan Ram, Pandit Nehru, Mr. Ghazanfar Ali Khan, Nawabzada Liaquat Ali Khan, Dr. R. Prasad, Sardar V. Patel, Sardar Abdur Rab Nishtar, Mr. I. I. Chundrigar, Mr. M. Asaf Ali, Mr. C. H. Bhabha.

about which apparently unimportant matter both parties seem very concerned.

From 4.30–6.30 p.m. we continued on that telegram to the P.M., and finally got it drafted. I fancy its contents will be a severe shock to the Cabinet. Then the S. of S. started again—with the support of Cripps who was present—on the matter of a further assurance to the Congress over the powers of the Interim Government. He wanted to discuss the whole matter again with Nehru and Azad. I deprecated this to the point of provoking an outburst from S. of S.; and said that on no account would I be a party to any further unilateral concession to Congress; if there was to be any convention or statement it must be jointly accepted by Congress and M.L. We had quite an unpleasant ten minutes, but I entirely refused to give way. The fact is, I am quite sure, that Cripps or S. of S. or both have committed themselves to Congress to secure some statement; S. of S. admitted to having written a letter to Nehru while up at Simla. It has, I think, been the bane of the Mission that it has been unable to keep away from continual personal contacts with Congress, and so have been unable to remain really impartial. S. of S. still goes for a walk with Agatha Harrison[1] nearly every morning, I believe. Alexander backed me. He dined alone with me afterwards, and said that Cripps was quite capable of making out at home, if the scheme failed, that it was because he, Alexander, had backed the Viceroy in being intransigent. I like Alexander very much, he is intelligent, honest and amusing; he has rather a surprising knowledge of poetry.

In a letter to the Secretary of State dated 2 June Wavell had strongly deprecated unilateral concessions to Congress in regard to the powers of the Interim Government for the reasons given in the following passage: 'It seems to me that there is a tendency to overlook the fact that the proposed Interim Government will be a coalition; and that these demands for conventions and concessions come at present from one party only. If we receive a combined request from both political parties with regard to the powers of the Governor-General or to the responsibility to the Central Legislature, we should obviously have to consider it very carefully; but these concessions to one party are merely likely to have the result of deterring the other party from joining the Interim Government.' The fact is that Jinnah and the Muslim League did not want the Governor-General's powers to be whittled away as they looked on these powers as affording some protection against Congress dictation.

[1] Miss Agatha Harrison was a friend of C. F. Andrews (a missionary and associate of Gandhi in South Africa and later in India), and through him had met Gandhi when he visited London in 1931 for the Round Table Conference. She was Secretary of a small group of Quakers known as the India Conciliation Group.

June 5

Council this morning had only four members: Srivastava, Khare, Azizul Huque, Hydari. We decided that Food should not be a weekly item any longer. J. P. S. who had been to the U.P. was suddenly optimistic again and rather loquacious.

June 6

The Muslim League has accepted by a large majority. Now the real battle begins, and the great question is whether the Delegation will stand up to Congress or not. Parity in the Interim Government may be the main issue. I am afraid that Cripps and P.L. are so much committed that they will be unable or unwilling to be firm with Congress.

We saw the Sikhs this afternoon, Tara Singh and Baldev Singh. On the whole I think it went fairly well. We told them that agitation and disturbances could only be harmful to their cause and would not be tolerated; and tried to persuade them that if they kept calm and used their influence they would be able to secure their position in the Punjab. The trouble is that the Sikhs have never forgotten that they once owned the Punjab, that they have been rather spoilt in the past, that they have no political sense, and an exaggerated idea of their own abilities and importance.

June 7

S. of S. came in for a talk about noon. He reverted to the suggestion that Maurice Gwyer[1] might be of assistance to me as an expert on Constitutional Law. He also recommended to me Ghosh,[2] whom he described as Gandhi's Mercury (he is an official in Tata's I believe). He said that he understood that my letter to Azad had been well received, but that Birla (I think probably at Patel's request) had been attacking on the parity issue. I said we must stand firm on this.

At 7 p.m. I had an hour with Jinnah on the Interim Government. Not very successful. He said the League would only come in on the 5 : 5 : 2 formula, on which he claimed I had given him an assurance. I said that I had not, though it was the formula to which I was still working.[3] He wanted the Defence Portfolio for himself, and Foreign Affairs and Planning for two of his followers.

[1] Sir Maurice Gwyer, having ceased to be Chief Justice, stayed on in Delhi as Vice-Chancellor of Delhi University.

[2] Sudhir Ghosh, a Bengali who as a student at Cambridge had been in touch with the Quakers' India Conciliation Group and later was associated with the Friends' Ambulance Unit in famine relief work in Bengal. Author of the book *Gandhi's Emissary* (London, 1967).

[3] See record of talk with Jinnah on pp. 267–8.

June 10

Azad and Nehru came to see the Delegation at 12 noon, and raised two issues, the vote of the Europeans in Bengal and the parity issue. The Delegation did not give way on either, though the Cabinet Ministers do not really believe in parity, and Congress is playing on this. Nehru struck me as a little unbalanced in some of his statements.

It is obviously more a matter of prestige now than anything else, and it looks rather like touch and go. Nehru said they could not possibly accept parity, but he said it rather with the air of the dealer who hopes for a slightly better bid.

I started to have a note drafted for the Delegation to take home.

Wavell began drafting this note at a moment when hopes ran high that the Delegation, due to leave for home before the end of the month, might witness an Interim Government in being before their departure and a Constituent Assembly summoned. He warned them that even if this much had been achieved the Indian problem would still by no means be solved. Both the Interim Government and the Constituent Assembly would be difficult to hold together and Congress and Muslim League would undoubtedly continue to pursue the conflicting aims they had never abandoned. In addition, there was a strong element in Congress that was likely to raise agitation in the States and in that case the Rulers might decline to enter into a Federation. H.M.G. must therefore have a policy prepared to meet a possible early breakdown and not wait until a crisis arose. He laid great stress on the weakness of the existing government machine, the dwindling number of British officers in the I.C.S., and the likelihood of divided loyalties in the Indian Army and Police. He also stressed that the Indian Interim Government would have to be handled with the greatest tact and forbearance. It would undoubtedly be provocative and tiresome in a great many of its acts and resolutions, and a great deal would have to be put up with that H.M.G. might neither approve nor consider wise.

He suggested that, if possible, H.M.G. should come to an understanding with the Opposition to take India out of party politics, anyway for the next six months.

June 11

At 10 a.m. the Delegation came and we talked for an hour and a half. P.L.[1] was all for seeing Gandhi. Alexander was bitterly opposed and went so far as to threaten to go straight home if P.L. insisted. Alexander is

[1] He had been informed by Miss Harrison and Sudhir Ghosh that Gandhi was likely to throw his whole weight against parity and that the only hope of preventing this was to see Gandhi.

completely mistrustful now of G. and all his ways. Cripps suggested an interview between myself, Jinnah and Nehru. None of the Cabinet Ministers are prepared to face a breakdown over the parity issue and were inclined to press me on it. I threw out the suggestion of a Cabinet on the British principle, with other Ministers not members of the Cabinet as a possible solution. Cripps was rather in favour of it.

We finally decided that I should see Jinnah and Nehru and try to arrange a Government; while P.L. went off determined to see Gandhi and A.V.A. stopped behind to tell me how much he disliked the idea. While we were talking, George Abell came in with a message that G. really wanted to see me, and A.V.A. at once said he had no objection to this.

G. turned up rather suddenly and unexpectedly at about 12.35 p.m. and I had about 40 minutes with him. He said he was thoroughly anxious for a settlement and agreed that a coalition was necessary. He said that parity was of no account nor whether the members belonged to the Congress or the League, provided they were the best men available. I suggested that perhaps the best course would be for me to see Jinnah and Nehru together and to endeavour to arrive at an agreed composition for the Interim Government with them. He agreed that the meeting should be between Jinnah and Nehru since he realized the difficulty of Azad meeting Jinnah. He advised me to pin them down to make a Government and not allow them to leave the room until they had done so.

It is always difficult to fathom how his mind is working, but he was quite friendly throughout and gave the impression that he would advise the Congress to come to terms and not to allow a breakdown on the parity issue.

At a Delegation Meeting at 6 p.m., we decided that Cripps should see Jinnah tonight to persuade him to meet Nehru and myself on the Interim Government.

June 12

A really hard—and very critical day. It began with a meeting of the Delegation at 9.30 a.m. to decide on measures to break the deadlock. It was agreed that I should write to Nehru and Jinnah and ask them to meet me in the evening to try and settle the Interim Government; Cripps had spent several hours with Jinnah last night and said that he had agreed to this. I was also asked to see Vallabhai Patel.

I then had a Council meeting of which the main item was an attempt to settle the threatened P and T strike.

After lunch I saw Vallabhai Patel.

I began by saying that I had asked to see him because I knew that acceptance of the Delegation's Statement and participation in the Interim Government by the Congress were hanging in the balance; and that my information was that he was opposed to acceptance. I said that I did not consider him a man who was likely to be persuaded of anything against his will, but that I should like to put before him something about the consequences that might follow rejection. I then spoke to him on the same lines as I had to Gandhi the day before of the problems facing India which required above all things a period of calm and constructive work. For Congress and the League to combine effectively in this work was the best way of removing the possibility of division and Pakistan, much rather than political manoeuvres or threats of civil war.

Patel said that I was quite correct in saying that he was opposed to the acceptance of the Statement, but so was the whole of the Working Committee, there was no-one in favour of it. I said that I thought there must be more moderation in Congress than that. He said that Gandhi had put forward all the arguments for acceptance, but had failed to convince the Working Committee; and Patel himself was all packed up ready to go to Bombay today when he had been asked to stop. It was quite impossible for them to accept the matter of parity.

We then had a discussion on the parity issue. I said that I entirely appreciated the Congress point of view but we had not adopted the parity solution in the Constituent Assembly or in the Union Legislature and there was no reason for fearing it as a precedent. He replied that it was being taken as a precedent even in villages and on municipal committees and so forth.

He then went on to say that Jinnah would only use his position in the Interim Government for purely communal and disruptive purposes and to break up India. I said that I was quite certain that that would not be Jinnah's attitude and that he could trust me to see that any attempt by Jinnah or either party to make the Interim Government a battle ground of communal politics instead of an instrument for administering India would be prevented.[1] Patel was not at all convinced, but said finally that if Jinnah and Nehru met and could agree on a list of names for the Government, he would be prepared to accept it. He said that it would be better if they sat alone, with no-one else.

He was quite friendly, although as bitterly hostile as usual to Jinnah and the League; and said finally that if Nehru and Jinnah could settle it, it might be all right.

[1] In the event Wavell was not really able to prevent this.

I then had a talk with Menon. He does not like the idea of an Inner and Outer Cabinet—no more do I—and thinks that I should press Jinnah to agree on 5 : 5 : 3 with the Scheduled Caste outside the Congress quota.

At 3.40 p.m., when I was due to see Nehru and Jinnah at 4 p.m., Cripps came in and told me that Jinnah would not come; he had written a letter earlier to say that he did not feel he could meet Nehru, unless the parity basis was conceded, and Cripps had gone to try and persuade him.

Saw Nehru at 4 p.m. and had 1¾ hours with him. He was attractive and interesting as usual, and we got as far as a list of names for Council. He produced a list of 15 names: 5 Congress (all Hindus), 4 Muslim League, one non-League Muslim, one non-Congress Hindu, one Congress Scheduled Caste, one Indian Christian, one Sikh, one Congress woman. I said that this list would be quite unacceptable to Mr. Jinnah, and I did not see how I could put it across to him. I promised to keep his list of names entirely to myself since, as he said, he was in a difficult position as he was not President of the Congress and Azad ought to have been in his place. He told me that they had had a letter ready to send me yesterday, more or less turning down the whole proposal, I gather; but Gandhi had intervened and it had not been sent. I asked him to see that no letters were sent to me for a day or two, while I saw how we could settle this business.

June 13

Delegation at 9.30 a.m. when we discussed the Interim Government and the European vote. At 11.30 a.m. I saw Jinnah and he agreed to accept (or rather to recommend to his Working Committee) 5 : 5 : 3 with the Scheduled Caste who would be a Congress nominee as one of the three. He also gave me some names for the Government if the League came in. After a short talk with the Delegation, I saw Nehru again at 3.30 p.m. I gave him a suggested list, with 5 Congress Hindus, 5 Muslim League, 1 Scheduled Caste (Congress), 1 Sikh, 1 Indian Christian. He seemed depressed, worked himself up to one outburst about Jinnah's refusal to meet Azad and described Jinnah as a wrecker. He promised to put the proposal to the Working Committee but without much hope of success.

After he had left, the Delegation assembled and were anxious that I should see Patel and try to enlist his support. I was a little doubtful about it but agreed. He came at 7.15 p.m., quite uncompromisingly hostile and very worked up, talked volubly without listening to any argument and sung a continuous hymn of hate against Jinnah and the League. He said the Working Committee had not taken five minutes to turn down the proposal I had given Nehru, and said that no Government formed by the Viceroy would be acceptable. It looks as if he had wrecked the whole proposal.

Sudhir Ghosh, by the way, who is so lauded by the S. of S., came to see me in the morning with a letter from Gandhi. He did not impress me as sincere at all, and I should place no trust in him. His claims to have told G. that he was wrong and to have corrected the errors caused by the worship of G.'s entourage are, I believe, mainly a device to create confidence with the Mission; and I should doubt if they were genuine. Cripps told me later that Lady C. distrusted him at once; and women are often better judges of character than men—so long as their affections are not involved.

> *Extract from Gandhi's letter to the Viceroy dated 13 June:* '*You are a great soldier—a daring soldier. Dare to do the right. You must make your choice of one horse or the other. So far as I can see you will never succeed in riding two at the same time. Choose the names submitted either by Congress or the League. For God's sake do not make an incompatible mixture and in trying to do so produce a fearful explosion. Anyway fix your time-limit and tell us all to leave when that time is over.*
>
> *I hope I have made my meaning clear.*'

June 14

Another of those sort of days of which I am getting very weary. We had a Delegation meeting at 10 a.m. on a Statement which it is proposed to put out if the negotiations fail, giving an Interim Government of 14: 5 Congress, 5 League, 4 Minorities. We had a good deal of discussion on the 14th Member and also on the 5th Congressman (to avoid Sarat Chandra Bose). We also discussed again the problem of the Europeans.

> *Since Congress were expected to reject the proposals for a Council of thirteen (5:5:3) and were demanding fifteen, it was decided in the projected Statement about the Interim Government to raise the number to fourteen (5:5:4) by the addition of either a Parsee, an Anglo-Indian, a non-Congress Hindu, or a non-League Muslim. In the end a Parsee, Sir N. P. Engineer, was selected.*

At noon I had an hour with Azad and Nehru: all the old ground was gone over again without much result. I had made a very stupid error yesterday in including Rajkumari Amrit Kaur[1] (again to avoid Bose) thinking she was a Hindu, while Nehru had apparently made an error in his representation of my proposals to the Working Committee. They went away finally saying they would recommend the proposal to the Working Committee without much hope.

---

[1] She was an Indian Christian (Congress); see footnote on p. 210.

June 15

Azad's letter received last night practically amounted to turning down both the Statement of May 16th and the Interim Government. Delegation met at 9.30 a.m. for a couple of hours and put the final touches on the new Statement about the Interim Government to be issued tomorrow—the European question intervening at frequent intervals.

We met again in the afternoon, registered the fact that the Europeans had made a statement which might or might not solve that part of the problem, and approved a reply to Azad.

The Europeans said that they would not nominate any person for election to the Constituent Assembly and would not vote for a European to sit in it.

June 16

Delegation meeting at 9.30 a.m. Cripps, as a result of talk with Rajagopalachariar, who is the blue-eyed boy of the moment with S. of S. and Cripps, tried to induce me to substitute the name of B. N. Rau for Engineer in the Interim Council list, so as to give an extra Hindu. I refused to agree and was backed up by Alexander (who was ill) and Croft;[1] and after some discussion S. of S. accepted my view that it would be a break of faith with Jinnah. We then drafted a letter to go to Azad and Jinnah with a copy of the new Statement.[2] S. of S. and Cripps then went off to get into a huddle with Rajagopalachariar again. S. of S. came back at 1.15 p.m. to seek my agreement to his seeing Gandhi again, on the advice of Rajagopalachariar, before the Congress Working Committee met on the new offer. I agreed that it could do no harm.

And so the Delegation's final (?) attempt to induce the children to play together is launched. I think the chances are 50–50 of its acceptance, perhaps. All this huckstering and bargaining by Congress has shown their complete inability to take a broad or statesmanlike view. Jinnah has shown up well in comparison.

June 17

Delegation at 9.30 a.m. S. of S. and Cripps in close touch with Congress camp as usual, via Agatha Harrison, Sudhir Ghosh and Co. S. of S. had seen Gandhi and Cripps was seeing Azad, so I had a message sent to Jinnah to say that all these interviews did not mean further concessions and that the Cabinet Ministers or myself would be very pleased to see him if

[1] Sir William Croft, Deputy Under-Secretary of State for India, 1941–7, on the staff of the Cabinet Mission.   [2] See Appendix VI.

he wished. Congress are apparently objecting to the inclusion of Nishtar and the exclusion of Bose.

Then a comparatively quiet time till the evening, when I had an interview with C.-in-C. on R.I.N. court-martials, which we decided must be postponed till the new Ministry takes office; Indian troops abroad; and some other matters.

Then a Council meeting on an attempted settlement of the Railway Strike.

June 18

A discouraging day, a little relieved by talk with Monty, who is refreshingly vital, self-confident and shrewdly egotistical.

Delegation met at 10 a.m. S. of S. reported conversations with Jinnah and Azad. Jinnah was anxious about portfolios and wanted a guarantee that the Muslims should have Defence even if Jinnah didn't come in. He also wanted a guarantee on the major communal issues, that they would not be decided against a Muslim majority vote. Azad grumbled about the nomination of Nishtar from the N.W.F.P., wanted Bose instead of Mahtab, and talked about the possible inclusion of Zakir Hussain.[1] Gandhi was reported in a bad mood, he still remains really the evil genius of the Congress: that stupid old man Abdul Ghaffar Khan is being brought down from the N.W.F.P. (by train, as his doctors are against his flying) on the Nishtar business; and it is alleged that I purposely indicated June 26 as the target date for the formation of the Interim Government, so as to saddle them with the responsibility for the railway strike due to begin on June 27!

I saw Azad and Nehru at 12.30 p.m. There was little new in what they had to say and after blowing off some steam on the new Statement it all came down to three points: the substitution of Sarat Bose for Mahtab which I agreed to after some discussion; their wish to include a non-League Muslim, possibly Zakir Hussain. This I pointed out would raise great difficulties but I said I would consider it; whether Abdul Ghaffar Khan would object to Nishtar: I said I could not accept his exclusion and they did not press this point.

Nehru is going off to Kashmir for the defence of Sheikh Abdulla.[2]

[1] Dr. Zakir Hussain, a pro-Congress Muslim and keen educationalist. President of India, 1967–9.

[2] Sheikh Abdulla, leader of the Kashmir National Conference, a pro-Congress political party, close friend of Nehru, became Premier of Kashmir on its accession to India, but was imprisoned by the Govt. of India in 1953. He had been arrested at this time in connection with an agitation that he was leading against the State Government, and was in gaol awaiting trial.

I told him I thought this was most unwise and not the period when he should absent himself from Delhi.

Monty turned up before lunch, and I had an hour's talk with him after lunch and another after dinner. He was in great form. He is an example of a happy man in that he has always known exactly what he wanted, has had complete self-confidence in his ability to get it, and had no outside distractions and no false modesty or self-consciousness.

In between my talks with Monty, I saw Hydari—another man with complete self-confidence and lack of modesty—who wanted to know about his future. He was quite content to take four months leave and wait. He thought Congress would come in; said the Mission had done well and was respected for its sincerity.

I also had a difficult and not very pleasant interview with Jinnah. The more I see of these Indian politicians, the more I despair of India. I began by telling him about my interview with Azad and Nehru this morning. He accepted the substitution of Bose for Mahtab but said that Zakir Hussain, whom he characterised as a Quisling, would be utterly and entirely unacceptable. He then objected to my including Nazimuddin in the Government, as he wished to propose him to the Nizam as Premier, and we had a long discussion about this. I said I should be sorry to lose Nazimuddin.

He wanted a guarantee about major communal issues not being decided against a vote of the majority of Muslims. I said I thought that there would be in practice no difficulty about the major communal issues, he agreed that the Viceroy would have to be the judge of what was a major communal issue. On portfolios he did not really seem to know his own mind and had not decided whether to come in himself or not. We discussed some names.

He said that the Working Committee were meeting tonight and would write to me; but indicated that he thought we were being very weak with Congress and giving way to them on every point, and that he himself was being 'ground down' beyond endurance. I am afraid it was not a very successful interview, Jinnah gave me the impression of being rather depressed and tired, and of feeling that he had been rather let down.

After this interview Jinnah wrote to the Viceroy to say that the substitution of Dr. Zakir Hussain would be totally unacceptable, and that the Muslim League would never accept the nomination of any Muslim other than a Muslim Leaguer. Jinnah's rigid insistence on this point, dating right back to the Simla Conference, requires a few words of explanation, as prima facie it would seem unreasonable that he should object to the inclusion of an extra Muslim in the

Government, which is what the substitution of Dr. Zakir Hussain for a Congress Hindu would have meant. His objection stemmed from his belief that the Muslims' only hope of resisting Hindu dominance was to put up an unbroken and united front, and that if any countenance was given to Nationalist Muslims, whom he regarded as Congress stooges, this would simply further the Hindu (Congress) aim of dividing the Muslims. In Sind, where the Muslims were in a clear majority, the Hindus, by exploiting Muslim divisions, had for several years during the war established what was virtually a Congress Government. More recently in the Punjab, by combining with the rump of the Unionist Party, they had successfully kept the Muslim League out of power in this important Muslim-majority Province. In Municipal Committees in West Punjab where they were in a minority, they had by similar skilful tactics habitually obtained for themselves control of affairs. Jinnah thought that if Muslims were allowed to attain high office as Congress (Hindu) nominees, then the Congress by subtle flattery or other more material inducements would win more Muslims to their side and fatally divide the Muslim ranks.

These reasons for Jinnah's intransigence were well understood by Wavell, but they were not easy to explain or defend in public, and at a later stage, when the Mission had gone home, he decided that it was impossible any longer to accept Jinnah's veto of a Nationalist Muslim.

June 19

Delegation met 10 a.m. as usual. The information (from Ghosh and Rajagopalachariar) was to the effect that the Congress Working Committee had decided, against the advice of Gandhi, not to put forward a Nationalist Muslim for the Interim Government and were going to accept subject to Abdul Ghaffar Khan raising no objection to Nishtar. Things looked hopeful, therefore, though the Muslim League was known to be asking for assurances. Vallabhai was reported to have opposed Gandhi on the Nationalist Muslim issue. Nehru has gone off to Kashmir in spite of much advice not to do so, and will quite likely run into trouble.

Later I had a long letter from Jinnah[1] complaining of the concessions to Congress, and asking for assurances and guarantees that there would be no more, much in the tone of his interview with me yesterday. Incidentally, Jinnah saw Monty yesterday and said that no Interim Government would last.

A. V. Alexander dined with Monty and myself, in very good form: talked of his early life, of his service in the first World War, of the Cooperatives and other matters. On the Indian situation, he was all for firm handling, equally so with the Jews in Palestine.

[1] This letter dated 19 June was subsequently published by Jinnah at a crucial moment and gave rise to a good deal of ill-feeling.

June 20

The situation seems to have gone all haywire again, thanks to Gandhi. We met at 10 a.m. and began to discuss my draft reply to Jinnah. S. of S. was all for being vague and indefinite, but I refused absolutely to give Jinnah a reply capable of misinterpretation later and insisted that we must be quite definite. Cripps and Alexander backed me. Then Woodrow Wyatt appeared with a message as a result of an interview with Rajagopal-achariar. He said that Rajagopalachariar had told him that Congress had gone back on yesterday's decision, on the instance of Gandhi, and were going to insist on the removal of Engineer's name, since he was an 'official',[1] and the placing of Azad in the Government (they would apparently suggest Dalal instead of Engineer). I said at once that both conditions were utterly unacceptable and that putting Azad forward was simply a manoeuvre to ensure Jinnah's refusal and thus put the onus of a breakdown on him. The Nishtar objection was gone apparently, since Abdul Ghaffar Khan, brought down at such trouble from Peshawar, had apparently said that the idea of participating in such a Government was nonsense anyhow, so what did it matter who was in it. We all agreed, I am glad to say, that there could be no question either of leaving out Engineer or including Azad or any other Congress Muslim. Cripps was anxious to see Azad and then if necessary Gandhi, before the meeting of the Congress Working Committee in the afternoon. Alexander protested loudly against anyone of the Mission ever seeing Gandhi again. I agreed with him, but S. of S. ruled that it could do no harm if Azad himself suggested it.

After lunch I had another talk with Monty, he seemed to have had satisfactory discussions with the C-in-C. He was amusing about his interview with Azad, he had asked him how soon he could get all the British troops out of India and the British officers out of the Indian Army, as he wanted them elsewhere; and Azad had said that they could not be spared for a long time.

The S. of S. turned up next, to tell me of Cripps' interviews with Azad and Gandhi. They had been quite fruitless; Azad was worn out and obviously bullied by Gandhi; Gandhi, with whom Cripps had spent an hour and a half, had been in his most tiresome mood, had expatiated on all the old themes and was obviously working for a Congress controlled Central Government, which I warned the Mission from the start was his objective.

Meanwhile Nehru has got himself arrested in Kashmir.[2]

---

[1] Sir N. P. Engineer was not an official, but he held at the time an official position, viz. the post of Advocate-General to the Indian Army.

[2] The Kashmir Government had banned Nehru's entry into the State, and when he

June 21

The usual meeting at 10 a.m. after a quiet beginning developed almost into a major communal issue on the question of what to do if the Congress refused. It was agreed that Jinnah should be asked to cooperate in a Government; Cripps was set on J. being actually asked to form a Government, in the obvious hope that he would fail or refuse, in which event he insisted that we should go back to Congress and ask them to form one even though they had refused the offer. This of course would give Congress exactly what they are working and hoping for, and would be manifestly unfair to the Muslim League. Cripps showed his Congress bias strongly, and said that he would, resign if this was not done. After over two hours talk it was left at that. Cripps threatens resignation freely, I think this is the third or fourth time he has spoken of it. I wonder how far he means it.

> In their telegram to the Cabinet dated 3 June the Delegation had proposed that if the League accepted the proposals for a Constituent Assembly and an Interim Government, but the Congress rejected them, then a Government should be formed of League representatives and representatives of the Minorities with seats reserved for Congress but held temporarily by non-Congress Hindus or officials. The Viceroy, the Secretary of State, and Mr. Alexander considered that this was how they should now proceed, on the assumption that the Congress were going to reject the proposals, rather than on the lines proposed by Cripps, and they all three agreed that to ask the Congress to form a Government would not be an acceptable solution.

Ambedkar lunched, he is off to Bombay tomorrow, another of my Council gone. He was quiet and depressed, obviously thinks his side has been let down by myself and the Delegation. His party was of course thoroughly defeated at the polls; whether the strange system of selection is fair or not I don't know. I do not know enough about the wrongs and disabilities of the Scheduled Castes to feel really sympathetic or sentimental about them, but I do know that they are not capable of supplying, for a very long time to come at any rate, the men of character, education and ability of whom India is so sorely in need. I should not feel inclined to hamper the progress of India by special measures for them at this stage, though they must be given their chance to develop gradually. Ambedkar is sincere, honest and courageous, but he is not an attractive personality.

persisted in crossing the frontier he was arrested and detained in a Rest House. Abul Kalam Azad got through to him on the telephone and persuaded him to agree to leave the State; and Lord Wavell sent an aeroplane to fetch him back.

Maurice Gwyer arrived and we talked for some time after dinner. He was very critical of Gandhi and the Congress. He does not think that I shall need additional advice on Constitutional matters; and I am sure that he would be quite misplaced on my staff.

June 22

Met Delegation at 11 a.m. over a suggestion by George Abell to write a letter to Azad to inform him that we could not agree to a Nationalist Muslim in the Government. We had some fireworks at first since Cripps produced an alternative draft which would probably have sent Jinnah in off the deep end (I wish I had a political pool with two shallow ends), as it suggested some further appeasement of Congress; but in the end we got a short and reasonable draft: though I am sure it will do no good, and by all accounts rejection by Congress is inevitable. They will of course put it down to Jinnah's intractability again. We then discussed our future course of action. The Mission decided to go off home on Thursday or Friday, so as to have time for full consideration with the Cabinet before Attlee goes off to Australia on July 29. Meantime I try to form a Government with Jinnah's participation, or failing that an official Caretaker Government. S. of S. asked wistfully for the inclusion of a woman if possible.

June 23

Last minute efforts to avert a breakdown. Delegation met 9.30 a.m.–12. S. of S. reported his interviews of yesterday and this morning. Earlier he had gone to Gandhi's prayers, with Agatha Harrison I suppose—a most unnecessary and undignified excursion to my mind, but I think it happens often; and had talked with Gandhi, Sarojini Naidu[1] and Patel, all quite assured on breakdown. Patel had gone right back to Simla in 1945, with incorrect ideas of what had happened there. He said, surprisingly, that Congress had accepted the long-term policy of the May 16 Statement.[2] Quite a number of Congress want to accept Interim Government, but their Working Committee as a whole is quite incapable of making a corporate decision. We discussed Rajagopalachariar's advice to see Gandhi and Azad, only Cripps favouring it; and then Alexander said very sensibly that if there were to be any more interviews, the Delegation as a whole should see the four leading members of Congress, with the principal object of removing any misunderstandings on our pledges to Jinnah and what

---

[1] Member of Congress Working Committee; poetess.

[2] It would seem that Patel had already decided in his own mind that Congress had better accept the Statement of 16 May and knew that they would do so.

I had said at various times, of which misleading versions were apparently being given. This was agreed, and we then spent some time discussing the line to be taken, turning up old correspondence with the Parties, records of interviews, etc. The interview was fixed for 2 p.m.

The interview lasted 2–3.20 p.m. Azad, Nehru, Patel, Rajendra Prasad came. S. of S. opened with an agreed statement to the effect that we had never accepted Jinnah's claims to represent all Muslims, but in this particular instance asked Congress not to press for a Nationalist Muslim. Discussion then proceeded on the old lines; that it was a matter of principle, that Jinnah had no right to question Congress nominations or to block progress etc. S. of S. and Cripps answered quite well. We then got on to the question of deciding major communal issues in Council; how Zakir Hussain's name had come to be mentioned; the position of the Viceroy— Nehru claimed that it was for the Parties to form the Government in consultation with the Viceroy. I said that was not the position at all, the Viceroy formed the Government in consultation with the Parties; and the objective was a united India and so forth. At this point the S. of S. lapsed into woolliness, and made several of his long-winded appeasement speeches; about the imminent transfer of power, the unreasonableness of Jinnah—and the implied reasonableness of Congress, etc. I felt I wanted a large piece of green baize, a knobkerry or some other extinguisher. He is curious: sometimes he makes quite concise, sensible, even statesmanlike contributions: and then he suddenly seems to turn into a gushing babbler, unable to control his tongue and quite incapable of stopping. He will not leave well alone. Apart from this, I think the interview was worthwhile. I do not think it will change their decision, they said so in fact, but they were friendly, and some misunderstandings were cleared up.

June 24

Delegation met at 10 a.m. S. of S. described the comings and goings of the evening and night before and this morning. Amrit Kaur had turned up at 9 p.m. as an emissary from Gandhi, very excited: she said that G. had gone completely off the deep end, as she herself had obviously done, over a paragraph in the instructions to Governors about elections to the Constituent Assembly. S. of S. says he lost his temper with her. Others who turned up to see various members of the Mission at intervals during the evening were Sudhir Ghosh, Patel and Rajagopalachariar; and the scene must have been rather like a French farce, as some of the visitors had come unbeknownst to each other, and had to be interviewed in separate rooms, sitting or bed. At 6 a.m. or 7 a.m. this morning Patel and Gandhi appeared (G.'s day of silence made discussions somewhat protracted) and talked on many matters. One of the latest ideas is apparently to put the Constituent Assembly on a legal basis, by Act of Parliament. S. of S. committed us to seeing G. again at 8 p.m.: his announcement of this led to a strong denouncement by Alexander of Congress and all its manoeuvres of the past weeks. We then turned to a discussion of our next meeting with Jinnah, which will obviously be an awkward one. S. of S. is inclined now to place the blame for failure on J.'s intransigence, which neither Alexander nor myself thought fair. Cripps now says that Congress while turning down the Interim Government will accept the May 16 Statement, the one thing which he assured me yesterday and the day before that they would never do; and which places us in a more awkward position with Jinnah. I am afraid that I would not put it past Cripps to have suggested to Congress in one of his many talks that they would put themselves in a better tactical position if they did so.

> The record of the meeting of the Delegation at 10 a.m. on 24 June shows that the various emissaries who had seen members of the Delegation on the previous evening had given them clearly to understand that Patel now wanted the Congress to accept the Statement of 16 May; and that when Gandhi and Patel appeared at 6.00 a.m., the Secretary of State had pointed out to them that if the Congress accepted the Statement of 16 May they would put themselves on the level with the Muslim League in respect of the Interim Government.
>
> Mr. Alexander expressed himself strongly on Congress manœuvres. He said that their acceptance of the May Statement would not be genuine, but a paper acceptance in order to get an Interim Government in which they would have control. 'He had come out to India quite unbiased and in the early stages had been somewhat exasperated with Mr. Jinnah's attitude. But he was bound to say that the behaviour of the Congress in the last six weeks seemed to him the most deplorable exhibition that he had witnessed in his political career.'

When the rest of the Mission had gone, the S. of S. came back again to the question of Maurice Gwyer, and I asked him bluntly what was behind it all, was it being suggested to him by Congress that I had nothing but official advice. He denied this, and said his desire was merely to help me, as I should have no-one to lean on for political advice after the Mission had gone! I said that I had had to rely on my own judgment for a long time before the Mission came, but that if H.M.G. or the P.M. would prefer to replace me by someone with more political experience, that would be quite all right by me.

During the afternoon I had a letter from Azad, to convey the Congress refusal to take part in the Interim Government.

The interview with Gandhi was, I thought, a deplorable affair; Gandhi was at his worst, yet the Mission was out to do everything possible to conciliate him. He began with the complaint that candidates for the Constituent Assembly were being compelled to sign a document which meant their acceptance of the principle of grouping Provinces in Sections for the determination of their constitution. He was given what seemed to me a dishonest assurance that this was not so; and when I said that the grouping was an essential part of the scheme, S. of S. asked me not to press the point.

Wavell was much disquieted by the lack of frankness to Gandhi on this matter. He wrote an important and telling note for the Delegation on the subject (Appendix VII) and, as will be seen, raised the matter at a meeting at 12 noon on 25 June, but without getting much satisfaction. Subsequent events showed that his apprehensions were fully justified.

G. then went on to the European question, on which propitiatory statements were again made to him. He next said that since negotiations for the Interim Government had failed all correspondence about it, including all assurances given to Jinnah, should be put on the scrap-heap. Just what the Congress want of course. He then wished the Constituent Assembly to be given legal status by Act of Parliament—this is a new Congress stunt. S. of S. burst into one of his long statements on the faith of the British Government being a greater safeguard than an Act of Parliament, etc; while Alexander contributed his favourite reference to the rights of Minorities and a treaty. The interview ended with Patel, who had hitherto sat silent, regarding Gandhi with some contemptuous tolerance, it seemed to me, bringing up the Europeans in Bengal again; but he did not press it. The meeting broke up with an air of heartiness on the part of the Mission towards G. which I did certainly not share. I have much more respect for Patel.

Sometime to-day I dictated a note to the Mission on the deplorable mess we had got into:

Congress manoeuvres have now put us into a very difficult position, both with Mr. Jinnah and as to the formation of an Interim Government.

Relying on a letter from Congress that the acceptance of the Statement of May 16th and the Interim Government hung together, and an assurance that there was no possibility of the Congress rejecting an Interim Government and accepting the Statement of May 16, we have committed ourselves, in paragraph 8 of the Statement of June 16, to forming an Interim Government with anyone who had accepted the Statement of May 16.

This paragraph was put in, perhaps rashly, because we felt that Mr. Jinnah, who had already accepted the Statement of May 16, should not be put at a disadvantage with the Congress, who had not; and in furtherance of our pledge that we would go ahead as far as possible with anyone who accepted the Statement of May 16.

We are now precluded from trying to form an Interim Government with the participation of the Muslim League, but without that of the Congress; and Congress will claim that in any fresh attempt all the original bases and the assurances given to Mr. Jinnah have disappeared. We have in fact been out-manoeuvred by the Congress; and this ability of Congress to twist words and phrases and to take advantage of any slip in wording is what Mr. Jinnah has all along feared, and has been the reason for his difficult attitude. The success of the Congress, which he will feel has been mainly due to their continuous contacts with the Mission, especially since the Statement of June 16, will increase his distrust, both of the Congress and of the Mission, and of the Viceroy.

In these conditions, I feel that it would be quite useless to try and press Mr. Jinnah to make the concession of accepting a Congress Muslim; and indeed I doubt whether Congress would now be prepared to come in if that concession were made. They would see their advantage, and would press it by demanding some further concession. The atmosphere for any sort of compromise is now, I think, more unfavourable than at any other time. Tempers are frayed; the Muslim League feel that they have been betrayed; and the Congress feel that they have gained an advantage of which they will not be slow to make capital.

The alternatives for an Interim Government therefore appear to be:

(a) To ask Mr. Jinnah to form a Government. I do not see how this could possibly be done, since both sides have now accepted the May 16 Statement; unless we decided that the Congress's is a dishonest one, as it in fact is, and refuse to regard it as an acceptance.

(b) To capitulate entirely to the Congress and ask them to form a Government, seeking the cooperation of the Muslim League on such terms as they judge right. It does not seem to me that this would be fair or honest to the Muslim League, and I could not accept it.

(c) To form a Caretaker Government of officials, to carry on for a short period while the Mission goes home for consultation; and everybody has a rest and recovers from the strain and heat aroused by the recent discussions and negotiations.

The solution depends on whether the Delegation propose to regard the Congress acceptance of the Statement of May 16 as genuine, in spite of their expressed intention to evade at least one of its essential provisions.

If the Delegation do not accept it, then Mr. Jinnah can be asked to participate in a Government as already agreed.

If the Delegation proposes to accept the Congress acceptance of the Statement, I think that the only possible solution is a temporary Caretaker Government of officials. It may not hold the situation for long, perhaps for not more than a few weeks, perhaps hardly that; but we have been manoeuvred into a position when it seems to be the only chance. However long it lasts, and whatever decision H.M.G. gives as to their general policy, I am quite certain that our last chance of getting a genuine Coalition Government for India has gone, for a very long time at any rate.

June 25

The worst day yet, I think. Congress has accepted the Statement of May 16, though with reservations on its interpretation. They did not intend to do so, having always said they would not accept the long-term policy unless they accepted the short-term one, Interim Government. Now Cripps, having assured me categorically that Congress would never accept the Statement of May 16, instigated Congress to do so by pointing out the tactical advantage they would gain as regards the Interim Government. So did the Secretary of State. When I tackled him on this, he defended it on the grounds that to get the Congress into the Constituent Assembly was such a gain that he considered it justified. It has left me in an impossible position vis-à-vis Jinnah.

We had a meeting with Delegation from 12–1.30 p.m. I challenged the assurance given to Gandhi last night on the matter of the undertaking to be signed by a Candidate for the Constituent Assembly as not quite honest, but these politicians can always out-talk me, and I had to withdraw. We then discussed the Congress letter of acceptance which is really a dishonest acceptance, but is so cleverly worded that it had to be regarded as an acceptance.

> In their letter the Congress referred to their Resolution of 24 May (see p. 277) in which they had pointed out what in their opinion were the defects in the proposals and had also given their interpretation of the provisions of the statement in regard to Grouping, and continued: 'While adhering to our views, we accept your proposals and are prepared to work them with a view to achieve our objective.'

Delegation met 3.30 p.m.–5 p.m., to discuss brief for interview with Jinnah. S. of S. showed his bias against Jinnah and wished to accuse him of having wrecked negotiations by giving out his letter of June 19[1] for

---

[1] See footnote on p. 297.

publication. I protested against this, saying that it was no use treating Jinnah in this way, and all agreed, but it did not in the event stop S. of S. doing so at the interview.

The interview with Jinnah (5.30–8 p.m.) was a deplorable one. It began with J. questioning the genuineness of the Congress acceptance of May 16. This resulted, quite unnecessarily, in a long argument about J.'s acceptance and the reservations[1] he had made. A little later S. of S., in spite of his agreeing not to raise the subject, attacked J. vehemently on the publication of his letter to me of June 19th and declared it to be the cause of the breakdown. There followed a long unseemly wrangle; and by the time we got down to real business, what to do next, J. was in a thoroughly evil mood; accused us of bad faith and of giving way to Congress, and considered that he should be given the opportunity of entering the Government. He finally left, asking me to write to him what we proposed to do.

We spent about ¾ of an hour drafting a letter to J. which I signed and sent off about 10 p.m. A sorry business, and I think we deserve some at least of J.'s strictures, though J. himself has not played his cards too well.

June 26

Delegation met at 9.30 a.m. and Congress (Azad, Nehru, Patel, Prasad) at 9.45 a.m. S. of S. was apologetic about the way he had handled the interview with Jinnah the evening before, but all the same was for keeping off anything which might annoy the Congress. I insisted that we should make it clear to Congress that we did not accept their interpretation of the Grouping business.

The interview went quite smoothly. Congress have a different technique to Jinnah, though more deadly in the long run. They agreed to the proposed interval, as they would naturally do. We had a little discussion on the publication of letters. Finally Nehru complained that Governors were thwarting Ministers in the Provinces and ought to give up all their special responsibilities etc. and do nothing except what their Ministers told them. I said Governors were doing their best to work with Ministers, but were bound to fulfil their duties under the existing Constitution.

After Congress had gone, we agreed that Alexander should see Jinnah and try to remove some of last night's unfortunate impression; dealt with

[1] In accepting the Statement of 16 May the Muslim League had declared that 'the attainment of the goal of a complete sovereign Pakistan still remains the unalterable goal of the Muslims of India' and that it was willing to co-operate with the proposed constitution-making machinery 'in the hope that it would ultimately result in the establishment of complete sovereign Pakistan'. The League also reserved the right to revise its policy and attitude at any time during the progress of the constitution-making body.

the paper on Minorities and Cripps' opinion on the grouping question; decided that we should have to go through all the correspondence and decide what should be published; and that a Statement of proposed action should be put out tomorrow. The Mission decided to go on Saturday.

Afterwards I had a talk with Alexander, and told him that I should normally ask to be relieved of my appointment after what had happened; that I thought I had been placed in an impossible position with the M.L., and that Cripps had not been quite straight; but that I did not want to embarrass H.M.G. He thought I ought to stay.

At 7 p.m. we drafted a short Statement on the proposed action, to be issued tonight; and heard Alexander's account of his interview with Jinnah, which had lasted 1½ hours. J. was naturally and justifiably sore; but A.V.A. had done something to calm him down. On the matter of a Congress or even non-League Muslim J. had spoken for over 20 minutes and had been absolutely and entirely adamant.

In their short Statement the Cabinet Mission and Viceroy expressed satisfaction that 'Constitution-making can now proceed with the consent of the two major parties and the States'. They regretted that it had not so far proved possible to form an Interim Coalition Government, but said that after a short interval, during which elections to the Constituent Assembly would take place, a fresh effort to do so would be made in accordance with Paragraph 8 of the Statement of 16 June. Meanwhile a temporary Caretaker Government of officials would be set up.

June 27

A comparatively short meeting of the Delegation this morning in which we approved replies to Azad and Jinnah, and discussed the publication of correspondence during the negotiations.

In the afternoon I saw Patel in view of a report that Nehru was off to Kashmir again.

I asked him to use his influence to prevent Nehru going as his visit would be most inopportune and could only do harm. It was surely better, I said, to negotiate with the Princes through their Negotiating Committee than to bring pressure to bear on individual States. Patel agreed with me and said he and Azad had done their best to dissuade Nehru from going. When I said that I had also tried to dissuade Nehru he said I should have done so more forcibly! I said I thought this would only be likely to rouse a spirit of opposition in N.

On the forthcoming A.I.C.C. meeting he told me Nehru would take over the Presidency. I then told him how disappointed I was that the recent negotiations had failed to secure a coalition government. I hoped Congress would come into any fresh negotiations in a constructive spirit and that they would not try to raise their price and make negotiations with the League difficult. He was non-committal, but said that he had no quarrel with Mr. Jinnah, and that communal feeling in the country at large would be stilled now that the long term policy had been accepted.

The conversation lasted for about half an hour. He was friendly and sensible.

In the evening Nehru came. He talked much of Kashmir and occasionally got wound up about the Princes. Then I had a dinner party, farewell for the Mission, at which everybody was rather subdued, except Alexander who was prepared to go on playing the piano and singing till early morning.

June 28

Delegation met from 10–11.15 a.m. on the publication of the correspondence which has passed during the Mission's negotiations. It was a waste of time so far as I was concerned. I said that I was prepared to abide by the dictum 'quod scripsi, scripsi', and was prepared for any letters of mine to be published. But the Mission, with an anxious eye on Parliament, debated the matter at some length. They were, however, forced to the conclusion that everything would come out sooner or later; and only made a reservation on the correspondence with Gandhi, about some of which some of them have, I think, a slightly uneasy conscience.

Later in the day I received a letter from Jinnah, accusing the Mission and myself of bad faith, in not at once forming a Government with him.

Jinnah had understood Paragraph 8 of the Statement of 16 June (Appendix VI) to mean that if the Congress refused to join an Interim Government composed as proposed in that Statement while the League agreed to do so, then the Viceroy would go ahead and form the Government as proposed, but without the Congress representatives. This was a possible, perhaps even the natural interpretation of the meaning of Paragraph 8. The Mission and the Viceroy interpreted it differently. They considered that since both parties had now accepted the Statement of 16 May Paragraph 8 required that fresh efforts should be made de novo to form an Interim Government. Jinnah said that this interpretation had been dishonestly 'concocted by the legalistic talents of the Cabinet Mission'.

June 29

I finished off a note for the Cabinet on the present position, so as to make it quite clear that the outlook was still unsettled and stormy.

This note was an expanded and slightly revised version of the note he had started drafting on 10 June, see p. 289.

At 11 a.m. S. of S. came to say goodbye. He read my note and said he thought it might be pessimistic. We had some talk on the past negotiations but nothing new was said. He thought Rajagopalachariar the biggest man in Indian politics, Nehru likeable but not courageous politically. He wanted me to give special facilities for Sudhir Ghosh to go home. I said I saw no reason to expedite a Congress agent and that S.G. was rather a snake in the grass. We parted on quite friendly but not cordial terms. I did not see Cripps.

Jinnah wrote again and I sent him a brief reply. The Mission departed, it looked at one time as if the weather might delay them. I will try to summarise my general comments on their work tomorrow.

June 30

Came up to Simla for a little change and rest, and to think out the next move.

With remarkable resilience Wavell on 28 June wrote a note for consideration by the P.S.V. on a possible new method of forming a Coalition Government, and in Simla he discussed the matter with Sir Evan Jenkins.

A Retrospect: Summary of Cabinet Mission's Work
(March–June 1946)

While the events of this period are fairly fresh in my mind, I want to set down my general impressions of what took place and the reasons for failure. I am doing so without any reference to documents, and mean simply to give my personal view. There will inevitably be a great deal of publicity and much controversy over this Mission, and I want to write before all this starts.

Firstly, the personnel of the Mission. The S. of S., old P.L., is a sentimental pacifist with a strain of rather pugnacious obstinacy if crossed, and I think a good deal of self-satisfaction and some vanity. He is more genuinely 'non-violent' than Gandhi, with him it really is a creed, while I believe that for G. non-violence is a political weapon far more than a creed. The approach of the S. of S. to these tough crafty Hindu politicians was often too abject, I thought; but he undoubtedly convinced them of his genuineness and honesty of purpose. He could make a very sensible little speech or pronouncement; but too often lapsed during interviews and discussions into an apparently uncontrollable cascade of words, delivered at a tremendous pace, often not very well thought out and always largely repetitive and redundant. He was a very bad draftsman of a document, wordy and indefinite.

Cripps was much the ablest of the party, with an extremely acute legal intellect, very quick to seize on a point, very persuasive, convinced of his ability to make both black and white appear a neutral and acceptable grey, a clever draftsman and very good at finding a compromise solution to any problem. But he is an ambitious man and was quite determined not to come away empty-handed this time; and this made him over-keen and not too scrupulous. My predecessor told me, à propos of the Cripps Mission of 1942, that C. was 'not quite straight under pressure', and he was right.

Alexander was straight, sensible and honest, the very best type of British Labour, the best we breed. At the beginning he knew nothing of India and the ways of Indian politicians, and sat back. At the end he really had a surer and more realistic grasp of the situation than either of the other two. He had a tendency to appeal to the strict letter of his instructions or of any document and obviously liked to have definite 'sailing orders' on which to base his opinions and actions.

Of the officials, Croft was rather disappointing and did not exercise much influence. He was rather too narrow and old-fashioned in his views, I do not think the S. of S. set much store by his advice, and his unquestioned ability was rather wasted. Turnbull was a very good secretary and produced good summaries of discussions etc. Joyce[1] on publicity was I think no more than adequate, he never seemed to have any special ideas for guiding the Press; but he may have been working behind the scenes. And I doubt whether the most skilled of snake-charmers could do much with the cobras and karaits of the Indian Press.

I think the unofficial excrescences were unfortunate. I do not approve, of course, of the political practice of using hunting jackals to nose out scraps of information behind the backs of the principals to a negotiation. I was rather shocked at it in 1945 when I was at home and found that certain members of the India Committee approached members of my Executive Council who were at home and even members of my staff in order to try and ascertain from them whether they agreed with views I had expressed. (I first struck this attitude of mind when Hore-Belisha became War Minister, and on meeting me for the first time—I was a divisional commander—endeavoured to get me to criticise the views of

[1] A. H. Joyce, Adviser on Publicity, India Office.

the A.G. and give him my own, and seemed rather surprised when I refused to do so.)

But far more unfortunate than these was the presence of Agatha Harrison and Horace Alexander,[1] who lived in the Congress Camp, were completely sold to Gandhi, and saw the S. of S. almost daily. No wonder that Jinnah and the Muslim League distrusted these unofficial connections with the Congress, I wonder whether I should have been more vigorous about it.

Phase I was the discussions of the Mission with myself at the end of March. I was worried by the lack of positive approach to their task on the part of the Mission; they seemed to be purely opportunist and content to wait on the discussions rather than direct them, though I sensed from the first that Cripps would take and encourage the Congress point of view (I knew that he had been in private correspondence with Nehru about the objectives before the Mission came out—a proceeding which I should not call strictly honest, though to a politician it seems quite normal). My suggestions for a firm line and possible threat of a big stick were received with shocked disapproval by the S. of S. It became clear to me during this Phase that the Mission had no real plan (though Cripps may have had a private plan): and that they would not therefore take charge of discussions and direct them, but would simply wait on events and were likely to be influenced by the loudest tongue. I was discouraged by the S. of S. lack of 'Commonwealth' backbone.

Phase II—the discussions with selected persons or groups—was, in my view, an almost complete waste of time. All the stale old Party slogans and dogmas were delivered in different forms; there was no sign of constructive statesmanship or compromise; no Hindu admitted that a Muslim could possibly have a grievance or any reason for mistrusting the 'democratic' predominance of the Congress, no Muslim would admit any possibility of justice or fairness from Hindu hands. The only people who put their case in some spirit of moderation and realism were the Princes, one or two of their Diwans, and Griffiths on behalf of the Europeans.

I thought the Mission handled the interviews in a thoroughly unbusinesslike manner, as was perhaps inevitable since they had no plan. Those interviewed were allowed to deliver long harangues, instead of being kept to the point; since the Mission, without a definite scheme, hardly knew where the point lay. The S. of S. was incapable often of asking a simple question without delivering an almost interminable little

[1] H. G. Alexander, a lecturer at Birmingham was, like Agatha Harrison, a member of the Quakers' India Conciliation Group. Along with Sudhir Ghosh and a group of young British pacifists of the Friends' Ambulance Unit he had been engaged on famine relief work in Bengal in 1942–3. He saw himself as an intermediary between Gandhi and the world of British officialdom in succession to C. F. Andrews.

speech; and every interviewer had to be assured, almost abjectly, of our desire to part with power and 'Quit India'. Cripps often got involved in lengthy legal discussions on details of constitutional questions which seemed to me waste of time at this stage. Alexander was still a little 'at sea' and did not make much contribution. The Indian politicians showed up as a sorry lot.

I was frankly shocked at the deference shown to Gandhi by Cripps and S. of S. The second round of these discussions, with the leaders of the Congress and Muslim League, was equally fruitless; and to my military mind equally mishandled owing to a lack of a definite plan. It was obvious that we should have to lead ourselves, and at least to make a plan, which should have been done at the beginning.

Phase III was the period before and after the Mission's recess in Kashmir and ended with the decision for the Simla meetings. I felt at this time that the discussions had shown that there was no hope of reaching agreement between the Parties; and that we should have to take a decision. I thought the Mission made rather heavy work of doing so, and that it was absurd to say that we must never speak of an 'award', only of recommendations and suggestions. We had the germ of a good and workable compromise in the 3-tier scheme, and my personal view was that had we boldly set it out, and had an alternative breakdown scheme definitely planned and approved by H.M.G., if the Congress hesitated, we should have had a good chance of its being accepted, and need not have been afraid to call it an award. I thought the manoeuvres by which the two parties were induced to go to Simla were not very dignified and a little disingenuous. I suppose it was a success in a way for the Mission; but from the point of view of a military observer it meant that we had shirked giving a decision and surrendered the initiative.

Phase IV I thought that the chief value of Simla was not the negotiations themselves, I did not think they ever had a hope of success, but the time it gave us to draw up the Statement of May 16. I doubt whether we should ever have arrived at as good a Statement down in Delhi. The discussions went on too long, they should have been broken off at once when Jinnah and Nehru reported that they had been unable to agree on an arbitrator. We went backwards after that; and the request to both Parties to put their claims on paper was, I thought and still think, a stupid blunder; and the long wrangle about the publication of documents was quite unnecessary and avoidable. That the negotiations should still have gone near to success in spite of them is I think a testimony to the anxiety of everyone for a settlement.

Phase V May 16 Statement was a good one, E. and O.E. We made a mistake over the Europeans; we gave the Congress lawyers a loophole for misinterpretation—quite wilful on their part, of course—between paragraphs 15(4) and 19(5); and perhaps we might have done something more to satisfy the Sikhs. Possibly too the condemnation of Pakistan was rather too sweeping. But on the whole it was a great tribute to the Constitutional ingenuity of Cripps and Rau.

Could we have kept the initiative after its issue, and forced a reply within a limited period? Only I think if we had really had a definite plan of action from the first. The long period of argument, quibbling, huckstering and hesitation by Congress was deplorable; and I think it ought somehow to have been prevented. The Mission's continuous touch with Congress during this period and the pathetic anxiety they showed to persuade them to accept was to my mind all wrong. It was, I think, both undignified and unprofitable; and I am not sure that it was always quite honest.

Phase VI The negotiations for an Interim Government were going on concurrently with Phases IV and V. I am not very proud of the way I conducted these, though I am not sure that I could have done any better. I was hampered by two things, that it was impossible to keep the Interim Government separate from acceptance or rejection of the long term policy; and that I never quite knew what was going on behind the scenes. I think perhaps I was wrong to begin with the 5 : 5 : 2 formula, also not to press Jinnah more strongly about a Congress Muslim from the very start. Still it is difficult to deal with people who continually change their ground, who give you to understand that only one point requires to be settled, and as soon as they get some satisfaction or concession on that, raise another, and so on. Thus the Congress first concentrated on the powers of the Government, then made an issue of parity, and finally of the Congress Muslim. Still I feel that I should somehow have been cleverer about it; and a little firmer with Jinnah.

I think the Statement of June 16 was on the right lines but perhaps Engineer was a mistake. If Anthony[1] had been suitable it would have been better to have included an Anglo-Indian. But the really unfortunate mistake was Paragraph 8, which was meant to help Jinnah and has caused him such irritation and enabled him to accuse us of bad faith. I wonder if Cripps foresaw from the first the way that would, or might, work out. At any rate it was, I think, definitely sharp practice on his part, after having several times assured me, when I raised the point, that there was no possible chance of Congress accepting the May 16 Statement, unless they came into the Interim Government, to point out to the Congress, as I am sure he did, the tactical advantage they would gain by accepting the May 16 Statement, even with reservations, and thus preventing Paragraph 8 of

[1] Frank Anthony, President-in-Chief of the Anglo-Indian Association and a member of the Central Legislative Assembly.

June 16 being operated in Jinnah's favour. And the S. of S. did so too. They played too keen a game, at the most charitable view. Cripps even said, with some satisfaction, that it was Paragraph 8 which had brought about Congress acceptance of May 16 Statement.

Whether Gandhi's final spanner could have been kept out of the works, if Jinnah had not published his letter; and whether Jinnah could have been restrained from publishing his letter, if we had kept in touch with the Muslim League as some of the Mission did with Congress, it will never be possible to say; but I do blame myself for not having had some line to Jinnah to re-assure him a little.[1]

Anyway, the third attempt which I have seen, and in which I have taken some part—a very minor role in the Cripps offer, the leading part in 1945, and a large but unsatisfactory role in this Cabinet Delegation business— has ended in failure; and perhaps a worse failure than ever before. What were the main causes?

As I have indicated, I think at the root of the failure lay the fact that H.M.G. and the Delegation never had any definite basic plan; and so could never keep the initiative. They negotiated as supplicants asking for favours, rather than as masters granting them. And we are still masters of India, even if a little precariously. We showed ourselves much too eager to make a bargain, almost at the price of honour and peace. I still believe that a firmer, more masculine attitude would not only have been more befitting a great people, but would have paid a better dividend.

It was quite wrong for the Mission to have had such constant contacts with the Congress camp, and especially with Gandhi. They put exaggerated faith and belief in him and showed him absurd deference. Sudhir Ghosh, Gandhi's emissary, is I believe a snake in the grass; and I would certainly never have trusted him. Even Rajagopalachariar would I am sure let them down if it suited his book or that of the Congress; and was throughout a propagandist of the Congress case.

Gandhi ran true to form and was the real wrecker. His one idea for 40 years has been to overthrow British rule and influence and to establish a Hindu raj; and he is as unscrupulous as he is persistent. He has brought to a fine art the technique of vagueness and of never making a statement which is not somehow so qualified or worded, that he cannot be pinned down to anything definite. His practice of mixing prayers with politics, or rather of making prayers a medium of political propaganda, is all a part of the make-up. He is an exceedingly shrewd, obstinate, domineering, double-tongued, single-minded politician; and there is little true saintliness in him.

---

[1] One of Cripps's assistants, Woodrow Wyatt, was on good terms with Jinnah and not unsympathetic to the Muslim League. Wavell might have made more use of him as a line to Jinnah, but did not feel complete confidence in him. He regretted that he did not keep in closer touch with Jinnah through members of his own staff.

With very few exceptions, the Congress Working Committee are not an impressive lot; while there is a good deal of cleverness there is no statesmanship amongst them. Azad came out well, he is honest, moderate and a gentleman; but not a strong character. Nehru is sincere, well-educated and personally courageous, but lacks balance and political courage. Patel is more like a leader than any of them, and might become the easiest to do business with. I liked Mahtab of Orissa, earnest but inexperienced.

Jinnah over-called his hand in the end, and was too uncompromising on the non-League Muslim issue; but he is straight compared with Congress, and does not constantly shift his ground, as they do, though he too drives a hard bargain.

Such is the judgment of one trained as a soldier on some very well intentioned but in the end a little sordid, political manoeuvres. I somehow feel that I ought to have been able to keep them on firmer and straighter lines; but it would have been difficult. And I was in agreement with most of what they did, it was their dilatory, too conciliatory, rather tortuous methods which I thought wrong; and I do not think I could have changed them.

I am depressed at the future prospect. Congress have been encouraged and will set their claims higher than ever. The suspicion and dislike of Jinnah for the Congress have been enhanced; and to them is added, I fear, a mistrust of H.M.G., and perhaps of myself. Further negotiations will not be easy.

(July 1 1946)

I picked up Alice through the Looking Glass one evening shortly before the end of the Mission and wrote the parody below; I put it down here, but doubt whether it is really worth preserving.

JABBER-WEEKS

(from Phlawrence through the Indian Ink)

Twas grillig; and the Congreelites
Did harge and shobble in the swope;
All Jinsy were the Pakstanites,
And the spruft Sikhs outstrope.

Beware the Gandhiji, my son,
The satyagraha, the bogy fast,
Beware the Djinnarit, and shun
The frustrious scheduled caste.

He took his crippsian pen in hand,
Long time in draftish mood he wrote,
And fashioned as his lethal brand
A cabimissionary note.

And as he mused with pointed phrase,
The Gandhiji, on wrecking bent,
Came trippling down the bhangi ways,
And woffled as he went.

Ek do, Ek do, and blow on blow
The pointed phrase went slicker snack;
And, with the dhoti, Ghosh and goat, he
Came chubilating back.

And hast thou swoozled Gandhiji!
Come to my arms, my blimpish boy!
Hoo-ruddy-ray! O Labour Day,
He shahbashed in his joy.

Twas grillig; and the Congreelites
Did harge and shobble in the swope,
All jinsy were the Pakstanites,
And the spruft Sikhs outstrope.

'It's very interesting', said Phlawrence a little wearily, 'but it's rather hard to understand'.

'So is nearly everything in this country', answered Hobson-Jobson. 'Shall I explain some of the difficult words for you?'

'Yes, please', said Phlawrence.

'Well, grillig is in the hot-weather at Delhi, when everyone's brains are grilled before 2 p.m. and don't get ungrilled till 2 a.m. Congreelites are animals rather like conger eels, very slippery, they can wriggle out of anything they don't like. Harge is a portmanteau word, it means to haggle and argue; to shobble is to shift and wobble; a swope is a place open to sweepers. Pakstanites are rather fierce noisy animals, all green, they live round mosques and can't bear Congreelites. Spruft means spruce and puffed up; outstrope means that they went round shouting out that they weren't being fairly treated and would take direct action about it'.

'That seems a lot for one word to mean', said Phlawrence.

'The Sikhs don't quite know what it does mean yet', said Hobson-Jobson.

'Well, anyway, the Gandhiji seems to have been swoozled, whatever that means', said Phlawrence, 'and I expect that was a good thing'.

'But he wasn't', said Hobson-Jobson, 'they found out afterwards that he had swoozled everyone else'.

'Thank you very much for your explanation', said Phlawrence after a pause, 'but I am afraid it is all still very difficult'.

13

THE INTERIM GOVERNMENT

July 4 (Simla)

Some comparatively peaceful days since I came up here. On the 2nd Evan Jenkins came in for a talk, he is looking very well and in good heart, less need as a Governor to overwork himself, I expect. He said the Sikhs were very excited, were talking wildly, had no leadership and might do something stupid. We talked of Nehru's visit to Kashmir; of possible means to resume negotiations for an Interim Government—which he thought more important than the Constituent Assembly; of the Services; about food procurement, which is going much better in the Punjab; and about the possibility of a Governors' Conference.

This morning I had the first meeting of the Caretaker Official Council. It will certainly be easier to do business with, but this morning there was practically nothing to do. Hutchings made a statement about Food, and seemed to think we should pull through all right with luck. Bengal is now the danger point.

Members of the Caretaker Council
Field Marshal Sir Claude Auchinleck, Commander-in-Chief, War
Sir Eric Coates, I.C.S., Finance
Sir Eric Conran-Smith, I.C.S., War Transport, Railways, Ports, and Air
Sir Akbar Hydari, I.C.S., Labour, Information and Arts, Health
Sir Robert Hutchings, I.C.S., Food and Agriculture
Sir Arthur Waugh, I.C.S., Home and Supply
Sir Gurunath Bewoor, I.C.S., Commerce and Commonwealth Relations
Sir George Spence, I.C.S., Law and Education

July 8

Nothing but routine papers from Delhi the last few days, and not too many of them. I have written a periodical letter to the King, describing the negotiations with the Cabinet Mission; P.S.V. thought it good, Q. thought poorly of it.

H.M. King George VI, in handing this letter to his Private Secretary, Sir Alan Lascelles, said 'And a damned good letter it is.' Sir Alan said that

it was all this and more—'a state and historical document of the first import-
ance.' Although it duplicates to some extent the summing up of the Cabinet
Mission given in the Journal, it is such a good letter that with Her Majesty's
gracious permission it is reproduced with only slight omissions as Appendix
VIII. The portion omitted contains brief comments on some individual Rulers.

July 10

Council had only two items; the release of ex-enemy technicians to
remain in India for jobs instead of deportation; and the date of the next
meeting of the Legislature. Conran-Smith made a statement about the
strike of postmen, due to start tomorrow, which it is proposed to fight,
and will be a half-hearted affair, it is hoped.

July 11

Wylie, Dow[1] and Twynam arrived yesterday; and I had a two-hours
conference with them this morning and two hours in the afternoon. In
the morning we discussed the protection of the Services against victimization for the 1942 disturbances. It was agreed that the question of an enquiry
into 1942 would undoubtedly depend on the attitude of the Congress
High Command; that the Services must be protected from such an Enquiry
even at the risk of a showdown with Congress; but that individual cases
brought against officers would have to be dealt with in accordance with
the law.

All agreed that compensation terms for the Services should be published
as soon as possible; that officers should be allowed to go on these terms if
they wished; and that the S. of S. Services would have in any event to be
wound up within a very limited period. It was decided that, if the S. of S.
agreed, Governors should approach their Ministries and ascertain whether
they wished to keep on the existing S. of S. officers.

In the afternoon, after a short discussion on the I.N.A. I gave Governors
an outline of the breakdown plan I had put to H.M.G. and their reaction.
The Governors had not much comment, they were all agreed on the
necessity for H.M.G. to have a definite policy; they thought they could
at present suppress a Congress movement, except in Bihar; but none of
them could answer the question of where we went from there.

Governors had no special problems otherwise. Evan Jenkins was rather
shocked at the deterioration of the administration in the Punjab in the last
10 years; he said it was now definitely an oriental standard. He was
apprehensive of communal trouble, especially from the Sikhs.

[1] Now Governor of Bihar. Mudie had taken his place as Governor of Sind.

July 12

All the Governors except Dow left early this morning. I had an hour's talk with Dow. He has a cynical contempt for Bihar and its politicians, but is holding his own with them, I think. He thinks his police unreliable. I believe even Congress think poorly of their supporters in Bihar; it has always been a difficult Province.

July 16

Left Simla yesterday and called in on H.H. of Patiala at Chail on the way down. I had an hour's talk to him about possible grouping of Sikh States and the problems of the Sikhs generally. He was sensible but nothing new came out of it.

S. of S. sent a very woolly reply to the telegram I sent from Simla about the Services, after my discussions with the Governors, to the effect that it 'raised serious issues,' 'would require earnest consideration by H.M.G.,' etc. Even worse, just as I had approved a final draft of letters to Nehru and Jinnah, reopening negotiations for an Interim Government, I had a letter from S. of S. saying that H.M.G. were about to send me instructions about the Interim Government. I almost decided to send my letters and turn a blind eye to his, but eventually cabled home text of letters and said I should send them unless I received orders to the contrary.

> *H.M.G. agreed to the issue of these letters and the one addressed to Nehru was given to him when he saw Lord Wavell on 22 July.*

July 17

The principal item in Council was a review of all the plans for the five year period ahead put forward by the Centre and Provinces, with an estimate of their cost. This produced a very interesting discussion; and the general result was that the financial resources could probably be provided, but that it was most unlikely that the necessary material resources—steel, bricks, machinery, coal, cement, etc.—would be available, or the skilled personnel required; so that an attempt to carry out the whole programme would merely result in competition for the limited material and a rise in prices, so that we should get no more done than our resources in material permitted but that the cost might be 50% or more higher. It was agreed that an estimate of our material resources was necessary before a realistic programme could be drawn up and priorities decided. The discussion was a good one and it is certainly easier to get business done expeditiously in an official Council.

July 18

S. of S. telegraphed instructing me to give that little snake Sudhir Ghosh a priority passage, which I had refused, and I sent back a telegram accepting his directions but registering a very strong protest; these unofficial political lines are all wrong and do a lot of harm.

I had a string of interviews in the afternoon. Conran-Smith spoke of the Post and Telegraph adjudication and wanted it approved by Council at once, so as to get it out speedily.

We had an emergency Council meeting at 7.30 p.m. and accepted the Post and Telegraph adjudication, with some misgiving at the probable effect on Railways and other Government Departments, who are likely also to demand to share in the hand-out.

July 22

Today, I had a fairly busy morning with papers, and an afternoon of interviews.

Smith, D.I.B., gave a most gloomy forecast of the law and order situation, said he considered the country ripe for serious trouble, thought that the Constituent Assembly would be made the instrument for a coup d'état by Congress, which would declare the C.A. to be a sovereign body and set it up as a parallel Government. I wonder how far his judgement is sound.

Then 40 minutes with Nehru. I discussed among other things the question of the Services and the demand for a general enquiry in the U.P., Bihar and C.P. into the 1942 disturbances. Nehru was very reasonable about this, said that he did not wish any general enquiry, and that his advice was against it. Public feeling was, however, strong, especially against certain individuals; would it be possible to retire these individuals? I said that if he would advise Premiers against any general enquiry, Governors would be prepared to discuss with them individual cases where there was well substantiated evidence that the bounds of duty had been exceeded in any way. Nehru was very quiet and sensible about this, and I hope that he may succeed in preventing any general enquiries.

By handing him at the end of the interview a letter with proposals for an Interim Government, which have also been sent to Jinnah, I began a fresh attempt to form a coalition of the two main Parties. But I am very far from being sanguine of success.

Meanwhile the Postal Strike worsens, the Sind Government is very rocky, the Sikhs are still sullen or worse, the Governor of the N.W.F.P.

and the Political Department want to start a war with the Mahsuds,[1] our efforts to get rice out of Java seem doomed to failure, and Jinnah is fulminating against the Nizam's appointment of Mirza Ismail as his Premier. Such is a selection from my daily cares.

July 23

A comparatively quiet morning till 12.30 p.m., when Weightman[2] came about the proposal to take action against the Shabi Khel section of the Mahsuds, who recently kidnapped Donald, the Political Agent. In order to rescue Donald we advanced 110,000 Rs. to the Mahsud jirga,[3] which they paid over to the Shabi Khel to deliver up Donald. We now propose to demand from the Shabi Khel the return of the 110,000 Rs. plus 250 rifles plus hostages. The ethics of this procedure seem to me doubtful but it is apparently in accordance with frontier procedure and code. If the Shabi Khel do not comply, as they almost certainly will not, it is intended to proscribe a certain area, and after due warning to destroy villages by bombing. Now I am rather doubtful of our ability to do this. Our resources available are three squadrons of Spitfires flown by Indian pilots. To expect an Indian pilot to fly low enough in a Spitfire in a narrow valley among those hills to hit the target is unduly optimistic. I sent for Carr the A.O.C.-in-C. who confirmed my misgivings about the likelihood of the action being effective. He said that the Spitfires in these hills were an untried weapon with doubtful pilots. We agreed to get the A.O.C. down to discuss the question.

Weightman was very insistent that it would be fatal not to take immediate action, but I am sure that to take ineffective action will be worse; and I decided to get down Olaf Caroe and discuss matters with him and C-in-C.

After lunch came Coates and Conran-Smith about the P. and T. strike, and it was decided that we must fight their impossible demands.

Just before dinner I got Nehru's reply to my proposal about the Interim Government. It practically amounted to an ultimatum, almost a declaration of war, by Congress. The Viceroy was to be a complete cipher in the Government, merely a figurehead, and the appointment of the Minority representatives would not be for him to have any say in, etc., etc. I wired the answer home and said I would comment on this 'ultimatum' tomorrow. I had not anticipated that the show-down with Congress would come quite so soon.

[1] One of the wildest tribes of the N.W.F.P.
[2] Sir Hugh Weightman, I.C.S., Secretary, External Affairs Department, 1946–7.
[3] Council of elders.

July 24

At Council this morning Conran-Smith made a statement on the P. and T. strike, there seemed to be a great many fingers in the pie now, with Jinnah, Patel, Nehru and perhaps Gandhi offering advice to the strikers or Government. It is perfectly clear that we must stand pat.

After lunch I had a conference on the proposed air proscription of the Shabi Khel. Carr had got down Long, the A.O.C., from the N.W.F.P. He seemed good and sensible and after hearing his views on the effort involved, the probable effect, and the skill and morale of the R.I.A.F. pilots, I decided to give approval to the proposed action, without waiting to see Caroe.

I sent a telegram to S. of S. about Nehru's letter, George Abell and Menon, as usual watered down my draft a little. I shall get a washy procrastinating reply from H.M.G., I am sure that they will not really face the issue.

> *In this telegram Wavell said that he proposed to see Nehru on the 29th and that if it became clear that Congress would not participate in the Interim Government except on condition that absolute power was handed over to them and the Governor-General's special powers abrogated he would speak to him in very clear terms. 'I would say that H.M.G. have the fullest intention of handing over power to Indians and wish a united India. But they do not recognise Congress as representing all India and have no intention of handing over power to Congress alone. While they are prepared to consider any modifications in the working of the Interim Government which are desired by both main parties H.M.G. will not accept unilateral demands by Congress.'*
>
> *In regard to the Constituent Assembly he proposed to tell him that if Congress did not intend to work the Statement of 16 May sincerely on the lines laid down therein, H.M.G. must reconsider the whole position.*
>
> *He also pointed out that if, as seemed possible, Congress decided to challenge H.M.G., then H.M.G. must make up their minds whether to abdicate or to accept the challenge. He himself had no doubt that the challenge must be accepted.*

July 25

Comparatively quiet day. No reaction yet from H.M.G. on any of my recent telegrams. The P. and T. strike continues.

July 27

I had a long and rather pussy-foot telegram from S. of S. in reply to mine about Nehru's letter; they are obviously in alarm lest I should say something uncompromising to Nehru. I sent a reply, George drafted it this time and I hotted it up.

Wavell in his reply said that he had no desire or intention to break with Congress if this could be avoided, but that he had wanted assurances that H.M.G. would stand firm on two essential matters, (i) that the Interim Government would function under the existing constitution, (ii) that the procedure for constitution-making laid down in the Statement of 16 May would be adhered to. He was glad to note that H.M.G. were prepared to stand firm on (i), but perturbed that their answer on (ii) was rather indefinite. He repeated his request that H.M.G. would decide their policy in the event of a direct challenge by Congress.

The whole situation was, however, just about to be radically altered by the Muslim League's withdrawal of their acceptance of the Statement of 16 May, as recorded in the last paragraph of the next Journal entry for 29 July.

July 29

I had a telegram from H.M.G. outlining their Palestine policy, and asking me for my comments. I thought their proposals quite disastrous and said so in very plain language. The effect in India at this juncture will be deplorable.

This morning I had a letter from the P.M., pressing on me again Maurice Gwyer as Political Adviser. He has obviously been told that I receive nothing but official I.C.S. advice and that my political judgement is therefore unsound, i.e. not sufficiently pro-Congress. I think my judgement is better than H.M.G.'s and shall say so; and tell him that if H.M.G. don't like it their duty is to find another Viceroy, as I will not be a figure-head.

So the Muslim League has run out; thanks to the Mission living in the pocket of Congress while out here, the dishonesty of Cripps, my stupidity and weakness in not spotting his dishonesty earlier and standing up to it, and the irresponsibility of Nehru in making the statements he has since the Mission left. I do not feel guilty about paragraph 8, I have always thought our interpretation correct; but I do feel guilty of not seeing through Cripps' manœuvres and refusing to be a party to Congress' insincere acceptance of the statement of May 16, and the dishonesty of Cripps and P.L. in instigating Congress to make such an acceptance. It was the one important point throughout the negotiations on which Alexander refused to support me, and I rather weakly gave way.

On 29 July the Council of the Muslim League at a meeting in Bombay resolved to withdraw its acceptance of the Cabinet Mission's proposals set forth in the Statement of 16 May and to resort to 'Direct Action' to achieve Pakistan. The League was moved to do this mainly by a number of rash statements made by Nehru. He publicly declared that the Congress had agreed only to go into the Constituent Assembly and to nothing else, and that, in his opinion there would probably be no Grouping (to which the League attached the greatest importance), and that what the Cabinet Mission thought or intended did not enter into the matter at all.

Jinnah had all along maintained that the Congress's acceptance of the Cabinet Mission's proposals was not genuine. Nehru's statements confirmed him and the League in this view. It was quite clear, they declared, that Congress had not really accepted the proposals at all.

The League Council also complained of the 'fantastic and dishonest construction' that the Viceroy and Cabinet Mission had put upon Paragraph 8 of the Statement of 16 June.

The last sentence of the above Journal entry and a passage in a subsequent telegram to the Secretary of State dated 31 August show that Wavell was under the impression that he had strongly opposed treating the Congress's acceptance of the Statement of 16 May as genuine. He had certainly expressed the opinion that it was insincere and that an acceptance which they meant to break was worse than a refusal. But both the Journal and the Cabinet Mission records indicate that he agreed with the Members of the Mission that because of its clever wording it had to be treated as a genuine acceptance. He did, however, urge that the Congress should be firmly told that the procedure laid down for the Constituent Assembly in the Cabinet Mission's proposals could only be altered by a majority of both communities, and it was on this point that Alexander did not support him and he gave way.

July 31

Yesterday morning I had one and a quarter hours with Nehru. I got the impression that he had been rather shaken by the Muslim resolution and realised that it was partly at least due to his hasty and intemperate statements. I don't think that his recent visit to Kashmir was a success. Anyway he seemed very subdued. I said to him that Congress now had a chance of showing real statesmanship and of giving the Muslim League assurances that would bring them into the Constituent Assembly. Nehru said that he did not quite see what assurances could be given to them, they certainly could not be given assurance of Pakistan. I replied that the principal grievance of the League was that the statements of Congress leaders made them believe that it was not intended to give the Group system, on the basis of which they had agreed to join, a fair chance. I referred specially to the Congress reservations in their acceptance of the Statement of May 16th. Nehru said that the Muslim League had also made reservations. I pointed out that these were long-term reservations, on a possible Pakistan a number of years ahead; whereas the Congress reservations were short-term ones and affected the immediate issue.

On the matter of the formation of an Interim Government, I said that I was still most anxious to form one as soon as possible, but that H.M.G. was quite clear that it was impossible to go beyond the assurances given in the letter of May 30th to Azad;[1] and there would be no question of an 'independent' Government, whether the Muslim League took part in it or not. Nehru made no comment on this.

Tuker dined, on his way home for 5 months leave. He is an attractive personality. On something that cropped up during dinner, I asked him and Charles Gairdner,[2] if they were given another chance of life and offered the choice of three qualities to have in that life—one moral, one physical, one artistic—what they would choose. I think we all three chose courage as the moral quality; Tuker and Charles chose good health as the physical quality, (Tuker has suffered much from ill-health), I chose vitality or (if vitality was considered a moral and not a physical quality) horsemanship; for art I chose an understanding of music which I have never had, Tuker wanted to be a master of the violin, and Charles G. to draw and paint well.

S. of S. telegraphed for an immediate appreciation of the situation caused by the Muslim League withdrawal which has obviously greatly perturbed them, and I sent a reply.

> *Wavell replied that the League's resolution would certainly increase communal tension which was already acute, and that the general situation was most unsatisfactory. There was widespread labour trouble, encouraged by the left-wing of Congress which believed in revolution. The right-wing wanted to secure power by constitutional means, but were keeping revolution in reserve in case constitutional means failed. 'Nehru,' he wrote, 'was probably elected President because he has the best chance of keeping a foot in each camp, though having no balance he will usually be on one leg and never on the same one for long.*
>
> *'The most urgent need is for a Central Government with popular support. If Congress will take responsibility they will realise that firm control of unruly elements is necessary and they may put down the Communists, and try to control their own left-wing. . . .*
>
> *'I dislike intensely the idea of having an Interim Government dominated by one party, but I feel that I must try to get Congress in as soon as possible.'*

[1] See p. 280.
[2] General Sir Charles Gairdner, Prime Minister's Special Representative in the Far East, 1945-8, Governor of Tasmania, 1963-8.

It was not, however, possible, he said, to go beyond the assurances given to Azad in the letter of 30 May, and if the Congress would not come in on these terms, the Caretaker Government would have to govern firmly even at the risk of a clash with left-wing elements.

He proposed that places should be kept for the Muslim League in the Interim Government in the hope that they would come in later, and that these should either be left vacant or filled temporarily by non-League Muslims.

He thought that he would have to go ahead and summon the Constituent Assembly as already arranged, though without the League Constitution-making for the Muslim majority Provinces would obviously be a farce.

August 1

Business began, for what will probably be a very disturbed month, with a wire from S. of S. suggesting that I should send for Jinnah at once and try to induce him to join a Coalition Government. I replied that I thought very poorly of this idea which would look like panic, would only increase J.'s intransigence and lead to no result; I would propose to leave Jinnah alone for the moment.

My afternoon began with Yeatts,[1] who begins an interview by taking out his watch and laying it in front of him, he then chatters uninterruptedly till the scheduled time is over, then replaces his watch, says regretfully: 'My time is up,' and takes his leave. His subjects today were disposal of surplus stores; the Hindustan Factory railway coach; the Sindri fertiliser factory; and the price of raw cotton.

Kharegat does not actually use a watch, but he times himself over the course pretty accurately, and keeps up a steady flow of measured and precise statement, usually of delays and difficulties rather than of accomplishment.

Conran-Smith was quick and businesslike. P. and T. strike seems likely to be off, and Railwaymen apparently satisfied with their terms; but Calcutta Port is on strike.

August 2

A comparatively quiet day.

Menon deprecated my proposal to keep the C-in-C as War Member if I formed a Government from Congress, since he thought it would give a handle to the Left Wing of which Nehru is very alarmed. Menon himself also thinks that Communism is a real danger in India. He advised that

[1] M. W. W. M. Yeatts, I.C.S., Secretary to the Government of India, Industries Department.

I should write to Gandhi to inform him of the negotiations for an Interim Government.

S. of S. telegraphed H.M.G.'s approval to my proposals for formation of an Interim Government. I also had a reply from Jinnah to my original letter, not perhaps as uncompromising as it might have been.

August 3

I had an interview in the morning, with Reid of the Daily Telegraph.

Reid whom I had not met before seemed quite intelligent and good but has not been long in India. He had recently had an interview with Jinnah, and had some interesting impressions. He is sure that J. wants a settlement and thinks that J. himself does not believe in Pakistan. Contrary to the general impression he does not think that J. dominates his Working Committee but that it dominates him. Nishtar impresses him as one of the strongest characters on it. We had a long discussion on J.'s interpretation of Clause 8 (which Reid shared) and his accusation of bad faith. I said that I had never had any doubts on the interpretation of Clause 8, once it was agreed that the Congress acceptance of the Statement of May 16 was to be regarded as genuine; it was on this point that I had my doubts. From what Reid said, it was obvious that Jinnah knew all about Cripps' interviews with Gandhi and Patel and the way in which Congress acceptance of the May 16 Statement was obtained. It was obvious also that the disastrous interview of June 26 had completely upset Jinnah who complained that he had been 'bullied'. Reid also mentioned an interview with Gandhi, at which Reid had said something to him about; 'Your relations with those other celebrities, the Mission and the Viceroy'. Reid said that Gandhi turned on him and said with great malevolence and venom: 'They are not celebrities'.

I decided to consult Council tomorrow on the negotiations to form an Interim Government, the latest proposal is to put the onus on Congress to approach the Muslim League.

August 4

I held an informal Council meeting and explained to them my proposals for trying to form an Interim Government. The members present—Waugh, Spence, Conran-Smith, Bewoor, Coates—approved unanimously. So I telegraphed for S. of S. approval. So begins yet another attempt to induce these irresponsible Indian politicians to show some sense and responsibility. I have no great hopes of success.

On 5 August Wavell received information 'from an unimpeachable source' about the attitude of Vallabhbhai Patel which led him to think that after all there was quite a chance of success. His informant told him that if Congress were asked to form an Interim Government Patel would insist that they should agree to do so and that they should not break over the issue of the status of the Interim Government. He considered that they should accept as the basis the letter to Azad of 30 May and he was prepared to resign from the Working Committee if his view was not accepted. He was convinced that the Congress must enter the Government to prevent chaos spreading in the country.

August 6

S. of S. cabled approving my proposed approach to Nehru. I don't like it, but I think it is the only possible move. I have a bad hour or two every morning now, when I wake early and think over the general state of India and the lack of a definite policy by H.M.G. and the virtual certainty of serious trouble, and the way all constructive work I have been able to do in the last $2\frac{1}{2}$ years seems likely to be wasted. However, after a ride and breakfast I cheer up again. I want a rest badly but see no prospect of getting one.

August 8

A busy day with conference of five Governors whom I have summoned for consultation: Burrows (Bengal), Wylie (U.P.), Jenkins (Punjab), Mudie (Sind), Caroe (N.W.F.P.).

At the morning session I gave some account of the Mission's negotiations, and explained the present situation and proposals. The Governors of these largely Muslim Provinces naturally did not like the idea of a Ministry at the Centre or the possibility of a Constituent Assembly which the Muslim League did not attend; and anticipated that there might be serious repercussions. But neither in Bengal nor Sind did the Ministries wish to go out of office, and it was obvious that the League had at present no organised plan for direct action. Caroe was the most worried, about the Tribes. Caroe himself has never yet really reconciled himself to the idea of our leaving India. Generally the Governors thought that they could hold the situation and were not able to contribute very much towards the solution of the present problems. Burrows was as solid, imperturbable, and quietly humorous as ever; he is really a complete Conservative in his ideas, and thinks the Grenadier Guards the finest body ever collected. Evan Jenkins had come in from tour, says the villages are all as friendly as ever and not much interested in politics. Shortages of cloth, kerosine, and sugar are their worries.

On the whole I think the conference was worth while, though nothing very concrete came out of it. No one likes the present or prospective situation, but no one has any new ideas for dealing with it.

August 10

Dictated a note in the morning on the breakdown plan, copy enclosed [below]:

Note for P.S.V.

1. I think the outcome of the present political situation may very well be that Congress will not reach any agreement with the Muslim League, either on the Interim Government or the Constituent Assembly; and that they may put forward proposals for an Interim Government which I shall feel unable to accept. If we in this way reach a deadlock, I imagine that it is quite probable that H.M.G. will summon me home for consultation. I want to be prepared with a definite plan in as much detail as possible.

2. As I said in my last telegram home, I can see no better breakdown solution than the one I put forward in paragraphs 11 to 14 of my Appreciation of last May, i.e. that we should hand over, after a stated period, the Congress majority Provinces to Congress, but maintain the present constitution and our own control in N.W. and N.E. India. If this is the best plan, and I can think of no better, we must have it worked out in as great detail as possible. I think this should be done as soon as possible, and secretly, by a small body. I suggest that this body should consist of: the Deputy Commander-in-Chief, Coates, Spence, Waugh, and yourself, working under my directions. What I want to get clear is whether the plan is practicable and what steps should be taken to put it into effect, if the necessity arises.

3. If H.M.G. were persuaded to adopt the plan, which could, I think, only be done in consultation with the leaders of the Opposition, and probably of the Dominions, they would have to make an announcement something to this effect:

(A) His Majesty's Government sent out a Cabinet Mission to endeavour to produce by agreement between the main parties a solution for a free and united India. As a result of those negotiations and the subsequent developments, it is clear to H.M.G. that it is at present impossible to reach any solution to which the two main parties will agree, and H.M.G. has to take a fresh decision.

(B) H.M.G. cannot consent to hand over India under conditions which are likely to produce civil war and disturbance. The chief obstacles to agreement lie in the north-western and north-eastern areas of India where the main Muslim populations are. These are also the areas of greatest importance for the defence of India's frontiers. The situation in the southern and central portions of India is less complex, since the population is more homogeneous.

(C) H.M.G. have therefore decided to withdraw all British officials and troops within six (?) months from the following Provinces of British India: Bombay, Madras, Orissa, C.P., Bihar, U.P.; and will hand over control of these Provinces to the Congress Working Committee.

(D) The present constitution and control will be maintained in the following Provinces: N.W.F.P., Punjab, Sind, Bengal, Assam, the Chief Commissioner's Province of Delhi, and the Agency of British Baluchistan, until some permanent solution for an Indian Union can be reached. The British will assist these two groups of Provinces in the N.W. and N.E. to reach agreement on a constitution and to arrive at terms with the remainder of India. They will then withdraw completely from India.

(E) The boundaries between the Provinces handed over to Congress, which may be referred to as Hindustan, and the Provinces remaining under British control, may be adjusted if necessary, by mutual agreement.

(F) H.M.G. will undertake responsibility for the defence of N.W. and N.E. India, and will by agreement, assist Hindustan in external defence if desired.

(G) The exercise of paramountcy over the States which lie within the boundaries of Hindustan will be relinquished by the Crown from the date when British control of the provinces of Hindustan is handed over. Paramountcy will continue with those States which lie within the boundaries of N-W and N-E India still remaining under British control. Those States which lie between Hindustan and the proposed areas under British control will be free to adhere either to Hindustan or to the British controlled area.

(H) During the period before control is handed over, H.M.G. shall make it clear that they will maintain law and order throughout India by all means at their disposal, and will not tolerate any revolutionary action.

4. The above is of course the merest skeleton; and there is a whole host of problems which would have to be solved. In the next paragraphs I outline a few of them. There are many others which will naturally occur.

5. *The Army.* One solution would be for the British at Delhi to retain control for the defence of the whole of India. This would avoid splitting

up the Army and would keep the door open for a subsequent Union of India and common defence arrangements. It would undoubtedly be the best arrangement, if Congress could be persuaded to accept it. I think it is quite conceivable that the Army might also accept it, but there would have to be some readjustments and redistribution of troops; and officers and men should probably have an option to resign. The C.-in-C. will have to advise on this.

6. *Foreign Affairs.* The same applies here as to the Army; i.e. it would be much better to keep these under Central control if possible.

7. *Communications.* Again these should be centrally controlled if possible. It would always be open to Congress, if they felt bloody-minded, to make the maintenance of communications practically impossible; but if the British Government were really firm, it could retort by cutting off external communications to Hindustan.

8. What form should the Central Government at Delhi take? It might have to be purely British, which would not be satisfactory; or it might be possible to negotiate some *ad hoc* Government to deal with agreed Central subjects until some permanent arrangement could be made.

9. Other difficulties would be currency, finance, customs, etc.; and there are doubtless many others.

10. I believe myself that this scheme would work, provided H.M.G. was quite firm on it, and was prepared to carry it out with a high hand if necessary. For this reason I have suggested that the consent of the Opposition and the Dominions should be obtained; and that Congress should be presented with a plan which had the full backing of the British Empire. I think it is possible that knowledge of such a plan might be sufficient to induce a reasonable mood in the political parties.

The plan would of course not be possible in face of determined opposition by the Muslim League; but I do not think it is likely that this would occur; in fact the Muslim League would presumably welcome the plan.

11. Please think this over and discuss it with me as soon as possible.

August 11

There were plenty of green boxes, mostly routine work. I was amused by Dow's note on the attitude of University students towards examinations for degrees. If they are unable, by bribery or theft, to obtain copies of the papers before the examinations, a very large proportion fail. They consider this most unjust and have put forward the following argument: 'Bihar wants more educated men, therefore examinations must be made much easier.' Q.E.D.

I had a special meeting of Council at 6.30 p.m. which lasted for nearly two hours.

We decided to grant certain reliefs to all grades of Government servants in conformity with the concessions recently granted to P. and T. and Railways, in order to forestall a possible strike.

August 12

Nothing during the week-end except a telegraphed letter from Nehru, agreeing to make proposals for an Interim Government. I cabled a draft reply to S. of S. who agreed to it at once.

The Nawab of Chhatari came to see me about the position of the 'loyalists' who had always helped the British; were we really going so soon and leaving them at the mercy of Congress, who had always been anti-British; and now we had got at odds with the Muslim League too; and what were our friends to do? Did I advise them to surrender their titles, as they were being pressed to do by Jinnah? Couldn't we stop another 10 years or so anyway, the Labour Government was surely going much too fast in handing over India. These interviews, of which I had already had a number and shall doubtless have many more, are rather trying and very painful. Some of the so-called 'friends' of the British have done nothing more really than support us because we kept order and enabled them to draw their rents from the land in ease and safety; few of them have been good land-lords or looked after their tenants; and not one of them hardly has had the political courage to come out into the open and oppose Congress. I have not a great deal of sympathy for them. But some like the Nawab are really genuine and are great gentlemen, and I am sorry for them. I always feel it is better to be honest and to say that we are going to hand over power; that it is right that we should do so and leave Indians to govern themselves; that while the Congress is not a body one would have chosen as the representatives of the great mass of the Indian people, it is the body that the Indian people have chosen for themselves and we have to do business with the men of their choice. The Nawab agreed to all this; and I gave him such comfort as I could by saying that the experience of history was that people became much more moderate when they got power and became responsible and did not do nearly all the violent things that they threatened. I said I saw no reason why they should give up well-earned honours at Mr. Jinnah's bidding but that was for them to decide. I explained to him frankly and fully what happened about paragraph 8 of the June 16 Statement and that Jinnah was not justified in his accusations.

August 16

Rather a depressing sort of day. Jinnah and Nehru have failed to agree about the Interim Government; Nehru has held a Press Conference and as usual has made some stupid remarks; and there has been some violent rioting in Calcutta.

August 17

In the afternoon I saw Nehru about the formation of an Interim Government. He said he had had a long and quite amicable discussion with Jinnah, but that it did not lead to any result. He had made him an offer of 5 seats in an Interim Government of 14 and told him that any names proposed by the League would be accepted by Congress. Jinnah had complained that under the proposed arrangement it would be open to Congress to nominate a non-League Muslim. Nehru had replied that he did not see how the League could object if it came out of the Congress quota.

Nehru told me that his idea was to propose the names of 6 Congress nominees and 3 Minority representatives, and to fill the 5 Muslim seats with neutral Muslims. I suggested the possibility of leaving them open for a time for acceptance by the Muslim League, but he said that he did not like this idea, as it would give the Government the appearance of instability.

I asked him what his views were about the summoning of the Constituent Assembly and he said he thought it should be summoned for about the middle of September.

The conversation lasted for an hour and a quarter and I suppose was reasonably satisfactory, but I am sure his 'neutral' Muslims won't work. He was very friendly and reasonable, but looked rather worn and tired. He told me that he was very much upset by his car having knocked down and killed a child a little while back.

Meanwhile in Calcutta the rioting continues on the most violent lines.

On 16 August, which the Muslim League had decided to celebrate as 'Direct Action Day' and which the Muslim League Government of Bengal unwisely declared a public holiday, there was an appalling outbreak of communal rioting in Calcutta that lasted several days. According to official estimates 5,000 people were killed and 15,000 injured.

August 18

Calcutta is as bad as ever and the death-toll mounts steadily. Sarat Chandra Bose rang up in the afternoon with a message of protest to me that the police were favouring the Muslims against the Hindus, whereas the Governor tells me the casualties are higher amongst the Muslims. Anyway it is a thoroughly bad business.

I saw Nehru again in the evening and told him that I thought I should see Jinnah and make a last appeal to him to join the Interim Government. I put forward the argument that it was just possible that Jinnah might feel more inclined to accept in view of the latest happenings; that a very grave responsibility would lie on us if we had not made every effort to secure his co-operation. Nehru was opposed to it and said it would be useless, but said he would put it to his Sub-Committee and write to me. I stressed particularly the danger of the Army breaking up. He produced a terrible list of Muslim names for the Government which I can certainly not accept.

Nehru informed Wavell on 19 August that his colleagues were also opposed to making a fresh approach to Jinnah, and Wavell himself concluded, in view of a statement by Jinnah published on the 19th, that it would be useless to send for him.

August 19

I sent S. of S. a telegram giving the probable composition of the Government which Congress would propose and saying that I did not think we should accept five Muslims. P.S.V. and Menon do not approve and think that we should not break with Congress over the Muslim issue.

I saw C-in-C who told me that there were already four British battalions in Calcutta and one more arriving, and two Indian battalions in and two more arriving, also a British Armoured Car squadron. I wonder what the situation would have been like if British troops had left India as Congress demanded. I sent a telephone message to Burrows later in the morning to ask if he would like me to go down, but he replied that it might embarrass him at the moment. The situation seems to be more in hand.

I had an hour in the afternoon with Azad about the Calcutta riots and the Interim Government. He criticized the Bengal Ministry severely, and said that although they had apprehended trouble they had not taken sufficient precautions; also they had been too late in enforcing a total curfew, and the troops had not been called out soon enough.

As regards the Interim Government, he said that it would be inadvisable for me to approach Jinnah direct, but would it be possible by indirect contact to give Jinnah some reassurance and persuade him to come in? I said that I would consider the matter, but that in the present mood of the League it might be difficult to give them sufficient assurances.

Azad is an attractive character and really a much truer representative of the Muslims than Jinnah. He was obviously very worried at the possible fate of the Muslims in such places as Cawnpore and Lucknow.

Smith, D.I.B., said that according to his information about the Congress Working Committee at Wardha,[1] Gandhi and Rajagopalachariar had drafted the resolution which was intended to appease the League, against opposition by Nehru and Patel; that Gandhi had rebuked N. and P. for the tactlessness of some of their recent utterances; but that he had agreed, in spite of his creed of non-violence, that force should be used against Muslims if they resisted a Congress Government—a typical piece of Gandhian hypocrisy. Smith said that in the Punjab Muslim feeling against Congress was growing, but that the Sikhs seemed to be tying up with Congress, and that the hot-heads amongst them were speaking of the 're-conquest of the Punjab'. Smith told me that he was disposing of certain dangerous C.I.D. records, in anticipation of a Ministry coming into office.

August 20

Ian Scott, usually cheerful and optimistic, was very depressing in a talk I had with him out riding this morning. Both he and George now seem to be convinced that our only course is to get out of India as soon as possible and leave her to her fate, which will be civil war.

At 5.0 p.m. I had an hour with the Committee[2] on my breakdown plan. They had produced a report, almost entirely on P.S.V.'s instigation, I think, which did not approve my plan and produced an alternative, with which I entirely disagreed. I turned them back again to my way of thinking, with the support of the Army representatives, Arthur Smith and Savory.

---

[1] In an attempt to repair the harm done by Nehru's irresponsible statements about the Constituent Assembly, the Congress Working Committee met at Wardha on 8 August and passed a resolution to the effect that they accepted the Cabinet Mission's constitutional scheme in its entirety. But they added that in their view 'provincial autonomy is a basic provision and each province has the right to decide whether to join a group or not'. This addition, in effect, nullified their acceptance of the scheme in its entirety; and the resolution did not satisfy the League.

[2] Wavell had suggested the formation of this Committee in Paragraph 2 of his note to the Private Secretary to the Viceroy on p. 330.

Just before dinner I received a letter from Nehru with his list for a Government. His Muslim names are terrible. Fazlul Huq, the most notorious crook in Bengal; Asaf Ali, whom I think contemptible; Sir Shafaat Ahmad Khan; Ali Zaheer, a Shiah; and one name not yet given. I cannot stomach Fazlul Huq, and shall tell him so; and the others will be passengers.

August 21

Congress proposal of Fazlul Huq as a member reminds me of a time when Mohamed Said (Mme. Sirry's father) was forming a Ministry and proposed a notoriously corrupt politician. To Allenby's remonstrances he replied: 'C'est un homme absolument sans principes; il nous sera très utile'.

A short meeting of Council this morning, perhaps the last of my official Council. How much easier and quicker and more effective it has been to do business with them. I shudder at the idea of dealing with a Political Council.

August 22

I saw Nehru for an hour this morning. I said that I could recommend to H.M.G. the six Congress names he had given me, viz: Patel, Rajendra Prasad, Rajagopalachariar, Bose, Jagjvan Ram and Nehru himself. I also agreed to the three Minority representatives: Baldev Singh (Sikh), Matthai (Christian), and Bhabha (Parsee).

We then turned to the Muslim representatives. I said that surely Fazlul Huq would let the side down badly, and that I advised Congress strongly not to include him. After a little discussion Nehru agreed to withdraw his name.

I again suggested the possibility of leaving the Muslim seats vacant, but Nehru said the Congress were not willing to agree to this. I then said that I was prepared to recommend Sir Shafaat Ahmad Khan, Sayed Ali Zaheer and Asaf Ali. The other two Muslim names were left over for the present. Azad had decided not to come in.

Nehru then pressed for a Council of 15 and the inclusion of Antony as Anglo-Indian representative. I said I should be very reluctant to increase the size of the Council, since I thought it would increase the suspicions of the Muslim League and make their joining more difficult. I would consider the matter of the Anglo-Indian representative, but I did not think I could agree to the increase of the Council to 15.

We had some discussion about portfolios. He said he thought that as War Member the Sikh representative might be suitable; that he himself would like to have External Affairs and that for Finance the choice seemed to lie between Rajagopalachariar and Matthai.

When we had completed our business, Nehru seemed reluctant to go and we had a general talk about methods of physical exercises in the morning, sport in India, and one or two other topics. He was quiet and friendly. I think that the prospect of responsibility has rather sobered Congress.

I had a few words with Arthur Smith who agreed that Baldev Singh was in the circumstances the best bet as War Minister.

I was sad to see a letter from the Nawab of Chhatari, renouncing his titles, I am sure he didn't really wish to; any more than H.H. of Bhopal really wishes to abdicate and become a private Muslim Leaguer, as he has proposed to me. I think both actions are part of a campaign of nerves instigated by Jinnah.

August 23

An interview with Nehru and preparation for a broadcast for tomorrow evening took up most of my time. Nehru looked tired and depressed, he is not looking forward to the responsibilities of office any more, I think, than I am to running the new Government. I told him that I had decided that the numbers of the Government must be restricted to 14, so a place could not be found for Antony. We agreed that the names of the members of the new Government should be announced tomorrow and that they should be sworn in on September 2nd.

August 24

After dinner, I got news that Sir Shafaat Ahmed Khan, a Muslim member of the new Government, had been murdered in Simla. An ominous start. (Actually he had not been killed, I heard later, only damaged.)

August 26

I got back tonight from 24 hectic hours in Calcutta. I left early yesterday morning, got to Calcutta about 1.30 p.m. and at once went on a two-hour tour of the scenes of the recent rioting. The city had been pretty well cleared up by this time and except for some burnt-out shops and houses there was not a great deal of evidence of recent occurrences. I spoke to some of the troops and thanked them, everyone agrees that they did magnificent work.

After a few minutes for a wash and change—Calcutta was as sticky as usual—I started a series of 3½ hours of interviews, 4.0 to 7.30 p.m. I saw first the Commissioner of Police, Hardwick, who gave me his account of what took place.

The chief points to my mind were Suhrwardy's continual presence in the Control room on the first day with many M. League friends and his obvious communal bias; that the victims were almost entirely goondas and people of the poorest class; that there were no attacks on the Police; and that any hesitation of the Police to open fire or take firm action was partly due to the political criticism directed against them after the riots of last February and November. Hardwick has only held this job for a few months, and seems perhaps to lack a little in toughness as well as in experience.

I then saw Bucher,[1] acting Army Commander, and Sixsmith, acting Area Commander, both good and sensible men who had done very well. They described events to me and the action of the troops. So far as I could see, their judgement and action had been correct and they had used the troops at the right time and in the right way. Bucher said the Indian troops, including Transport Companies (one manned by Mahsuds of the Shabi Khel whom we are now bombing) behaved very well indeed. He also said there was complete harmony between Civil and Military authorities during the disturbances. He commented on the completely communal attitude of the Chief Minister, Suhrwardy, when he had driven round with him on the 18th.

Then came the Chief Secretary, Walker, and his assistant, Martin. They agreed on the Communal bias of Suhrwardy, and said he had made continual allegations against the Chief Commissioner and his police. Walker said that S. was very worried but might be truculent when I saw him. He thought that Calcutta might get through the Id[2] without fresh disturbances unless Jinnah declared a jehad.[3]

After having a few words with Ranking, the new Area Commander, I had half an hour or so with the Governor. He outlined the position in the Assembly, where the Government was really dependent on the European vote and could be turned out; but there was no alternative Ministry and a Section 93 administration was not possible. He said that Suhrwardy had forfeited everyone's confidence and suggested the possibility of a Coalition Ministry under Aziz ul Huque. I told him that I had no great opinion of A. ul H.'s ability though he would be a pleasanter personality than S.

[1] General Sir Roy Bucher, who after Independence became Commander-in-Chief, Indian Army, 1948–9.   [2] A Muslim festival.   [3] A war against infidels.

I then had three quarters of an hour with Suhrwardy. He was polite and not at all aggressive and took in a subdued way a homily I delivered to him on his duties as Premier of Bengal. He suggested that the Chief Justice, Spens, should head an enquiry into the disturbances.

On the general political situation I said that I had done my utmost to secure a fair deal for the Muslims, but that I was quite unable to support Jinnah over the question of a Nationalist Muslim, and that I thought a Nationalist Muslim in place of a Hindu should be a source of strength to Jinnah rather than otherwise.

After dinner I had another hour with the Governor, who spoke of some of his troubles; Communists and Strikes; Sarat Bose and the I.N.A.; the danger of a really big flare-up at the Id with Hindus and Muslims, with Muslims the aggressors; the small numbers and low morale of the Calcutta Police, to whom he was giving a pep talk next day; and the dangers of famine. Burrows strikes me as being worried but still unperturbed.

And so bed, after an 18 hour day with no relaxation.

This morning I went out for an hour, to visit two Relief Centres; a Muslim one at the Lady Brabourne College and a Hindu one at the Asutosh College. These Centres, and there are very many others, brought home to one the misery caused by this communal frenzy; at each centre there were over 1,000 men, women and children, often injured, who had in many cases lost their relatives, their homes and possessions. At each place of course a large and voluble crowd of workers and others followed me round pointing out the results of the evil handiwork of the 'other party'.

Then I went back to Government House, and had a series of interviews with Hindus, Europeans and Muslims. Among the latter was Nazimuddin who made a statement on communal lines about the riots. He then spoke about the question of Grouping and its interpretation, and said that if it was quite clear that a Province could not opt out of a Group till after the Group discussions he thought that it might have a considerable effect on League policy. I had a final interview with the Governor; and then after a quick lunch flew back to Delhi. I found that Archie John and the new Governor of Burma, Rance,[1] had arrived that morning. I dined with them. Rance seems very sensible and capable. A.J. in good form.

I finished the evening with two very depressing telephone intercepts, showing Patel in very truculent mood and in touch through Ghosh with Cripps and P.L. (Apropos of the Shabi Khel mentioned above, they know that their homes are being bombed: they said to their officers: 'That is all

[1] Maj.-Gen. Sir Hubert Rance, Governor of Burma, 1946–8.

right, our people have been naughty and are being justly punished: but what are you going to do to these Hindus of Calcutta for all the murders they have committed?' A pertinent comment.)

According to V. P. Menon a definite change in Lord Wavell's attitude and policy was noticeable after his return from Calcutta. He had become convinced that unless some agreement was effected soon between the Congress and the League, the fearful Calcutta disorders would be repeated in other parts of India. He was also much struck by what Nazimuddin had told him about the attitude of the League towards participation in the Constituent Assembly. These factors account for his abortive attempt (recorded in the next entry) to induce Nehru and Gandhi to make a statement about the Constituent Assembly that would really satisfy the League.

August 27

I determined to make an attempt to induce the Congress to state clearly their intentions about Grouping in the Constituent Assembly, since this was obviously one of main obstacles to co-operation by the League. I therefore asked Gandhi and Nehru to come and see me in the evening.

Later, at 5.0 p.m. I had a meeting with the Committee on the breakdown plan. At the end I think we arrived at the outline of quite a reasonable plan, which will now be put into shape to go home.

The meeting with Gandhi and Nehru was not a great success. The old man was in a legalistic and malevolent mood, and Nehru was full of hate against the League. I told them that I thought the only chance of a peaceful transfer of power in India was if the Congress made a categorical statement that they would accept the position that the Provinces must remain in their Sections, as intended by the Mission, until after the first elections under the new Constitution. I said that I could not undertake the responsibility of calling together the Constituent Assembly until this point was settled. I handed them the draft of a statement which I asked them to make.

Gandhi went off into long legalistic arguments about the interpretation of the Mission's statement. I said that I was a plain man and not a lawyer, and that I knew perfectly well what the Mission meant, and that compulsory Grouping was the whole crux of the Plan.

The argument went on for some time, and Nehru got very heated. Gandhi said that if a blood bath was necessary, it would come about in spite of non-violence.[1] I said that I was very shocked to hear such words

[1] Lord Wavell always used to say that on this occasion Gandhi thumped the table and said, 'If India wants her blood bath she shall have it.'

from him. In the end they took away the formula, but I do not think there is much hope of their accepting it.

August 28

A very quick Council Meeting, presumably the last of the Caretaker Council which had lasted two months.

During the morning I received an abusive and vindictive letter from Gandhi, which he asked should be telegraphed home. Evidently my rebuke to him on his 'blood-bath' remark had gone home. It confirmed the view I have always held of G., that his professions of non-violence and saintliness are political weapons against the British rather than natural attributes. It looked like a declaration of war, and I wondered whether I really had held the last meeting of my Caretaker Council. However, I received later a letter from Nehru about nominations to the Peace Conference and U.N.O. Assembly, which seemed to show that Congress still intended to come into the Government.

Gandhi's letter was as follows:

28th August, 1946

Dear Friend,

I write this as a friend and after deep thought.

Several times last evening you repeated that you were a 'plain man and a soldier' and that you did not know the law. We are all plain men though we may not all be soldiers and even though some of us may know the law. It is our purpose, I take it, to devise methods to prevent a repetition of the recent terrible happenings in Calcutta. The question before us is how best to do it.

Your language last evening was minatory. As representative of the King you cannot afford to be a military man only, nor to ignore the law, much less the law of your own making. You should be assisted, if necessary, by a legal mind enjoying your full confidence. You threatened not to convene the Constituent Assembly if the formula you placed before Pandit Nehru and me was not acted upon by the Congress. If such be really the case, then you should not have made the announcement you did on 12th August. But having made it you should recall the action and form another ministry enjoying your full confidence. If British arms are kept here for internal peace and order your Interim Government would be reduced to a farce. The Congress cannot afford to impose its will on warring elements in India through the use of British arms. Nor can the Congress be expected to bend itself and adopt what it considers a wrong course because of the brutal exhibition recently witnessed in Bengal. Such submissions would itself lead to an encouragement and repetition of such tragedies. The vindictive spirit on either side would go deeper, biding for an opportunity to exhibit itself more fiercely and more disgracefully when occasion occurs. And all this will be chiefly due to the continued presence in India of a foreign power strong and proud of its arms.

I say this neither as a Hindu nor as a Muslim. I write only as an Indian. Insofar as I am aware, the Congress claims to know both the Hindu and Muslim mind more than you or any Britisher can do. Unless, therefore, you can wholly trust the Congress Government which you have announced, you should reconsider your decision, as I have already suggested.

You will please convey the whole of this letter to the British Cabinet.

I am, yours sincerely,

Sd/-M. K. Gandhi.

Just before going to bed, I received a letter from Nehru, but as it might have spoilt my sleep I left it unread.

August 29

Nehru's letter might have been worse, and it seems clear that the Congress will come into the Government all right, whatever I say about the Constituent Assembly. I answered it and said it was not a matter of legal interpretation but of practical politics. I had an almost panic-stricken telegram from the S. of S. asking me to do nothing rash with Congress.

> Nehru in his letter conveyed the refusal of the Working Committee to make an unambiguous statement about Grouping such as Wavell had requested. He said that the Congress had accepted the Cabinet Mission's scheme in its entirety, but 'they interpreted it so as to resolve the inconsistences contained in it. . . . They hold that Provincial Autonomy is a basic provision and each Province has the right to decide whether to form or join a Group or not.' Questions of interpretation could be referred to the Federal Court.

I had a talk with Spens about the possibility of the Federal Court being called on to interpret the Statement of May 16; and also about the Calcutta Enquiry. He was sensible and helpful.

August 31

I had another rather panic-stricken cable from S. of S., asking me on no account to do or say anything that might occasion a break with Congress. I sent back a telegram that I really should have sent long ago. I have been slow to realise: (a) that the real crux lies in the Grouping in the Constituent Assembly; (b) that Congress have never really meant to play over this;

(c) that Cripps and Co. had no intention of insisting on their (the Mission's) plan being carried out. I hope that I shall not be too late to see this put right.

> *In this telegram Wavell told the Secretary of State that the Interim Government would take office on 2 September, but that he did not think a single-party Government could control India for long without serious trouble arising.*
>
> *The compulsory Grouping of Provinces in the Constituent Assembly for framing both Group and Provincial constitutions was the crux of the matter, for unless the Muslim League were assured that this essential provision would be adhered to, it would be difficult to persuade them to enter the Constituent Assembly or to participate in the Interim Government.*
>
> *Wavell felt that after Nehru's wild statements in Bombay and the League's withdrawal from their acceptance of the Statement of 16 May he ought to have acted at once to get a clear decision on the Grouping question. He thought such a decision was essential before the Constituent Assembly was summoned— indeed, without it, 'the most essential part of the Mission's work on the long-term plan remains undone. The keystone of the arch is missing.'*

Dinner at night to say good-bye to my Caretaker Council. Hydari made quite a good little speech.

September 1

In the morning I dealt with the final draft of the Breakdown Plan.

> *The Breakdown Plan was sent to the Secretary of State on 7 September. It was based on the proposals contained in the 'Note for P.S.V.' dated 10 August, but some very important changes had been introduced.*
>
> 1. *The initial withdrawal of control was now to be only from the four southern Provinces of Madras, Bombay, Central Provinces, and Orissa and not also from Bihar and the United Provinces, as Lord Wavell had originally envisaged. (Retention of control in these two Congress (Hindu-majority) Provinces was considered advisable both from the point of view of communications and also to avoid the impression that control was being retained only in Muslim-majority Provinces so as to facilitate the creation of Pakistan.)*
>
> 2. *The initial withdrawal of control from southern India was to be followed by complete withdrawal from the whole of India by 31 March 1948.*
>
> 3. *This plan was not merely to be put into operation if a sudden crisis arose, but was to be announced and acted upon, whatever happened, not later than 31 March 1947.*
>
> *In forwarding to the Secretary of State this plan for the complete winding up of the British Raj within eighteen months Wavell requested that the orders of H.M.G. be passed on it at a very early date, and suggested that the Opposition*

and the Dominions should be consulted. He explained that unless H.M.G. were prepared to make a radical change of policy and announce their decision to remain in India for another fifteen to twenty years—which would immediately alter the whole position and rally support to their side—it would not be possible to exercise effective control over the whole of India for more than about eighteen months, and that therefore a programme of orderly withdrawal must be announced and acted upon very soon. He hoped that such an announcement might have the additional advantage of administering a severe shock and so induce the political leaders in India to adopt a saner outlook, but this was not the primary reason for putting forward this plan.

The first shock that was administered was to H.M.G. Wavell's proposals greatly perturbed them, and they concluded that they could not justify to Parliament so drastic a policy and that on this ground alone his plan was impossible. They said that if withdrawal from India became unavoidable, then withdrawal should take place from India as a whole as quickly as possible and without a long period of notice, and that there should be a military plan for the protection and evacuation of European personnel—quite a different matter from what Wavell had in mind, though such an emergency plan for the protection of Europeans in the event of an anti-European outbreak existed and had existed for years.

Wavell was not, however, to be put off and, as will be seen, continued to press his Breakdown Plan upon H.M.G., finally putting the whole position to them very plainly in a note which he delivered to them on his arrival in England early in December, see pp. 386–9.

In the afternoon I had an hour with Nehru over the Interim Government. We settled the distribution of portfolios and a number of other matters. I told him that I would have to appoint a Vice-President to act when I was absent, I gathered he would expect to be nominated himself. He also intended, apparently, to act as Leader in the Assembly. I mentioned the matter of interviews with Members and told him that I intended to discontinue the practice of Secretaries having access to the Viceroy, but that I wished to continue seeing all Members at regular intervals. He agreed.

I asked him, at the end, whether the Congress ban on accepting hospitality in the Viceroy's House was going to be raised, as I should like to be able to invite my Ministers. He said that he would consult the Committee and let me know, but that he himself anyway would have no difficulty in accepting an invitation. I then asked him and his sister, who is in Delhi, to dine on Tuesday night, and he agreed.

Nehru was quiet and friendly throughout and seemed anxious to make no difficulties. A.J. went off to Simla.

September 2

Arthur Smith came to see me in the morning and we discussed various matters. Then I swore in seven members of my new Government. Nehru added a soft 'Jai Hind' at the end of his oaths, but no one made any difficulty. I said a few words, and Nehru made a few quite conciliatory remarks. I believe there was quite a considerable crowd round about the Secretariat. On the whole, the inauguration of this new Government went all right, but I shall have some very tricky bowling to deal with in the near future.

September 3

No disturbance reported so far, except in Bombay.[1]

Spens, Chief Justice, came down from Simla about the enquiry into the Calcutta Riots, and I saw him this morning. He was sensible and practical.

Otherwise a quiet day. I sent a letter to Nehru to impress on him that I and not he was responsible for the vacant portfolios. I dealt with papers, and read a couple of very depressing reports on the communal tension from the Governors of the Punjab and U.P.

Nehru and his sister Mrs. Pandit dined in the evening. She is an attractive person.

September 4

The first Council meeting of the new Government went quite smoothly, and so far my Ministers are all sweet reasonableness. But I do not trust them a yard.

September 5

Vallabhai Patel came to dinner. He said he had broken all rules in doing so, but was very friendly and appeared to be in a mood to talk. At the end of dinner I said to him that in my opinion it was far more in the interests of Congress to get the League into the Constituent Assembly and Central Government than it was for the League to come in; it seemed to me in fact to be absolutely vital for the Congress, if they wished a united India and a peaceful transfer of power, and that it was well worth their while to go a long way to reassure the League. The first step was to reassure them on the matter of Grouping in the Constituent Assembly. I said I did not see how it could injure the Congress to carry out the intentions of the Mission's plan.

---

[1] It had been feared that there might be disturbances owing to adverse Muslim reactions to the assumption of office by a Congress Government.

Patel did not dissent from what I said, in fact he seemed to indicate agreement, but said that Jinnah was an impossible personality with whom to negotiate. If there was someone else in the Muslim League with whom they could talk, he thought that matters could be arranged.

On the matter of Grouping, he seemed to admit the meeting in Sections, but thought that each Province should vote as a Province. I said that this was entirely contrary to the intentions of the Mission, and would defeat its object. In neither 'B' nor 'C' Sections had the Muslims more than a narrow majority and this would make it impossible for them to do anything unreasonable. Patel said he had no great fears about Section 'B', but it was different in Section 'C' where Assam might be overwhelmed. I said that the Muslim majority was too narrow for there to be any chance of anything being done which would make the position of Assam impossible.

We left it at that. I do not know whether what I said made any impression, but he was very reasonable and sensible in his arguments and is certainly the most impressive of the Congress leaders and has the best balance. I asked how he was getting on with the D.I.B.; he said, 'Quite all right, they have destroyed all the compromising papers.' I said, 'Yes, I told them to make sure of that,' and he laughed.

September 6

I sent a telegram to the S. of S., saying that I hoped that the Press reports that he would be relieved by Cripps were not true and that if he did go I hoped that Alexander would succeed him.

September 7

I sent a letter to Nehru asking to see a copy of his broadcast before he delivered it. My staff were rather pussy-foot about this and thought I ought not to raise the issue, but I insisted. N. sent a copy at once, there was nothing really objectionable in it.

A long telegram from S. of S. about the Constituent Assembly, it was so full of references that I could not disentangle it, but it gave me the general impression of being both dishonest and cowardly.

Towards the end of this long, rambling telegram the Secretary of State said, 'We are still not clear whether your view is that we must stand for our own interpretation of Statement of May 16th, if necessary to the point at which Congress resign from Interim Government and presumably from Provincial Governments also'. Wavell replied firmly: 'In my view that Statement of May 16th is worthless if we have not the honesty and courage to stick to it, and I would rather lose the co-operation of the Congress at the Centre and in the

Provinces than go ahead with constitution-making on a one-party basis and in a way which the Mission never intended . . . I am quite clear we must grasp this nettle now and if we do it resolutely India may respond to our lead.'

Rajendra Prasad dined, he was almost embarrassingly deferential and quite friendly. I rubbed into him the importance from the Congress point of view of getting in the Muslim League. He said, rather surprisingly, apropos of his projected tour in the south: 'I suppose the Constituent Assembly will not meet before the middle of October.'

September 8 (Sunday)

The only event to record is an interview with Suhrawardy, the Premier of Bengal, who had gone to Bombay to see Jinnah, and was on his way back to Calcutta. He had obviously drawn a complete blank with Jinnah, who had refused to allow him to establish a coalition ministry in Bengal, unless there was a satisfactory coalition at the Centre. Perhaps he trusts Suhrawardy as little as I do. The Nationalist Muslim issue was raised of course, and I said that I could not support Jinnah on that point. Suhrawardy was obviously very worried. I dislike him and distrust him intensely. I have always thought him a dishonest and self-seeking careerist with no principles. I think Jinnah is worried too, but he seems as intransigent as ever.

September 9

A long unsatisfactory day. I despair of ever being able to make these Indian politicians see sense or lessen the tension between the communities. Nehru's quite fairly conciliatory reference to Grouping in his broadcast has merely drawn one of the most violent and bitter articles that Dawn has ever produced. And Nehru himself this evening was as communal as I have ever seen him.

Next was the Nawab of Chhatari, anxious to help if possible in resolving the relations between Congress and Muslim League, and full of the dangers of civil war or of another world war. He thought if it was made clear that H.M.G. meant to insist on their plan for the C.A., the League might be able to come in; but he admits the difficulties of dealing with Jinnah whose arrogant manners he considers atrocious. He emphasised the dangers of delay. He left with deep professions of loyalty to the British and of sadness that we were leaving India.

September 10

Mrs. Sarojini Naidu dined and we had a long talk on politics and of the necessity of getting Jinnah and the M.L. in and the difficulties of Jinnah's character. Mrs. N. spoke of Jinnah rather as of Lucifer, a fallen angel, one who had once promised to be a great leader of Indian freedom, but who had cast himself out of the Congress heaven.

September 11

The Cabinet Meeting was quite businesslike and sensible. I swore in four Ministers—Rajagopalachariar, Matthai, Sir Shafaat Ahmed Khan and Bhabha. The first two will obviously be a considerable addition to the debating and administrative strength.

After the meeting I saw Nehru and told him that I proposed to ask Jinnah to come and see me and make another effort to get him into the C.A. and if possible the Interim Government. I told him that I thought Jinnah would ask for certain assurances with regard to the work of the Constituent Assembly, especially the right of Sections to decide their own procedure. He demurred to this, and said that Congress was bound by assurances given to the Provinces, i.e. Assam. (I am told, however, that N. was not really speaking to Congress brief, and that the Congress is prepared to concede this point). N. was obviously reluctant to negotiate with the League at this stage, he wants to consolidate Congress power in the Central Government and the Constituent Assembly before dealing with the League. He tried to minimise the danger of communal trouble, and said that the Police could easily suppress it. I firmly disabused him of this idea. In the end, he said: 'If you want to see Jinnah, I can't prevent you.' I hope that the moderate members of Congress will be more forthcoming, but I expect that Gandhi will throw a spanner into the works in the end. N. then spoke of Sind and the alleged partiality of the Governor for a while; after which he turned to the iniquity of bombing the Shabi Khel, and wanted to discuss it at a Cabinet meeting.

(Fortunately I heard a few hours later that the Shabi Khel—or rather the Mahsud jirga on their behalf—had proposed terms which had been accepted).

September 12

Jinnah has agreed to come and is arriving on Sunday. I wonder what hope this eleventh-hour effort has. I am not very confident, I feel that the personalities of Gandhi and Jinnah will again prove insuperable obstacles.

September 13

In the Nationalist Press this morning it is claimed in headlines that Nehru has stopped brutal British bombing in Waziristan, while a leader in Dawn headed, 'Hands off the Pathan' implies that the first fruits of a Hindu Government have been the bombing of Muslims! Actually the bombing of Shabi Khel villages started more than a month ago, before the present Government came into power, and stopped just as Nehru made his protest, because the Shabi Khel had given in. Such is the accuracy of the Press in this country.

In the afternoon I had nearly an hour with Rajagopalachariar. In regard to the Constituent Assembly he said that Nehru was in a difficulty because of pledges he had given publicly to his supporters, and he therefore wished the decision about procedure in Sections, etc. imposed by the findings of some legal authority i.e. the Federal Court, even though he had no doubt the decision would be in favour of the Mission's interpretation. I said I saw the point. We left it at that.

We then went into the question of the Interim Government. I got the impression that there is a strong party in the Congress, led by Nehru and probably supported by Gandhi, to prevent the Muslim League from coming in, if possible, though they dare not say so openly and have to profess eagerness to get the League in.

My final interview was with Jagjiwan Ram,[1] the Labour Member, and I was rather pleasantly surprised. He had not made a great impression at first sight, he looked uncouth and unintelligent. But this afternoon he seemed to know his job and to be sensible on all the subjects we discussed; re-settlement of soldiers; labour unrest; the general position of the Scheduled Castes; the political situation.

September 16

A crowded and difficult day. I saw C-in-C at 10.0 a.m. He thinks that if Jinnah comes in and Government is reconstructed it will be better to stick to Baldev Singh now than to make a change.

Then a quick Cabinet Meeting. Nehru raised the question of a date for the meeting of the Legislature and wanted October 28 and that the first meeting of the Constituent Assembly should be postponed to first week of December, probably December 9.

After the meeting I had a talk with Nehru. He said his general programme for C.A. was to get a constitution in about 8 months—original meeting in December for a fortnight, two months for Committee work, another general meeting, submission of proposals to Provinces for

---

[1] Jagjiwan Ram, a member of a Scheduled Caste, continued after Independence uninterruptedly as a Minister of the Government of India. In 1972 he was Minister of Defence.

approval, and then final approval next autumn. Obviously very optimistic. I told him of the impending appointment of U.K. High Commissioner; and said that I did not propose to make my usual Calcutta speech to the Associated Chambers of Commerce, which he agreed was not a suitable forum. I told him the general lines on which I proposed to approach Jinnah. He obviously disapproved of my doing so at all.

I saw Patel at a routine interview an hour or so later. He had not a great deal to say about his Department but got off a good deal of communal hatred. I warned him very clearly of the dangers and consequences of civil war and of my determination to get the League in if possible. He took it quite mildly, but looked grim.

At 5.30 p.m. 1¼ hours with Jinnah. It went on the whole better than I had expected, and Jinnah was less aggressive and aggrieved than I had expected and easier to talk with. But it was all no more than preliminary sparring. Jinnah's 'no hope' at the end of it all was, I think, just a conventional way of ending the round before going to the corner to his seconds.

September 17

A comparatively quiet day.

I had 40 minutes with Matthai,[1] probably the most capable and intelligent of my Ministers. He thinks India's financial position has greatly deteriorated, and that there is serious danger of inflation. He is being pressed about the salt tax, but says, as I always told Gandhi, that it cannot be removed by a stroke of the pen, as Gandhi imagines.

September 18

Cabinet in morning dealt quite sensibly with problem of Burma rice price and other matters; but towards the end the matter of Indian troops in Indonesia and Burma cropped up, and Nehru became very eloquent and almost aggressive, rather to the embarrassment of some of his colleagues, I think.

I saw Nehru after the Cabinet and told him of my talk with Jinnah. He had to say that he welcomed a coalition but he obviously didn't. He challenged my contention that the Constituent Assembly must be summoned by me, but I stood firm on this.

[1] Dr. John Matthai, an Indian Christian, President of the Tariff Board, 1931–4, Director-General of Commercial Intelligence and Statistics, 1935–40. He was at first Finance Minister in the Interim Government, but later had to give place to Liaquat Ali Khan. He was Finance Minister again, 1948–50.

September 20

Day began with a Cabinet Meeting on trade controls, at which also food policy was discussed. Nehru looked a bit glum and hostile, I thought.

Next Sultan Ahmed came in to report a talk he had had with Jinnah, which almost makes it look as if a Settlement was in sight.

After lunch, Sarat Chandra Bose was my first visitor. He discussed the affairs of his Department with sense and with marked deference, all a part of the present Congress set-up to convince me what good boys they are. I was cynically amused to notice that his first reaction to a threatened strike of the Delhi electricity workers had been to make a plan for troops to be flown to Delhi to take over essential services and to summon certain British technicians. He then tried to put across Hindu propaganda on the origin of the Calcutta riots, but I cut him short at once by saying that it was for the judicial enquiry to determine responsibility. On the general political situation he brought up the 'divide and rule' insinuation. I said shortly that we were trying now to 'unite and quit', and that I was quite determined to get a coalition.

September 25

Cabinet meeting this morning lasted $1\frac{1}{4}$ hours and dealt with a number of subjects. Atmosphere was quite friendly and business-like.

After Council I saw Nehru and explained to him the lines on which I proposed to speak to Jinnah, and said that I was not trying to get the Muslim League in as a 'King's party' with the object of holding the balance of power but would like the Cabinet to work as a team.

Then in the evening the critical interview with Jinnah. It went as well as I could have expected. Jinnah was in quite a reasonable mood and is, I should say, really anxious to reach a settlement if it can be done without loss of prestige. But now will come the really critical business, getting Congress to *welcome* Jinnah in and make the way easy for him. I mistrust the influence of Gandhi and Patel.

September 26

Spent most of morning considering tactics for interview with Nehru this afternoon. Hearing that Gandhi was leaving Delhi tomorrow, I had asked if he would like to come and see me, and he had chosen 4.0 p.m., just after Nehru. I soon discovered that the old man had no intention whatever of leaving Delhi so long as any political negotiations are in progress.

I saw Nehru from 3.0 to 4.0 p.m., and Gandhi from 4.0 to 5.0 p.m. No progress, quite obviously they do *not* want Jinnah and the League in, and

Gandhi at the end exposed Congress policy of domination more nakedly than ever before. The more I see of that old man, the more I regard him as an unscrupulous old hypocrite; he would shrink from no violence and blood-letting to achieve his ends, though he would naturally prefer to do so by chicanery and a false show of mildness and friendship.

George Abell told me later that Baldev Singh gave him an account of Nehru's report to his colleagues after his interview with me. According to Baldev, they really are anxious for a settlement but are not going to make it too easy for Jinnah for fear that he will raise his price.

September 27

I saw Nehru again at 12 o'clock but did not make much progress. He said that Congress must put in a Nationalist Muslim. I asked him whom they proposed to put in and whom to omit. He said Asaf Ali, vice Rajendra Prasad; but on cross-examination I found that this was not a recent decision but one that they had considered some time ago. I told him to go and consider it again.

In the afternoon I saw Rajagopalachariar. He said Congress would have to insist on Asaf Ali, but I think that this was partly 'war of nerves'. He said he thought it would take 18 months at least to make a constitution.

Gandhi, typically, wrote me a letter giving his own account of our interview, and asking me to agree. I refused to be drawn into accepting a written record of a private discussion, beyond correcting an entirely false statement which he had put into my mouth.

According to Gandhi, Wavell had said that his 'leanings were towards the Muslim League'.

September 28

In the evening I saw Jinnah again. We did not make much progress but Jinnah quite friendly and obviously wants to come in. I said that I could hold out no great hope of Congress yielding on the Nationalist Muslim issue; and I had always told him that I could not support him to the end on this issue. I got the impression that he might in the end concede the Nationalist Muslim point rather than bring about a breakdown.

It is weary work negotiating with these people, it takes weeks or months to make any progress on a point which ordinary reasonable men would settle in an hour or so. How they will ever make a constitution at this rate I cannot imagine.

October 1

Made a note on line to take in bringing the present negotiations to a head.

Bhopal came at 11.30 a.m. He has apparently been trying to act as unofficial negotiator, and has seen Gandhi, Jinnah and Azad, but has obviously made no progress at all. He did not say much and seemed a little depressed.

October 2

Cabinet meeting took an hour, there was nothing controversial, but there are a lot of lawyers in this Cabinet and some rather technical points in the Bribery and Corruption Bill were argued at great length by Rajagopalachariar, who is always a bit garrulous, and Asaf Ali. These two are at present the chief talkers in the Cabinet.

At 12.0 noon I had the vital meeting with Jinnah; he said nothing at all on the Nationalist Muslim issue and did not attempt to argue it; but he said that if he was to have any chance of success with his Working Committee he must have some success to show on the other points he had raised e.g. the safeguard about being outvoted on major communal issues, the Vice-Presidency of the Council, and the question of Minorities. The matter of the Vice-Presidency was obviously the one to which he attached importance, from the psychological point of view. His argument was that with Nehru holding the office of Vice-President the Congress were in a superior position and that made the Muslim League inferior in status. I get the impression that Jinnah wants to come in, if his prestige can be upheld. It was agreed that he should send me a note setting out the points which we had discussed and asking for a decision on them.

October 3

In the evening I got Jinnah's promised letter, with the points on which he wants a decision before he meets his Working Committee on the 7th. I don't think they should present any really serious difficulty. We may be within sight of a settlement, though I shall not believe it till I actually swear the League in.

October 4

Spent some of morning preparing for interview with Nehru this afternoon and drafting replies to Jinnah's points. The Vice-Presidency is the most difficult one. I decided to try the rotational proposal on Nehru but without much expectation that he will agree, and I don't think it is worth while to force it on Congress.

Rather to my surprise he accepted all my replies to Jinnah except about the Vice-Presidency, without asking to consult his colleagues. So I sent my letter to Jinnah and a copy of the replies to his points to Nehru. This was rather better than I expected, George had prophesied a good deal more difficulty and objections, and was certain that Nehru would wish to consult his colleagues before agreeing. N. mentioned his proposed visit to the Frontier, and I said that if we have a coalition by then he might consider taking a Muslim colleague with him 'to show a united front'. He said he would consider it, but without any enthusiasm, as was natural.

So the prospects of a coalition are still alive but, as I said in my cable to S. of S. reporting progress, the issue rests on the knees of some very strange gods.

October 8 (Q.'s birthday)

Nehru was to have come in the afternoon, but there was some misunderstanding and he did not turn up. Negotiations between him and Jinnah are going on, and there seems optimism about.

George had an interview with Sudhir Ghosh, who has come back from England with a very swollen head. According to him, he had seen the P.M. and S. of S. frequently, had been sent to Paris at Government expense and to Switzerland to see Cripps; and had been consulted by the Times on all their leaders about India, and they had undertaken to remove anything of which he did not approve! He told George that he was mistrusted and unpopular! I always took a poor view of S.G.

October 9

Cabinet meeting after which I saw Nehru for a short time and asked him how the negotiations were going. He said that a good deal had been agreed but there were still some points outstanding. They had agreed that the arrangement of Vice-President should stand as at present but that the Vice-President need not be the Leader of the Assembly. They seemed also to have reached some sort of an agreement on the matter of major communal issues. They had not discussed portfolios nor the long-term issue. I said that the points outstanding must be very small. Nehru said: 'Yes, but seemingly small things sometimes become very big,' which is of course quite true with these people. Nehru looked rather tired and depressed, I thought, and was not very forthcoming.

Olaf Caroe was very worried about Nehru's proposed visit to the Frontier Tribes. I gave him what comfort I could and said that I hoped that a Coalition would be in existence before he went; and that I could not well stop him. He was chiefly concerned because Abdul Ghaffar Khan was going to accompany Nehru.

I saw Caroe again in the evening after his interview with Nehru. He had quite failed to shake N. in his intention to make the visit, but their discussion seems to have been amicable.

October 10

I cannot quite make out what is going on in these political negotiations but I am quite sure that Bhopal is being tortuous and evasive as usual. Sir B. N. Rau came round this morning with a message from Bhopal that there was only one point outstanding, that I should agree to consult the whole Cabinet over the appointment of a Minority representative and not the leaders of the two mains as I had said. I refused to budge, except to add that I hoped the leaders would by agreement recommend someone acceptable to the whole Cabinet. I am pretty sure that Bhopal was lying when he said that this was the only point outstanding, and that it was a try-on by him and Gandhi to get me to accept the principle of the Cabinet and not myself nominating members.

October 11

Bhopal asked George to see him and confessed that his attempt at negotiations had completely broken down. So far as I can make out, these so-called negotiations have in effect practically amounted to an attempt by Gandhi and the Congress to secure Muslim League compliance in an arrangement to eliminate the Governor-General's influence in the Cabinet and reduce him to a figure-head. The method appears to have been to offer Jinnah certain concessions provided that he agreed that the G.G. should never be allowed to interfere with the decisions of the Cabinet. The effort made yesterday to induce me to agree that the decision on Minority representatives should be made by Cabinet as a whole was just part of the plot and was not the last outstanding point, as I was told that Bhopal had promised. Now I shall have to get back to Jinnah again. Bhopal's intervention has not improved matters.

October 12

Spent most of morning on a reply to S. of S. comments on my Breakdown Plan, and produced a fairly stiff reply which was approved by George and later by C-in-C. I also began to draft a letter to the King.

Bhopal came in for a short time before lunch and told me about the recent negotiations, that Gandhi had drafted a formula, accepted by Jinnah, conceding that the Muslim League represented the overwhelming majority of Muslims, but Nehru and the Working Committee had refused to agree. A rider to the formula, that the Cabinet should work as a team and should agree never to permit interference by the Governor-General, was not accepted by Jinnah. Bhopal said that Congress had conceded Leadership of the Assembly to Jinnah in return for Nehru's continuance in the Vice-Presidency. There had apparently been some sort of agreement on the matter of major communal issues. The question of appointment of Minorities had remained unsolved, but I have never attached great importance to this. Bhopal was leaving by train this evening, but evidently would have liked to have been pressed to stay. I did not encourage him.

After lunch I saw C-in-C, who agreed with my draft reply to S. of S. on the Breakdown Plan. He told me the Cabinet was pressing for the release of all I.N.A. men. He confirmed that he would prefer to keep Baldev Singh as War Member rather than have Jinnah when the Cabinet was reformed.

At 5.30 p.m. came the crucial interview with Jinnah. Obviously the League have made up their mind to come in, obviously also there will be trouble inside the Cabinet, since Nehru and Jinnah have failed to agree. I am not sure yet how fast a one Jinnah's surprise ball about the inclusion of a Scheduled Caste in his quota is. George suggested that he might intend to put in Ambedkar!

Well, well, I suppose that is something of an achievement to have got so far, but I still see plenty of stiff fences ahead.

October 13

Shortly before lunch I received a letter from Jinnah. It was a typical acceptance by an Indian politician, in that the first two paragraphs set forth the reasons why he could not possibly accept the basis and arrangements of the present Interim Government, the final paragraph said that the League had decided to come in. I therefore wrote to him and to Nehru asking for their lists of names.

Later in the evening Jinnah asked to come and see me; and I saw him and Liaquat at 7.0 p.m. The subject about which they had come was the nomination of a non-Muslim Scheduled Caste Member in the Muslim League quota. Obviously what was in their minds was that if Congress did not nominate a Nationalist Muslim, they would refrain from including a non-Muslim Scheduled Caste Member. I told them that whatever the Congress did, it would be a mistake on their part to include a non-Muslim. It would mean that the two parties entered the Coalition Government in a mood of antagonism.

I then said I hoped they understood that the presence of the Muslim League in the Interim Government would be conditional on their re-consideration of the Bombay Resolution and acceptance of the Statement of May 16th. Jinnah said that he realised this, but that it would be necessary to secure certain guarantees from the Congress, and that the Council of the League would have to be called together. I said this should be done as soon as possible.

Now I shall have a difficult and unpleasant time with Nehru and the Congress, and I think it may be impossible to avoid a showdown and perhaps a breakdown. I am tired of dealing with these impossible people, and of knowing at the same time that I shall get only weak-kneed support from home.

During his interview with Nehru the next day, 14 October, Wavell showed him Jinnah's letter of 13 October which 'he read with some apparent amusement'. The letter was as follows:

The Working Committee of the All-India Muslim League have considered the whole matter fully and I am now authorised to state that they do not approve of the basis and scheme of setting up the Interim Government, which has been decided by you, presumably with the authority of His Majesty's Government.

Therefore, the Committee do not, and cannot agree with your decision already taken, nor with the arrangements you have already made.

We consider and maintain that the imposition of this decision is contrary to the Declaration of August 8th, 1940, but since, according to your decision we have a right to nominate five members of the Executive Council on behalf of the Muslim League, my Committee have, for various reasons, come to the conclusion that in the interests of Mussulmans and other communities it will be fatal to leave the entire field of administration of the Central Government in the hands of the Congress. Besides, you may be forced to have in your Interim Government Muslims who do not command the respect and confidence of Muslim India which would lead to very serious consequences; and, lastly, for other very weighty grounds and reasons, which are obvious and need not be mentioned, we have decided to nominate five on behalf of the Muslim League in terms of your broadcast, dated August 24th, 1946, and your two letters to me, dated 4th October, 1946, and 12th October, 1946, respectively, embodying clarifications and assurances.

October 14

I felt rather depressed early this morning, as I anticipated rather an unpleasant struggle with Congress over the entry of the Muslim League, especially as Nehru had written asking for Jinnah's names, so that he might submit them to the Cabinet! I sent a message asking him to come and see me, and prepared to be tough, if necessary.

The interview with Nehru went rather better than I had expected. And Vallabhai Patel, whom I saw after lunch, was almost effusive in his acceptance of the Coalition. I wonder how far the old villain was sincere, not very far I think.

October 15

Although I have at last succeeded in announcing a Coalition Cabinet, I feel no elation over it, rather depression over the difficulties still ahead. I wonder whether I can induce them to work together.

Jinnah's list of names came in late last night, just as I was going to bed. Since I did not wish to be kept awake by pondering on them, I only looked at them sufficiently to see that Jinnah had not included himself and had included a Scheduled Caste. When I studied it in detail, it was rather a disappointing list. Liaquat Ali Khan and Nishtar were certainties, but Chundrigar from Bombay and Ghazanfar Ali Khan from the Punjab are poor substitutes for Ismail Khan and Nazimuddin. I suppose J. was bound to put in someone from Punjab. I believe the Scheduled Caste, Jogendra Nath Mandal,[1] is not too bad.

I saw Nehru just before the Cabinet and gave him Jinnah's list confidentially. He promised me his list by the evening. He made little comment on J.'s names, did not object to the Scheduled Caste, but said it was not the best list that the League could produce. N. was obviously reluctant to discuss portfolios before he left for the N.W.F.P.; but I told him that the League must have one of the four 'key' portfolios previously held by Europeans—Finance, Defence, External Affairs, Home; and also one of the two portfolios Commerce or Industries and Supplies.

The Cabinet meeting passed off satisfactorily. The two principal subjects were the price of sugar and the reorganisation of the Salt Industry and the removal of the Tax on Salt for which Gandhi had been pressing for so long.

Nehru sent in his names in the evening. Of the three Muslims, Congress are keeping only Asaf Ali, and are dropping one Hindu, Sarat Chandra Bose. I had rather they kept Ali Zaheer than Asaf Ali, but Bose is the Hindu I had rather see go. N. showed no disposition to meet the League over portfolios, we shall have a struggle about this.

[1] Jogendra Nath Mandal had been included in Mr. Suhrawardy's Muslim League ministry in Bengal—the only non-Muslim in that ministry.

My chief difficulty today, however, was to get S. of S. to obtain the King's approval to Jinnah's list, which I had cabled early in the morning. He obviously mistrusted me and feared Congress, and wanted Nehru's approval to Jinnah's names rather than mine! I only got approval just before dinner.

Meanwhile very serious troubles seem to have broken out in Eastern Bengal with much killing of isolated Hindu communities by Muslim terrorists. A very inauspicious beginning to the new Government, I am afraid.

October 16

I had an hour with Jinnah this morning. He said with great emphasis that the spirit in which the Government at the Centre was conducted would all depend on whether Congress would get over the idea of the Muslim League coming in as subordinates in a Government run by Nehru. We had some discussion on the long-term issue and he said that there must be some agreement that the terms of the Statement of May 16th, as emphasised in the Statement of May 25th, would be observed by the Congress. Bose and Shafaat Ahmed came to lunch and Ali Zaheer came in afterwards. Then I had a talk with Patel mainly about events in Eastern Bengal. He started on rather a truculent note but was quite good-humoured. Nehru, Bose and Patel all very insistent about the riots in E. Bengal, but more for political reasons, I think, than with any real sympathy for the victims. Bucher thinks the killings have been exaggerated and that the matter is in hand, but I doubt if they really know in Calcutta what is going on.

October 20

Returned from a four-day visit to Bombay, which had as its objects to learn at first hand of the communal troubles in the City, and to collect Pam and my two grand-sons who were arriving from home in S.S. Andes, a liner normally on the South American run.

I flew down on the 17th, arrived about 2.0 p.m., and met the Ministers during the afternoon and evening.

On the morning of the 18th I did a tour of the parts of the city most affected by the disturbances. I had a surprisingly cordial reception from both Hindus and Muslims. I visited a hospital and saw some of the victims (last time I had been at this hospital it had been after the 1944 explosion).

I had a talk with Wilson, head of the Police, about the unhelpfulness of the public, and the instigation of some of the political people, notably the Mahasabha. Since September 1, when this trouble started there have been nearly 1,500 casualties, of which more than 360 have been fatal, about equally divided between Hindus and Muslims. Over 6,000 arrests have been made, more than half Hindus. There are certain quarters into which no Muslim can go without escort, and vice versa. A deplorable state of affairs, but not easy to remedy.

During the day I had two long talks with Archie Nye, mainly about the Breakdown Plan, on which he contributed some useful comments. He said all was going well in Madras and his relations with his Ministers were cordial. He thought the Province would just get through the food crisis.

October 21

I came back from Bombay feeling rather depressed, at the little progress we have made in settling the Indian problem, the great amount that remains to be done, the acuteness of the communal tension and the bitterness of feeling, the lack in the leaders of any sense of urgency or of any foresight, none seems able to look beyond the immediate party advantage. I believe Azad is in many ways the best of them all.

In the evening I had a talk with Patel. He blew off steam about Ghazanfar Ali's speech and about Eastern Bengal, and delivered a general hymn of hate against the Muslim League; but was reasonably friendly. He was as anxious as we are to get a decision from S. of S. about winding-up of S. of S. Services and terms of compensation for them. He said that he had advised Nehru not to make this N.W. Frontier trip.

October 22

A wearing day. I saw Jinnah in the morning, but it was not a very satisfactory interview, these people always go back to the same old arguments, and never seem to me to move forward at all. I have the impression that Jinnah is not so much in control of the Muslims as he was, that his preaching of Pakistan and Direct Action, which he meant more as political bargain counters than realities, has gone to the heads of the younger and more hot-headed, who want to translate them into action.

After lunch I saw Nehru, looking worn and tired after his Frontier experiences. He appeared to be less difficult about portfolios than I expected, but I daresay he will be difficult again tomorrow, after he has seen Patel.

I finished the day with a bad migraine.

Disregarding the advice of Abul Kalam Azad and others, Nehru had insisted on paying a visit to the N.W.F.P. On his arrival at Peshawar there was a hostile demonstration organized by the Muslim League. In tribal territory he was also given a hostile reception; the Afridis refused to meet him at all and at Landi Kotal and at the Malakand Pass stones were thrown at him and his party and they were extricated with difficulty. Some of the Congress Ministers of the N.W.F.P. unjustly blamed the local officials for these demonstrations. The effect of the tour was to weaken the Congress in the N.W.F.P. and to strengthen the League.

October 23

A really bad day. As I anticipated, Nehru had changed his tone after seeing his colleagues, and wrote me a long letter, which contained every possible reason for keeping the League out of the Government, unless they were prepared to crawl in apologetically.

Cabinet meeting considered Gurkhas, oil-seeds control, jute control and appointments of non-Indians. Nehru silent and sulky, Asaf Ali and Rajagopalachari loquacious as usual.

I saw Nehru after Council, and told him that the portfolios were for me to distribute, that the Muslim League must have their fair share, and that I hoped Congress were not going to wreck the only hope of peace for India. He listened but was not helpful and as usual accused Jinnah and the League.

Then I saw Jinnah, who brought Liaquat, and tried to persuade them not to insist on Home or Defence portfolios; but Jinnah was in one of his worst and most communal moods, as bitter against Nehru as N. had been against him. These people make me tired and discouraged.

So I wrote to Nehru to say that the League must have one of the principal portfolios; but I am afraid that we are in for a show-down. I warned S. of S. to this effect.

October 24

The Coalition Government is still alive at the end of the day, but only just, and it required something like artificial respiration this evening. It certainly does not look like outliving the cradle at present.

The morning began with a long letter from Nehru saying that Congress were unable to give up the External Affairs, Defence or Home portfolios, and containing the usual tirade about the Bengal disturbances, the speeches of the Muslim League leaders, their non-acceptance of the May 16 Statement, etc.; but offering the Finance portfolio if the League must have one of the major ones; and suggesting that it would be better if the League simply took the five vacant portfolios till the Legislative Assembly was over, and then reconsidering the matter later. I replied pressing for the Home portfolio. Nehru wrote just before lunch to say that Congress would resign from the Government sooner than agree to this, but that he would confirm this after consulting his colleagues. He confirmed it in the evening.

I then sent for Jinnah at 7.30 p.m., informed him of the position and asked whether the League would accept the Finance portfolio. J. was not in a very accommodating mood, and accused Congress of mutilating on the radio his statement about the Noakhali disturbances; but he agreed to the Finance and Commerce portfolios with three others, with the usual proviso that it was subject to the decision of his Working Committee. I then sent for Nehru at 9.30 p.m. and told him that the League would accept Finance, and asked him to let me know what alternative portfolio he proposed for Matthai. Nehru, who looked very tired and worn, accepted this quietly, and said he would let me know after consulting his colleagues. I had rather expected he might persist in resignation, and from previous experience shall not be in the least surprised if he comes back tomorrow with some new objection or proposal. I would not put it past Jinnah either to raise fresh difficulties. Neither party has the least trust in the other, and I am sure that Gandhi in the background is doing his best to wreck any hope of agreement.

During the afternoon, by the way, the Congress sent round Asaf Ali— on the pretext of his coming for his routine interview, half an hour late on what was obviously a reconnaissance of my position. After a little talk about his Department (proposal to construct locomotives in India) which was simply camouflage, he began by saying that he had proposed to retire from the Cabinet and let Azad take his place, but that the present time was not auspicious. After some talk about Jinnah and his previous friendship with him, which he said was broken in 1938, he launched out on the matter of portfolios and put out at me the same propaganda as had been in Nehru's letter. This was typical Congress technique, a would-be confidential and friendly approach to try and put me in a receptive mood, and then the proposition that Congress wanted to get across. I think I can recognise it readily now and am not easily deceived.

It is all very wearing; and for almost the first time in my life I am really beginning to feel the strain badly—not sleeping properly and letting these wretched people worry me. However, some courage and a sense of humour usually returns with the morning ride and carries me through the day.

October 25

After another day of excursions and alarms we have settled the difficult portfolio business. Nehru as usual opened the bowling with a fast one. He wrote that Matthai was taking the Industries and Supplies portfolio from Rajagopalachari, who would take Education; but that Bhabha would go to Works, Mines and Power, Now I told him last night that I was prepared to allot W.M.P. to Matthai if he wanted it but that otherwise I was committed to giving it to the League. So I sent George down to see Nehru and tell him that Bhabha should take Posts and Air or Health. No result. So I saw Nehru myself, again without result, except that he said he would put it to his colleagues. No result again. So I sent Ian Scott down to see Jinnah and offer him the other portfolios—Finance, Commerce, Posts & Air, Health, Legislative. Rather to my surprise Jinnah raised little protest, was friendly, accepted, and sent me a message of thanks.

So I have at last got a Coalition Government safely in office. But I am in no way inclined to optimism over the future, and do not feel in the least like 'celebrating the event', though I hope I may sleep better tonight. The new Government will be sworn in tomorrow under ominous auspices—the riots in E. Bengal, restlessness in Bombay and Calcutta, the resentment of Congress at having to take in the League without acknowledgment of Nehru's position as self-appointed Premier, the deep mistrust between the Party leaders. I shall have to be a very much better diplomatist and leader than I judge myself to be to make the Government work.

The correspondence over the distribution of portfolios shows the difficulty of settling matters between the two Parties, who cannot meet each other without immediate divergence. That an agreement has been reached at all is I suppose something of an achievement.

October 26

My apprehension that matters would not go smoothly for long received an immediate justification this morning. While I was waiting to go to the Cabinet to swear in the League members, George brought down a strongly-worded note from Patel, demanding that the Bengal situation should be discussed in the Cabinet this morning, and that the Centre should at once take over control of the disaffected areas from the Bengal Government. It was an immediate wrecking attempt before the new Government had even begun. I sent word at once that I refused to allow such discussion which was not within the competence of the Cabinet, unless I sought their advice which I had no intention of doing at present. I said that the meeting would be confined to swearing in the new members.

It had been the intention to discuss the Adjournment motions in the Assembly, but since a number of them dealt with Bengal, it would obviously have been dangerous, so on the grounds that I had only just seen the motions I said that I would discuss them with the leaders after the Cabinet and call another meeting later if necessary.

The new members were sworn in. Ghazanfar Ali, the only one I had not met, looks a rather irresponsible sort of buccaneer, I hope he will settle down. I made a short speech to them.

After the Cabinet I discussed the adjournment motions with Nehru and Liaquat and disposed of them satisfactorily, I hope. Then I had half an hour with Nehru, Patel and Rajagopalachari over Patel's note. I explained my view of the legal position. R. attempted to controvert it, but I refused to be drawn into a legal argument, and he had really no grounds for his argument and knew it. Then I said that quite apart from the legal point of view, it would be futile from the practical point of view to attempt to interfere from the Centre with the Government of Bengal, it would merely promote fresh conflict. Both Nehru and Patel got a little heated, they are obviously under strong pressure from their supporters; and there was at one time even a hint of resignation. But in the end we parted amicably. So that I was able for the first time this week to play a round of golf in the evening.

Chips[1] and Peter Coats arrived.

October 27

I spent the morning trying to get an appeal to end communal strife issued by the Party Leaders. Ian Scott went round to Nehru and Liaquat first of all; the difficulty here was that while both agreed with the appeal Nehru would not sign alongside Liaquat which would admit him to some sort of equality in the Cabinet; and suggested that either all members of the Cabinet should sign it, or that it should be issued over the names of myself, Gandhi and Jinnah. But Gandhi took refuge in his usual subterfuge that he was not even a member of Congress, and Jinnah would have nothing to do with anything signed by Gandhi, and so the proposal once again foundered on the rock of party jealousy and smallmindedness.

October 28

A comparatively quiet day.

I drafted a very short broadcast appealing for communal peace which

[1] Sir Henry Channon, M.P.

I delivered in the evening. It would have been better if my proposal of yesterday had succeeded, but my own appeal can at least do no harm.

October 29

First day of Assembly session seems to have passed off satisfactorily. Nehru and Liaquat sat side by side on the Government benches though I believe they did not exchange a word.

I saw Patel at 10.0 a.m. He was fairly friendly and reasonable, but pulled the usual fast one out of the bag at the end by producing a telegram from Pant to Congress asking permission to resign over the Measures case.

> *Sir Philip Measures, Inspector-General of Police in the United Provinces, learnt that the Congress Home Minister was corresponding direct with police officers instead of through him as Head of the Department; whereupon, without any reference to the Home Minister or to the Chief Minister, he issued a circular pointing out that such correspondence was irregular. The Home Minister, of course, was offended, and although Measures apologized, he gathered from Pandit Pant, the Chief Minister, that he had lost their confidence. He therefore tendered his resignation, and the Ministers wanted to accept it. But the Governor, Sir Francis Wylie, feeling that Measures was being forced out for a minor error of judgment, considered that in discharge of his special responsibility for the protection of the Services he should overrule his Ministers and refuse to accept Measures's resignation. Pandit Pant and the U.P. Ministry then threatened to resign, and Nehru threatened that the Congress Members of the Interim Government would do likewise. The matter dragged on for some days with recurrent threats of resignation. Ultimately on instructions from the Secretary of State the Governor gave way and Measures was allowed to proceed on leave preparatory to retirement.*

I saw Liaquat and spoke to him of the necessity for the Muslim League to accept the Statement of May 16 forthwith. He referred me to Jinnah. Liaquat seems a sensible level-headed person.

After lunch I had half an hour with Rajagopalachari talking about Education on which his views seem sound. But he gave me the impression of being depressed over the general situation. There is no doubt that Congress are bitterly disappointed over the entry of the Muslim League into the Government which checks their attempt to seize power.

October 30

Another of those sort of days. I had an interview fixed with Nehru for 10.0 a.m., but he apparently had a nervous breakdown and sent word that he could not come. I had Jinnah at 12.0 noon for one hour and ten minutes at his most Jinnah-ish, on the question of his calling his Council to accept the Statement of May 16th. It was completely unsatisfactory. Jinnah went over all the old arguments to the effect that the Congress acceptance of the Statement of May 16th was not a genuine one and should never have been accepted as such. His main theme was that he could not possibly get his Council to accept the Statement of May 16th unless Congress accepted the literal interpretation of the Mission's plan. His attitude was that 'if H.M.G. will not take a firm line and protect us, then leave us to our fate'.

It looks as if another long disputation was in sight.

In the evening I had the first meeting of the new Cabinet. The chief item was the proposal for a Consultative Committee with the States. Rajagopalachari was as usual very discursive and seemed to regard the Committee as a step towards a Federal Cabinet. Liaquat made on the whole the most sensible contribution.

In the evening Nehru sent from his sick-bed a rather plaintive indictment of the Governor of the U.P., the Muslim League and myself, and threatened resignations all round. War of nerves, I think.

Summary

These four months, from the departure of the Mission to the swearing-in of a Coalition Government, have been in many respects the most gruelling of my life so far. They are comparable to the four months from March to June in 1941 in the strain to which I was subjected; but then at least I was dealing in a medium to which I was trained, the conduct of war, and with people whom I could trust. These political negotiations are entirely foreign to my military training, and there seems no firm ground in political matters and no one whom one can trust.

The fatal weakness of the Mission in their abject attitude to Congress, and the duplicity of Cripps, left behind a legacy which it was beyond my power to counter-act. Congress realised that H.M.G. was afraid of them and would never really stand up to them—an impression which was increased by the treatment accorded to that little rat Sudhir Ghosh; while Jinnah and the League considered that they had been 'sold down the river' and were deeply suspicious. I have paid a heavy price for not being firmer in the last stages of the Mission and allowing myself to be double-crossed by Cripps. I don't believe that by his code he thought he was doing anything dishonest, he was merely being clever. But I am quite sure that cleverness does not pay with these people, they can be deeper and more dishonest still. Vallabhai Patel himself once remarked to me that they never knew where they were with Cripps, he said different things to different people. While Mrs. Sarojini Naidu said to one of my staff: 'We think very poorly of Sudhir Ghosh, but if he is the sort of person the Cabinet Mission like you cannot blame us for using him'.

I am very doubtful whether this Coalition will work, too much time has been wasted and things are moving too fast. The Congress is not interested in making a Constitution under British auspices, only in consolidating their power. The Mission gave away the weakness of our position, and our bluff has been called. Our time in India is limited and our power to control events almost gone. We have only prestige and previous momentum to trade on and they will not last long. My task now is to secure the safest and most dignified withdrawal possible.

I am sorry for the Muslims, they have more honesty, courage and dignity than the Hindus, but cannot stand up to the power of the rupee and the superior education and chicanery of the Congress. Up to a point Jinnah played his cards well, but I think he has been too unyielding.

14

THE LAST CHANCE
OF UNITY

November 3

Got back today from a short visit to Calcutta and East Bengal. I left Delhi
on the morning of October 31, and got to Calcutta in early afternoon.
Driving from the airfield at Dumdum, I found Calcutta streets dirty and
deserted, and the city looking more squalid even than usual. Buses and
taxis were on strike, most of the shops closed and barred and the streets
half blocked with refuse which had not been cleared for days. It seems that
no transport will run without escort.

I had a series of interviews in the afternoon about the disturbances in
East Bengal. They did little more than confirm my general impressions
about the course of events and the bitterness of communal feeling. The
Governor was calm and imperturbable but said in his slow fashion: 'I
realised that I was taking on an extremely difficult job, I did not realise
that I was taking on a practically impossible one.'

Next day, we flew over the area of the disturbances for an hour or so
and got a fairly good idea of the country and of the amount of damage
done. Then we landed at Dacca, lunched with the Commissioner (Holland)
and had a series of interviews. I had a telegram from PSV that all Congress
Ministries and Congress members at Centre were threatening resignation
over Measures case. After tea we drove to Narayangunge and embarked
on a river steamer for Chandpur.

We disembarked at Chandpur on the morning of the 2nd. More
interviews and an inspection of some refugee camps.

Meanwhile, I had a telegram that Nehru, Liaquat, Patel, and Nishtar
were flying together to Calcutta, which was welcome news.

We re-embarked about midday and steamed up river back to Dacca
and thence by plane to Calcutta where we arrived about 5.30 p.m.

I had a little talk with the Governor before dinner and again after dinner;
and at 7.0 p.m. saw Nehru and Co. I gave them my impressions of East
Bengal and cordially welcomed their initiative in coming down together.
They had nothing much to say about their mission, but seemed on quite

friendly terms with one another. I warned them against giving any countenance to Bose's proposed strike.

In my talks with Burrows he told me of the apparent hopelessness of arriving at a coalition at present (Roy, the Congress leader of the opposition, demands parity of seats with the Muslims except for the Chief Minister); of the danger of Bose's projected hartal,[1] which the Government will fight with all its resources; and of a difficulty about reinforcements for the Armed Police—Suhrwardy wants to enlist 500 Punjabi Muslims. I told him about my Breakdown Plan, with which he agreed, and said that he must know what plan he is carrying out. He said: 'I cannot carry Bengal for more than another 12 months, because after that it will not be there for me to carry.' He remarked that when he took on the job he thought he had one good asset, the Police Force, but found that it was now unreliable.

I left Calcutta this morning and touched down for 40 minutes at Bihta airfield near Patna, and saw the Chief Minister Sinha, some of his staff, the I.G. Police and the Sub-Area Commander. Sinha was definitely rattled; and it looks to me as if the troubles in Bihar were going to be worse than those in E. Bengal. The Premier of course wants more troops and aeroplanes.

A large number of Hindu refugees from East Bengal had made their way to Bihar, and their tales of woe excited Hindus of Bihar to murderous attacks on their Muslim neighbours which quite eclipsed in scale and savagery the slaughter in East Bengal.

The more I see of Bengal the more I dislike the country, the people, the climate. Most of Bengal is a swamp most of the time; the people are cowardly yet capable of terrorism and cruelty; the educated men are clever but in a soft superficial way; the climate is sticky and enervating. A deplorable part of the world.

Burrows remarked that it was costing more in casualties to hand over Bengal than it did to conquer it. The loss of life in the Calcutta riots was far greater than at the battle of Plassey.

November 4

One of those sort of days again. I puzzled over the problem of the League and the Constituent Assembly and wrote a note about it. It is sad to realise how the well-framed plan of the Mission has been ruined by the initial duplicity of Cripps and the failure to take a strong line in upholding our

---

[1] Hartal: the closing of shops as a political gesture.

intention. I hold myself to blame for this, but it is difficult to take a strong line with jellyfish.

The note was addressed to P.S.V. and is given below:

I am rather puzzled and worried about the matter of getting the Muslim League into the Constituent Assembly. Time is getting on, and we cannot delay sending out invitations much longer, if the C.A. is to meet on December 9th.

2. There are three parties to this impasse: the Muslim League (or rather Mr. Jinnah), the Congress, and H.M.G.

It seems impossible at the moment for me to move Jinnah in the matter; he professes that he could never get acceptance by the Council without further assurances, and is not willing to try. It is difficult to get at exactly what assurance Mr. Jinnah wants, but I think if it were definitely stated that the Sections will draft the Provincial Constitutions, this would satisfy him.

I do not see any possibility of persuading the Congress to give such an assurance; they are bound by frequent statements they have made, and always refer to their letter of acceptance to the Mission, which the Mission so wrongly accepted. They are apparently prepared to agree that the question of whether the Sections make the Constitution for the Provinces or the Provinces make their own, should be referred to the Federal Court; but this Jinnah will not accept. There is therefore an impasse also in this direction.

There remains H.M.G., who are to my mind absolutely committed to the League point of view, both by their statement of May 16th and by the assurance which Cripps and the Secretary of State gave to the Muslim League in the interview on May 16.[1] H.M.G. are, however, in my view, both cowardly and dishonest in this matter, and have so far refused to issue an unequivocal statement. Their attitude is that they dare not do anything which may upset Congress. There is therefore also an impasse in this direction.

3. The question is how to proceed: whether to try and work on Jinnah, on the Congress, or on H.M.G. We might perhaps get B. N. Rau to approach Jinnah, or try to induce the Muslim League Members of Government to influence him. I do not feel there is much hope in approaching the Congress. But if H.M.G. could only be persuaded to issue a clear and authoritative statement, I think that might satisfy Jinnah. I propose to send a telegram to H.M.G. to the effect that Jinnah is reluctant to call his Council until a definite assurance has been given him on this point; and

[1] The assurance was given during the meeting of Muslim League representatives with Cripps and Pethick-Lawrence briefly referred to in the Journal entry for 16 May, see p. 272.

that I consider that H.M.G., who are fully committed in honour on this issue, should make a statement to the effect that it was and still is an integral part of the scheme for the Constituent Assembly that a Section should make the Constitution for the Provinces inside that Section; and that a Province cannot withdraw from the Section (or Group if formed) until a later stage as laid down in the Statement.

4. The whole question is really academic, since the Constituent Assembly cannot work except by agreement; but unless we can get the Constituent Assembly together at an early date, the whole situation is bound to deteriorate, and there is a serious danger of the Government splitting up, since I shall have to bring pressure on Jinnah to call his Council or withdraw from the Government.

4/11/1946

At 10.30 a.m. I had a rather disturbing interview with the C-in-C. He goes too far in my view in subservience to his Minister, and has given the impression that he is quite prepared for the immediate withdrawal of all British troops, which will be very embarrassing for me. He left behind a note which he handed to Baldev in which he had spoken hypothetically of any British troops remaining in India after January 1, 1947. I have always maintained the attitude that British troops will not leave India until after the new Constitution is made. I wrote C-in-C a strongly worded letter.

We also discussed the N.W. Frontier, he is disturbed at the effect of Nehru's visit, does not think much of the Political Service, which he thinks has been going downhill for the last twenty years and has completely failed to change with the times.

At 3.15 p.m. I saw Vallabhai Patel and Liaquat Ali Khan on their return from Patna. They were sensible and seemed still on friendly terms, and impressed with the seriousness of the situation. This getting together of Congress and the League, if it continues and bears fruit, is the most hopeful feature of the political situation for a long time.

Afterwards I saw Jogendra Nath Mandal, the Scheduled Caste representative of the Muslim League, a smooth sort of Bengali, not very impressive.

November 6

The situation in Bihar seems quite out of hand. It is of course the result of the violent communal propaganda on both sides and of the lowering of the authority and morale of the services and Police by the Ministry. The question is when and how one can stop it. As I have warned H.M.G. on many occasions we have now the responsibility without the power, whereas the Indian Provincial Ministries have the power but little or no sense of responsibility.

I discussed with Weightman this morning Nehru's tour and his foolish and unrealistic note about it. Weightman said that Congress are 'gunning for' Olaf Caroe and will have him out if they can. W. says he can seldom get hold of Nehru, who is trying to do too much and is likely to have a nervous breakdown. He said that Cripps was in correspondence with Nehru and had written to him about Krishna Menon.[1]

The Muslim League members of my cabinet came to me about Bihar just before the Cabinet. Nishtar had returned that afternoon and they were all full of accusations against the Provincial Ministry and Congress; and wanted martial law, Muslim and British troops, and a visit to Bihar by myself. I decided that it might be a good thing if I went down tomorrow.

Cabinet meeting went off quite successfully in spite of the tension. We dealt with proposals for encouraging small savings; establishment of a Price fixing Committee; formation of a new Central I.C.S. and I.P. to replace S. of S. Services; rules for the admission of foreigners into India; instructions to India's U.N.O. Delegation about trying to secure a seat for India on the Security Council; and demobilisation. Then Asaf Ali made a statement about insecurity on the railways and wanted to establish a special armed force for protection of passengers and property—another symptom of the breakdown of law and order.

After Cabinet I had a few words with Patel and Liaquat about the Press and with the C-in-C about the Bihar situation.

Mandal, the Scheduled Caste representative of the League, was sworn in. Ghazanfar Ali will be a rather noisy and tiresome member of Cabinet, I fear.

November 9

Returned from a couple of rather harrowing days in Bihar where there has been an outbreak of savagery and bestiality even worse than the Calcutta killings and more terrible than the Noakhali riots for which they were a revenge. The victims are all Muslims.

I went off on the 7th and got to Patna after lunch. I had a series of interviews: with that gangster the Premier, Sinha; with Bowstead Secretary to Government and Creed the I.G. Police; with the military commanders, Bucher, Ekin and Russell; with Nehru and Prasad who have been doing their best to check the troubles and claim to be influencing a return to

[1] V. K. Krishna Menon, a Congress propagandist in the U.K. and a close friend of Nehru. After Independence he became High Commissioner for India in the U.K. and was later Defence Minister.

sanity; and then with three indignant and accusatory Muslims. The first of these Nauman, a central M.L.A., seemed to me a most unpleasant little man; it was only at the end of the interview that I realised he had some personal cause for his bitterness, as his property had been destroyed and relations killed. Mr. Hussein Imam, the local Muslim League leader was in a high state of indignation, demanding strong action, machine-gunning of crowds from the air, dismissal of the Government, etc. The third was Md. Yunus, a rather sad little man in European clothes with long bushy hair sticking out of his ears. His theme was the same but he was more restrained than the other two. The trouble is that there is little or nothing now that I can do to influence events. I cannot turn out the Government and run a Section 93 Administration. Machine-gunning from the air is not a weapon one would willingly use, though the Muslims point out, rather embarrassingly, that we did not hesitate to use it in 1942.

Yesterday I wasted my morning in a 3-hour flight over the affected area; one could see little or nothing of the damage done, even at a few hundred feet, and to all appearances the countryside was normal and peaceful. I took Nishtar with me, to whom I had given a lift in my plane from Delhi. I then went round the Patna Hospital, a poor old-fashioned hospital, and looked at riot victims.

In the afternoon I spent an hour looking at refugee camps, in buildings in Patna, a depressing sight. After that I had some more interviews.

Before I went off this morning, I had the Premier up to see me, and told him that his Government has disgraced and discredited Bihar; that it was criminal folly to allow Noakhali Day to be celebrated; and that the course of action of his Government, in insisting on the release of criminals, in persecuting Government servants and lowering the morale of the Police, and in failing to control the Press, had led directly to the present tragedy. I told him that he must give every support to the troops and police in restoring order, must stop the campaign of hatred in the Press, must see that offenders and instigators were punished, and must rehabilitate the sufferers. He took quite a considerable rocket meekly, but it will have little effect, and he left with a would-be propitiatory grin.

The communal trouble seems to have spread to U.P.[1] as feared.

November 10

Commemoration service in morning. Duty lunch party, went to finals of Delhi Tennis tournament for an hour; and finished the day with an

[1] Hindu pilgrims at the annual religious fair at Garmukteswar set upon Muslims and killed about 1,000 of them. Reports of these disturbances were fairly successfully suppressed.

interview with Nehru and Liaquat, which went stickily. I spoke of remedies for the present situation: control of the Press; coalition ministries in the Provinces; and proper support of officials and police. They listened calmly till I came to the matter of Provincial coalitions, when Nehru suddenly blew up as he so often does. He denied the existence of a Coalition at the Centre because the Muslim League members refused to recognise him as 'de facto' Premier and attend his tea-party Cabinets.[1] I reminded him of the Constitution, and he promptly offered his resignation, three times in five minutes. (N. had a very rough passage from some elements in Bihar, the ruffianly gangster side of Congress which had expected the Interim Government to be a Hindu raj which would suppress the Muslim League. He is obviously over wrought and not far off a nervous breakdown). After some talk on well-worn lines, he calmed down a little. Liaquat remained very quiet and self-possessed, said the Muslim League members were quite prepared to co-operate in the Cabinet but not to recognise Nehru as head of it; and to discuss conditions in the Provinces if it applied to all. In the end we discussed the question of the Honours list calmly and amicably. But I shall quite likely get one of Nehru's letters tomorrow, and possibly resignation. The aim of Congress has always been clear, to obtain power by eliminating the influence of Governor-General and Governors. A show-down is not far off, and I can still get no definite policy from H.M.G. I can bring about a crisis, indeed I shall find it difficult to avoid doing so, but I cannot solve it.

November 11

I meditated a little on the Breakdown Plan in the morning and wrote a note regarding some of the details of it on the assumption that H.M.G. agreed to the general principle.

Ghazanfar Ali Khan came in the afternoon and talked quite sensibly, for the irresponsible politician I believe him to be.

We had a Cabinet meeting on the Air agreement with U.S.A. which went quite smoothly, and I think arrived at a logical and sensible decision.

I had a violent headache and much bleeding of the nose during the evening, which Harold[2] attributed to over work and want of a holiday.

[1] When the Interim Government was first formed, Nehru arranged for all the Members to meet informally for discussion among themselves, usually in his room over a cup of tea, before the formal meetings at which the Viceroy presided. The object was to establish the convention that the Viceroy was only a constitutional figure-head. After the Muslim League representatives joined the Government, Liaquat and his colleagues firmly declined to attend Nehru's 'tea-party Cabinets' or to lend any countenance to his attempts to make himself, instead of the Viceroy, the real head of the Government.

[2] Lt.-Col. H. Williamson, I.M.S., Surgeon to the Viceroy.

He is quite right, but I don't think it is possible for me to leave my post at present. I cannot take a proper holiday in India, as papers are bound to follow me about, and the responsibility for what happens. And I do not want to go to England in the winter.

November 12

Matthai was my only visitor in the morning, as Jagjivan Ram was ill. We had a general talk at which I tried to put across my views about the necessity for coalitions in the Provinces as well as in the Centre and the absolutely vital need to make the present coalition at the Centre work. He said that if we could keep it together for the next month or two it might turn out all right.

In the afternoon I had three-quarters of an hour with Rajagopalachari. We dealt with the lack of any historic sense in India and the reasons for it. We came back inevitably to present-day politics at the end; and he held me responsible for all the recent disorders in India because I had not taken stronger action at the time of the Calcutta riots and dismissed the Bengal Ministry. I said that I wondered whether his views would have been the same if the Bihar riots had been the first to break out, and pointed out the difficulties of strong action with limited resources. Congress have of course been criticised by their supporters for not using the Bengal troubles to suppress the Muslim League; and they are not accustomed to criticism, so are naturally shifting the blame to Burrows and myself.

In the evening I had an hour with Patel on various matters: control of Press; private armies; the Assam evictions; and of course the recent disturbances. On the whole, I get on well with Patel, we speak our minds to each other without reservation, and he has more balance than Nehru though he is even more communal and anti-Muslim in his outlook. He finished up by saying that coalitions would never work, at the Centre or in the Provinces, and I said that I was going to keep on at them and would make them work.

November 13

Cabinet meeting in the evening went quite smoothly and the more of these we can get through on similar terms the better chance of the show settling down. Both Nehru and Liaquat speak sensibly. Rajagopalachari is loquacious—so is Nishtar—and Ghazanfar rather inclined at present to be an enfant terrible, the remainder are mainly silent.

November 19

Returned just before lunch from a tour to N.W. Frontier. I got to Peshawar soon after mid-day on the 14th. After lunch I had an hour of interviews, then a garden party and then the Khan Sahib and finally a dinner party.

It is evident that Caroe and the Khan Sahib are at odds, and Caroe is very much on edge, so too is the Khan Sahib. He is a pleasant well-meaning person, without the necessary force of character or wisdom to run a Province; and he and the Governor are entirely different types who are not likely to get on well together.

On November the 15 I motored to Landi Kotal and saw a jirga of the Afridis. Their representation was to the effect that if we were going we should hand them back the Khyber Pass, that they had no intention of being ruled by Hindus and resented Nehru's visit, and that anything in the way of a little extra cash would be very acceptable. I told them in effect to be good boys and that no one would interfere with their freedom and that they would have every opportunity to state their case to any future Government of India and make their own terms. The jirga was dignified and impressive.

After lunch we flew to Wana, where I saw a jirga of the Ahmadzai Wazirs. They were not so impressive as the Afridis and were more communal and less dignified in their outlook. I said to them much the same as I had said to the Afridis. I then had a series of interviews with the local commanders and officials, went to a drink party and dined in the Wana Brigade Mess.

On Sunday the 17th, we motored by Nowshera, Dargai, the Malakand Pass to Chakdarra, at the junction of the Dir and Swat Valleys. Here we had tea with the Nawab of Dir, a severe but competent looking person, who obviously does not believe in progress or change for his people, but apparently rules well. Then we went on to Saidu, the Capital of Swat. The Wali met us at the border of his State, a nice friendly old man. The Swat Valley is a lovely one, and the people seem reasonably prosperous. The State is progressive in its policy in contrast with Dir.

At the Malakand Pass I looked at the scene of the assault on Nehru and his party. The political agent, Mahbub Ali, whose conduct has been called in question, had met us at Dargai. While I think it is most unlikely that he instigated or was privy to the attack, it was inexcusable that he should have gone on down the hill as he did and not seen the party safely past what was obviously a danger point.

Next morning, the 18th, we had a chikore shoot at Swat, quite good fun but there were not many birds.

After lunch we motored back to Peshawar, about 80 odd miles, in a little over three hours. I came back to the atmosphere of political crisis, as P.S.V. had telegraphed the text of letters from Nehru and Jinnah, the former expressing great surprise that I had not already issued invitations for the Constituent Assembly, the latter protesting strongly against my doing so. It was an issue I knew would arise before long.

I left this morning after breakfast. It is always pleasant to visit the N.W.F.P., but it is not in a happy state at present. Caroe is highly strung and takes things too hardly and seriously. Nehru's visit has shaken the officials badly. The N.W.F.P. has been until lately out of the hurly-burly of Indian politics, and has run itself rather in the old fashioned way. The latest Congress Ministry and Nehru's visit has given them all a severe jolt and they are discouraged and resentful. But it had to come, and may possibly do good in the long run. Nehru, to judge by his last letter to Caroe, which I saw on return here, seems to have realised that the Frontier and the Tribes had better be left alone for the present.

I had long interviews with Jinnah and Nehru this afternoon and evening. I was not looking forward to either of them. I suppose they went as well as could be expected. J. gives me the impression of deliberately riding for a fall.

His whole theme was that a settlement between the two communities was *quite* impossible, and he went back to the history of Akbar and Aurangzeb to prove it. He said that it was no use the Muslim League coming into the Constituent Assembly, that the Muslims were being ground down, and that we could not help. He thought we should give them their own bit of country, let it be as small as we liked, but it must be their own, and they would live on one meal a day.

I told Nehru that it did not seem likely that the Muslim League would attend the Constituent Assembly if called now. On the other hand we could not put it off indefinitely, and if he advised me that he considered it should be called, I would issue invitations at once. Nehru said that if the Assembly were postponed now, there was no convenient date till April, by which time everybody would have lost interest in it. He therefore recommended that invitations should be issued at once. I said that I would have them issued. We then talked about several other matters including various diplomatic appointments. He said that he had Asaf Ali in mind for the Embassy at Washington (I refrained from comment).

Nehru was quiet and quite friendly throughout and remained at the shallow end of the pool.

November 20

A very busy harassing day without a moment's let up. I dealt with the usual accumulation of business, which is normal after a tour, had a number of interviews, a cabinet meeting and quite a house-party for dinner.

Khizar, the Punjab Premier, was my first visitor. If all Indian politicians were as sensible and attractive as he is, life would be much easier. He did not talk much about all-India politics, said I knew his views; that the British ought not to leave, in fact he did not see how they could leave, that Pakistan was nonsense and any idea about exchange of populations madness, that he did not see how the Constituent Assembly would work, but that if I felt I should call it that was my business, that Jinnah's policy was all wrong; and that the Punjab would get on perfectly well by itself if only it was left alone. He had only two matters he really wanted to speak about: that entry to the Indian War Academy should not simply be by competition, as it would then be filled by babus; and that I should not have taken away his British Chief Justice, as the standard was bound to deteriorate. I told him he must speak to the C-in-C about the Academy, he said he was going to take him to task most severely; also the Defence Member, who was bound to be sympathetic, since Sikhs were so stupid that they would never get in by competition. Khizar was in very good form. He said the Punjab would be prepared to keep all their British officials, on the same terms as the present S. of S. Services.

Khizar was followed by a Muslim deputation which had visited Bihar; Nazimuddin, Firoz Khan Noon and the Nawab of Mamdot. The last-named remained silent throughout and F.K.N. was comparatively subdued and said little, Nazimuddin was the spokesman and carried a good deal of conviction. He estimated the refugees as 70,000–80,000 in towns and camps and as many more still in the villages but unable to move without protection and short of food. They alleged that Hindus, with the complicity of government, were destroying bodies and evidence. They emphasised the brutalities and atrocities committed. They spoke of the size of the problem: the need for warm clothing and proper rations; the urgency of rescuing Muslims from the villages where they were marooned; the rescue of women who had been abducted; the harvesting of crops; the question of resettlement. All this was the responsibility of H.M.G. and myself who were still charged with the protection of Minorities; the Bihar Ministry would do nothing. There should be a judicial enquiry; they accused particularly the Finance Minister of the Government and the Deputy Commissioner, Patna. They said Nehru had done his best but had been mobbed at one of his later interviews.

I decided to send Ian Scott to Bihar to try and find details of the situation; and to raise at the Cabinet this evening the question of relief to Bihar from the Centre.

In spite of all the feeling between the parties, Cabinet meetings continue to go well and smoothly, and this evening's was no exception. I made a statement that I proposed to offer help to Bihar from the Centre which was well received by the League members and without evident disapprobation by the Congress. There was little on the agenda but it went all right.

Jinnah rang up to say he proposed to publish my last letter to him about the Constituent Assembly and his reply. I told P.S.V. to tell him that it would be much better if he did not and that it could not do any good. But he insisted. It is one of the difficulties of negotiation with these people that they insist on publishing all correspondence.

Lady Cripps wired from China that she proposed to stay with Nehru instead of us when passing through Delhi. It does not make matters any easier for me that Cripps advertises so blatantly his pro-Congress bias.

November 21

I had a talk with Rajendra Prasad about Indian agriculture generally, he is quite a friendly person.

In the evening I had a difficult interview with the four Muslim members of my Cabinet, who asked point-blank whether I and H.M.G. proposed to keep order in India and protect the Minorities or to give Congress a free hand. I was bound in honesty to confess our weakness.

Earlier we had had a luncheon party to which Liaquat Ali Khan and his wife, a woman of considerable intelligence and character, Ghazanfar Ali Khan and Bhabha came. There is no doubt that the Congress gain a considerable international advantage by the social qualities of their women-folk who are usually intelligent and attractive compared with those of the Muslims who are usually in purdah.

November 22

A depressing day, which made me feel that all my attempts to get the two Parties together have been quite fruitless and have failed. Nehru at Meerut made a bitter attack on me for not recognising him as a de-facto Premier —he did not actually say so, but that was what he meant. Jinnah in a statement he issued made an even more bitter attack on me for calling the Constituent Assembly. This means that I have been steering a middle course, which in theory is the right one with two conflicting parties; but it also shows that a middle course has little or no hope of success, especially when H.M.G. is so obviously committed to Congress.

During the day I had two, or perhaps it was three, letters from Nehru continuing the sapping process against my authority as Governor-General and Crown Representative; and one from Patel, bitterly communal, protesting against my sending Ian Scott to ascertain the situation in Bihar and saying that everything which the Bihar Government was doing must be right (because it is a Congress Government, I suppose) and everything the Bengal Government was doing in East Bengal was wrong.

I saw Jagjivan Ram and we talked of the affairs of his Department and of the Bihar disturbances—the latter on the lines of 'quidquid delirant reges, plectuntur Achivi,' which I translated to him as 'When the political leaders stir up violence, the Depressed Classes get it in the neck.'

In the evening we had a party for some of the Princes, about 50 or 60 people altogether, before dinner. It went quite well. Chips loved it and after dinner remarked naively, as he gazed at the invitation list, 'What a wonderful thing to be able to put in one's diary!'

November 23

I had an hour and 10 minutes with Liaquat Ali Khan in an attempt to induce the League to come into the Constituent Assembly. The result will be seen from my telegram to S. of S.

> *In this telegram Wavell said that he had told Liaquat that he could not agree to the League staying in the Cabinet without accepting the long-term plan. Liaquat had replied that the League members were prepared to resign whenever required, 'but they would not accept the long-term plan unless H.M.G. declared that the Provinces must meet in Sections,*
>
> *'that the representatives in the Sections would decide, by a majority if necessary, whether there would be Groups,*
>
> *'and that the Sections, again by majority if necessary, would frame the Provincial Constitutions and the Group Constitutions, if any.*
>
> *'Also H.M.G. must undertake not to implement the results unless this procedure was observed.'*
>
> *Liaquat had also said that 'if H.M.G. was afraid of the Congress and had not the courage or honesty to maintain their own Mission's plan, then the Muslims had been thrown to the wolves and must accept the position and do the best they could by themselves, for it was useless to expect any mercy from Congress'.*
>
> *Wavell said that he had argued with him for over an hour but failed to move him. He warned H.M.G. that he took a serious view of the situation, and*

*would send them his considered views after discussion with Jenkins whom he
had asked to fly down to Delhi from Lahore.*

It is clear that I cannot bring the parties together. The original cleavage
was deep enough; but the failure of the Mission, in which I weakly
acquiesced, to meet the Congress challenge last June, and the subsequent
lack of firmness and honesty on the part of H.M.G. has made the League
what one can only describe as mulish and bloody-minded.

I spent the afternoon drafting a telegram to H.M.G. and putting the
position to them; and decided to get Evan Jenkins down for an hour or
two tomorrow and put the position to him.

November 24 (Sunday)

While I was continuing my draft to H.M.G., a telegram came from S. of S.
proposing that I should go home with two representatives of the Congress
and two of the Muslim League for a discussion at home.

Evan Jenkins arrived about mid-day and left again soon after 3.0 p.m.
He did not think a statement by H.M.G. that would satisfy the League
would be of any use now, as Congress would not accept it. He was doubtful of the value of a visit home but thought it worth trying. He said
Khizar's impressions of his visit to Delhi were that the two communities
were determined to fight it out and that Congress feel that they have
H.M.G. in their pocket. I showed him the Breakdown plan and he agreed
with it. He agreed with me that a Sikh should be added to the party invited
home. He thought that he could hold the Punjab if his Ministers did not
interfere too much. I completed the telegram to H.M.G. and we talked a
bit about other Punjab matters: shortage of wheat, insufficient cloth and
sugar; the services; Khizar's wish for more British troops.

So begins yet another effort. I am doubtful whether Congress will accept
the invitation to U.K. They will certainly be angry with me and attribute
it to my machinations in favour of the League.

During an interview before dinner, my visitor said very slowly and
solemnly, while I was discussing some point: 'I am not sure that I should
mention this matter at the moment, Sir, and I am sure you will forgive me
if I interrupt at an inappropriate moment, but there has been a mouse
running about your table for the last five minutes!'

November 25

A comparatively quiet day but plenty of green boxes as usual and one or
two more of Nehru's querulous and aggressive letters. A cabinet meeting

in the evening on Telecommunications which went all right. Nishtar knew his brief and was sensible. Then there looked like being a communal row over Ian Scott's report on Bihar which I had circulated, so I cut short the meeting before it could develop.

Mrs. Sarojini Naidu dined, she is always good value. (One of her wise-cracks was about Gandhi: 'If only that old man knew how much it costs us to keep him in poverty.')

Times of India has published what I naturally think sensible leading articles, defending me against the accusations of both parties.

November 26

H.M.G.'s answer to my telegram came in the form of an invitation for two representatives of Congress, two of Muslim League and one Sikh to fly home at once for discussions in London. I got hold of Nehru at about 11.30 a.m., he was as I expected not at all enthusiastic but said he would consult his colleagues and let me know in the evening. Liaquat thought it a very good idea but had of course to consult Jinnah and flew off to Karachi to do so. Later on in the afternoon I saw Baldev, who was quite prepared to accept if Congress did so but thought they would refuse.

Earlier on I had seen Patel who was frankly communal as usual. To him control of the Press means the suppression of Dawn, prohibition of private armies, the dispersal of the Muslim Guards, and rehabilitation that of E. Bengal only; although of course he professes complete impartiality.

In the evening came the Congress reply to H.M.G.'s invitation, a refusal as I had expected.

November 27

Cabinet Meeting in the morning went off quite amicably, although there were one or two contentious subjects. Nehru's proposal to send K. P. S. Menon[1] to Moscow and Krishna Menon to other European capitals was naturally likely to be unpalatable to the Muslims, since Krishna Menon is a notorious Congress propagandist. Nehru was conciliatory and although Nishtar and Ghazanfar stated their objections they did not press them. The proposal to negotiate an agreement for Australian wheat caused little trouble. If only the leaders were as reasonable outside Cabinet as inside it.

After lunch I saw Corfield. He showed me a letter from Bhopal in which for the third time in the last few months he wished to resign the Chancellorship, abdicate, and 'fight to the death for the Muslim cause.'

[1] K. P. S. Menon, I.C.S., Agent-General for India and later Ambassador in China, 1943–8, Ambassador to U.S.S.R., 1952–61.

He wrote very bitterly about the abandonment by H.M.G. of both the Princes and the Muslims. The trouble about Bhopal is that he tries to stand in with everyone at once—his brother Princes, Congress, League, H.M.G., myself; is not really straight with anyone and is trusted by no one.

I spoke to Corfield about the Breakdown Plan and gave him an outline. He agreed that it was the only course.

Baldev Singh followed the Congress lead of refusing H.M.G.'s invitation and took the opportunity to condemn the Muslim League and all its works.

In the evening a large party of the members of two conferences: Railway Board and Irrigation Branch, about 250 people, mostly Indians. Chips a little horrified, not at all his sort of party, no lovely Maharanis or high-born gentlemen. Asaf Ali took occasion to whisper his 'willingness' to be nominated as Ambassador to Washington.

Liaquat came back from Karachi and saw me in the evening and said that he and Jinnah would come to London. I agreed to start on Saturday instead of on Friday.

November 28

As I rather expected, H.M.G. came back with a personal appeal by the P.M. to Nehru. Congress considered it all day and in the evening N. sent a letter recounting all the objections but saying that he would go if the P.M. made a special point of it. Baldev will I expect come too. So we shall have a party in London after all, though I think H.M.G. will be disillusioned if they think they will get any solution or induce the Muslim League to come into the Constituent Assembly. But Cripps may contrive to put Jinnah in the wrong.

The Colvilles arrived just before lunch.

In the afternoon little Menon poured out to me what practically amounted to a brief for Congress. I think George has trusted too much to Menon for advice; he is a good little man and honest but he is really bound in the end to turn to the Congress side; and I think he has for some time past been too much the mouthpiece of Vallabhai Patel.

November 29

I wanted a quiet day to get my things packed and hand over. I didn't get it. I spent a good deal of the morning with Colville explaining the Breakdown Plan to him. He was distressed by it but like everyone else can produce no alternative. I also had to deal with the S. of S. latest reply to my letter on the Breakdown Plan of October 23. It was, as usual, a deplorable bit of woolly and wishful thinking, but did admit at last the necessity for a plan of some kind; and I hurriedly drafted a letter to the C-in-C to tell him to get on with planning.

Nehru and Baldev have decided to come, rather unwillingly and ungraciously. Nehru sent me three letters on other subjects, Liaquat also wrote me two or three, Patel at least one; and what with answering them and an unending stream of green boxes I never had a moment's peace.

After dinner, just as I was going to finish packing and tidying, George came in with the news that Jinnah had now run out! What an impossible set of people they are! I sent Ian Scott off to see Liaquat; and by midnight he returned to say that we had got this far, that Liaquat had agreed to come with us to Karachi tomorrow to see Jinnah and try to persuade him to come. I rather expected that the news of J.'s decision would mean that Nehru and Baldev would run out; but apparently they still mean to come. I got to bed about 1.0 a.m., with the comment of Shakespeare's Bastard, Falconbridge, running in my head: 'Mad world, mad Kings, mad composition.'

November 30

Left Delhi in a York at 9.0 a.m. Omens rather more favourable this morning: Liaquat came, obviously dressed for Europe; Jinnah has had a telegram from Attlee which should satisfy him, though it may well have the opposite effect on Nehru; and Jinnah has made no public announcement about a refusal to go.

Got to Karachi about 12.30 p.m. and found a good guard of Honour of my Regiment. Governor reported all quiet in Sind. After lunch Jinnah came to see me and announced that he and Liaquat would go. His refusal seems really to have been what Her Ex. would call 'a bit of pretty Fanny,' perhaps he thought that as Nehru had had a personal appeal from the P.M., it behoved his dignity to have one too.

I saw the 2nd Bn.[1] on parade in the afternoon, quite a good-looking lot of officers and men, but at least 50% English, a very different type from the short, stocky men we used to have.

December 1

We left Karachi at 7.0 a.m.: Nehru, Jinnah, Baldev and several Secretaries. Jinnah rather late. A crowd, organised by the League, I suppose, was gathered outside to shout 'Pakistan Zindabad'.

[1] Black Watch.

Twelve hours flying to Cairo, with one hour at Basra. These York Machines are terribly noisy.

December 2

Left Cairo 4.30 a.m., Jinnah late again. Arrived Malta about 9.30 a.m. local time, on three engines. My usual experience of these breakdowns confirmed, i.e. R.A.F. (or in this case B.O.A.C.) said repairs would be effected in 40 minutes, and admitted an hour or two later that the plane would not go at all. Another plane was summoned. We left Malta about 1.0 a.m. on December 3 and arrived London 9.0 a.m.

At 11.00 a.m. on 3 December Wavell saw the P.M., the Secretary of State, and A. V. Alexander and handed over to them the following note in which he analysed the situation and suggested various possible courses of action.

Short-term Issue

1. The Cabinet Mission Plan was as good as could have been framed in the circumstances and could have been put through with firmness, but neither the Mission nor H.M.G. adhered to their original intentions with sufficient directness of purpose. In particular the Mission gave Jinnah pledges on May 16, which they have not honoured.

Congress has been reasonably honest in that they never meant to carry out the plan as the Mission intended, unless they were forced to, and said so.

League also have been reasonably honest and would have attempted to carry out Mission's Plan had H.M.G. stuck to it firmly.

2. Present situation is that Congress feel that H.M.G. dare not break with them unless they do something quite outrageous. Their aim is power and to get rid of British influence as soon as possible, after which they think they can deal with both Muslims and Princes; the former by bribery, blackmail, propaganda, and if necessary force; the latter by stirring up their people against them, as well as the other methods above.

They will continue a gradual process of sapping and infiltration against the British, the Muslims, and the Princes by various insidious methods for as long and so far as they are allowed, until they consider themselves strong enough to take more direct measures, such as an open revolt against British rule.

Congress are not really interested in the Constituent Assembly as conceived by the Mission, except as a means of getting rid of the British, and gaining more prestige and power for themselves. Though the sensible and moderate ones realise that they cannot get a united India without Muslim goodwill, or at least acquiescence, the Congress will not seriously negotiate with the Muslim League so long as they feel they can get what they want by pressure on H.M.G.

3. The Muslims are thoroughly alarmed and many of the leaders are getting desperate. They trusted to the British to give them a fair deal and feel that owing to the weakness and duplicity of H.M.G. they are not getting it.

They will not come into the Constituent Assembly unless they get a very definite pledge that it will be worked in the way they were promised and that H.M.G. will not recognise the results otherwise.

4. The Sikhs have been negotiating with both Congress and the League, but as the result of recent events have come down on the side of Congress, because they feel that Congress are the stronger and that H.M.G. dare not oppose them.

5. There are stresses inside Congress, League and the Sikhs.

Congress has a powerful Left Wing led by such as Jai Prakash Narain and Mrs. Asaf Ali, with no constructive programme but capable of stirring up the worst elements of the country and doing a great deal of destruction and mischief. They are already preaching that a revolt against the British will be necessary. The Right Wing, which used the Left Wing to create unrest and discredit the old Government, cannot now control it. Nehru is the unstable link between Right and Left.

Gandhi feels that his life work of driving the British from India is almost accomplished; and he knows that his political weapon of 'non-violence'—it was always really a weapon more than a gospel—is out of date. It was a weapon for the use of the weak against the strong; and now that the strong have become weak, more direct weapons will be used, which he cannot control.

Gandhi will remain in the background, will continue to deplore violence, but will do nothing to check it, since he knows he cannot.

6. The Muslim League leaders raised the cries of Pakistan and Islam in danger originally to enhance their prestige and power and thus their bargaining values as a political party. They have now so inflamed their ignorant and impressionable followers with the idea of Pakistan as a new Prophet's Paradise on earth and as their only means of protection against Hindu domination, that it will be very difficult to satisfy them with anything else. I think Jinnah is honest in saying that he had great difficulty in putting across the Mission Plan with his party, though he was probably wise enough to recognise it as a reasonable compromise worth trying at least for a period.

Hence his anger when he found that the Mission had double-crossed him, as he considered. He probably meant to use his Council meeting at

Bombay as a lever to force H.M.G. to announce their adherence to the promises on which he had accepted the scheme; and found his hand forced by his extremists into entire repudiation.

7. The internal stresses of the Sikhs are of a different kind, a struggle for power between various sections. But the Sikhs as a whole will back the party which they feel to be the strongest party and can give them most. This used to be the British, they now believe it to be the Congress.

8. On the short-term issue, i.e. persuading the Muslim League to enter the Constituent Assembly, I am confident that H.M.G. can only succeed by stating quite openly and firmly what they intended by their plan as to the method of drawing up Group and Provincial Constitutions within the Sections, and that they will not recognise a Constitution arrived at otherwise. I am sure that the League will come in on no other terms; and that no further arguments, formulas, legal sophistries or pleadings will have any effect.

The Congress of course would be furious, but I am not sure that they are ready yet for an open breach with H.M.G. Such a breach is however a possibility; and we can only face it if we have a definite policy and a Breakdown Plan. This leads us to the long-term issue.

PART II

The Long-Term Plan

9. Unless during the present discussions we can get back to acceptance by Congress and League of the original plan of the Mission as intended by the Mission and not as intended by the Congress, H.M.G. must accept the fact that the Mission Plan is dead. They must also accept the fact that we have only a very limited period and a very limited power to substitute fresh arrangements.

10. The following courses are open to H.M.G., on the failure of the Mission Plan:

A. To re-establish their own authority and rule India for a further period. This course they have already ruled out as politically impossible.

B. To attempt to negotiate a fresh settlement. This could only be some sort of Partition, and would at once bring us into conflict with Congress. It would imply our remaining in India to set up the Partition, it might be for some years.

I do not think that this is a practicable policy.

C. To surrender to Congress as the Majority party, to acquiesce in all it does, while using the little influence which will remain to us for a little time to try and secure what fairness we can for the Minorities, the States and the Services.

I do not think this an honourable or a wise policy; it will end British rule in India in discredit and eventually in an ignominious scuttle or dismissal by Congress. There is no statesmanship or generosity in Congress.

D. To announce that, having failed to bring about a settlement, we propose to withdraw from India in our own method and in our own time, and with due regard to our own interests; and that we will regard any attempt to interfere with our programme as an act of war which we will meet with all the resources at our command. But we should of course do our best to secure agreement while we remained, and in any event to hand over to established authorities, e.g. Provincial Governments.

This is in effect the Breakdown Plan; but it is intended for use not merely when widespread disorder has broken out, but for use in the event of a political breakdown and *before* disorder has broken out. The existence of this plan will also enable us to take a firm line with Congress, since we have a reasonable alternative on which to fall back; and may thus enable us to avert a political breakdown.

11. I recognise H.M.G.'s political difficulties; but Parliament must soon be informed of the realities of the Indian situation. I do not consider it is fair to leave Parliament, on whom the ultimate responsibility rests, to believe that the present situation can continue indefinitely; nor to His Majesty's servants in India to allow matters to drift on without a definite policy.

12. I therefore recommend H.M.G. to make the fullest use of the present discussions to try and restore the Mission plan to its original basis *as intended by the Mission*. If it fails in this, it must choose one of the courses outlined in para. 10 above. But it must be quite definite in its choice. Neither I nor the Governors nor any responsible officials can act with any confidence or decision unless we know, quite clearly, what policy H.M.G. proposes to follow.

It will also, I feel, be impossible to carry out the present negotiations with any hope of success, unless H.M.G. have made up their mind whether or not they are prepared to stand up to the Congress.

December 5

Since arrival in London I have hardly had one moment to make an entry. It has been one continued rush of conferences or official engagements. Immediately after a hurried bath and breakfast went to 10, Downing Street, and had conference with P.M., S. of S., Alexander.

I handed over to them the note I had already written. There was a general discussion on it.

The P.M. then went into the difficulty of putting the Breakdown Plan into operation, since legislation in Parliament would be necessary before the announcement. There was some discussion on the Breakdown Plan, which showed that the Ministers were at least beginning to realise the necessity of having such a plan.

Later I went to see the King, who seemed in good form and well posted on the Indian problem. The P.M. was there for the first ten minutes of my audience and I then had about 20 minutes with the King alone. He was very complimentary about my letters to him and said they gave him a better idea of affairs in India than anything else.

Ended with an official dinner to Jinnah and Liaquat at Lancaster House: Alexander, Samuel, R. A. B. Butler, Addison, Listowel, Eden and some Secretaries. I found Addison[1] sensible about the Indian problem and inclined to accept my views on what should be done. R. A. B. Butler said the Opposition had been very forbearing in not pressing Government on the Indian question, but that Winston was anxious to make it a party issue.

On the 4th I had conferences all morning and most of the afternoon. At 9.30 a.m. there was a meeting with the P.M. and the members of the Cabinet Mission at which the P.M. reported the result of his talks with Nehru and Baldev Singh, and the Secretary of State his with Jinnah on the previous day. Both had found them quite obdurate and had made no progress. The line they took fully bore out my note to the P.M. and Ministers of which I gave a copy to Cripps, who had not been present on the previous day. He read it, and, rather to my surprise, said that he agreed with the general analysis in it.

A discussion of nearly two hours with Nehru did not get us much further. Nehru charged the Muslim League with seeking to obtain its ends by violence, and went on to complain that the League was never prepared to cooperate in the Interim Government (which of course means, to him, submission to the Congress point of view). A remark by myself on the constitutional position led to one of his sudden outbursts, he said that he would put everything to the vote in Cabinet and make my position impossible; and complained that the approach to the Muslim League to join the Interim Government had been made over his head.

We then went on to the matter of the forming of Provincial constitutions within Sections. Nehru made another outburst, to the effect that never under any circumstances would Congress admit that Sections could form the Provincial constitutions. There was a long duel between him and

[1] Viscount Addison of Stallingborough (Dr. Addison), Secretary of State for Commonwealth Relations, 1945-7.

Cripps on the legal niceties in the interpretation of the May 16 Statement; it got us nowhere. At one time Nehru made the declaration about Congress that 'we are a revolutionary party'.

The only constructive part of this long discussion came in a suggestion by the Secretary of State towards the end that the question of procedure inside the Sections should be raised at the first meeting of the Constituent Assembly and referred to the Federal Court. Nehru agreed that this might be possible.

When we saw Jinnah and Liaquat, Jinnah was asked whether the League would come into the Constituent Assembly, if, on a reference to the Federal Court, the decision was favourable to the League, or if Congress were brought to accept the Mission's and the League's interpretation of the Statement of May 16. Jinnah would not commit himself, except that he would be prepared to call his Council and explain the position to them. He argued that there was no chance of agreement between the two parties and that, whatever happened, Congress in the Constituent Assembly would succeed in whittling down the Cabinet scheme, that H.M.G. would eventually be faced with a fait accompli, and would not have the courage to act against it.

Liaquat asked pertinently what H.M.G. would do if the decision of the Federal Court were unfavourable and pointed out what an awkward position they would be in. Both Cripps and the Secretary of State were evasive on this point. Liaquat also put very plainly the real point from the Muslim League point of view, that H.M.G. have not had the courage to stand up to Congress over the interpretation of their own scheme, so what guarantee had the League that H.M.G. would reject an unsatisfactory Constitution. The attempts by Cripps to deal with this were rather disingenuous.

It became quite obvious that we were going to make no progress in reconciling Congress and League. All the efforts of P.M., S. of S. and Cripps to find formulas for agreement or to persuade the leaders that their differences could be reconciled were completely fruitless, and they had to admit entire failure. Two lines of a poem of Browning's came into my head as appropriate:

> Now enough of your chicane of prudent pauses,
> Sage provisos, sub-intents and saving clauses.

I remembered too that the poem begins, ominously:

> Let them fight it out, friends: things have gone too far.

Another official dinner at Lancaster House, for Nehru and Baldev, much the same party.

Another long day to-day (5th). We began with a meeting 9.0 to 11.0 a.m. at 10 Downing Street. Cripps reported that he had sat up till 1.0 a.m. with Nehru, a proceeding which I mistrust. N. apparently proposed a reference by C.A. to Federal Court on main points at issue with League. Decision should be reached early January and meeting of Sections should be deferred till then. I emphasised importance of terms of reference if this were done. Question of acceptance by H.M.G. if against their view was then raised. After the discussion had proceeded some while, I had to put in a reminder of the realities of the situation and the need for a Breakdown Plan. Then for the last hour or so we had a really valuable discussion on the Breakdown Plan. P.M. emphasised the Parliamentary difficulties and world opinion, and Alexander was anxious about the effect on the Muslim world if we withdrew from India. The possibility of a reference to U.N.O. was raised. I stuck to my points, and in the end no one had really shaken my Plan and P.M. seemed prepared to accept it in principle. Cripps as usual had some simple sounding modification which I suspect of being a disguised attempt to alter it to his way of thinking. But on the whole I felt I had got H.M.G. down to face realities at last.

I went to lunch at Buckingham Palace.

The next item was a Conference at 10 Downing Street to discuss a Statement to be issued on the results of the visit of Indian leaders, the principal item in which was the matter of reference to the Federal Court of the clauses under dispute between Congress and League. It was a colourless statement, and I was by this time rather too discouraged to take much interest. There was some general discussion on the Breakdown Plan and Alexander came out strongly for taking a firm line.

December 6

The final day of these Conferences and a very heavy one. We began at Downing Street at 10.15 a.m. on the draft statement. Encouraged by the P.M.'s attitude I questioned the whole tone of it as being much too timid and too much on the Congress side. In the discussion which followed we lined up in the old way—Cripps and S. of S. for complete acceptance of the Congress view and fear of offending them; Alexander and self for justice to the Muslims. The P.M. rather came out on our side, and the statement was put back for re-drafting.

At 11.15 the Mission met Jinnah and Liaquat, and we talked for an hour, the last 15 minutes being only because the S. of S. would go on talking when there was obviously nothing more to be said. The main point was whether the League would come into the C.A., if the Congress accepted H.M.G.'s interpretation of the disputed clauses. J. as usual would not commit himself. He then said that there must be a body to prevent the C.A. making other flagrant breaches of the Mission plan, and there was considerable talk on whether the Federal Court was not the most obvious and appropriate body. Jinnah showed some signs of his usual tactics of possibly making some concession at the final moment.

I lunched with Halifax, who cross-examined me closely, speaking obviously to the Conservative brief, on recent happenings in India and the general situation.

Nehru came at 2.30 p.m., and we went over much old ground. He spoke with the usual complete self-righteousness of the Congress, implied that any recognition that H.M.G. had the right to interpret their own Mission's statement would be a concession to the violence and threats of force of the League (!) completely disregarding Bihar of course; and himself used his usual vague threats of outside forces beyond the control of Congress. But he seemed to raise no objection to the Federal Court acting as arbiter to the Constituent Assembly and interpreting the Statement; and was reasonable about the intentions of Congress at the first meeting of the C.A.—places would be left for the League in the Committees, etc. The interview ended with an appeal by Alexander to prevent civil war.

Then back to Downing Street, where we spent two hours mainly on re-drafting the Statement to be made on the outcome of the visit. It was, as usual, a complicated process, and the result a mixture of three drafts— by Cripps, Alexander and myself. It might have been worse.

In this Statement of 6 December H.M.G. said that the Cabinet Mission had throughout held the view that decisions of Sections, in the absence of agreement to the contrary, should be taken by simple majority vote of representatives in the Sections. This had been accepted by the Muslim League but not by the Congress.

H.M.G. had taken legal advice which confirmed that the Statement of 16 May meant what the Cabinet Mission had always said was their intention. This part of the Statement as so interpreted should therefore be accepted by all parties in the Constituent Assembly.

If, in spite of this reaffirmation of the intention of the Cabinet Mission, the Constituent Assembly should desire that this fundamental point be referred for the decision of the Federal Court, such reference should be made at a very early date.

The hope was expressed that if, as was likely, other questions of interpretation of the Statement of 16 May arose, the Muslim League would agree to accept the decision of the Federal Court as Congress had already agreed to do.

At 6.0 p.m. came the final act, when Nehru, Jinnah, Liaquat and Baldev came in. The P.M. spoke quite well, concisely and clearly and on the right lines. (He begins to impress me as likely to be a notable P.M.).

The others listened quietly but Nehru scribbled it all down. At the end Jinnah seemed quite prepared to accept the Statement, so long as it was recognised that the League would be no party to any reference of the disputed clauses to the Federal Court. Nehru spoke at considerable length. He said that this statement was an addition to the Statement of May 16 and created an entirely new situation, which the Congress would have to consider very closely. He elaborated the Congress position on the usual lines. He ended on a more co-operative note, and said that he did not take a dismal view of the present or future. But co-operation must be real and not 'an armistice in preparation for future conflict.' He complained, with obvious reference to myself, that Congress had not had 'a free hand' (i.e. been allowed complete power at once). The P.M. replied briefly to N. and refuted his argument that the new Statement was an addition, it was merely the maintenance of the view H.M.G. had always held. He also denied that there had been any outside pressure. Baldev then said that the Statement would worsen the position of the Sikhs and would be quite unacceptable to them; the reaction would be serious, though he would do his best to persuade them to be reasonable. Liaquat endorsed Jinnah. The P.M. then called on each of the Mission and myself for a few 'kind words'.

So ends this phase of the long-drawn-out drama of negotiations with India. On the whole a better curtain than seemed likely at one time. But the next Act will probably show all the Parties going right back to their original positions.

December 9

I had 40 minutes with the S. of S. about future procedure. He agreed that the whole policy must be settled before I went back, and that it might be difficult to get it all done this week. I impressed on him the necessity to fix a date for the winding up of the Services, which he seemed reluctant to do. On the Breakdown Plan he said that he did not see how the Central Government would work, especially as regards Finance, collection of Revenue, etc. I said that it was obviously impossible to say in detail what would happen, but if we got our plan settled in principle it would be then possible to work out the method and arrangements; the Plan was intended as an alternative to chaos and civil war, a great many things might be untidy and not work well, but if there was civil war they would not work tidily either, in fact they would not work at all.

December 11

I worked in the I.O. in the morning.

A meeting at 10 Downing Street lasted two hours and discussed the Breakdown Plan in rather a desultory way. Those present were P.M., S. of S., Cripps, Alexander, Addison, Ellen Wilkinson, Listowel, Henderson. It was on the whole useful, I think, in educating some of the Cabinet. Addison for example had no idea that the Sikhs lived in the Punjab, and Ellen Wilkinson had no idea that we only had some 500 British officials. Addison's reaction to the Plan was typical, he was shocked at the idea of withdrawing from India but had no idea of any alternative plan.

December 12

Worked at I.O. in the morning. Went to Peers Gallery after lunch to hear debate on India. Heard end of Cripps' speech and Winston's, latter in quite good form but no real fireworks.

Dined with Monty who was in his usual form and talked continuously; about the situations in Burma, Palestine, and Greece; about the Army at home; various other military topics.

December 16

Did a little shopping in the morning of 14th and a little work, on two notes for the Cabinet with reference to the Breakdown Plan; and then motored down to the Rodneys[1] at Penshurst, giving Julian[2] a lift down. I found Leo already there, and sighed, though I am very fond of Leo, because I knew he would want to talk a lot about India, and I wanted to forget about India for the week-end.

On Sunday morning I went for a walk with Leo, he is very slow and now has to pause often for breath—sad when he has been such a wonderful walker and climber. He still talks of going back to the House of Commons, but I am sure that the Conservatives must keep any seats available for younger men. His views on India are not up to date with the pace things have been going, and are still tinged with Imperialism, but he has plenty of common sense about it all.

[1] Capt. the Hon. and Mrs. Simon Rodney. Mrs. Rodney was a sister of Mrs. Amery.
[2] Julian Amery, son of Leopold Amery.

Linlithgow came to lunch with me at the Club and talked India, he was going down to speak in the Lords. He had apparently come to much the same conclusion as I had, i.e. that unless we were prepared to change our policy and hold on to India for a number of years we had to clear out at an early date; his chief point was that we ought to run no risk of India becoming a second Palestine for us on a larger scale.

December 17

Meeting at 10 Downing Street 10.0 a.m. to 12.0 noon. P.M., India Cabinet Committee, and Dalton. We discussed Breakdown Plan and S. of S. Services. We got to no decisions on former but made some progress. They were concerned more with justification to Parliament and with Constitutional procedure than with more practical considerations of the actual withdrawal.

P.L. began by commenting on Lords' Debate, mentioning especially Linlithgow's speech. My plan was then attacked on the basis of handing over power to Provinces without guarantees for Minorities, etc. After about 1½ hours rather desultory discussion, nothing was decided about date or form of announcement, but the plan of withdrawal by two stages beginning with South India seemed to be more or less accepted. Alexander intervened with a pessimistic forecast but had no alternative to propose. Addison kept harping on Parliamentary difficulties.

We then turned to the question of the Services with reference to Patel's note. It was at least decided that H.M.G. would stick to the principle of compensation; and that the U.S. of S., Henderson,[1] should go to India to discuss the question.

December 18

Did a certain amount of work at the I.O. and saw a few friends. No further meeting until tomorrow, I wish they would get on faster.

I gave Alan Moorehead[2] lunch and put him right on a passage in his book on Monty which had aroused controversy; he had represented me as opposing the expedition to Greece and Eden as having deceived me as to the possibilities of Turkey coming into the war. I told him neither was correct.

[1] Arthur Henderson, M.P., Parliamentary Under-Secretary of State for India and Burma, 1945–7.
[2] Alan M. Moorehead, Australian journalist, War Correspondent, and writer.

December 19

Work at I.O. in morning, preparing brief for this evening's meeting.

Saw the S. of S. after lunch, and impressed on him the necessity for me to get a decision and definite policy to-day or tomorrow, and emphasised the amount of time I had been kept hanging about. He spoke of their other cares, especially Burma, about which he is very worried.

I then went over to see Alexander and spoke to him on the lines that I must get a decision, that I realised his dislike of the plan, but that if no one had a better plan to propose I thought they should support it. He was pleasant and sensible as usual, but is really imperialistic in his outlook and hates the whole idea of handing over India.

The meeting at Downing Street which followed, 5.0 to 7.15 p.m., was disastrous. There were the P.M., Cripps, Alexander, S. of S., Ellen Wilkinson, Dalton and Listowel. Two hours desultory discussion resulted in no progress at all, with the P.M. now definitely hostile to the Breakdown Plan. They are all frightened of anything which involves Parliamentary legislation, and therefore tried to make out that the Plan was either unnecessary or misguided. It was all very disheartening, once again they have run out. Dalton's main contribution was an attack on S. of S. and myself for allowing women and children to continue coming to India, but we repulsed this. It was decided to meet again at 9.15 a.m. tomorrow and that I should first see the P.M. at 9.0 a.m.

December 20

I saw the P.M. at 9.0 a.m. and told him that I thought I had been very discourteously treated. It was a fortnight since the discussions with the Indian leaders, and in that time there had been only three conferences held. To enable Nehru to get back for the Constituent Assembly, three or four meetings a day had been held for three days, but the Viceroy was kept hanging about without any consideration for his convenience. P.M. made a rather lame excuse. I then said I could not go back without some definite policy. P.M. said he thought he could accept my Breakdown Plan in principle, but dilated on the difficulties of handing over the Centre, especially the I.A.

At 9.30 a.m. the India Committee assembled, less Cripps who had gone off to meet his wife. P.M. stated that he thought he could accept my plan in principle if it was put in a different form, not requiring Parliamentary legislation, but stressed the difficulties about the Centre and the I.A. Things seemed to be going reasonably well, when the S. of S. raised the point that legislation would be required about the Services. This led to an hour's indeterminate talk at which all the objections against the Plan were raised again and always came back to the rock of Parliamentary legislation, the idea of which always seems to send them into a panic. At 10.45 a.m. the P.M. left to make a Statement on Burma in the House, with nothing whatever settled. We then had a good deal of talk about another meeting. Everyone seemed to be breaking away for Xmas; but I said quite firmly that I must see the P.M. again anyway and that we must get something decided. It was eventually agreed that we should try to get another meeting for this afternoon with the Lord Chancellor to give an opinion on legal questions.

At 3.30 p.m. we had another two hours with the Cabinet Committee, plus Lord Chancellor[1] and Dalton. Lord Chancellor gave an emphatic view that nothing could be done without legislation; but later agreed that it would be possible to proceed by a resolution, with legislation later; and that even if the House of Lords rejected the Resolution we could still proceed if the Commons passed it. This seemed to satisfy everybody's difficulties; and we ended with a draft Resolution produced by Cripps, which I was assured would give me what I wanted, and would apparently satisfy Parliament. It was agreed to submit this to the Cabinet after Xmas. I asked the P.M. whether he wished me to remain for this. He said he would rather I returned to India. I then asked for a reply to a letter I wrote him after the first meeting this morning. He said the decision of the meeting just held covered it, but I pressed for a reply which he promised. I then said good-bye, he was not at all gracious, I am not sure that he has it in him to be so, or he doesn't like me, probably the latter.

I wonder whether I am wise to go back. I think I have got most of what I wanted, if they do not reverse their decisions when I am gone. I do not trust Cripps. But there is a lot to do at the other end, and I want to get back to Q. and the family.

I was impressed by the Lord Chancellor, he seemed knowledgeable, sensible and decided. The India Committee as a whole do not greatly impress me. S. of S. carries no weight, Henderson is futile, so is Listowel, I think, Ellen Wilkinson does not really understand it all, and Alexander does not like it. Cripps is of course the directing brain, and I repeat that I do not trust Cripps.

The P.M.'s ungracious manner is explained by the fact that two days earlier he had asked Lord Mountbatten to take over as Viceroy. He must, therefore, have felt some embarrassment in talking to Wavell and been guiltily conscious

[1] Viscount Jowett.

of a lack of candour towards him. The letter to which Wavell asked for a reply was as follows:

My dear Prime Minister,

If I am to return to India on Sunday to undertake the very serious responsibilities there, with no settled policy after nearly three weeks at home, I feel I should have your personal assurance on certain points, i.e.:

(a) That H.M.G. does recognise that we must make arrangements with a view to the transfer of power in India not later than March 31, 1948.

(b) That you accept in principle my general plan of withdrawal by stages, subject to further examination in the next few weeks, here and in India.

(c) That any legislation found necessary will be placed before Parliament at the beginning of next Session, and that I should be summoned home, if necessary, to discuss the final plan to be submitted.

(d) That you agree to the need for making a very early announcement about the winding up of the Secretary of State's Services.

I propose to leave my Private Secretary at home for the present to represent my point of view in the discussions here.

Yours sincerely,
Wavell

December 24

Got back to Delhi yesterday evening in time for dinner after a very good journey in the P.M.'s plane.

On Saturday morning 21st, I cleared up at the office, then lunched with A. V. Alexander at the R.A.C. and went with him to see Chelsea play football, he is a director. He is an enthusiastic football fan, shouting 'foul,' 'play the game,' 'don't mess about,' etc. as loudly as any one.

I had a message that Bevin would like to see me at Alexander's Flat at the Admiralty. I had about 1½ hours there. Bevin like everyone else hates the idea of our leaving India, but like everyone else has no alternative to suggest. He was pessimistic about our position generally, said that everyone was kicking us around, in Palestine, Egypt, Sudan, India and that our international prestige was very low. He said that the U.S.A. were very worried about India. I pointed out how they had encouraged Congress and pilloried us as imperialists, and could hardly expect us to face another Palestine in India because it suited their commercial interests that we should remain. I told Bevin the realities of the Indian situation, or rather Alexander did and I confirmed. He seemed to accept the picture. Both he and Alexander are in reality imperialists and dislike any idea of leaving India. I then finished packing and got to bed about 12.45 a.m.

D d

I had decided to leave George Abell behind to watch my interests with the Cabinet.

I had a long talk to Colville this morning about the Plan. Like everyone else he hates the idea of our leaving India, but again like everyone else can see no alternative. He suggested that the date should be put back to Jan. 1, 1949, or later, if the Indian parties wanted it, and says that he thinks there is a growing sense of responsibility in Congress. Colville is sensible and pleasant, and has obviously got on well with the Indians.

Spent rest of day clearing up and sorting out and picking up the general thread, as usual after an absence.

December 27

After a quiet Boxing Day I got into political harness again with two interviews with Ministers and one with the C.G.S.

The C.G.S. produced an appreciation of the Breakdown Plan from the point of view of military administration. It was quite useless since it advocated withdrawing from the north first and took no account of political situation. Claude Auchinleck is not really very helpful over this sort of planning, and I feel I shall have to do most of it myself.

Bhabha gave me the impression of being fed up with politics. His business friends in Bombay had obviously given him a roasting; and he talked of their feeling of insecurity and the lack of stability in the Government. He asked me whether I thought the present Government efficient. I said that six months ago I could have told him pretty well how all Departments of Government were working, since I saw Secretaries as well as Ministers; but that now, since I saw only Ministers and they either did not know what was going on in their Departments, or did not confide in me, I could not say so readily. But that since Ministers spent most of their time on politics rather than administration and let political considerations override those of administrative efficiency, I should be much surprised if administration had not much deteriorated. He said that he agreed. He is certainly out of place and not big enough for his job, and I think he would like to get back to business.

Chundrigar talked about cotton, business interests had obviously got hold of him, and he was proposing the export of more cotton and the raising of prices. He then went on to propose Nazimuddin as High Commissioner in London,—this is obviously a League riposte to the appointment of Asaf Ali to Washington. He also proposed to reverse a decision of Nehru that the Indian delegation to the International Trade Conference should not attend the preliminary meeting of the British Empire delegates.

He said that Jinnah was waiting for the decision of the Congress A.I.C.C. on January 5 before deciding whether to call his Council and recommend attendance at the Constituent Assembly.

December 30

My only official visitor was Nishtar, who had recently returned from the N.W.F.P. He tried to make out that the recent raid of tribesmen on the Hazara frontier should be excused and not punished, or only very lightly, on the grounds apparently that the victims were only Hindus, that the news of the Bihar massacres had excited the tribes and that 'boys will be boys'. I merely said that the Tribes must be kept in order and that I approved the measures being taken.

Francis Wylie arrived in the evening, and I put to him an outline of the Breakdown Plan and the recent discussions in London. He obviously did not like it, and said that the U.P. would not really run without our help, but could see no good alternative. He said he would think it over and give me his views tomorrow.

December 31, 1946

Wylie did not produce any new ideas on the Breakdown Plan this morning. He agreed that we must have a plan, that we must set a limit to our remaining in India, and that March 31st, 1948 was, if anything, rather beyond the date at which our control could have any effect, though he thought that our influence might still be valuable. His chief concern was with the technique of the announcement; would it not be possible to inform Nehru and Jinnah well in advance, at least 48 hours, of any announcement in Parliament and try to persuade them to agree to coalition governments in all Provinces and to some common line of action. I said that I realised the advantage of cushioning the shock of a sudden announcement in Parliament by preliminary warning; the trouble was that neither Nehru nor Jinnah was capable of committing his Party to anything, even if his own mind were made up, without consulting his colleagues; and that inevitably meant loss of secrecy, and it would be fatal if Parliament heard the news from India before they had been consulted. He agreed. He was pessimistic about the future of India, said that the Congress leaders were quite incapable of running the country, and knew that they were not really equal to the job; and that there was a complete lack of harmony and discipline in the Congress High Command, Patel with Birla's backing was trying to break Nehru, and that they were all frightened of the left wing.

Baldev Singh did not turn up, he had apparently simply forgotten his appointment, an increasingly bad habit with my present Ministers.

So ends 1946, the most gruelling year I have ever had, and I think in some ways the most unhappy.

I have been at full strain pretty well all the year; preparation for the Cabinet Mission; the shock of Simon's death; the three months of the Mission; the threat of famine in Southern India and the struggle to avert it; the efforts to bring the parties together after the Mission, and the discouraging experience of the complete lack of any statesmanship, toleration or generosity amongst the Indian leaders; the riots and massacres in Calcutta, Bombay, East Bengal, Bihar, U.P.; the visit home and the task of trying to put my views across to a reluctant and not very realistic lot of Ministers. They have left their mark and I feel depressed.

The Cabinet Mission was really our last chance to bring about a settlement in India, a temporary one which would have enabled us to leave India with peace and dignity. I have commented on its proceedings in a previous portion of this journal. I think it might have succeeded, had its attitude been less apologetic, and had Cripps and P-L. not been so completely in the Congress camp and had remained more neutral.

The result has been that I have had to deal for the rest of the year with an arrogant Congress, convinced that it had H.M.G. in its pocket; a suspicious and resentful Muslim League, feeling that it had been betrayed; and resentful Princes, who thought that H.M.G. should keep all their old privileges and way of life without change. It has not been easy.

Meanwhile the administration has declined, and the machine in the Centre is hardly working at all now, my ministers are too busy with politics. And while the British are still legally and morally responsible for what happens in India, we have lost nearly all power to control events; we are simply running on the momentum of our previous prestige. The loyalty of the Police is doubtful in some of the Provinces, they are tinged with communalism; fortunately the Indian Army seems unaffected so far, but it can hardly remain so indefinitely, if communal tension continues.

The British I.C.S. is disheartened and looking over its shoulder. The delay in settling terms of compensation, date for winding up and future prospects has had an adverse effect. I wonder whether I could have done more to prevent this, if I had been more sympathetic. I have been inclined to feel that the I.C.S. has been in some ways rather too highly privileged.

I have now committed myself, and very nearly committed H.M.G. to a plan of announcing a definite date of termination of our control of India and of withdrawing on a definite plan. I think I am right, and that this is the only way to avoid a worse disaster. But I have not that convinced certainty of my wisdom that Monty has for instance and have not really got my heart in it. It has been my fate for the last 5 or 6 years to have to conduct withdrawals and to mitigate defeats, and I have had no real opportunity of a success. This is inevitably depressing. Continual hard work, and almost continual failure. No rest, no success.

Personally too I have had rather an unhappy year. While I have not had a day's real illness, I have never really been 100% fit. The main trouble has been that I have been sleeping badly, waking up too early, to be assailed by doubts, fears and problems, official and private.

It is a great strain on a small man to do a job which is too big for him, if he feels it too big. Health and vitality suffer.

I am afraid that 1947 may be even more difficult, and more of a strain.

15

DISMISSAL

January 1

My first interview of the year, with Nehru, was not very satisfactory. Congress are obviously very annoyed at H.M.G. standing up to them at last in the statement of December 6. They had obviously been led to believe by their contacts with Cripps and P.L. that they never would do so. The pity is that H.M.G. did not do so long ago, as I repeatedly urged them to. Nehru was polite, but his chagrin was obvious.

At one point he worked himself up into a denunciation of H.M.G. and said that he would sooner India was divided into a hundred parts than that they should in any way abandon their principles and give in to the Muslim League. The whole attitude of the Muslim League, he said, was based on their knowledge that H.M.G. would support them to the end. I merely said that the Muslim League took entirely the opposite view and thought that H.M.G. had given unqualified support to Congress.

In the evening came a telegram from George Abell to report that the Cabinet had failed to come to a decision yesterday and had decided to hold another meeting in a week's time; but that the reception of the proposals was less unfavourable than expected.

Ian says his Committee on the Breakdown Plan met for 7 hours today, I wonder what they have produced.

January 2

I had an hour with Rajendra Prasad. After disposing of the business of his Food Department—he agreed that India was free for the moment of the famine threat, though he wanted Turkish wheat urgently—we discussed at some length the political situation, with special reference to H.M.G.'s statement of December 6, the meeting of the A.I.C.C. on January 5, and the position of Assam. I tried to convince him that it was manifestly to the interest of Congress to accept H.M.G.'s statement and try to get the Muslim League in, and that Assam's fears were groundless. Rajendra Prasad is sensible and moderate, and would, I think, be all for a reasonable settlement, but he has not very much force of character.

January 3

Un jour très mouvementé (is that reasonable French?). Cabinet meeting was very communal and inclined to be stormy. It lasted 10.30 a.m.–1 p.m. We discussed Press Ordinance, which was directed mainly against Dawn, and seemed unnecessarily drastic. An ordinance to possess ourselves of some jute required to pay for grain from the Argentine, had a comparatively easy passage. But the matter of the Salt tax, the repeal of which Liaquat as Finance Member wished to defer till the whole Budget was considered, led to a sudden outburst by Nehru against Liaquat and the whole Finance Department. I prevented it developing too far, and some of N.'s colleagues tried to spread oil on the troubled waters; but it is not a good augury for future relations, and I wonder how much longer the present Cabinet will hold together.

January 4

Very busy day for a Saturday. I began with a Cabinet meeting—9–10.30 a.m.—to try and finish yesterday's business. We dealt with the extension of the right of premature retirement to the S. of S. Services at the Centre; and with a threatened strike in the Government Presses. I think we reached reasonable decisions in the end, but the discussions in Cabinet tend to proceed more and more on communal lines.

After Cabinet I had a talk with Matthai, about the most level-headed of all my Ministers. He did not see much daylight ahead, agreed that the Congress was very short-sighted in its policy, but said that the chief trouble was personal antagonisms—Nehru versus Liaquat, Patel versus Nehru, Gandhi versus Jinnah. He had no good solution for the present situation, said that Great Britain and India were very closely tied by commercial interest, but that a stable and united India was necessary for this interest to operate, and that he did not see how this could be evolved.

Britter, the Times Correspondent, was my next visitor, a sensible and competent observer. He took a gloomy view of the political situation, thought that the Congress completely lacked any spirit of compromise or generosity, and that their internal dissensions were acute. He said that there was still mistrust of our intentions, that the Services were completely disgruntled and only anxious to go, and that to fix a definite date for our departure was probably the best thing we could do.

I then saw the Khan of Kalat, a stout middle-aged old-fashioned gentleman, who impressed on me his dislike of change, his loyalty to the British, and that Baluchistan had no real connection with India.

Arthur Henderson and his party, to negotiate a settlement of compensation for the I.C.S., arrived before lunch, and I had a talk with him in the evening. I doubt whether he will get much change out of Patel.

January 6

I saw C-in-C this morning. Chief subjects of discussion were the proposal put forward that I.N.A. convicts should be released, this we agreed must be resisted; the release of a large number of junior British officers from the I.A. and their replacement by Indian officers, which seems inevitable but will obviously weaken the I.A. and tend to make it more susceptible to communal influence; the visit of Aung San; and Defence Member's proposal to bring before the Cabinet a recommendation that all British troops should be withdrawn as soon as shipping could be made available, C-in-C had not been consulted on this.

A.I.C.C. seem to have passed a resolution accepting H.M.G.'s statement of December 6, but as usual with many reservations; and I rather doubt whether it will be enough to bring in the Muslim League.

> The A.I.C.C. while agreeing 'to advise action in accordance with the interpretation of the British Government in regard to the procedure to be followed in the Sections', could not refrain from adding the following reservations:
>
> 'It must be clearly understood, however, that this must not involve any compulsion of a province and that the rights of the Sikhs in the Punjab should not be jeopardized.
>
> 'In the event of any attempt at such compulsion, a province or part of a province has the right to take such action as may be deemed necessary in order to give effect to the wishes of the people concerned.'

January 7

I busied myself with consideration of the Breakdown Plan most of the forenoon, and then had $1\frac{1}{4}$ hours with Liaquat Ali Khan. We had a good deal of discussion about his estimate of the Budget deficit and other financial matters. I then spoke to him about the Congress Resolution, accepting H.M.G.'s statement of December 6th and said I very much hoped the Muslim League would now call their Council and come into the Constituent Assembly. He said that it was not a true acceptance by Congress and that they did not really mean to be honest about it; and that we ought to restore our authority and rule India for a further period of years, until the parties agreed. I pointed out that we could not break our pledges to give India self-government at an early date. He said that it would be very wrong to leave India to chaos in this way; but that if we were going to do it we should 'leave fair chaos for both parties', and not remain to establish the Hindus in power.

In the afternoon I saw Rajagopalachari. As usual, he knew nothing very much about the work of his Education Department, but was interesting about affairs in general. He admitted that it might have been better had the Congress acceptance of the Statement of December 6 been quite unequivocal, but stressed their difficulties with their followers, and said that it was only Nehru's personal efforts which had secured acceptance at all. We discussed Assam's attitude, which he agreed was unnecessarily apprehensive and unrealistic. Finally he mentioned Burma and said rather surprisingly that Burma's political leaders suggested gang leaders to him rather than statesmen—this was in reference to Aung San's visit—and that it was a pity that Burma had ever been separated from India.

Later I saw C-in-C about two proposals by Defence Member—one about withdrawal of British troops, the other about release of I.N.A. convicts. Congress are apparently alarmed at Sarat Chandra Bose's assuming leadership of the I.N.A. under the mantle of his deceased brother, and think they can appease him by release of the I.N.A. convicts (sentenced for murder or cruelty) and restoration of their pay to all of them. The next step would be of course to demand their reinstatement in the Army. I said I should resist any demand for concession to I.N.A.

January 8

Cabinet this morning lasted $2\frac{1}{2}$ hours. It was quite amicable and sensible on the whole. The first item was the Report on the R.I.N. Mutiny, which was accepted with some discussion. The next item on the Coal Report went through peacefully, though Nehru raised the matter of thorium and uranium in Travancore, which might, I thought, have provoked some awkwardness. Proposals for the protection of coated abrasives, whatever they are, and hurricane lanterns, a peculiarly Indian product, presented no difficulty. Liaquat then embarked on a statement in reply to some remarks by Nehru at a previous Cabinet meeting. I was apprehensive that this might provoke a communal riot, but all went well. Liaquat's statement was moderate and sensible; and he and Nehru almost, but not quite, purred at one another.

After lunch I had 45 minutes with Suhrwardy, the Bengal Premier whom I dislike. He was sulky, shifty and unattractive as usual. After a little talk on the Damodar Valley project, which was the ostensible reason for his visit to Delhi, he embarked on his normal hymn of hate against the Hindus, with reference to Bihar; Calcutta and East Bengal had of course been gentlemanly differences of opinion, in his view, compared with the Hindu retaliation in Bihar. He complained that we were strengthening the hands of the Hindus against the Muslims; and drew a most gloomy picture of Bengal after our departure, with Darjeeling annexed by Nepal or Sikkim etc. I gave him my usual line, that Hindus and Muslims had got to live together in India on some terms and that the sooner they got together to settle them, the better, etc. S. ended by admitting that H.M.G.'s statement of December 6 was fair, and that he would recommend to Jinnah that the League should enter the C.A. Jinnah was calling his Working Committee at Karachi for January 19.

George Abell telegraphed to say that the Cabinet at home has gone back completely and refuses to have anything to do with the Breakdown Plan, so he is returning at once. I thought they well might run out after I had left, they seem quite unable to face an awkward decision.

January 9

A very busy and rather tiresome day. It began with Baldev Singh coming at 10.30 a.m. about the I.N.A. He said that Sarat Chandra Bose was holding an I.N.A. meeting in Calcutta on Jan. 23; and that a Resolution would be moved in the Assembly early in February demanding the release of all I.N.A. prisoners under sentence—there are about 10 or a dozen, all convicted of murder or cruelty—; the payment of I.N.A. men of their pay for the time that they were fighting us; and that this was certain to be followed by a demand for their reinstatement in the Army. I naturally reacted very strongly and told him that such action would make it impossible for British officers to continue to serve and would destroy the I.A. He promised to put this to the political leaders, but did not seem very hopeful that they would agree, as they seemed anxious to appease the I.N.A. I then wrote to C-in-C, to see whether he was prepared to stand firm, and arranged to discuss it with him this evening.

After lunch I saw V. P. Menon, who has become rather the mouthpiece of Vallabhai Patel, I fancy. He said he thought the League ought to go into C.A., but was not hopeful of an agreed Constitution being evolved. He said that Congress leaders were losing popularity and that there were serious internal troubles in Congress and great fear of the Left Wing; and that the danger of labour difficulties was acute. Patel is very annoyed at Nehru for making the appointment of Asaf Ali without consulting his colleagues. Menon also said that Gandhi had proposed a most mischievous resolution about H.M.G.'s statement of December 6, but that Patel had opposed him strongly and was unpopular with G. at present.

Menon was very perturbed at the decline of the Administration—Ministers too busy with politics to pay much attention to their Departments; he outlined the chief dangers as Food distribution breaking down, lack of Textiles, Labour troubles, and slowness of the Development plan. I think he was echoing Patel. Finally, he described an interview with Aung San, which had shown that young tough's complete ignorance of financial, constitutional and economic questions.

At 6.30 p.m. I saw C-in-C about the I.N.A. problem. He told me that, after consultation with his senior officers, he was determined to stand, up to the point of resignation, on the first issue, the release of the prisoners. We shall have a first-class row with Congress, I expect, but I think we shall get away with it.

January 10

My sister Molly[1] arrived this morning, and General Tuker and George Abell. The latter returned very disappointed with the P.M. and Members of H.M.G. and the way they had gone back on their promises. He said that he was really horrified at their lack of realism and of honesty. I read later on some papers he brought back, he had kept his end, or rather my end, up very well but apparently to no purpose. I have not had one word from the S. of S. about the result of the Cabinet meetings on India; but he has telegraphed that an important letter from the P.M. is on its way to me. I must wait for that.

I saw Chundrigar in the afternoon. He said Jinnah was a sick man; and the meeting of the Working Committee not till January 29.

Sunday, 12 January

Tuker came in to see me before his departure from Calcutta. I like him, he has many more interests than soldiering, in fact his defect as a soldier is probably the same as mine, that soldiering rather bores him and books and history and art interest him more. We discussed the general situation, he eulogized the I.C.S. and their work, spoke of the break-up of the Congress, of the decline of Hinduism, and of the dangers in front of India. Nehru, Rajagopalachari and Baldev Singh came to lunch.

[1] Miss L. M. Wavell.

The luncheon party went off quite well. Nehru was friendly and talked freely, he is sometimes apt to be reserved and on the offensive-defensive, as at Buckingham Palace.[1] The gardens had been opened to the public and we walked in them afterwards, I think N. may have rather suspected it had been specially arranged to impress him, but it was in fact part of our normal winter programme.

I had a letter from the P.M., telling me that the Cabinet had rejected my plans. The letter was cold, ungracious and indefinite, the letter of a small man. It proposed that I should go home in the near future for further discussions, but I cannot see any value in doing so and shall reply to that effect. It is possible that the idea is to get me home and force my resignation.

January 13

I agreed with the C-in-C to produce a directive on which a combined civil and military staff would prepare a plan for a breakdown.

Nehru was due for an interview but did not turn up, an increasingly common habit on the part of my Ministers.

January 14

A long day in the office, with a number of interviews. I began with Jagjivan Ram, the Labour member. He talked of labour troubles, strikes and threatened strikes, at Karachi, Coimbatore, Cawnpore and elsewhere, and ascribed them largely to Communist agitation.

Nehru was next, and apologised for his absence yesterday, and was quite friendly. We talked of foreign affairs; of Travancore minerals, and other matters.

Baldev had not much to say, I told him that H.M.G. would not consent to the removal of British troops till a new constitution had been made, so that it was no use bringing his proposal to do so before Cabinet, as I should only have to overrule my colleagues if they passed it. He said that he and the Congress members quite understood this, but he implied that they wanted to clear themselves with their followers.

I worked on a planning directive for the Breakdown Plan, and drafted an answer to the P.M., which I thought was mild but which George apparently considers too drastic.

---

[1] Wavell had gathered that Nehru gave this impression when he was invited to Buckingham Palace during his visit to U.K. in December.

Wednesday 15th January

At his interview Patel began by complaining of H.M.G.'s decision of December 6 as unfair to Congress, I said that it was not unfair at all, it was merely that H.M.G. were saying what they meant, and that the only criticism could be that they ought to have done it months before. He agreed with this last part. He then spoke at some length (a propos of my question whether Jai Prakash Narain was still a member of the Congress Working Committee) about the danger of the Communists. I got the impression he would like to declare the Party illegal, he said that many young but misguided men of family and education were behind the movement.

The C-in-C agreed to the terms and to the composition of the Planning Committee on Withdrawal.

He told me that he had lunched with Nehru and Baldev and had discussed the I.N.A. question. He said that N. was quite friendly but that neither convinced the other.

Maulana Azad was moderate and sensible, and will I hope be a good influence in the Cabinet.[1] We discussed the general political situation. I said that I hoped that Nehru's resolution on a Republic would not be pressed in the C.A. on January 20, and Azad said that it might perhaps be postponed but he could give no guarantee. He deplored the lack of social contact between the political leaders, and said that communal feeling was running so high that Muslim League would not meet Congress.

Cabinet meeting lasted two hours 6–8 p.m. The Report on Planning was discussed in quite a reasonable spirit.

January 19

Got back this evening from a short shooting trip to the Dehra Dun jungles. This was originally to have been in December, but had been postponed on account of my visit to U.K. I began it inauspiciously by slipping in the aircraft when I was walking to the exit at Saharanpur—the floor is steel uncovered by a mat and I forgot I had nails in my shoes—and landing a terrific crack on my back. I thought I should be unable to do much, I felt so shaken and bruised, but I went on into the jungle and found I was able to move better than I had expected. Jim Corbett, the man who wrote Maneaters of Kumaon,[2] was running the shoot, with Yakub Khan[3] and

[1] He had taken the place of Asaf Ali.
[2] Jim Corbett, *Man-Eaters of Kumaon*, 1946.
[3] Captain Sahibzada Mohd. Yakub Khan, Adjutant to the Bodyguard. He later became a Lieutenant-General in the Pakistan Army, and Pakistan Ambassador in Paris.

some of the Bodyguard. His talk on tigers and jungle life is of extraordinary interest, and I wish I could have had more of it. He has rather pessimistic views on the future of tigers; he puts the present tiger population of India at 3000–4000 (I was rather surprised at the smallness of this estimate) and thinks that in many parts of India tigers will become almost extinct in the next 10 or 15 years; his chief reason is that 'Indian politicians are no sportsmen and tigers have no votes, while the right to a gun licence will go with a vote.'

January 20

Most of my day was taken up over an impending crisis about the I.N.A. which has been on the horizon for some time. Baldev Singh put up a summary for Cabinet recommending release of all I.N.A. men, convicted for brutality or murder, and restoration of pay for the period during which they were serving our enemies. He wanted it taken in Cabinet at once, in order that these concessions might be announced before January 23, when Sarat Chandra Bose is holding a meeting at Calcutta to assume the mantle of his brother as leader of the I.N.A.

I saw C-in-C at 10.30 a.m. and found he was still firm on the matter, he said he was determined to resign sooner than acquiesce in the proposals about the I.N.A.

So I wrote a note on Baldev's summary for Cabinet and told George to draft a telegram to S. of S. to warn him of the approaching crisis. I believe myself that if we all stand firm—H.M.G., C-in-C, myself—my Cabinet will not force the issue and they may even be encouraged to stand up to the Left Wing—J. P. Narain and Bose.

Ghazanfar Ali was my visitor in the afternoon. He is the worst representative of the League in the Cabinet (except Mandal)—intensely communal and rather stupid. He seemed completely hazy about Pakistan and its implications, and admitted that he did not understand the economy of it. I find him rather a trial, inside and outside the Cabinet.

Arthur Henderson dined, he is off tomorrow, having made no progress at all in his Mission, but having perhaps learnt a little about India.

January 21

Ian Scott had some political gossip out riding this morning. Menon, who is now very much in Patel's pocket, claims to have seen a letter from Gandhi to Patel, abusing him for supporting acceptance of H.M.G.'s statement of December 6, which G. had wished to reject. I have always regarded G. as our most inveterate, malignant and rather hypocritical enemy. Ian also had a story of an interview between Sultan Ahmed and Nehru, in which S.A. had intimated that the passing of N.'s Republic Resolution in the C.A. might make it difficult for the Princes to negotiate. According to the story, N. had blown up into one of his outbursts and said he did not care a damn for the Princes, to which S.A. had replied that the Princes did not care a damn for him.

I spent some of the morning over a telegram to the S. of S. to warn him of the I.N.A. crisis.

Azad came after lunch. He had one or two small matters on his Department; then spoke of the relations between the communities and advocated improvement in social contacts between the Members of the Cabinet. He is in favour of Coalition Governments in all Provinces, but says that it is no use to approach the subject unless the atmosphere at the Centre improves. I asked him about Nehru's Republic Resolution and he thinks it will be passed, though he sees the danger of doing so, and has advised against it, I gather.

Earlier Arthur Henderson had come to say goodbye. He had breakfasted with Nehru, who was very worried, he said, over the possibility of serious labour troubles and apprehended a railway and coal strike. N. made the usual complaint of non-cooperation on the part of the League members of the Cabinet. Henderson said he would recommend to Cabinet that the sooner the S. of S. Services were wound up the better.

Three-hour meeting of Cabinet 4–7 p.m. The matter of a Press Ordinance for the Commissioners Provinces, i.e., Delhi for all practical purposes, took nearly $1\frac{1}{2}$ hours, though it had been twice before Cabinet already. The Muslim League is convinced that it is simply a device of Patel's to muzzle Dawn, and they may have some reason for apprehension. I think, however, that the stand they have made may protect them to some extent.

The rest of the proceedings were less controversial, though the communal element obtruded itself. The League members do not show up well in Cabinet discussions, except Liaquat, who always talks good sense. Chundrigar is slow and dull, Nishtar loquacious and not very clever, Ghazanfar always communal and pugnacious. Congress can always make dialectical rings round them and appear reasonable and moderate.

January 22

I had a talk with Benthall, who has been co-opted into the Breakdown Plan Committee to represent the European Community. I put the position before him frankly and plainly, he was obviously rather shaken at the idea that we might withdraw so soon, but had no alternative plan.

After lunch I had three Sikhs—Harnam Singh, Kartar Singh and Ujjal Singh—who talked for 45 minutes about their requirements for safeguards in the Constitution without making it very clear to me what they did want, and I am not sure that they were really clear themselves. But they were friendly and only wanted sympathetic noises from me really, I think.

Cabinet, 6–7.15 p.m., went quite well. The difficult item was the demand for withdrawal of British troops but they obviously never really expected it to be accepted, and seemed quite satisfied. Ghazanfar's item of the export of Rhesus monkeys to South Africa proved quite a good comic interlude.

Thursday, 23rd January

Interview with Khizar who, if his heart was really in it, would be the best leader of the Muslims in India, but he does not like politics and would prefer to be out of it all.

Mandal who succeeded him is the poorest Member I have ever had in the Government, and I find great difficulty in understanding his English.

I had a telegram from S. of S. to say that H.M.G. would support me over the I.N.A. question, which was quite a pleasant surprise. I also had a telegram suggesting that I should go home again for discussions, which seems quite unnecessary.

I discussed with C-in-C at 6 p.m. the line to take at the conference which has been arranged tomorrow with Nehru, Liaquat and Baldev on the I.N.A. question.

January 24

A busy but interesting morning. At 10 a.m. I had a discussion of the I.N.A. business with Nehru, Liaquat, Baldev and C-in-C. On the whole it went better than I had expected. The discussion was conducted in quite a friendly spirit and was argued without heat of any kind, but what the eventual outcome will be it is hard to say.

January 27

For once in a way I had a comparatively peaceful Sunday yesterday, though the action taken in the Punjab against Muslim Guards seems to have raised a storm.

Lord Wavell, London, 1946

Liaquat Ali Khan and Mr. Jinnah in London, December 1946

On *24 January the Punjab Government, alarmed at the collection of arms by quasi-military organizations, operating under the direction of political parties, passed an order declaring the Muslim National Guards and the Rashtriya Swayam Sewak Sangh—a militant Hindu organization—unlawful bodies. The Muslim League leaders in the Punjab seized the opportunity to stir up agitation. There were demonstrations by Muslim mobs and after a few days the Punjab Government rescinded its order. This did not, however, prove to be the end of the matter.*

This morning I had an hour with the C-in-C on the reports of the Joint Planning Committee on our withdrawal from India, and various smaller matters. The Committee has recommended a phased withdrawal of authority instead of the phased geographical withdrawal which I originally recommended to H.M.G., i.e. a withdrawal first of the S. of S. Services, or rather their transfer to the Central and Provincial Governments, and then at a later date of British troops, thus leaving the Governor-General and Governors in position with no means of enforcing their orders. I don't much like it, nor does C-in-C.

Then came Liaquat with whom I had a long talk. Liaquat is always sensible and well-balanced but is firmly determined that cooperation with Congress is not possible.

Nishtar did not turn up for his interview in the afternoon.

Cabinet meeting in the evening (6–7.30 p.m.) was quite a surprise. I expected a long contentious sitting and much communalism, as there was plenty of material for display of feeling. But all the items went off in a peaceful and almost friendly atmosphere. Ghazanfar Ali was absent, and I suppose the League must have passed the word round to hold their fire.

January 29

Comparatively quiet morning. Dickie Mountbatten telegraphed that Archie John had been given a belated Military Cross, Mike Calvert told me some months ago that the original recommendation had gone astray and that he was putting it in again but I did not think there was much chance of it at this late stage.

Thursday, 30th January

Day began with Hutchings who is just off to London on food matters. We are all right for rice for the moment but very short of wheat. On the general situation, H. said he thought there was a section of Congress, and Gandhi himself, who did not really want a peaceful hand over but to claim that they had ejected the British by force; perhaps there is something in this.

January 31

C-in-C and three Army Commanders—Lockhart, Tuker and Messervy—
came to lunch and I gave them a sketch of the political situation.

February 1

The Muslim League Resolution seems to shut the door completely on
their participation in the Constituent Assembly and creates a difficult and
perhaps an ugly situation. I decided to send for Nehru and discuss it with
him this evening.

> *By a Resolution passed on 31 January the Working Committee of the*
> *Muslim League decided not to call the Council of the League to reconsider its*
> *withdrawal of its acceptance of the Cabinet Mission Plan. It declared that the*
> *A.I.C.C. by its reservations had conferred a right of veto within a Section 'on*
> *a Province and—what is more absurd—on a part of a Province, as well as on*
> *the Sikhs in the Punjab', and that these reservations completely nullified the*
> *'so-called "acceptance" by the Congress of H.M.G.'s December Statement'.*
> *The Working Committee called on the British Government to declare that*
> *the Cabinet Mission Plan had failed because the Congress had not really*
> *accepted it, nor had the Sikhs nor the Scheduled Castes.*

I saw Vallabhai Patel, who was more silent and restrained than usual,
and obviously did not wish to discuss the political situation, though I gave
him an opening. We spoke of the Bihar Government's reluctance to
reserve places in the Provincial service for ex-Service men, on which
Patel promised to help; and a number of other matters. He was friendly
and sensible.

In the evening I saw Nehru for half an hour. I said that the League
resolution created a very difficult situation, both for the Constituent
Assembly and the Central Government. There was of course no question
of H.M.G. going back on their policy or dissolving the C.A.; but it was
obvious that the C.A. without the League and possibly without the States
could not make an acceptable constitution for the whole of India. As to
the Central Government, the Congress was in a position to force the
resignation of the Muslim League members, but they would be well
advised to consider the matter very carefully; since the Muslim League in
active opposition might make the administration of the country even
more difficult than now. The crisis had come at an unfortunate time, just
as the Budget session of the Assembly was beginning. Nehru was subdued
and obviously realised the seriousness of the position. He said that the C.A.
would go on, but obviously could not force a constitution on unwilling

provinces. He hoped that the States, or at least a proportion of them, would join the C.A. As to the Cabinet, the matter would require serious consideration. Apart from the fact that the League had not joined the C.A., the policy of the Party, unless the Bombay decision last July were withdrawn, was direct action, i.e., active opposition to the Government of which they at present formed part. He would consult his colleagues and give me his views.

In the evening I got one of the S. of S. panic-stricken cables, deploring any initiative on my part in seeing Nehru. Too late, anyhow, and it would not have influenced me, I think, even if it had come earlier.

February 4

Harold Macmillan has been staying and I had a talk with him this morning before his departure for Calcutta. He had seen most of the Indian political leaders (he dined with Nehru last night) and had formed a fairly shrewd appreciation of them. He found Nehru charming but nervy, and said that he would not stand the racket of great events. He recognised in Patel much greater qualities of leadership, and compared him to Bevin as against Nehru for Herbert Morrison. He thought Liaquat easier to talk with than any Hindu, but could get little out of him beyond the usual party line, except that he apparently thought that H.M.G. ought to make a new start altogether.

Just after lunch I had a letter from the P.M. by special messenger, dismissing me from my post at a month's notice. Not very courteously done.

Azad told me he had settled the teachers' strike at Delhi, and then at once embarked on politics. He thought that the League rank and file wish to come in, and that H.M.G. should bring pressure on the Muslim League to reconsider the Karachi decision.

February 5

Quiet day, which I spent in composing a reply to P.M.'s letter[1] with the assistance of Q. and P.S.V.

February 6

As I had expected I had a letter this morning signed by all the Congress members of my Cabinet demanding the resignation of the Muslim League members. I wired it to H.M.G., it crossed a telegram from S. of S. asking me to 'gain time' if the Congress did put forward such a demand. But they

---

[1] See Appendix IX for Attlee's letter and Wavell's reply.

will not be able to put off a decision for long, and I do not see quite how the Congress demand can be resisted.

V. P. Menon, whom I saw this afternoon, usually so optimistic, was gloomy about the position and thinks that the partition of India is now inevitable. He says the League reckon on this, and expect to capture the Punjab Government soon.

February 8

Cabinet meeting again went quite smoothly. The main item was the strength of the post-war Indian Army. It became clear that India could afford not much more than half the annual amount that Defence Department had originally asked for. At the end of an hour's discussion I undertook to draw up a draft directive to the Defence Department to make plans for a smaller Army. We then considered the formal statement of the Budget figures, showing a deficit of 60 to 80 crores. Finally we passed the draft Air Agreement with the Dutch.

This morning I drew up the draft directive for the Defence Department and later discussed it with the C-in-C. We also spoke of the proposal to release the I.N.A. convicts on which he still remains firm; and plans for an emergency withdrawal of Europeans. I told him of the P.M.'s letter and my removal, since he was off on a week's tour and I did not want him to learn of it by a Press announcement; he seemed very upset.

I had a telegram from H.M.G. in the evening, with reference to the Congress request for the removal of the League members from the Government. As usual, it was indefinite, but H.M.G. apparently contemplate making an early statement about the termination of our rule.

On 9 February Wavell informed the Secretary of State that in his judgement neither side wanted an open breach and that both of them were hoping for some move from H.M.G. that would get them out of their difficulties. He therefore strongly advised that a final attempt should be made to bring all parties into the Constituent Assembly before taking the decisive step of announcing a date for the withdrawal of British authority. On 11 February he telegraphed the draft of a statement which he thought, if made by H.M.G., would offer a chance, though perhaps a slender one, of getting the League into the Constituent Assembly. Wavell's advice was not accepted.

February 11

I had nearly an hour with Nehru. I threw a fly over him on the matter of trying to get the League into the Constituent Assembly and keeping them in the government, but he did not rise. He seemed subdued.

Later Baldev came. His chief point was on the release of the I.N.A. convicts. The Resolution comes up in the Assembly on the 18th and he wanted the matter taken in Cabinet. I said I should have to over-rule the Cabinet, if they decided on release, and he said he would consult his colleagues. He then discussed the political situation and said that Jinnah did not want a settlement. He had had discussions with him in London but had got nowhere, and Jinnah offered no assurances to the Sikhs even if they supported Pakistan.

February 12

Saw Liaquat on the Budget proposals. The new taxes proposed are a Business Profits Tax (the peace time equivalent of the E.P.T.) estimated to produce 30 crores; increase of one anna in Corporation tax to produce 4 crores; some changes of super-tax to produce $2\frac{1}{3}$rd. crores; a Dividend tax, yield uncertain but not large; Capital Gains Tax (equivalent to a tax on Unearned Increment) to produce $3\frac{1}{2}$ crores.

He proposes a high-powered tribunal to deal with tax evasion.

I arranged that the Budget proposals should be discussed with Nehru and Matthai early next week.

Cabinet meeting in evening went smoothly. On the first item, Protection of the Leather Industry, Chundrigar was argumentative; there was a moment of light relief when he argued that 'hides were thicker in the Punjab than elsewhere'.

February 13

In the afternoon I had a talk with Matthai, who is always sensible and interesting. He deplored the leadership both of Gandhi and of Jinnah, but like all other moderates in India seemed to accept them as inevitable evils, whose influence could not be opposed.

In the evening I saw Nazimuddin about the Punjab situation, at the request of Evan Jenkins in a telegram. N. was moderate and quite willing for compromise, if the Punjab Government would make concessions over political meetings and processions. I like honest fat little Nazimuddin and wish Jinnah had put him in the Government. He told me something of the Karachi meeting, I think he may have been for joining the C.A. himself.

A longish telegram from the P.M., to say that they propose to make an announcement next week on India and include the change of Viceroy; and that Dickie Mountbatten had been appointed. An unexpected appointment but a clever one from their point of view; and Dickie's personality may perhaps accomplish what I have failed to do.

February 14

Of my visitors, the first were two representatives of a big British business firm, and left on me the impression that British business-men in India have not moved with the times; their chief plea was that they should still have, after the transfer of power, their own settlements, their own clubs and should in fact keep themselves to themselves.

After lunch I saw Jagjivan Ram, who was comparatively optimistic on the Labour troubles; but pessimistic on the political situation. He said that a fresh effort by H.M.G. was required, and that the departure of the League from the Interim Government was no solution (why then did he sign the Congress letter demanding it? These Indians have no political courage).

Big dinner party in evening in Banqueting Hall, the last I shall hold there.

February 15

Nazimuddin asked to see me again about the Punjab situation. He merely said that he had been in communication with Jinnah, that a settlement might be possible if the Punjab Government withdrew the ban on political meetings and processions, and that he was going to Lahore tonight. He also complained of a provocative statement by Tara Singh.

Late in the evening, J.P.S.V. (John Christie)[1] came back from Bengal with a long appreciation from Burrows. B did not know H.M.G. proposed to make an immediate statement giving a final date for transfer of power, but was very strongly opposed to any such statement at present and drew a gloomy picture of its effect on Bengal. He recommended, as I have done, a last effort to get the League into the C.A. and the winding up of the S. of S. Services as the immediate steps required. I telegraphed the gist of Burrows appreciation to S. of S. P.S.V. will go to Lahore tomorrow to see Jenks and get his reactions to the issue of a statement. I do not think it will be favourable.

February 16 (Sunday)

George Abell came back from Lahore with a note from Jenkins even more damning than that of Burrows. I then sent for C-in-C, showed him H.M.G.'s statement, and the notes of Burrows and Jenkins. I also told him the name of my successor. He was considerably shaken at H.M.G.'s action.

---

[1] W. H. J. Christie, I.C.S., Joint Private Secretary to the Viceroy, 1947. He had been Deputy Private Secretary to the Viceroy in Lord Linlithgow's time.

February 17

I sent a telegram to H.M.G. urging them to postpone their main announcement, and merely to announce on Thursday my replacement, their views on the differences between Congress and League, making a last effort to bring them together into the C.A. (though I do not think it will succeed), and if possible some decision about the Services. I said that I thought it was only fair on my successor to let him have a week or two to study the situation before the final date was announced; and on me that I should not have the responsibility in my final weeks of office of carrying out a policy which I thought mis-judged and ill-timed.

I saw C-in-C again, at his normal interview, and he produced a gloomy view of the results of the announcement the gist of which I cabled home.

Patel was pleasant, and we discussed a variety of matters: the slowness of H.M.G. in dealing with the question of the Services; the situation in the Punjab; Pakistan, he was quite prepared to let the Muslims have the Western Punjab, and Sind and N.W.F.P. if they wished to join, and Eastern Bengal; the question of language on the A.I.R.; the enquiries into the Calcutta and Bihar riots, he agreed with me that these enquiries were too late and too long and that any enquiry should be immediate and short.

In the evening I discussed the Budget proposals with Liaquat, Nehru and Matthai; all went well, the meeting was amicable and the proposals were accepted.

February 18

One of my visitors was Hutchings, just back from London who had had interviews with S. of S. and P.M. He regarded P-L as completely useless and dithering, and could get no sense or decision out of him over shipping or the Services. The whole attitude of the Cabinet to India was conditioned, as I found last December, not by any consideration of what was good or expedient in India, but by what they could put across in Parliament. Also they were thinking not about India but about coal, electricity and Palestine.

February 19

H.M.G. telegraphed adhering to their announcement; and also sent a long telegram of self-justification and accusation of myself as inconsistent, to which I think I can make an effective reply.

H.M.G. accused Wavell of inconsistency because, having strongly pressed when in London that a final date should be announced for the transfer of power, he had later transmitted reports from Burrows and Jenkins opposing such a course and predicting calamitous consequences in Bengal and the Punjab, and had himself urged that the announcement of the date should be postponed.

It does not appear that Wavell ever sent his 'effective' reply. Probably he would have pointed out that in forwarding the reports of Burrows and Jenkins he had expressed the view that they were unduly pessimistic; that he had only asked for a temporary postponement of the announcement in order to make one final effort to bring the Congress and the League together in the Constituent Assembly and that from the point of view of staving off a crisis there was no longer any immediate hurry to make the announcement, since neither party really wanted to precipitate a break; and finally that, in his view, before making the announcement, H.M.G. should have some definite plan for demitting power by the due date and that they had rejected his Breakdown Plan, but had not put forward any other.

I spent the afternoon working on papers. Cabinet meeting in the evening lasted $2\frac{1}{4}$ hours, but was very friendly. There was one very contentious item, the amalgamation of the External Affairs and Commonwealth Relations Departments, and the transfer of the High Commissioner in London from the Commerce to the External Affairs Department, but I managed to skate round the really contentious part—very skilfully, George Abell said. The other items—tariffs on bicycles and woodscrews, regulation of dentists, note by Nehru on Scientific Manpower, Land Requisition went almost hilariously. They are curious people, these Indians.

Late in the evening I was told that there had been leakage in London and the Press obviously had had the text of the Statement and the name of my successor.

Thursday, 20th February

Felicity's wedding[1] went well and smoothly, thanks to Q.'s weeks of hard work and the efficiency of the staff.

In the evening I had short interviews with Nehru and Liaquat and handed them H.M.G.'s Statement. Liaquat seemed to be genuinely sorry that I was going, and Nehru was polite.

The Statement announced that it was H.M.G.'s definite intention to effect the transfer of power to responsible Indian hands by a date not later than June 1948. If by that date no authorities had been established under a new Constitution worked out by a fully representative Constituent Assembly in accordance

---

[1] Felicity Wavell married Captain Peter Longmore, M.C., son of Air Chief Marshal Sir Arthur Longmore, G.C.B., D.S.O.

with the Cabinet Mission Plan, H.M.G. would have to consider to whom the powers of the Central Government should be handed over, whether as a whole to some form of Central Government for British India or in some areas to the existing Provincial Governments, or in such other ways as might seem most reasonable and in the best interests of the Indian people.

As regards the Indian States, the statement that had been made by the Cabinet Mission that H.M.G.'s powers and obligations under paramountcy would not be handed over to any Government of British India, was reiterated.

It was also announced that the war-time appointment of Lord Wavell as Viceroy was being terminated and that Lord Mountbatten was being appointed in his place.

February 21

A longish day. I saw Wylie in the morning and Colville in the afternoon. The first reaction of both to H.M.G.'s Statement had been to offer their resignations but I told them that they should carry on, and they agreed, though Colville apparently proposes to write to the S. of S. and offer his resignation if required.

Bhabha and Chundrigar had nothing much to say, I never linger over an interview with these rather dull personalities, and it never develops into a general talk on affairs or ethics or literature as with Rajagopalachari or Azad or Nehru or Liaquat.

In the evening I had about an hour each with Nehru and Liaquat. They were both friendly, both I think quite impressed by the Statement. Nehru described it as a courageous document which would have far-reaching effects, but he went on to speak of its lack of definition on many points. As regards the Muslim League members remaining in the Central Government he said that the Congress would not press for an immediate answer to their request that they should go, but that the issue would have to be faced in the near future.

Liaquat said that the Statement wanted very careful consideration, but was not hopeful of any Hindu–Muslim rapprochement.

February 23

I had quite a cordial telegram from the P.M. in reply to one I had sent deprecating any party controversy over my removal. I have had nice letters from Rajagopalachari, Azad and Nehru about my work.

February 26

Baldev Singh had no knowledge of Sikh reactions to H.M.G.'s Statement, since he had been away, but said that the rift between Sikhs and Muslim

League was wider than ever. He was perturbed at the idea of all British officers leaving I.A. in a year's time. He said nothing about the I.N.A. resolution, I am told that it has been postponed till April; I thought we should get away with it if we stood firm.

Cabinet meeting this evening. One would certainly never imagine from the atmosphere of friendly discussion that each side was demanding the withdrawal of the other; nor that they were likely to initiate a civil war.

February 27

Rajendra Prasad thought it was blowing up for another food crisis; and unfortunately at the same time our control over the Provinces and the Provinces' control over procurement and distribution is weakening, owing to the general preference for politics over administration.

In the afternoon I had three-quarters of an hour with Dr. Matthai, practically all on the general political situation and Indian mentality. He does not think that the Muslim League will come in, mainly because of Jinnah's personality and of the Congress arrogance in 1937–39, which persuaded the Muslims that they would never get a fair deal. He said that the Hindu did not naturally lack generosity, but that the Congress was swayed by the 'Gujerati mentality' of the leaders, i.e. that of a trader driving a hard bargain.

February 28

From an exchange of telegrams with London I learn that Mountbatten may arrive in Delhi on March 22 and that I shall leave next day. M–B has also wired that he will keep on the whole of the Personal Staff at any rate for the next three months.

We had a Cabinet meeting at 10.30 a.m. to hear the Budget proposals. They went down quite well. Rajagopalachari was rather talkative, but otherwise there was not much question. George says the Budget is a clever one, in that it drives a wedge between Congress and their rich merchant supporters, like Birla, while Congress cannot object to its provisions; but I doubt whether Liaquat had any deliberate intention of doing this, I think he took the advice of his officials, which I think was sound.

I saw Liaquat for a few minutes after the meeting, about the date for M–B's arrival. He said the League would certainly not have taken a decision by then, that Jinnah was a sick man and would not be in Delhi before the middle of the month at the latest.

After lunch I talked with Jagjivan Ram, whom I like and think the most sensible of the Scheduled Castes I have met. He said that H.M.G.'s Statement threw the S.C. to the mercy of the Majority Communities; that they would miss British protection and British justice and would have preferred that we should remain for another 10 years or so; but admitted the difficulties.

March 5

Lawson and Griffiths of the European Association came to see me. They were friendly and complimentary, and did not seem unduly apprehensive about the safety of Europeans or the prospects of British business. Griffiths was clear that the decision to fix a definite date was the right one.

I spoke to Patel on the Punjab situation and asked him to use his influence to stop the proposed anti-Pakistan demonstrations on March 11. He promised to help.

Nehru, Patel and Bhabha have sent in minutes, dissenting from the record of the Cabinet meeting at which Liaquat explained his taxation proposals. The record says the proposals were 'approved'. These minutes now say that their writers do not agree that they were approved. Poltroons, especially Nehru! They now find that the Budget is not popular with their big business supporters and are trying to rat or hedge. I drafted a stiff reply, but perhaps P.S.V. will tone it down.

I saw Liaquat just before lunch, and told him of the objections, not naming the objectors. He claimed, not unnaturally, that it would be an impossible position if the Budget were held to be the responsibility of the Finance Member alone and not of the whole Cabinet. Liaquat is going off to Dehra Dun for a rest. I asked him when the League Working Committee would meet, and he said he had no idea, he thought that perhaps the debate in the House of Commons would elucidate the position a little more. I tried to impress on him a sense of urgency.

After the evening Cabinet meeting, which went well enough, I got P.S.V. who had just returned from Lahore to explain to Liaquat the seriousness of the situation and to suggest his intervention with the Punjab Muslim League. Liaquat's attitude was inclined to be, what could one expect after such a damfool Statement by H.M.G.; but he will do his best to help, I think.

Although the Punjab Government had rescinded its order against the Muslim National Guards, the Muslim League continued their agitation and for over a month defied with impunity a government ban on meetings and processions. Eventually a compromise was reached, the League leaders in the Punjab agreeing

*to end the agitation if all those who had been arrested were released and the
ban on meetings was withdrawn. The impotence of the Punjab Government in
face of a Muslim League challenge was thus starkly revealed and on 3 March
Khizar submitted his Cabinet's resignation.*

*The League's agitation had so inflamed communal feeling that the mere
rumour that the League would now form a Ministry—it proved, in fact, unable
to do so and the Governor took charge under Section 93—evoked demonstrations
by Hindus and Sikhs; and these at once touched off violent communal rioting in
Lahore, Amritsar, Rawalpindi, and other smaller towns. The disturbances
spread to rural areas and there were heavy casualties.*

March 6

I saw Baldev Singh in the morning about the Punjab situation. He would
be prepared to go to Lahore if Governor wanted him, but says that there
can be no coalition between the Sikhs and the Muslim League. He harked
back to the days of the Moguls and the old feuds between Sikhs and
Muslims. I am afraid that communalism is rampant in the Punjab.

Jenkins does not want me to go there at present. He says that Mamdot
cannot form a stable ministry, and advocates keeping in Section 93 for the
present.

March 8

Yesterday was a quiet day, with no interviews for a wonder. This morning
I held my last Investiture (about 200 to be decorated) and dubbed my last
knight. There were a lot of the Household receiving awards appropriately
enough, Archie John, Peter Longmore, David Walker, my Surgeon
Taylor, Blake my Tour Superintendent.

Maulana Azad came to see me before lunch. We discussed the Punjab
situation, the failure of the Bihar Ministry over rehabilitation, a new
approach by Congress to the League. Azad is always for moderation but
I am doubtful how much influence he exercises.

March 10

After a quiet Sunday I had a fairly busy day. I saw C-in-C, who was rather
depressed about the Indian Army.

I then said goodbye to J. P. Srivastava, he always had rather more
character and guts than most of my Executive Council, though I fancy
his business methods may have been shrewd rather than scrupulous.

Then I saw Nehru, who was quite friendly. He agreed that the Cabinet
Mission Plan was the best solution if it could be carried through; and that
the only real alternative was the partition of the Punjab and Bengal. He

was quite sober and realistic in what he said, but did not seem really hopeful of a settlement with the League. When I said that I hoped my successor would succeed where I had failed, in bringing the two Parties together, he said that failures and successes were only relative and that some failures were greater than successes.

March 11

Mainly a military day. I presented five George Crosses, all posthumous except Durrani, at a parade near the Memorial Arch. It went off quite well. Then I was photographed with the Bodyguard. We had a dinner party in the evening and went to a Military Dance Festival at the Stadium, good but rather too long.

March 12

Council (I beg its pardon, Cabinet) went quite smoothly and in a friendly atmosphere.

Meanwhile things go badly in the Punjab.

March 13

Hutchings came to say goodbye. He was gloomy about the Food situation, as there seems to be a world shortage, and the harvests in India do not promise too well, as the wheat in Central India has been ruined by rust. We had a long general talk. He does not think that many of the Services will stop in India after June 1948. He agrees with many of the better men in the Services that the compensation claim is wrong but that Government should find employment for the Indian Services. He says that in England all the employees on Railways etc. are asking for compensation on being nationalised. We discussed Indian mentality and character, Hindu and Muslim and the future of India. Hutchings is one of the ablest I.C.S. men I have had under me.

After lunch Evan Jenkins who had been to Rohtak, came in. He was as calm and clear as usual, but took a serious view of the Punjab situation. The cities are more or less under control but the trouble in rural areas is spreading and is of course more difficult to check. He has no idea of what casualties yet are, but there may be a total of 1000 killed in the whole Province. The trouble in getting any settlement is that both the Congress and Muslim League are controlled from outside, from Delhi and Bombay; while the Sikhs, who are in a position to negotiate on the spot, are disunited and poorly led, Master Tara Singh is stupid and emotional. The local Muslim League leaders are poor: Mamdot is hopelessly stupid and

Firoz Khan Noon is trusted by no-one and cuts no ice. Khizar's resignation was prompted largely by the Statement of February 20.

Evan wants an extra brigade of troops from the south. He is rather afraid of the trouble taking an anti-European turn, and thinks it possible that we may be forced to evacuate the Punjab before the rest of India— just the reverse of what my plan proposed. I told him of Nehru's proposal to visit the Punjab, which he did not like but said could not be prevented: Baldev's visit had done more harm than good.

At 3.30 p.m. Nehru came in and we had about 40 minutes talk. N. began by recrimination against the methods of the Muslim League; Evan pointed out that they had used exactly the technique practised by the Congress in their agitations of 1921 and 1930. He also said that the trouble at Amritsar had been started by non-Muslims. Nehru showed signs of working up for one of his outbursts but the unruffled calm and in-controvertible statements of Evan kept him in check. No conclusion was reached, but N. gave the programme of his visit. He said nothing about going to Peshawar, and I hoped he had abandoned this idea, but I gathered later in the evening that he still might go there.

In the evening Burrows arrived, he had come up to say goodbye, a little reproachful that I had not gone to Calcutta. He was gloomy about prospects in Bengal, did not think that there was much hope of its holding together, unless he could get a Coalition Ministry in the next six months, and he saw little chance of that. He said that Suhrwardy was a very frightened man, that he was almost the only Indian politician he knew capable of taking a long view, but that he was a cad and untrustworthy. Burrows liked what he had seen of Liaquat. We had some discussion of all-India politics and agreed that the personalities of Gandhi and Jinnah had been the determining factors in preventing a solution of the Indian problem. He was very relieved that G. had left Bengal,[1] it had taken 20 of his best police to protect him; and he was sarcastic over an American correspondent's article headed 'Gandhi walks alone'!

Burrows is a really sterling character, the best type of Englishman we breed; and I think he was genuinely sorry at my departure.

March 14

I sent a message to Nehru asking him not to go to Peshawar and he agreed though protestingly. I think this will relieve Olaf Caroe's mind.

---

[1] After the outbreak of communal rioting in East Bengal Gandhi had undertaken an extensive tour on foot through the affected area in the hope of reconciling the two communities.

March 15

The President of the Council of State, Hossain Imam, came ostensibly to say goodbye, but occupied 15 minutes by a hymn of hate against Congress, especially on the score of lack of generosity to Muslims; this is of course true and is where Congress have shown such short-sightedness, they could have appeased the Muslims without really giving away anything essential for the good of India or their cause, but they have the mentality of the small lawyer who will hold on to the smallest point of his argument and of the bania who will not give up one anna of his bargain.

Spens, Chief Justice, came to say goodbye and we had a long talk. He says that the Calcutta Enquiry will show that there was Hindu incitement and a sudden and concerted attack without provocation on the Muslims in the north of Calcutta; that the Ministry will come out of it all right; that there was delay in bringing in the military owing to faulty information; and that Bucher and the military were magnificent when called in.

March 17

Claude Auchinleck came for his last official interview. He certainly regrets the change. He says he can get no decisions from Baldev Singh who is always away on political tours and anyway is afraid to give decisions by himself.

Then came Patel. We discussed the appointment of a D.I.B. vice Smith, Patel wants to put in an Indian I.C.S. man on the grounds that there is no Indian policeman good enough (actually there is a good Muslim but Patel will not have him and he will not serve under Patel). I said that it would be bad for police morale if the plum appointment in the I.P. went to an outsider. P. took the usual communal line about the Punjab and accused the officials and police, who are mainly Muslim, of bias. He had written to me advocating martial law, but I explained to him the disadvantages. We then got on to the Budget against which he declaimed very hotly; it has obviously got Birla and 'Big Business', with whom P. works closely, very much on the raw, and they are using every means to get it amended. P. wants the whole Budget taken again in Cabinet, I said we must wait now for the Select Committee's report. Patel was very friendly at the finish and we have always dealt on frank terms and have respected one another. He is entirely communal and has no sense of compromise or generosity towards Moslems, but he is more of a man than most of these Hindu politicians.

The vanguard of Mountbatten's large staff turned up.

March 18

I fell behind all the time today and never got abreast of the work. There was a continual succession of files and visitors.

I had a long talk with Liaquat mainly about the Budget. He said that it would have been perfectly easy for Nehru to come and see him if the Congress wished to propose any modifications in the Budget. The fact was that Big Business, headed by Birla and Dalmia, had got at the Congress High Command; and that instead of coming to him direct they had intrigued behind his back in the Select Committee. Actually he had now carried his proposals through the Select Committee with some modifications of the Business Profits Tax.

I have always liked Liaquat and thought him full of common sense, but he has no use for Hindus. Still if he had been in Jinnah's place I think we could have got a solution.

Azad spent most of his interview after lunch about the records of the Political Department. Congress have an idea that we are destroying all inconvenient or compromising files about the States and our relations with them, and want to try and have a finger in the matter. I lent him Arthur's[1] book on his pilgrimage to Mecca, and he said that it was a very fair and accurate account and that Arthur had gained a great insight into the manners and customs of the Arabs. (Azad was born in Mecca and spent many years there.)

In the evening I saw Matthai, the ablest and most impartial of my Ministers. We talked mainly of the Budget, I think he really approves the proposals and realises the difficulties Congress is in, if they back Birla and Co, but he had to put across the party line of modification of the proposals. On the question of British withdrawal he was gloomy on the future prospects of India, but said our real mistakes began 40 years ago, especially with Curzon's bureaucratic centralization and worship of efficiency, instead of putting Indians gradually into the saddle and accepting a lower standard of efficiency.

March 19

I had one of Nehru's rather intemperate letters on my request to him not to go to Peshawar; it ended with a demand for the resignation of the Governor. I sent a soothing reply and said nothing about his demand with regard to the Governor.

[1] Major A. J. B. Wavell, M.C., F.R.G.S., a cousin of Lord Wavell, went to Mecca and Medina in 1908 and wrote *A Modern Pilgrim in Mecca* (London, 1912). He was killed in East Africa in 1916.

A morning ride

The Viceroy greets his successor Lord Mountbatten

Cabinet meeting in the evening began with the I.N.A. case. I saved discussion on it by saying that I assumed that Cabinet supported the demand for the release of the prisoners; and when they assented I announced my intention to over-rule my Cabinet for the first time in my Viceroyalty, at what will probably be my last Cabinet meeting. Only Mandal tried to start an argument on the merits of the case, and I stopped him. Nehru said that my decision would have serious consequences but on the whole they took it quite well. After that we got through quite a lot of business.

March 20

A day of farewells and packing. Two Nepalese generals came to give me a farewell message from the Maharaja of Nepal.

Then Mandal gave me a half-hour discourse on the disabilities of the Scheduled Castes, their regret that the British are going and their fears for the future. It was all on the usual lines; but Mandal spoke with obvious sincerity and showed up better than at previous interviews when I have found him tiresome. I think part of his trouble is that his command of English is poor. And he is not clever.

Little V. P. Menon came in the afternoon. He has always been an admirer of mine, I think, and regrets my going.[1] Always an optimist, he thinks the budget dispute will be settled by Liaquat giving way. He gets this from Patel, I expect.

In the evening a farewell party for the Staff, about 300, I don't think I have ever properly realised the size of the Vice-regal household. Then Mavlankar, President of the Legislative Assembly, and his wife came in to say goodbye, quite a gesture I think from a very confirmed Congressman.

Finally a farewell dinner-party to the Cabinet, which went quite well. Nehru was quite genial and talkative, he is apt sometimes to be silent and aloof at these gatherings. I gathered from Liaquat that compromise on the Budget is possible.

March 22

My last day. A good turn-out for the last morning ride from Hauz Khas, 12 of the Personal Staff, Felicity and the Policemen.

Ismay, Mieville and some of M-B's staff turned up for lunch and I had about an hour with Pug Ismay and Mieville after lunch. They do not

---

[1] V. P. Menon *was* a great admirer of Lord Wavell and always stressed what a 'good' man he was.

seem really to know very much about it or to have any very new or
definite policy.

Then came the ceremonial arrival of the M-Bs, the Bodyguard in full
dress looked well and he was very pleased with them.

I talked with Dickie M-B from about 4.30 p.m. to 7 p.m. He began by
telling me that the P.M. had sent for him and asked him to take on the job
either before or at the time I left England last December. So that Attlee's
assurances at that time and subsequent letters were completely insincere.
He said that Attlee had been quite moved by my telegram assuring him
that I had no intention to make trouble for the Government and was well
disposed.

He then talked of the I.N.A., having in mind apparently to reduce the
sentences of those serving sentences for brutality as 'part of a political
gesture'. He also proposed to write to Gandhi and Jinnah to ask them to
come and see him, one more Viceroy, I suppose, who hopes to reconcile
these intractable personalities. He seems to have succeeded in getting
compensation for the Services, thanks partly, I think, to my cables to him
not to come out without settling this.

He also talked of his hope of getting India to accept some form of
Dominion status.

At 7.15 p.m. I saw Liaquat about the Budget crisis. He was prepared to
consider the compromise I suggested,[1] but only to prevent my successor
from the embarrassment of a contentious Cabinet meeting at once, and
provided Congress agreed to support all other Budget proposals, otherwise he would fight out the battle in the Assembly and 'I am on a strong
wicket', as I think he is. We parted on very friendly terms. I like Liaquat
and have a high opinion of him.

We dined alone with the Mountbattens. After dinner Pug Ismay,
Mieville and George Abell came in and we talked politics for about an
hour and a half.

March 27 (Claridges Hotel)

The departure ceremony from Delhi on 23rd went off all right. The M-Bs
contrary to precedent came to the airfield to see us off, which was friendly.
On arriving at Karachi, I paid a short visit to the 2nd Bn., (Black Watch)
and we then flew on and got to Habbaniyeh at 11.30 p.m. and stayed at
the A.O.C.'s house. Next day we flew on to Rome, arriving about 4 p.m.
local time. Next day (25th), we spent most of the morning at the Vatican,

---

[1] Liaquat accepted a reduction of the rate of the proposed Business Profits Tax from
20 per cent to 16½ per cent. He had originally proposed 25 per cent in the Budget.

mainly in the Sistine Chapel, and took off at 11.45 a.m. We got to North-holt at about 4 p.m. P-L, A. V. Alexander met me from the Government, Cripps sent the excuse of pressing business. At Joyce's pressing request I said a few innocuous words to the Press, very haltingly. We then went off to Claridges where the Government had booked us a suite for 10 days.

The only thing I have to record from the India angle in the next few days is a talk with one of my staff. He said that there had been a leak from P.S.V.'s office; that George Abell's Indian stenographer, whom he trusted absolutely though I had once or twice questioned the advisability of trusting any Indian with really secret stuff, had been passing copies of George's letters out to Congress; that Nehru had brought some home and showed them to Cripps as evidence that my staff was at heart biased against Congress; and that this was largely responsible for my dismissal. Now if there is any truth in this, it does show an amazing mentality on the part of the Cabinet Ministers concerned. Instead of warning P.S.V. or myself of the leakage; and, if they considered that the letters which were produced showed disloyalty to H.M.G.'s policy on the part of P.S.V. or myself, confronting us with them and asking for an explanation, they allow the leakage of secret correspondence to go on—or at least fail to warn us—and make arrangements to replace me more or less at Nehru's bidding. 'Politics is a dishonest business', R. A. B. Butler said to me in 1943. It certainly does change the ethical code of men who would, I suppose regard themselves normally as men of honesty and principle. I am glad that I have finished with politics.[1]

March 28

I went round to Downing Street this morning by request to meet the India Committee—P.M., Cripps, Alexander, P-L, Listowel, Addison. They questioned me for about 40 minutes in a rather routine and per-functory fashion, as if they knew all the answers already. Towards the end the S. of S. said: 'Is there any general advice you can give us on how to proceed?' I said that I had given them advice and that they had not liked it, that they had presumably given my successor full instructions, and that anything that I was likely to say could hardly have any influence. For what it was worth, however, I could only recommend them to make a last

---

[1] It is indisputable that there was a leak from the P.S.V.'s office not only of Sir George Abell's letters but also of top secret documents and that this came to the notice of Cabinet Ministers in the U.K. They did not disclose the leak to Lord Wavell, but as a result of the knowledge of it British stenographers were employed to handle secret correspondence when Mountbatten became Viceroy. There is no reason to suppose that the leak was responsible for Wavell's dismissal.

effort to bring the Parties together, and if that failed, as it seemed likely to do, to start on detailed arrangements for the partition of India, so as to avoid confusion when we leave, and in the hope that there may be some last-minute arrangement about Defence etc. Shortly afterwards the P.M. said: 'Well, thank you, that is all, I think'; and bowed me out without one single word of thanks or commendation. He is a singularly ungracious person. I had no desire for an insincere little speech and was glad to be spared it, but it was not a good exhibition of manners.

March 31

I think I had better close this record of my time in India at this point. I had a talk on India with Bobbety Cranborne today, and he said that it was a great pity that H.M.G. had not taken my advice and consulted the Opposition on Indian affairs. The Lords had always found it almost impossible to extract information about India from P-L, who was vague or evasive in his replies. This was one of the reasons why they had intended to press the debate in the Lords to a division. It was the speech of Halifax that had led them to re-consider the decision.

R. A. B. Butler said that my final broadcast had created great impression, and was simple and dignified.

I dined with Monty, who talked mainly about forthcoming Conference, Spearhead.

I am not going to attempt any summary here of my Viceroyalty. My last letter to the King was something in the nature of that. Whether I shall ever have the time or inclination to go through all these journals again and comment on them, I am rather doubtful. I think I have always been honest in the entries and have tried to represent accurately the events, discussions and impressions of the time. Perhaps they may be of interest to my family, or to some future historian many years hence. It has been interesting to write them down though rather a burden at times.

16

THE LAST THREE YEARS

*Wavell lived for rather more than three years after his return to England.
Though he received many honours—he was made Constable of the Tower,
Lord Lieutenant of London, and Chancellor of Aberdeen University—and was
appointed the London Vice-Chairman of the South African diamond Company
of de Beers and was much in demand as a lecturer, he was not very happy and
felt that he was spending his time unprofitably. If his health had not deteriorated,
he would probably have settled down to some serious writing. He left by his
bedside in hospital chapter headings for his memoirs and was planning to write
a detective story during convalescence.*

*When he left India in March 1947 he for a while gave up keeping his
Journal, but in August he decided to start it again and continued making entries
at irregular intervals till March 1950. Though he still had a good many public
and official engagements, he no longer held high office and so not many of
the entries are of historical interest; but a few have been selected for inclusion
in this volume that have a bearing on Indian affairs or that chronicle his last,
and ultimately successful, battle with H.M.G. over the grant of proportionate
pensions to British members of the lower grades of the Indian services, or that
give a good picture of his interests and activities during these closing years.*

He restarted the Journal on the day of Indian Independence.

August 15, 1947 (Indian Independence Day)

I gave up keeping a journal when I got back from India in March. But it
may be worth while to continue it on a reduced scale; and I will briefly
summarise the 4 or 5 months since I came home.

The Duke of Gloucester (acting for the King in S. Africa) and Queen
Mary saw me on April 2 and questioned me generally on Indian affairs,
but there was nothing of any moment in these interviews.

Then I went up to St. Andrews for a month. St. Andrews University
gave me an honorary degree, at the same time as they made George
Cunningham Rector.

During June I took my seat in the House of Lords as an Earl. I took
honorary degrees at Cambridge and Oxford and attended meetings and
receptions of various bodies and societies. Nearly all these involved
making speeches, which is not a thing I do easily or well.

All this time I was trying to find something to do, since until this was more or less settled it was not much use to look seriously for a house.

Listowel, now S. of S. for India, asked me to come and see him on July 11; and we had an hour's general talk on the situation in India. He said that it was only my visit home at the end of 1946 that had driven the Government into a policy and saved the situation by preventing drift. I said I thought I had perhaps been a bit too rude and uncompromising, and had annoyed Ministers. He said that this was so, but that nothing else would have made them do anything definite.

Q and Joan and I went up to Scotland on July 15th for the Highland Brigade Gathering and Ball at Edinburgh, a Royal Garden Party at Holyroodhouse, and the presentation by the City of Perth of its Freedom to The Black Watch and to myself. We had a fine day for the Perth ceremony, at which the Queen was present, and all went well.

Next I went to Germany to see the 1st Battalion (Black Watch). Just before I started off I had an offer of an appointment with de Beers, the big diamond concern in South Africa. After seeing Sir Ernest Oppenheimer, the head of de Beers and practically of the diamond concerns of the world, I gather, I agreed to take the appointment.

I flew over to Germany on the afternoon of August 5, and spent the night near the Minden Gap. It was near here that the famous disaster to Varro's legions had halted for ever the spread of Roman civilisation to Eastern Europe.

Next day I flew to Duisberg and carried out a strenuous programme with the 1st Bn.; then on to Luneberg and finally Berlin, where I had not been since 1936.

October 14

Q's strenuous flat or house-hunting has not been very successful and we are still homeless, but are in negotiation for a flat in Kingston House, Knightsbridge, not very attractive but possible.

I saw Evan Jenkins, and on the 11th had a long talk with Ismay, home for a short visit, on Indian affairs. He put the Punjab tragedy down to the failure of the Indian Army in the Border Force to take action against their own community, and the organisation by the Sikhs who had obviously made great preparations. Nehru and Liaquat did their best and the former especially showed great personal courage and considerable statesmanship.

October 31 (International Sportsmens Club)

On October 21, I carried the Sword of State at the Opening of Parliament,

Andrew Cunningham carried the Crown and Portal the Cap of Maintenance.

I went off the same night to St. Andrews, where I gave the Walker Trust lecture on Leadership on the evening of the 22nd. I had a very good and attentive audience.

On the 24th I went on to Aberdeen, and next day was my installation as Chancellor. It went well and my rather light-hearted address on games and athletics was very well received. As was inevitable, I suppose, the Press seized on my somewhat controversial remarks about waste of time at cricket and in football pools and gave them full publicity, while they entirely ignored for the most part my much more important speech at St. Andrews.

November 20 (Royal wedding)

Today we had seats in the Abbey for the wedding which went well. The King had ordained that Field Marshals should carry their batons, even if they were only in Service dress, and wear two stars of orders. Perhaps the only time I shall carry my baton.

I had about an hour this evening with Dickie Mountbatten. He was as voluble as ever and full of confidence and personality, but had evidently had a gruelling time. He paid a great tribute to George Abell and his staff. He said my stock stood high in India and that all the political leaders respected my integrity. He has very much gone over to the Congress side, as was I suppose inevitable in his position; says Jinnah has become an impossible megalomaniac; and that Nehru has shown himself a really great man. He thinks Liaquat the only man on the Muslim side who has shown sense and some statesmanship, which about tallies with my judgement. But Liaquat is a sick man and may collapse, which will leave Pakistan barren indeed. The bitterness of feeling between Hindu and Muslim is worse than ever before and neither side trusts or believes the other about anything.

On Dominion status, Dickie thinks that both wish to retain connection with the Commonwealth but India will have to do some sort of face-saving, in view of the declared resolution to become an independent Republic. I said I thought it would be highly dangerous to have Pakistan in the Commonwealth and India out of it. M.B. said he entirely agreed but that the Service chiefs at home seemed to him to be playing with the idea of making a base of Pakistan and letting India go, if she wished. I said I thought such a policy would be suicidal.

We had some talk of his Despatch and my criticisms of it, in the course of which he warned me again, as he had done at Delhi, that Winston was no friend of mine and had never been loyal to me.

November 30

On the 27th I took an honorary degree at London University, a good ceremony. But it brought me a great disappointment. I mentioned to the Vice-Chancellor at dinner that, having already four Degrees in Law, I had nearly asked for a D.Litt. when London University offered me another Degree in Law. He said: 'I do wish you had, and I do wish we had thought of it for ourselves'. I had not liked to ask for it, but I might have had it—and had it alongside Masefield.

December 1

The U.N.O. decision on the partition of Palestine is a sad business—not so much the decision itself, though that I am sure is bad, as the method of reaching it. It has been decided not on its merits but by a process of dishonest and discreditable lobbying among the smaller powers. It is disgraceful that a vital question like this should be decided by the venal votes of such countries as Haiti, Liberia, Paraguay. The Times reports that partition could have been carried in no other city than New York where Jewish influence is so strong.

December 7

The flat in Kingston House is finally taken, but we are neither of us at all enthusiastic about it. We shall be cramped in it and we don't really like London, but anyway it is some place of our own at last. I have been made Constable of the Tower when Philip Chetwode vacates next March.

December 31 (Selham House)

The second load of furniture came into the flat on the 23rd, and on Xmas Eve we motored down here, where we have spent a very quiet week indeed.

So ends 1947—a thoroughly bad year. I think on the whole I am well out of India, though I hated the way they chucked me out and should have liked to see the thing through. I have been rootless and unhappy ever since I came home, unable to settle down to anything or to make a plan; taking things as they come, accepting invitations to lecture, to dinners, and to functions of all kinds without really wanting to do any of them;

undecided where to live or what to do. There seems to be no prospect of getting down to some writing which might I think interest me. I can only hope that some of the things I have done in my various responsibilities have been of some use to someone.

And I have lost my best friend, Arthur Wauchope, and have not felt really well all the year. However, the family on the whole are flourishing, and Archie John will be home soon.

1948

January 29 (In plane between London and Tripoli)

The last four days have been a terrible rush, just before departure for S. Africa. Amongst other engagements Q and I lunched at the House of Lords, and I then asked a question about the unprotected European civil servants, whose case I am trying to get reconsidered.

Last night I never went to bed at all, what with packing, tidying up, finishing off my outstanding correspondence and talking with Archie John.

February 1st (Forest House, Federation Road, Johannesburg).

The journey out was uneventful and dull. We got to Johannesburg about 7 p.m. I was greeted with the news of Gandhi's assassination, an unexpected end for a very remarkable man. I never accepted him as having much of the saint in his composition but he was an extremely astute politician. Whether he did more harm or good for India it would be hard to say, but Indians will have no doubt, and he certainly hastened the departure of the British, which was his life's aim. But he wrecked the plan of the Cabinet Mission which might possibly have secured a united India and saved all the massacres. I do not believe that he really worked for an understanding with the Muslims, when his influence might have secured it. He was always the lawyer and the bania who would drive a hard bargain and then find some legal quibble to deprive his opponent of what he had seemed to gain. I always thought he had more of malevolence than benevolence in him, but who am I to judge, and how can an Englishman estimate a Hindu? Our standards are poles apart; and by Hindu standards Gandhi may have been a saint; by any standards he was a very remarkable man.

I have had two crowded days here.

February 3 (Blue Mountains, Beach Road, Muisenberg)

I flew down yesterday from Johannesburg, about 3 hours. Sir Ernest

Oppenheimer and Lady O. met me and brought me out here, a house they have built by the sea.

I motored in to Capetown this morning and saw Smuts and Hofmeyer. Smuts looks as young in mind and body for his age as ever. We talked of the state of Europe and he then went on to speak of the problems of Indians in S.A. and his hopes of arranging a round-table conference, but said that the Indians themselves were divided into a moderate and extreme element.

February 15 (Kimberley)

I left Capetown on the 12th with the Oppenheimers.

Everyone in S. Africa talks with apprehension about the Indian problem and the Native problem. The sanctions put on by India have hit S.A. badly as regards jute, which is badly wanted for bagging the grain crop; and Smuts is now anxious for a Round Table Conference, to which I tried to get him to agree before the sanctions, when I was Viceroy.

Smuts and his supporters, or most of them, would also like a liberal policy as regards the natives. But how even the most liberal policy is going to secure the permanent domination of a mere handful, comparatively speaking, of white men in a country of predominantly black men, who are becoming conscious of their numerical advantage and of the happenings in Asia, no-one can quite foresee.

> *Wavell remained in South Africa until the end of February, carrying out a full programme in connection with the business of de Beers, visiting mines and factories, attending meetings, and meeting many of the staff and officials of the company.*
>
> *On 29 February he flew to Rhodesia where he attended a variety of functions at Salisbury and Bulawayo and met many old friends. After another short visit to Johannesburg he returned home on 6 March.*

March 15

I found it had taken poor Q all the 5 weeks I was away to get permits for decorating the flat, so the painters were only just beginning. She had, however, got more bookshelves up. There was an enormous mass of correspondence waiting for me.

March 31

Worked away at the case for House of Lords on April 7. John Colville (Clydesmuir) and Scarbrough and Ismay will speak in support of me, I think.

April 10 (Kingston House)

Not much to record except the debate in the House of Lords on pensions for British officials outside the Secretary of State Services. This has been taking up a good deal of my time since last November when I saw Mountbatten and found that his representations had had no effect. I wrote to Cripps and got nothing but a blank refusal, then tried Noel-Baker and got a polite but non-committal reply, then asked a question in the House of Lords and got an official sort of answer. In the motion for papers which I moved on the 7th I was supported by Linlithgow, Clydesmuir, Scarbrough and Ismay. Listowel replied for the Government and put up a poorish case. I think we may get something done in the end.

May 31

One official activity during this month was to ask a question in the House of Lords on the uncovenanted Civil Servants so as to keep the ball rolling. I got an unsatisfactory reply from Listowel, so wrote him a letter asking him whether the Government did propose to do anything for these men in the end or not, and saying that I must adopt more forthright methods unless I got a satisfactory reply.

June 30

During June I did a good deal of Regimental work, and was very busy with my campaign on behalf of the uncovenanted Services in India. This culminated in a high-power Delegation to the Minister, Noel-Baker, probably the highest-powered Delegation which a Cabinet Minister has ever received: 4 ex-Viceroys,—Halifax, Linlithgow, Mountbatten and self; 7 ex-Governors of Provinces—Scarbrough, Burrows, Jenkins, Twynam, Caroe, Hallett, Lewis; Auchinleck, Ismay, Stanley Reed, Emerson (Railways). John Colville (Clydesmuir), John Anderson and Amery would also have been with us but for unavoidable engagements, and Wylie if I had had his letter in time. Though we got nothing definite out of N-Baker, I think that he was impressed and that we shall succeed in time. Our main opponents are Patel in India, and the Chancellor of the Exchequer[1] at home. The idea now is that Mountbatten and I should have a meeting with the Finance Ministers of India and Pakistan, who are in London for the discussion of the sterling balances.

Archie John went off to the School of Army Education at Castle Buchanan. I don't like his becoming so taken up with Education, but it

[1] This was now Sir Stafford Cripps.

seems to be what he likes. He has been with us for quite a long time—always good tempered and charming, thoroughly efficient, and lamentably untidy.

July 8

Noel-Baker sent a message to ask if I would come and see him, but on ringing him up I found that Cripps would not be there and that he merely wished to explain to me the difficulties in persuading the Indians to pay proportionate pensions to the non-S. of S. Services. I told him that whatever the Indians did or did not do, the men were our men and H.M.G.'s responsibility. I had a message later that he would try to arrange a meeting with Cripps next week.

July 21

Another hectic ten days or so. I went off on the 9th to Germany to visit the Regiment. I think the battalion is in good shape and the National Service men seem a good lot. Today we lunched at House of Lords with Mountbattens. The Duke of Edinburgh and he were being introduced into H. of L. After the introduction ceremony I went off to see Noel-Baker in his room at the H. of C. On the way I met Winston in a passage and had a talk, he was very affable. N-B admitted that we had won our case over the non S. of S. Services and that something was bound to be done for them. The strength of our Deputation had convinced even Stafford Cripps.

October 5

I spent September in Scotland, shooting, stalking and playing golf at St. Andrews. The news of Jinnah's death came while I was at St. Andrews. I never liked Jinnah, but had a certain reluctant admiration for him and his uncompromising attitude. He certainly had much justification for his mistrust of Congress and their leaders.

> *At various dates during October Wavell had several long talks on India with Indian and other personalities. The talks were interspersed with many other activities—his work for de Beers, regimental affairs, lectures either given or attended, golf and shooting, when time permitted, and a visit to Denmark.*

October 16

I had half-an-hour's talk with J. P. Srivastava at the Athenaeum on Wednesday; and with Nye next day I had nearly an hour on the affairs of

India. He tells me they had something very like a serious famine in Madras last winter but suppressed the news; had we been still in charge it would have had headlines. He thinks that relations between India and Pakistan might become reasonably good and things settle down if the Kashmir dispute were out of the way.

October 31

I had dinner with Liaquat last Sunday at Claridges, no-one else there except Rahimtoola, the High Commissioner, who hardly spoke. L. held forth almost continuously for 3 hours, he is in good form, looking well and very friendly. He told me of his discourse to the Premiers Conference, advocating much closer relations, now that the Dominions were not all of the same race; and of a long audience with the King, whom he found well-informed and friendly. We spoke of Kashmir, which he said was the only bar now to better relations with India; discussions with Nehru had led nowhere and Pakistan would never agree to Kashmir's accession to India. L. was obviously bitter about Mountbatten, though he said little. He told me the circumstances of Jinnah's sudden death. We then discussed some personalities: Nazimuddin; Bhopal, of whom he asked me my opinion which I gave him frankly; Ghazanfar Ali, who had blotted his copybook as a Minister by too much jobbery and had been sent as Pakistan's representative in Iraq; Firoz Khan Noon, whom he obviously regarded as a lightweight; Gracey, Mudie and Dundas, with all of whom he seemed happy; and some others. He described his own Cabinet as not brilliant but honest, and said, quite truly I believe, that Pakistan had faith in itself and would get along all right.

I asked him about proportionate pensions for the non S. of S. Services, and he said it had never been mentioned to him while he was over, but that Pakistan was quite ready to do the right thing by their British personnel.

On Monday I had tea with Nehru, also in his room at Claridges. He was less forthcoming than Liaquat, less friendly though quite pleasant, and less buoyant. He looked in fact rather worn, but said he was well, and ascribed it to his practice of standing on his head for a few minutes every morning. Nehru seems to me to be afflicted with something like an inferiority complex when he comes to England, I felt the same when he came over at the end of 1946. I think it requires an applauding crowd or a hostile reception to stimulate Nehru and he gets neither in London. He spoke on a variety of subjects—Kashmir, Hyderabad, inflation, shortage of food, personalities—but none very widely or deeply. He said he thought inflation the main danger to India at present and admitted that they had made a great mistake in taking off controls a year ago (I was told elsewhere that Gandhi was responsible for this), and had had now to reimpose them. It was interesting to find that he was disillusioned about Russia and that the Indian representative, his sister, had no more freedom of movement or action than the other foreign representatives. I asked him about proportionate pensions, and he told me that it had been settled 'according to Mountbatten's formula', but either did not know or would not disclose details.

That evening I saw Noel-Baker at an evening party of Pakistan, and tackled him about the settlement. It was fairly obvious, though he pretended ignorance, that the concession was *not* retrospective and did *not* include any compensation. I warned him that that would not satisfy us. I must look into this.

Summary of 1948

I suppose 1948 has been a better year than 1947 in that we have got somewhere of our own to live. But I dislike a flat and wish we lived out of London. Life is so difficult nowadays, however, that I daresay we should find ourselves worse off in the country. I have too much to do in London to live a long way out, and Q has always hated the idea of the country within 20 or 30 miles of London. So I suppose we shall have to carry on as we are.

I have had an aimless, purposeless, unprofitable year, and have settled down to nothing. I spend most of my time in dealing with matters of little importance, answering a large correspondence, refusing or accepting invitations, and so on. I spend much time on Regimental affairs, but am not sure that the Regiment would not get on just as well by itself. Except for the visit to S. Africa, de Beers has taken up very little of my time. I have succeeded in getting something for the non-Secretary of State Services in India, which has meant quite a bit of work. I, who am no speaker, have spoken far too often in public, over 50 times this year. Even when the material is good, my delivery is I know unattractive and I would be much better not to do it.

I wish I could find some real object, such as a book to write, and I wish I lived by a golf course and could get more opportunity to play.

During 1949 Wavell's activities were much the same as in 1948. He gave a number of lectures and addresses on military and literary topics, made innumerable speeches at dinners and other functions, went to Canada in November to see the Black Watch of Canada, visited the Black Watch in Germany, and played a good deal of golf. He also brought to a successful conclusion his long struggle with H.M.G. to get pensions for British members of the subordinate Indian services with retrospective effect from 15 August 1947. In his Journal he briefly records that he moved a resolution on the subject in the House of Lords on 6 July and 'had a rather unexpected success'. The Times *came out with a leader next day on 'Tardy Justice' and the* Daily Telegraph *commented:*

'Lord Wavell has won many battles, but none so long drawn out as that won in the Upper House yesterday. For 18 months he has fought for pension rights for certain of the lower grades of the Indian services. Time after time he has raised the matter on the floor without decisive result.

'It seemed yesterday as if he was going to carry his campaign into the division lobbies. He had formidable support . . . Lord Addison must have felt relieved that he was not called on to contest the case. He announced the acquiescence of the Government amid cheers.'

Throughout this year Wavell felt increasingly unwell, but on consulting a doctor he was told that there was nothing wrong with him and that he was remarkably healthy; and he stood up to the trips to Germany and Canada, which were rather taxing, better than he expected. In an entry dated 31 December summing up 1949, he complained, 'My digestion has given me a lot of bother and my golf is as bad as ever. I have done no writing worth while.'

The last entry that Wavell made in his Journal was dated 15 March 1950 and briefly described the visit of President Auriol of France whom as Lord Lieutenant of London he had to meet on arrival. In April he fell ill and underwent an operation. He seemed to make a good recovery and was beginning to think of plans for his convalescence, when he had a relapse and died on 24 May. There was a State funeral, and an offer was made of burial in Westminster Abbey near Allenby's grave,[1] but in view of his family's long connection with Winchester special permission was sought, and granted, for him to be buried in the chantry cloister of Winchester College of which as a boy he had been a scholar.

[1] See p. 11 entry for 15 July 1943.

EPILOGUE

THE SOLDIER–VICEROY

The selection of Wavell for appointment as Viceroy was, as he himself realized, a left-handed compliment. His own preference would have been for some high military command that would have given him the chance of redeeming previous defeats by winning victories over the Japanese. He rightly saw himself as the obvious choice for the post of Supreme Commander, South-East Asia. But Churchill did not want to give him this command; nor were the Americans keen that he should get it. Earlier they had held a high opinion of him; but during the 'Trident' conference, in Washington in May 1943, the advice that he gave created a bad impression. He pointed out—quite correctly, as it proved—that it would be impossible to launch from India a successful offensive against the Japanese without far greater resources than were likely to be available in the near future. This appraisal of the situation was unwelcome, and both the Americans and Churchill preferred to ascribe to Wavell undue pessimism than to recognize the unpalatable facts. Not for the first time, nor for the last, he was unjustly held to be a defeatist.

His reputation was, however, still high in military circles in Britain and in the country at large. The memory of his great victories over the Italians that had lightened the gloom of the winter of 1940–1, had not yet faded, and many Englishmen still regarded him as their best general. To keep him on as Commander-in-Chief, India, with mainly administrative duties and to entrust to another Commander the active direction of operations against the Japanese was out of the question. If someone else was to be appointed Supreme Commander, then a way had to be found for the honourable removal of Wavell from the military scene. His appointment as Governor-General of Australia was mooted; but a better means of evading his claims to high military command was afforded by the vacancy in the post of Viceroy. No other suitable candidate was readily available and Wavell's recent experience in India gave him some special qualifications for the post. So in the middle of war Britain's best general was told to put on civilian clothes and become a proconsul.

As Wavell remarked in his Journal, Churchill intended him simply to keep things quiet in India till the war ended. No move or initiative on his part towards solving the political problems was expected or desired. He was to be a stop-gap Viceroy who in the political field would just maintain the *status quo*. But Wavell was hardly the man cast for such a role, and it is somewhat surprising that Churchill did not realize this. It is true that at the time when he chose him to be Viceroy he had not read his biography of Allenby and was unaware of his rather progressive views as disclosed in that book. Their revelation a few weeks later came to Churchill as a great shock and caused him so much annoyance that he almost refused to attend the Cabinet's dinner to Wavell on the eve of his departure for India. But aside from these liberal sentiments of which Churchill was at first ignorant, it is difficult to understand how he could have imagined that such an intelligent and remarkable man as Wavell who, moreover, had been a close witness of Allenby's handling of political problems in Egypt after World War I, would be content passively to contemplate the Indian scene and make no endeavour to find answers to the challenging political problems that it presented.

Wavell of his own volition addressed himself to these problems from the very start; later when the war was over, he could not escape them and they engrossed most of his time and thoughts, robbing him of much of his enjoyment of his administrative work as Viceroy. Though the heavy burden of routine was often wearisome, he found a great deal of the administrative work intensely interesting and would have liked to have been able to give more undivided attention to it. Even as it was, the energy and enterprise that he showed in the discharge of this part of his duties was remarkable. He did more touring of the Provinces and States of India and saw a wider cross-section of the people than any of his predecessors. During his first six months of office he went to all the eleven Provinces of British India (to Bengal three times), spending not less than a week in each of them and visiting villages, agricultural stations, mines, factories, and other establishments besides granting a great many interviews. On one visit to Madras he saw all the Collectors (Heads of District) of the Province—probably an unprecedented performance. This extensive touring was made possible by the increased facilities for air travel, of which full advantage had not previously been taken, but to which Wavell, from his experience as a military commander, was well accustomed.

The Journal gives a good idea of one of his main administrative achievements—his prompt and firm handling of the Bengal famine and the success of his dogged and determined efforts to prevent its repetition. Another considerable achievement, touched on occasionally in the Journal but not particularly emphasized, was the progress made at his instance in the preparation of plans for post-war economic development. This was a subject in which he took a great deal of interest. He favoured projects that would advance the material prosperity of the people rather than grandiose plans for extending education. Full bellies, he said, must come before full minds. Largely as a result of his prompting and prodding, by 1946 the Provincial Governments, many of the Indian States, and the various Ministries and Departments of the Central Government had put together quite an imposing array of development projects and pro-grammes; and these, after some delay owing to the dislocation caused by Partition, were utilized by both India and Pakistan; indeed they became the main substance of India's first Five-Year Plan—small in scale, no doubt, compared with what was to follow, but perhaps the most successful of all the Plans.

The extent of Lord Wavell's personal initiative as Viceroy was not fully appreciated outside the narrow circles of New Delhi. He was popularly thought of as a fine old soldier who, being deficient himself in knowledge and understanding of the work of Viceroy, was content to be steered along by Sir Evan Jenkins (renowned for his ability) and other highly competent civil servants. Wavell himself testifies that he leaned quite heavily on Jenkins during his first two years of office; and he was in the habit of consulting Governors and other highly placed officials. But he was a man of far too outstanding intellect, ability, and character to be guided only by the opinions of others. Having listened to advice, he formed his own judgements and took his own decisions. Throughout his tenure of office he was a vigorous and effective Viceroy who did not let the grass grow under his feet, did not shirk awkward fences, and worked exceedingly hard. He said that he had never worked longer hours in all his life, not even when he was Commander-in-Chief, Middle East. It is remarkable how many letters, notes, and memoranda he undertook to draft himself instead of only touching up the drafts of others. As will be seen from some of the examples printed in this volume, he was a good draftsman and could sum up a situation and make his recommendations with great clarity and logical force—sometimes with too much force and his drafts had to be 'watered down' by his staff. No wonder he complained of Pethick-Lawrence's wordy and woolly drafting and grew impatient with the diffuse and futile rigmaroles that flowed from his pen!

Among the notes that Wavell himself drafted was one for a talk that he gave to Army Commanders at the end of January 1947.[1] This note outlines the political strategy that he had followed since his appointment

[1] Much of this note was later incorporated in his final letter to H.M. the King.

as Viceroy, and provides a useful review of the political side of his work. The first principle, he said, that he established in his mind was the vital necessity to the British Commonwealth (and to the whole world) of a united, stable, and friendly India. The obvious difficulty was that unity and stability seemed only possible if the British retained control; but if they did so, they were most unlikely to secure the friendliness at any rate of the educated part of the population. Moreover he was convinced that at the end of the war it would not be possible to induce the British people to make the effort that would be required to retain control of India against the wishes of a large part of its people.

He examined carefully whether it would be possible to make the more moderate elements in the country, who had supported the British during the war, the basis for a stable and friendly India. Such elements would have included the moderate political leaders who during the war had served in the Executive Council and National Defence Council, the Princes, the landowners, and many of the industrial and commercial magnates who wanted a peaceful transfer of power and a continuation of the British connection. He very soon perceived that this would not be feasible. Few if any people would have the courage boldly to stand out against the leaders of Indian nationalism as represented, antagonistically, by the Congress and the Muslim League, unless they were assured that the British would continue their rule indefinitely; and no such assurance could be given.

He therefore came to two conclusions: first that the attempt must be made to build up a stable and friendly India in conjunction with the existing leaders of Indian nationalism, particularly the Congress leaders, however unpromising this line of action might appear to be; and secondly that a start in this direction must be made well before the end of the war, since an Executive Council dominated by the political leaders would be much easier to handle while the war still provided valid excuse for fairly close control by the Viceroy.

These conclusions, which he conveyed to Churchill in his letter to him of 24 October 1944, were the basis of the Simla Conference in the summer of 1945. The Conference ended in failure and was followed immediately by two rather unexpected events, the collapse of Japanese resistance at least a year earlier than had been foreseen, and the complete victory of the Labour Party in the General Elections in the U.K.

A fresh start had to be made, and as a preliminary, General Elections were held throughout India. The results confirmed that Jinnah had greatly strengthened his position and now had the backing of nearly all the Muslims. Before these results were fully known, Wavell drew up proposals for making a second attempt to form a Congress–League Coalition Government and also for starting constitutional discussions and for tackling decisively the Pakistan issue, if Jinnah pressed it. The decision to send out the Cabinet Mission caused these proposals to be put aside, and there followed the Mission's interminable discussions which in the end left the Congress and the League even more embittered and exasperated than they were at the beginning and achieved no real agreement of any kind. But the Mission had the merit of producing what *appeared* to be a workable constitutional plan that both the Congress and the League could be induced to accept. Wavell considered that real success might have been achieved, if this plan had been put forward firmly as the award of the Power in possession rather than merely suggested as a basis for discussion. But the Mission, reflecting presumably the wishes of the British Government, were unwilling to take the stronger line that he recommended.

Wavell felt that the Mission's plan was Britain's last throw in India and that there must be some agreed strategy in case it failed. It would be fatal, he argued, for the British to hang on to responsibility when they were rapidly losing the power of exercising it, and to run the risk of becoming involved in a civil war or in anti-European troubles and of being eventually forced to scuttle out ignominiously. The strategy he therefore advocated, if the Mission's plan was not accepted by the parties or failed in its working out, was voluntarily to relinquish control in India by stages, handing over in the first instance the southern part of the country, where the communal problem was not acute, and remaining in the northern part for a further limited period only. He put forward this 'Breakdown Plan' while the Mission was still in Delhi; but he could not persuade the British Government to make up their mind about it. Later, in September 1946, when it had become obvious that the Mission's constitutional plan had a very poor chance of success, he pressed his Breakdown Plan on the British Government again, giving now a precise time schedule—withdrawal was to be announced and to begin early in 1947 and was to be completed by 31 March 1948. Again the British Government stalled.

In December 1946 he went to England and personally put before the Government the absolute necessity for a definite policy of some kind. He suggested four possible courses of action (including his own Breakdown Plan), if, as by this time seemed almost certain, no progress could be made with the Mission's plan. After many hours of conference he failed to get the Government to commit themselves to any definite course. It turned out in the end that the only firm decision they had reached was to dismiss him from the office of Viceroy.

It is very clear from this review that throughout his Viceroyalty Wavell had a firm grasp of the political situation and well-conceived, logical plans for dealing with it. But unfortunately he never had a free hand. He was continually obstructed and thwarted, first by Churchill's predominantly Tory Government and then by the Labour Government of Mr. Attlee. Consequently he was rarely able to take at the appropriate time the steps that he saw to be required. It is remarkable that despite all the hindrances put in his way by successive British Governments and their failure to support him at critical moments he came as near as he did to achieving the almost impossible task of bringing Independence to India in a manner satisfactory to all parties. Without these hindrances he might well have been successful.

The founders of British power in India, Clive, Warren Hastings, and Wellesley, would never have achieved what they did if in those days the Home Authorities had been able to exercise the same close control over them as they could over Wavell in the twentieth century. They would have liked to exercise such control, but the slowness of communications between India and England two hundred years ago precluded them from doing so and enabled, and at times compelled, the men on the spot to act on their own responsibility as they thought best. The Directors and the Board of Control might later complain that they had disregarded instructions, and might criticize, censure, and disgrace them; Warren Hastings was impeached; Wellesley was recalled. But what they had done could not be undone.

In our own day the British Government were all too slow to realize that in carrying out the difficult and delicate task of relinquishing power in India they must trust the man on the spot, give him ample authority and, when necessary, support, and if they did not trust his judgement, must replace him. Attlee's Government did not fully trust Wavell and did not fully support him; and when at last, belatedly, they decided to replace him, all chance of transferring power in India without disaster had vanished. His successor wisely insisted that more ample authority should be granted to him.

This disharmony between Wavell and two successive Governments in the U.K. was frustrating for him personally and calamitous for India. It made partition with all its disasters inevitable. What were the reasons for this disharmony?

Wavell's differences with Churchill's Government are easily comprehensible. They were not his fault. Promises had been made to India of

Independence, but Churchill's Government as a whole did not sincerely intend to try to fulfil them and habitually disregarded India's needs and aspirations, blocking even small concessions to Indian sentiment that Wavell proposed. He soon discovered that the Cabinet was not 'honest in its expressed desire to make progress'. The outgoing Viceroy, Lord Linlithgow, also observed that a chief factor in the problem of Indian political progress was 'the dishonesty of the British'. These judgements of two Viceroys go a long way to justify the deep Indian suspicion of British intentions. Amery, who was at any rate honest in his intentions, put the position very plainly in a letter to Wavell of August 1944.

You and I both genuinely mean to implement the Government's pledges, if they can be implemented, and at any rate to make quite clear that we are sincerely doing our best to promote a solution. . . . The Prime Minister passionately hopes that any solution involving the fulfilment of our pledges can still somehow or other be prevented, and with that in view naturally makes difficulties at every stage. In between come the Cabinet, most of whom agree with us in their hearts, and would do so even more if it became a question of stating a policy in public. But when in the Cabinet room a particular question crops up, they are overborne by the Prime Minister's vehemence and are glad to find an escape from open disagreement with him by accepting arguments against a particular matter brought up, whether it be an Indian Finance Member, Bajpai's status, or the terms of an answer to Gandhi. We have just to be patient and carry on as best we can.

Wavell was both patient and persistent, and ultimately extracted from Churchill's Government permission to make a political move; but only after eight months' delay, with the result that when the move, i.e. the Simla Conference, failed, there was no time for him to try again before the war came to an end.

In retrospect it seems doubtful whether in his dealings with Churchill's Government Wavell could have done much better than he did; but he probably made a mistake in raising with the Cabinet at the very beginning, before he had even got out to India, the question of a political move. He himself wanted to make such a move, not, indeed, immediately, but well before the war ended. Would this be acceptable to his masters, the British Government? His instinct as a soldier was to put the question and seek a directive; and it was natural that his Private Secretary, Sir Evan Jenkins, trained as a civil servant, should encourage him to do so. But politically it was unwise, and Amery, the politician, should have headed him off it. He should have told him that the Cabinet did not want to be bothered with India and would only be irked by any suggestion of a political move; and that he should first get himself well into the saddle as Viceroy and then, after six to nine months, come forward with his proposals which he, Amery, would fully support and which the Cabinet, at that stage, would find it difficult to reject.

This sort of advice was given by Mr. R. A. (Lord) Butler. In an interesting talk with Sir Evan Jenkins at the Cabinet's Farewell Dinner to Lord Wavell, he expressed the view that Wavell was wrong in trying to get guidance from the Cabinet; that in politics there can be no long-term planning or 'grand strategy'; that the political art is necessarily empirical and in a sense dishonest; and that Wavell's right course was to go to India without settled ideas, in the knowledge that the Cabinet would in fact try to act on any recommendation he might make.[1] This was sound advice, but it came too late. The matter had already gone to Cabinet and aroused Churchill's wrath.

The ill effects of this mistake were at most marginal. It may have enhanced Churchill's prejudice against Wavell and against India and contributed slightly to his reluctance eighteen months later to agree to the proposals for the Simla Conference; but it did not appreciably influence the course of events.

Wavell's differences with Attlee's Labour Government were more complex, more damaging in their effects, and require more detailed analysis. Attlee, while in Churchill's Cabinet, had never been very helpful to Wavell over India and, as records now reveal, had tended to be critical of him, bewailing the fact that he was not a politician. Wavell was unaware of this criticism and readily overlooked Attlee's previous failure to give him firm support. He welcomed the more sympathetic attitude towards India's problems that, with the advent of the Labour Government, immediately became apparent in Whitehall, and his relations with the new Cabinet Ministers were at first quite happy. But *ab initio* the Labour Government, particularly their chief India expert, Sir Stafford Cripps, were far too deeply committed to the Congress point of view and far too prone to give ear to Congress propaganda. This was the real source of the disharmony that developed. All along Cripps was in contact with Nehru either directly or indirectly through Congress agents and propagandists in the U.K., notably Krishna Menon, whose information and advice Cripps seemed in course of time to prefer to that of Wavell himself. This excessive readiness to rely on what was said by Congress became evident as early as Wavell's visit to England in August–September 1945. The

[1] From a note recorded by Sir Evan Jenkins at the time.

Labour Government, under Cripps's guidance, wanted to renew and enforce the Cripps offer of 1942, having been informed that this would be acceptable to Congress. They overlooked the fact that it would be totally unacceptable to the Muslim League.

During the Cabinet Mission this bias in favour of Congress was ill concealed. The results were unfortunate. By the time the Mission left, Jinnah and the League, aware that Congress were now, by a strange paradox, the favourites of the British Government, had become suspicious and resentful; while some of the Congress leaders, feeling that they had Cripps and the British Government in their pocket and that Wavell was the one obstacle to their having everything their own way, started a subtle, insidious propaganda, readily swallowed by Cripps, that Wavell was in the hands of I.C.S., and so, by implication, of anti-Congress, advisers. This led to Attlee's not very tactful suggestion that Wavell needed Sir Maurice Gwyer as a political adviser. Sir Maurice, who had the highest opinion of Wavell, ridiculed the suggestion; and it seems that Cripps and Attlee had forgotten that among Wavell's close advisers was V. P. Menon, the Reforms Commissioner, a Hindu official who had risen from the ranks and who, though a most loyal and admirable civil servant, could not be accused of being 'anti-Congress'.

Wavell consistently tried to remain impartial and to hold the balance evenly between the Congress and the League. He wanted to deal fairly, but firmly and decisively, with both parties. He was at one with Congress in desiring that power should be transferred to a *united* India. He never favoured Pakistan, and was as anxious as Congress and the British Government to avoid the partition of the country. When he went to England in December 1946, partition was one of the four possible courses that he proposed to the British Government; but he did not recommend it. Only when he came home for good at the end of March 1947 did he say that if a final effort to bring the parties together failed, arrangements should be put in hand for partition.

But Pakistan was, in his judgement, an issue that had to be faced. The demand for it was not just bluff, which could easily be called, as Nehru and many of the other Congress leaders liked to imagine. As late as January 1946 Nehru was writing to Cripps that if the British Government made it clear that it would in no way encourage Pakistan, then agitation for it would rapidly collapse, and that the Muslim League leadership were incapable of any form of direct action or of instigating any real trouble, though there might be petty riots in some cities.[1] This was a complete

[1] Letter from Nehru to Cripps dated 27 January 1946.

misreading of the situation, which Wavell could not accept. But he did intend to grasp the Pakistan nettle firmly, and he proposed to do so by telling Jinnah that if he persisted in the demand for Pakistan, all he could get would be a 'truncated' Pakistan with only half of Bengal and half of the Punjab. The Cabinet Mission agreed to take this line, whereupon, as Wavell had hoped, Jinnah opted for the loose Indian Union adumbrated in the Mission's Plan.

It was, however, essential to be ready also to take a firm line with Congress, and over this Wavell was completely let down by the British Government. His proposal for dealing with Congress's intransigence was his Breakdown Plan. It served two purposes; since it was likely to result in the division of India, it was a lever against Congress, if they withheld acceptance, or genuine acceptance, of the Mission plan or otherwise threatened trouble; and it prepared the way for an orderly withdrawal of British control. The existence of this Breakdown Plan would enable a firm line to be taken with Congress, since in the event of a breach with them there would be a reasonable alternative on which to fall back. Without its acceptance in principle there could only be weakness and indecision. Wavell wanted to be able to speak to the Congress leaders, if they were obdurate, in the following terms:

We have done our best to bring about a settlement and have given you what we think to be in the circumstances the best and fairest constitutional plan. Since you refuse genuinely to accept it, we propose now to begin withdrawal of our control from India in accordance with a planned programme of our own and with due regard for our own interests. We shall first relinquish control in the south of India; we shall retain control in the northern Provinces for a limited period, and so long as we do so, we shall continue to try to secure agreement for a united India; but we shall not allow failure to reach agreement or anything else to interfere with our programme for withdrawal from the whole of India within a short period of time.

If a firm attitude like this had been taken, it is probable that the Congress leaders would have been more reasonable and that all the months of haggling, amid growing ill will, over the interpretation of the Mission's plan would have been avoided. But the British Government's excessive deference towards Congress prevented them taking Wavell's advice and led them into fatal weakness and procrastination—besides antagonizing the League. They were afraid of anything being said or done that might offend Congress. When Wavell wanted to point out to Gandhi that the interpretation he sought to put on the Mission's plan was inadmissible, he

was asked by Pethick-Lawrence not to press the point. When later he
tried to get the British Government to state categorically that the Congress's interpretation of the Mission's plan was wrong and that the work
of the Constituent Assembly could not go forward until they accepted the
correct interpretation, he was rebuffed. The British Government would
not risk a break with Congress, although this cowardice reduced them to
virtual impotence and made them ridiculous in the eyes of the League; for
if the British Government would not stick up for their own interpretation
of their own plan, what would they stick up for?

In retrospect, it seems fairly clear that the bold, forthright, masculine
approach that Wavell wished to adopt towards both parties would have
paid greater dividends than the coaxing and wheedling of Congress and,
at times, dishonest cringing that Cripps favoured; and that if the British
Government had given Wavell a freer hand and stood four-square behind
him, there would have been a better chance of shepherding both the Congress and the League into a Constituent Assembly. Whether they would
ever have produced an agreed and workable Constitution is another matter;
but at least a fully representative sovereign body would have been brought
into existence to which the British could have fairly handed over control.

The difference of approach of Wavell and the British Government
became apparent at the time of the Cabinet Mission. It gave rise to some
stormy scenes, and near the end Wavell contemplated resignation. The
difference continued after the Mission had gone home. The Government
feared that Wavell might precipitate a breach with Congress; and they
were irked by his pressure on them to be honest about the Mission's plan
and by his growing insistence on his own Breakdown Plan. Wavell felt
frustrated by the Government's vacillation and by their unwillingness to
follow the course that he advised or to put forward any alternative.
Meanwhile, it seems,[1] Congress emissaries in England fed Cabinet
Ministers with Congress propaganda which was not always favourable to
Wavell. Even after Jinnah's call for Direct Action and the Calcutta
killings, Nehru still nursed the illusion that the Muslim League were on
the run and could cause no serious trouble—though in fact the country
was heading for civil war. He was therefore annoyed with Wavell for
boosting their morale by bringing them into the Interim Government,
especially without any cast-iron guarantee that they would enter the
Constituent Assembly. Their entry, however, depended on Nehru and
the British Government rather than on Wavell, and neither Nehru nor

---

[1] See, for instance, Durga Das, *From Curzon to Nehru and After* (London, 1969), p. 234,
and Sudhir Ghosh, *Gandhi's Emissary* (London, 1967), pp. 20–2 and 46–8.

the British Government would make their entry possible, the former by accepting without qualification the Mission's plan, the latter by confirming unambiguously the League's interpretation of it.

Matters came to a head in December 1946 during Wavell's visit to London. The British Government were at last induced to make an unambiguous statement about the Mission's plan; and his own Breakdown Plan now became the main bone of contention. The dogged, uncompromising manner in which he demanded that it should be accepted and a date announced for the ending of British rule in India put the British Government in a quandary. They shrank from facing Parliament with a proposal to leave India by a fixed date without any assurance of the peaceful transfer of power to an established authority; and some Ministers, e.g. Bevin and Alexander, began to feel a John Bull-ish unwillingness to let the Indian empire slip from their grasp. But the Government could put forward no alternative to Wavell's proposals, and they did not have the courage to tell him that they would look for another Viceroy who might think up something better. After many days of discussion the India Committee of Cabinet seemed at last more or less to agree to the Breakdown Plan and to the fixing of 31 March 1948 as the date for final British withdrawal; and Attlee assured Wavell that he had got all that he wanted. But after he had returned to India, they went back on their decisions.

What followed was a striking *reductio ad absurdum* of His Majesty's Government. They had rejected Wavell's demand for the fixing of a date and had decided to dismiss him from the post of Viceroy, only to find that his proposed successor made exactly the same demand and would not agree to take office unless it was granted. So Attlee and his Government capitulated, and soon were quite happy to take credit for a decision that had in fact been forced upon them.

Some of those who were close to these events have felt uncertain whether it was conflicts of policy or conflicts of personality that were mainly responsible for Wavell's dismissal. It seems clear that both played a considerable part. Though there was no disagreement over the basic objective of policy, namely to transfer power, if possible, to a united India, there were, as has been shown, grave divergences over the methods to be adopted in handling Congress and over the steps to be taken to liquidate British rule, if no agreement between Congress and the League could be reached. These divergences were aggravated by certain aspects of Wavell's personality. He was too forthright, blunt, and uncompromising to deal successfully with British politicians. He disliked and despised their 'polite prolixities' and had no aptitude for employing them himself.

His mind may have been, as he said, slow-moving—with the result that he was better on paper than in debate or at the conference table—but it was clear and powerful and went straight to the heart of a matter. He was impatient of the quibbles, petty objections, and sometimes dishonest evasions of lawyers and politicians; and both in correspondence and in debate was apt to treat them brusquely. He himself in his Journal wonders whether during the Cabinet Mission he had not on occasion been too rough with Cripps and Pethick-Lawrence; and he told Lord Listowel that he thought he had been too rude and uncompromising in his discussions with Cabinet Ministers in December 1946, and had annoyed them. Listowel confirmed that this was so. Cabinet Ministers found him disconcerting. Sometimes at meetings, having discharged a heavy broadside, he would relapse into grim silence, unwilling or unable to reply to the sniping of objectors on points of detail. If someone made a fatuous suggestion, instead of flattering the speaker by saying that it was a wonderful idea, though it might perhaps on examination be found to present certain difficulties, he would ignore it altogether and remain silent. The Ministers complained that he was too inflexible, whereas he would have considered that he was merely being straight with them. His roughness with them certainly contributed to his removal from the scene, though Listowel may well have been right in saying that nothing else would have made them do anything definite.

To all this was added the personal antipathy that developed between Wavell and Cripps. Having both been at school at Winchester, they should have imbibed similar traditions; but there was a natural disharmony between the straightforward soldier and the rather slippery lawyer and politician; and by the end of the long, testing Cabinet Mission negotiations their relations were far from cordial. Wavell distrusted Cripps. In his Journal he conceded that Cripps had done nothing dishonourable by his own standards; but they were the standards of a politician, not Wavell's standards. It is probable that if the report that Cripps was going to take Pethick-Lawrence's place as Secretary of State had proved true, Wavell would have tendered his resignation; and Cripps would have been glad to see him go. When, towards the close of the Cabinet Mission, he was known to be thinking of resignation, Cripps was not at all sorry and already had Lord Mountbatten in mind as his possible successor.[1] In the ensuing months, as the situation in India deteriorated and Wavell kept hammering on his Breakdown Plan, Cripps, who disliked it, must have

[1] He mentioned this possibility in a conversation with Major Short and the present editor in New Delhi at the end of June 1946.

felt more and more convinced that if only Wavell could be displaced, Mountbatten with his charm and nimble wit would be able to find some more acceptable solution.

Wavell more than once told Pethick-Lawrence that if he and the Cabinet distrusted his judgement and were disinclined to accept his advice, they should replace him. They did not take him up on this at the time. At the beginning of August 1946, in the course of a letter to Attlee, he pointedly remarked that if they wished to have a politician rather than a soldier as Viceroy and to end his wartime appointment, he would of course accept their decision without question. Attlee in replying made no reference at all to this matter, so Wavell wrote to him again, saying that he assumed from his silence that they wished him to continue. Attlee did not reply.

This was the position when Wavell was summoned home in December. Attlee's obvious disinclination to state positively that he wished him to remain at his post suggests that, prompted perhaps by Cripps, he was already thinking of making a change; and it seems clear that during the wearisome meetings in London in December, when Wavell insisted uncompromisingly on his Breakdown Plan, Attlee, Cripps, and other leading members of the Cabinet became as much fed up with him as he was with them, and they concluded, not perhaps altogether incorrectly, that he was tired and stale and that a fresh eye and mind was needed for the intractable problems of India. He had borne very heavy burdens for too long and met with little but defeat and disappointment. As he wrote in his Journal, 'Continual hard work, and almost continual failure. No rest, no success. . . . This is inevitably depressing.'

In all the circumstances, especially the lack of confidence and the frayed relations that had come to exist between him and the Cabinet, the decision to replace him was not wrong. He himself, though he was greatly disappointed at not being allowed to complete his task, would not have denied this; a younger man and a fresher mind, he said, were needed. It was the manner of his dismissal that really hurt him. It came to him as a shock to discover that Attlee had approached Mountbatten to take over the Viceroyalty on 18 December 1946 while he was still in England, yet had not had the courage or courtesy to say anything about it to him, and that the correspondence that thereafter for over six weeks Attlee and Pethick-Lawrence had kept up with him was entirely insincere. The only comment in the Journal on the abrupt termination of his services was 'not very courteously done', but this terse understatement concealed intense indignation at the way in which he had been treated.

The dismissal of a great public servant like Lord Wavell was a difficult operation but, having decided that it was necessary, Attlee's Government should have gone out of their way to make his departure as easy for him as possible. Instead of arranging everything behind his back and then suddenly confronting him with dismissal at short notice, they should have conveyed to him at an early stage what they had in mind and endeavoured in consultation with him to ease him out of office with the minimum injury to his feelings and the maximum of honour and glory and public expressions of gratitude for his great services. He would certainly have smoothed their path by tendering his resignation. But, apart from the conferment on him of an Earldom and a perfunctory reference to his having discharged the office of Viceroy with a high sense of duty, the Labour Government left all these things undone; and some years later Attlee unjustly labelled him an advocate of scuttle and a defeatist. A truer description of him would be that given by Horace of Ulysses, 'adversis rerum immersabilis undis'.[1]

By the canons of behaviour that ordinarily govern human relations the Attlee Government's treatment of Wavell was lamentable. But politicians are a race apart and a law unto themselves; as he wrote in his Journal, politics change the ethical codes of men who would normally regard themselves as men of honesty and principle. The final episode of the leak from the P.S.V.'s office, of which Cripps became aware but which he did not disclose to him, was only a straw, but it was the last one. After this, well might he exclaim, 'I am glad I have finished with politics.'

Cripps is said to have remarked: 'The trouble about Wavell is that he is no politician'—a remark that Wavell regarded as rather a good testimonial for honesty. The criticism reflected a belief among British Ministers that as they found him difficult to understand and to get on with, the same must be true of Indian politicians. This judgement, based on their own experience, was not entirely correct. His lack of the arts and graces required for charming British politicians into harmony with his views and his avoidance of all tricks of ambiguity and evasion went along with qualities of character that were of more importance in his dealings with Indian than with British politicians. As Viceroy, he had to be the impartial arbiter between the competing claims of the Congress, the Muslim League, the Untouchables, the Princes, and other sections of Indian society. He was not an equal negotiating with colleagues but an outside authority standing above them; and in this role his absolute integrity was an

---

[1] 'Never overwhelmed by the tides of misfortune.' Long after Wavell's death Sir Evan Jenkins pointed out that this quotation fitted him most aptly.

invaluable asset. They knew for certain that his Yea was Yea and his Nay was Nay and that he would not try to mislead them with half-truths and false promises. Some of the Congress leaders would have liked him to be more pliant to their wishes, but they all felt respect and some of them also affection for him. There was by no means such a lack of understanding and intimacy between him and Indian political leaders as some members of Attlee's Government imagined.

It is, however, true that it would have been an advantage if his integrity had been combined with more of the superabundant charm of his successor. His reticence, taciturnity, and occasional grimness of manner were certainly handicaps. He could talk freely with those who were congenial to him, but was apt to remain silent with others. The European members of the Assembly, who used to have interviews with the Viceroy from time to time, found that whereas Linlithgow would have long chats with them and give them a survey of the war, Wavell, having listened to what they had to say, replied, 'I see', and the interview ended without any talk or discussion. The Journal entry for 21 February 1947 reveals his willingness to talk with some, but not with others. He never lingered, he wrote, over interviews with rather dull personalities like Bhabha and Chundrigar, whereas interviews with Rajagopalachari, Azad, Nehru, or Liaquat might develop into general talk on affairs, ethics, or literature.

Nevertheless Wavell's relations with most of the leading Congress and League politicians were friendly. He disliked Jinnah, but got on tolerably well with him, completely ignoring his deliberate bad manners. He also disliked Gandhi and wholly distrusted him; but there was no unpleasantness between them till the interview on 27 August 1946 when Gandhi is alleged to have thumped the table and afterwards accused Wavell of being minatory. Wavell once wrote that he put the composition of Gandhi's character as 70 per cent extremely astute politician, 15 per cent saint, and 15 per cent charlatan. Most people would consider that Gandhi had more of the saint in him than Wavell allowed and that he was not 'malevolent' or 'malignant', as Wavell often described him. His actions were sometimes unpredictable and productive of calamitous consequences, but they were not prompted by malevolence. In judging, or perhaps one should say misjudging, Gandhi, Wavell was strongly influenced by his recollection that in 1942, when he as Commander-in-Chief was trying to secure India against Japanese invasion, Gandhi had let loose the 'Quit India' rebellion which for some weeks paralysed communications with the Eastern Front. Wavell conceded later that Gandhi had not deliberately intended this as a stab in the back, but this is what in effect it was. Wavell was never able to rid his mind of the memory of it and it coloured his judgement. Gandhi's capacity for mischief, unintended though it might be, was well illustrated towards the close of the Cabinet Mission. If it had not been for his last-minute intervention, the Congress would have accepted the Mission's proposals for an Interim Government and, with a Congress–League Coalition Government installed in office at the beginning of July, the communal outbreaks of the next few months would never have occurred. Even Cripps and Pethick-Lawrence by the time they left India had begun to share some of Wavell's mistrust of Gandhi.

Of the other Indian political leaders, Wavell had a high opinion of Liaquat and a considerable liking for him which was reciprocated. He also liked Nehru, though he had differences with him and sometimes found him lacking in judgement. Nehru undoubtedly preferred Mountbatten to Wavell, but he stated publicly that he had a high regard for the latter and was in many ways sorry to part with him. It was Nehru, too, who made the consoling remark to him that some failures were greater than successes. Wavell and Vallabhbhai Patel respected each other and in matters of business got on well together, as Patel was eminently practical and a realist.

A number of the lesser Congress figures had warm feelings of regard for Wavell, but the two who best appreciated his services to India and his efforts to hold the scales evenly between the Congress and the League were Maulana Abul Kalam Azad and Rajagopalachari. They were better judges of his fairness than the communally minded Patel, the unbalanced Nehru, or the far from impartial British Labour Government. Rajagopalachari in a charming farewell letter ending 'Yours affectionately', paid a high tribute to the justice, firmness, patience, and ability with which he had worked for an honourable settlement and said that it was a misfortune to all of them that he was leaving. Azad wrote him a long letter of appreciation, one sentence from which has been quoted earlier. He said that he had been deeply impressed by Lord Wavell's sincerity right from the time of the Simla Conference, and that he felt his departure as the loss of a personal friend who had done immense service to India.

Wavell's mention in his Journal that his official interviews with Azad, Nehru, and others sometimes developed into talks on ethics and literature is a reminder that he was a very well-read man with a wide knowledge of history and literature and a special interest in poetry, long passages of which he knew by heart. Despite his notorious silences and occasionally rather grim manner, he was normally of a gay and cheerful disposition, and in congenial company could be talkative and amusing. He had a fund of good stories and was an excellent raconteur. He liked rhymes and jingles and enjoyed writing parodies and doggerel and inventing light-hearted mnemonics. To remind himself of the order of precedence of the five biggest Princely States in India, he coined 'Hot Kippers Make Good Breakfast' (Hyderabad, Kashmir, Mysore, Gwalior, Baroda), and for the Mogul Emperors, 'Best Horses And Jockeys Seen Ascot' (Babar, Huma-yun, Akbar, Jahangir, Shah Jahan, Aurangzeb). An example of his parody is given in the Journal at the close of the Cabinet Mission, written after twelve gruelling weeks of heat and strain.

This was the lighter side of a remarkable man who, whatever future verdicts history may pass on him as Military Commander and as Viceroy, must always be ranked as a leading and heroic figure on the British side in the period of World War II. In all the high posts that he filled he in-variably had to battle against heavy odds with quite inadequate resources and without steady, firm support from the British Government. Yet he remained undaunted, and in both military and civil capacities displayed in a high degree, boldness, energy, and enterprise and—in adversity—courage, patience, and resolution. During his time as Viceroy it was he, not the British Government, who supplied the driving power behind successive efforts to break the deadlock between the Congress and the League; and it was he who saved India from a repetition of the Bengal famine.

Wavell was the only soldier to hold the office of Viceroy after the Crown took over control of India from the East India Company in 1858; and he was also one of the few Viceroys to be drawn not from the aristocracy, but from an upper-middle-class family—the class of society that was the mainstay of the British Raj and was largely responsible for its character. He typified the best qualities of this class and the best qualities of the Raj. First and foremost was his deep sense of public duty and public service; next his straightforwardness and complete integrity; and next his energy and capacity for hard work. But he also possessed some rarer qualities to which the younger of Nehru's two sisters, Krishna Nehru Hutheesing, has drawn attention. He was a good Viceroy, she has written,[1] and besides being conscientious was 'understanding and humane'. In his possession of these qualities Lord Wavell was in the tradition of the greatest line of British administrators in India, Warren Hastings, Munro, Malcolm, Sleeman, and Henry Lawrence, all of whom respected the people over whom they ruled, sympathized with their feelings, and tried to understand them.

[1] *We Nehrus*, p. 186 (I.B.H. Publishing Co., Bombay).

If Wavell had had a little luck or even if he had been allowed to finish his task, he would have been acclaimed a great Viceroy, not merely a good one. As it is, in the long roll of Viceroys and Governors-General his name will stand high, and though he may not be ranked with the greatest of them, Wellesley, Dalhousie, and Curzon, from each of whom he differed widely in character and achievement, he will be held in honour by Indians and Pakistanis no less than by his own countrymen.

Wavell was very fond of some words of Sir Walter Scott: 'Without courage there cannot be truth; and without truth there can be no other virtue.' Those who knew him best would say that these words were the motto of his life and believe that history will adjudge him a great and a good man—'the greatest and noblest man that it has been my fortune to encounter', one of them has written. The reader of this Journal will be able to form his own estimate.

APPENDICES

APPENDIX I

Lord Wavell's Note to the Private Secretary to the Viceroy Designate, 20 August 1943

I have been turning over in my mind how I should approach this question of finding a solution of the Indian problem if I discarded all normal methods and trusted entirely to my own common sense (such as it is) and my previous experience and training. As a result I have evolved the following scenario, on which I invite your opinion. It will probably appear to you fantastical, impossible or inadvisable; you will certainly consider it unorthodox, as it is.

I collect by summons, invitation or other means, with the greatest possible secrecy the following ten individuals to the Viceroy's House:

Gandhi
Nehru
Jinnah
Ambedkar
Rajagopalachariar
*Savarkar (Mahasabha)
Jam Sahib
Mudaliar
Zafrullah Khan
*Representative of big business (? Birla or head of Tatas)
(* I am a little doubtful about these two.)

I proceed to address them somewhat as follows:
I have collected you here, gentlemen, to debate the problem of India's future and to advise me on the solution of the present deadlock. I regard you as a representative selection of India's political and older leaders as near as I can assemble within the compass of a body small enough to deal with really important questions, i.e. a body approximately the size of the British War Cabinet or the present Executive Council. It is my experience that any body larger than this is too unwieldy to arrive at a decision. I believe that a vital decision in matters of government—and I am asking you to make a vital decision for India —can be arrived at only by a few selected men of wisdom and good will, not by counting votes. Your selection is purely my personal one, as is the idea of this conference. I am the man primarily responsible in this country for its government at present and for finding a means of improving that government.

I will outline to you briefly the reasons that have guided me in summoning this conference and in my choice of you to form it.

I have no axe to grind, I have no political career to make, I have little know-ledge of politics, I am here to do my duty to His Majesty the King Emperor who has honoured me by this appointment, to carry out the pledges of His Majesty's Government of self-government for India, and to do my best for the Indian people, for whose welfare Great Britain has been responsible for nearly two hundred years. I have been trained in a profession where it is necessary to take some action in a crisis, and where one has to take big risks. I have perhaps more experience of practical government in crises than most soldiers, in Egypt and Palestine and now here. I am quite clear that any government that is prepared to govern, whether it is autocracy, democracy or any other, is better for a country than no government or than a government too weak to carry out its decisions. We have a government in India at present that is prepared to govern and able to do so and until some better government, that is equally prepared and able to govern, can be formed, I do not propose to be any party to abro-gating that government, which I consider to be dealing with India's needs in a workmanlike and efficient manner in the present difficult conditions.

I can give you a definite pledge that His Majesty's Government is prepared to give self-government to India as early as possible, and that this is the earnest wish of the people of Great Britain and of the British Empire. I may also add that I have, for some reason, a certain prestige in Great Britain and the confi-dence of a large proportion of the people and that any solution of the Indian problem which I recommend will receive earnest consideration.

There are only two qualifications to His Majesty's Government's offer of self-government, and they are, I admit, most important ones. The successful ending of the war, in which we have made such sacrifices and overcome such odds, with much aid from India, must be an overriding consideration; and secondly, we must be satisfied that we are handing over India to a government that can govern and enforce its decisions to the same extent as the present government. The whole British people, and indeed the opinion of the United Nations, are behind these reservations. We do not intend simply to abrogate government and leave India to chaos; and we do intend to defeat the Japanese menace as completely as we are now doing the German.

I will now give you brief reasons for your selection by me and what I hope you will do. The present deadlock in Indian politics is caused by the inability of Indian leaders to reach an agreed solution (though there are a number of inde-pendent solutions by various parties) and by their rejection of any solution proposed by His Majesty's Government, while at the same time there is a demand that the British Government should take the initiative to find a solution. This conference represents my personal initiative to help Indian leaders to find a solution. As I have said, I do not believe in any large body taking a decision but I do hope that you, whom I have chosen as the best representatives of Indian opinion, may at least be able to offer me profitable advice on the line of action I should take during my Viceroyalty.

Mr. Gandhi, you command the trust and respect of the largest numbers in India, and have been the protagonist in India's search for self-government; you are the acknowledged, if not the official, leader of the largest political party. I have given you your ablest lieutenant *Pandit Jawaharlal Nehru* to assist you in representing Congress.

Mr. Jinnah, you are the leader of the next largest party and represent the Moslems of India.

Dr. Ambedkar and *Mr. Savarkar*, you have both large followings whose interest must be considered in any settlement.

Mr. Rajagopalachariar, you may have no large political following, but you have great political experience and you represent, in my mind, the views of a large body of enlightened Indian opinion. I feel I should like your advice.

Your Highness the Jam Sahib, I have invited you to hold a watching brief on behalf of the Indian States. I do not expect that you can commit them in any way, but in any solution of the Indian problem their interests must obviously have full consideration.

I should like you also, as an old soldier, to represent, as necessary, Indian military opinion and the interests of the Indian Army.

Sir R. Mudaliar as a Member of the present government may be said to voice official opinion, but I have added him mainly because of his recent experience in the War Cabinet in Great Britain, his knowledge of present British political leaders and opinion, and his own wisdom and judgment.

I have asked *Sir Zafrullah Khan* because in a body like this I think a legal mind and judicial outlook has value, also Sir Zafrullah Khan has, like Sir R. Mudaliar, great experience and judgment.

My final selection (*? Birla*) represents Indian business. India's future and the welfare of her rapidly growing population in this bustling go-ahead world must depend greatly on her industrial development, and I think it is right that you should have someone who can speak for Indian business.

There are certain most important bodies who are not represented, e.g. the Sikhs, the Anglo-Indians and the British in India. I believe that to increase your numbers would make a solution more difficult, and that I can trust you to remember absent friends.

I leave you to devise your own procedure and methods of debating the problem of India's future and advising me on it. Any assistance I or my staff can give you is at your service. We will provide any Secretariat, books of reference or so forth, and I am always available if you wish to question me or refer to me. I must, however, make it a condition that I hold you 'in purdah' for the period of your deliberations. I feel that the success of my experiment will be impossible if the influence of outside opinion, political followers and the Press is introduced. I hope you will consent to accept my conditions of this conference, i.e. no contact with outside opinion until you have reached a decision, and that you will meanwhile enjoy the hospitality of my house.

I hope you will not merely put forward political slogans such as 'Quit India', 'Immediate declaration of Pakistan', 'Release at once of all political prisoners'. These are incidental to your recommendations. As I have said, we are ready to hand over India to self-government as soon as practicable; if Pakistan, or some similar device, is essential for the welfare of India and can be made a practical solution, you will tell me so; I can assure you that I have no desire to hold anyone in prison for a day longer than is necessary for the security of the State.

The Cripps' proposals still hold good and may serve as the basis of your discussions. I have had prepared for you, should you desire them, notes on other systems of government, such as the Swiss Federal System, the American System and others, which may possibly be appropriate to India's problems.

I do not expect from you, nor is it possible for you to produce, a detailed solution or Constitution for India. What I want is a practical programme to give India self-government as soon as possible after the conclusion of hostilities, and to secure in the meantime the best government to carry the war to a successful conclusion, to deal with the many and urgent day-to-day problems of India, and to prepare for self-government after the war. If you fail to produce for me any practical programme, I shall carry on with the present methods and present government, which I may remind you is mainly Indian, and do our best for the progress of India in the many matters in which progress is possible without a political solution.

Gentlemen, the step I have taken in summoning you here is the best I can devise to help India after much thought. A heavy responsibility lies on you and on me for the future welfare, security and happiness of India, which is the end at which we are all aiming. May I in conclusion remind you that no political progress has ever been made without the spirit of compromise.

Above is of course only a very crude outline of what is in my mind. Is any such procedure a possibility? I have always been in military matters an upholder of unorthodox methods when orthodox methods have failed, as I think they have in India. Before I go any further, or submit my ideas to the Secretary of State or anyone, I should like your comments.

I naturally should not propose to take such action immediately on arrival in India, but to have it in mind after I had taken soundings.

20th August, 1943

APPENDIX II

Statement by the Cabinet Delegation and His Excellency the Viceroy

1. On March 15th last just before the despatch of the Cabinet Delegation to India Mr. Attlee, the British Prime Minister, used these words:

'My colleagues are going to India with the intention of using their utmost endeavours to help her to attain her freedom as speedily and fully as possible. What form of Government is to replace the present regime is for India to decide; but our desire is to help her to set up forthwith the machinery for making that decision.'

★ ★ ★ ★ ★ ★ ★ ★ ★ ★ ★ ★ ★

'I hope that India and her people may elect to remain within the British Commonwealth. I am certain that they will find great advantages in doing so.'

★ ★ ★ ★ ★ ★ ★ ★ ★ ★ ★ ★ ★

'But if she does so elect, it must be by her own free will. The British Commonwealth and Empire is not bound together by chains of external compulsion. It is a free association of free peoples. If, on the other hand, she elects for independence, in our view she has a right to do so. It will be for us to help to make the transition as smooth and easy as possible.'

2. Charged in these historic words we—the Cabinet Ministers and the Viceroy—have done our utmost to assist the two main political parties to reach agreement upon the fundamental issue of the unity or division of India. After prolonged discussions in New Delhi we succeeded in bringing the Congress and the Muslim League together in Conference at Simla. There was a full exchange of views and both parties were prepared to make considerable concessions in order to try and reach a settlement but it ultimately proved impossible to close the remainder of the gap between the parties and so no agreement could be concluded. Since no agreement has been reached we feel that it is our duty to put forward what we consider are the best arrangements possible to ensure a speedy setting up of the new constitution. This statement is made with the full approval of His Majesty's Government in the United Kingdom.

3. We have accordingly decided that immediate arrangements should be made whereby Indians may decide the future constitution of India and an Interim Government may be set up at once to carry on the administration of

British India until such time as a new Constitution can be brought into being. We have endeavoured to be just to the smaller as well as to the larger sections of the people; and to recommend a solution which will lead to a practicable way of governing the India of the future, and will give a sound basis for defence and a good opportunity for progress in the social, political and economic field.

4. It is not intended in this statement to review the voluminous evidence that has been submitted to the Mission; but it is right that we should state that it has shown an almost universal desire, outside the supporters of the Muslim League, for the unity of India.

5. This consideration did not, however, deter us from examining closely and impartially the possibility of a partition of India; since we were greatly impressed by the very genuine and acute anxiety of the Muslims lest they should find themselves subjected to a perpetual Hindu-majority rule.

This feeling has become so strong and widespread amongst the Muslims that it cannot be allayed by mere paper safeguards. If there is to be internal peace in India it must be secured by measures which will assure to the Muslims a control in all matters vital to their culture, religion, and economic or other interests.

6. We therefore examined in the first instance the question of a separate and fully independent sovereign State of Pakistan as claimed by the Muslim League. Such a Pakistan would comprise two areas; one in the north-west consisting of the Provinces of the Punjab, Sind, North-West Frontier, and British Baluchistan; the other in the north-east consisting of the Provinces of Bengal and Assam. The League were prepared to consider adjustment of boundaries at a later stage, but insisted that the principle of Pakistan should first be acknowledged. The argument for a separate State of Pakistan was based, first, upon the right of the Muslim majority to decide their method of Government according to their wishes, and secondly, upon the necessity to include substantial areas in which Muslims are in a minority, in order to make Pakistan administratively and economically workable.

The size of the non-Muslim minorities in a Pakistan comprising the whole of the six Provinces enumerated above would be very considerable as the following figures* show:

North-Western Area	Muslim	Non-Muslim
Punjab	16,217,242	12,201,577
North-West Frontier Province	2,788,797	249,270
Sind	3,208,325	1,326,683
Br. Baluchistan	438,930	62,701
	22,653,294	13,840,231
	62·07%	37·93%

* All population figures in this statement are from the most recent census taken in 1941.

	Muslim	Non-Muslim
North-Eastern Area		
Bengal	33,005,434	27,301,091
Assam	3,442,479	6,762,254
	36,447,913	34,063,345
	51·69%	48·31%

The Muslim minorities in the remainder of British India number some 20 million dispersed amongst a total population of 188 million.

These figures show that the setting up of a separate sovereign State of Pakistan on the lines claimed by the Muslim League, would not solve the communal minority problem; nor can we see any justification for including within a sovereign Pakistan those districts of the Punjab and of Bengal and Assam in which the population is predominantly non-Muslim. Every argument that can be used in favour of Pakistan, can equally in our view be used in favour of the exclusion of the non-Muslim areas from Pakistan. This point would particularly affect the position of the Sikhs.

7. We therefore considered whether a smaller sovereign Pakistan confined to the Muslim majority areas alone might be a possible basis of compromise. Such a Pakistan is regarded by the Muslim League as quite impracticable because it would entail the exclusion from Pakistan of (a) the whole of the Ambala and Jullundur Divisions in the Punjab; (b) the whole of Assam except the district of Sylhet; and (c) a large part of Western Bengal, including Calcutta, in which city the Muslims form 23·6% of the population. We ourselves are also convinced that any solution which involves a radical partition of the Punjab and Bengal, as this would do, would be contrary to the wishes and interests of a very large proportion of the inhabitants of these Provinces. Bengal and the Punjab each has its own common language and a long history and tradition. Moreover, any division of the Punjab would of necessity divide the Sikhs leaving substantial bodies of Sikhs on both sides of the boundary. We have therefore been forced to the conclusion that neither a larger nor a smaller sovereign State of Pakistan would provide an acceptable solution for the communal problem.

8. Apart from the great force of the foregoing arguments there are weighty administrative, economic and military considerations. The whole of the transportation and postal and telegraph systems of India have been established on the basis of a united India. To disintegrate them would gravely injure both parts of India. The case for a united defence is even stronger. The Indian armed forces have been built up as a whole for the defence of India as a whole, and to break them in two would inflict a deadly blow on the long traditions and high degree of efficiency of the Indian Army and would entail the gravest dangers. The Indian Navy and Indian Air Force would become much less effective. The two sections of the suggested Pakistan contain the two most vulnerable frontiers in India and for a successful defence in depth the area of Pakistan would be insufficient.

9. A further consideration of importance is the greater difficulty which the Indian States would find in associating themselves with a divided British India.

10. Finally there is the geographical fact that the two halves of the proposed Pakistan State are separated by some seven hundred miles and the communications between them both in war and peace would be dependent on the goodwill of Hindustan.

11. We are therefore unable to advise the British Government that the power which at present resides in British hands should be handed over to two entirely separate sovereign States.

12. This decision does not however blind us to the very real Muslim apprehensions that their culture and political and social life might become submerged in a purely unitary India, in which the Hindus with their greatly superior numbers must be a dominating element. To meet this the Congress have put forward a scheme under which Provinces would have full autonomy subject only to a minimum of Central subjects, such as Foreign Affairs, Defence and Communications.
Under this scheme Provinces, if they wished to take part in economic and administrative planning on a large scale, could cede to the Centre optional subjects in addition to the compulsory ones mentioned above.

13. Such a scheme would, in our view, present considerable constitutional disadvantages and anomalies. It would be very difficult to work a Central Executive and Legislature in which some Ministers, who dealt with Compulsory subjects, were responsible to the whole of India while other Ministers, who dealt with Optional subjects, would be responsible only to those Provinces which had elected to act together in respect of such subjects. This difficulty would be accentuated in the Central Legislature, where it would be necessary to exclude certain members from speaking and voting when subjects with which their Provinces were not concerned were under discussion.
Apart from the difficulty of working such a scheme, we do not consider that it would be fair to deny to other Provinces, which did not desire to take the optional subjects at the Centre, the right to form themselves into a group for a similar purpose. This would indeed be no more than the exercise of their autonomous powers in a particular way.

14. Before putting forward our recommendation we turn to deal with the relationship of the Indian States to British India. It is quite clear that with the attainment of independence by British India, whether inside or outside the British Commonwealth, the relationship which has hitherto existed between the Rulers of the States and the British Crown will no longer be possible. Paramountcy can neither be retained by the British Crown nor transferred to the new Government. This fact has been fully recognised by those whom we interviewed from the States. They have at the same time assured us that the

States are ready and willing to co-operate in the new development of India. The precise form which their co-operation will take must be a matter for negotiation during the building up of the new constitutional structure, and it by no means follows that it will be identical for all the States. We have not therefore dealt with the States in the same detail as the Provinces of British India in the paragraphs which follow.

15. We now indicate the nature of a solution which in our view would be just to the essential claims of all parties, and would at the same time be most likely to bring about a stable and practicable form of constitution for All-India.

We recommend that the constitution should take the following basic form:

(1) There should be a Union of India, embracing both British India and the States, which should deal with the following subjects: Foreign Affairs, Defence, and Communications; and should have the powers necessary to raise the finances required for the above subjects.

(2) The Union should have an Executive and a Legislature constituted from British Indian and States representatives. Any question raising a major communal issue in the Legislature should require for its decision a majority of the representatives present and voting of each of the two major communities as well as a majority of all the members present and voting.

(3) All subjects other than the Union subjects and all residuary powers should vest in the Provinces.

(4) The States will retain all subjects and powers other than those ceded to the Union.

(5) Provinces should be free to form Groups with executives and legislatures, and each Group could determine the Provincial subjects to be taken in common.

(6) The constitutions of the Union and of the Groups should contain a provision whereby any Province could, by a majority vote of its Legislative Assembly, call for a reconsideration of the terms of the constitution after an initial period of 10 years and at 10 yearly intervals thereafter.

16. It is not our object to lay out the details of a constitution on the above lines, but to set in motion the machinery whereby a constitution can be settled by Indians for Indians.

It has been necessary however for us to make this recommendation as to the broad basis of the future constitution because it became clear to us in the course of our negotiations that not until that had been done was there any hope of getting the two major communities to join in the setting up of the constitution-making machinery.

17. We now indicate the constitution-making machinery which we propose should be brought into being forthwith in order to enable a new constitution to be worked out.

18. In forming any Assembly to decide a new Constitutional structure the first problem is to obtain as broad-based and accurate a representation of the whole population as is possible. The most satisfactory method obviously would be by election based on adult franchise; but any attempt to introduce such a step now would lead to a wholly unacceptable delay in the formulation of the new Constitution. The only practicable alternative is to utilize the recently elected Provincial Legislative Assemblies as the electing bodies. There are, however, two factors in their composition which make this difficult. First, the numerical strengths of the Provincial Legislative Assemblies do not bear the same proportion to the total population in each Province. Thus, Assam with a population of 10 millions has a Legislative Assembly of 108 members, while Bengal, with a population six times as large, has an Assembly of only 250. Secondly, owing to the weightage given to minorities by the Communal Award, the strengths of the several communities in each Provincial Legislative Assembly are not in proportion to their numbers in the Province. Thus the number of seats reserved for Muslims in the Bengal Legislative Assembly is only 48% of the total, although they form 55% of the Provincial population. After a most careful consideration of the various methods by which these inequalities might be corrected, we have come to the conclusion that the fairest and most practicable plan would be—

(a) to allot to each Province a total number of seats proportional to its population, roughly in the ratio of one to a million, as the nearest substitute for representation by adult suffrage.

(b) to divide this provincial allocation of seats between the main communities in each Province in proportion to their population.

(c) to provide that the representatives allotted to each community in a Province shall be elected by the members of that community in its Legislative Assembly.

We think that for these purposes it is sufficient to recognise only three main communities in India: General, Muslim, and Sikh, the 'General' community including all persons who are not Muslims or Sikhs. As the smaller minorities would, upon the population basis, have little or no representation since they would lose the weightage which assures them seats in the Provincial Legislatures, we have made the arrangements set out in paragraph 20 below to give them a full representation upon all matters of special interest to the minorities.

19. (i) We therefore propose that there shall be elected by each Provincial Legislative Assembly the following numbers of representatives, each part of the

Legislature (General, Muslim or Sikh) electing its own representatives by the method of proportional representation with the single transferable vote:

Table of Representation

SECTION A

Province	General	Muslim	Total
Madras	45	4	49
Bombay	19	2	21
United Provinces	47	8	55
Bihar	31	5	36
Central Provinces	16	1	17
Orissa	9	0	9
Total	167	20	187

SECTION B

Province	General	Muslim	Sikh	Total
Punjab	8	16	4	28
North-West Frontier Province	0	3	0	3
Sind	1	3	0	4
Total	9	22	4	35

SECTION C

Province	General	Muslim	Total
Bengal	27	33	60
Assam	7	3	10
Total	34	36	70
Total for British India			292
Maximum for Indian States			93
Total			385

Note. In order to represent the Chief Commissioners' Provinces there will be added to Section A the Member representing Delhi in the Central Legislative Assembly, the Member representing Ajmer-Merwara in the Central Legislative Assembly, and a representative to be elected by the Coorg Legislative Council.

To Section B will be added a representative of British Baluchistan.

(*ii*) It is the intention that the States should be given in the final Constituent Assembly appropriate representation which would not, on the basis of the calculations adopted for British India, exceed 93, but the method of selection will have to be determined by consultation. The States would in the preliminary stage be represented by a Negotiating Committee.

(*iii*) The representatives thus chosen shall meet at New Delhi as soon as possible.

(*iv*) A preliminary meeting will be held at which the general order of business will be decided, a Chairman and other officers elected, and an Advisory

Committee (see paragraph 20 below) on the rights of citizens, minorities, and tribal and excluded areas set up. Thereafter the provincial representatives will divide up into the three sections shown under A, B, and C, in the Table of Representation in sub-paragraph (*i*) of this paragraph.

(*v*) These sections shall proceed to settle the Provincial Constitutions for the Provinces included in each section, and shall also decide whether any Group Constitution shall be set up for those Provinces and, if so, with what provincial subjects the Group should deal. Provinces shall have the power to opt out of the Groups in accordance with the provisions of sub-clause (*viii*) below.

(*vi*) The representatives of the Sections and the Indian States shall reassemble for the purpose of settling the Union Constitution.

(*vii*) In the Union Constituent Assembly resolutions varying the provisions of paragraph 15 above or raising any major communal issue shall require a majority of the representatives present and voting of each of the two major communities.

The Chairman of the Assembly shall decide which (if any) of the resolutions raise major communal issues and shall, if so requested by a majority of the representatives of either of the major communities, consult the Federal Court before giving his decision.

(*viii*) As soon as the new constitutional arrangements have come into operation, it shall be open to any Province to elect to come out of any Group in which it has been placed. Such a decision shall be taken by the new legislature of the Province after the first general election under the new constitution.

20. The Advisory Committee on the rights of citizens, minorities, and tribal and excluded areas should contain full representation of the interests affected, and their function will be to report to the Union Constituent Assembly upon the list of Fundamental Rights, the clauses for the protection of minorities, and a scheme for the administration of the tribal and excluded areas, and to advise whether these rights should be incorporated in the Provincial, Group, or Union constitution.

21. His Excellency the Viceroy will forthwith request the Provincial Legislatures to proceed with the election of their representatives and the States to set up a Negotiating Committee. It is hoped that the process of constitution-making can proceed as rapidly as the complexities of the task permit so that the interim period may be as short as possible.

22. It will be necessary to negotiate a Treaty between the Union Constituent Assembly and the United Kingdom to provide for certain matters arising out of the transfer of power.

23. While the constitution-making proceeds, the administration of India has to be carried on. We attach the greatest importance therefore to the setting up

at once of an Interim Government having the support of the major political parties. It is essential during the interim period that there should be the maximum of co-operation in carrying through the difficult tasks that face the Government of India. Besides the heavy task of day-to-day administration, there is the grave danger of famine to be countered; there are decisions to be taken in many matters of post-war development which will have a far-reaching effect on India's future; and there are important international conferences in which India has to be represented. For all these purposes a Government having popular support is necessary. The Viceroy has already started discussions to this end, and hopes soon to form an Interim Government in which all the portfolios, including that of War Member, will be held by Indian leaders having the full confidence of the people. The British Government, recognising the significance of the changes in the Government of India, will give the fullest measure of co-operation to the Government so formed in the accomplishment of its tasks of administration and in bringing about as rapid and smooth a transition as possible.

24. To the leaders and people of India who now have the opportunity of complete independence we would finally say this. We and our Government and countrymen hoped that it would be possible for the Indian people themselves to agree upon the method of framing the new constitution under which they will live. Despite the labours which we have shared with the Indian Parties, and the exercise of much patience and goodwill by all, this has not been possible. We therefore now lay before you proposals which, after listening to all sides and after much earnest thought, we trust will enable you to attain your independence in the shortest time and with the least danger of internal disturbance and conflict. These proposals may not, of course, completely satisfy all parties, but you will recognise with us that at this supreme moment in Indian history statesmanship demands mutual accommodation.

We ask you to consider the alternative to acceptance of these proposals. After all the efforts which we and the Indian Parties have made together for agreement, we must state that in our view there is small hope of peaceful settlement by agreement of the Indian Parties alone. The alternative would therefore be a grave danger of violence, chaos, and even civil war. The result and duration of such a disturbance cannot be foreseen; but it is certain that it would be a terrible disaster for many millions of men, women and children. This is a possibility which must be regarded with equal abhorrence by the Indian people, our own countrymen, and the world as a whole.

We therefore lay these proposals before you in the profound hope that they will be accepted and operated by you in the spirit of accommodation and goodwill in which they are offered. We appeal to all who have the future good of India at heart to extend their vision beyond their own community or interest to the interests of the whole four hundred millions of the Indian people.

We hope that the new independent India may choose to be a member of the British Commonwealth. We hope in any event that you will remain in close and friendly association with our people. But these are matters for your own free choice. Whatever that choice may be we look forward with you to your ever increasing prosperity among the great nations of the world, and to a future even more glorious than your past.

New Delhi, 16th May 1946

APPENDIX III

Gandhi's Letter to the Secretary of State

Valmiki Mandir,
Reading Road,
New Delhi.
May 20th 1946

Dear Lord,

As the matters we discussed yesterday morning and the day before were very important and affected and still affect my attitude and corresponding action, I think it worth while to reduce a summary to writing. You can correct me if there is misunderstanding. This may even help you, wherever necessary.

I may add that I have conveyed to the Working Committee of the Congress, the purport, to the best of my ability, of our talks.

With this preface I proceed to give the summary.

1. You were good enough to assure me that you will see to it that European members of Provincial Assemblies, neither voted at the elections of delegates to the Constituent Assembly nor expected to be elected by the electors of non Muslim delegates.

2. Election of the possible 93 delegates on behalf of the States would be determined by the Nawabsahib of Bhopal and Pundit Jawaharlal Nehru. In the absence of an agreed solution, there should be no election of delegates on behalf of the States, the function of looking after the interests of the Princes and their people devolving upon the Advisory Committee referred to in clause 20 of the State Paper.

3. In view of the fact that there is no machinery in British Baluchistan analogous to the Provincial Assemblies, it should be treated as the special concern of the Constituent Assembly, and should be included in the function of the Advisory Committee. Meanwhile it should be the duty of the Interim National Government to set up machinery to bring Baluchistan on a par with the other provinces.

4. I ventured to suggest that Paramountcy should cease even while Independence is at work in fact, though not in law, till the Constituent Assembly has finished its labours and devised a constitution. Sir Stafford saw danger in acting upon my suggestion. I hold the opposite view. Acceptance of my proposal would vivify the people of the States as if by a stroke of the pen. And the Interim Government would be a boon to the Princes who, though the creation of the

paramount Power and dependent on it for the continuance of their existence, still chafed under its heavy hand. The immediate end of Paramountcy would test the sincerity alike of the Princes and the paramount Power.

But if this Indian feeling did not find an echo in your hearts, I personally would be satisfied with Sir Stafford's view that Paramountcy which had been admittedly used to protect the Princes against their people in the shape of suppressing their liberty and progress, should for the time continue for the protection and progress of the people. If the people of the States are backward, it is not because they are different in kind from the people of the direct British parts of India but because they have been groaning under a double yoke. I endorsed also the suggestion that Paramountcy should be exercised in consultation with the National Government.

5. I have written to you on my difficulty on grouping, I need say nothing more on the subject, pending reply to it.

6. Whilst I appreciate your and Sir Stafford's frankness, I would put on record my conviction that Independence in fact would be a farce, if the British Troops are in India even for peace and order within, or danger from without. The condition of India after the labours of the Constituent Assembly are over will in this respect be no better than now. If the position about the Troops persists, 'Independence next month' is either insincere or a thoughtless cry. Acceptance of 'Quit India' by the British is unconditional, whether the Constituent Assembly succeeds or fails in bringing out a constitution. A drastic revision of the attitude is a necessity in every case.

Finally, it can in no way be contended that in the face of the Troops there would be natural behaviour in the Constituent Assembly.

7. As to the Interim Government, the more I think and observe, the more certain is my feeling that a proper National Government responsible in fact, if not in law, to the elected members of the Central Legislative Assembly should precede the summons for the election of members of the Constituent Assembly. Only then, and not before, can a true picture of coming events be presented. The food crisis demands immediate formation of a strong, capable and homogeneous National Government. Without it, deep and universal corruption cannot end, without it the psychological effect will not be produced in spite of the landing on Indian shores of expected grain from outside. Every day's delay in forming such a government is agony to the famished millions of India. There can be therefore no question of parity, whether the Government is allowed to be formed by the Congress or the Muslim League. The best and incorruptible men or women from India are wanted for the purpose. I was therefore glad to find that the Viceroy was already moving in the matter as quickly as possible.

Yours sincerely
sd. M. K. Gandhi

To The Rt. Hon'ble Lord Pethick-Lawrence

APPENDIX IV

Lord Wavell's Appreciation of Possibilities in India, May 1946

1. The Cabinet Delegation have asked for an appreciation of the situation likely to arise if our present proposals fail, and for a general policy for India in that event. . . .

2. The general political situation in the country may be briefly described as follows. The principal party, the Congress, which has long been a purely revolutionary movement, devoted almost entirely to agitation, suddenly sees power within its grasp, and is not quite able to believe it yet. The leaders are still mistrustful of our intention, and believe that we may take away from them what is offered and start another period of repression if we do not like what they do. They are therefore determined to grasp all the power they can as quickly as possible, and to try to make it impossible for us to take it back. It is as if a starving prisoner was suddenly offered unlimited quantities of food by his gaoler; his instinct is to seize it all at once and to guard against its being taken away again; also to eat as much and as quickly as possible, an action which is bound to have ill effects on his health. . . .

The real objective of the Congress, certainly of the Left Wing extremists, is not, at the present, so much to make a constitution, as to obtain control and power at the Centre. Their plan is to delay the formation of a constitution until they have obtained control at the Centre, have succeeded in getting British troops and British influence removed from the country, and have gained over the Indian Army and the Indian Police forces as their instrument. They then intend to deal with the Muslims and the Princes at their leisure, and to make a constitution that accords with their ideas. They will not swerve from this objective. Whether the moderate element in the Congress can control them, or wishes to, is uncertain.

3. The Muslim League is deeply suspicious of Congress under its present leadership, and more particularly of Mr. Gandhi. I think the Muslim League would be prepared to work with the moderate Congress element, if it could get rid of its extreme Left and of Mr. Gandhi's influence. The former is only likely to be removed by a violent conflict, the latter only by the normal process of a non-violent old age. So long as the Left-wing of Congress continue to exercise influence, and Mr. Gandhi throws his authority unaccountably to one side or

the other, it is going to be almost impossible to obtain Muslim–Hindu co-operation.

4. Of the minorities, the Sikhs are the most important from the point of view of this appreciation, since they occupy a key position in the Punjab and can be dangerously violent. They are much divided in both politics and in space; and their reactions are never easily discernible. They are an important element in the Indian Army.

5. The great mass of the Indian people desire to go about their affairs peaceably, few of them have any real feeling against the British, whom they have looked upon as protectors for many years; they do not realise what is happening, or what disorder or misfortunes threaten the country if law and order break down. They are, however, ignorant, and easily and suddenly swayed to violent passion and action; and there is, in every large town and in many country districts, a dangerous element who are accustomed to live and profit by violence and are ready tools in the hands of any agitator. Hatred against the British could soon and easily be roused; and there would then be considerable danger to isolated British officials, planters, etc.

6. The Rulers of States are perplexed and anxious; they realise that their former protectors, the British, are going, that they will be subject to the agitation of Congress, and that the end of their autocracy and easy living is in sight.

In any conflict or disturbances, the States would in all probability remain generally friendly to the British. . . .

7. It is impossible to tell how or when trouble is likely to come. It may take the form of very serious communal rioting, owing to the Congress and the Muslim League being quite unable to come to terms. The chief areas would probably be the Punjab, the U.P. and Bengal. Rioting in the Punjab would be likely to take the most severe form, since the peoples of the Punjab are more naturally violent than elsewhere in India. It would also be serious in the U.P. and Bihar, and these two Provinces, which might be termed the 'Mutiny' Provinces, where the trouble was greatest both in 1857 and 1942, are probably more anti-British than any others, with the C.P. a good third. Communal rioting in Bengal would take place mainly in the large cities, e.g. Calcutta and Dacca, since in the countryside the two communities are generally separated. . . .

Or trouble may take the form of a mass movement against British authority, either by Hindus or Muslims, or by both. . . .

A widespread mass movement, sponsored by the whole force of the Congress, would be likely soon to take a violent form, even if nominally begun on non-violent lines; and it would probably be beyond our resources to suppress it, at least without very considerable reinforcements of British troops. . . .

.   .   .   .

10. If it were the firm policy of His Majesty's Government that, in the event of the main parties failing to agree and either or both launching a movement

against the authority of the existing British rule, it should be suppressed, I should be prepared to attempt this, and believe it would have a chance of succeeding, if His Majesty's Government would support me with all forces they could make available and give me a free hand to take all measures necessary to restore order, e.g., the proclamation of Martial-law and the use of all force at my disposal. It would be essential for His Majesty's Government to make a clear statement of this policy and of its determination to enforce it.

I assume, however, that in the state of public opinion, at home and abroad, His Majesty's Government would not wish to adopt such a policy.

A policy of immediate withdrawal of our authority, influence and power from India, unconditionally, would to my mind be disastrous and even more fatal to the traditions and morale of our people and to our position in the world than a policy of repression. I could not consent to carry out such a policy.

It remains to examine whether any middle course between 'repression' and 'scuttle' can be found, if we are unable to persuade the Indians to agree to a peaceful settlement of their Constitution.

11. We must at all costs avoid becoming embroiled with both Hindu and Muslim at once. Nor do I think that we can possibly accept the position of assisting the Hindus, that is the Congress, to force their will on the Muslims; that would be fatal to our whole position in the Muslim world, and would be an injustice.

The alternative is that, if we are forced into an extreme position, we should hand over the Hindu Provinces, by agreement and as peaceably as possible, to Hindu rule, withdrawing our troops, officials and nationals in an orderly manner; and should at the same time support the Muslim Provinces of India against Hindu domination and assist them to work out their own constitution.

If such were our general policy, we should make it quite clear to the Congress at the appropriate time that this would be our policy and that it would result in the division of India. This might compel them to come to terms with the Muslim League.

12. There are obvious difficulties and dangers in such a policy. It is possible that the Muslims might decline our assistance, though I think it is unlikely; it would mean the division of the Indian Army; and our military position in the N.W. and N.E. of India would be weak, as a permanency, as the Commander-in-Chief has pointed out. The actual military operation of withdrawal from Hindustan into Pakistan would be difficult and possibly dangerous.

Further, we should have the large minorities, Hindus and Sikhs, to deal with in the Muslim Provinces; and we should have had to abandon our responsibility to minorities, and our own interests, in Hindustan.

Nevertheless, I can see no better policy available; and if it were carried out firmly, I think it would succeed.

13. . . . It is not suggested that this arrangement should be a permanency; and

that we should maintain indefinitely what would amount to a 'Northern Ireland' in India. We should endeavour to bring about a Union of India on the best terms possible; and then withdraw altogether.

14. The formation of an Interim Government is likely to be the crux of the whole problem.

If both the main parties come in, and really try to work the government, all may go well.

I think we may dismiss the contingency of the Muslim League agreeing to participate in the Interim Government, while the Congress declines, since I cannot conceive that a Government formed without Congress agreement could exercise authority in the Hindu Provinces.

The difficult situation will arise if the Congress agrees to take part in an Interim Government while the Muslim League declines. It will be very difficult to refuse to form a Government with Congress members and again to allow Jinnah to hold up all progress. At the same time to give control of all-India to a Government in which Muslims refused to take part would be very dangerous. It would be likely to lead to grave disorders in the Punjab and Bengal, and would be injurious to our whole position in the Muslim world. I could probably get a number of non-Congress non-League Muslims to join the Government, but with the League standing out the writ of such a Government would probably not run in the Punjab or Bengal; and there would be serious disorders.

It might be possible to form a Government temporarily, with non-League Muslims taking the seats reserved for the Muslim League, in the hope that this might induce the League to break away from Jinnah's control, or make Jinnah reconsider his refusal.

If this fails, a possible solution might be to allow the Hindus to form a Hindustan Government for all the Congress Provinces; and the League to form one for the Muslim Provinces; while the Centre was a purely official Government, carrying on as a Union Government, until the two Hindustan and Pakistan Governments could agree on terms of Union or Separation.

The dangers of such a solution are obvious, but it might be possible to work out a temporary arrangement on such lines.

15. Even supposing that we succeed in forming a Coalition Interim Government and (that) the Constituent Assembly (is) formed, our troubles will by no means be over. There is also sure to be in an Interim Government controlled by the Congress a continuous attempt to sap British authority in every possible way. A real Coalition Government might avoid this, as the Muslims and other Minorities would not wish British influence to be lessened or removed. It is, however, likely that it will be difficult to hold together either the Interim Government or the Assembly. All we can do then is, I think, to fall back on the policy outlined in paragraphs 11–13.

W, 30–5–46

APPENDIX V

Statement issued by the Cabinet Mission in New Delhi on 25 May 1946

The Delegation have considered the statement of the President of the Muslim League dated 22nd May and the resolution dated 24th May of the Working Committee of the Congress.

2. The position is that since the Indian leaders after prolonged discussion failed to arrive at an agreement the Delegation put forward their recommendations as the nearest approach to reconciling the views of the two main parties. The scheme stands as a whole and can only succeed if it is accepted and worked in a spirit of co-operation.

3. The Delegation wish also to refer briefly to a few points that have been raised in the statement and resolution.

4. The authority and the functions of the Constituent Assembly and the procedure which it is intended to follow are clear from the Cabinet Delegation's statement. Once the Constituent Assembly is formed and working on this basis there is no intention of interfering with its discretion or questioning its decisions. When the Constituent Assembly has completed its labours, His Majesty's Government will recommend to Parliament such action as may be necessary for the cession of sovereignty to the Indian people, subject only to two matters which are mentioned in the statement and which, we believe, are not controversial, namely: adequate provision for the protection of the minorities (paragraph 20 of the statement) and willingness to conclude a treaty with His Majesty's Government to cover matters arising out of the transfer of power (paragraph 22 of the statement).

5. It is a consequence of the system of election that a few Europeans can be elected to the Constituent Assembly. Whether the right so given will be exercised is a matter for them to decide.

6. The representative of Baluchistan will be elected in a joint meeting of the Shahi Jirga and the non-official members of the Quetta municipality.

7. In Coorg the whole Legislative Council will have the right to vote but the official members will receive instructions not to take part in the election.

8. The interpretation put by the Congress resolution on paragraph 15 of the statement, to the effect that the Provinces can in the first instance make the choice whether or not to belong to the Section in which they are placed, does not accord with the Delegation's intentions. The reasons for the grouping of the Provinces are well known and this is an essential feature of the scheme and can only be modified by agreement between the parties. The right to opt out of the groups after the constitution making has been completed will be exercised by the people themselves, since at the first election under the new provincial Constitution this question of opting out will obviously be a major issue and all those entitled to vote under the new franchise will be able to take their share in a truly democratic decision.

9. The question of how the States representatives should be appointed to the Constituent Assembly is clearly one which must be discussed with the States. It is not a matter for decision by the Delegation.

10. It is agreed that the Interim Government will have a new basis. That basis is that all portfolios including that of the War Member will be held by Indians and that the members will be selected in consultation with the Indian political parties. These are very significant changes in the Government of India and a long step towards independence. H.M.G. will recognise the effect of these changes, will attach the fullest weight to them and will give to the Indian Government the greatest possible freedom in the exercise of the day-to-day administration of India.

11. As the Congress statement recognises, the present Constitution must continue during the interim period and the Interim Government cannot, therefore, be made legally responsible to the Central Legislature. There is, however, nothing to prevent the members of the Government, individually or by common consent, from resigning if they fail to pass an important measure through the Legislature or if a vote of non-confidence is passed against them.

12. There is, of course, no intention of retaining British troops in India against the wish of an independent India under the new Constitution; but during the interim period, which it is hoped will be short, the British Parliament has under the present Constitution the ultimate responsibility for the security of India and it is necessary, therefore, that British troops should remain.

APPENDIX VI

Statement by Cabinet Delegation and His Excellency the Viceroy, 16 June 1946

1. His Excellency the Viceroy, in consultation with the members of the Cabinet Mission, has for some time been exploring the possibilities of forming a coalition Government drawn from the two major parties and certain of the minorities. The discussions have revealed the difficulties which exist for such a Government.

2. The Viceroy and the Cabinet Mission appreciate these difficulties and the efforts which the two parties have made to meet them. They consider however that no useful purpose can be served by further prolonging these discussions. It is indeed urgently necessary that a strong and representative Interim Government should be set up to conduct the very heavy and important business that has to be carried through.

3. The Viceroy is therefore issuing invitations to the following to serve as members of the Interim Government on the basis that the constitution-making will proceed in accordance with the Statement of May 16th:

Sardar Baldev Singh	Dr. John Matthai
Sir N. P. Engineer	Nawab Mohammed Ismail Khan
Mr. Jagjivan Ram	Khwaja Sir Nazimuddin
Pandit Jawaharlal Nehru	Sardar Abdur Rab Nishtar
Mr. M. A. Jinnah	Mr. C. Rajagopalachari
Nawabzada Liaquat Ali Khan	Dr. Rajendra Prasad
Mr. H. K. Mahtab	Sardar Vallabhbhai Patel

If any of those invited is unable for personal reasons to accept, the Viceroy will, after consultation, invite some other person in his place.

4. The Viceroy will arrange the distribution of portfolios in consultation with the leaders of the two major parties.

5. The above composition of the Interim Government is in no way to be taken as a precedent for the solution of any other communal question. It is an expedient put forward to solve the present difficulty only, and to obtain the best available coalition Government.

6. The Viceroy and the Cabinet Mission believe that Indians of all communities desire to arrive at a speedy settlement of this matter so that the process

of constitution-making can go forward and that the Government of India may be carried on as efficiently as possible in the meantime.

7. They therefore hope that all parties especially the two major parties will accept this proposal so as to overcome the present obstacles, and will co-operate for the successful carrying on of the Interim Government. Should this proposal be accepted the Viceroy will aim at inaugurating the new Government about the 26th June.

8. In the event of the two major parties or either of them proving unwilling to join in the setting up of a coalition Government on the above lines, it is the intention of the Viceroy to proceed with the formation of an Interim Government which will be as representative as possible of those willing to accept the Statement of May 16th.

9. The Viceroy is also directing the Governors of the Provinces to summon the Provincial Legislative Assemblies forthwith to proceed with the elections necessary for the setting up of the constitution-making machinery as put forward in the Statement of May 16th.

APPENDIX VII

Lord Wavell's Note for Cabinet Mission, 25 June 1946

1. I feel that I must know exactly how we stand with regard to the question of Grouping, i.e. paragraph 19 (v) of our Statement of May the 16th.

2. I understood from last night's interview that Mr. Gandhi, on the telegram from Assam, raised objections that representatives elected to the Constituent Assembly were being asked to commit themselves to acceptance of paragraph 19 before becoming eligible for election to the Constituent Assembly. He was apparently given reassurances on this point; and this is the subject of headlines in today's Press. I attempted to have it made clear that acceptance of paragraph 19 (v) of our Statement was an essential part of the Delegation scheme; but was asked by the Secretary of State not to press the point.

3. In our instructions to Governors, which were passed by the Delegation (though I believe Sir Stafford Cripps was not present), we made it perfectly clear that acceptance of paragraph 19 was a condition of eligibility for election to the Constituent Assembly; and laid down that a candidate was required to sign a declaration to this effect.

In the form issued by the Bengal Government, it appears that this provision did not appear; and that all the candidate was asked to do was to sign a declaration that he was elected with a view to forming a Constitution. I do not know why the Bengal Government substituted this for our instructions; but there is surely no guarantee that other Governments have done, or will do the same; and it is impossible to get over the fact that our instructions to Governors have laid down that section 19 must be accepted in full. It seems to me therefore that the reassurance apparently given to Mr. Gandhi last night may subsequently lead to an accusation of bad faith on our part, since it is obviously impossible that our instructions to Governors should remain a secret, and I believe that they have in fact been already published.

I am very concerned about this, since if my understanding is correct, I consider that there has either been a reversal of policy which has not been agreed, or that the assurance given to Mr. Gandhi is not entirely an honest one.

4. I also wish to be quite clear as to our policy with regard to section 19 (v). I understand from the Press today that Congress may accept the Statement of May the 16th, provided that they are allowed to interpret the provisions of the Statement in their own way, i.e. that Provinces may elect to opt out of the

sections in which they have been placed *before* those sections have been formed and have decided upon the matter of grouping. I take it that this cannot be regarded as an acceptance of the Statement of May the 16th, and that the Delegation will say so clearly.

5. The Cabinet Mission will remember that I raised the point of what would happen in the event of Congress attempting to obtain a legal decision in favour of their own interpretation of our Statement of May 16th. My point was that the Statement is not a legal document and that its interpretation must depend on the intentions of those who framed it. I therefore suggested to Sir Stafford Cripps that the Cabinet Mission, before leaving India, should draw up a paper stating clearly what the intentions of those who framed the document were in this respect; so that I could produce it as evidence of our intentions if the document were challenged in court, or elsewhere.

I do not quite understand the paper which has been drawn up by Sir Stafford Cripps; but I gather from it that he considers that the document may be challenged legally, and that its interpretation is open to question; and he proposes that a tribunal should be set up by the Constituent Assembly to interpret the document. As a Layman, I do not understand this; and I cannot accept that our clear intentions should be open to interpretation by another body.

W, 25–6–46

APPENDIX VIII

Lord Wavell's Letter to H.M. the King, 8 July 1946[1]

Viceregal Lodge
Simla
July 8th, 1946

Your Majesty,

I last wrote just before the arrival of the Cabinet Mission. In this letter I will give some account, from my personal point of view, of the $3\frac{1}{2}$ months of negotiations which have taken place, and of their results. I shall write quite frankly, as I conceive is my duty to Your Majesty, and shall not conceal such differences of view as there were between some members of the Mission and myself.

2. I will begin by saying that I do not think any men could have worked more wholeheartedly and with greater patience and good temper than did the Mission. It is not really questionable which is the more trying to the temper and patience, the climate of Delhi in the hot weather, or the quibblings, hagglings, tergiversations, and small-mindedness of Indian political leaders, especially of the Congress—the latter have it by a distance; but to have suffered the combination of the two over a long period without loss of courtesy or hope was a fine tribute to the Mission.

3. Their achievements were also very considerable. They certainly convinced Indian opinion, except perhaps the most extreme, that we really do intend to give India her freedom as soon as possible; they persuaded the Congress and Muslim League leaders to meet at Simla; they produced an admirable compromise plan in the Statement of May 16th; and succeeded, after some almost interminable haggling on the part of Congress, in getting it accepted by the two main Parties—though both had, I am afraid, more than mental reservations in their acceptance.

4. The failure to secure an Interim Government was perhaps more my fault than theirs, since I conducted most of the negotiations to this end. They came near success, I think. But at the last moment Gandhi, whose conduct, as always, was quite unpredictable, threw a spanner in the works at the Congress end; and Jinnah chose that moment to give to the Press an intemperate letter he had written to me about the attitude of Congress, before I had ever received it. And Nehru at the same critical juncture went off on a quite unnecessary and

[1] Reprinted, with slight omissions, by gracious permission of H.M. the Queen.

provocative expedition to Kashmir, mainly for reasons of personal prestige and vanity. Such are the irresponsibilities of the leaders with whom we have had to deal.

5. Any differences of view that I had with the Mission were on the methods of reaching our ends, not on the ends themselves, on which we were in full agreement. We are bound to fulfil our pledges to give India her freedom as soon as possible—and we have neither the power nor, I think, the will to remain in control of India for more than an extremely limited period, without a complete reversal of policy; we must try to leave India united; and we must secure the co-operation of the Congress which represents the great majority of Indian political opinion, whatever our views on the past record of that Party.

We are in fact conducting a retreat, and in very difficult circumstances. Now my military instincts when retreating—and I am afraid I have had to make a number of retreats—tell me to show as bold a front as possible and to try to simulate reserves of strength, so as to prevent being pressed too closely. I thought the Mission was too prone to parade the weakness of our position; and did not make enough of our strength—India is not yet able to stand without us and I feel that this should have been brought home more clearly to her rather irresponsible leaders; also what the consequences of attack on the British in India would be likely to be. I considered that the Mission should have taken and kept the initiative more; and should not have been so dependent on the shifts and changes of a set of inexperienced, short-sighted and sometimes malevolent politicians. After all, we are still in charge of India, and are giving a boon rather than asking one. Further, I thought it was a mistake that the Mission should have had, outside the official discussions, such a continuous and close touch with one of the two main Parties, the Congress; this naturally aroused the deep suspicion of the Muslim League, and was probably a cause of that letter of Jinnah's which contributed to the breakdown on the Interim Government.

I may be quite wrong in all this. Military ideas and methods may not be applicable to political negotiations; and perhaps the rather more summary methods I should have preferred would have failed completely.

Finally, I can never entirely rid my mind of the recollection that in 1942, at almost the most critical period of the war for India, when I was endeavouring as Commander-in-Chief to secure India with very inadequate resources against Japanese invasion, the supporters of Congress made a deliberate effort to paralyse my communications to the Eastern Front by widespread sabotage and rioting.

6. I will not trouble Your Majesty with any details of the various phases of the protracted negotiations; but I think that you may be interested in some estimate of the performance of the principal Indian personalities concerned, and in an appreciation of where we stand now.

Gandhi ran entirely true to form: his influence is still great; his line of thought and action at any given moment and on any particular issue is as unpredictable as ever; he never makes a pronouncement that is not so qualified and so vaguely worded that it cannot be interpreted in whatever sense best suits him at a later stage; but however double-tongued he may be, he is quite single-minded on the one objective from which he has never swerved in the last 40 years, the elimination of the hated British influence from India. My distrust of this shrewd, malevolent, old politician was deep before the Conference started; it is deeper than ever now. One of the Mission also came to distrust him at an early date, and I think all did at the end. Incidentally, he looks much tougher and in better health than since I first knew him. And I was persuaded that he was at death's door when I released him over two years ago. Curiously enough, I lately found an appreciation of the Indian situation sent to me by a friend in India ten years ago; he wrote that everyone was agreed that Gandhi could not live more than six months!

I have much sympathy with Jinnah, who is straighter, more positive and more sincere than most of the Congress leaders; but he overcalled his hand in the end, and thereby, I think, missed the opportunity of having a more favourable share in an Interim Government than he is likely to get again. He was naturally disappointed, and indulged in an unjustified outburst against the good faith of the Mission and myself. He is a curious character, a lonely, unhappy, arbitrary, self-centred man, fighting with much resolution what I fear is a losing battle.

Azad, the Congress President, did well. He is a gentleman and stood for good sense and moderation as far as he was able, in spite of poor health and a naturally weak character. But up against Gandhi he was as a rabbit faced by a stoat.

Congress, most unwisely brought up to the Simla Conference two Muslims out of their four representatives. Azad their President naturally had to come; but the presence of Abdul Ghaffar Khan, from the North-West Frontier Province, whose intelligence and grasp of English are both limited, was regarded by Jinnah as a gratuitous and deliberate provocation.

I have seen much of Nehru and cannot help liking him. He is sincere, intelligent, and personally courageous. But he is unbalanced—witness his ploy in Kashmir—and also lacks the political courage to stand up to Gandhi when he knows he is wrong.

Sardar Vallabhbhai Patel is the recognised 'tough' of the Congress Working Committee, and by far the most forcible character amongst them. I have a good deal more respect for him than for most of the Congress leaders, and he is probably the only one of them capable of standing up to Gandhi. If he takes the line of constitutional progress, he may be valuable; if he goes to the Left, he will be formidable.

The rest of the Congress Working Committee are poor stuff, except that possibly one of the younger ones, Mahatab, Premier of Orissa, who is earnest and likeable, may in time become a capable administrator.

8. Of the immediate future in India it is difficult to write with much confidence. I am left with one rather sickly infant, the Constituent Assembly, which I shall find much difficulty in nursing through its childhood; and one still-born babe, the Interim Government, which I am expected to resuscitate by some means. The Sikhs, who have always more conceit than political sense, are threatening to make trouble; Jai Prakash Narain and the Congress left wing will certainly do so if they see a chance; the Services, on whom the good government of India depends, are tired and discouraged; the loyalty of the Police and Indian Army in face of a really serious challenge to British rule is problematical; and the Congress are convinced that immediate power is theirs for the asking. This has always been their real objective, and they will concentrate on it rather than on constitution-making; that is in their eyes a sequel to the seizure of power, not a preliminary. The Congress is, however, by no means a united body and a considerable proportion are in favour of constitutional progress rather than violence. We may be able to secure an orderly withdrawal from our rule over India without a rebellion or civil war; but it is likely to be a close-run thing. And no-one can feel much confidence in the ability of the Indians who will take over from us to make a strong or prosperous new India. Still, if we play our hand well, they are likely to continue to lean on British help, and may maintain some connection with the Commonwealth; but these three months close contact with Indian politicians have certainly not enhanced anyone's opinion of their political wisdom or foresight. We shall know more of their immediate policy after the meeting of the All-India Congress Committee at Bombay this week.

Monty, who spent a few days with me last month, had rather an amusing interview with Azad. He pretended to be anxious for the immediate return to the U.K. of all British troops in India, and the withdrawal of all British officers from the Indian Army. Officially these are two of the most insistent demands of Congress; but Azad, quite taken aback, said that neither British troops nor British officers could be spared for some time to come.

9. Outside politics, I have little to tell Your Majesty. It looks as if we may just scrape through 1946 without famine, though Bengal is now causing some anxiety; and the threatened railway strike has been averted for the time being—at a cost.

I am taking a fortnight's comparative rest in Simla before descending again into the sticky and unpleasant heat of Delhi and of political discussion.

I have the honour to be,

SIR,

Your Majesty's humble and devoted servant,

WAVELL.

APPENDIX IX

Mr. Attlee's Letter of 31 January 1947 and Lord Wavell's Reply

PRIVATE AND PERSONAL   31st January, 1947

My dear Viceroy,

I have your letter of the 19th in reply to mine of the 8th. It is clear from what you say with regard to Government policy that there is a wide divergence of view as to the course which should be followed during the interim period. I had hoped that it would have been possible for you to have returned here during January to discuss the situation which has arisen.

I am very conscious of the heavy burden which you have carried and of the great services which you have rendered during this difficult period. I know that you undertook this task from a high sense of duty.

You were, I understand, informed that your appointment was a war appointment and that while the usual term for a Viceroy is five years, this might not apply. I think that three years was mentioned. This has now expired. I know, of course, that prior to your appointment as Viceroy you had had the heavy strain of high commands in war and, as you say in your letter, you have had no rest. I appreciate that you desire a month or two's leave at home.

But the Indian problem is entering on a new phase, which will be very exacting and may be prolonged. The next few months are of great importance.

In view of all these circumstances and of the fact that it is specially necessary that the Viceroy should be in full agreement with the policy of His Majesty's Government, I think that you may agree that the time has come to make a change in the Viceroyalty.

I recall that you expressed your readiness to retire in the event of disagreement on policy and this would seem to me to be the appropriate course to follow.

An announcement should be made with as little delay as possible in order to allow time for the appointment of your successor and for him to take over at the end of February or early in March. The normal announcement about your successor would be prefaced with the statement 'Field-Marshal the Viscount Wavell who accepted the Viceroyalty as a war appointment is now retiring.' I have not looked into details, but if as a result you are denied any leave of absence which you would normally have had, you may be sure that you will not suffer financially.

I should like to submit your name to His Majesty for the dignity of an Earldom in recognition of the self sacrificing and loyal service which you have displayed in your long and distinguished career in India both to the Indian people and to this Country and the Commonwealth.

Yours sincerely,
C. R. Attlee.

5th February, 1947

My dear Prime Minister,

I have received your letter of January 31, in which you inform me of your intention to advise his Majesty to terminate my appointment as Viceroy in a few weeks time.

As you say, my appointment was a war one and no fixed term of office was given me. I think you are in error about a term of three years having been mentioned;[1] but the point is immaterial, since the three year term passed several months ago without your giving any indication of wishing to make a change.

You are causing me to be removed because of what you term a wide divergence of policy. The divergence, as I see it, is between my wanting a definite policy for the Interim period and H.M.G. refusing to give me one. I will not at this time enter into further argument on this.

I do not of course question your decision to make a change. I have no desire except to serve the State to the best of my ability; obviously I cannot continue to do so if I have not the confidence of the Government in power.

I think, however, that I am entitled to observe that so summary a dismissal of His Majesty's representative in India is hardly in keeping with the dignity of the appointment. It has been usual to give a retiring Viceroy six months' notice of his replacement. I may recall to you that I wrote to you six months ago, at the beginning of August last, suggesting that you might now wish to replace the soldier by a politician, but that you gave no indication of any desire to make a change. Whether my conduct of my office since then has deserved dismissal at a few weeks' notice is for others to judge.

You can hardly have failed to appreciate the inconvenience and expense which you are causing to me and to the whole of my large personal staff by directing me to leave at such short notice; and I hope that I shall be given at least till the second week in March, to avoid the indignity, as well as the inconvenience of a scuttle. I note what you say about my entitlement to leave. I too have not looked into details on this matter, but will do so and will communicate with the Secretary of State. I hope that the expense and dislocation unexpectedly caused to my personal staff will be recognised and considered.

---

[1] Churchill told Wavell that he wished to be free to make another appointment after three years, if that should be necessary, but that he hoped it would not be. Apart from this, no exceptional limit was placed on his tenure as Viceroy. Normally the post was held for five years.

It is desirable for official and personal reasons to know the name of my successor, who has presumably been selected, as early as possible. You will of course give me advance notice of date and terms of announcement.

I thank you for what you say about my services, and will gladly accept your proposal to submit my name for the dignity of an Earldom.

Yours sincerely,
Wavell.

LIST OF ABBREVIATIONS

A.G.	Adjutant-General
A.I.C.C.	All India Congress Committee
A.I.R.	All India Radio
A.J.	Major A. J. A. Wavell
A.O.C.-in-C.	Air Officer Commanding-in-Chief
A.V.A.	A. V. Alexander
C.A.	Constituent Assembly
C.G.S.	Chief of General Staff
C.I.G.S.	Chief of Imperial General Staff
C.-in-C.	Commander-in-Chief
C.M.B.	Constitution-making Body
C.O.S.	Chiefs of Staff
C.P.	Central Provinces / Congress Party
D.C.I.G.S.	Deputy Chief of Imperial General Staff
D.G.I.M.S.	Director General, Indian Medical Service
D.I.B.	Director Intelligence Bureau
D.P.S.V.	Deputy Private Secretary to the Viceroy
E.P.T.	Excess Profits Tax
F.B.I.	Federation of British Industries
F.K.N.	Firoz Khan Noon
F.M.	Finance Member
F.O.	Foreign Office
G.	Gandhi
G.C.I.E.	Grand Cross of the Indian Empire
G.C.S.I.	Grand Cross of the Star of India
G. of I.	Government of India
H.M.G.	His Majesty's Government
I.A.	Indian Army
I.A.F.	Indian Air Force
I.C.S.	Indian Civil Service
I.M.S.	Indian Medical Service
I.N.A.	Indian National Army
I.O.	India Office
I.P.	Indian Police
J.	Jinnah
J.P.S.	J. P. Srivastava

L. of C.	Lines of Communication
M.B.	Mountbatten
M.L.	Muslim League
M.L.A.	Member of the Legislative Assembly
M.O.I.	Ministry of Information
M.S.	Military Secretary
N.D.C.	National Defence Council
N.W.F.P.	North-West Frontier Province
P. and T.	Post and Telegraph Department
P.L.	Pethick-Lawrence
P.M.	Prime Minister
P.O.	Post Office
P.S.V.	Private Secretary to the Viceroy
Q.	Queenie (Lady Wavell)
Q.M.G.	Quarter Master General
R.I.A.F.	Royal Indian Air Force
R.I.N.	Royal Indian Navy
S.E.A.C.	South East Asia Command
S. of S.	Secretary of State for India
S. of S. Services	Secretary of State's Services
U.P.	United Provinces
W.V.S.	Women's Voluntary Service

INDEX

The official designation, e.g. C.-in-C., has been added in square brackets after the names of those persons who are sometimes referred to in the text by designation instead of by name. Wavell has been abbreviated to W.